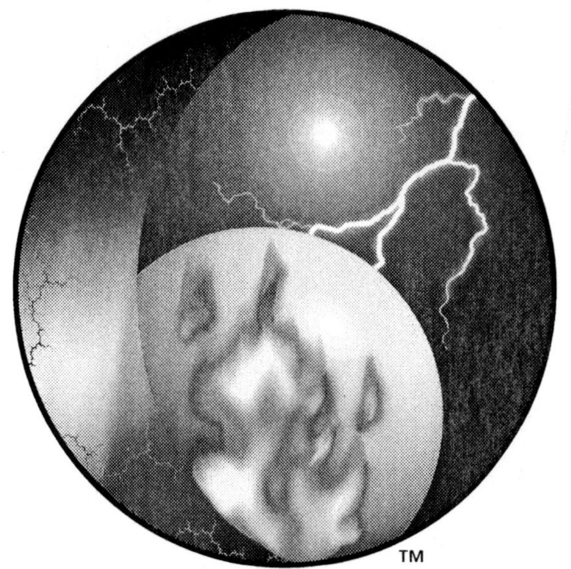

MYSTIC FORCES

BY

ACKNOWLEDGMENTS

Special Thanks
God
My wife
Elliot Randall Meade
Daniel Cox
Will Nezbitt

Game Concept
Lonie Joe Meade

Design
Lonie Joe Meade

Layout
Daniel Cox
Lonie Joe Meade

Artwork
Steven Corder
Matt Slone
Joey Hall
Lonie Joe Meade

Cover Illustration
Douglas Shuler

Play-testers
Adam Goble
Alex Locklear
Ashley Lykins
Billy Howell
Bo Tackett
Bradley Gearheart
Brian Mullins
Daniel Cox
Darren Gearheart
Fred Conn
Jamie Robinette
Joey Hall
Kenny Hamilton
Michael Carroll
Pat Tackett
Paul Funk
Ronnie Mullins
Shannon Ferrell
Steve Brashear
Steve Mitchell
Tim Martin

MYSTIC FORCES ™ is a Trademark of
Positive Role-Playing Inc.

ISBN 0-9701874-0-8

Printed in the United States by Morris Publishing
3212 East Highway 30, Kearney, NE 68847
1-800-650-7888

CONTENTS

CONTENTS

CONTENTS

ABOUT ROLE-PLAYING GAMES

It seems that a large portion of the general population has serious misunderstandings as to just what role-playing and role-playing games are, and most of these misunderstandings are in the line of thinking that role-playing games are evil or are a type of brainwashing. Such attitudes certainly stem from a lack of knowledge or experience with the role-playing genre altogether. Role-playing games are just that; games. They are no more negative or harmful than any other type of card or board game, and in many respects are no different than any other type of entertainment media. To say that all role-playing games are constructive and have no indecent or inappropriate material would be as untrue as saying that there are no movies with indecent or inappropriate contents. Certainly there are role-playing games on the market that have some pretty harsh or indecent contents but there are many out there that are very clean and respectable. Like so many things in life you simply have to be careful with what you buy or entertain yourself.

SO WHAT IS A ROLE-PLAYING GAME?

The basic concept of a role-playing game is taking a fictional character and placing him into a world of adventure where you get to decide how that character reacts to his surrounding and what he does. You as a player dictate the actions of your character within the game. Thus, you take on the role of the character in that you determine his every action within the game as you play ("role-playing").

There will be a group of players, normally four to six, who all have fictional characters that they will play and there will be one player who is the Game Master (or GM). The GM describes the surroundings and situation that the characters are in; what they see, hear, smell, etc., and the players in turn tell the GM how they would like for their characters to react to the situation at hand. A good deal of storytelling and improvisation in conjunction with certain rules and dice rolls determine the outcome of any given situation.

In many ways the traditional role-playing game is like a video game. With a video game you see your character on the TV screen and control his actions with a game controller. In a role-playing game you envision your character in your mind (or occasionally with the aide of miniatures) and control his actions through informing the GM what you would like your character to do and with the dice rolls and or game mechanics of the particular role-playing game. Instead of a video game projecting the images and sound of each scene or encounter that your character has, with a role-playing game the GM describes each scene and encounter to you and plays the part of the creatures and opposition that your character faces (the GM is a player too, but instead of just controlling one character as the other players do he controls every creature or other being that the players' characters encounter).

The actual abilities and details of the characters that the players control and the non-player characters and creatures that the GM controls are listed on paper either on a Character Sheet or in this rulebook itself. The stats and abilities of the characters and creatures in conjunction with the game mechanics laid out in this rulebook (which are often resolved with dice rolls) allow the characters to perform numerous tasks which can be resolved in an exciting and realistic manner.

Role-playing takes a bit more time to set up and play than does many other types of games, but it offers a level of group interaction and long-term playability that most other games don't even approach. There aren't very many types of games that you can play for four or five hours a week year after year and never have two gaming sessions be alike and never get bored with them. Most role-playing games, including **Mystic Forces**, can do just that.

So gather up some friends and start enjoying the endless hours of gaming enjoyment that role-playing has to offer.

GAME TERMS

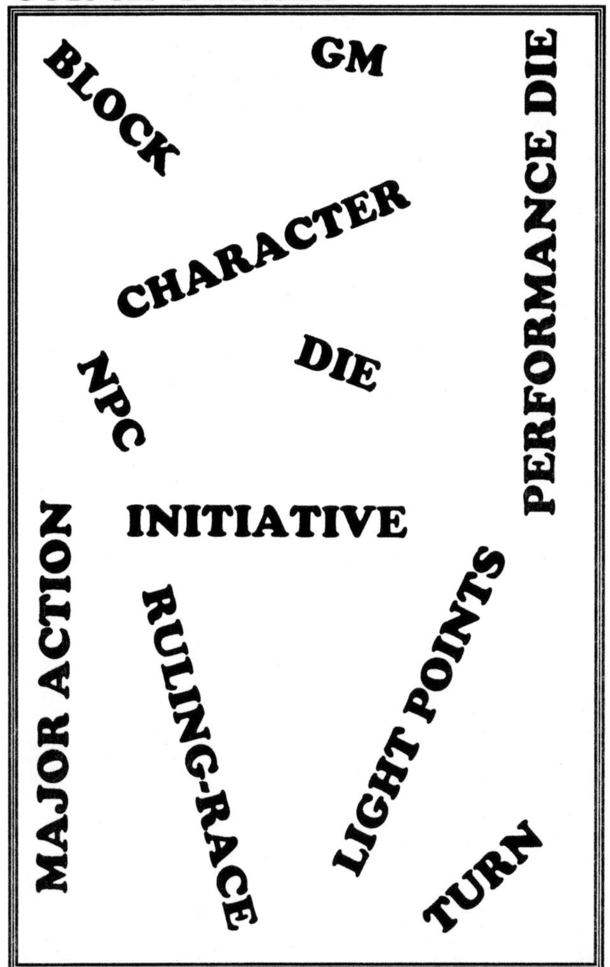

There are several different terms used throughout this rulebook that you will need to become familiar with in order to get the most out of **Mystic Forces** and to better understand and utilize the rules and concepts of the game. Many of the terms are common among many different types of role-playing games and others are unique to **Mystic Forces**.

The following is a list and definition of the various terms that you will need to know in order to fully understand and play **Mystic Forces**.

Block

A block is a unit of time that is equal to twenty five days. It is sort of our equivalent of a month.

Character

A "character" is a fictional being within the game that either the player or the GM controls. Characters that players control in the game are known as player characters and the characters and creatures that the GM controls in the game are known as non-player characters (or NPCs).

Die

Die is the singular form of dice. For example, you have many dice or one die.

In regards to dice there are some abbreviations that are used throughout this rulebook that you will need to understand. The dice that match the various Levels, as well as the dice to be rolled for events in the game, are written in an abbreviated form like 2D10 or 1D8. The "D" stands for die or dice. The number before the D is the number of dice to be rolled and the number after the D is which die is to be rolled. So 2D10 is the abbreviation for two ten-sided dice. 1D8 is the abbreviation for one eight-sided die and so on. Sometimes there won't be a number in front of the D. This means that you only roll one of the dice indicated after the D. So 1D6 and D6 are both abbreviations for one six-sided die.

Sometimes there will be values to be added to or taken away from the result of the dice rolls. For example, 2D20 +15 would mean that you will roll two twenty-sided dice and add 15 to the combined result of the two rolls. 1D4 -1 would mean that you would roll one four-sided die and then subtract 1 from the result.

To play **Mystic Forces** you will need a full set of dice which should include one of each of the following: 1D4, 1D6, 1D8, 1D10, 1D12, 1D20, and a percentile die to be used with the 1D10 for generating percentages. This dice abbreviation system is heavily used throughout the game.

GM

Short for Game Master, the GM is the player who takes on the responsibility of running the game and reffing all of the rules and controlling all of the NPCs that the player characters encounter.

For more information of Game Master and the GM's role go to the "GAME MASTERING" Section.

Initiative

This is a term that is used basically in reference to who is acting first in a Turn. Basically whoever's character has the highest Initiative acts first and then the next highest and so on.

For more details on the various types of Initiative and exactly how they are calculated and used within the game go to the "COMBAT" Section.

Light Points

Light Points are points that are awarded to characters for promoting the Light and vanquishing evil. Light Points are spent by the player to increase the various aspects of his character.

For more information on Light Points see "Awarding Light Points" in the "GAME MASTERING" Section.

Shadow Points

Shadow Points are points that are awarded to characters for any actions that defy the Light or are considered evil or un-Lightworthy. Shadow Points hinder characters by giving them penalties. The more Shadow Points that a character accumulates the more severe the penalties become.

For more information on Shadow Points see "Awarding Shadow Points" in the "GAME MASTERING" Section.

Character Points

Character Points are points that are awarded to characters for intelligent and creative role-playing. Character Points are used to purchase Universal Talents and can also be converted into Light Points.

For more information on Character Points see "Awarding Character Points" in the "GAME MASTERING" Section.

Major Action

A Major Action is an action that a character can perform that takes approximately three to five seconds to perform. Common Major Actions would be to make an attack or to climb or some similar action. Under normal circumstances player characters can only make one Major Action per Turn, though some NPCs, especially creatures, have the ability to make more than one *attack* per Turn, and have it considered to be a single Major Action.

Minor Action

A Minor Action is an action that a character can perform that takes approximately two seconds or less to perform. Common Minor Actions include shouting an order, drawing a weapon, or sheathing a weapon. Characters can make several Minor Actions each Turn, though the GM should limit the number of Minor Actions to no more than three in a single Turn. The main thing is that the sum of all Minor Actions taken in a single Turn should not add up to more than two seconds worth of action.

Performance Die

Performance Die is another name for a twelve-sided die (1D12). The D12 is very often used in **Mystic Forces** to determine how well that a character is performing on a scale of 1 to 12, thus the name Performance Die.

It is often used to determine the performance of attacks, Defenses, actions requiring a good deal of skill, and the success of Talents.

Player Character

One of the five ruling-races that a player controls in the game.

Re-roll on Max Roll

This term is applied to a bonus that players occasionally receive where one or more dice may be re-rolled one additional time with the new results being added onto the previous.

Ruling-race

Any one of five highly intelligent and civilized races of beings that inhabit Oryathar. Players may choose for their character to be any one of these five races. The five ruling-races are Brightling, Grak, Loremek, Valkin, and Warlum. Each of the ruling-races are described in detail in the "RUL-ING-RACES" Section.

Turn

One Turn equals five seconds of in-game time (that is time relative to the characters of the game not the players). One Turn within the game may actually take ten or twenty minutes to play out in real time.

All characters and NPCs can perform a certain number of tasks each Turn. These tasks typically include, but are not limited to, performing one Major Action, one or more Minor Actions, moving, and setting one or more Defenses.

NPC

Short for non-player character, NPCs are the characters that the GM controls in the game. NPCs are often the creatures that the player characters encounter but may also be other ruling-races that can act as either enemies or allies.

Test

Tests are exactly what they sound like. They are tests that challenge a character and require him to perform or react with a certain degree of effectiveness in order to be successful at the task being attempted.

Characters will be required to make Tests within the game for various reasons. Either to determine the effectiveness of an attack or to see whether or not that they avoid an oncoming attack or if they are able to climb a wall for instance, or a number of other challenges. Typically, whatever the task or challenge at hand is becomes the name of the Test that the character has to make. So to determine the value of a character's attack he must make an attack Test. To determine whether or not a character is able to swim across the river he must make one or more successful swimming Tests.

The different types of Tests that characters can make are based on the current Level of their attributes. Tests or events that call for a high degree of Agility will require an Agility-based Test. Events or challenges that require a good deal of perception or thought process will require an Intelligence-based Test. The GM has the final say as to what type of Test is necessary for the different actions that a character may wish to perform.

For a detailed description of the different types of Tests that characters can make and exactly how they are made see the "Tests" in the "GAME MASTERING" Section.

Each Turn your character can;

1. Perform 1 Major Action (Major Actions are actions that generally take 3 seconds or longer to perform. Some examples Include physical attacks, utilizing a Force-effect, climbing, or swimming).

2. Perform 1 or more Minor Actions (Minor Actions are actions that generally take less than 2 seconds to perform. Some examples include shouting a command, drawing a weapon, or throwing down an object). Total sum of all Minor Actions taken in a Turn should not add up to more than 2 seconds unless some of the Minor Actions can be performed simultaneously with the Major Action (shouting a command while attacking with a sword for ex.)

3. Move

4. Set one or more Physical Defenses

5. Set one or more Mystical Defenses

Tests

Three basic types of tests.   (The word "attribute" is substituted with one of the 6 actual attributes)

1. Attribute/Performance Test (ex. Agility/Performance Test) = roll 1D12 (the Performance die) and add the current Level of the appropriate attribute to the result (only Agility & Sixth Sense have attribute/Performance Tests)

2. Attribute Test (ex. Strength Test) = roll dice for the current Level of the appropriate attribute and add the attribute's current Level to the result

3. Random-roll attribute Test (ex. Random-roll Intelligence Test) = roll dice for the current Level of the appropriate attribute

Attacking

1. Physical attacks = Agility/Performance Test + any appropriate bonuses
2. Mystical attacks = Sixth Sense/Performance Test + any appropriate bonuses

Defending

1. Physical Defense (used against physical attacks) =Agility/Performance Test + plus any appropriate bonus due to type of Physical Defense used

The 3 types of Physical Defenses are Block, Dodge, Parry

  a. Block (shield intercepts attack) = may add Bulk Rating of shield to the defense + 1 point per Technique Point with shield used & 1 point if shield is green-steel

  b. Dodge (completely dodge attack) = no additional bonuses

  c. Parry (weapon or non-shield item intercepts attack) = may add 1point per Technique Point with weapon. used, 1point if weapon is of your character's Specialty, 1 point if proficient with the wpn., and 1 point if wpn. is green-steel

2. Mystical Defense (used against mystical attacks) = Sixth Sense/Performance Test

Pros&Cons for the 3 Types of Physical Defenses

Block; Pros = bonuses to Defense   Cons = opponent can possibly slip past shield & hit regardless of Defense & can possibly receive dmg. even though the Defense was successful. Not effective against all types of attacks

Dodge; Pros = equally effective against all types of physical attacks   Cons = no added bonuses to Defense

Parry; Pros = bonuses to Defense   Cons = can be disarmed. Wpn can be damaged. Not effective against all types of attacks

Determining Attack Success

If attack value exceeds target's Defense, the attack is successful

Determining Dmg. From Attacks

1. Physical attacks = # of points of dmg. equal to double the Level of Strength applied + Dmg. Yield of wpn. & any bonuses that may apply
2. Mystical attacks = varies according to each type of mystical attack (see specific Force-effect's description)

Movement

Maximum Speed = the fastest speed that your character is capable of moving

Action Movement = the maximum # of feet that your character can move in a single Turn & still have time to perform a Major Action

Gaining Force Knowledge

Dragonknight characters; 1 hr meditation + expenditure of 1 Light Point = gain Force Knowledge equal to the lowest result in common of a random-roll Intelligence Test & a Random-roll Sixth Sense Test

Enchanters; 30 minutes meditation + expenditure of 1 Light Point = gain Force Knowledge equal to the lowest result in common of a Random-roll Intelligence Test & a Random-roll Sixth Sense Test

Force Energy = Total Force Energy divided by 2 (round up) + Innate Force Energy

Recovering Force Energy

Dragonknights; 1 hr meditation = gain Force Energy equal to the lowest result in common of a Random-roll Intelligence Test & a Random-roll Sixth Sense Test times 2

Enchanters; 30 minutes meditation = gain Force Energy equal to the lowest result in common of a Random-roll Intelligence Test & a Random-roll Sixth Sense Test times 2

Enchanting Strength; characters have 1 point of Enchanting Strength for each 50 Total Force Energy

Recovering Enchanting Strength

30 minutes meditation +5 Light Points = recover 1 point of Enchanting Strength

Mystical Attuning Points

A number of points equal to the number of Mystic Forces controlled +1

Health

1. Receiving an amount of dmg. in one blow equal to or greater than character's **Injury Rating** = character receives an injury
2. Acquiring amount of dmg. equal to or greater than character's **Force Failure** = character blacks out (goes unconscious)
3. Acquiring amount of dmg. equal to or greater than character's **Life Force** = character is dead

Injury; -2 Level penalty to attribute
Critical Injury; -3 Level penalty to attribute
Fatigue; -1 Level penalty to attribute per Fatigue Point
Knockdown; any Physical Defense as well as the results of any Agility-based Tests are cut in half (round down)
Knockout; complete unconsciousness for 1D4 Turns
Stun; -4 point penalty to all Tests except End. & Willpower-based Tests (normally lasts 1 Turn)

Healing Damage

3 Recovery Tests per day + 1 instant damage recovery made by expending 1 M.A.P.
3 Fatigue Points to a single attribute or any current dmg. other than injury dmg. will put your character in recovery
Once in recovery your character receives 1 Recovery Test every 2 hours
Recovery Test = Random-roll Endurance Test + any bonuses that may apply. Result is # of points of dmg. healed

Each Recovery Test removes 1 Fatigue Point from every attribute as well as recovering dmg.

Learning Force-Effects

Expend required Unapplied Force Knowledge while drawing upon the Mystic Forces contained within the Force-effect to be learned & make a successful Sixth Sense/Performance Test against the listed Learning Difficulty Value

Novice Factor = 20% chance of automatic failure

Learning Ranks in Skills

Train for the required time and then make the required attribute and/or attribute/Performance Test (known as Progress Tests when training for a Skill). The result of each subsequent Progress Test must be 1 point higher than the last. When all three Progress Tests are passed the Rank in the Skill is learned
There is no set # of Skills that your character can use in a single Turn

Learning Talents

Expend the required amount of Light Points
Your character can normally only use 1 Talent per Turn. Talents defined as "Permanent" can be used in the same Turn as another Talent

Learning Universal Talents

Expend the required amount of Character Points
Your character may use up to 3 Universal Talents per Turn, but may not use more than 1 Universal Talent marked with a * in the same Turn

Raising Attributes

Expend the required amount of Light Points based upon the # of times that attribute has been raised
 (see the "ATTRIBUTE COST" table on page 246). Mark a line in the box to the left of the attribute for each increase

Oryathar was once a planet of abundant life and splendor. Brightling, Grak, Loremeks, Valkin, and Warlum, known as the ruling-races, lived in relative peace with each other and the land, with no regard to prejudice or racial differences. Wars were virtually unheard of and the few that did spring up were more of a short brawl than a war.

Oryathar was rich with mystical beings and creatures of all types. The land flourished with a multitude of plant and animal life. Villages, towns, and cities thrived and enjoyed an unnaturally peaceful existence. Life for the ruling-races was good.

The ruling-races enjoyed the balance between the Light and the Shadow. All things are a result of these two supreme powers. The magical energies of these two powers are believed to be the core of all existence. The ruling-races were quite familiar with both of these powers. They knew death, disease, despair, loneliness, fear, and all of the wrongful and dreadful things that a being could experience, and knew that these were the work of the Shadow. They also knew hope, life, joy and love, and acknowledged that these virtues are the work of the Light; the counter-force to the Shadow.

Everything that exists is a result of these two supreme entities. There is no death without life, and all that which lives will someday die. The world exists because of the balance between these two forces; but this balance never remains constant, for the Shadow always strives to throw the balance in its direction, and is always countered by the Light. The hand of the Shadow and the Light are constantly at work upon the world. All that which is bad being a product of the Shadow, and all that which is good being a product of the Light. Thus is the continual struggle of good and evil.

The prosperous and rich lives led by the ruling-races, and all of Oryathar, was not pleasing to the Shadow. Its hatred of all that which is good compelled it to tip the balance between good and evil. Vile and loathsome creatures were born unto Oryathar, serving no other purpose than to kill and destroy. These creatures were filthy and horrid looking. Some were small leathery skinned beasts with long fangs and claws, some were huge scaly creatures with slimy poisonous skin, some looked like large birds with long whip-like tails tipped with stingers, just to name a few, but one thing they all had in common was their profound evil and lust to kill.

These unholy creatures multiplied and produced many more of their foul kind. New species began to appear as these evil creatures raped those of the natural world. All of these Shadow-spawned creatures became known as Shadow-kin. They came forth from the forests, swamps, and caves, that were often their homes, to destroy and lay waste to villages, towns, and anyone that got in their path. The homes of the innocent were descended upon and the lives of the ruling-races were claimed in mass by the Shadow-kin. Their lust for blood seemed endless and the killing grew to devastating proportions. Oryathar was no longer the safe and peaceful place it had once been.

There was resistance as the ruling-races of Oryathar fought back against their unnatural foes, but they were no match for supernatural beasts spawned from the Shadow; but as always the Light was ready to combat the forces of evil and restore the balance.

The females from each of the five ruling-races began bearing children with a special ability. These children had the ability to sense and control the powerful mystical energies of Oryathar, known as the Mystic Forces. The five Mystic Forces are *Air*, *Fire*, *Land*, *Spirit*, and *Water*. As these children grew into adulthood their abilities grew stronger and they became aware that they could sense things that others could not (the Mystic Forces). Through meditation they learned how to become more aware of and in tune with the Mystic Forces, steadily increasing in knowledge and eventually learning how to control them.

Those of the ruling-races gifted with this special ability learned to combat the Shadow-kin by conjuring the Mystic Forces into effective offensive and defensive weapons, such as summoning and controlling lightning, causing landquakes, summoning explosive balls of fire, and many more extraordinary feats. Some of these gifted ones were even able to transform themselves into powerful dragon-like forms, while others had the gift to enchant objects.

With the passing of years many more with this gift were born, and each became an effective weapon against the Shadow-kin.

This period of time when the Shadow-kin began to emerge and ruling-races began controlling the Mystic Forces became known as "The Awakening". So important to the ruling-races was the Awakening that it became their reference for all future years. All years past that point are now marked "AA", (After the Awakening), and all years previous to the Awakening, which were before recorded only as a number, are now marked "BA" (Before the Awakening). This changing of the calendar took place in the year 1650, or what is now referred to as the year 1650 BA.

Organized parties of these ruling-races who could conjure soon began gathering together in an effort to seek out and destroy the wretched abominations that now plagued the land. Those who were able to manipulate and conjure the Mystic Forces began to be called Shinkai, the Brightling word for hope or light. The Shinkai that could transform into the dragon-like form became known as Shinkai Dragonknights, and those with the ability to enchant objects became known as Enchanters. As many Shinkai that could be found were asked to join in the task of ridding Oryathar of Shadow-kin.

Soon these groups of Shinkai began to organize themselves in a military style. Before long they became very powerful and effective units of soldiers, and in the year 26 AA named themselves the Clan of Justice.

The Clan of Justice continued to grow in number and support all across Oryathar. The Shinkai that had the ability to create magical weapons and items used their gift to aid all those who were willing to fight. These weapons and items were very powerful and aided greatly to the battles against the Shadow-kin.

The dedicated efforts of the Shinkai proved not to be in vain, for the number of Shadow-kin slowly began to decrease. The raids came less frequently and with less intensity. The Clan of Justice definitely seemed to be making progress in restoring the balance between good and evil.

For years the Clan of Justice operated out of their own homes or make-do shacks. In the year 60 AA the kings of all the lands increased their assistance to the Shinkai by constructing forts for members of the Clan of Justice. This lead to a more organized and effective means for the Clan of Justice to protect the villages, towns, and cities from the Shadow-kin raids, and offered their members a safer place to train and recruit members.

The Clan of Justice continued to grow and thrive, and in the year 72 AA their name was changed to the Defenders of the Light.

The Defenders of the Light gained ever-increasing support, financially and morally, and the forts that became home to the Shinkai spread all across Oryathar. Soon great cities ded-icated to the upkeep of the forts and the support of the Defenders therein were formed, and the mere forts became fort cities. The Defenders of the Light became a very powerful and respected military organization, dedicated to the fight against the Shadow. Their efforts to stamp out all Shadow-kin never ceased over the next hundred years and it finally seemed that the forces of the Shadow were falling to the Defenders of the Light.

It was in the year 173 AA that the sudden twist in events occurred. The raids from the Shadow-kin abruptly ceased. No Shadow-kin sightings were reported anywhere; it was as if they had all vanished. This worried the Defenders of the Light greatly, and their efforts at finding and destroying every last Shadow-kin was doubled; but to no avail. No Shadow-kin were to be found.

For the next several years the silence and peace continued; the Defenders of the Light no longer seemed necessary, but with unerring faithfulness they continued to recruit those who could conjure and train them in the art of combat, both physically and mystically.

In the year 188 AA the silence ended. Waves of Shadow-kin descended upon the lands. Thousands upon thousands of these horrible beasts sprang forth as if from nowhere. The land was sent into a panic as the blood-thirsty Shadow-kin began pouring into the weaker areas of defense. The villages and towns furthest from the Defender's forts were crushed beneath the hungry waves of Shadow-kin.

The greatest shock was not from the Shadow-kin themselves, however, but from the Defenders of the light. As the Defenders of the Light began to form their defense against this onslaught a truly horrible act of violence and betrayal took place; an act that would forever taint the reputation of Shinkai.

Many of the Defenders of the Light began helping the Shadow-kin. They turned their abilities into weapons of destruction against their own people. These venomous traitors brought particular disgust to the ruling races which still followed and upheld the ways of the Light, for they are not merely creatures created by the Shadow, but intelligent beings who once stood together with the other ruling-races of Oryathar to form a common alliance against the forces of evil; now they fight against their own kind as they are filled with greed and lust for the gifts promised them by the Shadow. The term Shadow-sworn was given to those of the ruling-races who serve the Shadow, and a name for Shinkai who turned to the Shadow was also born. Korgathool, which is Valkin for "Dark *Gift*", became the name for any Shinkai who has turned Shadow-sworn. The name Korgathool would strike fear in the hearts of many for centuries to come.

Those who had not sworn over to the Shadow fought with all the strength and courage that they possessed, for they knew the fate of Oryathar was now hanging by a thread. They remained true to the Light and stood together to combat this common enemy.

The entire planet turned into a massive and bloody battleground as the two forces continued to wage merciless war among themselves. Fire, lightning, storms, and landquakes ravaged the land as the Mystic Forces were wielded by the Shinkai.

The war raged on for several years. The Shadow-kin alone claimed a tremendous number of lives, but with the aid of their Shadow-sworn allies and the Korgathool the Defenders of the Light, and all Light following beings, were very hard pressed. It became painfully obvious that this battle would surely be lost to the Shadow unless they came up with some way to even the odds; and quick!

The Defenders of the Light formed a desperate plan, which if successful, would bring a swift victory for the Light. Ten of the most powerful Shinkai known, that were still faithful to the Light, were brought together to carry out this plan.

Using an enchanted crystal that enhances and strengthens flows of the Mystic Forces, they would attempt to unite their powers to banish all Shadow-kin (if not kill them) back into their dark holes forever. The only problem with this plan was that nothing even close to this magnitude had ever been attempted, and they weren't even sure that it was possible. With no other options available the Defenders of the Light set their plan into motion. Even a flawed plan was better than no plan at all, and time was running out.

Outside of one of the Defenders of the Light forts marched forth an army of Shinkai and other courageous soldiers ready to do battle with the approaching onslaught of Shadow-kin, Shadow-sworn, and Korgathool. With this army marched ten of the most powerful Shinkai on Oryathar, armed with an enchanted crystal. Each of the ten carried a weight greater than any mountain, for the fate of Oryathar depended upon their success.

High atop a snow-covered hill overlooking a valley swarming with approaching Shadow-kin, the ten formed a circle around the enchanted crystal and began to draw upon the Mystic Forces. The rest of the army fought with wreckless

abandon to hold off the enemies for as long as they could; hopefully long enough for the ten to complete the banishment.

The ten Shinkai, later to be named the "Moaja", which means "circle of ten", drew upon the Mystic Forces as strongly and deeply as they safely could, focusing the energies into the enchanted crystal. The crystal vibrated with energy and began to glow faintly. The Shadow-kin still came on strong, battling and killing.

Each one of the ten could feel that it wasn't working. Their eyes met as if to confirm the thoughts that each now held. With a nod of agreement the ten drew even deeper upon the Mystic Forces; deeper than their bodies could withstand. With a shattering scream of agony and victory all ten erupted into blazing, golden flames and fell dead, completely consumed by the raging flood of mystical energies coursing through their bodies; but not before their goal was completed.

The crystal raged to life with a blazing brightness so intense that all near it were blinded. Streams of golden light shot out from the crystal in a thousand directions, striking any and every Shadow-kin that lived. Many of the Shadow-kin dropped dead where they stood and those that didn't turned and fled. The Shadow-sworn that remained were easily taken by the Defenders of the Light, for the biggest part of their strategy depended upon the help of the Shadow-kin.

Messages from other Defenders of the Light all across Oryathar reported the same event; streams of golden light coming from nowhere and everywhere striking the Shadow-kin, either killing them or causing them to flee.

Within the next one hundred days all Shadow-sworn resistance was crushed. Shouts of victory rang out all across Oryathar. It was the year 198 AA and the end to the long, bloody war had come.

The aftermath of the war was truly horrifying. The population of the entire planet had been brought to a mere speck of its former self. Both the Shadow-kin and ruling-races alike had suffered astonishing losses; but neither side had been eliminated. The Shadow-kin that were not killed by the Moaja's efforts withdrew into seclusion underground and within remote caves. The ruling-races had hope that the Shadow-kin would never return again, but the fear and dread of the possibility always lingered like a hungry wolf in the shadows.

This brutal war became know as the War of Betrayal, and although the war was over the ruling-races were not without troubles. Homes and livestock had been totally wiped out, and most every family that had survived was no longer whole. The number of Shinkai remaining after the war was pitifully low and in the years that followed their numbers grew less and less until there were no Shinkai left on the face of the planet.

For several hundred years the survivors of the War of Betrayal continued to rebuild their land and live in peace without the threat of the Shadow-kin. With the efforts of the ruling-races the cities and towns were again made strong, however the fort cities in which the former Defenders of the Light had flourished were never rebuilt. They lay toppled and destroyed, a legacy to the lands salvation, and destruction. It seemed that the horrible events of the past could finally be forgotten, but the story of the ten Shinkai who boldly gave their lives to banish the Shadow-kin would be retold for centuries to come.

The ruling-races truly believed that the threat of the Shadow-kin was over, until the year 560 AA when small groups of Shadow-kin began to be spotted wandering near many villages and towns. Many people began to fear that the banishment was breaking down and that the Shadow-kin would again roam the lands in mass.

Their fears were soon brought to reality when the Shadow-kin raids began to occur once more.

Their numbers were few at first and most of their attacks were repelled, but as the years passed they began to come forth in larger and larger numbers. Their raids became more frequent and intense, and the number of lives claimed by their evil kind climbed at a horrifying rate. And as before, there were those of the ruling-races who stood against the forces of good and promoted the ways of the Shadow, whose corruption is an ever present and deadly threat against those who stand for the Light. Blending into civilization and lying in wait to carry out their evil deeds, the Shadow-sworn became as feared as the Shadow-kin creatures themselves. For as all know, the most dangerous enemy is the one not seen.

As the raids continued the forces of evil began to gain the upper hand. Without the abilities of the Shinkai the Shadow-kin, Shadow-sworn, and Korgathool began to take control of the lands once more. Many believed that the Light had forsaken Oryathar for their actions in the War of Betrayal, and that is why Shinkai became extinct. Others believed that the ability to conjure was taken away because it was too powerful and too easily abused to be in the hands of the ruling-races. Whatever the reason for the extinction of the Shinkai, it happened, and the ruling-races simply accepted it as part of life.

With the increase of raids from the Shadow-kin and Shadow-sworn, the hopes of all Oryathar began to dwindle. It seemed that the Shadow would surely defeat the Light, a thought that sent a chill through many hearts. It was at this time, when the hopes of the world were at their lowest, that events began to change once more.

It was the year 575 AA that the rebirth of a lost gift reappeared. The ability to conjure began appearing among the young adults of the ruling-races once more. This brought a wave of hope and excitement, and for the first time in many years the ruling-races felt as if the world was not lost, and that the Light may yet prevail. But the rebirth of the Shinkai also brought fear to many hearts for it was the wielding of the Mystic Forces by the ruling-races that brought such destruction and death to Oryathar once before. Many feared that the Shinkai would side with the Shadow and lay waste to the land once again.

The ruling-races would not be caught off guard this time though, for they knew all too well the seductive abilities of the Shadow. They would be constantly aware and on the lookout for those who would swear allegiance to the Shadow. Quick justice would be dealt to those who would betray the Light.

It is now the year 600 AA and the struggle to reclaim Oryathar from the grip of the Shadow is in full flight. Kings of all lands are pouring their resources into the restoration of the Defenders of the Light and the once mighty fort cities. The forces of the Light are still greatly outnumbered, but with the rebirth of the Shinkai events are bound to change.

You as a character in the world of **MYSTIC FORCES** are Shinkai. Born with the ability to wield the Mystic Forces, the core energies of all existence, your destiny is to combat the forces of evil. The land may yet fall to the Shadow, but not without a fight, not as long as you, Shinkai, still retain hope. You have been born to come forth and reclaim the lands from the Shadow and restore the true name of the Defenders of the Light! You have the ability to stand against the Shadow and to see that the Light prevails once more! But be careful, for the influence of the forces of evil are great, and you too could fall into the hands of the SHADOW!

The following is an excerpt from a scroll recovered from the ruins of Fort Northwood, a former fort city of the Defenders of the Light.

"With honor and pride I serve the Light, knowing that all my strengths and abilities have been granted me by the grace thereof. For the ways of the Light I shall gladly lay down my life, for there is no greater cause than that which I serve. The Light shall illumine and overpower the Shadow, for my life is a testament thereto. The Light shall prevail!"

THE SHADOW'S HOST

Torch in hand Pendrule and his two companions slipped into the narrow opening in the massive wall of rock - the last dying rays of the sun weakly sifting through behind. They walked in silence for nearly ten minutes, slowly winding deeper and deeper into the cold bowels of the mountain.

"I don't like this place", said Krelg, rubbing his hands together nervously. It was then that he noticed he could see his breath rising as he spoke, and realized how cold it had suddenly become. Apparently he wasn't the only one who felt so. Pendrule and Olbreh were pulling their cloaks about them tighter and rubbing their arms in an attempt to warm themselves.

Pendrule raised an arm and the party halted.

"What is --"

"Shhhh", scolded Pendrule, cocking his head to the side, intently listening for something further down the narrow passage. The three stood motionless, the only movement was the flickering dance of the torch's flames. Nothing sounded in the distance, at least nothing that Krelg and Olbreh were aware of.

Pendrule handed the torch to Olbreh and motioned for the two of them to stay put (Pendrule being a Valkin had no need of a torch, having perfect night vision, and carried the torch only for the benefit of Olbreh and Krelg), then graceful as a tiger and silent as a shadow, Pendrule turned and headed down the tunnel. His long stag-handled dagger whispered from its leather sheath and stood ready to perform at its master's will. The unnaturally sharp blade, forged from green-steel, had tasted the flesh of many a foe unfortunate-or foolish- enough to cross Pendrule.

Krelg and Olbreh remained where they were, though neither liked taking orders from Pendrule. He wasn't even a Defender of the Light. However, it was their orders from Colonel Crauwold that they do as Pendrule instructed. He was the one who found the entrance to the lost fort city, and supposedly knew the way into it.

There was no denying Pendrule's exceptional talents. When it came to slipping around in the shadows, there was no one better. It is also a well known fact that Pendrule is Shinkai, a name given to those with the gift to conjure the Mystic Forces, and even rumored to be Dragonknight; yet despite the pleas from every fort city in the Northern Realm, Pendrule would not join ranks with the Defenders of the Light. What a waste. With the help of the Defenders of the Light Pendrule could be ten times the man he is now. Krelg, being Shinkai himself, knew this from personal experience. Since he had come to Fort Algusta, just two years earlier, his skill with the Mystic Forces had grown considerably. He could now control *Fire*, *Land*, and *Spirit*, not to mention how much more proficient he was in all of the physical aspects of his life.

"There is nothing like life as a Defender of the Light to bring out the best in a person - Shinkai or not." At least that is what his Lieutenant always said.

"I just want to confirm this location and get out of here", mumbled Olbreh, but not too loudly for fear of disturbing whatever Pendrule had slipped off to investigate.

"Me too", answered Krelg. "Something about this place doesn't feel - well, natural."

They exchanged expressionless gazes for a moment then suddenly spun in unison to face the dark corridor where Pendrule had disappeared. A single bat fluttered overhead, past the two of them. Both sighed heavily in relief and relaxed their white-knuckled grip on the handles of their swords. The air seemed so cold and heavy, and still. Even the smoke from the torch seemed to struggle to ascend. Something was not right about this place. No, not right at all.

"What's keeping Pendrule? I wish he would hurry up and get back here." Olbreh shifted nervously from side to side, often turning about to ensure no one, or thing, was sneaking up from behind. Krelg made no reply, but the deep lines that crossed his brow told Olbreh that his companion was no less worried than himself.

The air was cold and thick with a foreboding and sense of dread which Pendrule had felt only one other time in his life, when he had wandered into this same area two weeks earlier. It was much stronger this time though, hungrier.

He surveyed the area with scrupulous Valkin vision, attempting to locate the source of this pervading evil. Two tall oak doors stood proudly, marking the entrance to the once great fort city of Woodform. Much of the stone walls to either side of the doors had long since fallen away, but remarkably the huge oak doors stood, as if in proud defiance of reality. One now remained half open, giving the appearance of recent use.

Pendrule held his stag-handled dagger at the ready, the veins of his battle hardened arms raised in response to his tense poise. A soft whisper drifted out to him from the darkness beyond the fort city's entrance, raspy and cold, yet somehow inviting . "Come to me."

Instantly Pendrule was drawing upon the Mystic Force of *Fire*, its radiant warmth coursing through every inch of his body. As the Mystic Force raged into Pendrule's body so did an eagerness for combat. A feeling of near invincibility laced his tongue like the sweet nectar of life itself. His left palm hovered in front of him, fingers spread wide, ready to conjure a searing ball of fire at his will.

"Come to me." The cold voice- no, not a voice, but a thought again drifted to him deep from within the remains of the city. Still drawing upon *Fire* he stepped through the opened door and slowly began to pick his way through the rubble and debris of the buried city. The air grew colder with every step, yet a trickle of sweat managed to escape down his brow.

"Who are you?" whispered Pendrule, as much to himself

as to his beckoner. There came no reply. Nothing stirred in the distance, yet Pendrule was sure that he felt the presence of someone, or thing, not far ahead; he continued forward.

A thick blanket of frost clung to the walls of the well, a product of the unnatural cold that seethed up from its depths. Once a source of refreshing water, this well was now home to a brooding evil; a dark and soulless embodiment of the Shadow itself. It was a host that this evil Shadow-spawn craved, and with its probing darkness it had found not one, but three such beings who could fulfill its desires. It was the closest one, though, that it desired. What strength this one held, and a spark of defiance that made him that much more appealing. Yes, he would make a perfect host. Pendrule would not be the first such victim of this evil thing. His body would be used as a means to move about the land, slaying others for the pure delight that killing brought, and when Pendrule's body gave in to the corruption inside and finally died, it would simply move on to someone or something else. A near silent footstep sounded about thirty yards from the well, but even the most stealthy approach couldn't escape the Shadow-spawn's senses. Closer, just a little closer.

Suddenly Pendrule jerked stiffly as if he had been struck in the head with an icy pick. The Mystic Force of *Fire* on which he was drawing leaped from his grasp. Desperately he tried to hold on to it, but it was like trying to hold the wind. The evil that was growing stronger with every step now seemed right upon him. His eyes scanned the area where he stood and froze upon a small stone-walled well. A thin layer of shimmering frost clung to the rim of the ancient-looking well. He had found the source of the cold and the pervading evil; the very thing that he sensed far back in the main tunnel where Krelg and Olbreh now waited. Pendrule tried again to draw upon the Mystic Forces, first *Fire*, then *Spirit*; nothing. He could sense them, but trying to embrace them was impossible. He wasn't sure of what was happening, but he was sure that the culprit resided within the well that now held his gaze. Probably just waiting to leap out and attack him. He fingered the handle of his dagger nervously. "Looks like its up to you", he thought to himself.

Pendrule took another cautious step forward, keeping his eyes locked on the rim of the well. "All right, come on out and play", he whispered, though in the stillness of this desolate place it seemed to carry forever. He gave a start as something suddenly moved upon the surface of the well. It looked like a swirling cloud of darkness, only distinguishable from the surrounding darkness by the small flashes of red that danced within its form.

Pendrule tried to back away from the thing but his legs would not move. A wave of fear and panic washed over him like he had never known. The entity continued to swirl over the surface of the well, continuously changing form. One moment tall and thin, the next short and wide. A long snake-like tendril of the unnatural darkness stretched out toward Pendrule, reaching for him. Pendrule wanted to move, want-

ed to shout, anything but stand there like a helpless lamb awaiting slaughter, but his body was no longer his to control. The tendril of darkness now danced mere inches from his face. Still, Pendrule made not a move. His breath was coming in labored gasps and his heart raged inside his chest as if it would burst any moment.

"So strong and feared in the world of mortals, but now you cower in the face of true strength." The thoughts slid from the shadowy extension like blood from a blade. "My fear leaves you powerless, yesss?"

Pendrule's mouth twisted as if to scream, but no sound escaped his lips. The terror in his eyes could have been no greater as the tendril of darkness reared backwards like a snake preparing to strike.

Krelg and Olbreh jumped in unison as a single, blood-curdling scream echoed through the tunnel from the darkness beyond; a sound of pain and torment that would be expected in a torture chamber. They both stared down the tunnel where Pendrule had gone, wide-eyed and hearts racing.

Olbreh swallowed hard. "By the Light, what was that?"

Krelg turned to face Olbreh, face pale, as if all of the blood had drained from him. "Perhaps we should find out. Be prepared for anything." Krelg took the torch from Olbreh and began down the tunnel. After a moments pause, Olbreh exhaled deeply and followed.

Pendrule moved about the grounds around the well as if testing his legs for the first time. An expression of anxiousness painted his face. Occasionally a flicker of red appeared in his eyes, then disappeared. Many of the soulless creature's powers would be limited or useless now, but it had gained many new abilities as well; the ability to move about freely, to feel- to kill. The long green-steel dagger flashed forward in a stabbing motion, then recoiled with lightning speed, twirled easily around Pendrule's hand before being sheathed. The creature that was now Pendrule smiled evilly then trotted off up the corridor in the direction of the other two mortals that had entered its home.

Pendrule's mortal mind and thoughts still lingered somewhere within his body, but they were no longer in his control. The creature tasted of them as if to sense their intent, their purpose. The thoughts that once belonged to Pendrule were now just toys for the creature to play with and destroy at its leisure. One thought slid to the surface and caught the creature's attention. "Must warn General Tirey, and the others."

The creature pondered the thought for a moment and apparently found it amusing. "I don't think so, but I do think a visit to this General would be worth my time." It was Pendrule's mouth that moved, but the voice that came out was cold and raspy, none at all like the smooth, casual tone that belonged to the former man.

Pendrule moved swiftly and eagerly along the narrow corridor that led up to the surface, stopping at every side tunnel to feel for the two mortals. He yearned for the taste of death with an intensity no less than a ravenous wolf would crave the tender flesh of a young lamb. It had been far too long. He continued on up the lightless corridor, the only clue of his presence was the occasional flicker of unnatural red in his eyes.

Krelg and Olbreh slowly descended down the twisting tunnel, occasionally calling for Pendrule as loudly as they dared. Both feared the worst, but neither spoke it, as if avoiding it would somehow make it not so. If the deathly scream was from Pendrule, then surely he must be dead, and who or what killed him they did not look forward to finding.

The tunnel suddenly forked in front of them, with no sign of which way Pendrule had taken. Krelg knelt and examined the floor carefully, holding the torch low searching for some clue as to which way Pendrule had gone. Nothing. Krelg stood and peered down both tunnels.

"He could have gone either way. The floor is so dry and rocky, I can't make spit of it." Krelg sounded disgusted. Olbreh placed a hand on his shoulder to ease him. The situation was unsettling to say the least, but they needed to stay calm and focused.

"It's OK Krelg. Let us choose either one for a distance. If we don't see any sign of Pendrule quickly, then we'll simply try the other. He can't have gone far."

"Of course," agreed Krelg. He took one last glance down both tunnels before heading to their left, mumbling something to himself. The only words that Olbreh caught were, "Pendrule", and "sticking together."

The two hadn't gone far at all when the tunnel stretched open into a wide cavern, at least a hundred paces wide, and just as far to the back wall. They turned about slowly surveying the area, looking for any sign of Pendrule's passing.

"This place is huge," breathed Olbreh as he gazed up at the rock ceiling far overhead, huge stalactites hanging from it like giant spears.

Krelg was already making his way across the expanse, head turning from side to side, carefully surveying the area for any signs of movement, or anything else that could pose a threat.

Krelg's time at Fort Algusta had taught him much about such things. His superiors were quite proud of him, and it was even rumored that he was being seriously considered for promotion to Lieutenant. He enjoyed being a Defender of the Light, and would hopefully live out the rest of his days being just that. As far as Krelg was concerned, there was nothing more important, or rewarding, than being a servant of the Light.

As Krelg searched the darkness he softly spoke to himself, reciting the words that all Defenders of the Light held as their creed, drawing strength from them to combat the sense of evil that seemed to hang in the air like the stench of a rotting corpse. "With honor and pride I serve the Light, knowing that all my strengths and abilities have been granted me by the grace thereof. For the ways of the Light I shall gladly lay down my life, for there is no greater cause than that which I serve. The Light shall illumine and overpower the Shadow, for my life is a testament thereto. The Light shall prevail!"

Olbreh, realizing that he was being left behind, quickly scrambled to catch up with Krelg.

As they approached the far side of the cavern the silence was broken by the sound of water dripping. Krelg held the torch out to reveal a large pool of water occupying nearly thirty paces of the cavern floor. The water seemed to be undisturbed except by the occasional drop of water slipping from the stalactites overhead.

A disturbing thought suddenly came to Krelg. He had heard of places, mostly in underground caverns such as this, where it was not possible to draw upon the Mystic Forces. Krelg instantly let his senses become receptive to the Mystic Forces, the very energies of all creation, of life itself. Flows of *Air*, *Fire*, and *Spirit*, the only Mystic Forces that he was able to control, rushed through him like a hurricane. His body felt lighter than air, so in control, so powerful. Holding the Mystic Forces made him feel safe. He felt as if no one in the world could harm him at this moment. Of course drawing on the Mystic Forces did not make one all powerful, but it could sure make you feel as though you were; a false sense of security that was the undoing of many a novice Shinkai. Krelg was aware of such things, and was never one to underestimate any opponent. His ability at conjuring the Mystic Forces into Force-effects was remarkable. Many who have seen him conjuring the Mystic Forces in combat undoubtedly think him to be all-powerful, or the next thing to it.

After a moment Krelg let the Mystic Forces go. He was completely oblivious to the signal he had just sent out to the creature that was already stalking him and Olbreh. If it didn't know exactly where they were before, it did now.

"I don't think Pendrule came this way" said Olbreh.

"I think you're right. We'll try the other tunnel."

Just as they turned to head back out of the cavern Olbreh stopped suddenly and drew his sword up before him. "Something isn't right. Do you feel it?"

Before Krelg had time to reply a tall figure stepped into the cavern from the same tunnel where they had entered just minutes before. Instantly Krelg was drawing deeply upon *Fire* and *Spirit*, torch held wide in one hand and a broadsword in the other. Olbreh was gripping his sword tightly ready to do combat. The figure continued on into the room and they quickly realized it was Pendrule that approached.

Both sighed with relief and visibly relaxed, though for some reason Krelg chose to hold on to the Mystic Forces for a moment longer. "I was hoping that it was you. Where have you been, and what was that horrible scream...." Krelg's words trailed off as he stared at Pendrule's eyes. He could have sworn that- yes, there was tiny bursts of glowing red coming from his eyes. Krelg took a step back.

"What is the matter? You do not look well." The voice was cold and had a harshness to it that reminded Krelg of a file sliding across steel. Olbreh was right, something was definitely wrong.

Krelg gave Pendrule a questioning stare. "Answer me. Where have you been?" Krelg knew that something was very wrong. A sense of evil seemed to roll from Pendrule so strongly that it made Krelg's hair stand.

Olbreh stepped up to Pendrule and extended a hand toward his shoulder. "What is wrong with you Pendrule? Didn't you hear what Krelg jus-" The words caught in Olbreh's mouth as the long cruel blade of a green-steel dagger slid up under his ribs. Reflexively Olbreh grabbed at the dagger that had impaled him, his eyes were rolling back wildly and his mouth contorted in agony.

Pendrule, or more correctly the soulless creature that now inhabited his body, wrenched the dagger free. Several fingers dropped to the floor just before Olbreh collapsed to his knees. Blood now poured heavily from his mouth and made a horrible gurgling sound as he struggled to breathe. Pendrule's lips curled in an evil smile of enjoyment.

Krelg couldn't believe what he was seeing. He just stood there with a look of shock on his face. It seemed to him as if everything was moving in slow motion. What was Pendrule doing?

Krelg blinked and gained control of himself as Pendrule knocked Olbreh on to his back with a forceful kick in the face, then stepped over him, dagger twirling and dancing around his hand. Krelg met Pendrule's cold gaze hate for hate. "You're mad!"

Pendrule lunged forward at Krelg slicing at his face with the razor-edged dagger. Krelg fully expected as much and leaped backwards easily avoiding the blade. Pendrule pressed on, dagger slicing and darting, each time being met by the blade of Krelg's sword. Krelg stepped in and feigned a thrust for Pendrule's head, instead he dropped low to the ground sweeping out and forward with his left leg. Pendrule saw through the ruse, but not in time to dodge Krelg's kick. Both of Pendrule's leg were knocked out from under him, landing him hard on his back. Krelg spun on around with the momentum of the kick stopping in a low stance facing his downed adversary. Without hesitating he dropped his torch and a brilliant flash of silver blue lightning exploded from his finger tips, brightly illuminated the entire cavern.

Pendrule somehow managed to roll aside just in time to avoid the lethal blast of lightning, which slammed into the ground with a violent explosion. Bits of rock and dirt flew in all directions leaving a deep smoldering hole where Pendrule had fallen.

Pendrule used the momentum of his roll to spin himself up onto one knee, coming up facing Krelg with one hand extended in front of him. A crackling ball of white-hot fire streaked from his open palm, leaving a long tail of flame to mark its flight. Krelg dropped to the ground. The ball of

flame singed his hair as it missed the top of his head by a fingers width and slammed into the back wall of the cavern, sending a shower of sparks hissing down into the water below.

Krelg wasted no time in drawing on the Mystic Forces once again, this time he drew upon *Air*, conjuring an invisible shield of solidified air. He lunged forward into Pendrule, slamming the shield forward into his chest. A lengthy blade of green-steel sunk deep into the invisible barrier right over Krelg's heart. The force of Krelg's momentum knocked Pendrule completely off of his feet, sliding him across the hard floor on the flat of his back. Krelg looked down at the blade suspended in the air, its tip just inches from breaking through to his chest. That was close.

There was a flicker of light as the torch on the floor sputtered and ate at the last bit of its fuel. Krelg had no desire to fight Pendrule in complete darkness, no that would be more than foolish. Krelg conjured again and the room was suddenly illuminated with a bright golden glow from a sphere of pure light hovering high overhead.

By this time Pendrule had made it back onto his feet. Not breathing hard or paying any attention at all to the steady drip of blood coming from a gash in his chin, he waded forward toward Krelg. The only emotion detectable was a look of enjoyment.

Krelg released the air shield and caught the stag-handled dagger as it fell. Unlike Pendrule, he was breathing hard now, but his concentration was needle sharp. He couldn't understand why Pendrule was doing this, the man was perfectly sane less than an hour ago. Krelg eased backwards, giving ground to Pendrule. "Why are you doing this Pendrule? I am not your enemy!" No response. "Don't make me kill you!"

Pendrule laughed loudly. "You, kill me? You flatter yourself mortal." The words were so cold and deep, not at all like Krelg remembered Pendrule's voice to be, and that last thing that he said, "Mortal"? A look of enlightenment and fear flashed across Krelg's face. This was not Pendrule he was fighting. At least, not Pendrule alone.

Krelg set his feet and prepared to cut Pendrule down if he came any closer. Pendrule came on, never slowing. A raging sword of fire suddenly burst to life in one hand and then he was in melee with Krelg once more. Swords met again and again, sending sparks flying with each clash of steel against fire. Krelg fought vigorously to hold his ground. He didn't know how much longer he would be able to continue this pace. Pendrule still came in strong, not seeming to tire in the least. Both of Krelg's blades whirled and slashed, dived and thrust, but Pendrule avoided them all with unnatural speed. Krelg just stepped up his performance all the more. Finally, a break in Pendrule's defenses. Pendrule's own dagger buried deep into his side. With a twist Krelg pulled it free and leaped backwards, expecting Pendrule to fall from the obviously fatal wound.

Pendrule looked down at his side. Blood poured heavily from the wound, steam rising from it as it rushed out to meet the cold air of the cavern. Krelg nearly fell over with disbelief as Pendrule slid the blade of his flaming sword across the wound. Blood and flesh hissed loudly, bubbling under the tremendous heat of the sword. Pendrule just looked back up at Krelg and smiled. "Now that wasn't very nice." On he came.

This was too much. How was he to beat such an adversary? Krelg's mind raced for an answer and suddenly a desperate plan formed. He didn't have enough energy to keep conjuring for long, but if his plan worked he would only have to do so twice more.

Krelg turned and ran for the water, its surface shimmering with a golden reflection from the orb above. He only hoped that it was deep enough to serve his purpose. Without slowing, Krelg dived in head first and quickly began swimming for the middle of the pool. The water was very deep for at no time did Krelg touch the bottom. Perfect!

Pendrule paused for a moment at the edge of the water, tilting his head to one side, seeming confused. He seemed reluctant to enter the water.

Krelg was now in the middle of the pool, paddling to keep afloat. "Come on," he silently mouthed. Suddenly a ball of fire was flying towards him. With a gasp he plunged under the water. The ball of fire exploded into the water with tremendous force. Water and steam raged high into the air. Two more searing fireballs followed in quick succession pounding the water. Silence followed, and for more than thirty seconds nothing moved in the water, then Krelg broke the surface sucking in air with a loud gasp.

Pendrule looked disgusted. A growl rumbled through gritted teeth, and then he plunged forward, the flaming sword disappearing just before he hit the water. At the same moment that Pendrule jumped into the water, Krelg began drawing upon *Air*. He made no attempt to flee or engage, just paddled water and waited for Pendrule to get out a little farther from the bank, where the water should be well over his head. Just when Pendrule was about five feet or so from him, Krelg conjured an air bind around Pendrule's entire body. Pendrule froze in mid-stroke as if he had been turned to stone. Instantly he began to sink. Not a word or sound did he make as he disappeared under the surface of the water, nor did he break eye contact with Krelg.

Krelg shivered hard, as much from the sight of Pendrule sinking to his death as the bitter cold of the water. Without wasting another moment Krelg was swimming hard for the bank, making sure he held tight to the flow of *Air* that held the air bind around Pendrule. With no little effort he pulled himself up onto the cold, but dry floor of the cavern. He stood and stared into the water where Pendrule had sunk. Water trickled down his face, a look of steel determination beset him. He never enjoyed killing, but sometimes it was just unavoidable.

Slowly he raised an arm toward the water, pointing his fingers to the very spot where Pendrule should be resting on the bottom. Once again the cavern exploded to life with the silver blue flash of lightning. The entire pool seemed to light up as the lightning stabbed down into its depths, but Krelg could see no sign of Pendrule. The water must be incredibly deep. Krelg sighed deeply and knelt to the ground. He felt so tired. Using as much of the Mystic Forces as he had was beginning to take its toll. Using a technique that he had recently learned back at Fort Algusta, he tied off the flow of the Mystic Force that was holding the air bind around Pendrule. That would hold the bind without him having to continue conjuring, at least for a few more minutes. Krelg was quite sure that Pendrule was dead by now, but he wasn't taking any chances; not after what he witnessed just moments ago.

Krelg now got back to his feet and walked over to Olbreh who was lying flat on his back in a pool of his own blood, eyes staring blankly. Krelg ran a hand over Olbreh's face, closing his eyes for eternity. He bent low and scooped him up into his arms. He would take him back to Fort Algusta where he could be laid to rest properly.

Behind Krelg, a shadowy tendril quietly broke the surface of the water.

General Tirey sat comfortably in his high-backed chair in front of his marble-topped desk. His quarters were lavishly furnished with the finest of furniture and tapestries. He had just dipped the tip of a blue tinted quill into a bottle of ink when a young knight rapped gently at the door before stepping in, immediately saluting. General Tirey waved him to ease.

"General Tirey, sir, Knight Krelg Talvnon is here and wishes to speak with you." He paused for just a moment before continuing. "He says that he has a report on a very important mission that he must give to you in person." The Knight's facial expression made it clear that he did not think the General would recognize the name or give him the time if he did. It was not a common practice for knights to request a personal audience with the General.

General Tirey casually placed the quill into a holder inlaid with gold. "Knight Krelg, ah yes. Send him in."

The young knight seemed surprised, but did not hesitate to comply. Seconds after he marched out of the room a tattered and tired looking Krelg came walking in, stopping just short of the general's desk. General Tirey immediately noticed the failure to salute and was just about to let Krelg know of it, but something curious caught his attention. The General stared up at Krelg intently, studying the unnatural flicker in his eyes.

"What is the matter General? You do not look well."

Oryathar, a planet of mystical splendor and untold beauty has slowly begun to succumb to the evils and decay of the Shadow. Only time will determine whether the forces of the Light can rescue this dying planet from the clutches of the Shadow.

Following is a description of the various aspects and features of Oryathar that may be of interest to you. They include physical description, habitat, calendar, phenomenon, and influencing planets and stars.

PHYSICAL DESCRIPTION

Oryathar is a round planet hovering in a distant mystical universe. Unlike earth, Oryathar doesn't orbit but rather floats in a stationary position. Similar to earth, Oryathar has many individual bodies of land that are surrounded by vast bodies of water.

There is a multitude of plant life that grows on Oryathar. Some are simply mundane plants and trees while some plants are very exotic and possess mystical properties. The ruling-races have learned to grow and harvest many of the different types of plants, fruits, and vegetables that grow on Oryathar. Though not as abundant as before the pestilence of Shadow-kin, Oryathar still maintains an adequate variety of flora with which the ruling-races can sustain themselves.

Oryathar has a single golden sun that warms the planet and provides it with light. It hovers directly above the northern-most region of Oryathar. This area of Oryathar closest to the sun is extremely dry and hot with temperatures reaching as high as two hundred degrees. Because of its extremely hot nature this area of Oryathar has become known as the land of fire. The sun's rays are so intense and bright here that everything seems to be bathed in a bright golden glow. The combination of the intense light and heat make the land of fire an unsuitable environment for ruling-races. Only the creatures suited to withstand these severe conditions reside here.

In contrast to the land of fire, on the opposite side of Oryathar (southern-most region), there is a region of land known as the ice-land. Because this area of Oryathar is on the opposite side of the planet as the sun, it gets virtually no sunlight. For this reason it is almost completely dark in this region as well as bitterly cold. Temperatures frequently reside and often fall below negative one hundred degrees. Extremely few ruling-races can tolerate the harsh conditions of the ice-land and subsequently it is a barren and frozen wasteland. Only strange creatures suited for the cold dark climate reside there.

All regions of Oryathar with the exception of the land of fire and ice-land experience varied weather conditions throughout the year. Hail storms, heavy rains, storms producing high winds and lightning, droughts, and snow storms are just a few of the common weather anomalies that can be experienced on Oryathar.

AREAS OF INTEREST

There are many areas of interest on the planet of Oryathar. It would be impossible to list and describe them all within this book, however all of the major areas of interest that lie within a region of land known as the Ellabrian Realms will be described in detail in this Section. Most all of the initial adventuring and exploring that characters will do, at least in the beginning, will be within the Ellabrian Realms.

ELLABRIAN REALMS

The Ellabrian Realms was given its name in 216 BA by King Wasbry Holpras who was the king of this region at this time. His wife whom he loved dearly took ill and died only two years after he assumed the throne. Her name was Ellabria, and so in her memory he named the entire region of land under his reign the Ellabrian Realms. The name has remained unchanged unto this day.

The boundaries of the Ellabrian Realms extend from a point 255 miles west of the south-western edge of the Skarz Forest in the Volthic Sea eastward for 520 miles, and then extends due north for 398 miles before turning west where it extends for 520 miles and then turns south where it extends for another 398 miles and connects with the starting point in the Volthic Sea. The Ellabrian Realms take in approximately 200,000 square miles of land. It would take roughly eleven days of travel on horseback to travel from the western border of the Ellabrian Realms to the eastern border and approximately nine days to travel from the southern border to the northern border, assuming that a minimum of ten hours a day was spent traveling. (A complete map of the Ellabrian Realms can be found in the back of this book.)

The Ellabrian Realms are now under the reign of King Dalksten Lorsprit, an elderly Loremek. King Lorsprit assumed the throne in 580 AA and has won the hearts of all who dwell in his kingdom. King Lorsprit has done much to support all those in his kingdom and without his support the fort cities of the Defenders of the Light would not be in operation. King Lorsprit has generously funded and supported the rebuilding and operation of all of the old Defender of the Light fort cities as well as helping in the construction of new ones. He has great respect for Shinkai and believes that without them the fight against the Shadow is certain to be doomed. King Lorsprit, as well as many of his own personal military, known as the King's Guard, are Shinkai. Like the Defenders of the Light, the King's Guard are well trained soldiers who eagerly take up the fight against the Shadow and any who would oppose the Light.

Every major city and town in the Ellabrian Realms has posts where units of King's Guards reside, protecting and giving aid to the citizens. The King's Guard are renowned throughout the land for their persistence and precision in combat. They are truly an elite and formidable army only equaled by the Defenders of the Light. In many ways the King's Guard and the Defenders of the Light are much the

same. The major difference is that the Defenders of the Light are more specialized in the training and recruiting of Shinkai.

Black Mountains

The Black Mountains are located in the south-western region of the Ellabrian Realms approximately forty miles off the coast of the Volthic Sea. The Black Mountains are so named due to the fact that a large percentage of its ominous rock formations and cliffs are very dark in color. They are the third largest mountain range in the Ellabrian Realms.

These mountains are home to a diversity of plants and trees as well as a host of natural creatures. Though there are some Shadow-kin that reside in these mountains the number of Shadow-kin are much lower within the Black Mountains than they are in other mountain ranges throughout the Ellabrian Realms. Many believe that this is because of the proximity of the mountains to Fort Kengra and Helmsrink. Regardless of the reason, and despite their foreboding appearance, the Black Mountains are by far the safest of the four mountain ranges within the Ellabrian Realms. For this reason the Black Mountains are home to numerous small villages, most of which make their living by trapping and hunting.

Bone Island

This small island is located in the Volthic Sea approximately forty miles west of the Westpoint Peninsula. It is approximately fourteen miles wide and fourteen miles long. The island gets its name because of the large number of deaths that occurred there in the year 303 AA. During this time the island was heavily populated with many villages and towns. The civilization of the island was flourishing and its appearance was that of a pristine and thriving land. A host of fishing boats owned by the locals brought much prosperity to the island through supplying the inland trade centers with silver fish, a very common and popular type of fish found in abundance near the island.

A terrifying phenomenon that would forever change the livelihood of the island occurred during the first grey season of the year 303 AA. Every single inhabitant of the island, ruling-race and creature alike, dropped dead within a matter of minutes. For two days anyone or thing that set foot on the island fell dead within moments. The only explanation that could be supplied was that the entire island must have experienced a Force drain of the Mystic Force of *Spirit*.

For several years no one dared to set foot on the island for fear of dying. The dead simply decayed where they fell. The massive number of skeletons scattered across the island gave rise to its current name, Bone Island.

Though there are a few small villages on Bone Island today, the current population is only a fraction of what it once was. The island has very little vegetation and the main source of food and commerce for the inhabitants of the island remains silver fish. Though trade ships still make routine trips to and from Bone Island many hold to the belief that the island is cursed. The mere mention of the island still conjures up thoughts of death and fear to this day.

Grey-ridge Mountains

The Grey-ridge Mountains are the overall smallest of the four mountain ranges in the Ellabrian Realms but has the highest peaks of all of the mountains. Some of the peaks in the Grey-ridge Mountains reach towering heights of fifteen miles.

The Grey-ridge Mountains are located in the far south-eastern border of the Ellabrian realms. There are no villages, towns, cities, or other types of civilizations within several days ride of the mountains. This is largely due to the fact that the Grey-ridge Mountains are home to more Shadow-kin than any other mountain range in the Ellabrian Realms. Virtually every type of Shadow-kin known can be found in and around the Grey-ridge Mountains. It's not very common for ruling-races will travel into these treacherous mountains, but on rare occasions they do.

The Grey-ridge Mountains are known to be a very rich source for a mineral known as summit emerald. Summit emerald is a rare and valuable mineral used in alchemy. Many are willing to pay high prices for this mineral and for this reason some ruling-races are willing to risk their lives to collect it.

Grosh Swamp

The Grosh Swamp is a dark and murky swampland, home to a myriad of Shadow-kin and other foul creatures. It is located in the southern-most region of the Ellabrian Realms on the western border of the Skarz Forest.

The Grosh Swamp covers an area of approximately nine hundred square miles, most of which is filled with stagnant mosquito-infested water and a numerous amount of quick-sand pits. Black and twisted trees and vines stretch up out of the tainted waters, moss and mold clinging to their cold surfaces. Travelers who haplessly wander into its filth-ridden bogs rarely make it back out.

Kreggin Desert

The Kreggin Desert is a large area of dry and barren land located just to the west of the Lava Mountains. The Kreggin Desert occupies approximately 8,100 square miles of territory. Very little plant-life grows in the Kreggin because of the extremely dry climate and the fact that the ground in the desert consists mostly of sand or hard baked dirt, neither of which is very productive for plant growth.

Because of the inability to grow crops there, the Kreggin Desert has only a few scattered villages and towns inhabiting it. Another reason for the small population of the Kreggin Desert is that the ground there is ideal for the lairs of a type of deadly Shadow-kin known as the rasp-worm. Large numbers of these Shadow-kin live in and travel through the Kreggin Desert in search of any wandering beings that they can make into their lunch.

Because this area of the Ellabrian Realms is so dry and humid, water requirements for ruling-races traveling or residing in the Kreggin Desert is double that of the normal requirement. It is very easy to become dehydrated in this region. Also, because the terrain of the Kreggin Desert is very flat and has virtually no trees or other notable landmarks it is extremely easy to get lost there. Travelers in this area should make preparations and take special precautions in order to overcome its many dangers.

Kreymid Forest

The Kreymid Forest is located in the north-western region of the Ellabrian Realms between the Lava Mountains and the Volthic Sea. This massive forest covers an area of approximately 2,500 square miles. The Zurrod River which flows out of the Lava Mountains winds it way through the western-most part of the Kreymid Forest supplying the inhabitants of the forest with an abundant source of fresh water.

The Kreymid Forest has the most abundant supply of natural creatures of any forest in the Ellabrian Realms. Like all areas of Oryathar it also has its share of the filthy creatures that plague the land, but overall it is a peaceful and thriving forest.

There are many small villages in and around the Kreymid Forest. The abundant resources of the forest have made trapping a common occupation in the area. A large quantity of the furs and food that supplies much of the Ellabrian Realms comes from the Kreymid Forest, and also the Windy Forest to the far south.

Larrow's Hills

This massive expanse of hills is located on the eastern region of the Ellabrian Realms just south of the Rocklid Mountains. Though not nearly as tall or large as the mountain ranges found in the Ellabrian Realms Larrow's Hills are fairly impressive in height.

The hills were named after a Valkin who discovered that there were several deep and extensive caves within the hills. Some of these caves are merely cubby holes in the hillsides but others extend for miles beneath the hills and surrounding lands. Many of these caves contain vast amount of green-steel which has proven to be a very reliable source of wealth for the Ellabrian Realms. Unfortunately the caves are also ideal lairs for many types of Shadow-kin. Many ruling-races have lost their lives in the caves of Larrow's Hills, but the allure of the green-steel to be harvested keeps a constant supply of willing ruling-races frequenting its perilous caverns.

Lava Mountains

The Lava Mountains, located in the north-western region of the Ellabrian Realms, is considered by many to be the most dangerous mountain range in the realms. The Lava Mountains are home to countless active volcanoes and lava pools and streams. There is one pool of churning lava so large that it has been named the Lake of Fire. It is approximately 22 miles in diameter.

The activity of the volcanoes causes constant rockslides and landquakes not to mention the deadly lava, ash, and hot rocks that the volcanoes send spraying into the air. These mountains are also home to a host of Shadow-kin and aggressive mystical creatures as well. For these reasons very few ruling-races dare to venture into the Lava Mountains.

Rocklid Mountains

The Rocklid Mountains are the largest mountain range in the Ellabrian Realms. They cover a staggering 3,550 square miles. The Rocklid Mountains are located in the north-eastern region of the Ellabrian Realms just north of Larrow's Hills. The Rocklid Mountains have an abundant diversity of plant and animal life.

The Rocklid Mountains are home to numerous Warlum villages. These Warlum live high in the mountain's peaks and rarely come down into the flat-lands. They live off of the land, gathering fruits and nuts and hunting the many species of natural creatures that live in the mountains.

Skarz Forest

The Skarz Forest is located in the far southern regions of the Ellabrian Realms just east of the Grosh Swamp. It is the largest forest in the Ellabrian Realms and has also earned the reputation of being the most dangerous forest in the Ellabrian Realms.

The Skarz Forest is home to more Shadow-kin than any other one area in the region. There are many river boats that

travel the Valenth River, which runs through the western edge of the Skarz Forest, but none of these boats pass through the forest except for on the rarest of occasions.

The Shadow-kin that inhabit the Skarz Forest seem to be exceptionally aggressive in comparison to Shadow-kin in other areas. The exact reason for this behavior is unknown, but all who have traveled through the Skarz Forest report that the forest itself seems to resonate with an evil presence. It is the belief of many that the forest has been cursed by the Shadow.

Syldryn Lake

Syldryn Lake, located just north-east of the Black Mountains,s is the only lake in the Ellabrian Realms. It is approximately 15 miles long and 12 miles wide. The Dark River flows into Syldryn Lake giving it a constant supply of fresh water. The lake is a gathering place for local fisherman and is also commonly used for leisurely swimming. It also serves as the water reserve for the Ellabrian Realms during the occasional droughts of the Light season. During the Shadow season it is not uncommon for the lake to freeze over solid. This is a welcomed event for the local children who enjoy skating and playing on the ice.

Volthic Sea

The Volthic Sea is a massive body of salt water that encloses the entire continent on which the Ellabrian Realms are located. Large ships carrying precious cargo travel the Volthic Sea making their way around the continent and even from one continent to another. Large fishing vessels traveling the Volthic Sea import a large percentage of the food supply to the Ellabrian Realms.

Although the sea is a valuable resource it can also prove deadly. Occasionally powerful hurricanes will roll in from the Volthic Sea bringing devastating winds, heavy rains, and massive tidal waves. Ships and boats sailing the sea also occasionally fall victim to whirlpools or pirates. But beyond the danger and destruction that the Volthic Sea brings, the life-giving resources that it provides make it an extremely valuable asset to the Ellabrian Realms, and all other realms as well.

Windy Forest

The Windy Forest is located in the south-western region of the Ellabrian Realms just south of the Black Mountains. It is the second largest forest in the realms. The forest gets its name because of the frequent winds blowing through it from the nearby coast.

Many small villages and towns border the Windy Forest and several villages are located deep within the forest itself. The Windy Forest isn't known to have a large quantity of Shadow-kin residing within it, but like any place on Oryathar there is always those that wander through or take up temporary residence.

The Windy Forest is an exceptionally dense forest and has an abundance of plant and animal life. Timber harvested from this forest is used to make most all of the ships and docks along the neighboring coast.

INFLUENCING PLANETS AND STARS

As mentioned previously, Oryathar has a single golden sun. This sun resides far above Oryathar and like the Oryathar itself, it simply floats in a stationary position. The intensity of the sun changes from hour to hour throughout the day. At approximately half way through the seventh hour the sun reaches its brightest and hottest state. At approximately half way through the nineteenth hour it reaches its weakest and coldest state, actually becoming black and giving off no light at all. Through the sun's consistent increasing and decreasing intensity day and night for Oryathar is formed.

At the twenty-fifth hour the sun's intensity has built up enough for very small amounts of light to reach Oryathar (this is dawn). The sun continues to grow in intensity and brightness until it reaches its peak at the seventh and a half hour. Its intensity then begins to fade. At the fifteenth hour its brightness has all but faded only giving off a very small amount of light and energy (this is dusk). By the sixteenth hour it has lost enough intensity that it no longer provides any visible light for Oryathar. It continues to lose strength until the nineteenth and a half hour at which time it begins to slowly regain strength and increase in intensity. It takes the sun exactly twenty-five hours to make one complete cycle.

Beings, plants, and all life forms that follow or are creations of the Light draw strength from the sun's energy, while creatures and beings of the Shadow draw strength and comfort from the night.

The vast skies of Oryathar are filled with countless stars. Some are bright white in color while others are blue and some are even red. There is one exceptionally large red star that can be seen in Oryathar's sky. It is so bright and radiant that it can be seen even on cloudy nights and can often be spotted during the day. It was traditionally called Sky-fire because of its fiery glow radiating into the sky, but today it is referred to as the Dream Star.

It has become common knowledge that gazing up at this star for long periods of time can induce vivid dreams to ruling-races that go to sleep shortly after observing the star. The dreams are often very pleasant and euphoric but are occasionally very nightmarish. (Characters that gaze at the Dream Star for twenty minutes or longer have a fifty percent chance of having a very vivid dream if sleep occurs shortly after viewing the star. If the percentile dice result is 20 or under the dream is very frightening and disturbing, but if the result is 21 to 50 the dream is extremely pleasant. It is the GM's choice as to the details of these dreams.)

Many ruling-races believe that the Dream Star is actually a planet from which mystical creatures travel to Oryathar.

Some creatures thought to be from the Dream Star are unicorns, white-wolves, and shawlesh. Though this theory can neither be proved nor disproved, it is an idea that is still very popular among the ruling-races today.

Seen only in the gray seasons is the solitary dark moon of Oryathar. Its color is a deep gray to almost black and its shape is round. This moon is seen high in the sky and always to the west of the sun. Like Oryathar and its

sun, the moon does not orbit but rather maintains a stationary position in the sky. It does not produce its own light as do the sun and the stars, but is only visible due to the illuminating rays of the sun.

Very similar to earth's moon Oryathar's moon goes through different phases. Sometimes the entire round moon can be seen and at other times only portions can be seen. Unlike earth's moon, however, Oryathar's moon does not cycle through its phases in any kind of predictable pattern. Instead it just randomly shifts through its different phases. It may be completely visualized one night and then only have a quarter or less visible the next night. The changes in the moon's appearance are believed to be due to the dark cloud-like gasses moving over the moon's surface. When enough of these clouds gather in one place over the moon's surface they completely absorb the sun's light and block them from illuminating that area of the moon.

HABITAT

Oryathar has an abundant number of creatures ranging from mundane animals to rare mystical beings. Many scribes and researchers have gone to great lengths to research and record information on a great number of Oryathar's inhabitants. In the larger cities and towns of Oryathar such scrolls and books can often be found, but are very scarce in the smaller towns and villages. Such information is invaluable to those who seek to adventure into the untamed regions of Oryathar. The King's Guard as well as the Defenders of the Light make it a point to have information regarding the various creatures of Oryathar readily available to their members.

All creatures of Oryathar can be divided up into three major categories; natural creatures, mystical creatures, and Shadow-kin.

Natural Creatures

The Shadow-kin that inhabit Oryathar are not the only creatures that are a threat to the ruling-races. Though many of the creatures that inhabit Oryathar are quite harmless others are extremely dangerous. There are many natural creatures that are deadly predators and though they may not intentionally seek out a ruling-race, some of these creatures will not hesitate to attack ruling-races if their territory is invaded or if they feel threatened.

A large number of the natural creatures of Oryathar are hunted and killed by the ruling-races as a food source as well as for clothing. Bear, rabbit, and deer are just a few examples of the types of creatures that are hunted by the ruling-races.

Some breeds of natural creatures have been domesticated by the ruling-races to be used for transportation, work animals, and even pets. Some such creatures include horses, bleyk, and dogs.

Mystical Creatures

There are a great many creatures of Oryathar that are not considered Shadow-kin or natural creatures. These are the mystical creatures. They possess mystical abilities that are not found among the natural creatures of Oryathar. The rarest and most revered of such creatures is the dragon. Known for its incredible size, strength, and ability to conjure, the dragon has been named the most powerful creature on Oryathar. Other examples of Oryathar's mystical creatures are the unicorn, fire bat, crystal serpent, and lava lizard just to name a few.

Though many Shadow-kin possess mystical abilities they differ from true mystical creatures in that they are still constructs of the Shadow and remain evil through and through. True mystical creatures are not inherently evil, though they can prove to be just as dangerous if threatened or provoked.

The ruling-races believe the mystical creatures of Oryathar

to be protected by the Light. For this reason mystical creatures are never hunted or attacked without just cause, at least not by those who follow the Light.

Shadow-kin

These are the evil and bloodthirsty creatures created by the Shadow. They exist only to kill and destroy. There are a multitude of different breeds and types of Shadow-kin, each type unique and possessing their own particular abilities and skills. Some Shadow-kin are very difficult to distinguish from natural creatures while others possess obvious mystical properties and abilities that quickly distinguish them as the Shadow-spawned creatures that they are. One common link between all Shadow-kin, however, is their lust for killing. Some Shadow-kin devour their prey and others kill and leave their victims lying. Regardless of killing style or motives all Shadow-kin have an inherent passion for killing.

As might be expected Shadow-kin have no sense of loyalty, even to their own kind. It is not unusual for Shadow-kin to attack and kill one another for no obvious reason.

As a matter of integrity and respect for the Light Shadow-kin are never eaten or used as a source of clothing, at least not by any respectable person.

CALENDAR

The time period of Oryatharian days, weeks, months, and years is different than that of earth's. Here is a quick breakdown of Oryatharian time and the Oryatharian calendar. There are sixty seconds in a minute, sixty minutes in an hour, twenty five hours in a day, twenty five days in a block, and sixteen blocks (400 days) in a year (blocks are the equivalent of months). The first day of the Light season is the first day of each new year.

There are four seasons in a single Oryatharian year. They are the Light season, first gray, Shadow season, and second gray. The Light season is earth's equivalent of summer, first gray is similar to fall, the Shadow season is similar to winter, and second gray is similar to spring. The Light and Shadow seasons are known as the extreme seasons and the first and second gray seasons are known as the neutral seasons. There are two blocks in the Light season and Shadow season and six blocks in the first and second gray seasons.

During the Light season temperatures are higher than normal and a general mood of goodness and well-being seems to be in the air. Storms are less frequent and Shadow-kin activity slows. Many mystical creatures as well as ruling-races seem to be noticeably stronger and healthier during the Light season, and Shinkai that are obedient to the Light become more proficient in handling the Mystic Forces during this time of year while those who are Shadow-sworn seem to become less proficient.

During the gray seasons the temperature and weather is generally mild. Storms and high winds occasionally blow across the lands, but with no real intensity. As might be expected with a name like the neutral seasons, the general mood of creatures and ruling-races remain unaffected during these seasons and maintain a normal disposition. Neither the Shadow nor Light seems to have the upper hand during these times of the year.

During the Shadow season temperatures plummet to bitter levels and icy winds persistently whip across the land. Storms of freezing rain, hail, and extremely high winds are common place. A mood of dread, depression, and paranoia hangs thick in the air throughout this season. In contrast to the Light season many mystical creatures as well as ruling-races seem to be noticeably weaker during the Shadow season. The Shadow-kin and followers of the Shadow, however, seem to become stronger and more confident during this time of year. Shinkai that are obedient to the Light become less proficient in handling the Mystic Forces during this time of year while those who are Shadow-sworn seem to become more proficient.

The different seasons of Oryathar are believed to be brought about due to the direct influence of the Light and the Shadow, though the exact nature and mechanics of this influence remains a mystery.

MYSTICAL PHENOMENON

Oryathar is a mystical planet that is full of magical energies and mystical phenomenon. The following will describe some of the more intriguing and significant of these phenomenon. Included are descriptions of the various mystical realms, Force surges and Force drains, Light and Shadow entities, gray death, natural enchantments, and black voids.

The GM can use these phenomenon to spice up his or her adventures and add exciting elements to their campaign.

Mystical Realms

Beyond the physical realm of existence there are six other mystical realms of existence. None of these mystical realms can support ruling-race life for more than a few short moments. Four of the five Mystic Forces have their own mystical realm where their energies are extremely intense and all elements of existence there are made up exclusively of that particular Mystic Force. Other than the mystical realms of *Air*, *Fire*, *Land*, and *Water* there are two more mystical realms; the Light and Shadow realm.

The mystical realms can only be reached by mystical means. It is not possible to physically locate or travel to a mystical realm without the aid of magic. Their true location is completely unknown to the ruling-races. Access to the mystical realms is achieved through portals that Shinkai are capable of creating through the use of runes. Once opened these portals allow access to and from Oryathar to the mystical realms.

Conjuring inside of the mystical realms is extremely dan-

gerous. Conjuring inside of a mystical realm is the equivalent of conjuring in an area undergoing a Force surge of that particular Mystic Force (automatic over-expenditure of Force energy by 3D20 points and Force burn. May also cause boosted effects of the Force-effect at the GM's discretion).

Only the Mystic Force that a particular mystical realm consists of can be conjured when inside of it. So, if your character were inside of the *Air* realm he could only conjure *Air*. If he were inside of the *Land* realm he could only conjure *Land*, etc.

Each of the mystical realms, with the exception of the Light and Shadow realm, have a myriad of mystical creatures that inhabit them. Some of these mystical creatures can be summoned and controlled by Shinkai. For a detailed description of some of these mystical creatures see the "CREATURE LORE" Section.

Each of the six mystical realms are described below.

Air

There are no solid objects within this mystical realm. It is composed completely of swirling currents of white mystical *Air*. The temperature of the *Air* realm is extremely cool. Occasional bursts of gale-force winds rip through this realm which are two to three times stronger than the strongest winds ever seen on Oryathar.

Oryatharian beings, that can not fly, that enter the *Air* realm drift about aimlessly without any control of their movement. The air of this realm is not the same as that of Oryathar and is not healthy for Oryatharian beings. Oryatharian beings that breath this air for more than 10 Turns will begin to suffocate, taking 1D20 points of damage per Turn as the mystical air begins disintegrating their lungs. If an Oryatharian being is within the *Air* realm during one of its notorious gale-force winds they will be violently slung across the realm for hundreds of miles and most likely be lost forever in the vastness of the realm.

Fire

This realm consists of nothing but mystical *Fire* and lakes and rivers of mystical lava floating within the flames. The temperature of the *Fire* realm is extremely hot, much hotter than the core of an Oryatharian volcano.

If an Oryatharian being was to enter the *Fire* realm they would be incinerated into ashes in a matter of seconds.

Land

Perhaps the most hospitable of the mystical realms, the *Land* realm consists of infinite brown mountain ranges, coarse brown soil, and rock-like formations of various shapes and sizes. The temperature of the *Land* realm is moderate and the air within this realm is very stale and damp.

Oryatharian beings can survive for as long as two to three days within the *Land* realm. Oryatharian beings experience extreme fatigue and loss of energy while within this realm. It is believed that the landscape itself drains the Life Force from Oryatharian beings. Remaining within the *Land* realm for more than a few hours will result in 1D10 points of damage per hour and 1 point of fatigue every five hours.

Water

There are no solid objects within this mystical realm. It is composed completely of blue mystical *Water*. The mystical waters of this realm are full of swirling vortex-like whirlpools. The water itself is very cold in most spots but there are a few limited areas where the water is warm.

Oryatharian beings entering the *Water* realm have no choice but to hold their breath for there is no sky or air there, only water. Beings caught in one of the *Water* realm's whirlpools will suffer 3D20 + 20 points of damage per Turn and must make a swimming Test against a Difficulty Value of 40 in order to swim out of the vortex.

Using the Force-effect "Water Breathing" is not advisable in the *Water* realm. The mystical waters of the *Water* realm are too pure and strong in their natural state to be introduced into Oryatharian being's bodies, whether by drinking *or* breathing it. Breathing this water by means of "Water Breathing" or drinking it will yield 2D20 + 20 points of damage.

Light

This realm is not accessible to the living. It is the dwelling place for the essences of those who followed and pleased the Light during their life. Some ruling-races who have died and then been ressurected claim to have glimpsed this realm and describe it as a wondrously beautiful land full of rich golden light and warmth with a gentle breeze that caresses the soul into euphoric bliss. All of the senses seem to be infinitely heightened. Colors are more vibrant, sounds are richer, and the countless beautiful flowers and plants give off the richest and most pleasant- smelling aromas imaginable.

In summation, the Light realm is a place of indescribable and eternal bliss, reserved for those who lived their lives in obedience to the Light. In this realm they enjoy the freedom and eternal bliss that only the Light can provide.

Shadow

The Shadow realm, like the Light realm, is not accessible to the living, but the similarities end there. It is the dwelling place for the essences of those who followed and pleased the Shadow during their life. Some ruling-races who have died and then been ressurected also claim to have glimpsed this realm, and describe it as a place of indescribable evils and terror. A sunless sky of morbid darkness envelops the land with a sense of despair and misery. The air is filled with the anguish-filled cries of the tortured souls who are imprisoned there.

In summation, the Shadow realm is a place of indescrib-

able horrors, reserved for those who lived their lives in service to the Shadow. In this realm they suffer the eternal agony and consequences of forsaking the Light, the evil and tormentive despair of the Shadow is their only companion.

Force Surges and Force Drains

The five Mystic Forces, *Air*, *Fire*, *Land*, *Spirit*, and *Water*, are invisible mystical energies that swirl and intertwine with every inch of Oryathar and the surrounding universe. These Mystic Forces flow and intertwine with one another as they move about in an endless and seemingly random pattern. Occasionally one or more of the Mystic Forces will pool up and become more condensed in a certain area. If enough of a particular Mystic Force and its inherent energies gather in a particular area it creates what is known as a Force surge. There is also times when one or more of the Mystic Forces shift away and become absent from a certain area. When there is a total absence of one or more of the Mystic Forces within a given area it creates what is known as a **Force drain**. Each of these two types of phenomenon can create drastic and often deadly consequences for the inhabitants of Oryathar.

Though a Force surge or drain can possibly consist of all five Mystic Forces it is extremely rare for a Force surge or drain to involve more than two of the Mystic Forces.

Force surges tend to produce more extreme results than Force drains, but this is not always so. The exact result of a Force surge depends upon which of the Mystic Forces are involved. Following is a list of the different Mystic Forces and the common effects produced by them if they are the cause of a Force surge.

Air; produces extremely strong winds and even tornadoes, and causes extreme drop in temperature.

Fire; produces extreme increases in temperatures, and may cause small streams, ponds, and rivers to rapidly dry up (drought).

Land; produces landslides and landquakes, and may cause small plants and vines to slither and move as if alive.

Spirit; produces irrational fear and panic among animals as well as ruling-races. Causes plants, weeds, and trees to grow wildly and rapidly. And undoubtedly the most disturbing effect of a Force surge of *Spirit* is the spontaneous resurrection of animals and ruling-races. Such resurrected beings no longer retain the intellect or emotions of their previous lives but are simply wandering, mindless zombies. They will return to their previous state of death once the surge ceases or if they wander or are removed from the surging area.

Water; produces mass flooding, mudslides, hail, and extremely heavy rains.

Aside from the possibilities already given for Force surges there are countless possibilities of effects when Force surges contain combinations of Mystic Forces. Force surges can also produce the same effects as some Force-effects.

To determine what possible Force-effect equivalent that a Force surge could produce just look at the Mystic Forces contained within certain Force-effects. If a Force surge contains the same combination of Mystic Forces that a particular Force-effect does, then it is possible that it could randomly produce that Force-effect.

For example, the Force-effect "Lightning" contains the Mystic Forces of *Fire* and *Spirit*. A Force surge consisting of *Fire* and *Spirit* may create frequent lightning. The Force-effect "Freeze (Inanimate)" contains the Mystic Forces of *Air* and *Water*, so an area undergoing a Force surge consisting of *Air* and *Water* may freeze up.

Force drains and Force surges can often produce the same effects, but there are many effects caused by Force drains that are not produced by Force surges. The exact result of a Force drain depends upon which of the Mystic Forces are involved. Following is a list of the different Mystic Forces and the common effects produced by them if they are the cause of a Force drain.

Air; causes animals and ruling-races to smother.

Fire; produces extreme drops in temperature.

Land; causes animals and ruling-races to experience unexplained weakness and loss in stamina.

Spirit; causes sudden unexplained deaths to plants, crops, animals, and ruling-races.

Water; produces droughts, and may cause small streams, ponds, and rivers to rapidly dry up.

The range that a Force surge or drain can cover can be as small as several hundred feet in diameter or as much as a hundred square miles. Most Force surges and drains only last for one to five days, though in rare instances they have been known to last as long as two weeks.

Light and Shadow Entities

Light and Shadow entities are an extremely rare phenomenon. They appear as floating globules of pulsing energy. The Light entities are bright golden light while the Shadow entities are a deep black absence of light. These entities pulse and shift in shape and size as they float silently through the air. They can pass through inanimate objects and materials completely unhindered and without harming the objects or materials themselves. Light and Shadow entities can be as small as one foot in diameter and as large as five feet in diameter.

Both the Light and Shadow entities are believed to be deposited energies from the Light and Shadow themselves. The creation of such entities has never been witnessed. The longest that either a Light or Shadow entity has ever been observed is for three days, after which time they simply vanish. Neither Light nor Shadow entities can be controlled, moved, or influenced in any known manner other than touching and absorbing them. Their movement is unpredictable and appears to be completely random.

Both types of entities have extremely powerful effects on living beings that come in contact with them. This applies to all creatures as well as ruling-races. Light entities generate a sense of goodness and warmth to all living beings within one hundred feet of them while Shadow entities generate a sense of evil and coldness to all beings within one hundred feet of them.

If a Light entity comes in direct contact with any living being it will immediately absorb into their body. The being is immediately overwhelmed with a sense of goodness, honesty, and morality. Their attitude toward the Light becomes significantly stronger and more positive than before, and their general compassion for others greatly increases. Their understanding of the ways of the Light increases significantly as well.

If a character comes in direct contact with a Light entity the GM should immediately award them with 2D20 + 5 Light Points and 2D20 + 5 points of Force Knowledge in each of the five Mystic Forces (Shadow-sworn and Korgathool receive similar bonuses when they come in contact with Shadow entities).

The touch of a Light entity can make even the most cold-hearted Shadow-sworn turn to the Light. Unfortunately it can not turn Shadow-kin from their evil ways, but it does have a severe effect on them. If a Shadow-kin comes in direct contact with a Light entity it will suffer 3D100 + 50 points of damage.

If a Shadow entity comes in direct contact with any living being it will immediately absorb into their body. The being is immediately overwhelmed with a sense of evil, distrust, and resentment for all life. Their attitude toward the Shadow becomes significantly stronger and more receptive than before, and their general compassion for others decreases drastically. Their understanding of the ways of the Shadow significantly increases as well.

If a character comes in direct contact with a Shadow entity the GM should immediately award them with 2D20 + 5 Shadow Points. This is more than enough to turn even the purest followers of the Light into Shadow-sworn.

Gray Death

Gray death is the single most destructive force on Oryathar. It is an extremely rare phenomenon that is the result of a Light entity and Shadow entity colliding with one another. When this happens the two entities merge and become one. This uniting of Light and Shadow creates an unstable creation of energy known as gray death.

After the creation of gray death the new entity rapidly grows into a destructive tornado-like vortex of energy that destroys anything and everything that it comes in contact with. Extremely high winds and a high pitched screams accompany this entity as it spins out its rage.

Gray death may become as large as two hundred feet tall and fifty feet in diameter. Just as the creating entities, gray death moves in a random pattern, but unlike Light and Shadow entities it does not pass through inanimate materials without harming them; it totally destroys them.

There have only been three documented cases of gray death on Oryathar. In all three cases there was absolutely nothing that could be done to stop them or change their course. They must simply run their course, which in all three documented cases took from ten to twenty five hours.

There is a story documented along with the accounts of one of the gray death sightings that indicates that the gray death was moving into the territory of a pair of dragons. These dragons summoned three more of their kind to do battle with the gray death to prevent it from destroying their home territory. The battle lasted only moments, during the course of which three of the dragons were torn to shreds by the gray death's destructive force and the other two were cast aside like dolls, critically injured. The gray death moved through unhindered and dissipated a few hours later.

Natural Enchantments

It is a well-known fact that some Shinkai have the ability

to create magical items or enchantments. They are able to do this through manipulating the Mystic Forces and infusing them into objects. What many people don't know, however, is that Shinkai are not responsible for the creation of *all* enchantments. There are particular types of enchantments known as natural enchantments.

Natural enchantments are items or materials that become enchanted without the aid or interference of Shinkai. The usual cause for the creation of natural enchantments is Force surges and Force drains. A natural enchantment could be anything from a small pebble or farm tool to a house or even a mountain side. Any inanimate object within the area of a Force surge or drain could possible become enchanted, the properties of which may vary widely.

Force surges and drains are not the only causes of natural enchantments. Some natural enchantments have sprung up in areas where no Force surges or drains have ever been documented. The creation of these unexplained natural enchantments is contributed to the mysterious workings of the Light and Shadow themselves.

Unlike the enchantments created by Shinkai, natural enchantments often serve no useful purpose and are generally unpredictable in how and when they work. Some natural enchantments have extremely powerful effects while others may do little to nothing. Many natural enchantments and their effects are permanent but there have been several cases where the natural enchantments only lasted for short periods of time before totally disappearing.

Some examples of what a natural enchantment may be could be a cave opening that causes anything that passes through it to freeze, or a stone that vibrates and moves on its own, or a section of ground that always glows with a warm orange light.

There are many areas and objects throughout Oryathar that have become natural enchantments. The exact effects and properties of any natural enchantment is totally up to the GM. So, if you are a GM feel free to make up as many natural enchantments as you like, giving them whatever effects and properties that you feel will work well with the particular campaign or adventure that you are running.

The cause for a natural enchantment being created and its effects can be virtually anything that the GM wishes. This element of flexibility allows for a great deal of creative freedom for the GM and the adventures that he might write or run. Have fun creating your own unique natural enchantments to challenge and intrigue your players.

Black Voids

Black voids are an extremely dangerous phenomenon that, thankfully to the Light, is a very rare occurrence on Oryathar. Black voids get their name due to the fact that they appear to be solid black areas of nothingness. They are round in shape and appear to be very thin disk-like voids of infinite blackness. They can be found on the ground, floating in mid-air, or on the face of a rock cliff, or virtually anywhere at all.

Anything that is placed into a black void is lost forever. It simply vanishes and ceases to exist, as if it had never been there. If your character were to stick his arm into a black void up to his elbow he would feel no pain or sensations at all, but when he pulled his arm back he would pull back a stub. His arm would be gone from the elbow down. It will be as if he were born without that area of his arm, and it can not be regenerated. No blood or scars, just a flat smooth stub. Placing objects partially into a black void results in the same effect. They are cleanly severed at the point where they make contact with the void. Any part that was placed inside the black void is simply gone.

Most black voids range in size from about three to eight feet in diameter. Once manifested they will remain for up to five days before disappearing.

No one knows for certain what causes black voids to be created. One theory is that they are caused by a Force surge of *Air*, *Land*, and *Spirit*. This theory has not yet been proven, however, there has been more than one account of black voids being found in areas that had recently experienced a Force surge of *Air*, *Land*, and *Spirit*. Another theory is that they are simply the work of the Shadow. Some ruling-races believe that if a living being falls or is thrown into a black void that there soul is trapped in the Shadow realm to suffer for eternity.

Whatever the cause of black voids they are extremely dangerous. Whenever a black void is located the King's Guard and the Defenders of the Light are always quick to secure and guard the area around it to prevent anyone or thing from falling or walking into it.

CREATING A CHARACTER

Before your character can begin exploring the world of Oryathar and set forth on his many legendary quests for adventure, you must first create a character with which to do so. This Section will take you step by step through the process of creating a character.

Though each step of creating a character will be explained, much of the terminology and details of the different aspects of a character is not described here. You may find it helpful to read the rules in their entirety before attempting to create a character.

There are many different strategies and methods for creating a character, most of which will only come with trial and error, and experience. The following information and example for creating a character should give you the basic understanding needed for creating whatever type of character you would like to play.

In order to create a character you will need a scrap piece of paper, a pencil, a Character Sheet, and the following dice; 1D4, 1D10, 1D12, and a percentile die (a die marked from 00 to 90 to represent the ten's place when rolled along with a normal ten-sided die).

Choose Shinkai Type

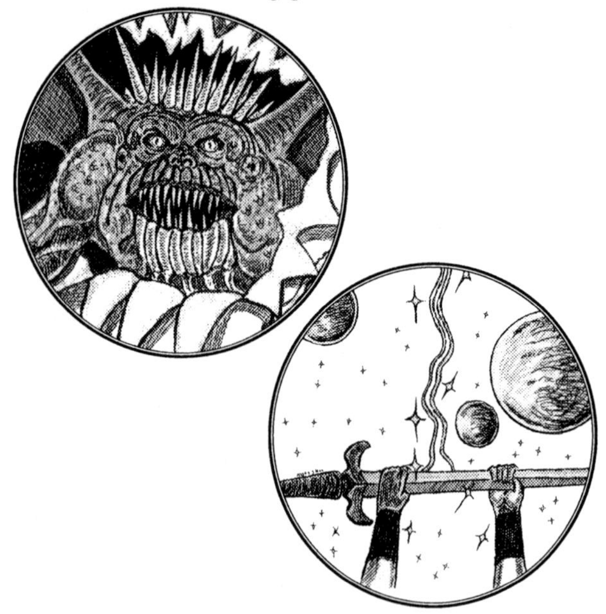

As a player in **Mystic Forces** you may choose what type of Shinkai you will play. Your character may be Shinkai Dragonknight or Shinkai Enchanter. If you wish, you may also choose for your character to be a normal Shinkai or just a normal ruling-race, but it is unlikely that you would choose to pass up the benefits of being Dragonknight or Enchanter just for the sake of doing so.

Joey has his pencil, paper, and dice and is ready to create his character. He isn't quite sure whether he wants to be a Dragonknight or Enchanter. He turns to the "DRAGONKNIGHT" Section of the rulebook and reviews all of the abilities of a Dragonknight, then reviews the "ENCHANTING" Section.

After a few moments of thought Joey decides that he would like to play a Shinkai Dragonknight. Joey selects the character sheet for Shinkai Dragonknight and moves on to the next step.

Choose a Specialty

There are seven different Specialties that you may choose from. They are **Archery**, **Defending**, **Edged Melee Weapons**, **Nature**, **Non-Edged Melee Weapons**, **Throwing Weapons**, and **Unarmed Combat**.

A Specialty represents an area with which your character has exceptional talent. You may only choose one Specialty for your character. The Specialty that you choose now will be the permanent Specialty for your character. It will reflect the area of expertise of your character. (You may not decide to change Specialties later.)

Each Specialty has ten separate Talents that can be learned. Each Talent gives your character certain benefits and or bonuses. Though it its possible to learn Talents from another Specialty you will have to pay twice as much to do so. It is recommended that you read through each Specialty and see which has the bonuses and Talents that would most interest you.

*Joey turns to the "SPECIALTY/TALENTS" Section of the rulebook and reviews the different Specialties and their Talents. He likes the excitement of close combat and has always had a fondness for bladed weapons. After looking through all of the Specialties Joey decides that **Edged Melee Weapons** is the Specialty that would best suit his character.*

Joey goes to the top of his character sheet and writes "Edged Melee Weapons" in the appropriate space provided. He is now ready for the next step, choosing a race.

Choose a Race

There are five separate ruling-races on Oryathar from which you may choose for your character. They are Brightling, Grak, Loremek, Valkin, and Warlum. The "RULING-RACES" Section describes each of these five races in detail.

Depending upon which Specialty you have chosen, you may wish to choose a race that will more easily accommodate the Talents of that Specialty. Though this is not necessary, it does add to the depth and realism of the game. For example, if you have chosen **Defending** as your character's Specialty you may wish to choose Brightling as your character's race, due to their small stature. This will make it easier for your character to sneak around and hide in even very small spaces. If **Unarmed Combat** is your character's Specialty, you may want to consider a Warlum or Grak as your character's race. Their stout build will lend itself nicely to unarmed combat situations.

Another interesting point to be made here, is that each of the ruling-races has their own unique innate abilities. You may wish to consider each ruling-race's innate ability as a factor in determining which of the races you would prefer to play.

Whichever of the ruling-races that you choose, choose one that you will enjoy playing, even if it doesn't seem to fit perfectly with the Specialty you have chosen. Who knows? You may end up with a combination that is far more exciting and interesting to role-play.

Joey wants his character to be stout and very battle-hardy. He turns to the "RULING-RACES" Section and reads through the descriptions and innate abilities of each of the five ruling-races and decides that he would like his character to be Grak. Joey writes down the race of his character in the appropriate space at the top of his Character Sheet and also records his races' innate ability, "Efficient Metabolism", in the appropriate space.

Determine Starting Attributes Points

There are six different attributes that make up the physical, mystical, and mental aspects of a character. They are Agility, Strength, Endurance, Willpower, Intelligence, and Sixth Sense. Each attribute serves a different purpose in the overall performance of the character.

As you progress your character through adventuring you will have the opportunity to increase these attributes (as you can afford it). At the start, however, you have a set number of points to assign among the six attributes.

To determine how many attribute points your character begins with, you will need 1D12 and a scrap piece of paper and a pencil.

You automatically receive 30 points, and now roll 5D12. Write down the result of each roll until you have the results of five separate rolls. You may now throw out the two lowest results and re-roll them, however, if the new result rolled is lower than the first, you must keep it.

Add the five rolled results together and then add your initial 30 to it. This is the number of points you now have to assign among the six attributes.

Joey has his pencil and paper in front of him and has dug through his dice bag to find his favorite D12. His first roll is a 5, the second is an 8, the third is a 2, the fourth is a 6, the fifth is a 10. Joey decides that he will re-roll the 2 and the 5. He rolls a 1 in place of the 2 and a 6 in place of the 5.

Joey adds all five of his adjusted rolls together for a total of 31. He adds his automatic 30 to this for a total of 61. Joey has 61 points to assign among the six attributes.

Assign Attribute Points

You may divide your character's starting points up among the attributes in any way that you like, with the exception that you may assign no lower than 5 points to any one attribute and no higher than 15 points. Racial modifiers may take the values that you assign below 5 or above 15, but you may not *assign* less than 5 or more than 15. (The racial modifiers for each ruling-race's attributes are listed with each ruling-race's description in the "RULING-RACES" Section.)

Before you begin assigning points, you most likely want to know what things that each attribute affects, which attributes are important to what kinds of actions, and which attributes are more important to the type of character that you plan to create. To answer such concerns each attribute is described in detail below.

Agility

Agility is a measure of how athletic and mobile your character is. The higher your character's Agility, the quicker and more agile he is.

This attribute is the single most important factor affecting physical actions. It affects how well your character can defend against physical attacks, how well he can perform physical attacks, and how well he can perform other physical feats such as swimming and climbing. It is one of two attributes that determines how fast your character can move and how high and far he can leap. It also affects your character's ability to learn many of the Skills.

In general, Agility greatly affects any feat requiring coordinated movement.

Strength

Strength is simply a measure of your character's overall muscular fitness. The higher your character's Strength, the stronger and faster he is.

This attribute affects how much damage your character can inflict with physical attacks, how much weight he can lift and carry, as well as being one of three attributes that determines his Life Force, Force Failure, and Injury Rating.

Endurance

Endurance is a measure of your character's physical toughness and how much physical stress he can endure. The higher your character's Endurance is, the more physical punishment he is able to withstand, and the quicker he is able to recover from physical stresses and damage.

This attribute affects how rapidly your character is able to recover from physical damage, determines his ability to resist being knocked out, and is one of three attributes that determines your character's Life Force, Force Failure, and Injury Rating.

Willpower

Willpower is a measure of your character's mental toughness and determination. How much mental stress he is able to endure, and how much physical stress he is able to ignore. The higher your character's Willpower is, the better he is at withstanding very stressing situations as well as mentally overcoming physical afflictions. In some ways it is very similar to Endurance, but with more emphasis on the character's mental toughness rather than physical toughness.

This attribute determines your character's ability to resist succumbing to Force Failure (going unconscious), and is one of three attributes that determines your character's Life Force, Force Failure, and Injury Rating.

Intelligence

Intelligence is a measure of you character's overall logic, reason, awareness, and recall. The higher your character's Intelligence is, the better he is at problem solving, recalling information, making casual observations and thinking in general.

This attribute is one of two attributes that affects how rapidly your character is able to gain Force Knowledge, and affects the learning of runes and some Skills. It also affects

the outcome of any situation that requires perception, understanding, or reason.

The "RULING-RACE INTELLIGENCE" table gives a basic description of a ruling-races' intelligence based upon their Intelligence Level.

RULING-RACE INTELLIGENCE	
Intelligence Level	**Description**
1-2	Unable to read or write
3-4	Able to read & write very basic word
5-6	Average intelligence/ Able to read & write well
7-8	Above average intelligence
9-up	Highly intelligent

Sixth Sense

Sixth Sense is a measure of your character's ability to effectively utilize the Mystic Forces as well as to sense things normally undetected by others, such as danger, evil, or the strong presence of the Shadow or the Light.

The Sixth Sense is present in Shinkai due to the *Gift* within them. The higher your character's Sixth Sense is, the better he is able to effectively utilize his *Gift*. The more in control or their *Gift* that a Shinkai is, the better they are at wielding Force-effects and the more sensitive they are to the presence of danger, evil, the Shadow, and the Light. A strong *Gift* in a Shinkai also makes them more capable of resisting and defending against mystical-based attacks. For more information about the *Gift* see the "MAGIC" Section.

Sixth Sense affects the learning and use of many Force-effects, determines your character's Mystical Defense, and is one of two attributes that affects how rapidly he is able to gain Force Knowledge.

Now that you know what the function of each attribute is, you need to assign your starting attribute points up among them. All starting attribute points must be assigned, and no attribute may be left blank. As noted before, you may assign no lower than 5 points to any one attribute and no higher than 15.

The areas that you feel are most important for your character's Specialty or style of play should be taken into consideration. Don't get worried if some of the attributes look pathetically low compared to others, or if none of your attributes at all seem to be that impressive. You can always build them up later through game play and the expenditure of Light Points.

Joey is now ready to assign values to each of his character's six attributes. He gets his scrap piece of paper and writes down all six attributes.

Joey decides that for now at least he is more interested in having a strong and quick character than one that is adept

mystically. Taking this into consideration he applies the following values to Intelligence and Sixth Sense.

For Intelligence he assigns 7, and for Sixth Sense he assigns 6, which becomes a 5 after deducting -1 from it because of the Grak's racial modifier. Joey writes down 7 beside of Intelligence and 5 beside of Sixth Sense. This now leaves Joey with a total of 48 points to assign among the remaining four attributes.

Joey's next concern is Agility. He would like his character's Agility to be at least Level 3, and after noting that Grak receive a -1 point penalty to Agility he will have to assign a value of at least 12 in order to obtain Level 3 (the 12 is modified to a 11, which according to the "LEVEL/DICE" table is the lowest value possible to still obtain Level 3). Joey writes 11 on his scrap paper beside of Agility. He has 36 points left to assign.

The last three attributes that Joey has yet to assign points to are the three attributes that make up his character's Life Force, and subsequently his Force Failure and Injury Rating.

The next attribute that Joey decides to assign points to is Strength. Joey wants his Grak to be very strong and battle hardy, so he decides to be fairly generous in the points he assigns to this attribute. He decides that he wants his character to have a starting Strength of Level 4. Taking into account that Grak receive a +2 point bonus to Strength, Joey will be able to assign 14 points to Strength and with his racial modifier obtain a Level 4 (the Grak's racial modifier to Strength modifies the 14 to a 16). He writes down 16 beside of Strength on his scrap paper. Joey now has 22 points to assign among the remaining two attributes.

Endurance and Willpower are the last two attributes to which Joey needs to assign points. As a Grak, Joey's character receives a +2 point bonus to Willpower. Joey decides that he would like Endurance and Willpower to be fairly equal. To Endurance he assigns 12, and to Willpower he assigns 10, which is modified to 12. Joey writes 12 beside of Endurance and 12 beside of Willpower.

Joey has now spent all of his starting attribute points, and is ready to fill in the "Value", "Level", and "Dice" spaces on his Character Sheet in the spaces provided beside of each attribute.

The following "LEVEL/DICE" table will give you all of this information.

Joey writes down all of his adjusted attribute values, their Levels, and the dice for each Level in the appropriate spaces on his Character Sheet.

Look to the right of your character's attributes value on the "LEVEL/DICE" table to see what Level each value falls in. Look to the right of the appropriate Level to see what dice are rolled for that Level. Record these on your character sheet in their appropriate spaces.

The "Range" column on the "LEVEL/DICE" table is a quick reference that shows the lowest and highest possible results for each Level on a Random-roll attribute Test.

LEVEL/DICE

Value	Level	Dice	Range
1-5	1	1D4-1	0-3
6-10	2	1D4	1-4
11-15	3	1D6	1-6
16-20	4	1D8	1-8
21-25	5	1D10	1-10
26-30	6	1D12	1-12
31-35	7	1D10+1D4	2-14
36-40	8	1D10+1D6	2-16
41-45	9	1D10+1D8	2-18
46-50	10	2D10	2-20
51-55	11	1D12+1D10	2-22
56-60	12	2D12	2-24
61-65	13	1D20+1D6	2-26
66-70	14	1D20+1D8	2-28
71-75	15	1D20+1D10	2-30
76-80	16	1D20+1D12	2-32
81-85	17	2D20	2-40
86-90	18	2D20+1D8	3-48
91-95	19	3D20	3-60
96-100	20	3D20+5	8-65

Every increase of 5 points is another Level. For each Level above 20, an additional +1 is added to the result of the roll.

Joey writes down 11 in the space provided under Value across from Agility on his character sheet. Looking to the "LEVEL/DICE" table, Joey sees that a value of 11 is classified as Level 3. He writes 3 in the space provided under Level across from Agility. In the space provided under Dice, across from Agility, he writes 1D6. The Penalty and Penalty Type spaces do not apply at this time, so they are left blank.

Determine Health Statistics

There are four main categories that fall under Health. They are Life Force, Force Failure, Injury Rating, and Recovery.

Life Force

Life Force represents the number of points of damage that your character can take before he dies. To find your character's Life Force value add his Strength, Endurance, and Willpower values together. This is your character's Life Force. As you increase your character's Strength, Endurance, or Willpower you will appropriately increase his Life Force so that his Life Force is always equal to the sum of these three attributes, unless unusual circumstances apply.

Joey's character has a Strength value of 16, an Endurance value of 12, and his Willpower value is 12. Adding all three together Joey determines that his character has a Life Force of 40. Joey writes down 40 in the appropriate space on his Character Sheet for his character's Life Force.

Force Failure

Force Failure represents the number of points of damage that your character can take before he becomes unconscious. To find your character's Force Failure value, divide his Life Force value by four (rounding up), then subtract this value, which is actually your character's Injury Rating, from his Life Force. The remaining value is your character's Force Failure.

Joey divides his Life Force (40) by 4 for a result of 10. He now subtracts 10 from his Life Force of 40 for his a result of 30, which is his character's Force Failure. Joey writes down 30 in the appropriate space on his Character Sheet for his character's Force Failure.

Injury Rating

Injury Rating represents the number of points of damage that your character must receive at one time, from a single source, in order to sustain an injury. To find your character's Injury Rating, divide his Life Force by 4 and round up.

Joey has already divided his Life Force by 4 as part of the process for finding his character's Force Failure, and found that it is 10. Joey writes down 10 in the appropriate space on his Character Sheet for his character's Injury Rating.

Recovery

Recovery represents the dice that you roll that determines how much damage your character is able to recover when he makes a Recovery Test. Your character's Recovery dice are normally equal to his Endurance dice.

When your character goes into recovery, caused by sustaining damage or fatigue, the Recovery dice is what you roll to determine how much damage is removed.

Joey looks across from his character's Endurance to the column labeled Dice and sees that the Endurance dice for his character is 1D6. Joey's character is Grak however, and has the Innate Ability of "Efficient Metabolism" which gives a +2 Level increase to all Recovery Tests. This modifies the 1D6 for Recovery Tests to a 1D10. This is the die that he will roll when his character makes a Recovery Test.

Joey writes down 1D10 in the appropriate space on his Character Sheet for his character's Recovery.

Determine Defense Bonuses

If your character's Agility or Sixth Sense is high enough, he receives Defense Bonus Points. Agility is the attribute that determines your character's Physical Defense Bonus Points, and Sixth Sense is the attribute that determines your character's Mystical Defense Bonus Points.

Once either your character's Agility or Sixth Sense Level reaches Level 5 or higher your character receives Defense Bonus Points. At Level 5 the bonus is +1, at Level 6 it is +2, at Level 7 it is +3, and so on. So, a character whose Agility is Level 5 and Sixth Sense is Level 8 would have a Physical Defense Bonus of +1 and a Mystical Defense Bonus of +4 (or plus 1 and plus 4 points). A simple method is to simply subtract 4 from your character's Agility or Sixth Sense Level. Any remaining value is his Defense Bonus Points.

Joey looks at the Levels of his character's Agility and Sixth Sense and sees that neither is Level 5 or higher, so he leaves the Physical and Mystical Defense Bonus spaces blank for the time being. When he raises either of these attributes to Level 5 or higher, he may then fill in the Defense Bonus spaces with the appropriate bonuses.

Determine Movement

There are two main categories of movement for your character. They are Maximum Speed and Action Movement.

Maximum Speed actually represents your character's top running speed. More precisely, it is the maximum number of feet that your character can move in a single Turn.

Action Movement is not representative of a speed, but rather a distance. It is the number of feet that your character may move in a single Turn and still have enough time to perform a Major Action.

A character's Maximum Speed and Action Movement is based upon a combination of Agility and Strength. Add the values of these two attributes together and then look to the following "MOVE & LIFT/CARRY" table to look up your character's appropriate movements.

Find the appropriate value for the sum of your character's Agility and Strength values under the column labeled "Value". Now move straight across to the next column labeled "Movement" to see your character's movement values. The number before the forward slash is your character's Maximum Speed, and the number after the forward slash is his Action Movement.

Joey adds his character's Agility and Strength values together for a combined total of 27. Looking this up on the "MOVE & LIFT/CARRY" table Joey sees that his character's Maximum Speed is 110 feet per Turn, and his Action Movement is 37 feet. Joey records these values in their appropriate spaces on the front of his Character Sheet.

MOVE & LIFT/CARRY

Value	Movement	Lifting/Carrying Capacity (Lbs.)
1-5	60/20	175/44
6-10	70/24	225/50
11-15	80/27	275/69
16-20	90/30	300/75
21-25	100/34	325/82
26-30	110/37	350/88
31-35	120/40	375/94
36-40	130/44	400/100
41-45	140/47	425/107
46-50	150/50	450/113
51-55	160/54	500/125
56-60	170/57	550/138
61-65	180/60	575/144
66-70	190/64	600/150
71-75	200/67	625/157
76-80	210/70	675/169
81-85	220/74	700/175
86-90	230/77	725/182
91-95	240/80	750/188
96-100	250/84	775/194
101-105	260/87	800/200
106-110	270/90	825/206
111-115	280/94	850/213
116-120	290/97	900/225
121-125	300/100	950/238
126-130	310/104	1000/250
131-135	320/107	1050/263
136-140	330/110	1100/275
141-145	340/114	1150/288
146-150	350/117	1200/300
151-155	360/120	1250/313
156-160	370/124	1300/325
161-165	380/127	1350/338
166-170	390/130	1400/350

Determine Lifting Limit & Carrying Capacity

There is a maximum amount of weight that your character can lift and carry. These values are based on your character's Strength value.

The Lifting Limit is the maximum amount of weight that your character can pick up. This amount of weight is too great to move with, so your character is unable to move with this amount of weight. He or she is only able to lift it.

The Carrying Capacity is the maximum amount of weight

that your character can actually carry around without being considered "encumbered". Your character can *actually* carry an amount of weight equal to twice his listed Carrying Capacity, but receives penalties for doing so (this is discussed later).

To find your character's Lifting Limit and Carrying Capacity, turn to the "MOVE & LIFT/CARRY" table on page 38. Find your character's Strength value under the column labeled "Value". Now move straight across to the column labeled "Lifting/Carrying Capacity (Lbs.)". The number before the forward slash is your character's Lifting Limit and the number after the forward slash is your character's Carrying Capacity.

Joey's character has a Strength value of 16. He looks down the "Value" column until he finds the row containing a value of 16, then moves across that row to the "Lifting/Carrying Capacity (Lbs.)" column and sees that his character's Lifting Limit is 300 pounds and his Carrying Capacity is 75 pounds. Joey records these values in their appropriate spaces on the front of his Character Sheet.

Determine Starting Silver Coins

All characters start out with one hundred to four hundred silver coins with which to make initial purchases.

To determine how much silver your character receives to make these initial purchases roll 1D4 and multiply the result by one hundred. This is how many silver coins your character begins with.

Joey rolls 1D4 and gets a result of 3. He has 300 silver coins that his character can spend. Joey writes this amount down on his scrap sheet of paper. Much of this coin will be spent purchasing initial items and equipment for his character. He will wait until he sees how much is left before he actually writes his coin on his Character Sheet.

Purchase Equipment and Weapons

As of now your character has no clothes, weapons, or items of any kind. It is up to you to clothe and equip him. You may purchase any equipment, items, or weapons out of the "EQUIPMENT & MERCHANDISE" and "WEAPONS & ARMOR" Sections of this rulebook that you like, with the exceptions of green-steel and enchanted items. These types of items must be purchased through actual game-play. The cost of all items and weapons (which is listed under Coin) is in silver coins, and the weight is in pounds, except where otherwise noted.

The amount of silver that you rolled up in the last step is all that you have to spend on your character at this time. You may not borrow coin from other players for the initial equip-

ping of your character. After you begin playing your character may borrow anything he likes from other characters, provided they are willing, but not at this stage of the game.

It is very important that you keep up with the weight and bulk of each item or weapon that you purchase for your character. As noted previously their is a maximum amount of weight that your character can carry, and coincidentally there is a maximum Bulk Rating that your character may carry (34 for all races except Brightling, which is 30).

If the total Bulk Value of all items that your character is carrying exceeds 34 (30 for Brightlings) your character will be penalized. For each Bulk Value of 1 beyond the maximum allowance, your character will receive a -1 Level penalty to his Agility and a -10 feet per Turn penalty to their Maximum Speed.

It is suggested that you write down the weight and Bulk Value of each item that you purchase as you go. This will make it much easier for you to figure up your character's Load (amount of weight he is packing) and Total Bulk Value. The Equipment Sheet is designed specifically for keeping track of this information.

Joey gets out the Equipment Sheet for his character and turns to the "EQUIPMENT" Section of the rulebook. Joey decides that he will start with the "EQUIPMENT" table and buy all of the basics for his character, then worry about weapons and armor after he sees how much silver he has left.

The first thing Joey decides that he wants to buy for his character is some clothes. Looking down the equipment list Joey chooses the following items to purchase: boots, breeches, a shirt, and underclothes. He writes the items, their Bulk Value, and their weight down on his Equipment Sheet. Then on his scrap piece of paper he subtracts their cost from his total silver. After clothing his character with these items Joey has 276 silver coins left to spend.

He decides that his next priority is to buy some basic equipment. After looking through the equipment list for any items that he feels that his character may need during the course of his travels and adventuring, Joey purchases the following items: A backpack, compass, flint and steel, leather pouch (for his remaining coin), three days supply of trail rations, two small sacs (for small items), three torches, one waterskin, and a whetstone.

Joey writes down all of this equipment on his Equipment Sheet as well as the Bulk Value and weight of each item. Next he subtracts the coin that he just spent to make sure that he hasn't overspent. He also decides that he had better add up the Bulk Value of all of his items to determine that he hasn't exceeded his allowable Total Bulk Value of 34, as well as adding up the weight of all of the items to be sure that his Load does not exceed his character's Carrying Capacity.

After subtracting the coin and adding up the Bulk Values and weights for his items, Joey's character still has 213 sil-

ver coins left, his Total Bulk Value is currently 12, and his Load is 19 pounds and 5 ounces. He is well within his limits and has a pretty handsome sum of silver left as well. But, he has yet to purchase any weapons or armor, and he knows that is where he will run into the more expensive items with high Bulk Values and heavy weights

Now for the exciting part, Joey gets to choose weapons for his character, and possibly some armor if he has enough coin. Since Joey's character's Specialty is **Edged Melee Weapons** and he receives a bonus when using weapons of his own Specialty, he has already decided that the first weapon he will buy is an edged melee weapon.

Turning to the "WEAPONS & ARMOR" Section Joey locates the "EDGED MELEE WEAPONS" table and begins looking for a weapon that he would like to buy. He sees that the highest Minimum Strength requirement for any of the edged melee weapons is Level 4. His character's Strength is Level 4, so his character meets the Strength requirements for any of these weapons.

Joey decides that he wants the highest damage yielding weapon that he can buy for the lowest possible price. It takes only a moment to decide. Joey chooses a battle-axe. This weapon requires both hands to wield it, but Joey doesn't mind. He adds it to his Equipment Sheet along with its Bulk Value and weight in the same manner as the previously purchased items.

Joey now subtracts the cost of the battle-axe from his character's remaining silver and sees that he has only 38 silver coins remaining. He decides that he would like to have some sort of shield to offer his character some protection until he can afford to buy some decent body armor. The only type of shield that can be used with a two-handed weapon such as a battle-axe is a buckler. Besides that, a buckler is the only type of shield that he can afford at this time.

Joey adds the buckler to his Equipment Sheet and now has 18 silver coins left. He decides to buy a knife and a sheath (the sheath is found on the "EQUIPMENT" table) as his last purchases, which will leave him with 8 silver coins. Joey records his character's remaining 8 silver coins in the appropriate space on his Character Sheet.

Joey again totals up the weight of all his character's items and adds all of the Bulk Values together. The total weight of all of his items is 33 pounds and 13 ounces, which Joey writes in the space beside of Load at the bottom of his Equipment Sheet. The Bulk Values of all of his character's weapons and items comes to a total of 23, but he hasn't placed any items in his backpack or sacs yet.

Joey decides to place the compass, flint & steel, three days supply of trail rations, three torches, and whetstone into the backpack. A backpack can hold up to 24 Bulk Value worth of items. The total Bulk Value of all the items placed into the backpack at this time is 7.5, which is less than half of the backpack's capacity. The Bulk Value of the backpack and all of its contents is only 2. If the backpack is empty or half-full or less, its Bulk Value is 2, if it is over half full then it and its entire contents have a Bulk Value of 4.

Joey subtracts 7.5 (the total Bulk Value of all items placed into the backpack from the initial Bulk Value of 23 (which he did not account for items being placed into the backpack) for a total of 15.5.

Joey's character's Total Bulk Value at this time is 15.5, which he writes in the space beside of Total Bulk Value at the bottom of his Equipment Sheet. Had Joey decided that his character would carry all of the items loose, his Bulk Value would have been 23. So by using a backpack to place many of his smaller items into he reduced his character's Total Bulk Value by 7.5 points.

Fill in Weapon Statistics

The Weapon Statistics area of your Character Sheet is designed to readily provide you with the necessary information for determining the attack and damage from various weapons that your character may use. Though it is not necessary to fill in this section of your Character Sheet, it is extremely helpful for keeping up with the adjusted attacks and damages of any given weapon based upon your character's attributes and the various bonuses that he may have when using that type of weapon.

Start by writing down the names of the weapons that your character intends to use, or has a good possibility of using, under the heading "Weapon Type". "Tech.", short for technique, is left blank at this time (Technique Points must be earned through actual game-play).

The next heading is "Attack". This space is provided to give you the exact value that you will add to your character's Performance Die result when attacking with that particular weapon. It takes into account any Technique Points that your character may have with that weapon as well as his Attribute Level, and any other bonuses that he receives when using a weapon of this type (or this particular weapon). Such bonuses include green-steel bonuses (green-steel adds +1 to attacks and +1 Levels to the weapon's Damage Yield), Specialty bonuses (when using weapons of your character's own Specialty you may add +1 to attacks with that weapon and increase the Damage Yield of the weapon by 1 Level), proficiency bonuses (if your character is proficient with a particular type of weapon you may add +1 to attacks with that weapon and increase the Damage Yield of the weapon by 1 Level), Technique Point bonuses (every Technique Point that your character has with a particular weapon type adds +1 to attacks with that type of weapon), and enchantment bonuses (enchantments may alter or change the effects of a weapon or item in any number of ways).

Since starting characters do not have Technique Points, proficiencies, green-steel, or enchanted items, it is fairly simple to determine the attack for your character's weapons at this time. The base value is equal to your character's

Agility Level. If the weapon is of your character's Specialty add 1 to the base value. This is the value that you will add to your Performance Die when you attack with this weapon.

If your character later acquires Technique Points with a weapon, you will add 1 point to the attack for each Technique Point. If the weapon is made of green-steel you will add 1 point to the attack. If your character becomes proficient with the weapon you will add 1 point to the attack. Enchantment bonuses are also added in accordingly, the effects of which are nearly limitless (every enchantment is different and has different effects).

For example, a character with an Agility of Level 5 has a green-steel short-sword, 2 Technique Points with short-swords, **Edged Melee Weapons** is his Specialty, and he is proficient with short-swords. His attack would be 10. When attacking with a short-sword he would add 10 to the result of his Performance Die roll for his total attack value.

The next heading is "Dmg. Yield". This is used to predetermine the total Damage Yield of the weapon, based upon the weapon's normal Damage Yield plus any bonuses that your character may have with the weapon. Such bonuses include green-steel bonuses, Specialty bonuses, proficiency bonuses, or enchantment bonuses (Technique Points do not increase the damage of an attack, only the attack value).

Since starting characters do not have proficiencies, green-steel, or enchanted items, it is also fairly simple to determine the Damage Yield for your character's weapons at this time.

For simplicity, you should write the dice to be rolled under the "Damage Yield" heading. If you don't have a problem remembering what dice apply to the different Levels, then feel free to write the Level of the Damage Yield instead of the dice.

The base Level of damage that a weapon does is the Damage Yield of the weapon as listed on the appropriate weapon table. If the weapon is made of green-steel you will add 1 Level to the Damage Yield (this 1 Level increase is already factored in on the green-steel weapons table. If your character is proficient with the weapon you will add 1 Level to the Damage Yield. Enchantment bonuses are also added in accordingly. After adding all bonus Levels into the weapon's normal Damage Yield Level, look this total adjusted Level up on the "LEVEL/DICE" table to see what dice are rolled for that Level.

For example, a character has a war-hammer with which he is proficient and **Non-Edged Melee Weapons** is his Specialty. The Damage Yield of that weapon would now be Level 8 for this character instead of Level 6.

"Damage Received" is the last heading. This is used to record any damage the weapon has received. Since the weapons that characters begin with are new and have no damage, this space is left blank. As the weapon takes damage it should be recorded here.

The only weapons that Joey has purchased for his charac-

ter are a knife and a battle-axe. He knows that since his character has these two weapons in his possession, there is a good chance that he will be using them. He decides to go ahead and record them under "Weapon Statistics".

Under "Weapon Type" Joey writes the names of his character's weapons (knife and battle-axe). Joey skips "Technique" because his character does not yet have technique with any weapons. Across from his knife under the "Attack" heading Joey writes 4, the Level of his character's Agility plus 1 Level because his character's Specialty is Edged Melee Weapons and a knife is an edged melee weapon and .

Looking to the "EDGED MELEE WEAPONS" table Joey sees that the normal Damage Yield for a knife is Level 2. Joey adds 1 Level to this because a knife is a weapon of his character's own Specialty ("Edged Melee Weapons") for a total of Level 3. Under "Damage Yield" Joey writes 1D6, the dice for Level 3.

Now for the battle-axe. Across from his battle-axe under the "Attack" heading Joey writes 4, the Level of his character's Agility plus 1 Level because his character's Specialty is "Edged Melee Weapons", and a battle-axe is an edged melee weapon.

Looking to the "EDGED MELEE WEAPONS" table Joey sees that the normal Damage Yield for a battle-axe is Level 5. Joey adds 1 Level to this because a battle-axe is a weapon of his character's own Specialty ("Edged Melee Weapons") for a total of Level 6. Under "Damage Yield" Joey writes 1D12, the dice for Level 6.

Joey skips "Damage Received" because these weapons do not yet have any damage.

Fill in Armor Statistics

Find the type of armor or shield that your character is equipped with on the appropriate "ARMOR" or "SHIELDS" table. For armor other than shields look across to the column labeled "Protection Rating" to see how much protection that particular piece of armor offers. For shields look across to the column labeled "Destroyed" to see how much damage the shield can take before it is destroyed.

Now write down the type of armor or shield that your character has under "Armor Type" on the bottom right hand side of your Character Sheet under the "Armor Statistics" section. "Tech.", short for technique, is left blank at this time (Technique Points must be earned through actual gameplay). "P.R./Destroy" is where you will write the Protection Rating value of the armor and/or the amount of damage that it takes to destroy it. If the armor has an Agility or movement penalty, which will be listed on the "ARMOR" or "SHIELDS" table, write it under "Move/Agil. Penalty." "Dmg. Received" is also left blank at this time (the armor is new and has no damage), but as your character's armor does take damage you will keep record of it here.

The only item in the armor category that Joey's character currently possesses is a buckler. He writes buckler down under the armor type. Looking to the "SHIELDS" table Joey finds that a buckler has a Destroyed Rating of 160. He writes 160 under "Destroy". A buckler has no movement or Agility penalties so Joey is finished logging the armor statistics for the buckler.

Determine Protection Ratings

There are basically five different zones of a ruling-race that can have separate sources of protection (armor) applied. They are head/neck, arms, torso, pelvis, and legs.

If your character has armor, he will need to determine how much protection he has to each zone, or area, of his body. Each type of armor, or section of armor, offers protection to different zones of the body. Look to the "WEAPONS & ARMOR" Section to find exactly which zones of the body that the various types of armor can protect, and refer to the "ARMOR" table on page 224 of the "WEAPONS & ARMOR" Section for detailed information on each piece of armor such as weight, Protection Rating (P.R.), and Agility and movement penalties.

If more than one type of armor is covering the same zone of the body, then the Protection Ratings of the overlapping pieces of armor are added together.

Look up the Protection Rating of each article of armor your character is "wearing" and write its P.R. value beside of the zone that it is protecting in the section of your Character Sheet titled "Protection Rating".

For example, if your character has a steel helm on his head (P.R. of 5), a chain mail long-shirt with sleeves (P.R. of 6), and leather breeches (P.R. of 3), you would record his P.R. values like this:

Head/Neck: 5

Arms: 6

Torso: 6

Pelvis: 9

Legs: 3

The Pelvis zone has a P.R. of 9 because it is being protected by both the chain mail long-shirt (P.R. of 6) and the leather breeches (P.R. of 3), for a total P.R. of 9.

You must also record any Agility or movement penalties that wearing the armor may render in the appropriate areas on your Character Sheet.

Joey does not have any armor to wear at this time, so he leaves the zones under "Protection Rating" blank for now.

Determine Mystical Attuning Points

Mystical Attuning Points are directly linked to the number of Mystic Forces that a character controls. Mystical attuning is an ability that helps any Shinkai more effectively utilize his *Gift* as well as allowing them to instantaneously recover a small amount of damage, fatigue, or Force Energy.

To determine your character's Mystical Attuning Points, simply add a value of 1 to the number of Mystic Forces that your character controls. All starting characters will have 1 Mystical Attuning Point (they don't yet control any of the Mystic Forces).

For more information about Mystical Attuning and Mystical Attuning Points see "Mystical Attuning" in the "MAGIC" Section.

Write your character's Mystical Attuning Points in the blank space beside of M.A.P. on your Character Sheet.

Joey writes 1 down beside of Total M.A.P. and beside of Current M.A.P. and Total M.A.P. on his Character Sheet.

Determine Prowess Ratings

Prowess Ratings are simply a rating of how talented or skilled a person or being is in a given area. There are two different types of Prowess Ratings, Physical and Mystical.

For the purpose of determining Prowess Ratings for Dragonknight characters, the attributes of the ruling-race form are always used. Regardless of whether a ruling-race is in Dragonknight form or not, their Prowess Ratings are determined by their ruling-race form's attributes.

Physical Prowess is comprised of Agility and Strength. It is a general measure of your character's skill in all aspects of physical abilities.

To determine your character's Physical Prowess, add his Agility and Strength Levels (of his ruling-race form) together. Find this Level on the "PROWESS RATING" table on page 248 to see what the rating is for that Level.

Write this rating down in the blank space beside of "Physical", under the heading "Prowess Rating", on the front of your Character Sheet.

Mystical Prowess is comprised of Intelligence and Sixth Sense. It is a general measure of your character's skill in all aspects of mystical abilities.

Mystical Prowess is determined in the same manner, except Intelligence and Sixth Sense are used instead of Agility and Strength.

Write this rating down in the blank space beside of "Mystical", under the heading "Prowess Rating", on the front of your Character Sheet.

Joey adds his character's Agility Level of 3 to his Strength Level of 4 for a total of 7. He now finds Level 7 on the "PROWESS RATING" table. The rating for Level 7 is "Amateur".

Joey's character has a Physical Prowess of Amateur at this time. He writes Amateur down in the space provided for

Physical Prowess.

Joey now adds his character's Intelligence Level of 2 to his Sixth Sense Level of 1 for a total of 3. Looking to the "PROWESS RATING" table Joey sees that the rating for Level 3 is also "Amateur".

Joey's character has a Mystical Prowess of Amateur at this time. He writes Amateur down in the space provided for Mystical Prowess.

Determine Innate Force Energy

Innate Force Energy is the amount of Force Energy that your character possesses even before he begins to gain Force Knowledge. If your character is Brightling he will have 3D10 +10 points of Innate Force Energy. If your character is any race other than Brightling, he will have 1D10 +10 points of Innate Force Energy.

Roll the appropriate dice for your character's race. The value rolled is your character's Innate Force Energy, which you will write down in the appropriate space on the top, back side of your Character Sheet. This value will never change.

Joey's character is Grak, so he will roll 1D10 +10 to determine his Innate Force Energy. Joey rolls 1D10 for a result of 8. He adds 10 to his result of 8 for a total of 18. Joey's character has an Innate Force Energy of 18. He writes this down in the space provided on the back of his Character Sheet.

Determine Vertical & Horizontal Leap

There is a maximum distance that your character is able to leap vertically and horizontally based upon his or her Agility and Strength Levels.

To determine the leaping ability of your character add his Agility and Strength Levels together. This Level is the maximum number of feet that your character can leap horizontally (as long as he has a running distance of at least thirty five feet). Without at least a thirty-five foot running start, your character's maximum Horizontal Leap is one-half (rounded down) of its normal distance.

Your character's maximum Vertical Leap is determined by dividing his Horizontal Leap by four, rounding any remainders to fi foot.

Joey adds his character's Agility and Strength Levels together for a total of 7. His character can leap as far as 7 feet horizontally.

To find his character's Vertical Leap, Joey divides his character's Horizontal Leap by 4 for a result of 1.75. The .75 is simply rounded to fi foot. His character has a Vertical Leap of 1 and fi feet.

Joey writes his character's Horizontal and Vertical Leap

distances in the provided spaces on the back of his Character Sheet.

Determine Personal Flaw

A personal flaw is simply an odd or unusual trait that your character possesses. Having a personal flaw doesn't limit your character's ability to be an affective member of society, but rather opens the door for interesting and creative role-playing.

There is only a twenty percent chance that your character has a personal flaw. This is determined by rolling the percentile dice, or die if you have a one hundred-sided die. A result of twenty or lower means that your character has a personal flaw.

To determine exactly what your character's flaw is, simply take the number that you rolled on the percentile dice, and look it up on the following "PERSONAL FLAW" table.

Remember, having a personal flaw doesn't mean that you have a substandard character. It simply means that you have a more interesting character. If taken advantage of, a personal flaw can be an excellent springboard for earning Character Points.

Joey picks up his percentile dice and gives them a roll. He rolls a 15. Since a result of twenty or lower means that the character has a personal flaw, this means that Joey's character has a personal flaw. Joey immediately looks to the "PERSONAL FLAW" table. Finding 15 on the table Joey sees that his character is extremely laid back, and never gets in a hurry.

Joey records the description of his character's personal flaw in the space provided for notes on the back of his Character Sheet.

PERSONAL FLAW

1	Too ready to do battle, even when it may not be the best answer.
2	Constantly worries over physical appearances (has to look good all of the time).
3	Finds it nearly impossible to turn down a personal challenge.
4	Will do nearly anything for a pretty face.
5	Has a moderate fear of conjuring.
6	Hard of hearing.
7	Very quiet and hates engaging in idle conversation.
8	Has a fear of tight or enclosed spaces.
9	Very untrusting of all strangers.
10	Wasteful with coin.
11	Can't turn down someone in need, even very minor needs.
12	Extremely tight with coin. Hates to spend coin on anything unless it is absolutely necessary.
13	Very impatient.
14	Loves to joke around excessively, and often very inappropriate moments.
15	Extremely laid back. Never gets in a hurry.
16	Very careless about their own physical appearance (sloppy).
17	Has little care about their own personal safety. Will risk their life without hesitation if necessary.
18	Has a speech impediment.
19	Afraid of the dark.
20	Gets extremely nervous when preparing to fight.

Determine Physical Characteristics

Now is the time to determine your character's physical characteristics. This includes your character's height, weight, age, skin, eye, and hair color.

Each of the five ruling-races has their own unique physical features. Refer to the description of the race you have chosen for your character in the "RULING-RACES" Section. There you will all of the physical characteristics that are normal for each race. You should try to stick to the characteristics and averages given with your race's description, but at the GM's discretion you may decide that you want your character to have one or more characteristics that are *not* normal for that particular race.

For example, if you have chosen Grak as your character's race, but are bent on your character having blue eyes, you may do so as long as the GM doesn't have a reason for disallowing it. It is recommended though, that this not be made a regular practice. After all, what it the use of each ruling-race having their own unique characteristics if no one uses them?

Joey turns to the "RULING-RACES" Section and reads through all of the different physical traits for Grak. He wants his character to be of average height and weight for his race. He decides that his character will be five feet tall and weigh two hundred seventy five pounds. He notes that Grak reach physical maturity at around sixteen years of age and decides that he wants his character to be seventeen years of age.

Joey still has to determine his character's eye, hair, and skin color before his character's description is complete. After reading through the choices Joey decides that he wants his character to have red eyes, black hair, and will of course have ash-green skin (the only color of skin that Grak can have).

Joey records all of this information under "Character Description" on the back of his Character Sheet.

Determine Stats for Dragonknight Form (if your character is Dragonknight)

If you have chosen Dragonknight as your character's Shinkai Type, then you will need to determine what all of the stats are for him when he is in Dragonknight form.

This is actually quite simple. It is merely a repeat of the same steps that you used to determine the stats for your character's ruling-race form, but instead of rolling and assigning new points for your character's Dragonknight attributes, everything is based upon the attribute values of your character's ruling-race form.

The first step is to determine exactly what your character's attribute values are when he is in Dragonknight form; all other stats are based upon this. Since your character's Dragonknight form is physically larger and more powerful than his ruling-race form, most of his attribute values will increase when he transforms into Dragonknight.

When your character is in Dragonknight he becomes less in tune with the Mystic Forces. For this reason your character's Sixth Sense lowers when he transforms into his Dragonknight form. Your character's Intelligence doesn't change between forms.

How much each attribute's value changes when your character transforms into Dragonknight is given on the following "DRAGONKNIGHT ATTRIBUTES" table. The Level, Dice, and other factors affected by the change in each attribute's value should be noted and adjusted in the Dragonknight area of your Character Sheet.

An attribute's Value can never be lower than 1. So, a character whose Sixth Sense Value in ruling-race is 5 would still have a value of 1 after transforming into Dragonknight form.

Start with your character's Agility and work down until you have determined each attribute's value when in

Dragonknight. Record each value as you determine it in the appropriate space beside of each attribute under "Dragonknight Form" on the back of your Character Sheet.

DRAGONKNIGHT ATTRIBUTES

Attribute	Value Change
Agility	+10 Points
Strength	+10 Points
Endurance	+10 Points
Willpower	+10 Points
Intelligence	No Change
Sixth Sense	-5 Points

Joey is ready to determine the Values for his character's attributes in Dragonknight form. His character's Agility Value is 11. According to the "DRAGONKNIGHT ATTRIBUTES" table Agility Value increases by 10 points when going to Dragonknight form. This would mean that his character's Agility Value will be 21 in Dragonknight .

Joey writes 21 down as his character's Agility Value when in Dragonknight. Referring to the "LEVEL/DICE" table Joey now fills in the Level and Dice for his Dragonknight's Agility. Looking up a value of 21 on the table (Level 5) Joey sees that the dice for that Level is 1D10. He records his Dragonknight's Agility Value, Level, and Dice in the appropriate spaces on the back of his Character Sheet.

Joey now determines the Value, Level, and Dice for his character's Strength, Endurance, and Willpower while in Dragonknight in the same manner as he did for Agility and records them in the appropriate spaces.

Intelligence does not change when in Dragonknight form so Joey records the Value, Level, and Dice for his Dragonknight's Intelligence just as they are for his character's ruling-race form.

The only attribute remaining is Sixth Sense. When in Dragonknight form this attribute drops by 5 points (1 Level). His character's Sixth Sense Value is 5. Since an attribute's value can't be lower than 1, it is decreased to 1. Joey's character has a Sixth Sense Value of 1 when in Dragonknight form.

Referring to the "LEVEL/DICE" table Joey sees that the Level for a Value of 1 is 1 and the Dice for Level 1 is 1D4-1. He records this information in the appropriate spaces.

All of the Health statistics, Defense Bonuses, Lifting Limit, Carrying Capacity, and Horizontal and Vertical Leap for your character's Dragonknight form are found in the same manner as described for your character's ruling-race form, except you use the Dragonknight form's attribute values instead of the ruling-race's. Movement is the only category that is determined somewhat differently.

There are two main categories of movement in Dragonknight; Ground and Flight. Ground movement represents your Dragonknight's movement upon the ground whereas Flight movement refers to your Dragonknight's movement while flying.

Ground movement is found in the same manner as movement for the ruling-race form. Add your Dragonknight's Agility and Strength values together and then look up this value under the column labeled "Value" on the "MOVE & LIFT/CARRY" table. Now move straight across to the next column labeled "Movement" to see your Dragonknight's movement values. The number before the forward slash is your Dragonknight's Maximum Ground Speed, and the number after the forward slash is his Action Ground Movement.

Your Dragonknight's Maximum Flight Speed is exactly double your Dragonknight's Maximum Ground Speed. Your Dragonknight's Action Flight Movement is one third, round up, of his Maximum Flight Speed.

Joey adds his Dragonknight's Agility value of 21 to his Strength value of 26 for a total of 47. According to the "MOVE & LIFT/CARRY" table this means that his Dragonknight has a Maximum Ground Speed of 150 feet per Turn, and an Action Movement of 50 feet.

Now to find his Dragonknight's Maximum Flight Speed. Joey doubles his Dragonknight's Maximum Ground Speed of 150 feet per Turn to get 300 feet per Turn. To get his Dragonknight's Action Flight Movement he divides 300 by 3 for a result of 100. Joey's Dragonknight has a Maximum Flight Speed of 300 feet per Turn, and an Action Flight Movement of 100 feet.

Joey now finishes determining the remaining stats for his character's Dragonknight form (Health statistics, Defense Bonuses, Lifting Limit, Carrying Capacity, and Horizontal and Vertical Leap) in the same manner as he did for his character's ruling-race form.

Since your character is just starting out, he does not yet have any breath attacks. "Breath" is left blank for now. When your character learns the various breath attacks for his Dragonknight form they will be recorded here.

Play

Now you're ready to head out into Oryathar's Shadow-tainted lands and face the enemy. Proving that the Light is not defeated and fighting to see that it will prevail over the Shadow.

Reclaim the glory that once belonged to the majestic lands of Oryathar and restore the balance of good and evil.

"May the Light guide you to your destiny."

Player Name: _Joey Hall_

Character Name: _Kargolius_

Race: _Grak_

Specialty: _Edged Melee Wpn_

Gender: _Male_

Innate Abilities: _Dragonknight Efficient_

MYSTIC FORGES

	Attribute	Value	Level	Dice	Penalty	Penalty Type
☐	Agility	11	3	1D6		
☐	Strength	16	4	1D8		
☐	Endurance	12	3	1D6		
☐	Willpower	12	3	1D6		
☐	Intelligence	7	2	1D4		
☐	Sixth Sense	5	1	1D4-1		

Health
Life Force: 40
Force Failure: 30
Injury Rating: 10
Recovery: 1D10

Prowess Rating
Physical: Amateur
Mystical: Amateur

Total M.A.P. 1   Current M.A.P. 1

Defense Bonus
Physical:
Mystical:

Total Light Points:
Current Light Points:
Character Points:
Total Shadow Points:
Current Shadow Points:

Protection Rating
Head/Neck:
Arms: Torso:
Pelvis: Legs:

Maximum Speed: 110 ft/T
Action Movement: 37 ft
Lifting Limit: 300 Lbs
Carrying Capacity: 75 Lbs

Coin
Gold:
Silver: 8
Copper:

Weapon Statistics

Weapon Type	Tech.	Attack	Dmg. Yield	Dmg. Received
Battle-axe		4	1D12	
Knife		4	1D6	

Armor Statistics

Armor Type	Tech.	P.R./ Destroy	Move/Agil. Penalty	Dmg. Received
Buckler		160		

Mystic Forces
- ☐ Air
- ☐ Fire
- ☐ Land
- ☐ Spirit
- ☐ Water

Force Knowledge

Unapplied Force Knowledge

Technique

Total Force Knowledge: _______

Innate Force Energy: **18**

Total Force Energy: **18**

Notes	Talents	Skills	Universal Talents
Personal flaw; extremely laid back. Never gets in a hurry.			

Character Description

Height: **5'** Skin: **Ash-green**
Weight: **275 lbs** Eyes: **Red**
Age: **17** Hair: **Black**
Other: _______________

Max. Horizontal Leap: **7 ft**
Max. Vertical Leap: **1½ ft**

DRAGONKNIGHT FORM

Attribute	Value	Level	Dice	Penalty	Penalty Type
Agility	21	5	1D10		
Strength	26	6	1D12		
Endurance	22	5	1D10		
Willpower	22	5	1D10		
Intelligence	7	2	1D4		
Sixth Sense	1	1	1D4-1		

Health
Life Force: **70**
Force Failure: **52**
Injury Rating: **18**

Advanced Combat ☐

Scale Color: **Ash-green**
Protection Rating: **3**
Scale Damage: _______

Defense Bonus
Physical: **1**
Mystical: _______

Breath

Horizontal Leap: **11 ft**
Vertical Leap: **2½ ft**
Lifting Limit: **350 lbs**
Carrying Capacity: **88 lbs**

Maximum Ground Speed: **150 ft/T**
Action Ground Movement: **50 ft**
☐ Maximum Flight Speed: **300 ft/T**
☐ Action Flight Movement: **100 ft**

RULING-RACES

RULING-RACES

There are five different races from which you can choose to create your character. They are the Brightling, Grak, Loremek, Valkin, and Warlum. Each of these five races, known as the ruling-races, have their own unique physical characteristics and innate abilities.

This Section will explain each of the five ruling-races in detail. By the end of this Section you should know enough about each of the five ruling-races to decide which one you would like your character to be.

A well-rounded gaming group will often include one of each of the ruling-races. As you play **Mystic Forces** you will no doubt have a favorite ruling-race to play, but hopefully you will eventually give all of them a try.

As you will find later in this Section, each of the five ruling-races has their own unique abilities, strengths and weaknesses. Some of these strengths and weaknesses come in the form of attribute bonuses or penalties (to the assigning of initial attribute points only). Along with the description of each of the ruling-races is a list of the six attributes with a value following each one. These values are the number of points that you must subtract or add to that attribute at the time you create the character. These bonuses and penalties do not affect future increases to the attributes or to the Tests made by the attributes, only to the initial attribute values that you assign at the creation of the character.

LANGUAGE

Each of the five ruling-races speaks a universal language known as Oryatharian (English to us humans). In addition to Oryatharian each ruling-race also speaks their own personal language. So a Brightling, for example, would normally speak Oryatharian and Brightling. A Loremek would speak Oryatharian and Loremek; you get the point.

Along with each ruling-race's description is two language tables. One table lists fifty-four common words that might be useful for a character to know. The words are in Oryatharian (English) on the left side of the table and in the ruling-races' own language on the right side of the table. The other table has the Oryatharian alphabet listed down its left side and the ruling-race's own alphabet equivalent on the right side.

Though not necessary in order to play, the unique words and alphabets for the different ruling-races adds a bit of flavor to the game and allows players to actually talk and write in their character's own language. Some adventures may contain letters written in a particular ruling-race's own language and must be deciphered. It is a good idea for each player to make themselves a copy (feel free to photocopy) of their race's language tables so that they can easily translate and write their character's language. If a player's character learns to read and write another ruling-race's language, via the "Language" Skill, then they can make themselves a copy of that ruling-race's language tables as well.

Each of the ruling-races languages has a unique sound and look. After a little practice you will be able to distinguish between the different ruling-race languages and alphabets without the aid of the language tables.

BRIGHTLING

Attribute	Modifier
Agility	0
Strength	-1
Endurance	-1
Willpower	0
Intelligence	+1
Sixth Sense	+3

Brightlings are the smallest of the five ruling-races, and are known most for their exceptional sixth sense and closeness with the Mystic Forces. They range in height from four to four and a half feet, and weigh an average of ninety pounds. Their normal skin color is light gray or white. Their normal eye colors are white, blue, or green.

Brightling's have very unique facial features. They have no noses, but rather just a distinctive marking where the noses of other ruling-races would be. Their nostrils are located on their necks adjacent to the thin membranes on the sides of their faces.

The signature mark of Brightlings, and the reason for their name, is their vibrant hair colors. Their normal hair colors are white, silver, or gold. Brightlings have extremely long, pointed ears that stand straight up.

Brightlings are fairly long lived. Their natural life span ranges from one hundred to one hundred-fifty years. They reach physical maturity around twenty years of age.

The innate ability of Brightlings is "Sense Conjuring". They have the ability to sense conjuring, or even someone that is just drawing upon the Mystic Forces, up to one mile away. This sense is very keen and accurate. A Brightling can very accurately determine the direction from which the conjuring is coming from and how far away it is.

Another ability of Brightlings that is directly related to their "Sense Conjuring" ability, is their ability to sense if another being is Shinkai just by being close to that being. To do this, the Brightling must make a successful Sixth Sense/Performance Test against a Difficulty Value of 8. Success means that they are able to tell if the being is a Shinkai. Failure means they are unable to sense whether the being is Shinkai or not.

If a Brightling attempts to sense if another being is Shinkai and fails, they can not attempt to sense if that same being is Shinkai again until their Sixth Sense value has been raised by at least 1 point.

Brightlings are inherently more in tune with the Mystic Forces than any of the other ruling-races. For this reason they roll 3D10 +10 for their Innate Force Energy rather than just 1D10 +10. Also, Brightling character's can move two mystical attuning counters (or the same one twice) at the first hour instead of one.

Brightlings tend to be very calm and rational beings with a very high sense of logic and morals. Despite their size, they don't intimidate easily, and once enraged they prove to be as fierce an opponent as any.

Language

The Brightling language has a flow to their words and a pronunciation that is very similar to that of the oriental languages.

The Brightling alphabet has a distinctive pattern in that the majority of its letters consist of curved lines and semi-circle patterns.

A very interesting and unique thing about Brightlings that is in direct association with their language is the fact that Brightlings do not use their mouths to speak. They project their speech mentally. The sound travels and is heard by all other beings just as an actual spoken voice would be, except the sound is produced by mental energy rather than with vocal cords.

"ONCE THE BLINDING LIGHTNING AND RAGING WINDS HAD PASSED IT BECAME OBVIOUS TO THE UNFORTUNATE THIEVES THAT THE BRIGHTLING'S SMALL SIZE WAS IN NO WAY REFLECTIVE OF HIS ABILITY TO DEFEND HIMSELF"

BRIGHTLING

ORYATHARIAN	BRIGHTLING
Armor	Vosten
Attack	Lahari
Brightling	Batunara
Coin	Kairu
Cost	Lai
Dark *Gift*	Jen Ruka
Dawn	Kulonyn
Dead/death	Horita
Defender	Sodarden
Eat	Bai
Evil	Zirgob
Fear	Fura
Food	Shonfu
For	Bor
Fort	Teroken
Good	Gaben
Grak	Harook
Hate	Maruke
Heal/healing	Hafo
Help	Borosu
How much	Ben kyon
I	Makyn
Kill	Nebdo
King	Rikba
Large	Romesh
Light	Shinkai
Lormek	Denman
Love	Para
Need	Tenba
Night	Haraka
Of	Ot
Queen	Yoroki
Race	Gah
Retreat	Baroden
Ruling	Pesuno
Run	Kabaren
Shadow	Danu
Shadow-kin	Danukyra
Shall	Shashen
Sleep	Resuwa
Small	Lepo
Stop	Naros
Sun	Rikoda
Sworn	Wakuna
The	Tep
Valkin	Robala
Walk	Maro
Warlum	Wefuso
Water	Melsa
Weapon	Takronan
When	Dimen
Where	Rolebu
Who	Beroma
Why	Washu
You	Layden

A	
B	
C	
D	
E	
F	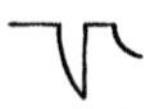
G	
H	
I	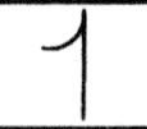
J	
K	
L	
M	
N	
O	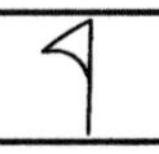
P	
Q	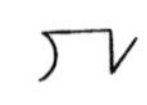
R	
S	
T	
U	
V	
W	
X	
Y	
Z	

GRAK

from fifty to sixty-five years. They reach physical maturity around sixteen years of age.

The innate ability of Grak is "Efficient Metabolism". This ability allows a Grak to go twice as long without food or water, without penalties, as any of the other ruling-races. Another benefit of this ability is that Grak recover from damage faster than the other ruling-races. As a Grak your character receives a +2 Level increase to all Recovery Tests. This also applies to the instant Recovery Test granted by spending a Mystical Attuning Point.

Grak are typically very easy going in nature but are not opposed in the least to resorting to physical conflict when necessary. Their brute strength and an unequaled determination are perhaps their strongest qualities. Rarely will you find a Grak that will give up on anything that he has set his mind to do, and rarely will you find someone foolish enough to try and stop them.

Language

The Grak language has a very short choppy sound to it. Their words are pronounced very harshly and with abrupt and stressed endings. Most Grak words have only one or two syllables.

The Grak alphabet consists of letters that are almost exclusively made up of straight lines and ninety degree angles.

Attribute	Modifier
Agility	-1
Strength	+2
Endurance	0
Willpower	+2
Intelligence	0
Sixth Sense	-1

Grak are short and very stout in stature. They have extremely wide and thick bodies, and are known for their exceptional strength and willpower. They range in height from five to six feet, and weigh an average of two hundred-fifty to three hundred pounds. Their normal skin color is ash-green. Their normal eye colors are brown, green, or red. Their normal hair colors are black or dark brown.

Grak have two small horns approximately an inch in length that protrude straight out from their forehead, just above their eyebrows. Their noses are wide and squared, and their ears are also large and square in shape. The overall appearance of a Grak reminds one of a giant stone block due to their wide and solid stature.

Grak are fairly short lived. Their natural life span ranges

"I HAD NEVER EXPECTED IT FROM MOLK, WHO WAS NEARLY AS WIDE AS HE WAS TALL, BUT HE HAD ACTUALLY OUT-LASTED AND OUTPERFORMED EVERY OTHER KNIGHT ON THE TRAINING GROUNDS. HIS SHEER WILLPOWER AND DESIRE FOR PERFECTION WOULD NOT ALLOW HIM TO COME SHORT OF ANY-THING BUT THE BEST. AT THE END OF THE WEEK THOSE WHO HAD LAUGHED AND JEERED WERE SITTING ASIDE AND WATCHING MOLK RECEIVE THE CROSSED SWORDS PENDANT THAT MEANT THAT HE HAD BEEN RAISED TO THE RANK OF LIEUTENANT."

GRAK

ORYATHARIAN	GRAK
Armor	Abkar
Attack	Akarak
Brightling	Bemtet
Coin	Kafkor
Cost	Seldka
Dark *Gift*	Em Slag
Dawn	Kenktan
Dead/death	Notansk
Defender	Tekwan
Eat	Kep
Evil	Brak
Fear	Sorek
Food	Zekba
For	Nafk
Fort	Bakneb
Good	Zakeb
Grak	Mysk
Hate	Rak
Heal/healing	Sarknas
Help	Bekek
How much	Hosk kek
I	Trike
Kill	Het
King	Saktz
Large	Pontet
Light	Dartquo
Lormek	Hablant
Love	Sharft
Need	Harftk
Night	Tednan
Of	Bar
Queen	Karb
Race	Iraka
Retreat	Ighak
Ruling	Tepnak
Run	Elrost
Shadow	Tank
Shadow-kin	Tanktyrak
Shall	Norok
Sleep	Fleek
Small	Jetdo
Stop	Hardoon
Sun	Kan
Sworn	Zydhar
The	Kask
Valkin	Vlak
Walk	Blefk
Warlum	Wasuka
Water	Watkure
Weapon	Krag
When	Fresk
Where	Dorak
Who	Nod
Why	Drot
You	Yek

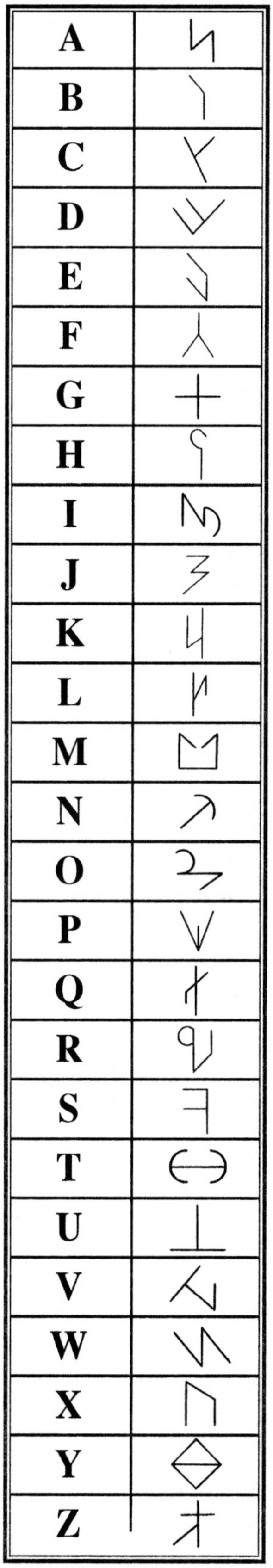

LOREMEK

Attribute	Modifier
Agility	+2
Strength	0
Endurance	-1
Willpower	0
Intelligence	+1
Sixth Sense	0

Loremek are tall and slender, with exceptionally long arms in proportion to the rest of their body. The legs of the Lormek bend opposite of the legs of the other ruling-races giving them the ability to move with extremely quick bursts of agility and speed, which is how they have earned the title of the quickest ruling-race. Their leg structure is very similar to that of a horse or deer and though their feet do not have hooves they are very tough. Many Loremek prefer to go barefoot instead of wearing anything on their feet.

Loremek have smooth, rounded facial features and their noses are moderately sized and their ears are small and rounded. Loremek have absolutely no body hair.

Loremek range in height from five and a half to six and a half feet, and weigh an average of one hundred sixty-five pounds. Their normal skin color is any number of shades of white or brown. Their normal eye colors are blue, brown, or green.

Loremek have an average natural life span ranging from seventy five to one hundred years. They reach physical maturity around eighteen years of age.

The innate ability of Loremek is "Graceful Movement". This ability allows them to move exceptionally fast. Due to this innate ability the Maximum Speed of all Loremek characters is 30 feet per faster than the listed movement (Action Movement is of course increased in proportion). This innate ability also allows Loremek to fall from as high as ten feet without taking any damage. If the fall is greater than ten feet, their innate ability doesn't help in any way; they will take the same amount of damage as any of the other races.

Generally speaking, Loremek have a neutral disposition. They are easy to get along with as long as they are treated well, but they have a fairly short fuse when it comes to being treated rudely or unjustly. Loremek definitely do not handle disrespect very well and it normally doesn't take much of it to make them fighting mad.

Language

The Loremek language is considered the most difficult of the ruling-race languages to learn. Loremek words have a very peculiar letter combination and very few vowels. This combination makes their words difficult to pronounce.

The Loremek alphabet has letters that are made up of squares and triangles. Their are no curves or circles at all in Loremek letters.

"I FINALLY CLIMBED THE LAST FEW FEET TO THE TOP OF THE CLIFF AND CAUGHT UP WITH THE LOREMEK SCOUT. I SIGHED WITH DEEP DREAD AS I REALIZED THAT ANOTHER EQUALLY DIFFICULT CLIMB FACED US JUST AHEAD. I HAD NOT REALLY BEEN AROUND MANY LOREMEK BEFORE AND COULDN'T HELP BUT WISH THAT I HAD THEIR LEGS AS I WATCHED THE SCOUT LOPE TOWARD THE CLIFF FACE AND BEGIN GRACEFULLY SCALING IT AS IF IT WERE NO MORE THAN A LEISURELY STROLL THROUGH THE COUNTRY-SIDE. TAKING IN A DEEP BREATH AND GRABBING UP MY PACK I JOGGED OFF AFTER HIM WONDERING WHAT I HAD GOTTEN MYSELF INTO."

LOREMEK

ORYATHARIAN	LOREMEK
Armor	Arktyn
Attack	Gardlny
Brightling	Cormdon
Coin	Quent
Cost	Karzt
Dark *Gift*	Myr Vnel
Dawn	Efklor
Dead/death	Relts
Defender	Kektsar
Eat	Mafryl
Evil	Skren
Fear	Emnerot
Food	Sormtet
For	Hompf
Fort	Hastz
Good	Palmsen
Grak	Gorft
Hate	Hekp
Heal/healing	Palknik
Help	Etla
How much	Asfertel
I	Dmal
Kill	Romnes
King	Glestern
Large	Barsdo
Light	Larkd
Lormek	Fyntid
Love	Krinis
Need	Motrod
Night	Byrndarsl
Of	Lsk
Queen	Kesdury
Race	Divixt
Retreat	Derstgler
Ruling	Nolbev
Run	Pelf
Shadow	Forskt
Shadow-kin	Forsktlynk
Shall	Kmelpt
Sleep	Brontle
Small	Ompt
Stop	Soolt
Sun	Norsb
Sworn	Calpry
The	Ftes
Valkin	Klimpfta
Walk	Mlomt
Warlum	Psefa
Water	Rampf
Weapon	Tesrinok
When	Kumtna
Where	Havsk
Who	Brom
Why	Quebl
You	Vyes

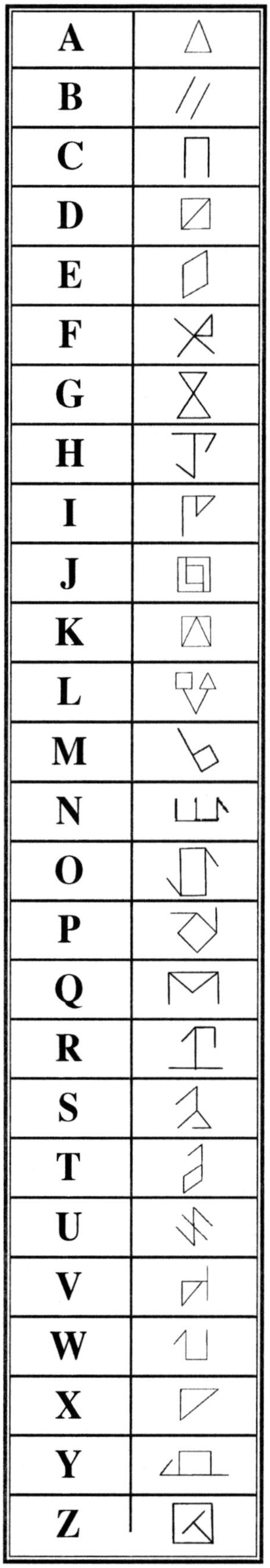

A
B
C
D
E
F
G
H
I
J
K
L
M
N
O
P
Q
R
S
T
U
V
W
X
Y
Z

VALKIN

Attribute	Modifier
Agility	+1
Strength	+1
Endurance	0
Willpower	-1
Intelligence	0
Sixth Sense	+1

Valkin are tall and somewhat slender, but not as slender as Loremek. Their eyes have vertical pupils like that of a cat and their teeth are sharp and pointed, and their noses are small and pointed as well. Their ears are short and mildly pointed and tend to get longer later in the Valkin' years. Valkin are known most for their ability to see in the dark, and their striking appearance, which many consider intimidating.

They range in height from five feet ten inches to six feet four inches, and weigh an average of one hundred-fifty pounds. Their normal skin colors are black, tan, or white. Their normal eye colors are black, blue, purple, or white. Their normal hair colors are black, gold, or white.

Valkin are fairly long lived. Their natural life span ranges from one hundred-fifty to two hundred years. They reach physical maturity around twenty-five years of age.

The innate ability of Valkin is "Night Vision". A Valkin can see quite comfortably in total darkness. One drawback to this ability is that it takes several seconds for the Valkin's vision to adjust from light to total darkness, or vice versa. If a Valkin that is in total darkness is suddenly subjected to light (it need not even be a very bright light) they experience a moment of blindness while their vision adjusts. It takes 3 Turns for their vision to adjust and return to normal. The same temporary blindness will also occur when stepping from any source of light into total darkness.

It doesn't take 3 Turns for a Valkin's vision to adjust if just going into or out of partial darkness. Their vision is just as keen in extremely low-light situations as it is in daylight, and doesn't require an adjusting period. It is the GM's decision as to whether or not a particular area is dark enough to warrant the adjusting period.

The attitude of Valkin is a peculiar one that many non-Valkin find hard to understand. They have a strange disposition that is often confused with rudeness and tend to state their opinions very boldly and often appear to be overly proud.

Language

The Valkin language is a very smooth language and its words have a rhythmic flowing sound that gives them a very soft and relaxing feel.

The letters of the Valkin alphabet consist almost exclusively of circles with some lines and curves frequently incorporated.

"I TURNED TO CHASE THE VALKIN ASSASSIN INTO THE NIGHT-BLACKENED FOREST BUT WAS STOPPED SHORT AS MY LIEUTENANT GRABBED ME BY THE ARM. "IT WOULD BE FOOLISH TO FOLLOW HIM NOW. AS WE STRAIN OUR EYES SEARCHING FOR HIM HE WILL BE STALKING US AS CONFIDENTLY AS A PANTHER. WE WAIT UNTIL MORNING." A SUDDEN CHILL CAME OVER ME AS I STOOD STARING BLINDLY INTO THE NIGHT. AT THIS VERY MOMENT THE ASSASSIN'S EYES COULD BE UPON ME. I WOULD WAIT TILL MORNING."

VALKIN

ORYATHARIAN	VALKIN
Armor	Egloban
Attack	Kleeban
Brightling	Blomylen
Coin	Kyl
Cost	Horbyl
Dark *Gift*	Korga Thool
Dawn	Hilodel
Dead/death	Domys
Defender	Shoros
Eat	Bulo
Evil	Gardeb
Fear	Molgel
Food	Blesyl
For	Rob
Fort	Flibas
Good	Ponma
Grak	Robla
Hate	Nablen
Heal/healing	Leelop
Help	Flydris
How much	Dar freer
I	Oolb
Kill	Preer
King	Henbish
Large	Sholar
Light	Sylmorn
Lormek	Nishbyn
Love	Vorboon
Need	Jorlys
Night	Desdoryl
Of	Ben
Queen	Oween
Race	Gool
Retreat	Phlyrin
Ruling	Bleegra
Run	Salbo
Shadow	Hoskryl
Shadow-kin	Hosdrylnos
Shall	Voryl
Sleep	Wogran
Small	Fisa
Stop	Mongry
Sun	Syldra
Sworn	Lefnan
The	Blem
Valkin	Smorbleb
Walk	Hanglom
Warlum	Mefor
Water	Nyrma
Weapon	Walydan
When	Morbry
Where	Dalwor
Who	Flom
Why	Mothris
You	Plob

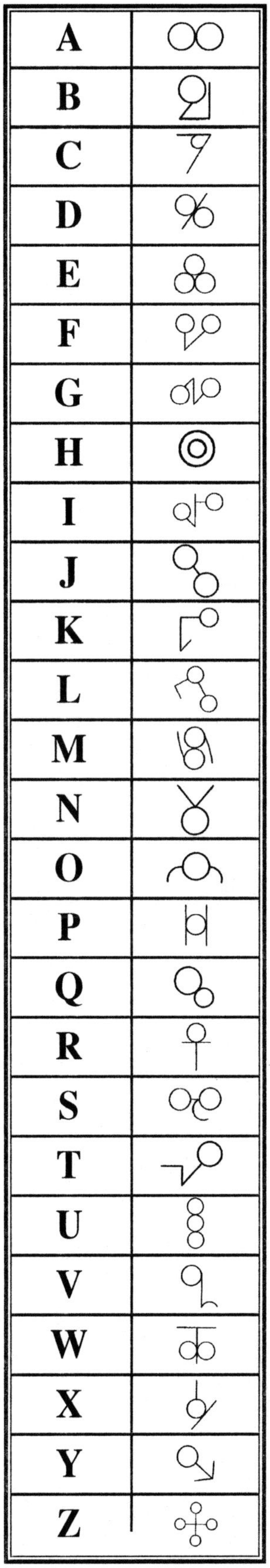

A
B
C
D
E
F
G
H
I
J
K
L
M
N
O
P
Q
R
S
T
U
V
W
X
Y
Z

WARLUM

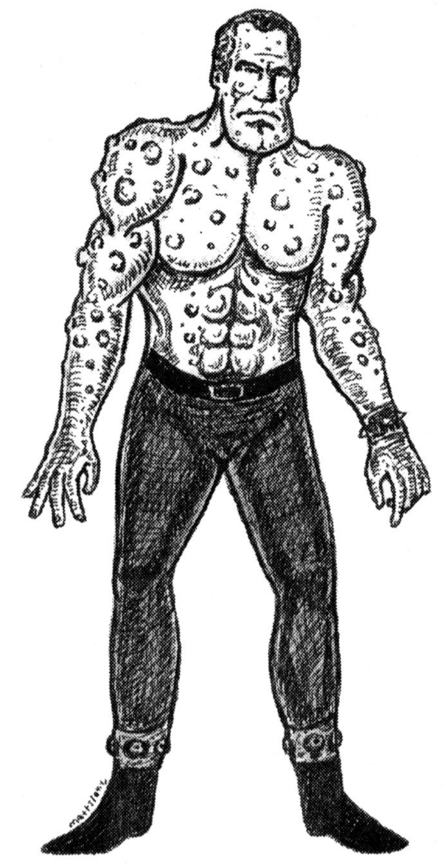

Attribute	Modifier
Agility	0
Strength	+2
Endurance	+2
Willpower	0
Intelligence	-1
Sixth Sense	-1

Warlum are very tall and stout in stature. They have a fairly wide chest and shoulders, and are known for their exceptional strength and endurance. Warlum have very wide and flat noses. Their eyebrows are very wide and thick. Their ears are fairly large and round, and lay flat against the sides of their head. Their lower jaw is very wide and strong. They range in height from six and a half to seven and a half feet, and weigh an average of two hundred to two hundred-fifty pounds. Their normal skin color is copper. Their normal eye colors are blue or brown. Their normal hair colors are black, brown, or sandy blonde.

Warlum are fairly short lived. Their natural life span ranges from sixty to seventy-five years. They reach physical maturity around thirteen years of age.

The innate ability of Warlum is "Stone Skin". They have extremely tough skin that is covered with many hard knots. This tough skin gives the Warlum a Natural Protection Rating of 2 to all zones.

Warlum are a very high-strung race. They are always aware of, and ready, for the possibility of combat. They have a very high sense of honor, and tend to hold grudges for a long time against those that offend them. They show little fear in the face of their enemies, regardless of how they may feel inside. The Warlum's ability to withstand physical abuse and endure even the harshest of climates has earned them the reputation for being Oryathar's toughest and most rugged ruling-race.

Language

The Warlum language has a very repetitive sound. Most of their words have only two syllables with the syllables usually rhyming with each other.

The Warlum alphabet has a distinctive double-line pattern to most all of its letters, which consist of a myriad of lines, circles, and triangles.

"IT WAS AT THE HEIGHT OF THE BATTLE WHEN THE BOTTLE OF GLOWING RED LIQUID CAME WHISTLING DOWN TOWARD US FROM THE CLIFFS ABOVE. THE EXPLOSION WAS TREMENDOUS AND DOZENS OF OUR TROOPS WERE KILLED INSTANTLY. THE OVERTURNED WAGONS THAT WERE BEING USED FOR COVER DISINTEGRATED UNDER THE FORCE OF THE EXPLOSION. SOMEHOW I MANAGED TO SURVIVE THE BLAST, THOUGH I WAS BADLY INJURED. IT WAS THE WARLUM OF OUR UNIT THAT FOUGHT OFF THE REST OF THE ATTACKERS AND CARRIED US TO SAFETY. THOUGH MOST OF THEIR CLOTHES HAD BEEN TORN OFF FROM FLYING DEBRIS THEY HAD HARDLY A SCRATCH ON THEM, AND THOSE THAT DID HAVE INJURIES DIDN'T SEEM TO NOTICE THEM."

WARLUM

ORYATHARIAN	WARLUM
Armor	Romra
Attack	Folwar
Brightling	Brenlo
Coin	Rop
Cost	Telp
Dark *Gift*	Gabra Hava
Dawn	Wal
Dead/death	Darp
Defender	Debned
Eat	Eften
Evil	Eknat
Fear	Komrom
Food	Dromo
For	Nyl
Fort	Krasha
Good	Vomga
Grak	Wadgla
Hate	Berzert
Heal/healing	Mehe
Help	Teknek
How much	Fer desmet
I	Srama
Kill	Lefk
King	Detret
Large	Drome
Light	Shrekmek
Lormek	Bararn
Love	Wevget
Need	Sneebreeg
Night	Papnap
Of	Rif
Queen	Mevlee
Race	Rala
Retreat	Bemled
Ruling	Zurune
Run	Daraf
Shadow	Sarkar
Shadow-kin	Sarkarver
Shall	Hafnaf
Sleep	Breegree
Small	Melel
Stop	Famglap
Sun	Zomnon
Sworn	Kromro
The	Kel
Valkin	Quemsem
Walk	Wromgra
Warlum	Strosbon
Water	Nayhay
Weapon	Flibkif
When	Derbrer
Where	Marglar
Who	Shro
Why	Glymlite
You	Eklek

DEFENDERS OF THE LIGHT

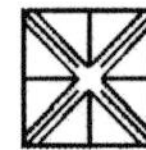

DEFENDERS OF THE LIGHT

The Defenders of the Light are a highly respected military organization dedicated to the fight against the Shadow. They are known mainly for their expertise in recruiting and training Shinkai. No greater concentration of Shinkai can be found anywhere else on the planet than inside the walls of the Defenders of the Light fort cities.

Being a Defender of the Light carries with it great responsibilities and sacrifice but it is far from a thankless job. Though the Defenders of the Light lead a very strict and intense lifestyle they also enjoy many benefits and receive great gratification from their service to the Light. The Defenders of the Light train very hard and put their lives at risk every day for the sake of others and for the greater good. They have earned the respect and admiration that now symbolizes all that the Defenders of the Light are.

You have a choice as to whether or not your character will become a Defender of the Light. Some like the idea of belonging to an organization and being part of the legend of the Defenders of the Light, while others prefer being a renegade that can come and go as they please without having to answer to anyone.

This Section will discuss many of the details and information that accompanies life as a Defender of the Light. By the end of this Section you should know whether or not you would like your character to enlist as a Defender of the Light or to remain a freelance adventurer.

The golden sun ebbs to rest above the jagged mountain crest. The Shadow wakes now death and fear spread like a fire to devour and kill.

With shining swords and fists of might rise to the call Defenders of the Light. Into the heart of night they ride to face the Shadow and restore their pride.

Black flesh and claws embrace shining steel the Light the Shadow desires to kill. Lightning and fire from fingers take flight creatures of darkness fall prey to the Light.

More innocent saved less Shadow alive, still more will come with each passing night. As long as there's evil and Shadow to fight they'll stand proud and true, Defenders of the Light!

Ara Kade

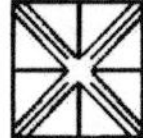

BENEFITS

There are many benefits that members of the Defenders of the Light enjoy. Many of these benefits make the choice of whether or not to become a Defender of the Light much easier, but hopefully the choice to enlist into this elite and honorable organization will be based on more than just physical rewards.

Discounts

All members of the Defenders of the Light receive a fifty percent discount on any non-green-steel or non-magical items that they purchase within any Defender of the Light fort city. Consequently, any non-green-steel or non-magical items that a member of the Defenders of the Light sells within a fort city will only bring half of its normal value.

Purchasing items within a fort city for half-price and then re-selling them in other towns or cities for full price is not a respectable practice for someone who has sworn to serve the Light. Such practices are frowned upon greatly and may be met with severe consequences. It is an unwritten code among the Defenders of the Light that any items purchased within a fort city with the Defenders of the Light discount only be re-sold or traded in a Defenders of the Light fort city.

Pay

Members of the Defenders of the Light are paid weekly. Payment is issued on the first day of the week. The amount of pay that Defenders of the Light receive is based upon their rank. The following list shows the base pay that Defenders of the Light receive based on their rank.

Knights = 25 sc per week

Lieutenants = 40 sc per week

Captain = 50 sc per week

Colonel = 70 sc per week

General = 100 sc per week

Knight are issued their pay by their Lieutenants. Lieutenants are issued their pay by their Captains, and so on. The General is responsible for obtaining his own payment from the fort's treasury.

There are means by which a Defender of the Light can increase his weekly pay. The more proficient and skilled that a Defender of the Light becomes the more pay that he will receive (to a certain extent).

For every Specialty that is mastered an additional 5 silver coins per week will be added to that Defender of the Light's pay. Specializing in calvary can also increase one's pay if he obtains the title of Cavalryman. Cavalrymen receive an additional 5 silver coins per week to their pay above what non-cavalrymen do.

Provisions

All new recruits to the Defenders of the Light are issued one full suit of padded leather armor (includes hood, arm-guards, chest/back-guard with pelvis skirt, and breeches), one pair of boots, two shirts, two pairs of breeches, two changes of under clothes, and one short sword or mace (knight's choice). These items once issued are property of the new recruit. If he loses them or they are destroyed or become in need of repair he is responsible for them. If a member of the Defenders of the Light were to have his issued weapons or armor destroyed, in combat for instance, he can borrow a replacement weapon or piece of armor from the fort's armory, at his lieutenant's discretion, until he could afford to buy his own.

All members of the Defenders of the Light receive two free meals a day served in the fort's dining hall at the 5th and 13th hours.

Residence

Members of the Defenders of the Light take up permanent residence within massive fortified cities known as fort city's. Knight's quarters are on the first floor where two or more knights are assigned to a single room. Lieutenants and other officers have private rooms on the upper floors. No fee is charged for this occupancy. It is one of the many benefits given to the Defenders of the Light.

Training

All Defenders of the Light have free access to any of the fort's many training grounds. In addition, all Defenders of the Light are required to train for a minimum amount of time each day. This training is done under the guidance and instruction of masters of every form of combat known, both physical and mystical. Such training by such experienced and skilled instructors can't be found for free just anywhere.

Generally eight hours of training a day is the required training for all knights. Lieutenants and officers of higher rank may not train as long each day as do the knights (they have many other duties and responsibilities to attend to).

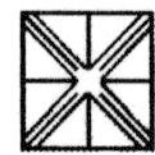

EXPECTATIONS

The Defenders of the Light are always under a watchful eye. Everyone expects them to be upstanding and loyal and to be there when needed. These high expectations from the public are taken very seriously by the Defenders of the Light. The expectations that the officers of the Defenders of the Light have for each and every member of its ranks is no less demanding and meets no lower of a standard.

Behavior

Every member of the Defenders of the Light, regardless of their rank, is expected to behave themselves in a professional and respectful manner at all times. Their attitude and demeanor should be such that their obedience to the Light should never be questioned.

Arrogance, hostility, lack of respect, disobedience, and dishonesty are just a few of the traits that have no place among the Defenders of the Light. Serving the Light is an honor and a privilege and the attitudes of those in the Light's service should reflect just that. Those who are not able to behave themselves in an appropriate manner may quickly find that they are no longer a member of the Defenders of the Light.

Commitment

All members of the Defenders of the Light have an extremely important role in restoring the balance to Oryathar. This task is not an easy one, but commitment to this goal is an absolute must. Though at times it is easy to become discouraged and it may often seem that the fight against the Shadow is all but impossible, we must realize that without a commitment to fight and a belief that the Light *will* prevail we have already lost.

More than anyone else the Defenders of the Light are looked upon as the focus of the fight against the Shadow. Never should any member of the Defenders of the Light allow his commitment to the Light or to the people of Oryathar to waiver.

Loyalty

Loyalty to the cause to which he serves is what makes a Defender of the Light more than just a soldier. The Defenders of the Light take pride in their job and show great respect for their superiors and fellow ruling-races. It is this respect and loyalty within the ranks of the Defenders of the Light that makes them such a strong and effective weapon against the Shadow.

All members of the Defenders of the Light are expected to display the utmost of loyalty to their superiors as well as to the cause for which they fight.

Role-model

Being a role-model is a large responsibility of each and every member of the Defenders of the Light. Regardless of where they are or what they are doing a Defender of the Light should carry himself in a manner that will bring honor to the Light and to the Defenders of the Light as a whole. More importantly than what a Defender of the Light may say to try to positively influence others is his actions and the example that he puts forth.

It is the responsibility of each and every Defender of the Light to be a positive example for others.

POLICIES

In order to run smoothly and efficiently there are many policies that the Defenders of the Light employ and to which they must adhere. Some of the more important and relevant of these policies will now be discussed.

Terms of Recruitment

Being a Defender of the Light demands a great deal of physical and mental endurance. For this reason not just anyone can become a Defender of the Light. Individuals who wish to join ranks with the Defenders of the Light must appear in person at the main fort of a Defender of the Light fort city. There they may request to speak with a recruiting officer, this is generally a lieutenant. The recruiting officer will give the possible recruitee a physical and mental examination. If there is reason to suspect that the individual can not perform within the expectations of the Defenders of the Light, either physically or mentally, they will be respectfully declined at this time.

If the recruiting officer feels that they meet the qualifications for a member of the Defenders of the Light they will be taken to one more of the fort city's training grounds where they will be asked to observe and train with knights for one

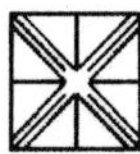

full day. During this time they will be given a room in the main fort and will be allowed to join the knights in the dining hall, free of charge.

The following morning, if the recruitee still wishes to become a Defender of the Light, he and all other potential recruits that have made it to this stage will be taken to meet the general of the fort city. The general will speak briefly with each recruitee and further explain the expectations and requirements of the Defenders of the Light before proclaiming them knights of the Defenders of the Light.

As a tradition as well as a pledge of faith and commitment each recruit is asked to recite the following creed of the Defenders of the Light.

"With honor and pride I serve the Light, knowing that all my strengths and abilities have been granted me by the grace thereof. For the ways of the Light I shall gladly lay down my life, for there is no greater cause than that which I serve. The Light shall illumine and overpower the Shadow, for my life is a testament thereto. The Light shall prevail!"

The new knights will then be shown to their quarters and issued their provisions. Their names as well as other personal information about each knight is recorded by a scribe and filed in the fort's hall of records.

Terms of Resignation

Any Defender of the Light that wishes to resign membership with the Defenders of the Light must request an audience with their general where they will give a full explanation for their actions. The general will determine whether or not there is any foul-play or outside influences in the Defender of the Light's decision to resign. If he can not change their mind or find any reason why they should not be allowed to resign the general himself will at this time decree their nullification as a Defender of the Light and they may go their way. The details of the meeting with the general will be recorded by a scribe and recorded in the fort's hall of records.

Leaving the ranks of the Defenders of the Light in any other manner (other than death of course) is unacceptable and is considered abandonment.

Any Defender of the Light that abandons their fort will be hunted down and brought to question before the general of their fort. If found guilty of abandonment they will be fined a sum equal to six weeks of their current pay and will be temporarily stripped of their rank as a Defender of the Light. Depending upon the reason for the abandonment it may be one to five weeks before the general will re-instate the offender, during which time they must remain within the fort city. If the abandoning Defender of the Light no longer wishes to remain a member of the Defenders of the Light or if the general so chooses he may permanently discharge the offender from the Defenders of the Light at this time.

If found guilty of abandonment a second time the Defender of the Light is again fined a sum equal to six weeks of their current pay and is immediately dishonorably discharged as a Defender of the Light. Reinstatement is only possible by the consent and approval of a general of the Defender of the Light, a kingsman of the King's Guard, or the king himself.

The fines for abandonment can either be paid in full up front or if the abandoning Defender of the Light does not have the coin, they can work off the debt within the fort. Pay for these services is normally two silver coins per day and the duties are determined by the general of the fort, or in the case of the King's Guard it is determined by the kingsman (or the king himself on rare occasions).

Promotion

All initial recruits into the Defenders of the Light enter at the rank of Knight. Anyone with a rank higher than Knight is considered an officer.

There are four ranks above Knight. In this order they are Lieutenant, Captain, Colonel, and finally General. The general is the highest rank attainable within the Defenders of the Light. (The King's Guard also has similar ranks starting at Guardsman then progressing to Legionnaire, Captain, Major, and finally Kingsman. Above all of these, including a general of the Defenders of the Light, is the king himself.)

If a member of the Defenders of the Light wishes to increase their rank they must submit a written letter to their immediate supervisor (in the case of knight's this would be their Lieutenant, for lieutenants this would be their Captain, etc.) explaining their desire to increase their rank as well as an explanation of why they feel they qualify for the promotion. A meeting with the general, who personally interviews all those seeking promotion, will take place and the decision to promote or not promote the individual will normally be given within one to two weeks.

Normally only knights and lieutenants actually leave the fort city to embark on missions and quests. Captains and colonels generally remain within the fort city to handle authoritive duties. This will likely make it undesirable to have a character ranked higher than Lieutenant. For this reason only the qualifications for Lieutenant are explained. If any player wants their character to obtain a rank higher than Lieutenant then the GM can simply make up his own qualifications for those ranks.

Characters may also choose to join ranks with the King's Guard, however they will not receive the specialized training that they need to hone their Shinkai abilities anywhere other than with the Defenders of the Light. But if players do want their character to join up with the King's Guard the qualifications for enlistment and for promotion through their ranks is essentially the same as for that of the Defenders of the Light.

It should be noted here that all players within the group should decide and agree whether or not their characters will join ranks with the Defenders of the Light or with the King's Guard (if either). Either choice is acceptable but it is advised

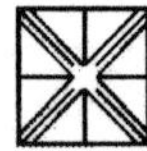

not to have half of the characters Defenders of the Light and the other half members of the King's Guard. It will be a very difficult and time consuming task trying to write or run adventures that will be able to keep the characters together or on the same mission. If all of the characters are Defenders of the Light or all of them are members of the King's Guard then it is much simpler and logical to keep them together and to run the adventures smoothly.

Qualifications for Lieutenant

1. Your character must know the first five Talents of his Specialty.

2. Your character must have Rank 2 or higher in the "Calvary" Skill.

3. Your character must have Rank 1 or higher in the "Climbing" Skill or must know the "Climbing" Talent

4. Your character must have all three Ranks of the "Traveling" Skill.

5. Your character must have been an active member of the Defenders of the Light for at least five blocks.

If your character meets all of these requirements he may apply for promotion to Lieutenant.

It is a good idea for one of the characters, and usually no more than one, in a gaming group to be a lieutenant. In most situations at least one lieutenant must accompany a troop of knights any time they are sent on a mission. If one of the player's characters is a lieutenant then he can assume that role and eliminate the need for the GM to run an npc lieutenant on every mission that the characters embark on.

Being a lieutenant means accepting a great deal of responsibility. The lieutenant has to be responsible for the actions of all of the knights under his supervision. He is expected to make sure that orders are followed and that any given mission is carried out as ordered. When a mission goes well the lieutenant is usually the first one to be congratulated but on the other hand when a mission fails or there are problems within his ranks he is the first one to catch the blame and brought to question.

Armory

Every Defender of the Light fort city has an armory in their main fort. This armory contains all of the weapons and armor that the fort possesses. The fort's armory is used to supply all of the members of the Defenders of the Light with the weapons and armor that they might need for any given mission or battle.

All weapons and armor acquired by any member of the Defenders of the Light while on a mission or in the service of the Defenders of the Light must be turned in to the fort. It will then be placed in the fort's armory and those responsible for acquiring the items will be given a bonus in their next pay (usually around ten percent of the value of the items turned in) for their contribution to the fort.

The Defenders of the Light have a very limited amount of

weapons and other resources and are often funded and supported by the king. All members of the Defenders of the Light are urged to purchase their own weapons and armor, but for those who can not yet afford needed weapons or armor they may temporarily borrow them from the fort's armory at the permission of their Lieutenant.

Treasury

Every Defender of the Light fort city has a treasury in their main fort. This treasury contains all of the coin and other valuables, such as diamonds and rubies and other valuable jewels that the fort possesses. The fort's treasury is used to supply all of the necessary supplies and expenditures for the fort. Such expenditures include the coin to pay the members of the Defenders of the Light, coin for food supplies as well as clothes, weapons, and armor. The general of the fort decides how the treasury's funds are distributed and regulated.

As with weapons and armor, all coin and other valuable items acquired by any member of the Defenders of the Light while on a mission or in the service of the Defenders of the Light must be turned in to the fort. It will then be placed in either the fort's treasury, or armory, as necessary. Those responsible for acquiring the coin or valuable items will be given a bonus in their next pay (usually around ten percent of the value of the items turned in) for their success and contribution to the fort. Those who think it unfair to only get a portion of what they discover or acquire should realize that without the training and assistance of the Defenders of the Light they would likely not have lived to acquire it in the first place. Beyond this, no one is forced to join the

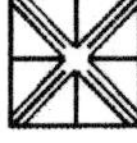

Defenders of the Light. If they don't agree with their policies they should not join.

REGULATIONS

In order to maintain their integrity and their ability to effectively maintain order as well as to remain an effective force against the Shadow there are many regulations that the Defenders of the Light strictly adhere to. Some of the more important and relevant of these regulations will now be discussed.

Code of Conduct

All members of the Defenders of the Light are to conduct themselves in a respectful and decent manner at all times. Additional respect is expected to be shown for one's superiors. Unless in hostile territory where it would not be wise to single out the superior or commanding officer all Defenders of the Light and members of the King's Guard are to salute their superior officers immediately upon entering their presence and are to hold the salute until the superior officer returns their salute or puts them at ease. (The salute used by the King's Guard and Defender's of the Light is performed by holding the right fist over the heart, palm-side facing the chest, with left hand held up beside of the left side of the head, palm facing forward.)

A common dismissal by officers as well as an accepted phrase used all across Oryathar is, "May the Light guide you to your destiny".

Failure to salute a superior will result in a stern warning by the superior officer. A failure to salute a superior a second time will result in a strict warning and the assignment of any physical duties that the superior officer feels is necessary, such as running laps on the training ground, doing pushups, running the training course repeatedly, etc. Failure to salute three or more times will result in a meeting with the general, or kingsman, to discuss the motives of the individual who is failing to follow regulations or show the proper respect to their superiors. This will normally include the use of the Force-effect "Lie Detection" and/or the Judgement Stone.

Upon the general's judgement the guilty individual may be fined, demoted to inactive status and given a term of penance, dishonorably discharged, or all of the above.

For reasons of security and organization, as well as respect, no member of the Defenders of the Light, or King's Guard, is to leave their designated area of the fort city without informing their superior.

The orders of a superior should be followed at all times unless the orders are in direct violation of the law or in direct conflict with the Light or the standing orders of a higher ranking officer.

Whether a member of the King's Guard or a Defender of the Light officers are due the respect they have earned and deserve. So if your character is a knight in the Defenders of the Light anyone within the Defenders of the Light with a rank of Lieutenant or higher is his superior and anyone within the King's Guard with a rank of Legionnaire or higher is his superior. There is no disrespect or competition between the King's Guard and the Defenders of the Light. Any member of the Defenders of the Light will show all the respect for an officer of the King's Guard as he would for an officer of the Defenders of the Light, and vice versa.

All members of the Defenders of the Light as well as the King's Guard are taught to respect and value life, especially the life of other ruling-races. Unless given strict orders by a commanding superior no Defender of the Light or the King's Guard will attack another ruling-race with the intent to kill unless there is no other alternative. All ruling-races, regardless of their crimes, are to be brought to justice either before the general of the Defenders of the Light or the kingsman of the King's Guard (or the king himself).

Curfews

Unless assigned to other duties all Defenders of the Light must be inside the main fort by the 16th hour, and unless assigned to other duties all Defenders of the Light are to be in their chambers by the 18th hour (they will need to get plenty of rest so that they will be ready to rise at the 25th hour and report for their daily duties and training).

Daily Regimen

At the sounding of the waking trumpet (25th hour) all Defenders of the Light will rise and report to their respective lieutenants either in the central meeting hall of the main fort or directly in front of the main fort (the exact area for reporting varies from fort city to fort city depending upon the size of the fort and number of recruits). Knights must report to their lieutenants in the designated area by the first hour.

The knights are then assigned to specific duties or tasks by

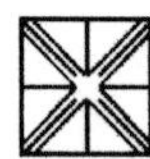

their lieutenants. These duties are generally for a duration of five hours, after which time all knights are to report to their lieutenants for further assignments, if the lieutenant has not already given assignments for their next task.

While not on specific assignments or duties knights, under the assistance of their lieutenant, are to train for a minimum of four hours a day in the various areas of the fort's training grounds. There is a different section of the training grounds designed for the training and development of each of the seven Specialties.

Knights that are Shinkai are also to receive a minimum of four hours of training with the Mystic Forces each day. This training takes place in an area within the fort known as Shinkai Hall.

Two meals a day are served in the dining hall within the fort. Breakfast is served from the 5th to 6th hour and dinner is served from the 13th to 14th hour.

Enforcement of the Law

The Defenders of the Light as well as the King's Guard are very strict and swift in dealing punishment to those who break the law. Violation of the laws of the land and acts of the Shadow are not tolerated to any degree. For the lesser crimes fines, forced labor, and imprisonment are often employed. However, crimes against the Light are dealt with much more seriously.

Any ruling-race found guilty of being Shadow-sworn will be brought before the entire city in the public square where the general, or kingsman, will formally charge the guilty. A circle of Shinkai, generally ten which are handpicked by the general or kingsman, known as the execution squad, will then bring sudden and swift death upon the guilty by means of the Force-effects "Air Bind", "Disintegration", and

"Decay". The current state of Oryathar and the well-known historical events that took place during the War of Betrayal have made such drastic measures necessary when dealing with those who serve the Shadow.

SUMMATION

This is only a few of the more important details that pertain to the Defenders of the Light. Feel free to create your own laws, regulations, policies, etc., or feel free to change those already given in this Section. If you find that a particular rule or regulation is not appropriate for your gaming group or playing style then just change it to whatever works for you.

This Section is simply a guideline to help you in understanding how the Defenders of the Light operate and what is expected of someone who is a Defender of the Light.

"May the Light guide you to your destiny"

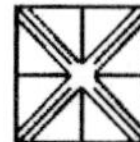

COMBAT

Though combat is not always the best solution, it is often necessary, especially where the Shadow is involved. The current state of Oryathar makes it nearly impossible for the ruling-races; especially the Defender's of the Light, not to occasionally find themselves in a combat situation.

This Section will describe all of the different types of combat in detail, including how to attack, how to determine the damage yielded from an attack, and much more.

At first glance it all may seem overwhelming, but be patient and read through all of the rules carefully. Once you've read through it once dive in and give it a try, referring back to the rules as needed. In no time at all your character will be slicing his way through the fiercest of battles with ease.

There are basically three major types of combat; Physical, Mystical, and Dragonknight. The following is a description of the more common elements of each of these three types of combat. Each individual type of combat will also be described in detail separately.

Initiative

Initiative is a term used to indicate who gets to initiate their actions first in a Turn. Each being involved in combat has an Initiative value that will determine at what point during the Turn their Major Actions are initiated. Though in reality most actions are all taking place simultaneously there must be a way within the game to determine whose attack goes first. That "way" is Initiative.

There are two types of Initiative, Physical Initiative and Mystical Initiative. Physical Initiative is used to determine the action order of physical actions and Mystical Initiative is used to determine the order of mystical actions.

Your character's Physical Initiative value is equal to his current Agility Level and his Mystical Initiative value is equal to his current Sixth Sense Level +2. So, if you want your character to use a Force-effect as his Major Action he will get to perform it at his Mystical Initiative value (Force-effects are mystical actions). If you want your character to attack with a sword or shoot a bow he will get to do so at his Physical Initiative value.

Major Actions begin with the being with the highest Initiative and then proceeds with the next highest and so on until all beings have performed their intended actions for the Turn. One exception to this rule that will often allow an individual with a lower Initiative to perform their Major Action before another individual with a higher Initiative is the concept of immediate actions verses immediate movement. All combatants who are performing their Major Actions before moving get to perform them before combatants who plan to move a significant distance before performing their Major Actions. The ideal here is that the combatant who is not moving before their Major Action is performing their actions while the other combatant is moving.

For example, Krag wishes to attack an approaching serpent-wolf with "Fire Lightning". The serpent-wolf begins the Turn eighty feet away. Eighty feet is within the serpent-wolf's Action Movement so it can get to Krag and attack him this Turn. The serpent-wolf wants to rush into melee with Krag and bite him. This is a physical attack so we will use the serpent-wolf's Physical Initiative value to determine at what point in the Turn it gets to attack. Krag wishes to use a Force-effect to attack the serpent-wolf. This is a mystical attack and so we use Krag's Mystical Initiative to determine at what point during the Turn his attack takes place.

Krag's Mystical Initiative is 12 and the serpent-wolf's Physical Initiative is 20. Had Krag and the serpent-wolf both been in melee with each other at the beginning of the Turn the serpent-wolf would have attacked first, but because the serpent-wolf doesn't have any ranged attacks it must close into melee before it can attack. While the serpent-wolf is moving toward Krag he can release his "Fire Lightning" (Krag has immediate actions verses the serpent wolf's immediate movement).

In short, Major Actions are resolved in the order of Initiative among those with immediate actions first and then among those who chose to move before performing their actions.

Lets say that in the above example Krag wanted to begin the Turn running for cover behind an overturned wagon, but he still wanted to attack the approaching serpent-wolf with "Fire Lightning". If Krag chooses to use "Fire Lightning" as soon as he begins moving and does so *while* moving, his attack will still come before the serpent-wolf's. Krag's actions are still considered immediate actions instead of immediate movement because he is not waiting until he has moved before performing his attack, but rather attacking *while* moving. The serpent-wolf, not having any ranged attacks, does not have this option and thus must wait until *after* it has moved the complete distance into melee before performing its action (attacking).

As an advanced rule it is possible for those with immediate movement to perform their Major Action before those with immediate actions if their Initiative is double or more of the being's Initiative who has immediate actions. So if my character's Physical Initiative is 16 and I want him to run toward a creature that is within range of his Action Movement and attack it with a sword, and a partner is standing by with his bow and wishes to shoot the same creature, normally he would go first regardless of Initiative Values (he has immediate actions verses my character's immediate movement). But let's say that his Physical Initiative is 8. My character's Initiative is double his, therefore he is able to rush the creature and attack it with his sword before he is able to get of a shot with his bow.

Using Initiative values to resolve the order of actions in combat is not a fool-proof method. There will be many situations in which you are not sure whether the Initiative value

accurately dictates the order of actions. My advice here is to simply take a logical look at the situation and determine the flow of events in the way that makes most sense. Initiative is only a guide not a written-in-stone law. Feel free to alter the order of actions whenever it seems appropriate, regardless of Initiative values.

One point to make here is that the GM's decision is final. Most GM's put a lot of hard work into understanding the rules of the game and making the gaming session as enjoyable as possible. They will do their best to make a fair and logical ruling on any of the situations that may arise. Their decision should be respected. Remember, its just a game and the purpose of playing is to have fun. Nobody likes a rules lawyer who wants to argue over every little detail of the game.

Attacking

Before your character can begin his glorious conquest to rescue Oryathar from the Shadow you will need to know how to walk him through combat. This begins with learning how to attack.

One of two attributes are used to perform attacks depending upon the type of attack that your character is making. "Agility" is used to perform physical attacks and "Sixth Sense" is used to perform mystical attacks. Dragonknight attacks, which are technically physical attacks, are in a category by themselves. Agility is the attribute used to perform Dragonknight attacks (breath attacks included). All types of attacks are Major Actions, unless otherwise stated .

An attack is not necessarily one hit or one strike with a weapon, but may be several slices, thrusts, or hits. But for simplicity of the game's sake it is all considered one attack. For some weapons, namely archery and throwing weapons, a single attack *is* a single hit, but for melee weapons a single attack may consist of a series of thrusts and slashes.

Though a single attack may technically consist of several hits to various areas of an opponent, the damage from one successful attack is applied to a single area. Think of this as the area of the opponent that took the hardest hit or most well-placed hit.

To perform an attack, find the current Level of the appropriate attribute for the attack. It may be necessary to adjust this Level up or down if your character is suffering from injuries, fatigue, and the like, or if he is being affected by a Force-effect or any other factors that affect the appropriate attribute. Modifiers that affect the attack value and not the attribute itself are added in last.

For example, Draven wishes to attack an approaching bristle-wolf with his dagger. He has an Agility (the appropriate attribute for a physical attack) of Level 8, but has an injury applied to his Agility, which is a -2 Level penalty. Draven currently has a rune drawn on him that increases his Agility by 3 Levels. These bonuses and penalties bring his Agility

for this attack to Level 9.

Once the attribute has been adjusted, the next step is to roll 1D12 which is referred to as the Performance Die. The Performance Die represents how well your character is performing. The number rolled on the Performance Die is now added to your character's current attribute Level. If your character has any bonuses, or penalties for that matter, that apply to the attack value they are now added to this total for the total value of the attack. Such bonuses often include Talents, Specialty bonus, Technique Points, "Proficiency", and bonuses from green-steel or enchantments.

Some exceptions to the method of determining your character's attack value are "Feeble Attempts" and "Flawless Performances". If you roll a 1 on the Performance Die it is called a "Feeble Attempt". You do not add the 1 to the attack and must now subtract 1D4 points from the attack value. If you roll a 12 on the Performance Die it is a "Flawless Performance". You not only add the 12 points to the attack, but also add an additional 1D4 points to the attack value.

If the total attack value **exceeds** the opponent's Defense value, then the attack is successful. The specific area of the target that is struck is determined by rolling percentile dice and consulting the "ZONE/STRIKE" table (this is explained a little later in this Section).

If your character's attack value doubles his opponent's Defense value, any dice rolled to determine the damage of the attack that roll the highest number possible may be rolled one additional time, adding this result in as well ("re-roll on a max roll").

If your character's attack triples his opponent's Defense, he receive all the benefits of doubling it as well as adding an additional 1D8 points to the damage of the attack (this 1D8 can also be re-rolled on a max roll).

Attacking vs. Movement

Attacks made while your character is moving at speeds of 35 feet per Turn or greater (running speed) will receive a -1D6 point penalty to the attack value.

Attacking a target that is moving at speeds of 35 feet per Turn or greater will also give your character a -1D6 point penalty to his attack value. So if your character makes an attack against a target that is moving 35 feet per Turn or faster while he himself is moving at speeds of 35 feet per Turn or faster he will receive a -2D6 point penalty to his attack value.

Damage

Once your character makes a successful attack you will need to determine how much damage, if any, he has inflicted. The amount of damage done with a physical attack depends upon the Level of Strength your character applied and the Damage Yield of the weapon used. The amount of damage done by a mystical attack varies widely according to

the particular Force-effect being used, and in the case of essence combat, it depends entirely upon the roll of the Force Energy Dice.

In the case of physical attacks you decide what Level of Strength you would like your character to apply to the attack. This can be any Level desired up to your character's current Strength Level. It may be necessary to adjust your character's Strength Level up or down if he is suffering from injuries, fatigue, and the like, or if he is being affected by a Force-effect or any other factors that affect his Strength Level.

For each Level of Strength that your character applies to the attack 2 points of damage are inflicted. Modifiers that affect the damage and not your character's actual Strength Level are added in last. Some examples of such modifiers may be Talents, enchanted items, or runes.

If a weapon is being used, the dice that match the Level of the weapon's Damage Yield are rolled and this value is also added to the damage of the attack.

For example, Draven has just delivered a successful broadsword thrust to a Bristle-wolf. He has a Strength of Level 7 and applied all 7 Levels to the attack. His broadsword has a Damage Yield of Level 4 and has also been enchanted so that its normal Damage Yield is increased by 4 points. Draven has an injury applied to his Strength which is a -2 Level penalty. After taking all of his bonuses and penalties into account Draven will be applying 5 Levels of Strength to the attack and will roll the dice for Level 4 (the Damage Yield of his broadsword) and add 4 points (the sword's enchantment bonus).

Unless the opponent is wearing armor or has a Natural Protection Rating on the area that they are hit, they will receive the full amount of damage rendered by the attack. If the opponent does have armor or a Natural Protection Rating, the amount of damage received from the attack will be lessened by a number of points equal to that being's Natural Protection Rating or the Protection Rating of the armor worn over that area.

Injuries

If a being receives an amount of damage, at one time, equal to or greater than their Injury Rating (after armor and or Natural Protection Ratings have been subtracted) they will receive an injury. Injuries will always affect either Agility, Strength, or Endurance. A good method of determining where the injury will be applied is to roll 1D6. A result of 1 or 2 and the injury goes to Agility, 3 or 4 and it goes to Strength, 5 or 6 and it goes to Endurance. Each injury gives a -2 Level penalty to the attribute to which it is applied. The penalty remains until the injury is healed.

At the time the injury is received the GM should apply a number of days that it will take for the injury to heal (see "Health" in the Section titled "SURVIVING ORYATHAR"

for more on healing injuries). One method that may be used to determine how long it will take an injury to heal is to roll 1D4, the result being the number of days it will take the injury to heal (without mystical intervention), or the GM can just assign a number of days depending upon the nature and seriousness of the injury.

If the amount of damage done by a single attack is double or more the value of the target's Injury Rating, the target receives additional penalties beyond just receiving an injury. If a being receives an amount of damage in a single attack that doubles their Injury Rating, they are knocked down and stunned, regardless of the area that received the damage. If the damage yielded by an attack triples an opponent's Injury Rating, the opponent is knocked down, stunned, and receives a "critical injury" instead of a normal injury.

Critical Injuries inflict 1D4 points of damage per Turn after the Turn that they are inflicted. This damage is commonly due to blood loss, whether internal or external, but could be due to any condition that the GM deems appropriate. This damage continues to be applied each Turn until the injury is treated (GM's discretion as to what is proper treatment). Critical Injuries normally take twice as long to heal than normal injuries (1D4 number of days times 2).

Defense

To avoid an attack your character will have to set an appropriate Defense. This is done by making either an Agility/Performance or Sixth Sense/Performance Test. Agility/Performance Tests are used to set Physical Defenses, which your character will use to avoid any type of physical attacks against him such as a creature's bite or claws or a sword attack, etc. Sixth Sense/Performance Tests are used to set Mystical Defenses, which your character will use to avoid any type of mystical attacks against him such as Force-effects or a creature's mystical abilities.

Physical Defenses are slightly more complicated than Mystical Defenses. This is because there are three types of

Physical Defenses that your character can use; block, dodge, or parry, and there is only one type of Mystical Defense. Each type of Physical Defense has its own benefits and down sides as well.

Your character may use a different type of Physical Defense (block, dodge, or parry) for each separate attack made against him in a single Turn.

For example, if your character is attacked by three separate enemies, you may declare that he will dodge for his first Defense, parry for his second Defense, and block for his third Defense.

There is a slight penalty to setting more than one Physical Defense or one more than Mystical Defense in a single Turn. The second Physical Defense that your character sets in the same Turn will receive a -2 point penalty, the third will receive a -3 point penalty, the fourth will receive a -4 point penalty, and so on. This applies equally to Mystical Defenses. The second Mystical Defense that your character sets in the same Turn will receive a -2 point penalty, the third will receive a -3 point penalty, etc.

For both Mystical and Physical Defenses there are Bonus Points that can be used to increase your character's Defense value, even after his Defense has been declared insufficient against an attack. These are listed on the Character Sheets as Physical Defense Bonus and Mystical Defense Bonus.

The value for your character's Physical Defense Bonus is derived from his Agility Level and the Mystical Defense Bonus is derived from his Sixth Sense Level (creatures as well as characters can have Defense Bonus Points, though Defense Bonus Points are not actually listed with the creature's stats). Your character can have a maximum of 15 Physical Defense Bonus Points and 15 Mystical Defense Bonus Points. To determine how many Physical Defense Bonus Points that your character has you simply subtract 4 from his Agility Level. Any positive value that you have remaining is the number of Bonus Points that your character has. Mystical Defense Bonus Points are determined in the same way except your character's Sixth Sense Level is used instead of Agility. So, if your character's Agility is Level 12 and his Sixth Sense is Level 9 he would have a Physical Defense Bonus of 8 points and a Mystical Defense Bonus of 5 points.

If your character's Physical Defense Bonus is 10 you have 10 points that you can use to increase your character's Physical Defense values by each Turn. Each Turn you may use any or all of your character's Defense Bonus Points, but you can only add up to 5 Defense Bonus Points to a single Defense.

One drawback to using Defense Bonus Points is that however many points you spend to increase your character's Defense value, his next attack, if made in the same Turn, is penalized by an equal number of points. Physical and Mystical Defense Bonus Points work entirely independent of one another. Physical Defense Bonus Points spent will only penalize physical attacks and Mystical Defense Bonus Points spent will only penalize mystical attacks.

You can add Defense Bonus Points to your character's Defense even after you have learned that your character's Defense is insufficient against his opponent's attack, but not after you have learned the exact value of the attack. So when your character attacks a foe don't immediately announce what his attack value is. Wait to hear what your opponent's Defense value is first and then tell them whether or not it is sufficient to avoid your character's attack (they may want to add Defense Bonus Points to their Defense and if you immediately announce what your character's attack value is they will know exactly how many points to add).

As mentioned previously, you may only add as many as 5 Defense Bonus Points to a single Defense once per Turn. For example your character has just set a Physical Defense (Dodge) against an attack from a wretchin. You roll your Performance Die and add the result to your character's current Agility Level for a Physical Defense value of 12. The GM announces that this is insufficient. Your character has a Physical Defense Bonus of 5, and you can add up to 5 points to a single Defense. You don't want your character's counter-attack to penalized too heavily so you decide to just add 2 Defense Bonus Points into his Physical Defense making it a 14. The GM announces that this is still insufficient. You may not add any more Defense Bonus Points to this Defense, but if your character were to get attacked a second time in this same Turn and set a Defense, you could add some or all of his remaining Defense Bonus Points for the Turn into this new Defense.

For example, if a second wretchin were to now attack your character, he would still have 3 Physical Defense Bonus Points left that you could add to his Physical Defense. At the beginning of the next Turn your character would have his maximum number of Defense Bonus Points back to spend all over again.

The following describes the pros and cons of each of the three types of Physical Defenses.

Block

This type of Defense is almost exclusively based upon the use of shields, or similar items. Weapons can not be used to perform a block (it is considered parrying when using weapons to intercept an attack).

With this type of Defense your character uses a shield to intercept the attack. Blocking can be used against any type of physical attack, unless stated otherwise.

If your character's Specialty is **Unarmed Combat**, and only if **Unarmed Combat** is your character's Specialty, he may perform a block with his hands/arms instead of a shield.

In the case of a weapon attack, when your character blocks a melee attack with his hands he is actually blocking the motion of the attacker's arms, not the weapon itself. Blocking attacks in this manner renders no damage to your

character, unless the GM decides there is some reason it should.

There is no way for a character to effectively block a ranged attack with his hands/arms. Your character would simply be blocking the attack itself, purposely taking the hit (he will of course be damaged accordingly).

When blocking with the hands/arms you may add 1 point to your character's Physical Defense for each Technique Point he has with his hands/arms, 1 point because **Unarmed Combat** is his Specialty, and 1 point if he is proficient with his hands/arms.

When blocking with shields you may add a number of points to your character's Physical Defense equal to the Bulk Value of the shield. You may also add 1 point to your character's Physical Defense for each Technique Point that he has with the type of shield that he uses to block with.

Even though your character may block an attack with his shield the impact of the attack may knock him down. Successfully blocking an attack with a shield that renders an amount of damage double to or greater than your character's Injury Rating will knock him down and stun him, though he will receive no damage from the attack.

Shields that block attacks take the full amount of damage dealt by the attack, unless the GM feels that the particular weapon or type of attack blocked would not be able to damage the shield. At the GM's discretion, minimal damage may be dealt to weapons or items that are blocked with a shield (1D4 would be appropriate in most cases).

Some attacks may also completely penetrate a shield without destroying it (such as an arrow shot from a heavy bow at close range). The holder of the shield in such cases may still take damage even though he intercepted the attack with his shield (the arrow may have come through and stuck in his arm). The GM may decide to reduce the amount of damage rendered from the attack due to the partial protection of the shield (perhaps it slowed the arrow down enough to reduce its damage).

Dodge

This type of Defense is very self-explanatory, your character simply dodges the attack. He completely avoids it by moving out of the way. Dodging is equally effective against all types of physical attacks, but doesn't offer the bonuses that can be given by blocking or parrying.

Parry

This type of Defense is almost exclusively based upon the use of weapons, or similar items. Shields can not be used to parry (it is considered blocking when using a shield to intercept an attack).

With this type of Defense your character actually intercepts or bats the attack away with a weapon or similar item. If your character attempts to parry a charge or dive attack his Physical Defense receives a -5 point penalty. If he attempts

to parry a ranged attack his Physical Defense receives a -10 point penalty.

If your character has technique with a weapon that he uses for a parry Defense, you may add 1 point to his Physical Defense for each Technique Point he has with that particular weapon. You may also add 1 point to your character's Physical Defense if he is proficient with the weapon, and 1 point if the weapon is of his Specialty. If the weapon is made of green-steel you may add another 1 point to your character's Physical Defense.

When your character successfully parries a weapon attack, your character and the attacker must immediately make a Random-roll Agility Test and a Random-roll Strength Test to determine if either of them are disarmed. If you roll lower on both Tests, then your character is disarmed. If your character's opponent rolls lower on both Tests, then he is disarmed. A character must lose on both the Random-roll Agility and Random-roll Strength Test in order to be disarmed. The result of the Random-roll Agility Test may be modified by +1 for each Technique Point that your character has with the weapon he is using and by another +1 if your character is proficient with the weapon. You may also add another +1 if the weapon that your character is parrying with is a weapon of his Specialty.

If your character is disarmed that means that his weapon is knocked 1D8 feet out of his hands in a random direction determined by rolling another 1D8 and consulting the scatter diagram below.

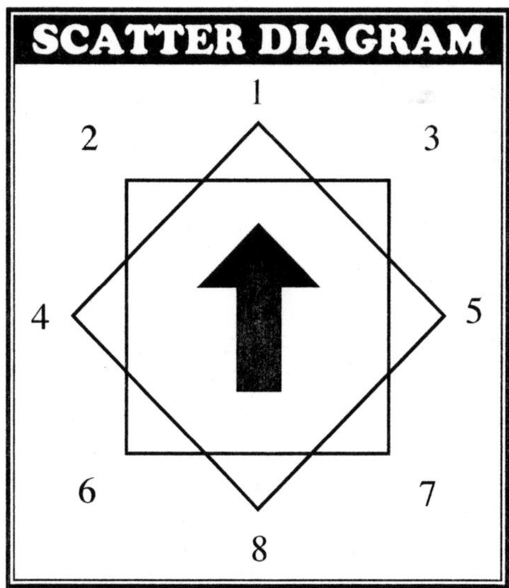

The arrow in the center of the scatter diagram indicates the direction your character is facing. So a result of 1 would indicate that your character's weapon was thrown, or knocked, straight ahead of him, a result of 8 means that it was thrown directly behind him, etc.

If an opponent is between your character and his weapon your character must outmaneuver him in order to retrieve it

(unless the opponent doesn't wish to stop your character from recovering the weapon). Your character and the opponent that your character is trying to outmaneuver must make a Random-roll Agility Test. The individual with the highest result has outmaneuvered their opponent. If your character outmaneuvers his opponent then he is able to get around him and get his weapon. If the opponent outmaneuvers your character then your character is unable to get around him to get his weapon. Outmaneuvering attempts and retrieving weapons, that are within your character's Action Movement, are generally considered Minor Actions.

Any weapon that is used to successfully parry against another weapon attack, or any attack with a very solid item or substance, will receive an amount of damage equal to the Damage Yield of the weapon that it intercepted (or a number of points of damage determined by the GM to be appropriate). The parried weapon or item will also receive an amount of damage equal to the Damage Yield of the weapon that parried it. When parrying a creature's attacks they will take a number of points of damage equal to the Damage Yield Level of the weapon used to parry the attack. The attacks from most creatures will not damage a weapon, but some may (GM's discretion as to whether or not parrying a specific creature's attack will render damage to the weapon).

Green-steel weapons receive half the damage that non-green-steel weapons do.

For example, Kargolius intends to use his broadsword to parry an attack from an opponent wielding a battle-axe. The broadsword has a Damage Yield of Level 4 and the battle-axe has a Damage Yield of Level 5. Kargolius successfully parries the attack from the battle-axe. His broadsword immediately receives 5 points of damage, and the battle-axe receives 4 points of damage. Both combatants would both have to make Random-roll Agility and Random-roll Strength Tests at this time to see if either of them are disarmed.

Only a single weapon, or item, may be used per parrying Defense. If your character has two separate weapons in hand and chooses to parry as his Physical Defense, you must declare which weapon is being used to parry. If your character is attacked multiple times in a single Turn, you may alternate which weapon that he uses for each separate parry.

COVER

In many combat situations it is beneficial to hide or take cover behind something. This is a wise strategy because cover gives bonuses to your character's Physical Defense. Cover can be anything from something as simple as a branch to a wagon.

There are three main categories of cover that add bonuses to the users Physical Defense. They are minimal cover, average cover, and optimal cover.

Minimal Cover

Minimal cover offers only a very small amount of protection or obscures only very minute portions of the target. Examples include thin branches or bushes, a small wagon wheel, or a small pile of rocks.

Minimal cover gives the being utilizing it a +2 point bonus to their Physical Defense.

Average Cover

Average cover offers a fairly significant amount of protection or obscures a significant amount of the target. Examples include small barrels, boulders, small trees or shrubs.

Average cover gives the being utilizing it a +3 point bonus to their Physical Defense.

Optimal Cover

Optimal cover offers a very significant amount of protection or nearly completely obscures the target.

Examples include large boulders, large trees, or another being.

Optimal cover gives the being utilizing it a +5 point bonus to their Physical Defense.

COMBAT TURN

The following is a list of the different phases or actions that occur in a single Turn (5 seconds) of combat. Each phase takes place in the order given unless stated otherwise. The details of each of these phases is explained a little later along with the description of each type of combat.

Phases of a Combat Turn

1. State your character's intended actions for the upcoming Turn
2. Perform actions in the order of Initiative, or in a logical order
3. Resolve the effects of the actions
4. * Set a Defense, if needed

5. * Move

6. Adjust any factors that changed during the Turn

* These phases do not always occur in the listed order

PHYSICAL COMBAT

This section will describe how to perform physical attacks and how to resolve and determine the results of those attacks, such as damage, injuries, knockdown, death, etc.

Physical combat is combat that is performed by physical means, such as sword fighting, wrestling, or archery. There are two basic types of physical combat; melee and ranged. Melee combat takes place any time the combatants are within five feet of one another. Combat is considered ranged when the combatants are more than five feet apart. Because there is differences in the way that melee and ranged combat is performed, each will be discussed in detail separately.

MELEE COMBAT

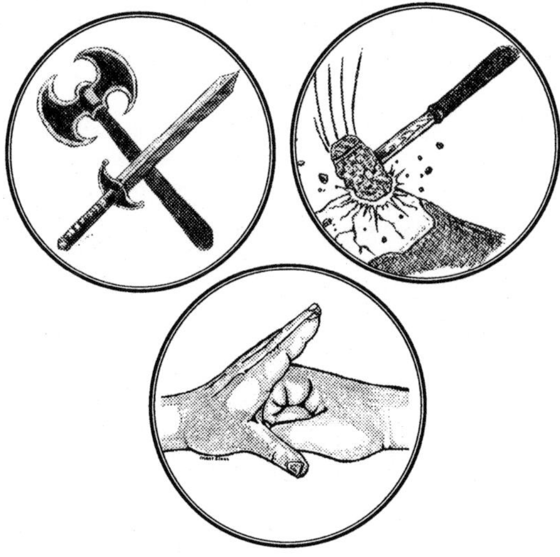

Melee is normally a very fast and furious type of combat. Those who are not very fond of hacking it out face to face with blood-thirsty Shadow-kin or a battle-axe-wielding maniac should consider other types of combat.

Combat is considered to be melee when combatants are within five feet of one another. Further, opponents must be within five feet of one another in order to use a melee weapon, unless they throw the weapon, but in such cases the attack would be classified as *ranged* instead of *melee*. There are some melee weapons that allow your character to make melee attacks even though he is further than five feet from his opponent. All such exceptions are discussed in detail in the specific weapon's description.

Naturally, it makes better sense to use weapons designed for melee when fighting in melee, but this is not absolutely necessary. Throwing weapons may be used in melee, but the Damage Yield for the weapon is then modified to the equivalent of its melee counter-part, or further if the GM sees fit. So a character could use a throwing dagger to fight with in melee, but its Damage Yield would be the same as a normal dagger, not a throwing dagger.

Outmaneuvering

Once engaged in melee with an opponent, or opponents, your character can not just simply break out of melee and move at will without risking leaving himself open to an attack, at least not as long as one or more of the opponents engaged in melee with him wishes to maintain melee. If your character wishes to effectively break out of melee with opponents who wish to maintain melee, he must outmaneuver them in order to do so, but that doesn't keep them from following your character.

Outmaneuvering someone uses ten feet of your character's movement for the Turn. When your character attempts to outmaneuver someone your character and those he is attempting to outmaneuver must each make a Random-roll Agility Test. If your character's result is higher, then he has outmaneuvered his opposition. If not, then he has been outmaneuvered. Even if your character isn't engaged in melee, but wishes to move past a being that is in front of him and that being doesn't wish for him to pass, he must outmaneuver them in order to pass them. If the being wishing to stop your character is further away from him than the range of their allowed movement for the Turn, then your character does not have to outmaneuver them (they are too far away from your character to stop him).

If your character wishes to break melee and is outmaneuvered by his opponent then he can not set a Defense against that opponent if that opponent immediately attacks your character as he is exiting melee.

Phases of Melee Combat

The following is a description of the different phases of melee combat. These phases are very often the same for all of the different types of combat or actions that take place in a Turn, with only minor differences distinguishing them.

The different phases of each Turn should flow into one another seamlessly, just as the action that is actually taking place is flowing from one action to another. So, in all reality, many of the different phases of a Turn are taking place at the same time. For example, a character runs toward his foe as he draws a dagger and then hurls it forward. Even as he is finishing the throw he suddenly spins to one side just in time to dodge a spear aimed for his heart. Events happen very fluidly and in rapid succession. His attacker didn't wait for him to run forward and throw his knife before deciding

to throw his spear at him; the actions were taking place at relatively the same time.

The events of a Turn have been broken down into phases for the sake of keeping actions in order and to help players keep organized. Initiative is simply a guideline. Also, the order of the phases may be changed at any time as the GM sees fit. It should also be noted that the phases will vary slightly from one form of combat to another.

Each individual moves through each of the 6 phases separately, so while your character is on phase 3 someone else will most likely be on phase 4 (if your character is attacking his opponent is most likely defending), so on and so forth.

Some phases, such as Move and Set a Defense are often repeated by the same individual during a single Turn (your character may move twice and set an infinite number of Defenses).

1. State your character's intended actions for the coming Turn

This is a detailed description of what actions your character would like to perform during the coming Turn. Some examples of intended actions may include what Talents, combat variants, and weapons, if any, will be used. What is your character's intended target or targets, etc.? Major *and* Minor Actions to be performed should be stated at this time.

Major Actions are actions that generally take three seconds or longer to perform, or require a great deal of concentration or movement. Some examples include attacking an opponent, using a Force-effect, drawing a rune, climbing, or running a distance greater than your character's Action Movement. Normally, your character may only perform one Major Action per Turn.

Minor Actions are actions that can be performed in two seconds or less and do not require a great deal of concentration or movement. Some examples include drawing a weapon, shouting a warning, or tossing off a helmet. There is no set number of Minor Actions that can be performed in a single Turn. However, the total amount of time spent on Minor Actions should not exceed two seconds.

CHANGING INTENDED ACTIONS

Your character may decide to change his declared course of action after the Turn has begun. Depending upon the differences in the actions, the GM may wish to assign penalties to the new course of action. An average penalty for changing intended actions is -1D6 points to the action being performed, though the GM may wish to assign a set number of points as the penalty.

Shannon announces that his character's intended action for the Turn is to charge an opponent and attack with his sword. After the Turn has begun Shannon decides that he wants his character to throw a spear at an opponent in an opposite direction from his initial target. The GM assigns a -1D6 penalty to the spear attack, due to the significant *change from the original course of action (Shannon's character has to completely stop his forward charge, change direction, and then alter his attack from melee to ranged).*

2. Perform actions in the order of Initiative, or in a logical order. (In the case of combat, the intended action is usually to carry out an attack)

"Initiative" is a guide for keeping events and actions flowing in proper order and sequence throughout a Turn. In this phase of the Turn the characters, foes, and other interacting beings attempt to carry out their intended actions. The normal way that these actions are carried out is by the character with the highest Initiative beginning their actions first, then the next highest, and so on. However, depending upon the nature of the events taking place, the GM may wish for some actions to take place out of the normal order of Initiative. Also, characters may wish to perform their action later in the Turn, even though they may have the highest Initiative.

Initiative for physical attacks or actions is equal to your character's Agility Level. Initiative for mystical attacks is equal to your character's Sixth Sense Level +2. If you choose, you may lower your character's Initiative. This is often done when your character wants to wait for a particular action from someone else before performing his Major Action. Say that your comrade has an Initiative of 9 and is going to shoot his heavy bow at a creature that you want your character to attack with his mace. Though your character's Initiative is 10 he may want to lower it to 8 so that his comrade gets his shot off before he rushes into melee and risks getting hit. Unlike changing intended actions, there is no penalty for delaying your character's Initiative.

Beings whose actions for the Turn do not include moving before their actions are to take place resolve their attacks or actions (in the order of Initiative) before those beings who will use movement before performing their actions. In most cases the persons with immediate actions will perform their Major Action before persons with immediate movement and *then* a Major Action.

Steve's character, Seb, has a Physical Initiative of 10. Steve wants Seb to hold his place and throw his enchanted spear at a charging kicker. Tim's character, Kromro, has a Physical Initiative of 12. Tim wants Kromro to run forward forty feet and attack another kicker with his enchanted broadsword. Daniel's character, Reptek, has a Physical Initiative of 7. Daniel wants Reptek to stand his ground and throw his arc-knife at another approaching kicker. All three kickers have a Physical Initiative of 8 and wish to charge in and attack Seb, Kromro, and Reptek.

The flow of events looks something like this; Kromro and all three kickers begin charging toward their targets while Seb and Reptek take aim and release their ranged weapons. Since Seb and Reptek are not moving or doing anything else

before their attack (they have immediate actions), they will perform their actions first. Seb's Initiative is higher than Reptek's so his spear is into the air before Reptek's arc-knife. Kromro's Initiative is higher than the kicker's so he would now attack the kicker he had charged. If any kickers are still alive and able they will now make their counter-attacks.

3. Resolve the effects of the actions

This phase is where the results of your character's actions are finalized. Did your character's attack succeed? Where did your character strike his opponent? How much damage did your character inflict? How far across the field did your character make it before he was knocked senseless? This phase is where all of your planning and skills come to bear.

Whether or not your character's attack succeeded is determined by comparing his total adjusted attack value to his opponent's Defense value (Physical Defense in this case, since we are talking about physical attacks). If your character's attack value exceeds his opponent's Defense value then the attack is successful.

The damage inflicted by your character's attack depends largely upon two factors; the Level of Strength that your character applied to the attack and the Damage Yield of the weapon that he used. For each Level of Strength that your character applies (which can be any Level you choose up to your character's current Strength Level) 2 points of damage are inflicted. If a weapon is being used, the dice that match the Level of the weapon's Damage Yield are rolled and this result is added to the damage of the attack.

If your character's opponent has a Natural Protection Rating or is wearing armor over the area that the damage is assigned, then the amount of damage that they receive is reduced by a value equal to the total Protection Ratings of all armor protecting that zone.

Once an attack has been declared successful you will immediately roll the percentile dice to determine where the damage of the attack will be applied. Percentile dice will generate results from one to one hundred. The result of the percentile dice determines where the opponent is hit. Generally speaking, the higher the result, the closer to the head the attack came. The lower the result, the closer to the feet or opposite end that the attack came.

The following "ZONE STRIKE" table shows what basic zone, or area, of the target that the damage is applied to depending upon the value rolled on the percentile dice. Also shown is the base percent chance of randomly striking that zone. The GM will decide the exact area within the zone or area that is struck.

If your character aims his attack for a certain area of his target, then the odds that he will strike that particular area are greater than if he rolled randomly with the percentile dice. "Aimed Attacks" are explained later in the "Combat Variants" area of this Section.

4. * Set a Defense if needed

If your character wishes to avoid an incoming attack, which is usually wise, he will need to set an appropriate Defense. Regardless of the phase of the Turn your character is currently in, he may set a Defense any time it becomes necessary.

In the case of physical attacks your character will be setting a Physical Defense. To do this he will make an Agility/Performance Test (roll the Performance Die and add the result to your character's current Agility Level). If you roll a 1 on the Performance Die (Feeble Attempt), you may not add that 1 point and must also now roll 1D4 and subtract the amount rolled from your character's Physical Defense value. If you roll a 12 on the Performance Die (Flawless Performance), you not only add that value (12), but may now roll 1D4 and *add* the result to your character's Physical Defense value.

* Your character may set a Defense at any time during the Turn that it becomes necessary.

Defense Bonus Points

You have the option of adding a portion of your character's Physical Defense Bonus Points into his Physical Defense, as described earlier, but doing so will penalize your character's counter-attack by that same value. You may only assign these Defense Bonus Points one time to each Defense that your character sets and no more than 5 points to a single Defense. So, if the GM informs you that your character's Physical Defense is insufficient to defend against the attack you may decide to add 3 of your character's Physical Defense Bonus Points into his Defense. If this is still insufficient you no longer have the option of adding more Defense Bonus Points to this Defense.

You roll and determine a separate Defense for each separate attack that your character wishes to defend against.

5. * Move

There are two different listings for movement on your character sheet; Maximum Speed and Action Movement. Maximum Speed refers to the fastest speed that your character can move under normal conditions as well as the maximum distance your character can cover in a single Turn, considering he spends the entire Turn running. Action Movement does not actually refer to your character's speed, but rather the distance that he can travel in a single Turn and

ZONE STRIKE		
% Die Result	**Zone Hit**	**Random Odds**
100-96	Head/Neck	5 %
95-81	Arm	15 %
80-41	Torso	40 %
40-26	Pelvis	15 %
25-1	Leg	25 %

still have time to perform a Major Action.

For example, Marcus has a Maximum Speed of 150 feet per Turn (abbreviated 150'/Turn), and an Action Movement of 75 feet. He may choose to only move a distance equal to his Action Movement (so that he may still perform a Major Action this Turn), but may choose to cover that distance at a speed of 150'/Turn.

Your character does not have to wait until his Initiative in order to move. Movement begins at the beginning of the Turn for anyone who has declared that they wish to move. If your character does not wish to move until after he has performed his Major Action for the Turn, then he must wait until his Initiative in order to perform his Major Action and then he could move.

You may divide your character's movement for the Turn into two separate movements, but the total of all movements in the Turn may not exceed your character's appropriate movement value (either Maximum Speed or Action Movement).

For example, your character has an Action Movement of 90 feet and he is forty feet away from an opponent that he wants to attack with a sword. Your character could close to melee with the opponent, attack, and then use the remaining fifty feet of his Action Movement to move to another area (though if the original target wished to maintain the melee he would have to out-maneuver them before he could break out of melee, or risk leaving himself open for an attack).

*Movement may take place at any time throughout the Turn.

6. Adjust any factors that changed during the Turn

In this phase you make sure that any penalties or bonuses acquired during the Turn, such as damage, injuries, fatigue, results of a Force-effect, etc. have been applied. Any damage to armor or weapons, any changes to you're character's Total Bulk Value, Load, or any other factors that may have changed during the course of the Turn should also be noted and adjusted at this time. This phase is essentially a follow through and clean up of Phase 3.

In short, the adjustment phase is the appointed time for you to make any adjustments or changes that may have occurred during the Turn.

COMBAT EXAMPLE

The following is a complete example of one Turn of melee combat.

In the previous example Steve, Daniel, and Tim's characters each attacked a kicker. Let's go through that combat Turn step by step.

We will begin this example with Steve's character because his character had the highest Initiative value among all of the participants with immediate actions.

Steve has already completed **Phase 1** (stating his character's intended actions). This is where he stated that he wanted his character to attack a kicker with his spear.

Phase 2 (performing actions). Steve's character, Seb, is now ready to perform his intended action, which is to attack. Seb makes an Agility/Performance Test. Seb's current Agility Level is 10. Steve rolls a 10 on the Performance Die (1D12) which is added to Seb's Agility Level of 10 for a result of 20. Seb's Specialty is **Throwing Weapons** which gives him a +1 bonus to the attack, and a +1 Level increase to the Damage Yield of any throwing weapon. Seb's spear is also enchanted to give him a +5 point bonus to any ranged attacks made with it. This brings Seb's total attack value to 26. The kicker that Seb attacks attempts to dodge for its Physical Defense, this is actually **Phase 4** for the kicker (setting a Defense). The GM rolls a 6 on the Performance Die for the kicker's Defense and adds this to the kicker's current Agility Level of 8 for a result of 14. Seb's attack value of 26 far exceeds the kicker's Physical Defense value of 14. Seb's attack is successful.

Steve is now ready for **Phase 3** (resolving the effects of his character's action). Steve rolls the percentile dice for a result of 79. Referring to the "ZONE STRIKE" table he sees that Seb's spear has struck the kicker in the torso. Steve is now ready to determine how much damage that his character's attack inflicted. Seb applied all 9 Levels of his current Strength to the throw. This is doubled for a result of 18. The spear that Seb is using has a Damage Yield of Level 4, but because it is a weapon of his Specialty, **Throwing Weapons**, its Damage Yield is increased to Level 5 for him.

The dice for Level 5 is 1D10. Steve rolls 1D10 for a result of 8. He adds this 8 to the 18 (determined from the Strength Level he applied) for a total of 26. Seb's attack inflicts 26 points of damage to the kicker. The kicker has a Natural Protection Rating of 5 so the GM subtracts this from the 26 points of damage for an adjusted total of 21. The kicker actually receives 21 points of damage to its torso area.

Now for Daniel. He has already completed **Phase 1** and is ready for **Phase 2** (performing Reptek's actions). Reptek now makes an Agility/Performance Test to attack. Daniel rolls the Performance Die for a result of 4 which he adds to his character's current Agility Level of 7 for a total result of 11. Reptek has no bonuses that will apply to this attack, so his final attack value is 11.

The kicker attempts to dodge (this is **Phase 4** for the kicker). The kicker's Performance Die result is a 12 (Flawless Performance). The GM immediately rolls 1D4 (the bonus for a Flawless Performance) for a result of 2 and adds this to the Performance Die result of 12 for a result of 14. The GM adds the 14 to the kicker's current Agility Level of 8 for a result of 22. The kicker's Physical Defense value of 22 is higher than Reptek's attack value of 11. Reptek's arc-knife

has missed the kicker.

Phase 3 (resolving the effects of the actions). Since Reptek missed the kicker and there were no other beings in melee with the kicker, the GM decides that the result of Reptek's action is that his arc-knife zips past the kicker and stabs harmlessly into the ground several feet to the left of the kicker.

Now for Tim. He too has already completed Phase 1 (stating that he wants his character, Kromro, to charge forward the approximate forty feet needed to close to melee and attack a kicker with his enchanted broadsword).

Phase 5 (move). Kromro has an Action Movement of eighty seven feet, so it is no problem for him to move the forty feet needed to close to melee with the kicker and still perform a Major Action (attack).

Tim is now ready for Phase 2 (performing Kromro's intended actions). Remember, the Phases don't always take place in order because movement and setting a Defense can take place any time during the Turn. Kromro makes an Agility/Performance Test to attack. Tim rolls the Performance Die and gets a result of 9. He adds this to his character's current Agility Level of 12 for a total of 21.

This kicker also attempts to dodge as its Physical Defense against this attack, this is actually Phase 4 for the kicker (setting a Defense). The kicker's Performance Die result is a 1 (Feeble Attempt). The GM immediately rolls 1D4 (the penalty for a Feeble Attempt) for a result of 3 and subtracts this from the kicker's current Agility of Level 8 for a result of 5 (because a 1 is a Feeble Attempt the kicker doesn't even get to add the 1 to its Defense). The kicker's Physical Defense is a 5, which is not even close to dodging Kromro's attack. Kromro's attack is more than triple the kicker's Defense. This means that he may add 1D8 points to the damage of his attack as well as getting to re-roll (1 time) any dice rolled for damage that roll the maximum number possible for that die ("re-roll on a max roll").

Tim is now ready for Phase 3 (resolving the effects of his character's action). Tim rolls the percentile dice for a result of 99. Referring to the "ZONE STRIKE" table he sees that Kromro has struck the kicker in the head. Now to determine how much damage his character has inflicted. Kromro's sword is enchanted to increase its Damage Yield to Level 10. The dice for Level 10 is 2D10. Tim rolls a 3 on one of the D10 and a 10 on the other. Tim immediately rolls that D10 again (one of the bonuses for tripling the kicker's Defense) for a result of 5. He now rolls 1D8 (another bonus for having an attack value that triples the kicker's Defense) for a result of 7. He adds all of this together for a combined result of 25. Kromro applied all 10 Levels of his Strength to the attack (this is doubled for a result of 20 points). Tim adds the 25 that he rolled for the weapon's Damage Yield to the 20 determined by the Level of Strength that his character applied for a result of 45 points of damage. After deducting 5 points for the kicker's Natural Protection Rating the kick-

er receives a total of 40 points of damage to its head.

This kicker's Injury Rating is 20. On the nose Kromro has inflicted a number of points of damage (in one blow) that has doubled the kicker's Injury Rating. This means that the kicker is automatically knocked down and stunned. The GM applies the injury to the kicker's Agility. Its Agility is lowered by 2 Levels until the injury is healed.

Phase 1. Now it is time for the kickers to attack. Kickers get two attacks per Turn. The GM announces that one of the kickers will attempt to kick Reptek for its first attack and then bite him for its second attack.

Phase 2. The kicker makes an Agility/Performance Test to attack. The kicker's Performance Die result is a 2 which is added to its current Agility Level of 8 for a result of 10. Kickers receive a +2 point bonus to all kick attacks which now brings its attack value to a total of 12.

Daniel decides that his character will use his buckler to attempt to block the kick (Phase 4 for Daniel). Daniel's Performance Die result is a 7 which he adds to his character's current Agility Level of 7 for a result of 14. A buckler gives a +2 point bonuses to blocking Defenses. This brings Reptek's Physical Defense value to 16. Reptek's Defense value of 16 is higher than the kicker's attack value of 12. He has blocked the kick with his buckler.

Phase 3 (resolving the effects of the kicker's attack). The force of the kick staggers Reptek slightly and stings his arm, but he receives no damage. His buckler, however, is a different story.

The kicker applied all 10 Levels of its Strength to the kick, which is doubled for a result of 20 points of damage. A kicker's kick has a Damage Yield of Level 10. The dice for Level 10 is 2D10. The GM rolls 2D10 for a combined result of 14. This 14 is added to the 20 for a total of 34. The kicker's stone-hard claws dig into Reptek's buckler rendering 34 points of damage to it.

For the kicker's second attack of the Turn it will attempt to bite Reptek (back to Phase 2 for the kicker because it gets two attacks per Turn). The kicker's total attack value is 20.

Daniel again decides that Reptek will use his buckler to block (back to Phase 4 for Daniel). Reptek makes another Agility/Performance Test. His Performance Die result is an 8 which is added to his character's current Agility Level of 7 for a result of 15. To this Daniel adds the +2 point bonus that a buckler adds to blocking Defenses for a result of 17. But because this is the second Physical Defense that Reptek has set in a single Turn he will receive a -2 point penalty to his Defense value. Reptek's total adjusted Physical Defense value for the Turn is 15. The kicker's attack value of 20 is higher than Reptek's Physical Defense value. Reptek's attempt to block the kicker's bite was unsuccessful.

Now back to Phase 3 (resolving the effects of the kicker's second attack). The GM now rolls the percentile dice to see where Reptek is bitten. The result is 89, which according to the "ZONE/STRIKE" Table indicates an arm. The GM

states that the bite was to Reptek's left arm (the arm that has the buckler attached to it).

The kicker applied all 10 Levels of its Strength to the bite which is doubled for 20 points of damage. The Damage Yield of a kicker's bite is Level 5. The dice for Level 5 is 1D10. The GM rolls 1D10 for a result of 9. This is added to the 20 for a total of 29 points of damage. Reptek isn't wearing any armor on his arms so he will take the full 29 points of damage. Reptek's Injury Rating is 22. The kicker has inflicted (in one blow) an amount of damage equal to or greater (in this case greater) than Reptek's Injury Rating. The bite has caused an injury to Reptek's arm.

The GM decides to apply the injury to Reptek's Agility. The GM now rolls 1D4 (a random method for determining the number of days for a normal injury to heal) for a result of 3. It will take three days for the injury to heal, unless mystical means of healing are used. Reptek's Agility is now 2 Levels lower until the injury is healed.

Phase 1. The GM announces that the the kicker attacking Seb will attempt to bite him for its first attack and kick him for its second attack.

Phase 2. The kicker lunges toward Seb in an attempt to bite him. The kicker makes an Agility/Performance Test to attack. The GM rolls the Performance Die for a result of 10 which is added to the kicker's current Agility Level of 8 for a result of 18. Kickers receive a +2 point bonus to all bite attacks. This brings the kicker's attack value to a total of 20s.

As a Minor Action Seb draws his short-sword and attempts a parry as his Physical Defense (**Phase 4** for Steve). Seb makes an Agility/Performance Test to parry. His Performance Die result is a 9 which is added to his current Agility Level of 10 for a result of 19. Seb has 1 Technique Point with short-swords so he adds 1 point to his Defense value for a total Defense value of 20. The kicker's attack value does not exceed Seb's Physical Defense value. Seb successfully parries the kicker's bite.

Phase 3 (resolve the effects of the kicker's first attack). It must now be determined whether or not the kicker's attack has disarmed Seb. Seb makes a Random-roll Agility Test for a result of 7 and a Random-roll Strength Test for a result of 9. Because Seb has 1 Technique Point with short-swords he adds 1 point to the result of his Random-roll Agility Test for an adjusted result of 8. The kicker also makes a Random-roll Agility Test for a result of 10 and a Random-roll Strength Test for a result of 13. The kicker has beat Seb on both Tests. Seb is disarmed (the force of the kicker's bite has knocked Seb's short-sword out of his hands). Seb's short-sword has a Damage Yield of Level 3, so the kicker takes 3 points of damage because it was parried with the short-sword. However, kickers have a Natural Protection Rating of 5, so its hide is tough enough that a parry from a short-sword will not harm it. It actually receives no damage from the parry.

The GM rolls 1D8 to determine which direction that Seb's

short-sword is thrown. The result is 8. Consulting the scatter diagram on page 73, the GM sees that a result of 8 is a direction directly behind Seb. To see how far Seb's short-word was thrown the GM rolls another 1D8. The result is 6. Seb's short-sword is knocked out of his hand and lands six feet directly behind him.

For the kicker's second attack it rears back on its tail and kicks out with both legs (back to **Phase 2** for the kicker). The kicker's total attack value for the kick is 28.

Steve decides that Seb will attempt to dodge this attack (back to **Phase 4** for Steve). He makes another Agility/Performance Test. He rolls a 3 on his Performance Die which he adds to Seb's current Agility of Level 10 for a result of 13. The kicker's attack value of 28 is higher than Seb's Physical Defense value. The kicker's attack is successful and is double Seb's Physical Defense value.

Now back to **Phase 3** to resolve the effects of the kicker's second attack. The GM now rolls the percentile dice to see where Seb has been kicked. The result is 54 which indicates the torso. The kicker plants both feet squarely into Seb's chest.

The kicker applied all 10 Levels of its Strength to the kick, which is doubled for 20 points of damage. The Damage Yield of a kicker's kick is Level 10. The dice for Level 10 is 2D10. Because the kicker's attack value is double Seb's Defense value any dice rolled for the damage of the attack that roll their highest number may be re-rolled, adding this result into the damage as well. The GM rolls a 5 on one of the 10 siders and a 7 on the other for a combined result of 12. This is added to the 20 for a total of 32 points of damage. Seb's Injury Rating is 26. The kicker has inflicted (in one blow) an amount of damage equal to or greater (in this case greater) than Seb's Injury Rating. The kick has caused an injury to Seb's chest.

The GM decides to randomly determine to which attribute the injury will be applied. He rolls 1D6 for a result of 5 (1 or 2 = Agility, 3 or 4 = Strength, 5 or 6 = Endurance). The injury is applied to Seb's Endurance. The GM now rolls 1D4 (a random method for determining the number of days for a normal injury to heal) for a result of 4. It will take 4 days for the injury to heal, unless mystical means of healing are used. Seb's Endurance drops by 2 Levels until the injury is healed.

Phase 1. The GM states that the kicker that Kromro has knocked down will attack him with its tail from the ground for both of its attacks instead of using its Major Action to get up (it is a Major Action to get up while stunned).

Phase 2. The kicker makes an Agility/Performance Test to attack. The kicker's Performance Die result is a 10 which is added to its current Agility Level of 6 (it is now 2 Levels lower than before because of the injury that Kromro inflicted) for a result of 16. Kickers receive a bonus of +3 points to all tail attacks which brings the attack value to 19, however, the kicker is attacking from a knocked-down position which cuts the result of any physical action taken by half,

round down. The attack value of 19 is cut in half and rounded down to 9. The kicker's final attack value is a 9.

Kromro attempts to dodge as his Physical Defense (this is **Phase 4** for Tim). Kromro makes an Agility/Performance Test in order to dodge. His Performance Die result is a 6 which he adds to his character's current Agility Level of 12 for a total Defense value of 18. Kromro has dodged the kicker's tail attack.

The kicker immediately rolls toward Kromro and launches another tail attack for its second attack (back to **Phase 2** for the kicker because it gets two attacks per Turn). The kicker's total attack value ends up being a 7. Tim decides that Kromro will try to dodge this attack as well (back to **Phase 4** for Tim). Kromro makes another Agility/Performance Test. His Performance Die result is a 5 which he adds to Kromro's current Agility Level of 12 for a result of 17. Because this is the second Physical Defense that Kromro has set in a single Turn he will receive a -2 point penalty to his Defense value. Kromro's total adjusted Physical Defense value for this attack is 15. This is still more than sufficient to dodge the kicker's tail attack value of 7. Kromro remains untouched for the Turn. Because the kicker's attack was unsuccessful there really isn't a **Phase 3** (resolve the effects of the actions) for the kicker. Its attack simply missed and there are no effects.

None of the combatants wish to move again this Turn. They decide to hold their ground and continue melee combat.

Phase 6 (adjust any factors that changed during the Turn).

During this phase Daniel will make sure that he has recorded the total damage that Reptek has taken for the Turn, the damage that his buckler has taken, and will record his injury as well as which attribute that it effects and how many days it will take to heal.

Steve will also make sure to record the total damage that Seb has taken for the Turn and will record his injury as well as which attribute that it effects and how many days it will take to heal.

The GM will record the damage and injuries inflicted to the kickers.

This is the end of the first Turn of Combat.

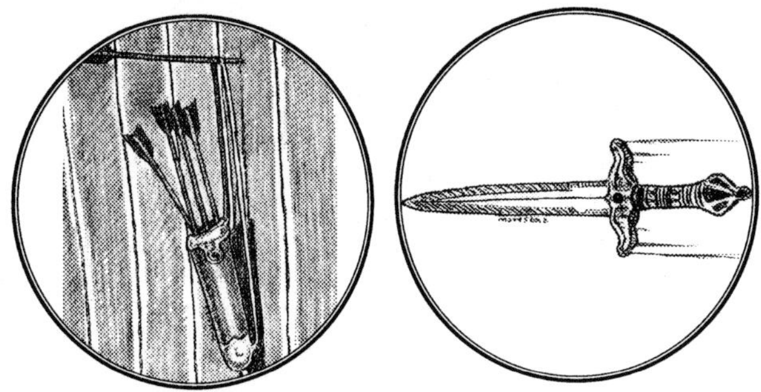

RANGED COMBAT

Combat is considered ranged any time the combatants are more than five feet away.

Many Force-effects are actually ranged attacks, but they will be discussed separately in the "Mystical Combat" part of this Section.

(Physical) Ranged combat mainly includes the use of archery and throwing weapons, but may include any weapon that is used to attack targets from a distance. Ranged weapons can be invaluable, especially if your character is the type who doesn't care for close encounters. If your character's opponent doesn't have a ranged weapon, then they can not counter-attack your character unless they can close to melee. Also, in many cases ranged attacks will take place before other attacks (your character can throw or shoot while his target is trying to move into melee).

Though ranged combat gives your character the comfort of attacking his opponent without having to get too close, it does have some draw backs when compared to melee.

The first drawback is that adding more Levels of Strength than the required Minimum Strength Level of an *archery* weapon does not increase the damage of the attack. If a bow is pulled back to full draw, then it will perform at its maximum. Applying more Strength than the listed Minimum Strength Level will just risk breaking the bow.

Secondly, when attacking with ranged weapons, whether with bows or throwing weapons, the target's size and distance from your character becomes a determining factor in the difficulty of the attack. The smaller the target and further away, the more difficult it becomes to hit. This added difficulty due to distance and size is reflected as penalties to your character's attack value.

RANGE MODIFIERS

If your character attempts to make a ranged attack subtract 4 points from his attack if the target is within "Normal" range of the weapon being used, or 8 points if the target is within "Long" range of the weapon. If the target is beyond "Long" range then the attack automatically fails.

SIZE MODIFIERS

If the target of a ranged attack is large enough your char-

acter will receive bonuses to his attack. These bonuses may, depending upon the size of the target, be enough to negate the penalty for the target's distance from your character (the -4 or -8 point penalty). In contrast though, if your character's target is small enough he will receive additional penalties to his attack.

To determine whether or not the target's size will give your character bonuses or penalties to his attack simply subtract 4 from the target's Bulk Value. Any points left over are added to the attack. Any negative values that you end up with are subtracted from the attack. For example, if a target's Bulk Value is 8 you would subtract 4 from this for a result of 4. You would add 4 points to your character's attack. If the target's Bulk Value is 2 you would subtract 4 from this for a result of -2. You would subtract 2 points from your character's attack.

One exception to the range modification rule is if the target is within twenty feet of the attacker. This is considered point blank range. In this case the attacker would not be penalized by the normal -4 points for the target being within "Normal" range.

Though it is possible to throw weapons at a target while they are within five feet of your character, throwing a weapon in melee is considered a melee attack, not ranged (the weapon is only traveling a few feet before it strikes its target, thus simulating melee enough for the attack to be classified as melee). The Damage Yield for the throwing weapon in this case is modified to the equivalent of its melee counter-part, or further if the GM sees fit. So your character could use a throwing dagger to fight with in melee, but its Damage Yield would be the same as a normal dagger, not a throwing dagger.

Reloading an archery weapon while engaged in melee requires your character to outmaneuver his opponent, or opponents, by a difference of at least 3. Failure means that he was unable to get his bow nocked or his crossbow loaded due to the action and stress of the melee.

This all may sound a little complicated at first, but you will find, after a little practice, that it is actually quite simple. Here are a couple of examples to demonstrate:

Kuldar spots a Shadow-kin and wants to attack it with his normal bow. Because this is a ranged attack Kuldar will receive penalties to his attack based upon the Shadow-kin's size and distance from him. The GM states that the Shadow-kin is sixty three feet away. This is within "Normal" range of Kuldar's normal bow and he decides to take the shot. The GM also states that the Shadow-kin has a B.V. of 6.

For the target being within "Normal" range Kuldar subtracts 4 points from his attack. Now to determine whether or not the Shadow-kin's size will give bonuses or penalties to his attack Kuldar subtracts 4 from the Shadowkin's Bulk Value of 6 for a result of 2. He adds 2 to his attack value. Kuldar receives a total penalty of -2 to his attack (-4 points for the target being in "Normal" range and +2 due the tar-

get's size for a total of -2). If the Shadow-kin had been two hundred and thirty feet away ("Long" range) he would have received a -6 point penalty to his attack (-8 points for the target being in "Long" range and +2 due to its size for a total of -6).

Using the same scenario as above, but with the Shadow-kin only seventeen feet away (point blank range) Kuldar would receive a +2 point bonus to his attack. Remember, point blank range removes the normal -4 point penalty for ranged attacks made within "Normal" range of the weapon. This would leave Kuldar with a +2 point bonus to his attack due to the Shadow-kin's size (Bulk Value of 6 - 4 = 2).

Whenever your character shoots or throws at a target that is within melee (five feet) of other beings there is a chance that if your character misses his intended target he will hit one of the other beings within melee of his target. The more beings in melee with your character's intended target the greater the chance is that he will hit one of those beings if he misses his intended target.

The following table shows the percent chance for hitting an unintended target depending upon the number of beings within melee of the intended target.

If the GM chooses he my allow the unintended target beings to set a Defense against the stray arrow or throwing weapon instead of allowing them to be automatically hit.

As an optional rule you can even use the "SHOOTING INTO MELEE" table for missed melee attacks as well.

SHOOTING INTO MELEE

# in Melee	% to Hit
1-2	25 %
3-4	50 %
5-6	75 %
7-8	90 %
9 or more	100 %

Phases of Ranged Combat

The following is a list and explanation of the different phases in a Turn of ranged combat. Some of the phases pertaining to ranged combat are the same as those for melee combat. The phases of ranged combat will be listed, but not described in detail when they are the same as previously described under "MELEE COMBAT". If you wish to see details of those phases please refer back to them in the "MELEE COMBAT" area of this Section.

1. State your character's intended actions for the coming Turn

2. Perform actions in the order of Initiative, or

in a logical order

This Phase is the same as Phase 2 in melee combat, but with the following exceptions. When attacking with ranged weapons, the target's size and distance from your character becomes a determining factor in the difficulty of the attack.

These differences have been described in detail in the beginning of this section.

3. Resolve the effects of the actions.

Damage from a successful attack with a throwing weapon is determined in the same manner as that for melee combat (a number of points equal to double the Strength Level applied plus the result of the dice rolled for the weapon's Damage Yield). If you wish, your character may apply any Level of Strength that you wish as long as it does not exceed his current Strength Level. Example, if your character has a Strength of Level 8 he may only wish to apply 5 Levels of Strength to the attack.

Damage from an attack with a bow or crossbow is determined in a different manner than with other types of weapons. To determine the damage yielded from a successful bow or crossbow attack you roll the dice for the Damage Yield of the weapon and add a number of points to the result equal to the Damage Yield Level of the weapon. So, to determine the damage from a successful attack with a normal bow you would roll 1D10 + 1D4 (the dice for Level 7) and then add 7 points to the result. To determine the damage from a successful attack with a heavy crossbow you would roll 1D10 + 1D6 (the dice or Level 8) and then add 8 points to the result

Here is another interesting exception for bows. If your character chooses, or is forced, to apply a lower Strength Level than the Minimum Strength listed for the archery weapon, the weapon's Damage Yield will drop in relation to the amount of Strength applied (lower amounts of Strength than the listed minimum indicates the bow is not being brought to full draw; the lower the Strength Level applied, the lower the Damage Yield). It also will not travel its normal distance and may cause the attack itself to receive penalties (GM's discretion as to the extent of these penalties).

4. * Set a Defense if needed

* Your character may set a Defense at any time during the Turn that it becomes necessary.

5. * Move

* Movement may take place at any time throughout the Turn.

6. Adjust any factors that changed during the Turn

MYSTICAL COMBAT

Mystical combat is the signature of Shinkai, for they are the only ones capable of this type of combat, with the exception of a few rare mystical creatures. Mystical combat usually refers to combat that focuses the energy of the Mystic Forces into what is known as Force-effects. Force-effects can be either ranged *or* melee. Another type of mystical combat is what is known as essence combat. This is when a Shinkai projects his very essence, or Life Force, out of his body. This essence can then do combat with other essence forms.

The use of Force-effects and essence in combat is described separately and in detail below. Many more aspects of Force-effects, such as a complete list of all available Force-effects, how to learn them, and a full description of each one is described in the "FORCE-EFFECTS" Section.

Force-effects in Combat

The use of Force-effects in combat takes in a wide variety of specific attack styles. Force-effects may be either melee or ranged depending upon the particular Force-effect being used. Each specific Force-effect will tell in its description whether or not it is melee or ranged, or both. Also included in each Force-effect's description is a full description of its effects, range, Defenses that are effective against it, Force Energy required, etc.

In order to use a Force-effect your character must expend a certain amount of Force Energy. This amount of Force Energy varies from Force-effect to Force-effect. A term that you will need to be familiar with is "conjuring". Conjuring is the act of converting the Mystic Forces into Force-effects.

Once you have chosen the Force-effect that you would like for your character to use you should make sure that he has enough Force Energy to accommodate that particular Force-effect. The Force Energy is expended during the conjuring of the Force-effect.

It *is* possible to perform a Force-effect for which your character does not have enough Force Energy. As long as your character has at least 1 point of Force Energy to initiate the conjuring of the Force-effect his Life Force may be used to make up the difference for the Force Energy that he lacks. This Life Force which is used as Force Energy will affect your character in the form of damage. The Force-effect literally drains his Life Force, and of course can kill your char-

acter if more points are drained than what he has available.

Because your character's Life Force is not the same as Force Energy, there is a chance that when it is used to substitute even 1 point of Force Energy, the attempt to conjure the Force-effect will fail. The chance of that failure is fifty percent. If you roll 50 or lower on the percentile dice the Force-effect automatically fails. The Force Energy and Life Force are still expended. If you roll 51 or higher the Force-effect works as it would have had normal Force Energy been used.

OK, so maybe you know what Force-effect you want your character to use and he is more than able to safely meet the required Force Energy. There are still a few more perils that could hinder the success of the conjuring. Some Force-effects have a Difficulty Value to overcome in order to be conjured successfully. If a Difficulty is given with the description of a Force-effect, then your character must meet or exceed the listed value on a Sixth Sense/Performance Test in order to successfully use the Force-effect. If the result is lower than the listed Difficulty value, then the conjuring failed, the Force-effect does not work, and the Force Energy is wasted.

NOVICE FACTOR

Another obstacle to overcome, especially for beginning characters, is if their Force Knowledge in any of the Mystic Forces used in a Force-effect is less than 100. If your character's Force Knowledge in a particular Mystic Force is less than 100, he is considered novice with that Mystic Force and novice with any Force-effect containing that Mystic Force.

Any Force-effect containing a Mystic Force in which your character is novice will require you to roll against the "Novice Factor" in order to successfully conjure that Force-effect. The Novice Factor is a twenty percent chance that the Force-effect will fail; because of the fact that your character is still a novice and may have made a slight error in the conjuring process (the Novice Factor does not apply to learning Force-effects; only to the use of them). A roll of 20 or lower on the percentile dice means that your character failed to conjure the Force-effect properly. The Force Energy required for that Force-effect is still expended.

Whenever your character succumbs to the Novice Factor (you roll 20 or under on the percentile die while your character is attempting to conjure Force-effects that he is novice in) you must immediately roll 1D20 and consult the following "NOVICE FACTOR" table to see the result of your character's conjuring attempt.

NOVICE FACTOR	
1	No Effect, Force Burn, & Overexpend Force Energy
2	Adverse Effect, Force Burn, & Overexpend Force Energy
3	Force Burn & Overexpend Force Energy
4	Adverse Effect & Force Burn
5	No Effect & Force Burn
6	Force Burn
7	Force Burn, & Underexpend Force Energy
8	Force Burn, & Underexpend Force Energy
9	Adverse Effect & Overexpend Force Energy
10	No Effect & Overexpend Force Energy
11	Adverse Effect
12	Overexpend Force Energy
13	No Effect
14	No Effect
15	No Effect
16	No Effect
17	No Effect
18	No Effect
19	Underexpend Force Energy
20	Underexpend Force Energy

The five basic categories of things that can result from succumbing to the Novice Factor are "No Effect", "Force Burn", "Adverse Effect", "Overexpend Force Energy", and "Underexpend Force Energy". Some results may include a combination of these effects.

No Effect is just that, nothing happens. The Force-effect completely fails and produces no effects at all.

Force Burn yields a number of points of damage to your character equal to the number of points of Force Energy required to conjure the Force-effect.

Adverse Effect is any unplanned or abnormal effect that the GM would like for the attempt to produce. Because the adverse effect is a result of succumbing to the Novice Factor, whatever the adverse effect is it should be unexpected and not the normal result of the Force-effect (be creative).

Overexpend Force Energy means that your character has drawn too deeply upon the Mystic Forces required to conjure the Force-effect and has consequently expended too much Force Energy. To determine how much your character has overexpended roll 1D20, the result is the number of points of Force Energy that he expended beyond what is listed in the Force-effect's description. Overexpending Force Energy does not in itself cause the conjuring of the Force-effect to fail (your character just spent more Force Energy than he really needed to). So even though your character may have overexpended Force Energy, the Force-effect will still work normally, unless it fails for other reasons.

Underexpend Force Energy means that your character hasn't drawn in enough of the Mystic Forces required to conjure the Force-effect and subsequently the Force-effect fails to be conjured. To determine how much your character has underexpended roll 1D20, the result is the number of points

of Force Energy that your character expended below what is listed in the Force-effect's description. Underexpending Force Energy always results in failure of the Force-effect.

Attacking

Some Force-effects are automatically successful if conjured properly while others must overcome a target's appropriate Defense or a set Difficulty Value. Each Force-effect's description will give this information.

If the Force-effect has a Defense that can be effective against it or if it has a Difficulty, it will be listed. Whenever your character uses a Force-effect that has a Defense or Difficulty listed you must make a Sixth Sense/Performance Test. If the result is equal to or greater than his opponent's Defense and/or the listed Difficulty, the Force-effect is successful, unless another factor hinders it.

Damage

The results of any particular Force-effect, whether damage yielding or not, are described in detail in the description of each individual Force-effect.

Phases of Force-Effect Combat

The following is a list and explanation of the different phases in a Turn of Force-effect combat.

1. State your character's intended actions for the coming Turn

2. Perform actions in the order of Initiative, or in a logical order

3. Resolve the effects of the actions

This phase of Force-effect combat is different than that of the other forms of combat. The results of some Force-effects may not be damage at all, and for those that are, the dice rolled to determine the result may vary widely. Each individual Force-effect's description will tell you what its specific effects are.

4. * Set a Defense if needed

* Your character may set a Defense at any time during the Turn that it becomes necessary.

5. * Move

* Movement may take place at any time during the Turn.

6. Adjust any factors that changed during the Turn

ESSENCE COMBAT

This form of combat is truly unique to all other forms of combat. The Shinkai actually separates his Life Force, or essence, from his body. The Shinkai's essence can then do combat with other essence forms. Projecting your character's essence is a Minor Action and does not require conjuring or the expenditure of Force Energy.

Essence forms can not directly harm anything other than another essence form. It is not possible to conjure, use Talents or Skills, or transform into Dragonknight while in essence form (unless stated otherwise in the specific Talent or Skill's description).

When your character projects his essence his body falls into a sleep-like state. Your character's essence form remains fully aware of his body and can sense if anything disturbs it.

If your character doesn't control any of the Mystic Forces his essence form will appear as a mist-like vapor in the shape of his own body. If your character controls one or more of the Mystic Forces his essence form appears as a swirling vapor-like mixture of the Mystic Forces that he controls; also in the shape of his own body (*Air* is white, *Fire* is red, *Land* is brown, *Spirit* is silver, and *Water* is blue).

Your character's essence form moves with a smooth gliding motion and may move in any direction that you desire, this includes the vertical plane as well as the horizontal. The maximum speed that your character's essence form can move in a single Turn is the same as his Action Movement in

normal ruling-race form. Your character's essence form also has the ability to pass through solid objects with the exception of enchanted objects, water, rock, soil, and living beings.

If your character's essence form comes close to another being, enchanted object, rock, etc., your character's essence form will be pushed away by an invisible force; much like pushing the like poles of two magnets together.

Passing through green-steel objects will yield Level 6 damage to your character. He suffers no visible damage, but does usually end up with a whopping headache.

Your character can speak in essence form, though his voice will not be very loud. Many describe the sound of speaking in essence as the sound of a subtle breeze.

The essence form is not always used for combat. As the previous description shows, it can be a very effective way of scouting out a room or tunnel with no fear of a physical attack (essence forms can only be harmed by other essence forms).

Your character may assume his essence form once a day by expending 1 Mystical Attuning Point. If your character remains in his essence form for more than 5 Turns, he will begin receiving fatigue at a rate of 1 Fatigue Point for every Turn past the fifth Turn that he remains in essence. He will continue to receive 1 Fatigue Point per Turn until he accumulates 5 (at which point he will collapse and automatically return to his body) or until he chooses to return to his body. If your character stays in essence form for more than 10 Turns, his body and essence will die.

In order for your character's essence to return to his body he can be no further from his body than a number of feet equal to his Current Force Energy. The returning of your character's essence form to his body is a Minor Action and happens almost instantly (once within range of his body).

Attacking

As noted previously, essence forms have the ability to attack and damage other essence forms. This is known as essence combat. In essence combat, the attack and damage are both combined into one step. Your character may only make one attack on a single target each Turn, though he can be attacked from multiple essence combatants in the same Turn.

To attack another being's essence your character must be in melee with their essence. Your character's essence must then actually strike the other being's essence in order to damage it.

To attack in essence form you roll the dice that match your character's Current Force Energy value on the following "ESSENCE COMBAT" table. The result is your character's attack value. If your character's attack value is greater than his opponent's Defense value then he has successfully damaged their essence form.

ESSENCE COMBAT			
F. E.	Level	Dice	Range
1-30	1	1D4-1	0-3
31-50	2	1D4	1-4
51-70	3	1D6	1-6
71-90	4	1D8	1-8
91-110	5	1D10	1-10
111-130	6	1D12	1-12
131-150	7	1D10+1D4	2-14
151-170	8	1D10+1D6	2-16
171-190	9	1D10+1D8	2-18
191-210	10	2D10	2-20
211-230	11	1D12+1D10	2-22
231-250	12	2D12	2-24
251-270	13	1D20+1D6	2-26
271-290	14	1D20+1D8	2-28
291-310	15	1D20+1D10	2-30
311-330	16	1D20+1D12	2-32
331-350	17	2D20	2-40
351-370	18	2D20+1D8	3-48
371-390	19	3D20	3-60
391-410	20	3D20+5	8-65

(Once beyond Level 20, every increase of 10 points is another Level. For each Level above 20, an additional +1 is added to the result of the roll.)

Only your character's *Current* Force Energy is used to determine the dice you will use in essence combat, often referred to as Force Energy dice. As your character takes damage in essence form his Current Force Energy will drop and thus the dice that you roll for attacking and defending drops.

Your character may choose to "hold" his opponent instead of attacking them. This is performed in the same manner as attacking, except that instead of draining Force Energy from the opponent (if your roll is higher) your character simply holds on to them. When your character successfully places a hold on another being's essence form he can keep them from moving or can force them to move where he moves. In order to break free from a hold you must roll higher on the Force Energy dice. Each Turn you must choose whether your character will attack or hold (he can not do both). If you choose for your character to hold his opponent you will roll the dice that match your character's Current Force Energy (just as if he were making an attack) and the opponent in the hold must also roll the dice that match his Current Force Energy (if he wishes to break free). If your character's result is greater than that of his opponent's then he maintains the hold, if not then the opponent has broken free. Remember, holding an opponent does not do damage to them.

If a being's essence form is within range of their body, holding them will not keep them from being able to return to

their body.

Defense

Setting a Defense in essence form is done differently than with any other type of Defense. To set a Defense you roll the dice that match your character's Current Force Energy, listed under "F.E." on the "ESSENCE COMBAT" table. The result is your character's Defense value. There is no limit to the number of Defenses that your character can set in essence form in a single Turn.

There are no bonuses that can be applied to Defenses while in essence form.

Damage

Damage rendered from a successful attack in essence combat is determined by multiplying the difference between the attacker's attack value and the defender's Defense value by two. This value is the number of points of Force Energy subtracted from the Current Force Energy of the being that is hit. If the amount of damage rendered is more than the being's Current Force Energy, then the remaining damage goes to their body (their Life Force is used in replace of Force Energy). If the damage caused from essence combat exceeds a being's Life Force, they will die (their Life Force is simply destroyed). So as you can see, essence combat does have the potential to be lethal. Immediately after being brought to 0 Current Force Energy a being's essence will return to their body.

Phases of Essence Combat

The phases of a Turn of essence Combat are considerably shorter, and simpler than that of the other types of combat.

1. State your character's intended actions for the coming Turn

2. Perform actions in the order of Initiative, or in a logical order

Mystical Initiative is used for all actions performed while in essence form. In most cases the intended action is to attack another essence form. Though it can be to hold another being's essence or to simply move to a different location or search a given area, etc.

7

3. Resolve the effects of the actions

This is where you will determine such things as how much damage if any that your character's attack did, if his opponent was forced out of essence combat, was he able to hold on to his opponent, etc.

4. * Set a Defense if needed

If your character is attacked by another essence form while he is in essence form he must set a Defense in order to avoid the attack. If your character chooses not to set a Defense against an essence attack his Defense value for that attack automatically becomes a 1.

* Your character may set a Defense at any time during the Turn that it becomes necessary.

5. * Move

* Movement may take place at any time during the Turn.

6. Adjust any factors that changed during the Turn

This may be recalculating your character's Current Force Energy or Life Force due to damage that he has taken or recording Fatigue Points for remaining in essence form for more than 5 Turns.

COMBAT EXAMPLE

The following is an example of one complete Turn of essence combat.

Iskrae has just projected his essence and is engaging two other beings in essence combat, Morbray and Kreylin. All combatants are within melee of one another.

Joe's character Iskrae decides to attack Mike's character Kreylin this Turn. Morbray, Pat's character, and Kreylin will both attack Iskrae. Iskrae's Mystical Initiative is 12. Morbray has a Mystical Initiative of 9 and Kreylin has a Mystical Initiative of 15. Since Kreylin has the highest Initiative he gets to attack first. Kreylin's Current Force Energy is 195. Looking to the "ESSENCE COMBAT" table Mike sees that the dice that he will roll to attack are 2D10. He rolls a 6 on one D10 and a 9 on the other. Kreylin's total attack value is 15. Iskrae now attempts to defend against the attack. His Current Force Energy is 140. Looking to the "ESSENCE COMBAT" table Joe finds that the dice that he will roll for Iskrae's Defense are 1D10 + 1D4. Joe rolls a 3 on the D10 and a 4 on the D4. Iskrae's total Defense value is 7. Kreylin's attack value is higher which means that Iskrae's Defense is insufficient. There is an eight point difference between the result of Kreylin's attack value and Iskrae's Defense value. We multiply this value of 8 by 2 for a total of 16. Iskrae takes 16 points of damage which is immediately subtracted from his Current Force Energy.

Iskrae has the next highest Mystical Initiative (12) so it is now his turn to attack. Iskrae's Current Force Energy is now 124. According to the "ESSENCE COMBAT" table the dice for for this value is 1D12. Joe rolls 1D12 for a result of 10. Kreylin will now set a Defense against this attack. His Current Force Energy is still 195 so Mike will roll 2D10 to determine his Defense value. He rolls a 2 on one D10 and a 6 on the other for a total Defense value of 8. This is insuffi-

cient against Iskrae's attack value of 10. Kreylin is hit. The difference between his Defense value and Iskrae's attack value is 2 so he takes 4 points of damage. Mike immediately lowers his character's Current Force Energy by 4 points.

Morbray may now resolve his attack (attacking Iskrae). Morbray has a Current Force Energy of 100. According to the "ESSENCE COMBAT" table the dice for this is 1D10. Pat rolls 1D10 for a result of 8. Iskrae sets another Defense in an attempt to avoid the attack. His Current Force Energy is 124. The dice for this value is 1D12. Iskrae rolls a 2 on the D12 for a Defense value of 2. Iskrae's Defense is insufficient by a difference of 6 so he takes 12 more points of damage that is immediately subtracted from his Current Force Energy.

End of combat Turn 1.

DRAGONKNIGHT COMBAT

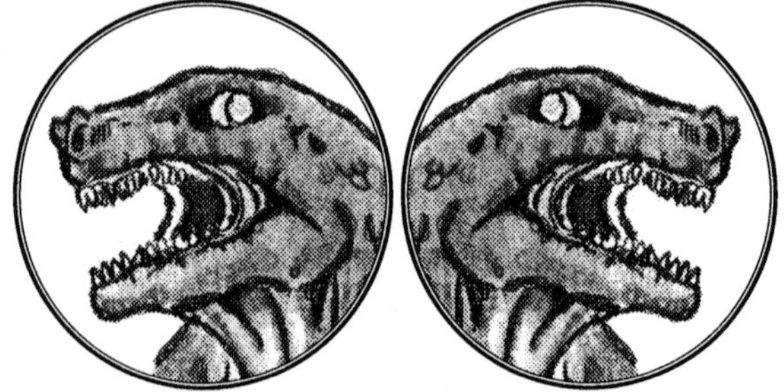

This is a very powerful form of combat that is not witnessed very often on Oryathar. The reason for this is that only about one in every five hundred ruling-races born is Shinkai Dragonknight. Of course every player in the game of Mystic Forces has the choice of being Shinkai Dragonknight, but you must realize that your character is compared to the rest of Oryathar's population, Shinkai or otherwise.

As with physical combat there are two major types of combat that fall under the category of Dragonknight combat; melee and ranged. Melee combat can be any type of physical attack that the Dragonknight can perform that takes place within five feet of the opponent (bite, claw, etc.). Ranged attacks for Dragonknights is their breath attacks, which can be used against targets that are more than five feet away.

Conjuring or projecting your character's essence form is not possible while in Dragonknight form, and only the Talents that specifically state so may be used while in Dragonknight.

Each aspect of the Dragonknight form as well as more details on combat in Dragonknight form is given in the "DRAGONKNIGHT" Section of the rules.

MELEE COMBAT

There are basically three types of melee attacks that Dragonknights can employ. They are bite, claw, and tail. The following will describe each type of melee combat in detail.

Bite

The powerful jaws and teeth of a Dragonknight are very effective weapons, capable of crushing foes with a single bite. The average Dragonknight's bite has a Damage Yield of Level 9, though the bite of some Dragonknights is less damaging and others are more damaging.

The details of Dragonknight bite attacks are discussed under each specific Dragonknight's description in the "DRAGONKNIGHT" Section.

Claw

The arms and legs of a Dragonknight are equipped with very sharp talons capable of tearing an enemy to shreds. The hands of a Dragonknight are not capable of grasping weapons effectively enough to use them, but the claws themselves are very lethal weapons. The average Dragonknight's claws have a Damage Yield of Level 7, though the claws of some Dragonknights are less damaging and others are more damaging.

The details of Dragonknight claw attacks are discussed under each specific Dragonknight's description in the "DRAGONKNIGHT" Section.

Tail

Dragonknights all have fairly long and muscular tails, which can be used to strike their enemies. The tails of Grak, Loremek and Warlum have a Damage Yield of Level 5 while the tails of Brightlings and Valkin have a Damage Yield of Level 6. Brightlings, Grak, and Valkin also have additional abilities in regards to their tails. These abilities are described in detail under their Dragonknight description in the "DRAGONKNIGHT" Section.

FLYING

Because Dragonknights can fly, they have the option of performing dive attacks. To perform a "Dive Attack" the Dragonknight dives down upon a target using the momentum of the dive to increase the impact.

Because of the speed and maneuverability of flying Dragonknights, it is possible for them to make a melee attack on a non-flying target and then fly out of melee before their opponent can counter-attack.

As long as the attacking Dragonknight has a higher Initiative than his opponent, he may try to exit melee before his opponent can counter-attack. If his Initiative is not higher than his opponent's then he may not enter and exit melee without his opponent having the option of attacking while he

is still in melee.

Let's say your character's Initiative *is* higher than his opponent's and your character wants to swoop in and out of melee without his opponent getting a chance to attack him in melee. To do this your character must outmaneuver his opponent. If he *does* out-maneuver him, then he may exit melee before his opponent can counter-attack. Your character's opponent could then only counter-attack if he had a ranged attack. But, if your character does not outmaneuver his opponent, then his opponent may counter-attack before he can fly out of melee.

See "Combat Variants" later in this Section for more on dive attacks.

RANGED COMBAT (Breath)

The only ranged combat that Dragonknights are capable of is their breath attacks (see "Breath" in the "DRAGONKNIGHT" Section for details of each type of breath attack). Your character may learn two separate breath attacks.

Breath attacks are considered to be a physical attack, much like a throwing weapon attack. The Dragonknight must quickly align his head with his target and release the breath with the right timing and speed.

Agility is the attribute used to perform breath attacks (Agility/Performance Test). Damage and effects of breath attacks are explained in detail in the "DRAGONKNIGHT" Section of the rules.

Breath attacks may be made against targets in melee as well as ranged targets. This does not affect the attack or damage in any way, and unlike throwing weapons in melee, the attack is still considered ranged.

Dragonknights are immune to their own breath, so using them in melee does not risk harming themselves. It should be noted that a Dragonknight is only immune to his or her own breath, they are not immune to the same type of breath coming from another Dragonknight.

The phases of ranged Dragonknight combat are the same as those for physical melee combat.

Phases of Dragonknight Combat (Melee & Ranged)

The following is a list of the phases for melee and ranged Dragonknight combat. The details of these phases are the same as that for "Physical Melee Combat", except Dragonknights do not use weapons (their bodies *are* weapons).

1. State your character's intended actions for the coming Turn

2. Perform actions in the order of Initiative, or in a logical order

3. Resolve the effects of the actions

4. * Set a Defense if needed

* Your character may set a Defense at any time during the Turn that it becomes necessary.

5. * Move

* Movement may take place at any time during the Turn.

6. Adjust any factors that changed during the Turn

COMBAT VARIANTS

Combat variants are simply modifications to an attack or Defense. Most combat variants are not Major Actions in themselves, but are ways of modifying other Major Actions, namely combat actions.

As long as there isn't a conflict in the description, combat variants may be used in conjunction with any Talent, Skill, Force-effect, or other type of ability that your character may wish to use in combat.

Up to three combat variants may be used in a single Turn, as long as they do not conflict with each other or the action being performed (GM has the final decision on whether a combat variant may be used or not). Using the same combat variant three times in a single Turn is the same as using three different combat variants. Or using the same combat variant twice in the same Turn is the same as using two different combat variants. The limit is still three whether by three different combat variants or the same one multiple times. "Surprise Attack" is an exception to the three combat variants per Turn rule. It may be used even if three other combat variants are already being used in the same Turn.

Another exception to the number of combat variants that can be used is that your character can not use two combat variants that are marked with an asterisk (*) in the same Turn.

Following is a list and description of the different combat variants. It does not cost anything to use a combat variant and they do not have to be learned as do Talents or Skills. Your character may begin using combat variants at any time that you feel comfortable in incorporating them into the game.

COMBAT VARIANTS

1. Adrenaline Rush
2. Aimed Attack
3. Charging *
4. Desperate Deed
5. Dive Attack (Dragonknight) *
6. Fake
7. Flat Blading
8. Iron Defense *
9. Meditation
10. Single Strike
11. Slipping Past Shields
12. Surprise Attack

Adrenaline Rush

"Adrenaline Rush" is a very useful boost that your character can use when in situations which produce high amounts of excitement, fear, or rage. You may declare that your character is using "Adrenaline Rush" at any time during the Turn. It need not be part of your stated intended action. However, your character can not wait for an action to be resolved and then decide to use "Adrenaline Rush". For example, you can't wait until you see that your character's attack successfully strikes his opponent and then declare that he will use "Adrenaline Rush" to boost his Strength. Or you could not wait until it has been determined that an attack has hit your character and then decide to use "Adrenaline Rush" to boost his Agility to help him avoid the attack. If you stated at the beginning of the Turn that your character is using "Adrenaline Rush" it will also increase his Physical Initiative value by 2 points.

When using "Adrenaline Rush" you add 2 Levels to your character's Agility or Strength, or both, for the duration of the Turn. But using it for both doubles the number of Fatigue Points received. On the Turn after "Adrenaline Rush" is used all attributes receive 1 Fatigue Point unless both Agility and Strength were affected, in which case 2 Fatigue Points are received.

"Adrenaline Rush" can not be used for more than 3 Turns in a row. There must be at least a 10 Turn wait before "Adrenaline Rush" can be used again if it is used for 3 consecutive Turns. If it is spaced out by at least 1 Turn in between uses, "Adrenaline Rush" may be used as many times as you wish, as long as the GM deems the situation appropriate. Your character can not receive more than 5 Fatigue Points from "Adrenaline Rush", or by any other means for that matter (a character will collapse if he accumulates 5 Fatigue Points to any single attribute other than Intelligence and Sixth Sense).

Aimed Attack

Quite often it is hard enough for your character to just hit his target, let alone hit the target in a specific or designated area. But sometimes it may be necessary that your character's attack strike a certain area of his target to be effective. It is called an "Aimed Attack" whenever your character attempts to pin-point his attack to a certain area of his target. You may, for example, declare that your character is aiming for his opponent's right ear, or his opponent's head/neck area. To do this your character must utilize the "Aimed Attack" combat variant.

"Aimed Attacks" are much more difficult than just swinging it out with a foe or letting an arrow or throwing weapon fly in their general direction. Imagine just trying to hit a creature that is jumping and moving and making attacks, and now imagine that you want to pin-point a certain area on that jumping and moving creature. It becomes obvious that this is no easy task.

Whenever your character makes an "Aimed Attack" the result of the Performance Die for the attack must be at least 5. Also, the attack itself is penalized by 5 points. If the GM feels that the area that your character is aiming for is particularly small or hard to hit he may increase the required result of the Performance Die to any value that he feels is appropriate. The penalty to the attack is also increased to the same value as the required Performance Die result. So, if the GM increases the needed Performance Die result to 8, the result of the attack is penalized by 8 points.

If your character makes an "Aimed Attack" and you do not roll the needed result on your Performance Die then the area of the target struck, assuming that your character's attack value exceeds the target's Defense value, is determined by rolling the percentile dice and consulting the "ZONE STRIKE" table (page 77).

Paul decides that his character, Felsar, will attack an approaching wolf with his normal bow. Paul declares that his character is aiming for the wolf's left eye (he is utilizing "Aimed Attack"). The GM decides that this is an exceptionally difficult shot and will require a Performance Die result of at least 10 (this also means that the attack value will be penalized by 10 points). Felsar's current Agility Level is 8, he has 2 Technique Points with a normal bow, and his Specialty is "Archery". Felsar's Performance Die result is a 9. Now to calculate his attack value. We start with his Agility Level of 8 and add 2 points to that for his 2 Technique Points with the normal bow and to that we add an additional 1 point because a normal bow is a weapon of his Specialty. To this we add his Performance Die result of 9 for a total 20. The wolf is within Normal range of Felsar's bow so only 4 points are subtracted from the attack due to the wolf's distance from felsar, and the wolf's Bulk Value is 4 so there is no bonuses or penalties to the attack due to its size. We must also now subtract 10 points from the attack because of this is an exceptionally difficult "Aimed Attack". This brings the attack total to 6.

The wolf's Defense value is 5. He has hit the wolf, but because his Performance Die result was not a 10 or better he

did not hit where he was aiming (the wolf's left eye). He must now roll the percentile dice to see where the arrow struck. He gets a result of 56. Referring to the "ZONE STRIKE" table he sees that a 56 is the Torso area. He has hit the wolf in its torso (chest). Had his Performance Die result been 10 or higher he would not have had to roll percentile dice; his attack would have hit where he was aiming.

Thoroughly confused? You'll get the hang of it. This example uses many different advanced and optional rules and circumstances. Not all combat situations are nearly this complex.

Charging

"Charging" is used when your character is riding upon large mounts, such as horses or bleyk, that are moving at a minimum speed of 200'/Turn. The momentum and strength of the mount increases the damage of a successful physical melee attack, but penalizes the attack itself.

A mount must move a minimum of thirty-five feet, from a dead stop, in order to reach any type of charging speed. Depending upon how fast the mount is charging, there are different bonuses and penalties that affect the attack and the damage of the attack.

The three categories of charging speeds are Minimal, Average, and Maximum. Minimal Charging Speed is 200' to 250'/Turn and gives a -1 point penalty to the attack and a +4 point bonus to the damage. Average Charging Speed is 251' to 300'/Turn and gives a -2 point penalty to the attack and a +8 point bonus to the damage. Maximum Charging Speed is 301'/Turn and above. It gives a -3 point penalty to the attack and a + 12 point bonus to the damage.

Charging is often a desirable combat variant to employ due to the fact that it can significantly boost the damage of attacks, but it also poses some risks. If your character utilizes "Charging" and successfully strikes his target he will absorb a great deal of the impact and therefore risk being disarmed or even knocked off of his mount.

On a successful attack from a charging mount your character must make an Agility/Performance + Strength Test against a base Difficulty Value of 16. The Difficulty Value changes according to the exact speed at which the charge is made. The Difficulty Value is 16 if your character is charging at Minimal Charging Speed. If your character charges at Average Charging Speed the Difficulty Value is 18, and if he charges at Maximum Charging Speed the Difficulty Value is 20. Success means that your character is able to hold on to his weapon; failure means that he is disarmed. If your character is disarmed roll 1D8 to determine how many feet away that the weapon is thrown. Roll another 1D8 and consult the scatter diagram on page 73 to see in what direction that your character's weapon is thrown.

Failing the Test with a result half or less than half of the required Difficulty Value will result in your character being knocked off of his mount as well as being disarmed.

If your character is knocked off of a charging mount he will receive a number of points of damage equal to the bonus points given for the charge. So, if your character was charging at Minimal Charging Speed and was knocked off of his mount he would receive 4 points of damage. If he was charging at Average Charging Speed he would receive 8 points of damage. If he was charging at Maximum Charging Speed he would receive 12 points of damage.

For example, John has just made a successful sword attack while on a mount charging at 275'/Turn (Average Charging Speed). He must now make an Agility/Performance Test and a Strength Test, adding the two results together. He needs a result of 18 to keep his sword from being knocked out of his hand. John adds his results together for a total of 12. The impact of his sword striking its target knocks his sword from his hand. John now rolls 2D8. He gets a result of 7 on the first D8 which means that his sword is thrown seven feet. He gets a result of 6 on the second D8. The scatter diagram indicates that the sword is thrown behind and to the left of John.

Had John had a total result of 9 or less he would not only have been disarmed, but he would have also been knocked off of his mount and would receive 8 points of damage from the fall (the same as the charge bonus for Average Charging Speed).

If your character performs a successful attack against an opponent who is charging him, he will receive the same bonuses to the damage of his attack that the charging being receives to his.

For example, Gronk is charging Eurik at Maximum Charge Speed. As Gronk closes into melee, Eurik attacks him with his quarter staff. The quarter staff strikes Gronk in the chest! Eurik will now add 12 points to the damage of his attack (the amount indicated by a Maximum Charge Speed attack). If able, Gronk may now follow through with his attack, applying -2 points to his attack and +12 points to his damage (as indicated by a Maximum Charge Speed attack). Notice that Eurik does not apply the -2 point penalty to his attack. He is not the one moving at over 250'/Turn.

Though not mentioned in this example, Eurik's attack would actually have been penalized by 1D6 points; because he is attacking a moving target (see "Attacking vs. Movement" at the beginning of this Section).

Only physical melee attacks may benefit from "Charging".

Desperate Deed

This combat variant allows your character to combine his Agility, Strength, and Willpower into one Test. This Test is treated as either a single Agility/Performance Test, Strength Test, or Willpower Test; you may choose which.

In order to perform a Desperate Deed you must first spend 5 Light Points and 1 Mystical Attuning Point at the time your character wishes to execute the Desperate Deed. You may then add the Levels of his Agility, Strength, and Willpower

together. This new Level is used to perform the Agility, Strength, or Willpower-based action of your choice. Talents, enchantments, or other modifiers may still be used to adjust the Level of the action.

Performing a Desperate Deed yields 2 Fatigue Points to all attributes at the beginning of the next Turn.

Dive Attack

Because of their ability to fly, Dragonknights are capable of making high speed dive attacks. "Dive Attacks" add damage to a successful physical attack, but may penalize the attack itself, because of the movement and speed of the Dragonknight as he performs the attack. Diving is very much like "Charging", except the attack is coming from the air instead of on the ground.

The Dragonknight must start the dive from at least thirty-five feet above his target in order to use "Dive Attack" (a minimal amount of speed must be reached). Depending upon how fast the Dragonknight is diving, there are different bonuses and penalties that could affect the outcome of the attack.

The three categories of diving speeds are the same as those for charging (Minimal, Average, and Maximum). Minimal Dive Speed is 200' to 250'/Turn and gives a -1 point penalty to the attack and a +4 point bonus to the damage. Average Dive Speed is 251' to 300'/Turn and gives a -2 point penalty to the attack and a +8 point bonus to the damage. Maximum Dive Speed is 301'/Turn and above. It gives a -3 point penalty to the attack and a + 12 point bonus to the damage.

If your character has the Initiative over another being that is performing a dive attack against him, he must wait until the diving opponent flies into melee with him before he can attack (unless your character has the means of performing a ranged attack). This delay means that your character is lowering his Initiative to the same value as that of the diving foe.

If your character performs a successful attack against the diving being, he will receive the same bonuses to the damage of his attack that the diving being receives to his.

For example, Boris who is in Dragonknight form is diving down at Maximum Dive Speed upon a Shadow-Sworn Grak. As Boris closes in, the Grak thrusts a spear at him. The spear strikes home! The Grak will now add 12 points to the damage of his attack (the amount indicated by a Maximum Dive Speed attack). If able, Boris may now follow through with his attack, applying -3 points to his attack and +12 points to his damage (as indicated by a Maximum Dive Speed attack). Notice that the Grak does not apply the -3 point penalty to his attack. He is not the one moving at over 301'/Turn. However the Grak's attack would actually have been penalized by 1D6 points for attacking a moving target (see "Attacking vs. Movement" at the beginning of this Section).

If a diving being is attacked before their attack can be carried out, as in the above example, and they set a Defense

against this attack, their dive bonuses and penalties are negated.

For example, Boris who is in Dragonknight form is diving down at Maximum Dive Speed upon a Shadow-sworn Grak. As Boris closes in, the Grak thrusts a spear at him. If Boris attempts to dodge the attack, meaning he sets a Defense, he will lose the "Dive Attack" bonuses (and penalties), but the Grak would also lose the damage bonus to his attack.

Though Dragonknights are used as the example to describe dive attacks, any large creature capable of flying can perform a "Dive Attack". A Bulk Value of 5 or higher is generally required in order to qualify for a "Dive Attack".

Fake

This combat variant can only be used with melee attacks. Its function is to deceive an opponent into thinking that the attack is being aimed for one area and then at the last instant the attack changes direction and strikes at another area.

In order to successfully fake an opponent your character must beat them on Performance Die results (the performance of your character's attack against the performance of their Defense).

Compare Performance Die results. If you declared that your character is using "Fake" and the Performance Die result for your character's attack is greater than his opponent's Performance Die result for their Physical Defense, then your character may add the difference to his attack value. If Performance Die results are the same then "Fake" doesn't work and your character's attack is neither penalized nor receives bonuses.

If you declare that your character is using "Fake" and his opponent's Performance Die result is greater than his, then your character's attack is penalized by the difference in Performance Die results.

For example, Jade is attacking a serpent wolf with a battle-axe and declares that he wants to use "Fake". The Performance Die result for Jade's attack is 9 and his total attack value is 22. The serpent wolf's Performance Die result for its Physical Defense (dodge) is 10 and its total Defense value is 21. Jade's Performance Die result is not higher than the serpent wolf's so his attempt to "Fake" has failed. Also his attack is now penalized by the difference in the Performance Die results, which is 1 point. Jade subtracts 1 point from his attack value bringing it to a 21. His attack value does not exceed the serpent wolf's Defense value so his attack misses.

Flat Blading

If you choose, your character may use the flat side of an edged weapon to reduce the damage done by a successful attack, as well as converting it into non-lethal damage. You must state that your character is using "Flat Blading" before attack success is determined. The result of the Damage Yield of the weapon is reduced by half (round down). The

Strength Level that is applied to the attack is still doubled, only the result of the dice rolled for the Damage Yield of the weapon is halved.

The edged weapon now yields non-lethal damage.

Iron Defense

This combat variant allows your character to assume a more effective defensive posture. "Iron Defense" gives your character the option of using his Defense Bonus Points in a way other than simply adding them to his Physical Defense value. Your character utilizes "Iron Defense" by rolling the dice that match a Level equal to his Physical Defense Bonus Points.

For example, Bane has a Physical Defense Bonus of 7. He may utilize "Iron Defense" by rolling the dice for Level 7 (1D10 + 1D4) and adding the result to his Physical Defense value.

If Defense Bonus Points have already been added to your character's Defense value, then "Iron Defense" can not be used that Turn.

No Major Actions can be taken in the same Turn that "Iron Defense" is used. If your character has already utilized "Iron Defense", then he may not perform any Major Actions (such as attacking) for the duration of that Turn. If your character has already performed a Major Action, then "Iron Defense" may not be used in that same Turn. In short, unlike setting a normal defense, "Iron Defense" is a Major Action.

Meditation

Sometimes you may find it helpful for your character to stop and focus for a moment on the task he is about to perform. If your character takes a few moments to focus and meditate on his upcoming action it will increase his chances of success.

If your character meditates for 1 Turn you may add 1 point to the result of your character's action. Meditating for 2 Turns gives a +2 point bonus, and meditating for 3 Turns or longer gives a +3 point bonus. Any Major or Minor Actions performed during meditation negates all meditation up to that point and your character must start over.

"Meditation" may not be used for learning Force Knowledge, Force-effects, Runes, Skills, or any other action that the GM deems inappropriate.

Single Strike

With this combat variant the combatant focuses the strength and energy of the attack into one concentrated strike. Normally when a character, or a creature, makes an attack there is more than one strike, bite, or blow made, but all of the strikes and hits for the Turn are considered a single attack. With "Single Strike" there is actually only one strike made for the entire attack, but it is more focused and more powerful than if several lesser strikes were made.

When making a "Single Strike" attack you may add 6 points to the damage of the attack, but the attack itself receives a -3 point penalty. You must declare whether or not your character is utilizing "Single Strike" before the attack is actually made. "Single Strike" can only be used in conjunction with **physical melee** attacks.

Though archery and throwing weapon attacks are inherently a single strike action, they do not qualify as a "Single Strike" attack as described by this combat variant.

Slipping Past Shields

When facing a foe that is wielding a shield your character has the option of attempting to place his attack in a way that it will slip past their shield, even though the shield would have normally intercepted the attack. Only **physical melee** attacks can slip past shields.

You must declare the use of this combat variant with your character's intended actions at the beginning of the Turn.

If your character's attack doesn't miss overcoming his opponent's Physical Defense (block) by more than 10 points, then he will slip past their shield as long as your Performance Die result is high enough. A Performance Die result of 7 will slip past a buckler, a result of 8 will slip past a half-shield, and a result of 9 will slip past a full-shield.

One drawback to using this combat variant is that the damage of the attack is penalized by 1D4 +6 points, regardless of whether the attack actually slips past the shield or not.

For example, Mike is preparing to attack an opponent who is armed with a half-shield. He declares that he will attempt to slip past his opponent's shield.

Mike's attack value is 16 (the Performance Die result was 8). His opponent's Physical Defense is 26. Since the attack didn't miss by more than 10 points, and the Performance Die result met the minimum requirement for slipping past a half-shield, the attack will slip past the shield. The damage yielded by Mike's attack is lowered by 1D4 +6 points.

Surprise

A being that is caught off guard by an attack is usually considered to be surprised (GM's decision as to exactly what will constitute a surprise). If the GM declares that a being is surprised, they receive a 1D4 +3 point penalty to their next Test of that Turn if it occurs immediately after being surprised.

For example, Ulric is walking around the corner of a building admiring the beautiful clouds when a wretchin suddenly jumps from out of nowhere and attacks him with a bone dagger. The GM rules that this constitutes a surprise so any Defense that Ulric sets against this attack will be penalized by 1D4 +3 points.

PERILS OF COMBAT

For many players the most exciting part of a role-playing game is the action of combat. Though this *is* a very exciting and challenging aspect of the game, combat is not without its risks to your character. There are many unfortunate and undesirable situations that your character may encounter or endure during the course of combat. This section of the combat rules will deal with some of the more common perils of combat.

Death

The most severe and dreaded outcome of combat is that your character is killed. If your character sustains an amount of lethal damage to a vital area that is equal to or greater than his Life Force he will die. Character death is a part of the game and though no player relishes the thought of losing a character that they have been playing for months or even years, they must remember that it is just a game. Characters die and life goes on. Roll up another character and jump back into the game.

Special Circumstances

In regards to character death there are a few factors that may actually allow your character to survive even though he has sustained a number of points of damage greater than his Life Force. These factors are; the type of damage rendered and where the damage is applied.

There are basically two types of damage that a character can receive. They are lethal damage and non-lethal damage. Lethal damage is damage that can potentially cause death to a character or creature. Examples of lethal damage would be being stabbed with a sword, being hit with "Fire Lightning", receiving Force burn, critical injury blood loss, Force Energy expenditure in excess of your character's Current Force Energy, or essence combat damage in excess of your character's Current Force Energy.

Non-lethal damage is damage that can harm or damage a character or creature but does not typically cause death. Examples of non-lethal damage would be a finger-prick from a briar, a slap in the face, damage from someone using "Flat-blading", or a bee sting.

If it is non-lethal damage that gives your character an amount of damage equal to or greater than his Life Force value it generally will not kill him. However, if even 1 point of lethal damage is received by your character after he has more damage than his Life Force he will immediately die.

Most sources of damage that your character will encounter during the game will be lethal damage, however there will be situations where your character will receive non-lethal damage. In the case that your character receives damage that you're not sure should be classified as lethal or non-lethal damage, the GM's decision will be the final and determining factor.

Another factor that affects whether or not your character dies after receiving an amount of damage equal to or greater than his Life Force value is where the damage is applied. There are basically two categories where damage to a character or creature is applied. They are vital areas and non-vital areas. Vital areas are areas of a being's body that contain vital or life-supporting organs, such as the head/neck, chest, or pelvis. Vital areas of a being are areas that the being can not survive without. Non-vital areas are areas of a being's body that are not absolutely necessary for survival, such as hands and fingers, ears, feet, etc. Though these areas of the body do serve functions and it is nice to have them, they are not vital for survival.

If it is damage to a non-vital area that gives your character an amount of damage equal to or greater than his Life Force value it generally will not kill him. However, if even 1 point of damage is rendered to a vital area of your character's body after he has more damage than his Life Force he will imme-

diately die. The head/neck, torso, and pelvis zones of ruling-races are considered vital areas.

Unless the GM rules that a particular situation calls for a different outcome, the damage received that takes your character's current damage equal to or above his Life Force value must be *lethal* damage to a *vital* area in order to kill him.

Force Failure

Whenever a character receives an amount of damage equal to or greater than his Force Failure he risks becoming unconscious. This is not technically a knock out, but it can be classified as such if the GM deems the situation appropriate. Generally Force Failure is considered to be the result of blacking out, passing out, fainting, or any other means of becoming unconscious that the GM deems appropriate due to the cumulative damage that the character has received.

Injuries

For each injury that your character has 1 point of damage can not be healed until the injury is healed; 2 points of damage can not be healed for each critical injury. An injury lowers the attribute to which it is applied by 2 Levels and a critical injury lowers the attribute by 4 Levels. Each injury to Agility or Strength decreases movement by 20 feet per Turn and each critical injury to Agility or Strength decreases movement by 40 feet per Turn.

When an injury is received the GM assigns it to one of three attributes; Agility, Strength, or Endurance. The GM should also assign a number of days that it will take for the injury to heal (naturally heal). The GM may simply choose how long the injury requires to heal, or as a recommended method of randomly determining healing time he or she may simply roll 1D4. The result is the number of days required before the injury can be healed naturally.

Injuries are healed with Recovery Tests just like damage. See "Recovering from Damage" in the "SURVIVING ORYATHAR" Section for more on healing damage and injuries.

Knockdown

Beings may be knocked down in several different ways, and depending upon how they are knocked down the event is handled differently. If a being is knocked down and stunned at the same time, usually the result of having their Injury Rating doubled by the damage of a single attack, it is a Major Action to get up as long as they remain stunned (which is normally the duration of that Turn).

If a being is knocked down by any other means, such as being tripped, then it is only a Minor Action to get back up. Regardless of how a being gets knocked down the total result of their Physical Defense and any physical actions is cut in half, rounded down, as long as they are down.

There may be certain circumstances where it is still a Major Action to get up from a knock down even if your character isn't stunned (the Talent "Throw" for example).

Flying beings that have their Injury Rating doubled by the damage of a single attack are knocked out of the air. All rules pertaining to a knockdown also apply here, the only difference being that they are considered knocked out of the air instead of knocked down.

Knock Out

A true knock out is quite different than going unconscious due to Force Failure. Your character doesn't have to have accumulated any certain amount of damage in order to be knocked out. Some types of attacks, especially those to the head/neck zone, can knock your character out regardless of whether he has reached Force Failure or not.

If your character receives an amount of damage to his head/neck zone that doubles his Injury Rating (meaning he is knocked down and stunned) he must immediately roll the percentile dice to keep from being knocked out. A result of 25 or under means that he is knocked out for 1D4 Turns.

If the attack in the above example was a Flawless Performance, your character is automatically knocked out for 1D4 (no percentile dice roll is necessary).

Critical injuries to the head/neck zone automatically knock out the recipient of the attack.

It is a Major Action to get up on the same Turn that your character becomes conscious after being knocked out.

Knocked out beings stay unconscious for 1D4 Turns unless they receive mystical intervention (Healing, Vitalize, etc…).

Stun

Beings are usually stunned by receiving damage to their head/neck area or receiving double their Injury Rating in damage in one blow, but other factors, such as being struck by lightning, may also stun them. A stunned being receives a -4 point penalty to all Tests, with the exceptions of Endurance and Willpower-based Tests, for the duration of the Turn, as well as having both their Physical and Mystical Initiatives lowered by 4 points.

If a being receives an injury to their head/neck zone, they must immediately make an Endurance Test against a Difficulty Value of 10. Failure means that they are stunned for the remainder of the Turn. If the attack was a Flawless Performance the opponent is automatically stunned.

If your character has a Flawless Performance on an attack that causes a stun, the target being does not get to make the Endurance Test; they are automatically stunned. In addition, the stun lasts 1 extra Turn.

SKILLS

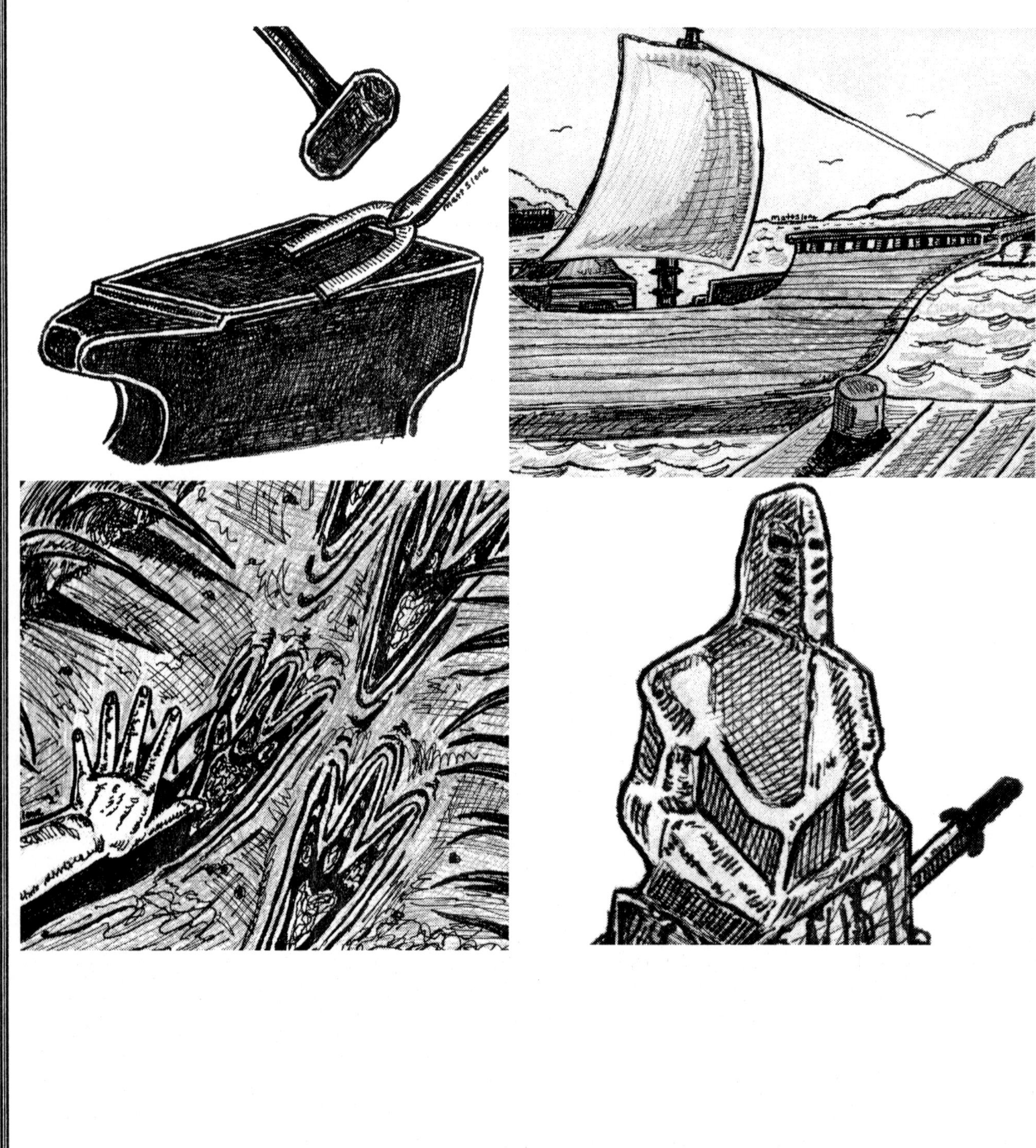

"Skills" are abilities that your character may learn through the course of adventuring. They are not purchased with Light Points as Talents are, but require actual training and practice in order to be learned.

Some of the Skills can not be learned without a trainer to teach and instruct your character. If a Rank in a Skill requires a trainer, an asterisk will appear after the Rank number. If there are any important details relevant to the training, it will be given in the Skill's description.

Your character may not use any mystical-based abilities or items to assist in the learning of Skills. This includes any type of Force-effects (such as "Rune Lore's" Agility rune), or enchanted items. Such methods of boosting attributes required for *using* a Skill is quite acceptable, once the Skill has been learned. It is just not allowed for the learning of a Skill (that must be done by your character's own natural abilities). Attempting to learn a Skill while under the influence of such mystical properties results in automatic failure of all Progress Tests made during that time.

Some Skills may have a similar counter-part in a Talent ("Climbing" and "Tracking" for example), but you will find that Talents are much more advanced than their Skill counterparts. Having both the Talent and Skill for the same types of abilities often has added bonuses.

Skills are not necessarily vital to your character's survival, but they can be very helpful. A smart gamer will make sure that his or her character doesn't pass up the opportunity to learn Skills.

"THE SKILLS OF A WARRIOR ARE WHAT DETERMINES HIS SURVIVAL OR DEFEAT, AND WHETHER OR NOT HE IS THE PREDATOR OR THE PREY."

There are five major categories that apply to the learning and use of Skills. They are Relevant Attribute (appearing in parentheses under the name of the Skill), Maximum Rank, Progress Tests per Rank, Training Time, and Starting Difficulty. Each of these categories is explained in detail below.

Test Type

Along with the name of each Skill appears one or more types of attribute Tests in parentheses. This is the type or types of attribute Tests (referred to as Progress Tests when made in the attempt to learn a Skill) made to learn and often perform the Skill (unless stated otherwise).

So, if the Test Type for a Skill is an Agility/Performance Test, then that means that your character must make Agility/Performance Tests for his Progress Tests. If the Test Type is an Intelligence Test, then your character must make Intelligence Tests for his Progress Tests.

The Ranks of some Skills require more than one attribute Test in order to learn them. If there is a + in between the two attribute Tests then you may add the results of the two Tests together to meet the Difficulty Value of the Test. If there is an & in between the two attribute Tests then you must make each Test separately and compare the results to the appropriate Difficulty Values listed beside of "Starting Difficulty". With Skills that require this type of Tests there will be two numbers listed beside of "Starting Difficulty". The number before the forward slash is the Difficulty Value for the Test Type listed before the forward slash beside of the Skill name. The number after the forward slash is the Difficulty Value for the Test Type listed *after* the forward slash beside of the Skill name.

So lets take the Skill "Fishing" for example. The listed Test Type for this Skill is an Agility/Performance Test & Intelligence Test. You will notice that the Starting Difficulty for all of the Ranks of this Skill have two numbers instead of one. The number before the forward slash is the Starting Difficulty for the Agility/Performance Test and the number after the forward slash is the Starting Difficulty for the Intelligence Test.

When two separate Tests with two separate Difficulty Values must be made in order to make Progress Tests for a Skill both attribute Tests are considered a single Progress Test. If either Test is failed then the Progress Test as a whole is failed and both Tests must be repeated (after the required Training Time has again been met) in order to pass that Progress Test. Also, the Difficulty Value for both Tests increases by 1 point even if only one of the two Tests was failed (remember, both Tests are treated as a single Progress Test).

Maximum Rank

The number that appears after "Maximum Rank" is the maximum number of Ranks that can be achieved in that par-ticular Skill.

Each rank represents a certain degree of proficiency with that Skill. The higher the Rank, the more potential benefits that characters can receive from the Skill.

Progress Tests

A "Progress Test" is simply an attribute Test made against a Difficulty Value assigned to a particular Rank of a Skill. Your character must make three successful Progress Tests in order to learn any given Rank of a Skill. The passing of these Tests demonstrates your character's progress at learning the Skill.

Every Rank of a particular Skill has a Starting Difficulty, which is the Difficulty Value of the first Progress Test. All subsequent Progress Tests for that Rank must be at least 1 point higher than the Difficulty Value of the previous Progress Test.

So, a Rank in a Skill that has a Starting Difficulty of 8, means that your character must make three successful Tests (with the appropriate Test Type) with the result of the first being at least 8, the second at least 9, and the third at least 10.

Any failed Progress Test can be repeated after repeating the appropriate amount of Training Time, but the Difficulty Value will increase by 1 point for each failed attempt. Failed attempts should be noted on your Character Sheet so you will have a record for what the next required Difficulty Value will be. The results of all subsequent Progress Tests (for that Rank) must be 1 point higher than the previous Difficulty Value.

Once your character successfully learns a rank in a Skill he is able to start training for the next Rank at the Starting Difficulty listed. Failed attempts in previous ranks do not affect the Starting Difficulties of subsequent Ranks.

Once all three Progress Tests for a given Rank have been successfully made your character has learned that Rank of the Skill.

The Starting Difficulty listed for each Skill is a base value and may be adjusted by the GM if he feels it is necessary.

Be sure to record any passed or failed Progress Tests in your notes on your Character Sheet for reference when attempting further Tests for that Rank again. Remember, the Difficulty Value increases by 1 for each failed attempt within a given Rank.

For example, my character has already learned Rank 1 in "Blacksmithing" and wishes to learn Rank 2. The Starting Difficulty for Rank 2 is 9. The Test Type is an Intelligence Test, so my character will need to make three successful Intelligence Tests in order to learn Rank 2 of this Skill. The Training Time is eight hours and because Rank 2 of this Skill has an asterisk beside of it my character must have a trainer in order to learn it.

After working up a deal with the local blacksmith he has agreed to train my character in the ways of blacksmithing.

After working for a total of eight hours with the trainer at his forge, which my character did over the course of three days, he has met the training time required to make a Progress Test. My character's Intelligence is Level 6, the dice for that Level is 1D12. I roll a 4 on 1D12 which is added to my character's Intelligence Level of 6 for a total Intelligence Test result of 10. The Starting Difficulty for this Rank of "Blacksmithing" is 9. My character passes his first Progress Test for Rank 2 of "Blacksmithing".

Over the next few days my character completes eight more hours of training at the forge. He is now ready for his second Progress Test. The result of this Test must at least 1 point higher than the required Difficulty Value of the last Test, which was 9. My character needs a result of 10 or higher in order to pass his second Progress Test. The result of my character's Intelligence Test is 12. He has passed his second Progress Test; one more to go.

Within four days my character has put in another eight hours of training with the blacksmith. He is ready to attempt the third and final Progress Test for this Rank. The Difficulty Value of this Intelligence Test is 11 (1 point higher than the Difficulty Value of the last Test). I roll a 1 on the 1D12 for a total Test result of 7. My character has failed this Progress Test. After eight more hours of training he is ready to try again. The Difficulty Value of the Progress Test this time is increased by 1 point beyond the required Difficulty Value of the last Test, which was an 11. I now need a 12 or better in order to pass this Test. I roll a 7 on the 1D12 for a total Test result of 13. My character has passed the third Progress Test. He now has Rank 2 in "Blacksmithing".

Training Time

This is the actual amount of time that your character must spend practicing and training for a Skill in order to make a Progress Test. Your character must actually train or practice what he is trying to learn the Skill for in order to obtain the Skill.

For example, to learn "Arm Wrestling" your character must actually spend the training time arm wrestling, for "Climbing" your character must actually spend the Training Time practicing climbing. If the title of a Skill makes it unclear as to what must be practiced during the training time, an explanation will be given with the description of that particular Skill. In Skills that require different types of training for its various Ranks, the training information will be listed with the training time information of each Rank.

Minimum Training Time

The amount of time required to train for each Progress Test may not be broken up by increments of less than one hour. Your character may not train for twenty minutes here and there and add it up to make enough time for a Progress Test. Your character must spend at least one hour at a time in training before the time is counted. Of course if your character

has less than an hour of training left, then he doesn't have to train for another hour. He may finish up the remaining training time, and then make his Progress Test.

For example, Ronnie is training for his first Progress Test for Rank 1 of "Creature Lore". He spends two and a half hours of consecutive training before resting. Two days later he is ready to complete his training. Only thirty minutes of training remains. In this case he does not have to spend an hour in training. He studies for the remaining thirty minutes and then makes his Progress Test.

If the listed Training Time for a particular Skill is less than one hour, then the Training Time must be met all at once.

For example, the listed Training Time for Rank 1 of "General Combat (Dragonknight)" is 5 Turns. If your character is training for this Rank of this Skill he must train the full 5 Turns at once in order for the time to be counted.

Maximum Wait in Between Training

There is a maximum amount of time that your character can wait in between training sessions and Progress Tests.

Your character may not wait more than five days in between training sessions for a Progress Test, and may not wait more than five days in between Progress Tests for any given Rank.

For example, Ronnie wishes to learn the first Rank of the Skill "Blacksmithing". The listed Training Time that must be met in order to make a Progress Test for Rank 1 is two hours. He must spend at least one hour at a time in training at a forge and may wait no longer than five days in between training sessions. Once a Progress Test has been successfully made Ronnie must begin training again within five days for the next Progress Test or lose all training time for that Rank.

If more than five days lapse in between training sessions or successful Progress Tests for a given Rank, then all the time spent in training as well as all Progress Tests for that Rank is erased and your character must start over. If your character is forced to start over for this reason, the Starting Difficulty for the first Progress Test is 1 point higher than that listed.

The Training Time listed for each Skill is an average and may be adjusted by the GM if he feels a particular character has special characteristics that would aid in the learning of a particular Skill.

* Indicates that your character must have a trainer in order to learn one or more of the Ranks for that Skill.

SKILLS

1. Alchemy *
2. Arm Wrestling
3. Black Smithing *
4. Bow & Arrow Making *
5. Cavalry *
6. Carpentry *

7. Carving/Sculpting
8. Climbing
9. Controlled Transformation
10. Creature Lore
11. Enchantment Buffering
12. Farrier *
13. Fishing
14. General Combat
15. General Combat (Dragonknight)
16. General Conjuring
17. Hunting
18. Language *
19. Rapid Transformation
20. Sailing *
21. Swimming
22. Tracking
23. Traveling

ALCHEMY Intelligence Test

(* = Intelligence Test + Sixth Sense/Performance Test)

In order to use this Skill you must first have a copy of the "ALCHEMY" sourcebook, which introduces all of the rules and applications for the use of alchemy in the **Mystic Forces** role-playing system.

Alchemy is the most complex and detailed Skill that your character can learn. This Skill gives your character the knowledge and ability to create a variety of potions and products; some with mere mundane properties, others having immense mystical powers.

All Ranks of this Skill can be learned through the study of books, scrolls, and examining actual ingredients and products. As long as the book, scroll, or information source adequately describes and explains the necessary information for the Rank a trainer is not necessary. However, Ranks 8, 11, and 12 are much harder to learn on one's own than with the assistance and guidance of a trainer who has already mas-

tered those Ranks. When attempting to learn Ranks 8, 11, or 12 without a trainer the listed Starting Difficulty increases by 5 points.

Due to the amount of detail and complexity involved with this Skill, there is a separate section of rules devoted entirely to the explanation and use of alchemy.

If you are interested in your character learning the art of alchemy you should read the "ALCHEMY" Section of the rules before having your character train for this Skill.

Maximum Rank: 12

(STAGE ONE)
Rank 1
Training Time: 1 hr
Starting Difficulty: 9

Your character gains a basic knowledge and understanding of the concepts of alchemy. Your character also learns the names and effects of 1D10 Stage One alchemy products.

Rank 2
Training Time: 1 hr
Starting Difficulty: 10

Your character learns the names and effects of all Stage One alchemy products and also learns 1D10 Stage One alchemy ingredients, including the ingredient's physical characteristics, where it can be found, and its availability.

Rank 3
Training Time: 1 ½ hrs
Starting Difficulty: 11

Your character learns detailed information (physical characteristics, where they're found, and relative availability) of all Stage One alchemy ingredients.

Rank 4
Training Time: 1 ½ hrs
Starting Difficulty: 12

Your character learns the process for creating all Stage One alchemy products, what their effects are, and any precautions for the creation or use of the products.

(STAGE TWO)
Rank 5
Training Time: 2 hrs
Starting Difficulty: 12

Your character learns the names and effects of 1D10 Stage Two alchemy products.

Rank 6
Training Time: 2 hrs
Starting Difficulty: 13

Your character learns the names and effects all Stage Two alchemy products and also learns 1D10 Stage Two alchemy ingredients, including the ingredient's physical characteris-

tics, where it can be found, and its availability.

Rank 7
Training Time: 3 hrs
Starting Difficulty: 14

Your character learns detailed information (physical characteristics, where they're found, and relative availability) on all Stage Two alchemy ingredients.

Rank 8
Training Time: 3 hrs
Starting Difficulty: * 25

Your character learns the process for creating all Stage Two alchemy products, what their effects are, and any precautions for the creation or use of the products. Your character also knows the effects of all Stage Two product's unstable forms as well as gaining the ability to recognize whether or not a Stage Two product is unstable. A close examination is required in order to detect whether a product is unstable or not.

(STAGE THREE)
Rank 9
Training Time: 3 hrs
Starting Difficulty: 14

Your character learns the names and effects of 1D10 Stage Three alchemy products.

Rank 10
Training Time: 3 hrs
Starting Difficulty: 15

Your character learns the names and effects all Stage Three alchemy products and also learns 1D10 Stage Three alchemy ingredients, including the ingredient's physical characteristics, where it can be found, and its availability.

Rank 11
Training Time: 4 hrs
Starting Difficulty: * 34

Your character learns detailed information (physical characteristics, where they're found, and relative availability) on all Stage Three alchemy ingredients. Your character also learns how to sense the Mystical Strength Value (M.S.V.) of the ingredients and know how low the ingredient's M.S.V. can be before the ingredient becomes unstable or useless for alchemy purposes.

In order to sense the ingredient's M.S.V. your character must be within close proximity to the ingredient (two feet or less) and draw in on *Spirit* while focusing on the ingredient. It takes only 1 Turn to detect the ingredient's M.S.V. and is considered a Major Action.

Rank 12
Training Time: 4 hrs

Starting Difficulty: * 30

Your character learns the process for creating all Stage Three alchemy products, what their effects are, and any precautions for the creation or use of the products. Your character also knows the effects of all Stage Three product's unstable forms as well as gaining the ability to recognize whether or not a Stage Three product is unstable. A close examination is required in order to detect whether a product is unstable or not.

ARM-WRESTLING (Strength Test)

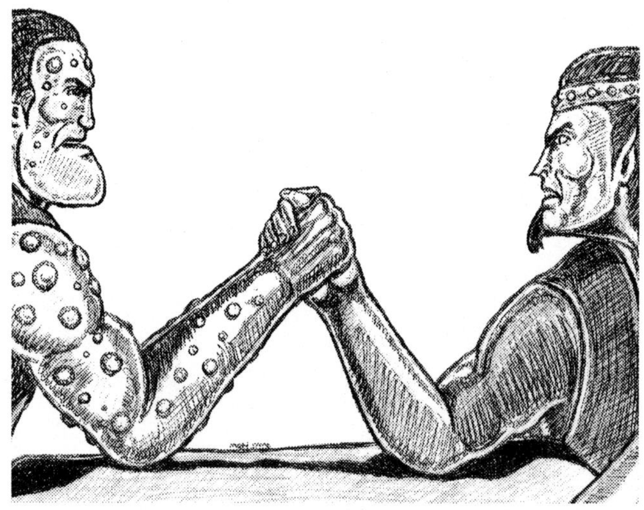

This Skill develops the specific muscles required to arm-wrestle and improves your character's technique, thus allowing him to be much better at arm wrestling than another person with the same Strength and no skill in arm-wrestling.

When arm-wrestling, both beings engaged make a Strength Test and compare results. The being with the highest result takes his opponent forty-five degrees (half way) in the desired direction. So from the starting position, it takes two consecutive wins to beat an opponent in arm-wrestling.

If your character has Technique Points with his hands/arms he may add 1 point to the result of his arm-wrestling Test for each Technique Point he has with his hands/arms.

Training Time for all Ranks of "Arm-wrestling" must consist of actually arm-wrestling with other ruling-races.
Maximum Rank: 3

Rank 1
Training Time: 30 min
Starting Difficulty: 5

Your character may add 1D4 points to the result of any arm-wrestling Test.

Rank 2
Training Time: 1 hr
Starting Difficulty: 7

Your character may add 1D8 points to the result of any arm-wrestling Test.

Rank 3

<u>Training Time</u>: 2 hrs

<u>Starting Difficulty</u>: 9

Your character may add 1D12 points to the result of any arm-wrestling Test.

BLACKSMITHING (Intelligence Test)

Your character learns how to operate a forge and create weapons and other items from raw metals.

The training for all Ranks of "Blacksmithing" requires actual hands on training and instruction in a working forge.

<u>Maximum Rank</u>: 4

Rank 1 *

<u>Training Time</u>: 2 hrs

<u>Starting Difficulty</u>: 7

Your character becomes familiar with and can operate a forge to a small degree. Your character also knows many details of the forging process and the types and applications of the different metals used in blacksmithing.

He can repair up to two Reduced Effectiveness (R.E.) ratings worth of damage to any metal weapon (not green-steel).

Rank 2 *

<u>Training Time</u>: 8 hrs

<u>Starting Difficulty</u>: 9

Your character can now repair any level of damage to non-green-steel weapons, can make basic styles of weapons up to a Bulk Value of 2, and can repair armor.

Rank 3 *

<u>Training Time</u>: 9 hrs

<u>Starting Difficulty</u>: 11

Your character can now make any size and style of weapon, and can make armor.

Rank 4 *

<u>Training Time</u>: 16 hrs

<u>Starting Difficulty</u>: 13

Your character can now repair and make green-steel weapons and armor.

For any of the Ranks of this Skill your character must, of course, have a forge and the needed tools and metals necessary to repair and/or make weapons and armor. It is left up to the GM's discretion as to how long it will take a character to make any given type of weapon or piece of armor.

BOW & ARROW MAKING

(Intelligence Test + Agility/Performance Test)

This Skill allows your character to make his own bows and arrows.

<u>Maximum Rank</u>: 3

Rank 1 *

<u>Training Time</u>: 3 hrs

The training consists of actual hands on practice and instruction with carving and shaping wood into arrows.

<u>Starting Difficulty</u> : 13

Your character can make arrows for all sizes and types of bows and cross bows. It typically takes two hours to make a single arrow once your character has become experienced with the process. The first several arrows that he makes may easily take six to seven hours each to create.

Rank 2 *

<u>Training Time</u>: 9 hrs

The training consists of actual hands on practice and instruction with shaping wood into bows.

<u>Starting Difficulty</u>: 14

Your character can now make all sizes and types of bow. It typically takes one week to make a bow from scratch.

Rank 3 *

<u>Training Time</u>: 4 hrs

The training consists of actual hands on practice and instruction with making crossbows.

<u>Starting Difficulty</u>: 16

Your character can now make or repair all sizes and types of cross bows. It typically takes a week and a half to make a crossbow from scratch.

CARPENTRY (Rank 1 = Intelligence Test, Ranks 2 & 3 = Intelligence Test + Agility/Performance Test)

Carpentry gives your character the knowledge to select and distinguish between the different types of woods and their uses and also how to make and repair wooden items such as wagons, houses, etc.

<u>Maximum Rank</u>: 3

Rank 1 *

Training Time: 1 hr

Training consists of studying carpentry tools and their applications with someone who is skilled with the tools.

Starting Difficulty: 5

Your character can recognize the different types of woods and carpentry tools and knows their basic uses.

Rank 2 *

Training Time: 5 hrs

The training consists of your character actually working on various simple wood projects under the instruction of a skilled carpenter.

Starting Difficulty: 8

Your character becomes competent with most carpenter tools and knows how to make most minor repairs as well as simple items such as axe handles, yokes, bowls, etc.

Rank 3 *

Training Time: 12 hrs

The training consists of your character actually working on various advanced projects under the instruction of a skilled carpenter.

Starting Difficulty: 11

Your character becomes a true carpenter capable of making and repairing detailed items from wood such as furniture, carts, barrels, and even large scale projects such as wagons and houses.

CARVING/SCULPTING

(Intelligence Test + Agility/Performance Test)

Your character learns to shape wood and stone into fashionable and/or useable items that may even be able to bring a handsome price at market.

Maximum Rank: 3

Rank 1

Training Time: 3 hrs

The entire training time must be spent actually carving and working on at least three separate wood projects. Your character must have a carving tool kit in order to train for this Rank.

Starting Difficulty: 10

Your character can competently carve wood into various shapes and forms.

Rank 2

Training Time: 4 hrs

The entire training time must be spent actually sculpting and working on at least three separate stone projects. Your character must have a sculptors kit in order to train for this Rank.

Starting Difficulty: 11

Your character can competently carve stone into various shapes and forms.

Rank 3

Training Time: 6 hrs

The entire training time must be spent actually sculpting and working on at least three separate stone projects and carving out at least three separate wood projects. Your character must have a sculptors kit and carving tools in order to train for this Rank.

Starting Difficulty: 12

Your character becomes very expert in both of the above Ranks and his work is of such quality that it can commonly be sold for a good price. The average price that can be expected for carvings and sculptures depends upon how much time and effort was put into the piece and the type of material the piece consists of.

The following is a rough average of what most merchants will pay for carvings and sculptures. These prices are just an average and should be adjusted by the GM if the item consists of precious stones, rare woods, etc, or if an extraordinary amount of time was put into the piece.

1 hours work: wood = 1 sc, stone = 2 sc

2 hours work: wood = 3 sc, stone = 5 sc

3-5 hours work: wood = 5-7 sc, stone = 6-9 sc

6-10 hours work: wood = 8-10 sc, stone = 10-13 sc

11 hrs or greater: wood = 11-15 sc, stone = 14-20 sc

CAVALRY (Agility/Performance Test)

This Skill develops your character's abilities in riding and performing various physical tasks from a mount. He gains more control while on any mount and learns the invaluable art of mounted combat.

If your character learns all five ranks of this Skill he is classified as a cavalryman. Cavalrymen that are Defenders of the Light receive an additional five silver coins in pay above what a non-cavalryman of equal rank would receive.
<u>Maximum Rank</u>: 5

Rank 1
<u>Training Time</u>: 3hrs

The training for this Rank requires persistent training with a horse or bleyk. Repetitive mounting and dismounting and attacking from the mount is the majority of the training for this Rank.

<u>Starting Difficulty</u>: 10

Your character's penalty for attacking from a mount drops from -1D6 points to -1D4-1 points. He can also mount up as a Minor Action.

Rank 2
<u>Training Time</u>: 3 hrs

As with Rank 1, the training for this Rank requires persistent training with a horse or bleyk. Repetitive mounting and dismounting and attacking from the mount is the majority of the training for this Rank.
<u>Starting Difficulty</u>: 12

Your character no longer receives any penalty for attacking from a mount. In addition, he receives a +3 point bonus to the result of the Agility/Performance + Strength Test made to resist being knocked off of his mount when making a successful charge attack.

Rank 3 *
<u>Training Time</u>: 3 hrs

The training for this Rank requires persistent training with a horse or bleyk. Repetitive mounting and dismounting and defending against attacks while on the mount is the majority of the training for this Rank.
<u>Starting Difficulty</u>: 11

Your character's penalty for setting a Physical Defense from a mount drops from -1D6 points to -1D4-1 points.

Rank 4 *
<u>Training Time</u>: 3 hrs

As with Rank 3, the training for this Rank requires persistent training with a horse or bleyk. Repetitive mounting and dismounting and defending against attacks while on the mount is the majority of the training for this Rank.
<u>Starting Difficulty</u>: 13

Your character no longer receives any penalty for setting a Physical Defense from a mount.

Rank 5
<u>Training Time</u>: 4 hrs

Your character must practice making ranged attacks from the mount while moving in excess of 35 feet per Turn for the duration of the training time.
<u>Starting Difficulty</u>: 12

Your character no longer receives the -1D6 point movement penalty to ranged attacks when exceeding speeds of 35 feet per Turn while on a mount (movement penalty would still apply if he is moving on foot).

CLIMBING (Agility/Performance Test)

Your character develops his climbing ability; increasing the speed and competency at which he climbs.

The duration of the training time for all Ranks of this Skill must be spent climbing various types of surfaces with varying degrees of steepness.
<u>Maximum Rank</u>: 3

Rank 1
<u>Training Time</u>: 1 hr
<u>Starting Difficulty</u>: 7

Your character is now able to climb an additional 5 feet per Turn and may add +1 to the result of any Agility-based Test that involves climbing.

Rank 2
<u>Training Time</u>: 1 hr
<u>Starting Difficulty</u>: 8

Your character is now able to climb an additional 10 feet per Turn instead of just 5 feet per Turn and may add +2 to the result of any Agility-based Test that involves climbing instead of just +1.

Rank 3
<u>Training Time</u>: 1 hr
<u>Starting Difficulty</u>: 9

Your character is now able to climb an additional 15 feet per Turn instead of just 10 feet per Turn and may add + 4 to the result of any Agility-based Test that involves climbing instead of just +2.

CONTROLLED TRANSFORMATION

(Sixth Sense/Performance Test)

Your character is now able to control his Dragonknight form in a new and more complete manner. He learns to bridge the gap between his ruling-race form and his Dragonknight form without fully transforming.

The duration of the training time for all Ranks of this Skill must be spent in uninterrupted meditation. If your character breaks meditation for more than 3 Turns at any point during the training for a particular Rank, he loses all training time and passed Progress Tests for that Rank and must start over (with the Starting Difficulty 1 point higher than it was at the time your character was forced to begin his training time over).

Maximum Rank: 3

Rank 1

Training Time: 3 hrs
Starting Difficulty: 10

Before your character can learn this Rank he must first have the maximum available number of Technique Points (5) with his Dragonknight's tail.

This Rank of "Controlled Transformation" allows your character to grow the tail of his Dragonknight form without actually transforming into Dragonknight. Only the tail is manifested. No attribute changes are made and no other aspects of the Dragonknight form can be used, including Advanced Combat.

The tail will, however, have a Protection Rating equal to the Protection Rating of the scales currently possessed by your character's Dragonknight form. If your character's Dragonknight form has gold scales, then his tail will also have its gold scales when grown in this manner.

The Force Energy requirements for growing only the tail by means of this Skill is the same as the Force Energy requirements for transforming into full Dragonknight form. This controlled transformation is considered a Major Action, unless your character has learned "Rapid Transformation".

Rank 2

Training Time: 4 hrs
Starting Difficulty: 11

Before your character can learn this Rank his Dragonknight form must be able to fly, and he must have both Technique Points in aerial combat.

This Rank of "Controlled Transformation" allows your character to grow the wings of his Dragonknight form without actually transforming into Dragonknight. Only the wings are manifested. No attribute changes are made and no other aspects of the Dragonknight form can be used, including Advanced Combat.

These wings will allow your character to fly, but because the ruling-race form is not nearly as strong as the Dragonknight form, or designed to support wings, the Maximum Flight Speed that can be reached using the wings in this manner is equal to your character's Maximum Speed in ruling-race form.

The Force Energy requirements for growing only the wings by means of this Skill is the same as the Force Energy requirements for transforming into full Dragonknight form. This controlled transformation is considered a Major Action, unless your character has learned "Rapid Transformation". Even if your character does have "Rapid Transformation" he can not grow the both the tail and wings of his Dragonknight form in the same Turn (until he learns Rank 3 of this Skill).

Ranged attacks made while flying (at any speed, even less than 35 feet per Turn) in this form receive a -1D6 penalty.

Rank 3

Training Time: 2 hrs
Starting Difficulty: 12

This Rank of "Controlled Transformation" allows your character to grow both the tail *and* the wings of his Dragonknight form at the same time. Your character can grow both the tail at wings at once, or grow one part one Turn and the other part on a subsequent Turn if he chooses. Whether your character grows only the tail or wings or both at the same time, the Force Energy for the transformation is the same as for transforming into full Dragonknight form and it is considered a Major Action, unless your character has learned "Rapid Transformation".

Transforming into *full* Dragonknight from a partially transformed form, such as already having the tail and wings, is no less strenuous or time consuming as transforming from normal ruling-race form. It still takes a Major Action to transform into Dragonknight from a partially transformed state, and no other actions can be taken while transforming.

CREATURE LORE (Intelligence Test)

Your character learns a great deal of useful information about all of the different types of natural creatures, Shadowkin, and mystical creatures found all across Oryathar.

Maximum Rank: 6

Rank 1

Training Time: 3 hrs
Starting Difficulty: 7

Your character now knows the names of most all species of natural creatures, and can recognize them upon sight as well as recognize their tracks or other signs of passing that such creatures may leave behind.

Rank 2

<u>Training Time</u>: 5 hrs
<u>Starting Difficulty</u>: 8

Your character learns a great deal of detailed information about most all species of natural creatures, such as their diet, migration (if any), disposition, areas where they can be found, etc. Your character also learns information on the creatures such as their strengths, weaknesses, Natural Protection Rating, Life Force, etc. The exact amount of knowledge that your character has about each creature is left up to the GM.

Rank 3

<u>Training Time</u>: 5 hrs
<u>Starting Difficulty</u>: 9

Your character now knows the names of most all species of Shadow-kin, and can recognize them upon sight as well as recognize their tracks or other signs of passing that such creatures may leave behind.

Rank 4

<u>Training Time</u>: 7 hrs
<u>Starting Difficulty</u>: 10

Your character learns a great deal of detailed information about most all species of Shadow-kin, such as their diet, migration (if any), disposition, areas where they can be found, etc. Your character also learns information on the Shadow-kin such as their strengths, weaknesses, Natural Protection Rating, Life Force, etc. The exact amount of knowledge that your character has about each type of Shadow-kin is left up to the GM.

Rank 5

<u>Training Time</u>: 7 hrs
<u>Starting Difficulty</u>: 11

Your character now knows the names of most all types of mystical creatures, and can recognize them upon sight as well as recognize their tracks or other signs of passing that such creatures may leave behind.

Rank 6

<u>Training Time</u>: 7 hrs
<u>Starting Difficulty</u>: 12

Your character learns a great deal of detailed information about most all types of mystical creatures, such as their diet, migration (if any), disposition, areas where they can be found, etc. Your character also learns information on the mystical creatures such as their strengths, weaknesses, Natural Protection Rating, Life Force, etc. The exact amount of knowledge that your character has about each type of mystical creature is left up to the GM.

ENCHANTMENT BUFFERING

(Sixth Sense/Performance Test)

Enchantments that have the exact same combination of Mystic Forces within them will have a reaction when coming within five feet of one another. Such reactions can cause what is known as an "adverse reaction", which can be very dangerous.

"Enchantment Buffering" allows Shinkai Enchanters to buffer the enchantments they create so that they will not react with other enchantments containing the same combination of Mystic Forces.

"Enchantment Buffering" works by slightly adjusting the way in which the Mystic Forces are infused into the item being enchanted. The easiest way to learn this process is by looking into the "Raging" of another Shinkai Enchanter while he or she creates a buffered enchantment. Without such a trainer to demonstrate the intricate techniques of this Skill it is much more difficult to master. If you attempt to learn this Skill on your own the listed Starting Difficulty for each Rank is increased by 5.

The listed Training Time for all Ranks of "Enchantment Buffering" is variable because the training is actually done by creating an enchantment. Any Rating of enchantment can be created to learn the various Ranks of this Skill, so the Training Time is equal to the amount of time that it takes to create the enchantment. Even if the creation of the enchantment fails your character can use the attempt as the required training to make a Progress Test.

Technique Points in the Mystic Forces will give bonuses to the Progress Tests made for this Skill. For each Technique Point that your character has in each of the Mystic Forces contained within the enchantment he may add 1 point to the result of the Progress Test made after attempting to create the enchantment.

For more information on enchantments and adverse reactions see the "ENCHANTING" Section of the rules.
<u>Maximum Rank</u>: 4

Rank 1

<u>Training Time</u>: Variable
<u>Starting Difficulty</u>: 17

Your character learns how to create enchantments that have a slightly reduced likelihood of causing an adverse reaction when brought within five feet of another enchantment containing the exact same combination of Mystic Forces. Though they will still glow and react when brought within five feet of another enchantment with the same combination of Mystic Forces, they will not cause external effects to manifest if the two enchantments have an adverse reaction with the result being "External Effects". If that result is rolled as the result for the adverse reaction, there is no adverse reaction, either in the buffered enchantment or the other enchantments with the same Mystic Force combination.

Rank 2

Training Time: Variable
Starting Difficulty: 18

Your character learns how to create enchantments that have a fairly reduced likelihood of causing an adverse reaction when brought within five feet of another enchantment containing the exact same combination of Mystic Forces. Though they will still glow and react when brought within five feet of another enchantment with the same combination of Mystic Forces, they will not cause external effects to manifest *or* a blinding flash of light and thunder clap if the two enchantments have an adverse reaction with the result being "External Effects" or "Blinding Flash/Thunder Clap". If either of those results are rolled as the result for the adverse reaction, there is no adverse reaction, either in the buffered enchantment or the other enchantments with the same Mystic Force combination.

Rank 3

Training Time: Variable
Starting Difficulty: 19

Your character learns how to create enchantments that have a significantly reduced likelihood of causing an adverse reaction when brought within five feet of another enchantment containing the exact same combination of Mystic Forces. Though they will still glow and react when brought within five feet of another enchantment with the same combination of Mystic Forces, they will not cause external effects to manifest *or* a blinding flash of light and thunder clap, *or* neutralize the enchantments if the two enchantments have an adverse reaction with the result being "External Effects", "Blinding Flash/Thunder Clap", or "Neutralize". If either of those three results are rolled as the result for the adverse reaction, there is no adverse reaction, either in the buffered enchantment or the other enchantments with the same Mystic Force combination.

Rank 4

Training Time: Variable
Starting Difficulty: 20

Your character learns how to create enchantments that will not react at all with other enchantments containing the exact same combination of Mystic Forces. The buffered enchantment will not even glow or have any other type of reaction, let alone an adverse reaction, with other enchantments with the same combination of Mystic Forces. The enchantment or enchantments with the same combination of Mystic Forces that come within five feet of the buffered enchantment will not react or show any signs of a reaction.

FARRIER (Endurance Test + Intelligence Test)

With this Skill your character learns how to properly shoe horses and take care of their feet.

The duration of the training time for this Skill must be spent actually shoeing horses under the instruction of a skilled farrier.
Maximum Rank: 1

Rank 1 *

Training Time: 6 hrs
Starting Difficulty: 14

Your character can properly shoe all sizes of horses and knows how to shape and manipulate the shoes and hooves for general and corrective shoeing and maintenance purposes.

FISHING (Agility/Performance Test & Intelligence Test)

Your character learns how to effectively catch fish using a line and hook. He learns the best types of water to catch the different types of fish in as well as how to clean and prepare the fish for eating.

The duration of the training time for all Ranks of this Skill must be spent fishing.

See "Fishing" in the "SURVIVING ORYATHAR" Section for details on how to fish.
Maximum Rank: 4

Rank 1

Training Time: 1 fi hrs
Starting Difficulty: 5/5

Your character is capable of utilizing a string and hook to catch fish and knows how to properly clean and prepare the fish for eating. You may add 3 points to the result of any fishing Test.

Rank 2

Training Time: 1 fi hrs
Starting Difficulty: 7/7

Your character increases his fishing skill allowing 1D4+1 people to be fed from each successful fishing Test.

Rank 3

Training Time: 2 hrs
Starting Difficulty: 8/8

Your character increases his fishing skill and may now add 6 points to the result of any fishing Test.

Rank 4

Training Time: 2 hrs
Starting Difficulty: 9/9

Your character increases his fishing skill and may now catch enough fish with each successful fishing Test to feed 1D6+1 people.

GENERAL COMBAT (Agility/Performance Test)

This Skill gives your character an extra boost to his physical combat prowess. This Skill does not affect your character's Dragonknight form.
Maximum Rank: 2

Rank 1 *

Training Time: 3 hrs

The duration of the training time for this Rank must be spent in combat training with another ruling-race that is already skilled in "General Combat". Your character will be concentrating his training efforts to defending against various styles and types of attacks.
Starting Difficulty: 10

Your character becomes more proficient in all types of physical combat (excluding Dragonknight), and may now add 1D4 points to the result of one Physical Defense per Turn.

Rank 2 *

Training Time: 3 hrs

The duration of the training time for this Rank must be spent in combat training with another ruling-race that is already skilled in "General Combat". Your character will be concentrating his training efforts to executing various styles and types of attacks.
Starting Difficulty: 10

Your character many now add 1D4 points to the result of any one physical attack Test per Turn, as well as to his Physical Defense.

For example, Draven has Rank 2 in this Skill. In the same Turn he may add 1D4 points to the result of one physical attack, which may be any weapon or style of attack he wishes, and 1D4 points to the result of one Physical Defense per Turn.

GENERAL COMBAT (DRAGONKNIGHT)

(Agility/Performance Test)

This Skill gives your character an extra boost to his physical combat prowess while in Dragonknight form.
Maximum Rank: 2

Rank 1

Training Time: 10 Turns

The duration of the training time for this Rank must be spent in Dragonknight form in combat training with another ruling-race that is already skilled in "General Combat (Dragonknight)" or "General Combat". Your character will be concentrating his training efforts to defending against various styles and types of attacks.
Starting Difficulty: 12

Your character becomes more proficient in all types of physical combat while in Dragonknight form, and may now add 1D4 points to the result of one Physical Defense per Turn.

Rank 2

Training Time: 10 Turns

The duration of the training time for this Rank must be spent in Dragonknight form in combat training with another ruling-race that is already skilled in "General Combat (Dragonknight)" or "General Combat". Your character will be concentrating his training efforts to executing various styles and types of attacks.
Starting Difficulty: 12

This Rank allows your character to add a 1D4 bonus to the result of any one physical attack Test per Turn, as well as his Physical Defense.

For example, Matusu has Rank 2 in this Skill. In the same Turn he may add 1D4 points to the result of one physical attack, which may be any style of attack he wishes, and 1D4 points to the result of one Physical Defense per Turn.

GENERAL CONJURING

(Sixth Sense/Performance Test)

This Skill increases your character's ability at conjuring any of the Mystic Forces. He learns how to more effectively and accurately initiate and perform conjuring.

Your character must initiate and release conjuring or draw upon and release a Mystic Force once every Turn for the duration of the training time.

Your character will be concentrating on drawing upon the Mystic Forces and studying the process of using his *Gift* to initiate and maintain their flow into his body.
Maximum Rank: 2

Rank 1

Training Time: 10 Turns
Starting Difficulty: 10

Your character receives a 1D4 point bonus to all Sixth Sense/Performance Tests for conjuring, the primary example being the learning and use of Force-effects. This bonus does not apply to Mystical Defenses, or learning Skills; only conjuring and learning of Force-effects.

Rank 2

Training Time: 14 Turns
Starting Difficulty: 12

Your character now receives a 1D6 point bonus to all Sixth Sense/Performance Tests for conjuring. As with Rank 1 this bonus does not apply to Mystical Defenses, or learning Skills; only conjuring and learning of Force-effects.

HUNTING

(Agility/Performance Test & Intelligence Test)

Your character learns how to locate and kill his own food with the weapon of his choice (GM's discretion as to which weapons are appropriate for hunting, but is usually limited to ranged weapons).

The entire training time for all Ranks of this Skill must be spent hunting.

See "Hunting" in the "SURVIVING ORYATHAR" Section for details on hunting.
Maximum Rank: 4

Rank 1

Training Time: 1 hr
Starting Difficulty: 5/5

Your character is capable of hunting and killing various types of game and knows how to properly clean and prepare them for eating. You may add 3 points to the result of any hunting Test.

Rank 2

Training Time: 1hr
Starting Difficulty: 7/7

Your character increases his hunting skill allowing 1D4+1 people to be fed from each successful hunting Test.

Rank 3

Training Time: 1 fi hrs
Starting Difficulty: 8/8

Your character increases his hunting skill and may now add 6 points to the result of any hunting Test.

Rank 4 *

Training Time: 1 fi hrs
Starting Difficulty: 9/9

Your character increases his hunting skill allowing 1D6+1 people to be fed from each successful hunting Test.

LANGUAGE (Intelligence Test)

With this Skill your character can learn to speak and write one or more of the five ruling-race languages, other than his own of course. Each of the languages is considered to be a separate "Language" Skill. So all of the following Ranks are the separate Ranks for each individual language. So, technically there are fifteen Ranks for the "Language" Skill (three Ranks for each of the five languages), but they begin anew for each individual language.

Your character may learn multiple languages without completing all three Ranks in any of the previously learned languages. So, your character may know up to Rank 2 in Valkin, Rank 1 in Loremek, Rank 3 in Brightling, and so forth.

At least half of the training time for each of the Ranks must be spent with another being who is capable of fluently speaking and writing that particular language. The other half of the training time can be met through studying scrolls or books on the particular language. Such books and scrolls are very rare and can generally only be found in the larger cities.
Maximum Rank: 3

Rank 1 *

Training Time: 8 hrs
Starting Difficulty: 8

Your character learns to read and write basic words of the language, however his vocabulary is very limited.

Rank 2 *

Training Time: 9 hrs
Starting Difficulty: 9

Your character is now capable of reading and writing most words of the language, he can understand and structure his own sentences in that language, and has a fairly extensive vocabulary.

Rank 3 *

Training Time: 10 hrs
Starting Difficulty: 11

Your character is now very fluent in reading and writing the chosen language, and possesses a very extensive vocabulary.

RAPID TRANSFORMATION
(Sixth Sense/Performance Test)

Your character is able to more completely and efficiently control the transformation process into Dragonknight.

Your character must change into his Dragonknight form a minimum of five times during training, which is every other Turn (1 Turn to change and 1 Turn to change back).
<u>Maximum Rank</u>: 1

Rank 1
<u>Training Time</u>: 10 Turns
<u>Starting Difficulty</u>: 11

Your character is now able to transform into Dragonknight much more rapidly (under 2 seconds). It is now only a Minor Action for your character to transform into his Dragonknight form or back into ruling-race form.

Your character can not transform into Dragonknight form and then back into ruling-race form in the same Turn.

SAILING (Intelligence Test)

Your character learns to manage and operate various styles and sizes of boats and ships.

The entire training time for all of the Ranks of this Skill must be spent on a boat or ship under the instruction of a skilled sailor (someone that has mastered the Rank for which your character is training).
<u>Maximum Rank</u>: 3

Rank 1 *
<u>Training Time</u>: 1 hr
<u>Starting Difficulty</u>: 7

Your character can manage and sail small *boats* and *crafts* in fair weather conditions.

Rank 2 *
<u>Training Time</u>: 2 hrs
<u>Starting Difficulty</u>: 9

Your character can now also manage and sail small *ships* in fair weather conditions.

Rank 3 *

<u>Training Time</u>: 4 hrs
<u>Starting Difficulty</u>: 11

Your character can now manage and sail all types of boats and ships in any type of weather.

SWIMMING (Agility/Performance Test)

Your character learns how to swim properly and is able to increase his swimming speed and capabilities in the water.

The duration of the training time for all Ranks of this Skill must be spent in the water practicing swimming.

See "Swimming" in the "SURVIVING ORYATHAR" Section for details on swimming.
<u>Maximum Rank</u>: 3

Rank 1
<u>Training Time</u>: 30 min
<u>Starting Difficulty</u>: 9

Your character learns the basic mechanics of swimming and is now able to swim an additional 10 feet per Turn (beyond that of someone without the "Swimming" Skill), as well as receiving a +2 point bonus on all swimming Tests.

Rank 2
<u>Training Time</u>: 1hr
<u>Starting Difficulty</u>: 10

Your character extends his swimming capabilities and is now capable of swimming an additional 20 feet per Turn (beyond that of someone without the "Swimming" Skill), and receives a +3 point bonus on all swimming Tests.

Rank 3
<u>Training Time</u>: 1 fi hrs
<u>Starting Difficulty</u>: 11

Your character is now a very expert swimmer capable of swimming an additional 30 feet per Turn (beyond that of someone without the swimming Skill), and receives a +5 point bonus on all swimming Tests. He is also able to fail three consecutive swimming Tests before suffering drown damage.

TRACKING (Intelligence Test)

Your character becomes competent at spotting the subtle signs or tracks that mark the passing of another being, and is able to accurately track them.

The training for both Ranks of this Skill requires your character to be outside actually examining tracks and observing tracks and other tracking signs being made.
Maximum Rank: 2

Rank 1
Training Time: 1 hr
Starting Difficulty: 7

Your character can more easily spot tracks and signs of another creature's passing than those who are not skilled in the ways of tracking can. Your character can distinguish between several different trails or tracks that may cross the same spot and which direction the being or creature that made it was traveling.

At the time that your character is looking for tracks or signs of a being's passing, or actually spot the tracks or signs, he must make an Intelligence Test. On results less than 15 he will not be able to determine the information normally discernable with this Rank of the "Tracking" Skill. On results of 15 or higher he is able to determine all of the tracking information that this Rank entitles him to. An area as large as twenty feet in diameter can be searched with a single use of this Rank of the "Tracking" Skill.

If your character also has the "Tracking" Talent you may add 3 points to the result of any tracking Test.

Rank 2
Training Time: 1 hr
Starting Difficulty: 8

Your character is now able to accurately determine whether or not that a being that made a particular track was running or walking, approximately how heavy the being is, and will also know approximately how old any particular track is.

At the time that your character is looking for tracks or signs of a being's passing, or actually spots the tracks or signs, he must make an Intelligence Test. On results less than 15 he will not be able to determine the information normally discernable with this Rank of the "Tracking" Skill. On results of 15 or higher he is able to determine all of the tracking information that this Rank entitles him to. An area as large as twenty feet in diameter can be searched with a single use of this Rank of the "Tracking" Skill.

If your character also has the "Tracking" Talent you may add 3 points to the result of any tracking Test.

TRAVELING (Intelligence Test)

This Skill allows your character to correctly read and interpret maps, compasses, and other traveling devices, determine directions by using the stars and other natural signs, and correctly determine travel routes and distances for any mapped destination.
Maximum Rank: 3

Rank 1
Training Time: 30 min

The training for this Rank requires your character to be outside actually using a compass. He will be practicing how to use landmarks to line up his compass and keep on the path he has chosen and in the direction that he wishes to travel.
Starting Difficulty: 6

Your character can correctly use compasses and other traveling devices to guide him from one point to another.

Rank 2
Training Time: 1 hr

The training for this Rank requires your character to be outside actually following coordinates on a map and determining how to turn the scaled distances on a map into useful travel information
Starting Difficulty: 8

Your character can accurately determine distances and travel time to and from any mapped location.

Rank 3
Training Time: 3 hrs

The training for this Rank requires your character to be outside studying the signs and landmarks of the land and sky that can accurately determine directions and locations from other given landmarks or anomalies.
Starting Difficulty: 9

Your character can accurately determine directions by using the stars and other natural bodies and landmarks, making it virtually impossible for him to get lost.

SPECIALTIES & TALENTS

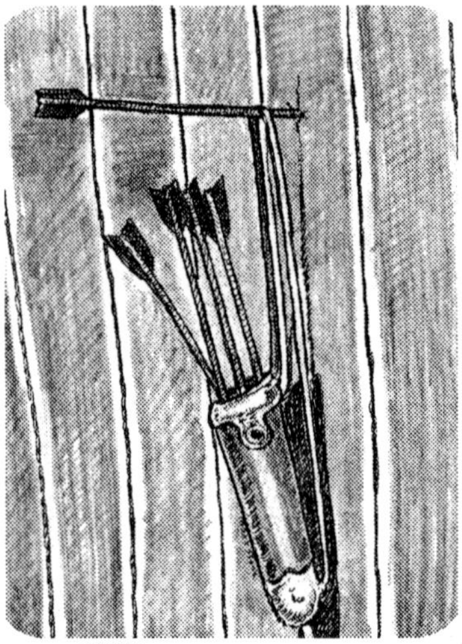

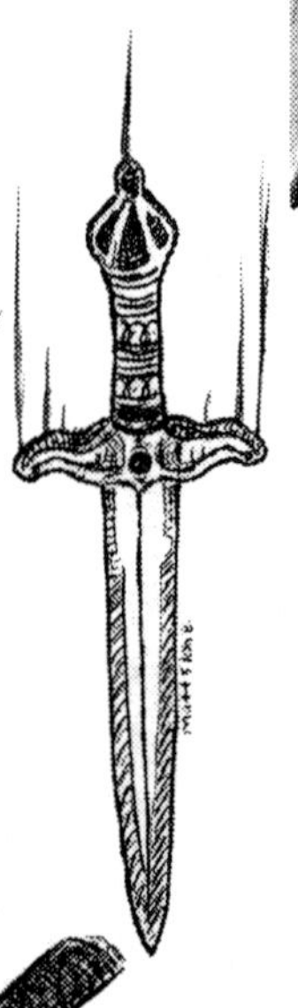

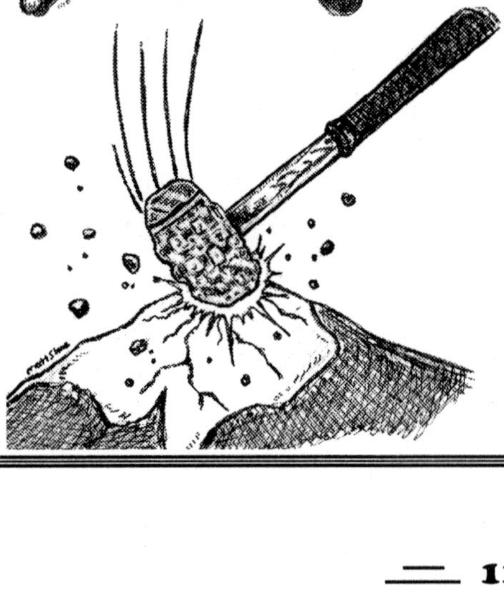

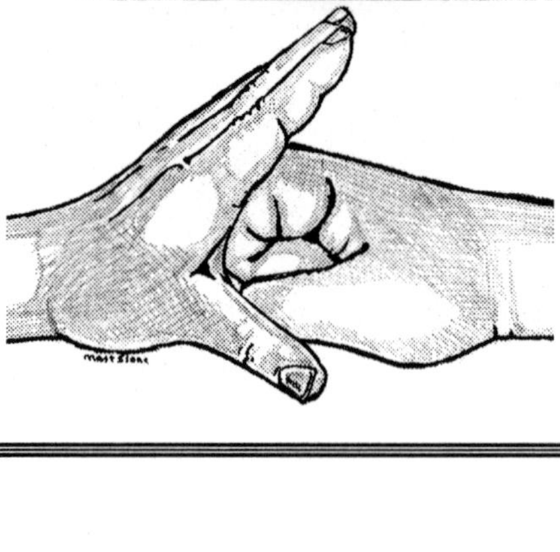

SPECIALTIES

There are seven different Specialties from which you may choose. Your character's Specialty represents a certain field that he is naturally gifted in. Your character will receive bonuses when operating within his own Specialty that someone that is not of that Specialty can never receive.

Once you choose a Specialty for your character it may never be changed. Each Specialty has ten Talents that your character may learn. Your character may also learn Talents from other Specialties but he will still only have one "Specialty".

Any character who has a weapon-specific Specialty, which is any of the Specialties except **Defending** and **Nature**, receives a +1 point bonus to their attacks and a +1 Level increase to the Damage Yield of weapons of their own Specialty. Characters of either of the two non-weapon-specific Specialties, **Defending** and **Nature**, receive special bonuses to the use of the Talents of their own Specialty; these special bonuses are described in the description of the individual Talents.

One special note in regards to the Specialty of **Nature** is that all characters of that Specialty receive the following additional bonus. There is an automatic fifty percent chance that mundane animals will not attack them. Unusual circumstances or being provoked by the character may negate this bonus (GM's decision).

TALENTS

Talents are purchased with Light Points, which represents the unleashing of your character's potential within his Specialty. Your character's potential continues to grow as he continues to promote the Light. Most Talents are not mystical abilities, but merely mundane talents potential to all of the ruling-races. Your character may learn as many as five Talents in a single day.

Talents must be purchased in order, thus to get the third Talent of a Specialty your character must first know the first and second Talents of that Specialty.

Some of the Specialties have one or more Talents with the same name, such as "Proficiency" or "Second Weapon". When learning one of these Talents it pertains only to the Specialty under which it is being learned, although all may be learned eventually. Meaning, if your character learns "Second Weapon I" under the Specialty of Throwing Weapons he can not use a non-edged melee weapon as the second weapon, unless he had learned the "Second Weapon I" Talent for the Specialty of **Non-Edged Melee Weapons**.

So, your character may actually learn several "Second Weapon" or "Proficiency" Talents, but for separate Specialties.

Exceptions to this rule are "Weapon Concealment", "Desperation Dodge", and "Desperation Parry". These Talents are learned once and count as being learned in all of the Specialties. If your character has one of these Talents, he would simply skip it when learning Talents from another Specialty that contains the duplicate Talent.

For example, Kambrok's Specialty is **Edged Melee Weapons**, and he knows his first five Talents (this includes "Desperation Parry"). He is currently learning Talents from the **Non-Edged Melee Weapons** Specialty. After Kambrok learns "Proficiency" he will skip to "Second Weapon II" because "Desperation Parry" is the same Talent in all Specialties and he has already learned it. Kambrok must still pay 16 Light Points for "Second Weapon II". Even though he was able to skip buying the fifth Talent, "Second Weapon II" still costs the same as it would if he had not.

Also, Talents that appear under a specific Specialty only work in regards to that Specialty. So if your character is using "Weapon Strike", which is a Talent of the **Non-Edged Melee Weapons** Specialty, he must be using a non-edged melee weapon, or if your character is using "Double Distance" he must be using the weapon of the Specialty in which that particular "Double Distance" was learned (though the name may be the same they are actually different Talents; "Double Distance" with a throwing weapon is different than "Double Distance" with an archery weapon).

Your character may only use one Talent per Turn, with the exception of permanent Talents, which can be used at any time even while using another Talent.

Maintaining a Talent is considered a use of a Talent. For example, a character who uses the Talent "Choke Hold" on an opponent and maintains the "Choke Hold" for subsequent Turns, is using their Talent for those Turns. The same also applies to the Talent "Grappling". By continuing to maintain a grapple on a target your character is considered to be using "Grappling" for each of those Turns, which means he may not use another Talent during those Turns (unless the Talent is a permanent).

Some Talents may only be used successfully if you roll above a certain value on your Performance Die. The minimum roll needed, if any, on the Performance Die to successfully perform a Talent is stated with the specific Talent's description (beside of the word "Performance"). For example, if your character is attempting to use "Accuracy" you must roll a 3 or better on the Performance Die.

If the minimum Performance Die value for a Talent is not rolled, then the Talent fails, or fails to yield its normal bonuses. The exact penalty for failing to meet the minimum Performance value for a Talent is left up to the GM. Normally, the Talent completely fails.

The Specialties and their respective Talents are all listed in this Section. The Specialties are in bold with their Talents listed below them. The title in parentheses beside of each Specialty is the title given to someone who has mastered that Specialty (meaning they have obtained all 10 Talents).

Your character is not given the title for a Specialty until he has learned all ten Talents of that Specialty. Those who adopt a Specialty title without actually mastering the Specialty (learning all 10 Talents) are usually looked upon with great disapproval.

The first Talent for any Specialty costs 3 Light Points, and each subsequent Talent costs 1 more Light Points than the last. So the second Talents costs 4 Light Points, the third costs 5, and so on.

To learn Talents from Specialties other than your character's own Specialty you must pay twice the normal Light Point cost. Your character must have all of the Talents in his own Specialty up to the number of the Talent he wishes to learn from the alternate Specialty. Your character must also have all of the Talents up to that point in the alternate Specialty as well.

For example, your character's Specialty is **Nature**, and he wants to learn the Talent "Climbing" which is the third Talent in the Specialty of Defending. He must already have the first three Talents of his own Specialty (**Nature**) as well as the first two Talents of **Defending** before this Talent could be learned.

The ✶ symbol beside of the names of certain Talents is there for the use of the Universal Talent "Double Talent".

ARCHERY (Bow Master)

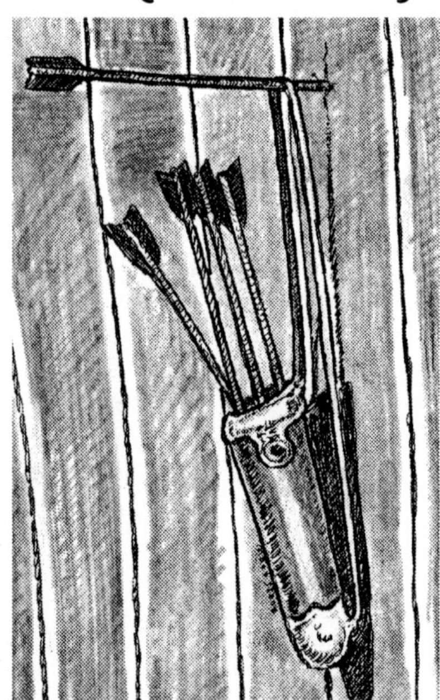

With keen eyes and a steady hand, those of the **Archery** Specialty prefer to keep a reasonable distance from the fray of melee, launching their silent missiles toward their enemies with lethal precision.

Those whose Specialty is **Archery** are gifted with in the use of all types of bows as well as crossbows and are a valuable asset to any combat unit.

1. Quick Shot ✶
2. True Aim
3. Moving Attack ✶
4. Proficiency
5. Double Distance
6. Unstable Shot
7. Drop Shot
8. Glance Shot
9. Speed Nock
10. Wicked Shaft

DEFENDING (Defender)

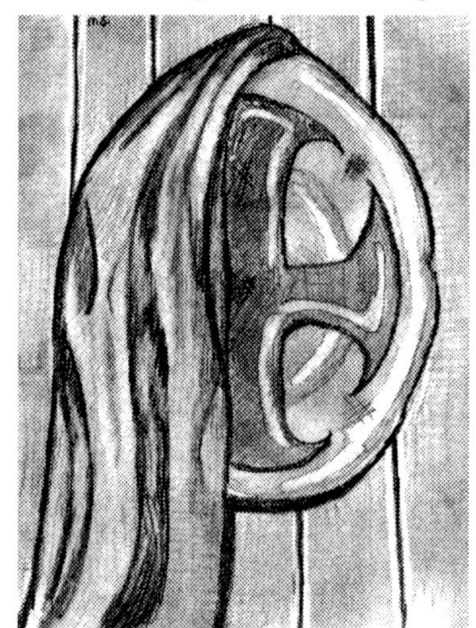

Slipping quietly through corridors without a sound and blending effortlessly into their surroundings is second nature to those whose Specialty is **Defending**.

Taking great pride in their abilities to lead a party through the most treacherous of areas, spotting traps and disarming them, picking locks and bringing their comrades safely to their destination is what being a Defender is all about.

1. Lock Picking
2. Weapon Concealment
3. Climbing
4. Proficiency
5. Desperation Dodge ✶
6. Locate/Disarm Traps
7. Silent Walk ✶
8. Cloaking
9. Lip-Reading
10. Fearless Attack

EDGED MELEE WEAPONS
(Blade Master)

Ringing steel and the whistling of a razor-edged blade slicing through the air are sounds of music to the ears of those of the **Edged Melee Weapons** Specialty. Preferring any edged melee weapon, those of this Specialty are truly formidable opponents in battle. With grace and lightning speed they are capable of cutting down the strongest of enemies.

1. Quick Hand ✶
2. Swift Strike
3. Second Weapon I
4. Proficiency
5. Desperation Parry ✶
6. Second Weapon II
7. Disarm
8. Strike Control
9. Blade Frenzy
10. Double Strike

NATURE (Naturalist)

Communing with nature and bonding with all living creatures, the Naturalist is a master of his domain. Capable of tracking the faintest of trails and picking up the scent of his quarry not many can escape the keen skills of those of this Specialty.

Those of the **Nature** Specialty have abilities that extend beyond the scope of the mundane. Feeling completely at home in the outdoors the Naturalist can survive indefinitely on their own in the harshest of natural environments. Only the uninformed or foolish challenge a Naturalist on his own turf.

1. Survival
2. Tracking ✶
3. Locate Water
4. Proficiency
5. Herb Knowledge
6. Scent Sense ✶
7. Animal Empathy
8. Animal Call
9. Plant Reading
10. One With Nature

NON-EDGED MELEE WEAPONS
(Bludgeon Lord)

Preferring the crushing power of non-edged melee weapons those of this Specialty blast their way through their opponents with brute force and heavy steel. Wielding their heavy, blunt weapons with deadly accuracy a Bludgeon Lord can easily crush and snap the bones of his opponents.

1. Stun
2. Knockdown
3. Second Weapon I
4. Proficiency
5. Desperation Parry ✶
6. Second Weapon II
7. Down Strike
8. Weapon Strike

9. Enhanced Defense ✷
10. Crushing Blow

THROWING WEAPONS
(Dagger Lord)

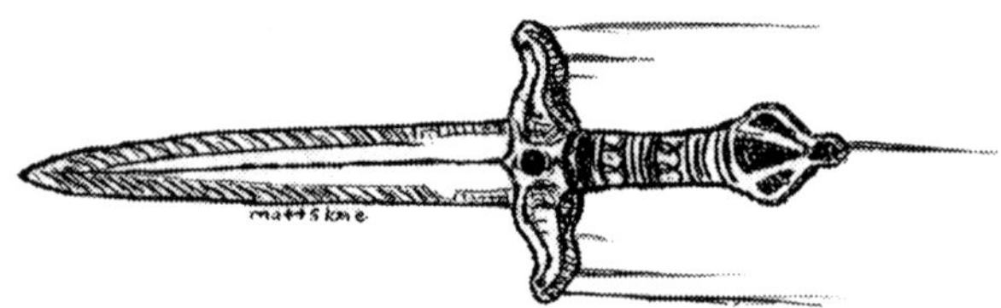

Lightning quick and deadly accurate, the Dagger Lord specializes in throwing weapons. The preferred weapons of those whose Specialty is **Throwing Weapons** ranges from small spiked balls to the heavy and deadly arc-knife.

Dagger Lords are known for their precision and speed. They can produce and send a weapon into flight faster than most can draw a sword.

1. Accuracy ✷
2. Weapon Concealment
3. Second Weapon I
4. Proficiency
5. Desperation Dodge ✷
6. Second Weapon II
7. Double Distance
8. Rolling Throw
9. Lethal Throw
10. Aerial Strike

UNARMED COMBAT
(Battle Master)

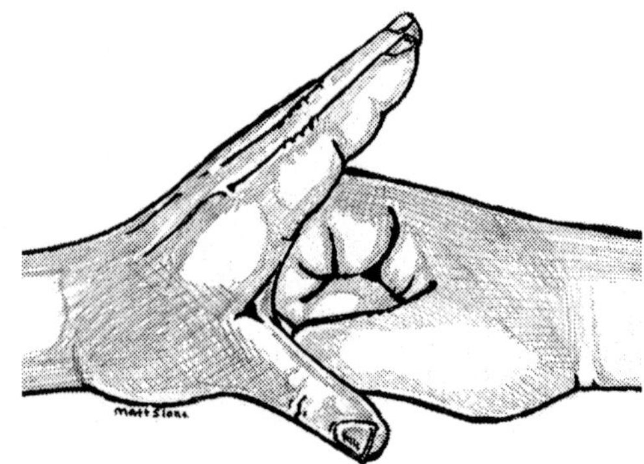

Never to be caught unarmed those of the **Unarmed Combat** Specialty use their own bodies as deadly weapons. Punches, kicks, holds, and unique fighting skills makes the Battle Master a true master of combat.

A Battle Master with the proper discipline and training can perform attacks with his or her own body that are just as deadly as any weapon of steel, capable of killing an opponent with a single strike. The head and hands/arms of a ruling-race has a Damage Yield of Level 1, and their feet/legs have a Damage Yield of Level 2.

Technique Points can be learned with the hands, feet, and head just as it can be with weapons. A maximum of 1 Technique Point can be learned with the head, 5 with the hands/arms, and 4 with the feet/legs.

1. Throw
2. Grappling
3. Choke Hold
4. Proficiency
5. Desperation Block ✷
6. Heart Strike
7. Fists of Fury
8. Power Kick
9. Stun Touch ✷
10. Focused Energy

Following is an alphabetical listing and description of all of the Talents of every Specialty.

ACCURACY (Performance = 3)

This Talent increases the accuracy and effectiveness of throwing weapon attacks. When using "Accuracy" your character receives a +3 point bonus to his attack value and a +1D4 bonus to the damage of the attack.

AERIAL STRIKE (Performance = 9)

This Talent allows your character to make a truly beautiful and deadly attack with a throwing weapon. Your character takes a few steps forward then leaps into the air, flipping forward into a somersault. As your character spins back into an upright position to land he releases the weapon. The momentum of the spin adds tremendous force and speed to the weapon's flight.

Any being struck by an "Aerial Strike" attack receives double the normal points of damage, and is automatically

knocked down and stunned.

Any Physical Defense that your character sets receives a +3 point bonus for the remainder of the Turn following a successful "Aerial Strike" attack.

ANIMAL CALL

With this Talent your character is able to understand and reproduce the language of animals. With "Animal Call" he can summon natural animals, up to one mile away, by imitating their call. Your character can also communicate basic requests or commands such as "run", "help", or "come".

To call or communicate basic requests to an animal requires an Intelligence Test against a base Difficulty Value of 6 (9 if **Nature** is not your character's Specialty). This difficulty may be raised at the GM's discretion depending upon the circumstances and complexity of the communication.

Immediately upon learning "Animal Call" you may choose three types of animals that your character can call. Your character will then be able (GM's discretion) to learn to call one additional type of animal each week thereafter.

If your character is proficient with this Talent he gains the ability to relay much more detailed information and commands to the animals that he communicates with. Such information and commands may be "chew the rope tied around my wrists into", or "follow me at a distance and protect me if I am threatened".

These are just a few examples, the GM has the final say as to what he will and will not allow a character to communicate to the animals.

ANIMAL EMPATHY

When using "Animal Empathy" your character is able to sense the feelings and basic intentions of animals, as well as relate his own feelings and basic intentions to animals (without verbally communicating) up to one hundred yards away. An animal that your character has empathized with may go out of its way to help him. The empathy is related from your character to the animal through scent, visual cues, and Sixth Sense.

For example, if your character is endangered by another being or creature he may relate his distress through empathy to a target animal. This animal might very likely come to your character's aid.

In order to successfully use "Animal Empathy" your character must make a successful Sixth/Sense Performance Test against a base Difficulty Value of 7 (10 if **Nature** is not your character's Specialty). The difficulty may increase or decrease depending upon the Aggression Rating of the animal.

The GM decides whether or not a particular type of animal can be empathized with or not.

This Talent does not work on Shadow-kin or mystical creatures.

If your character is proficient with this Talent any animal that he successfully empathizes with will develop an immediate and strong bond with the character. The animal will always go out of its way to help and protect the character, even if it has to endanger its own life to do so.

BLADE FRENZY (Performance = 8)

"Blade Frenzy" is a very ferocious and wild type of attacking maneuver. When using this Talent your character receives a +4 point bonus to his attack, but due to the wild and uncontrolled nature of the attack, the damage of the attack receives a -4 point penalty.

The recipient of a "Blade Frenzy" attack is pressed so hard and fast that their counter-attack, if available, receives a -4 point penalty. This penalty only applies if the counter-attack is made in the same Turn as the "Blade Frenzy" attack.

This Talent can not be used in conjunction with "Single-Strike" attacks.

CHOKE-HOLD (Performance = 4)

This is a maneuver that allows your character to place an

iron tight choke-hold around an opponent's neck. It takes only one arm to perform. It differs from grappling in that the being in the choke-hold can still perform Major Actions, which may be subject to penalties at the GM's discretion.

To break the choke-hold your opponent must beat your character on a Strength Test. This Test is considered a Major Action for the being attempting to free themselves from the choke-hold. It is also a Major Action to hold an opponent in a choke-hold (your character must make a Strength Test each Turn that he has someone in a chokehold).

A being in a "Choke-Hold" will suffer damage each Turn, and will black out for 1D4 Turns if they remain in the hold for 3 consecutive Turns, or longer. No Willpower Test can be made to resist this blacking out. The amount of damage rendered by the hold is equal to the result of the Strength Test that your character makes each Turn to hold the choke-hold.

If your character attempts to set a Physical Defense while maintaining a choke-hold on an opponent, his Defense value will be cut in half.

If a being currently being held in a choke-hold attempts to set a Physical Defense, their Defense value is cut in half (round down) plus receives a -1D6 point penalty in addition to that.

CLIMBING (Performance = 3)

With this Talent your character can climb much faster and with less effort, gaining a +2 point bonus to all climbing Tests. This Talent also gives your character the permanent ability to climb 10 feet per Turn faster than his normal climbing speed.

Only a +1 point bonus and 6 feet per Turn are all that is gained if **Defending** is not your character's Specialty.

If your character is proficient with this Talent the bonus to his climbing Tests is doubled (+4 points if **Defending** is your character's Specialty, +2 if it is not). Also your character can climb 15 feet per Turn faster than his normal climbing speed instead of 10 feet per Turn faster.

CLOAKING (Performance = 6)

Using this Talent your character can conceal himself in places that would seem impossible to hide. Whether it is shadows, trees, or a shallow dip in the ground, when using "Cloaking" your character is able to conceal himself nearly as well as a chameleon. He must, however, be dressed similar in color to his surroundings or in some cases the cloaking may not be successful.

Anyone attempting to spot someone using "Cloaking" must make an Intelligence Test against a base Difficulty Value of 15 to be successful. The difficulty is only 12 if **Defending** is not your character's Specialty. Regardless of the result of the Intelligence Test there is a ten percent chance that the cloaked being will still be spotted (no chance of spotting cloaked being if the being looking has an Intelligence of Level 2 or lower).

The Difficulty Value may be altered by the GM depending upon the specific circumstances or terrain.

If your character is proficient with this Talent there is no longer a random percent chance that he will be spotted (regardless of the Intelligence Level of the beings). Also, the Difficulty Value of the Intelligence Test to spot your character is increased by 3 points.

CRUSHING BLOW (Performance = 9)

This is a very powerful offensive Talent. A "Crushing Blow" attack adds 10 points to the damage of your character's attack, causes an automatic injury, and automatically stuns the victim regardless of whether the attack would normally have done so or not. "Crushing Blow" also automatically takes any armor struck down to its next Reduced Protection Rating.

In order to use "Crushing Blow" the attack must be a "Single-Strike" attack. The bonuses given by "Crushing Blow" already include the damage bonus for using a "Single-Strike" attack and also negate the normal -3 point attack penalty for using "Single Strike".

If "Crushing Blow" fails, the attack is still a "Single-Strike" attack and thus you may add 6 points to the damage of the attack but you also must subtract 3 points from the attack itself.

DESPERATION BLOCK

This is a defensive Talent used to avoid attacks at the last instant. Your character actually blocks or bats the attack aside at the last possible moment.

"Desperation Block" is used after an attack against your character is declared successful, but before any damage is dealt. If you wish for your character to use any of his Defense Bonus points, he must do so before using "Desperation Block" (this Talent can only be used after your character has finished setting a blocking Defense, and it has been determined to be insufficient). As with Defense Bonus points, these points are added in after all adjustments due to penalties or other bonuses are calculated.

The attacked character using "Desperation Block" rolls 1D10 and adds the result to their Physical Defense. If this adjusted Defense is greater than the result of the opponent's attack value, then the attack was blocked at the last instant.

If, however, the result is less than the result of the attack, then the character attempting the block does not avoid the attack and is also stunned by the attack whether it would normally have done so or not.

DESPERATION DODGE

This is a defensive Talent used to avoid attacks at the last instant. Your character completely dodges the attack at the last possible moment.

"Desperation Dodge" is used after an attack against your character is declared successful, but before any damage is dealt. If you wish for your character to use any of his Defense Bonus Points, he must do so before using "Desperation Dodge" (this Talent can only be used after your character has completely set his Defense, and it has been determined to be insufficient). As with Defense Bonus Points, these points are added in after all adjustments due to penalties or other bonuses are calculated.

The attacked character using "Desperation Dodge" rolls 1D10 (1D10 +2 if **Defending** is your character's Specialty) and adds the result to their Physical Defense. If this adjusted defense is greater than the result of the opponent's total attack value, then the attack was avoided (dodged) at the last instant.

If, however, the result is less than the result of the attack, then the character attempting to dodge does not avoid the attack and is also stunned by the attack whether it would normally have done so or not.

If your character is proficient with this Talent you may add an additional 2 points to the result of the 1D10 bonus given by this Talent.

"Desperation Dodge" can be used in Dragonknight form.

DESPERATION PARRY

This is a defensive Talent used to avoid attacks at the last instant. The character uses a weapon, or solid item with a Bulk Value of 1 or greater, to bat an attack aside at the last possible moment.

"Desperation Parry" is used after an attack against your character is declared successful, but before any damage is dealt. If you wish for your character to use any of his Defense Bonus Points, he must do so before using "Desperation Parry" (this Talent can only be used after your character has completely set his Defense, and it has been determined to be insufficient). As with Defense Bonus Points, these points are added in after all adjustments due to penalties or other bonuses are calculated.

The attacked character using "Desperation Parry" rolls 1D10 and adds the result to their Physical Defense. If this adjusted defense is greater than the result of the opponent's total attack value, then the attack was avoided (parried) at the

last instant.

If, however, the result is less than the result of the attack, then the character attempting to parry does not avoid the attack and is also stunned by the attack whether it would normally have done so or not.

If your character is proficient with this Talent you may add an additional 2 points to the result of the 1D10 bonus given by this Talent.

DISARM (Performance = 6)

This Talent is used to greatly increase the odds that your character will disarm his opponent, as well as help prevent him from being disarmed.

While your character is using this Talent he may add 5 points to both the Random-roll Agility Test and random-roll Strength Test for determining whether he is disarmed when he parries or is parried against. While using this Talent only one of these two Tests has to beat the opposing opponent's Test in order to disarm them (normally both Tests must beat the opponent's Tests in order to disarm them).

As soon as you declare an attack with an edged-melee weapon you must state at that time whether or not your character is using "Disarm". If your character's opponent parries against his attack, then the bonuses described previously apply to determining if either your character or his opponent is disarmed. If someone attacks your character, you must state at the moment you decide to parry against their attack (with edged-melee weapons only) whether or not your character is using "Disarm".

DOUBLE DISTANCE (Performance = 6)

The use of this Talent allows your character to greatly increase the range of his ranged attacks. Your character can calculate and effectively perform ranged attacks at double the listed range for the weapon he is using. "Normal" and "Long" range for any weapon used with this Talent is double the listed distances.

The target must still be within your character's range of sight in order to accurately utilize this Talent.

DOUBLE STRIKE (Performance = 9)

The name of this Talent may suggest that only two strikes are made, but this is not the case. The actual attack may consist of several strikes or a single strike. This Talent makes the attack or strikes from the attack doubly potent, thus the name "Double Strike".

When using "Double Strike" extra damage is rendered to an opponent's armor, if worn, and himself. When attacking with this Talent, set the attack as normal. If the attack is successful then determine damage as normal, but apply the entire amount of the damage to any armor struck. If the

armor still offers protection then subtract its Protection Rating from the damage and apply the remaining damage to the attacked being. If the armor is destroyed by the attack then the attacked being will also take an amount of damage equal to that dealt to the armor. If the attacked being has no armor, then they will receive double damage.

DOWN STRIKE (Performance = 7)

"Down Strike" is a powerful offensive Talent. When using this Talent your character leaps several feet into the air and use his falling momentum to make an extremely powerful attack. When using "Down Strike" add 10 points to the damage of the attack as well as making the dice rolled for the Damage Yield of the weapon re-rollable on a max roll. If the "Down Strike" attack strikes the opponent's head, then it adds 14 points to the damage of the attack instead of 10.

In order to use "Down Strike" the attack must be a "Single-Strike" attack. The bonus for the attack being "Single-Strike" is already included in "Down Strike's" bonus.

If "Down Strike" is used successfully (you roll a 7 or higher on the Performance Die) the attack is not penalized by the normal -3 points for using a "Single-Strike" attack.

If "Down Strike" fails, the attack is still a "Single-Strike" attack and thus you may add 6 points to the damage of the attack, but also must subtract 3 points from the attack value itself.

DROP SHOT (Performance = 7)

Using this Talent allows your character to use a bow or crossbow to perform a shot in which the arrow is shot up into the air and then falls down directly onto the target. This Talent increases the listed ranges of the weapon by 50 feet. It also cuts the Physical Defense value of beings attempting to evade the attack by half (round down).

This type of attack makes any type of cover, other than over-head cover, useless. One drawback to this Talent is that the target must remain stationary for the duration of the Turn in which the "Drop Shot" is performed or the attack automatically misses.

ENHANCED DEFENSE (Performance = 6)

The use of this Talent increases your character's combat prowess, allowing him to be much more efficient in defending against attacks.

When using "Enhanced Defense" the result of any type of Physical Defense that your character sets is increased by 8 points.

You must declare that your character is using this Talent before his Physical Defense value is determined.

"Enhanced Defense" can be used in Dragonknight form.

FEARLESS ATTACK (Performance = 10)

When using this Talent your character is so focused upon his attack that he can not be affected by any type of fear tactics, confusion, or any thing which affects mental alertness or awareness (whether mystical or mundane) for the entire Turn that it is used.

A "Fearless Attack" is so ferocious and focused that it gives your character a +7 point bonus to his attack and a +10 point bonus to the damage of the attack (only +4 points to the attack and +7 points to the damage if **Defending** is not your character's Specialty). This Talent only affects melee attacks.

"Fearless Attack" may be used while in Dragonknight form.

If your character is proficient with this Talent the Minimum Performance required to use it is lowered to 7.

FISTS OF FURY (Performance = 7)

This Talent imbues your character with the ability to throw a blinding fast stream of punches that is exceptionally hard to dodge.

When using "Fists of Fury" your character receives a +5 point bonus to his attack and a +6 point bonus to the damage of the attack.

This Talent can not be used in conjunction with a "Single Strike" attack.

FOCUSED ENERGY (Performance = 9)

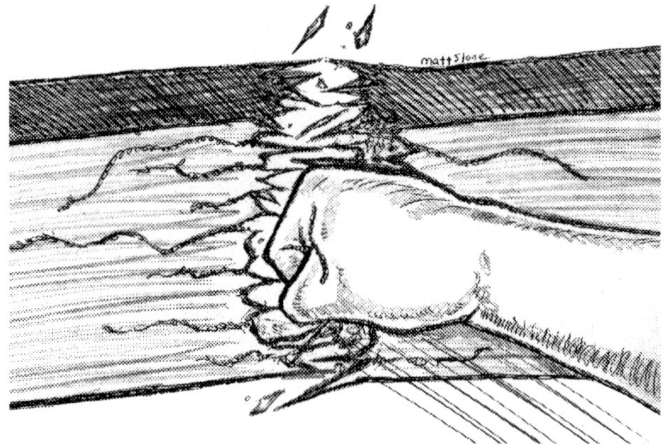

"Focused Energy" allows your character to make a truly powerful unarmed attack in which he summons all of his inner strength and concentrates it into one lethal blow.

"Focused Energy" adds 16 points to the damage of the attack. Also any being struck with a "Focused Energy" attack is immediately knocked down, stunned, and receives an automatic injury in addition to any inflicted by the damage yielded by the attack itself.

A "Focused Energy" attack must be delivered by a "Single-Strike" kick or punch. The +16 point bonus to the damage of the attack already includes the damage bonus for "Single-Strike".

If "Focused Energy" is used successfully (you roll a 9 or higher on the Performance Die) the attack is not penalized by the normal -3 points for using a "Single-Strike" attack.

If "Focused Energy" fails, the attack is still a "Single-Strike" attack and thus you may add 6 points to the damage of the attack, but also must subtract 3 points from the attack itself.

GLANCE SHOT (Performance = 7)

With this Talent your character can perform amazing glancing shots (archery only), without receiving penalty or increased difficulty. The arrow ricochets off of a solid object, such as a shield, tree, rock, wall, etc., and then strikes its target. The arrow can be deflected up to ninety degrees from its original direction of travel. Beings attempting to evade a "Glance Shot" attack receive a 1D10 +5 point penalty.

GRAPPLING (Performance = 3)

With "Grappling" your character uses a type of wrestling hold to lock onto and hold his opponent so that they can not move or counter-attack. When using "Grappling" your character may also inflict up to half of his Strength value in damage per Turn to a being that he has successfully grappled.

A grappled being can perform no other Major Actions (physical) other than trying to free himself. To do so, they must beat your character on a Strength Test. This Test is their Major Action for that Turn. It is also your character's Major Action to hold the grappled being.

The only Minor Action that can be taken while grappled is speaking, breathing, etc. A grappled being can not make a Strength Test to free himself in the first Turn in which he is grappled.

HEART STRIKE (Performance = 6)

With this Talent your character can perform a very powerful strike to an opponent's chest that will weaken and shock them for a short time.

In order for this Talent to be used successfully, the attack must be a punch or kick, and must be a "Single-Strike" attack. The attack must also strike the opponent in the torso area (near the heart).

An opponent that has "Heart Strike" used successfully on them has the results of all Agility-based Tests reduced by half (rounded down) for the next 2 Turns, and the results of all Strength-based Tests reduced by half (rounded down) for the next 3 Turns.

If "Heart Strike" is used successfully (you roll a 6 or higher on the Performance Die) the attack is not penalized by the normal -3 points for using a "Single-Strike" attack.

If "Heart Strike" fails, the attack is still a "Single-Strike" attack and thus you may add 6 points to the damage of the attack, but also must subtract 3 points from the attack itself.

HERB KNOWLEDGE

The use of this Talent allows your character to identify most all types of plant life. He knows where to locate these plants, and knows their basic uses, if any.

When attempting to identify a plant your character must make an Intelligence Test against a base Difficulty Value of 7 (10 if **Nature** is not his Specialty). If the Test is successful, he knows the nature and name of the plant, and its uses, if any. This Talent does not give your character knowledge of the alchemy uses for plants and herbs.

The Difficulty Value may be altered by the GM as he or she sees fit.

If your character has learned up to Rank 4 or higher in "Alchemy" he may add +2 to the Intelligence Test for identifying a particular type of plant. Also, by knowing this Talent your character may add +2 to any of the Progress Tests for learning Ranks 2 and 3 of "Alchemy".

If your character is proficient with this Talent the Difficulty Value of the Intelligence Test made to identify a plant is lowered by 2 points. Your character also knows whether or not a particular plant or herb is used in alchemy (though your character still will not know what its exact uses are, unless he has the appropriate Ranks in the "Alchemy" Skill).

KNOCKDOWN (Performance = 3)

The use of this Talent greatly increases the chance that your character's opponent will be knocked down. When attacking with the "Knockdown" Talent (non-edged melee weapons only) your character only has to inflict enough damage to *equal* his opponent's Injury Rating in order to knock them down. Any being knocked down in this manner is also stunned, regardless of where the damage is inflicted.

LETHAL THROW (Performance = 8)

This Talent is a very nasty and often lethal type of attack. When utilizing "Lethal Throw" your character receives a +12 point bonus to the damage of the attack. In addition, any being struck by a "Lethal Throw" attack receives an automatic critical injury.

LIP-READING

Using this Talent, your character can tell what another being is saying without being able to actually hear that individual. To use "Lip-Reading" your character must be able to see the target being's mouth and understand the language being spoken. The target being must be within "Normal" range of vision, but even then there is a twenty percent chance of automatic failure (thirty-five percent chance if **Defending** is not your character's Specialty).

The GM may require an Intelligence Test for reading the lips of non-ruling-race beings.

If your character is proficient with this Talent the percent chance of automatic failure for lip-reading is lowered ten percent (twenty-five percent if **Defending** is not your character's Specialty).

For obvious reasons this Talent does not allow a character to read the lips of a Brightling.

LOCATE/DISARM TRAPS (Performance = 5)

This Talent allows your character to effectively locate and disarm traps. When using this Talent for locating traps your character may add 3 points to the result of his Intelligence Test for locating them and 5 points to his Agility/Performance Test for disarming them.

If **Defending** is not your character's Specialty, the bonuses are only +1 and +2 points, instead of +3 and +5 points.

Locating and disarming are separate Major Actions. Disarming some traps may require more than 1 Turn.

If your character is proficient with this Talent the Minimum Performance is lowered to 3 and the bonuses to both the Intelligence Test for locating traps and the Agility/Performance Test for disarming them are increased by 2 points.

LOCATE WATER

The use of this Talent gives your character the peculiar ability to locate water. He makes a Sixth Sense/Performance Test against a base Difficulty Value of 6 (9 if **Nature** is not your character's Specialty). The Difficulty Value will vary according to the depth and/or amount of water in the area. If the Test is successful your character has located any sources of water within three hundred yards.

If your character is proficient with this Talent he can locate water sources within six hundred yards instead of three hundred yards. The base Difficulty for locating water is also lowered to 4 (7 if **Nature** is not your character's Specialty).

LOCK PICKING (Performance = 2)

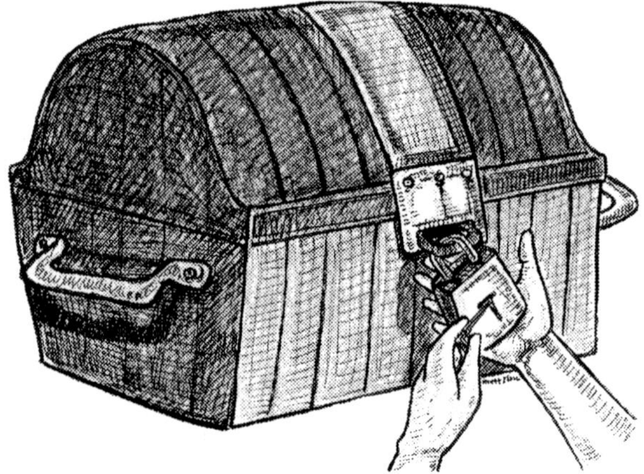

This Talent allows your character to accurately assess a lock and gives him the necessary skill to pick it. "Lock Picking" lets your character know the basic difficulty of picking any particular lock on sight (you know the base Difficulty Value).

Actually picking a lock requires your character to make a successful Agility/Performance + Intelligence Test against a Difficulty Value determined by the GM (20 is the base Difficulty Value for common locks). "Lock Picking" adds +5 points to the result of all lock picking Tests (+3 if **Defending** is not your character's Specialty).

The normal time for picking a lock is 2D4 Turns, but the use of this Talent drops the time to 1D4 Turns.

If your character is proficient with this Talent the bonus to his lock picking Tests is increased +8 points (+6 if **Defending** is not your character's Specialty).

MOVING ATTACK (Performance = 4)

This Talent allows your character to perform archery attacks against targets moving faster than 35 feet per Turn without the -1D6 penalty. It also allows your character to make archery attacks while he is moving faster than 35 feet per Turn without receiving the -1D6 penalty (even from a mount that is moving in excess of 35 feet per Turn).

If your character is moving faster than 35 feet per Turn while using this Talent, any Physical Defense that he sets is increased by 3 points for the entire Turn in which "Moving Attack" is used.

ONE WITH NATURE

This is undoubtedly the most unique, complex, and impressive of all the Talents. Only characters whose Specialty is **Nature** can learn this Talent.

This Talent allows your character to focus in on and draw upon a small portion of the natural energies and Life Forces of the surrounding area and its creatures. Every plant, tree, and mundane creature (Shadow-kin and ruling-races are not affected) within a number of feet radius equal to your character's Sixth Sense Level times 100 will relinquish a portion of their Life Force and energy to your character. This gathered Life Force and energy is referred to as "natural energy".

The amount of natural energy that your character can gather each Turn is an amount normally equal to his Sixth Sense Level. If the targeted area is extremely barren of mundane creatures and plant-life, then the amount of natural energy that your character can gather in may be much less (GM's discretion).

The maximum number of consecutive Turns that your character may use "One With Nature" is 5 Turns. If your character does use "One With Nature" for 5 consecutive, uninterrupted Turns he may add an additional 10 points to the number of points of natural energy that he drew in. So it is possible to draw in a number of points of natural energy equal to your character's Sixth Sense Level x 5 + 10.

The use of this Talent requires intense concentration. Your character may not perform any other Major Actions while using this Talent.

There are two main uses for the natural energy that is drawn in by means of "One With Nature". The first use is to assist in healing. Each Turn that your character uses "One With Nature" he may absorb this energy. This energy will then help your character to heal by adding a number of points to his next Recovery Test equal to the amount of natural energy absorbed. Using this natural energy to boost your character's Recovery Tests does not count as a use of mystical healing.

If your character currently has no current damage other than injury damage (he is not in recovery) this natural energy can not be absorbed. Once your character makes a Recovery Test all of the natural energy that he absorbed is used up. It is not possible to absorb more points of natural energy than a value equal to your character's Sixth Sense Level times 5 (+10) points.

The second use for this Talent is only available to Shinkai. So it is not possible for an NPC that is not Shinkai to utilize "One With Nature" in the manner described hereafter.

Instead of absorbing this natural energy as it is drawn in,

the Shinkai stores it within himself. This stored energy can be released in a single blast of invisible energy that will spread out in all directions from the Shinkai. This energy will do 1 point of damage per point of natural energy released to any living being in its path. This includes Shadow-kin, ruling-races, and all mundane creatures.

This blast of energy will travel out a number of feet, in all directions, equal to the Shinkai's Sixth Sense Level times one hundred feet. No natural armor protects against this energy blast. The Force-effect "Spirit Shield" will offer protection.

The Shinkai may not store this energy to be used at a later time. Unless the Shinkai continues using "One With Nature" into the next Turn, he must release the energy at the end of the Turn in which he draws it in. It is not possible to store more points of Natural Energy than a value equal to your character's Sixth Sense Level x5 +10 points.

If the Shinkai is distracted or attempts to perform another Major Action while using "One With Nature" all of the energy stored up to that point is released (an energy blast) in an uncontrolled fashion. This uncontrolled energy blast will do a point of damage to the Shinkai using "One With Nature" for each point of natural energy that is released as well as to all other beings within range.

If your character's Sixth Sense is Level 15 or higher he gains the ability to control these energy blasts with precision. Instead of the energy blast effecting all living beings within its path your character may target it to one or more specific targets or areas.

As mentioned previously, the use of this Talent drains Life Force and energy from all living creatures and plant-life in the targeted area. This drain is dispersed over the targeted area so that each creature, plant, or tree suffers only a minimal loss of life and energy. But if only one source of Life Force is within the targeted area, it alone will lose the entire amount of Life Force and or energy that is drained. If two sources of Life Force are within the target area, they will each take fi of the amount drained, etc. In most areas there is enough plants and creatures within range that no measurable damage is inflicted to any one being.

"One With Nature" is an extremely powerful Talent and should not be used carelessly. Anyone who abuses this Talent by needlessly draining, and possibly killing, the land and its creatures should be awarded with Shadow Points accordingly.

Both the draining of natural energy and the blast it can produce is considered lethal damage. So, if your character drains more natural energy from a creature or plant than it has Life Force, it will die. As an average most plants have a Life Force of 5 and most small creatures such as rabbits, fish, squirrels, etc. have a Life Force of 15.

If your character is proficient with "One With Nature" he can absorb a number of points of natural energy equal to his Sixth Sense Level times 5 (+20) instead of (+10), and he can

focus the blast of energy once his Sixth Sense reaches Level 12 instead of Level 15.

PLANT READING (Performance = 8)

All plants and trees are alive and aware of their surroundings and other beings. They are able to sense the presence of other beings and decipher the type and race of those beings. Plants are also very in tune with the weather and know as far as three days in advance what the weather will be like.

By using "Plant Reading" your character is able, in a sense, to communicate with plants and retrieve such information. To do this your character must physically touch the plant. The "Plant Reading" is done mainly through very subtle vibrations and Sixth Sense.

A successful Sixth Sense/Performance Test against a base Difficulty Value of 9 (13 if **Nature** is not your character's Specialty) must be made in order to successfully read a plant. Only one plant can be communicated with at a time, and it takes approximately 5 Turns of touching the plant, without interruption, before the Sixth Sense/Performance Test can be made.

The following information can be gained through the use of this Talent. The type, race, number, and Life Force strength (wounded, weak, healthy, etc.) of any beings who came within thirty feet of the plant within the past eight days, as well as the prediction of the weather up to three days in advance. Some trees have a much larger memory than of that listed above. Some of the larger ancient trees can recall specific data from events as long ago as three hundred years.

All trees and plants are able to communicate between themselves as long as they are no further than fifty feet apart. This could potentially allow your character to receive information from a tree or plant miles away from him by allowing the tree or plant that he is using "Plant Reading" on to communicate through the trees and plants within its range. As long as there is not a gap between trees or plants greater than fifty feet a chain-like link of communication can be established.

If your character attempts to use "Plant Reading" and the attempt fails, all further attempts to use "Plant Reading" on that particular plant for the remainder of that day will automatically fail.

If your character is proficient with this Talent he can make the Sixth Sense/Performance Test to read a plant after only 2 Turns of touching it. Also the Minimum Performance is lowered to 5.

POWER KICK (Performance = 7)

This Talent is just what it says; an extremely powerful kick. A well-placed "Power Kick" is capable of bringing down the strongest of opponents. The kick must be a "Single-Strike" in order to use "Power Kick". The bonus for the attack being "Single Strike" is already included in "Power Kick's" bonus.

When "Power Kick" is used successfully 20 points are added to the damage of the attack. Also, if "Power Kick" is used successfully the attack is not penalized by the normal -3 points for using a "Single-Strike" attack.

If "Power Kick" fails, the attack is still a "Single-Strike" attack and thus you may add 6 points to the damage of the attack but also must subtract 3 points from the attack itself.

PROFICIENCY

This is the only Talent common to all of the Specialties. It permanently improves your character's abilities in the specified field of your choice, with a few exceptions. Characters learning "Proficiency" in a weapon-specific Specialty (all but **Defending** and **Nature**) must choose a particular weapon of that Specialty to become proficient with.

When using a weapon in which your character is proficient he receives a +1 point bonus to the attack value of any attacks made with that weapon and a +1 Level increase to the Damage Yield of the weapon. Another bonus to "Proficiency", of any of the Specialties, is that when your character learns it his next two attribute increases may be purchased at half cost (round down).

Characters learning "Proficiency" in either of the two non-weapon-specific Specialties (**Defending** and **Nature**) choose a particular Talent of that Specialty to become proficient with. They may choose to be proficient in a Talent that they do not know yet. If so, then the proficiency is simply held until they learn that particular Talent and then it is applied; the attribute purchase bonus may be spent at any time. The bonuses for being proficient with a Talent from either the **Defending** or **Nature** Specialty will be described along with the Talent's description. Once you have chosen a Talent for your character to become proficient with you can not change it later. The proficiency is permanent.

If you choose for your character to learn the "Proficiency" of the **Unarmed Combat** Specialty your character may be proficient with his arms, legs, or head. Your character receives bonuses to any type of attack utilizing the body part with which he becomes proficient (+1 point to the attack and a +1 Level increase to the Damage Yield).

If your character is proficient with his arms he gets the proficiency bonus when punching, grappling, choking, arm-wrestling, etc. If your character is proficient with his legs he receives the proficiency bonus to kicking and grappling. Proficiency with the head gives bonuses to headbuts and bites.

QUICK HAND

This Talent allows your character to act faster and perform quicker melee attacks. When using "Quick Hand" your character receives a +2 point bonus to his Physical Initiative and a +1 point bonus to his first attack of the Turn.

QUICK SHOT

This Talent allows your character to draw and shoot much quicker than normal. When using this Talent your character receives a +1D4 point bonus to his Physical Initiative. The bonus is removed if your character's action is not an archery attack.

"Quick Shot" may not be used with a crossbow.

ROLLING THROW (Performance = 7)

With this combat maneuver your character dives into a roll, and as he comes out of the roll he releases his throwing weapon. This type of attack adds a great deal of momentum to the attack.

When using this Talent you add 5 points to the attack and 5 points to the damage of the attack. Also, the next Physical Defense that your character sets during the Turn in which "Rolling Throw" was successfully used receives a +3 point bonus.

SCENT SENSE

When using "Scent Sense" your character is able to pick up the scent of other beings in much the same manner that a dog or wolf does. These scents can be sensed up to nine hundred feet away. In order to pick up a scent, it must be no more than six hours old. Weather and climate conditions may alter the range and/or duration of a scent. "Scent Sense" also allows your character to identify the type of being from which the scent originated, if he has encountered that type of being before.

This Talent is very useful as it allows your character to track another being when physical tracks are not available or sight is impaired.

In order to successfully use "Scent Sense" a successful Sixth Sense/Performance Test must be made against a base Difficulty Value of 9. If your character is proficient with this Talent the Difficulty Value is reduced to 6.

The Difficulty Value may be altered by the GM depending upon the circumstances (wind condition, distance from the source, etc.) of the immediate area.

On exceptional Tests the GM may choose to allow a character to also sense the emotions of other beings within ten yards of him. A character should have a minimal Sixth Sense/Performance Test result of 14 in order to sense emotions (11 if your character is proficient with this Talent). "Scent Sense" can only be used once per hour.

"Scent Sense" can not be learned if **Nature** is not your character's Specialty.

SECOND WEAPON I (Performance = 4)

This Talent gives your character the ability to effectively wield two weapons at once, thus allowing him to make two attacks per Turn (both attacks are considered a single Major Action). The second weapon may not have a Bulk Value greater than 1.5, and the first weapon can not require both hands to wield. Both weapons used with this Talent must be of the same Specialty as the learned "Second Weapon I" Talent. Your character must actually use two separate weapons in order to use this Talent. He may not make the two attacks with the same weapon.

The second attack takes place immediately after the first (if your character's Initiative is 12, the first attack takes place at 12 and the second at 11). Each attack may target a different opponent as long as they are within five feet of one another.

You must set up each attack separately, including rolling a separate Performance Die for each attack, though the result of the first Performance Die will determine if your character is even allowed a second attack.

If the Minimum Performance Die result (of the first attack) is not met, then your character can only make one attack that Turn (you may choose which weapon performs the attack).

This Talent can not be used with a Charge or Dive attack.

SECOND WEAPON II (Performance = 7)

This Talent is merely an advance form of "Second Weapon I". The advantage over "Second Weapon I" is that with "Second Weapon II" the second weapon may have a Bulk Value as high as 3.

All other rules applying to "Second Weapon I" also apply to "Second Weapon II".

SILENT WALK (Performance = 6)

Using this Talent your character can move with extreme stealth and silence. When a character uses "Silent Walk" another being must make a successful Intelligence Test against a Difficulty Value of 15 in order to hear him. If **Defending** is not the Specialty of the character using "Silent Walk" then the Difficulty Value for hearing them is lowered to 12. When moving faster than 35 feet per Turn the Difficulty Value for hearing someone using "Silent Walk" is lowered to 11 (8 if **Defending** is not their Specialty).

The Difficulty Value may be altered by the GM according to the particular circumstances.

If your character is proficient with this Talent the Minimum Performance is lowered to 4, and the Difficulty Value of the Intelligence Test to hear him is increased by 2 points.

SPEED NOCK (Performance = 8)

With this Talent your character can draw and shoot a bow with exceptional speed. "Speed Nock" enables your character to get off two shots per Turn, in essence giving him two separate attacks per Turn (both attacks are considered a single Major Action). Each shot may be directed at different targets as long as they are within twenty feet of each other and each attack receives a +5 point bonus.

The second attack takes place immediately after the first (if your character's Initiative is 12, the first attack takes place at 12 and the second at 11).

You must set up each attack separately, including rolling a separate Performance Die for each attack, though the result of the first Performance Die will determine if your character is even allowed a second attack.

If the Minimum Performance value (of the first attack) is not met, then you fail to properly use "Speed Nock" and your character can only take one shot that Turn.

STRIKE CONTROL (Performance = 6)

This Talent gives your character more control over the placement and the effects of successful attacks. The Combat Variant "Aimed Attack" must be used in order for this Talent to work.

"Strike Control" negates the attack penalty (normally -5 points) to aimed attacks. Also, all dice rolled for the Damage Yield of the weapon used to perform a "Strike Control" attack may be re-rolled on a max roll. In addition to this, if the attack causes an injury you may decide to which attribute the injury is applied (Agility, Strength, or Endurance).

STUN (Performance = 2)

Normally a being is stunned by receiving an injury to the head/neck zone and then failing the Endurance Test to resist being stunned. This Talent forces the being to make the Endurance Test to resist being stunned if even 1 point of damage is inflicted to their head/neck zone. In addition the Difficulty Value needed to resist being stunned is increased to 12.

STUN TOUCH (Performance = 8)

With this Talent your character learns to utilize pressure points to execute incapacitating attacks. A being struck by a "Stun Touch" attack is automatically stunned for 2 Turns and also receives an amount of damage equal to the Strength Level your character applied times 2 (+16) points. So if you apply 8 Levels of Strength, "Stun Touch" will inflict 32 points of damage.

In order to use this Talent the attack must be made with the hands (punch, knife-hand, choke, etc.) and must strike a vital area.

SURVIVAL

This Talent permanently gives your character all of the basic knowledge that he will need to survive in the wild. Your character knows most all types of common flora and fauna. He knows which are edible, which are not, how to cook and prepare them, etc.

If your character is proficient with this Talent and **Nature** is his Specialty, there is a seventy percent chance that mundane creatures will not attack him, unless provoked. If your character is proficient with this Talent and **Nature** is *not* his Specialty, there is only a thirty percent chance that mundane creatures will not attack him.

SWIFT STRIKE (Performance = 3)

The use of this Talent allows your character to perform extremely swift and impressive maneuvers with edged melee weapons that often intimidate any would-be foes.

When your character uses "Swift Strike" all opponent's (maximum of five) watching him must make a Willpower Test against a base Difficulty Value of 8 or receive a -3 point penalty to the result of all attribute Tests made for the rest of that Turn.

Due to the extreme swiftness of a "Swift Strike" attack your character receives an additional 1D4 points to the result of his attack, but the extreme speed of the attack somewhat hinders the amount of strength behind it. For this reason the damage of the attack is penalized by a number of points equal to the number of points gained to the attack.

THROW (Performance = 2)

This combat maneuver allows your character to sweep his opponent completely off of his feet and throws them forcefully to the ground. Any being successfully hit by an opponent using "Throw" is thrown to the ground.

A being that is successfully thrown is automatically knocked down, and if an injury was caused they are also automatically stunned. They will also suffer an amount of damage equal to double the Strength Level that your character applied to the throw. Armor does not reduce the damage received from being thrown by the use of this Talent.

It is a Major Action for a being to get up in the same Turn in which they are thrown, even if they are not stunned.

TRACKING

This Talent allows your character to find and track the trails left by other beings. To do so your character must make a successful Intelligence Test against a base Difficulty Value of 10 (13 if **Nature** is not your character's Specialty). This Talent also gives your character the ability to efficiently cover his own tracks, making it much harder for him to be tracked.

On a successful Test your character can recognize most all types of tracks and can distinguish between several different trails or tracks that may cross the same spot. He will know how old any particular track is, which direction the creature or being that made it was traveling, and also facts about the being's weight and condition.

If your character has the appropriate Ranks in the "Creature Lore" Skill he will also know exactly what type of creature made any particular track. This Talent is superior to the "Tracking" Skill, but if your character also has the "Tracking" Skill you may add 3 points to the result of any tracking Test. Each tracking Test allows your character to search an area as large as twenty feet in diameter.

Depending upon the terrain or other circumstances the GM may assign a higher or lower Difficulty Value for successful tracking.

If your character is proficient with this Talent the base Difficulty Value for successfully tracking is lowered to 7 (10 if **Nature** is not your character's Specialty).

TRUE-AIM (Performance = 4)

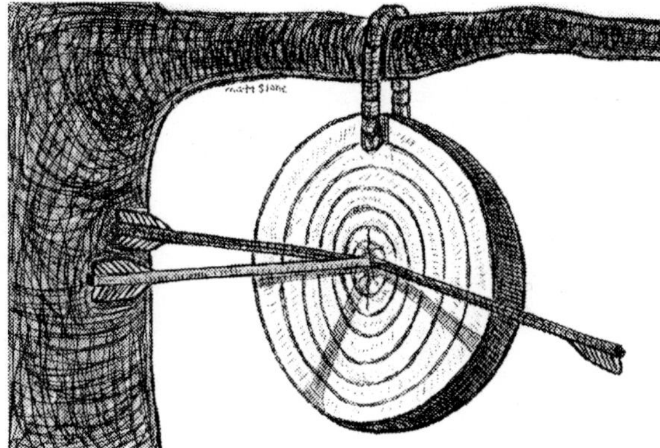

"True-aim" allows your character to make a more focused and steady shot with an archery weapon, thus improving his chance of hitting his target as well as increasing the damage done by a successful hit.

When using "True Aim" your character may add 3 points to his attack value and 1D4 points to the damage of the attack. Also, characters who successfully use this Talent and are also utilizing the combat variant "Aimed Attack" to pinpoint an area of their target only need a minimum Performance Die result of 3 and only receive a -3 point penalty to the attack instead of the normal 5 Performance Die result and -5 point penalty.

UNSTABLE SHOT (Performance = 6)

When using this Talent your character may perform archery attacks while knocked down or in any number of awkward positions or situations (hanging upside-down, seated on a mount, etc.) without penalty to the attack.

WEAPON CONCEALMENT

This Talent gives your character the permanent ability to conceal weapons under his clothing in such a fashion that they are undetectable by others without a close physical examination. Your character can conceal a various number of weapons or items with the following restrictions. None of the items concealed may have a Bulk Value higher than 2, and the total Bulk Value of all concealed items may not exceed 8 (may not exceed 5 if **Defending** is not your character's Specialty).

It is a Major Action to conceal a single item, but if your character is proficient with this Talent he can conceal an item as a Minor Action (maximum of three items per Turn).

WEAPON STRIKE (Performance = 6)

This Talent allows your character to concentrate the damage of an attack to an opponent's weapon instead of the opponent himself (the difficulty for hitting the opponent's weapon is the same as hitting them).

All damage done by a "Weapon Strike" attack goes to the attacked weapon. Even if the damage done is greater than the weapon's Destroyed Rating, the weapon's wielder does not receive any damage from the attack.

Even if an opponent intentionally parries against a "Weapon Strike" attack, their weapon still receives the entire amount of damage yielded by the attack.

Regardless of whether or not the opponent attempts to parry against a "Weapon Strike" attack, they must make the Random-roll Agility and Random-roll Strength Tests to resist being disarmed. Further, a being whose weapon receives a "Weapon Strike" attack has a much higher chance of being disarmed than they normally would. In such cases the being wielding the weapon that receives the "Weapon Strike" receives a -3 point penalty to both their Random-roll Agility and Random-roll Strength Tests to keep from being disarmed.

WICKED SHAFT

Your character must first have learned Rank 1 in "Bow and Arrow Making" before he can learn this Talent.

This Talent gives your character the permanent ability to craft exceptionally well-balanced and lethal arrows. These arrows must be fastened with green-steel broadheads before they can be considered to be wicked shafts.

A target struck with a wicked shaft takes double damage. Wicked shafts penetrate all types of armor instantly (the armor absorbs none of the damage), with the exception of green-steel armor, and some being's natural armor or hide, such as a dragon's scales or kruelin hide, all of which offer protection as normal. Armor stuck with a wicked shaft instantly drops to its next Reduced Protection Rating (R.P.R.) in addition to any R.P.R.s that it drops due to actual damage sustained.

These arrows are weighted and designed differently than normal arrows and are much more difficult to shoot. For this reason *anyone* shooting a wicked shaft must reduce their attack value by 2D4 points (only 1D4 points if they know the "Wicked Shaft" Talent).

Due to the complicated process in making these arrows, it takes approximately six hours to fashion one wicked shaft. At the end of the six hours your character must make an Agility/Performance + Intelligence Test Test against a base Difficulty Value of 23. If he passes, the arrow is created successfully. If he fails, the arrow was ruined in the creating process and is worthless as a weapon.

Universal Talents are Talents that can only be purchased with Character Points. Most Universal Talents are permanent, meaning that the abilities they give your character are permanently in effect. You do not have to declare that your character is using them, and it is not considered a use of a talent to use them, unless the specific Universal Talent states or implies otherwise.

Some Universal Talents, however, are not permanents. You must state when you would like your character to use these Universal Talents. Universal Talents that are not permanents will not say permanent in their description and will require your character to spend a Mystical Attuning Point in order to use them. Like other special abilities granted by the expenditure of a Mystical Attuning Point, the Universal Talents that require Mystical Attuning Point expenditure can only be performed once per day.

Your character can't use more than three Universal Talents that require Mystical Attuning Point expenditure in the same Turn. In addition, your character can't use two Universal Talents that have an asterisk (*) beside of their name in the same Turn. The Universal Talents that have an asterisk beside of their names are "Auto-Talent", "Double-Talent", "Iron-Will", and "Sixth Sense Attuning".

Below is a list, and description, of the nineteen Universal Talents available to your character.

Feel free to use the following as examples for creating your own unique Universal Talents. Part of the fun of running a campaign is having it custom tailored to the playing styles of your particular group of players.

UNIVERSAL TALENTS

1. Attack Control
2. Auto-Talent *
3. Blood of the Ancients
4. Crisis Control
5. Double-Talent *
6. Essence Projection
7. Force Sight
8. Heightened Senses
9. Iron Will *
10. Lure of Alchemy
11. Master's *Gift*
12. Master's Touch
13. Mind Focus
14. Persuasion
15. Quick Skill
16. Rapid Healing
17. Second Wind
18. Sixth Sense Attuning *
19. Soul Search

ATTACK CONTROL

Learning Cost: 15

Allows your character to increase his attack or damage result. For every point that the attack is decreased, the damage of the attack may be increased by 1 point, up to a maximum of 4 points, and vice versa (the damage may be decreased in order to increase the attack value).

Which attribute that will be increased and which is to be decreased must be declared before the attack takes place.

AUTO-TALENT *

Learning Cost: 12

This Universal Talent allows your character to bypass the Minimum Performance normally required to successfully use a Talent; the Talent automatically succeeds. Your character may not attempt to use a Talent and see whether or not he fails the Minimum Performance before deciding to use Auto-Talent. You must declare that your character is using Auto-Talent before the Performance Die is rolled.

This Universal Talent requires the expenditure of 1 Mystical Attuning point.

BLOOD OF THE ANCIENTS

Learning Cost: 10

This powerful Universal Talent increases the number of points that an attribute is raised by when paying to increase it. Instead of rolling 1D4 and getting a 1 point increase on results of 1 or 2 and a 2 point increase on results of 3 or 4, the attribute is increased by 1D4 +1 points.

CRISIS CONTROL

Learning Cost: 17

Allows your character to perform a "Desperate Deed" without paying any Light Points to do so. This can only be done if the you roll a 50 or under on the percentile dice.

This Universal Talent requires the expenditure of 1 Mystical Attuning point.

DOUBLE-TALENT *

Learning Cost: 15

This Universal Talent allows your character to use two different Talents in a single Turn. However not just any Talents may be used in the same Turn.

In the "TALENTS" Section there is a star (★) beside the names of certain Talents. At least one of the two Talents that are to be used in the same Turn must have a star beside of their name.

Even if one of the two Talents does have a star beside of it your character may not use two Talents that conflict with each other. The most common method of conflicting Talents is by trying to use Talents from two separate specialties at the same time. Many Talents only work with weapons of that particular specialty. One example of a conflict is trying to use "Accuracy" and "Fearless Attack". "Accuracy" is for use only with throwing weapon attacks and "Fearless Attack" can only be used with a melee attack (obvious conflict).

This Universal Talent requires the expenditure of 1 Mystical Attuning point.

ESSENCE PROJECTION
Learning Cost: 10

This Universal Talent unleashes your character's potential to project his essence. Rules for projecting and using your character's essence form are given in the "COMBAT" Section of the rules.

This Universal Talent requires the expenditure of 1 Mystical Attuning point.

FORCE SIGHT
Learning Cost: 10

This Universal Talent gives your character the permanent ability to see and distinguish the Mystic Forces when a Shinkai is conjuring or simply drawing upon them, even in Dragonknight form. The Mystic Forces are seen as a very faint glowing aura around the conjuring Shinkai's body. Your character can distinguish which of the Mystic Forces that are being drawn upon and possibly what Force-effect is being produced by them. If your character knows a particular Force-effect, then when viewing the Mystic Force that are pulled into a Shinkai using that Force-effect he will recognize it. Even if the Force-effect is unknown your character will still be able to determine the basic nature of the Force-effect.

The Force-effect "Wind Missile" is being conjured by Bane. Felsar is observing Bane with "Force Sight", but does not know the Force-effect "Wind Missile". Felsar would still know that the flow is of Air and that the effect is offensive and possibly damage inflicting.

Flows that have been tied as well as wards can be seen with "Force Sight", but they give off a very faint and distinctive aura, much less recognizable than the flows of the Mystic Forces as they are actually being drawn upon.

The glow around a conjuring Shinkai that can be seen with "Force Sight" is simply a visible form of the Mystic Forces that already bathe and surround us all at any given time. It is made visible to "Force Sight" because of the additional energies produced by the Mystic Forces connecting themselves to the *Gift*.

HEIGHTENED SENSES
Learning Cost: 10

This Universal Talent improves your character's ability to use his *Gift* thus allowing you to move two attuning counters, or the same one twice, at the first hour instead of just once. Brightlings, who can normally move two attuning counters at the first hour can move three times with "Heightened Senses".

IRON WILL *
Learning Cost: 5

A character with "Iron Will" gains the ability to more effectively resist blacking out due to damage he has received. Characters with "Iron Will" add 2 Levels to all Willpower Tests made to resist Force Failure. This bonus is only for Willpower Tests made to resist Force Failure.

So, if your character's Willpower is Level 3 and he has "Iron Will", his Willpower Test to resist Force Failure will be made at Level 5.

LURE OF ALCHEMY
Learning Cost: 10

This Universal Talent gives your character the understanding and potential for creating Stage Two and Three alchemy products. Without knowing this Universal Talent your character can't learn past Rank 4 of the "Alchemy" Skill.

The rules and applications for the use of alchemy in the **Mystic Forces** role-playing game are available in a separate sourcebook called "ALCHEMY".

MASTER'S GIFT
Learning Cost: 25

Before this Universal Talent can be learned your character must first be non-novice in all five of the Mystic Forces and must have a Legendary Mystical Prowess.

The effects of this Universal Talent are permanent. It allows your character to learn up to 6 Technique Points in each of the Mystic Forces instead of just 3. The Difficulty Value for the Sixth Sense/Performance Test to learn the sixth Technique Point is 23 and the Training Time is fifty eight hours.

MASTER'S TOUCH
Learning Cost: 20

Before this Universal Talent can be learned your character must have a Legendary Physical Prowess.

The effects of this Universal Talent are permanent. It doubles the Maximum Technique that your character can learn with any weapon, shield, or other item (also applies to

Technique Points in the various aspects of a character's Dragonknight form). So if a weapon normally has a Maximum Technique of 5 a character with "Master's Touch" can learn up to 10 Technique Points with it.

Each Technique Point above the fifth requires an additional ten hours of training beyond the Training Time required for the previous Technique Point. The Difficulty Values for Agility/Performance Test required to learn Technique Points above the fifth continue to increase by 3 points as normal.

The following table shows the Difficulty Values and Training Times for the sixth through tenth Technique Points.

Technique Point #	Difficulty Value	Training Time (hrs)
6	23	58
7	26	68
8	29	78
9	32	88
10	35	98

MIND FOCUS

Learning Cost: 17

This Universal Talent helps your character to become more in tune with the Mystic Forces and to their own Sixth Sense in general. "Mind Focus" gives your character a +20 point bonus to the 1D20 points of Force Energy that he can regain at the first hour of each day (will also give a +20 point bonus to the instant 1D20 Force Energy recovery that is granted by the expenditure of a Mystical Attuning Point).

"Mind Focus" also allows the Performance Die for all Sixth Sense/Performance Tests to be re-rolled (one time) on a maximum roll.

PERSUASION

Learning Cost: 5

Persuasion helps characters improve their social interactions with others. Characters with Persuasion add 1D4 points to all Intelligence Tests for purposes of persuasive interactions. Some examples are haggling, obtaining information, obtaining favors, etc.

QUICK SKILL

Learning Cost: 15

"Quick Skill" greatly increases your character's potential for learning Skills and thereby allows him to learn them much quicker and more efficiently than those who do not know "Quick Skill". Characters with "Quick Skill" can learn Skills in half the normal Training Time and may add 2 points to the result of any Progress Test.

RAPID HEALING

Learning Cost: 11

This Universal Talent improves your character's general health, and helps him to recover from damage more quickly.

"Rapid Healing" raises all Recovery Tests by 2 Levels.

SECOND WIND

Learning Cost: 12

Allows your character to remove 1 Fatigue Point from all attributes at will. "Second Wind" can be used instantly and at any time.

This Universal Talent requires the expenditure of 1 Mystical Attuning point.

SIXTH SENSE ATTUNING *

Learning Cost: 10

This Universal Talent gives your character the ability to gain insight into any particular situation or event. If your character has this Universal Talent you may roll 1D4 once per day. A result of 1 or 3 means that your character must make a Random-roll Sixth Sense Test against a Difficulty Value of 9, while a result of 2 or 4 means the Random-roll Sixth Sense Test is made against a Difficulty Value of 5.

Success on this Random-roll Sixth Sense Test means the GM will give you insight into the immediate surroundings and/or situation (GM's discretion) due to your character's extra-perceptive Sixth Sense.

SOUL SEARCH

Learning Cost: 12

"Soul Search" extends your character's awareness and control of his essence form, thereby allowing him to be more effective in controlling and utilizing it.

"Soul Search" gives your character a +1D10 point bonus to all attack Tests made in essence combat.

DRAGONKNIGHT

"Dragonknight" is a name given to the dragon-like form that some Shinkai are capable of transforming into. Only Shinkai are capable of becoming Dragonknights and only about ten percent of Shinkai are Dragonknights. The Defenders of the Light have done an excellent job of seeking out and recruiting Shinkai Dragonknights. There are generally four to five Shinkai Dragonknights in the service of any one Defenders of the Light fort city. Fort Blazing Stone, however, currently has fifteen Shinkai Dragonknights enlisted as Defenders of the Light and have had as many as twenty two.

The transformation of a ruling-race into their Dragonknight form is a truly awesome sight. The following is an exert from a journal kept by King Lorsprit when he was twenty years old. It is an account of his memories of the first time that he ever witnessed the transformation of a ruling-race into their Dragonknight form.

"Never in my life had I ever been as awestruck or captivated as when I first witnessed the transformation of a ruling-race into the Dragonknight form. In a few short seconds the body of a tall and youthful female Valkin distorted and transformed into a massive dragon-like creature. Her poise was like that of a stalking lion. Massive muscles rippled and flexed across her beastly form. The scales that covered her entire body reflected the sun like a polished emerald. I stood speechless as the Dragonknight began to speak to the crowd that had assembled for the demonstration. Her voice, though still feminine, possessed an intimidating strength and emanated with such volume that I could feel the vibrations in my chest.

After a few moments of describing to the onlookers some of the feelings and abilities that she possessed in her Dragonknight she crouched low and then sprung up into the air leaping at least ten feet or more before her massive wings exploded to life, blasting her up into the morning sky. My body tingled with excitement and wonder as I watched her elegant form disappear into the horizon."

THE TESTING

Although you as a player know that your character is Dragonknight, your character doesn't know until someone informs him, or he is able to find out on his own. It's the GM's choice as to whether or not new characters already know whether or not they are Dragonknight.

The Defenders of the Light have developed an accurate method for testing Shinkai to determine whether or not they are Dragonknight. The process requires that someone uses focused conjuring to direct the Mystic Force of *Spirit* into both eyes of the Shinkai to be tested (the eyes are the window to the *Gift*). A minimum of 20 points of Force Energy must be expended at this time in order for the testing to work properly. If the Shinkai being tested is Dragonknight their skin will take on a scaly appearance, much like what the initial scales of their Dragonknight form looks like.

This testing serves a vital purpose for the Shinkai Dragonknight. It not only lets the Shinkai know that he is Dragonknight but also unlocks his potential for transforming into his Dragonknight form. Until the Shinkai has been tested he is unable to feel the presence of the dormant alternate form that resides within him. The testing makes the Shinkai aware of his potential Dragonknight form and gives him enough understanding of its presence to allow him to attempt a transformation. Actually transforming into the Dragonknight form is another matter.

Transformation

Transforming into the Dragonknight form requires different amounts of Force Energy depending upon the seasons. During the Light season it take 5 points of Force Energy in order to transform, and 2 points of Force Energy per Turn thereafter to maintain it. During the neutral seasons (first and second grey) 10 points of Force Energy must be expended in order to transform into Dragonknight, and 5 points of Force Energy per Turn thereafter to maintain it. During the Shadow season it take 15 points of Force Energy in order to transform into Dragonknight, and 7 points of Force Energy per Turn thereafter to maintain it.

Transforming into Dragonknight is a Major Action and no other actions may be taken while transforming. Transformation begins at the transforming character's Mystical Initiative.

First Transformation

Your character's first transformation into his Dragonknight form, assuming of course that your character is a Dragonknight, is not without difficulty. When your character first attempts to transform into his Dragonknight form he must make a successful Sixth Sense/Performance Test against a Difficulty Value of 10. Failing this Test means that the transformation attempt was unsuccessful and the Force

Energy required to make the transformation is wasted. This Sixth Sense/Performance Test must be made each and every time that your character attempts to transform in his Dragonknight form until he is successful. Once your character makes a successful transformation he no longer has to make the Sixth Sense/Performance Test in order to transform.

Until your character has a Total Force Energy of 200 or higher there are additional difficulties to overcome when attempting to transform into his Dragonknight form. As long as your character's Total Force remains under 200 you must roll 1D12 each time that he attempts to transform into Dragonknight. If he has not yet successfully transformed into Dragonknight for the first time the Performance Die (1D12) rolled as part of the required Sixth Sense/Performance Test will substitute for this 1D12. On a result of 1 the transformation attempt completely fails and the required Force Energy for the transformation is wasted. On results of 2, 3, or 4 the transformation is successful, but only if three times the normal required Force Energy is expended. So if it normally takes 10 points of Force Energy to transform and you roll a 2, 3, or 4 it will require 30 points of Force Energy in order to make the transformation (maintaining the Dragonknight form costs the same as it always does. Only the cost for the transformation is increased by three times). Results of 5 or higher on the 1D12 means that the transformation attempt has occurred as normal.

Once your character's Total Force Energy is 200 or higher you no longer have to roll the 1D12 when attempting to transform. Transformations occur normally and for the normal Force Energy requirement.

At the beginning of each Turn the Force Energy for transforming or maintaining Dragonknight form must be expended or the Shinkai will immediately begin transformation back into their ruling-race form (this is also a Major Action). Your character may not substitute Life Force for Force Energy in order to transform into or maintain his Dragonknight form.

During transformation to or from Dragonknight form the Shinkai is very vulnerable. No controlled movements, such as setting a Defense or running, can be performed during this time of transformation. The transformation process is very uncomfortable and intense, but once completed no ill effects are retained.

Any damage or effects sustained during transformation from ruling-race to Dragonknight goes to the character's ruling-race form. Any damage or effects sustained during transformation from Dragonknight to ruling-race goes to the character's Dragonknight form. This same concept applies to characters that set a Mystical Defense while transforming. If transforming *from* Dragonknight *to* ruling-race, the Mystical Defense is set using the Sixth Sense of the Dragonknight form. If transforming *from* ruling-race *to* Dragonknight form, the Mystical Defense is set using the

Sixth Sense of the ruling-race form.

Any armor worn will still offer its normal protection to your character during the Turn that he is transforming into Dragonknight. Though the body is increasing in size and changing shape for the duration of the Turn, armor is not considered destroyed until after transformation is complete.

Along the same lines, a Dragonknight's scales offer their normal protection during the Turn of transformation back into ruling-race.

Shinkai Dragonknights preparing to transform into their Dragonknight form should take some precautionary measures before doing so, such as taking off any armor or clothing that they do not wish to be destroyed.

When Shinkai Dragonknights assume their Dragonknight form they not only change drastically in shape and appearance, but size as well. The size of the Dragonknight form is calculated by doubling the height of the Shinkai Dragonknight's ruling-race form and adding an additional five feet. The weight of a Dragonknight is approximately double that of their ruling-race form. So it is easy to see why anything worn at the time of transformation into Dragonknight will most likely be destroyed.

During transformation into Dragonknight form 1D20 + 1D10 +30 points of damage is exerted on anything that restrains the Shinkai's body from transformation, such as armor or another being holding the Shinkai. If it is another being holding onto the Shinkai, the 1D20 + 1D10 +30 points of damage is translated into points of strength. The being holding the Shinkai that is attempting to transform into Dragonknight must immediately make a Strength Test. The result must be greater than the number of strength points exerted by the Shinkai's transformation in order to hold onto them. If it is an object that is restraining the transformation into Dragonknight then the number of strength points exerted by the Shinkai's transformation must be greater than the object's Shatter Threshold or enough to take the object beyond its Destroyed Rating.

If the restraining object or force is not immediately removed or broken through, then the transformation will stop and the Shinkai will immediately return to his or her ruling-race form. The Force Energy for transformation is still spent regardless of transformation success.

At the GM's discretion damage may be taken by Shinkai Dragonknights whose transformation is restrained (this depends largely upon the source and strength of the restraint).

A Shinkai who is killed or reaches Force Failure while in Dragonknight form will immediately transform back into their ruling-race form. This transformation also takes 1 full Turn to complete.

Dragonknights have many abilities that are much akin to those of true dragons, some of which are the ability to grow very tough protective scales, the ability to fly, and various types of breaths that can be used as effective weapons

The Dragonknight form is physically superior to that of the normal ruling-race form. Dragonknights are very powerful and possess many exceptional abilities. With this power comes responsibility. Running your Dragonknight is not as simple as it may first appear. There is much to consider, such as the fact that a Dragonknight must eventually return to his ruling-race form, which is not nearly as strong as that of the Dragonknight form. Damage taken in Dragonknight will soon come over to the ruling-race form. Much disaster can come to a character that carelessly uses his Dragonknight abilities.

When a Shinkai changes into his Dragonknight form his attributes change as well. The attribute values for a Shinkai's Dragonknight form are derived from those of his or her ruling-race form. The following "DRAGONKNIGHT ATTRIBUTES" table shows what changes are made to the character's attribute values when in Dragonknight form.

DRAGONKNIGHT ATTRIBUTES	
Attribute	**Value Change**
Agility	+10 Points
Strength	+10 Points
Endurance	+10 Points
Willpower	+10 Points
Intelligence	No Change
Sixth Sense	-5 Points

The Life Force, Force Failure, Injury Rating, Movement, Lifting Limit, Carrying Capacity, etc. for the Dragonknight form are then calculated as normal from these attribute values. The Protection Rating of the initial scales for all of the Dragonknight forms is 3.

DRAGONKNIGHT FORMS

There are five types of Dragonknight forms, one for each of the ruling-races. Each of the five types of Dragonknights have their own unique innate abilities just as each of the ruling-races have their own unique innate abilities. The Dragonknight forms of each ruling-race are just as unique and varied as the different ruling-races themselves.

The following is a detailed description of each of the five types of Dragonknights.

Brightling Dragonknight

The Brightling Dragonknight is the smallest of the four forms, as is the Brightling's normal form. They are very slender and have a smooth body. Their tails end in a very sharp stinger that has a Damage yield of Level 6, and can inject a burning venom in those struck by it. This poison takes effect immediately, yielding Level 7 damage and causing agonizing pain for four to six hours.

If a being is struck by a Brightling Dragonknight's tail, they must immediately make an Endurance Test against a Difficulty Value of 10. If the victim's Endurance Test is successful, they only suffer the effects of the venom for the duration of the Turn in which they are stung. If they fail the Test, they will suffer the effects of the venom for the duration of the Turn they are stung as well as the following Turn.

Brightling Dragonknight teeth are very small but are needle sharp. A Brightling Dragonknight's bite has a Damage Yield of Level 8. The small and razor-sharp claws of a Brightling Dragonknight have a Damage Yield of Level 6.

Their initial scale color is gray, often with silver streaks throughout.

Due to their body shape and weight Brightling Dragonknights are exceptional flyers, capable of extremely quick maneuvers and high speeds (they receive a +30 feet per Turn bonus to their Maximum Flight speed).

Grak Dragonknight

Grak Dragonknights have very stout and thick bodies, and are fairly short, much like their ruling-race form. They are not the most graceful of flyers, but can fly well enough. Their most prominent feature is the two long horns that protrude straightforward from their forehead. These horns are about three feet in length. The Grak Dragonknight are very skilled with using these horns to impale foes. These horns have a Damage Yield of Level 8.

Grak Dragonknights also have exceptionally powerful tails. Their tails are somewhat shorter than that of the other Dragonknights, but are much thicker and muscular. Their tail has a Damage Yield of Level 5, but its most impressive feature is that any being struck by a Grak Dragonknight's tail must immediately (regardless of the damage received from the attack) make a Random-roll Agility Test against a Difficulty Value of 8, and a Random-roll Endurance Test against a Difficulty Value of 8. Failure of the Agility/Performance Test means the opponent is knocked down, and failure of the Endurance Test means they are stunned for the remainder of the Turn.

Grak Dragonknights have fairly long teeth set in a wide jaw. Their bite has a Damage Yield of Level 9. Their claws are very strong and sharp and have a Damage Yield of Level 7. Their initial scale color is ash-green.

Lormek Dragonknight

Loremek Dragonknights are fairly slim with a very balanced and toned body. They are exceptional flyers and have arms that are longer than those of the other Dragonknight forms. These exceptionally long arms make Loremek Dragonknights capable of performing faster and more powerful claw attacks. The Loremek's exceptional flying ability is demonstrated through the fact that they must receive (at one time) a number of damage points that triples their Injury Rating, instead of doubling it, before they can be knocked out of the air.

When attacking with their claws Loremek Dragonknights receive a +1D4 point bonus to their attack value. Their claws have an impressive Damage Yield of Level 8.

The tails of Loremek Dragonknights are of average length

and have a Damage Yield of Level 5. Their head and teeth are very much equivalent in size to that of the Valkin Dragonknight. Their bite has a Damage Yield of Level 9. Their initial scale color is light brown.

Valkin Dragonknight

The Valkin Dragonknight is fairly long, and has a very beautiful and proportionate shape. Their tails are exceptionally long, ending with a very sharp and stiff spike that is covered with many razor-sharp barbs. This tail has a Damage Yield of Level 6.

When a Valkin Dragonknight makes a successful attack with their tail the sharp barbed tip of their tail detaches and remains in the unfortunate victim. This spike is very hard to remove due to the curved barbs covering its surface. This spike is also hollow, with many small holes throughout its surface.

As long as this spike remains in a living being it causes that being to suffer 1D4 points of blood-loss damage per Turn. Removing the spike does an additional 1D8 points of damage due to the razor-sharp barbs that tear at the flesh as it is removed.

A Valkin Dragonknight will re-grow a lost tail spike at the beginning of the Turn following its loss.

Valkin Dragonknight teeth are of average size and are very sharp. They have a Damage Yield of Level 9. Their claws are also very sharp and have a Damage Yield of Level 7. Their initial scale color is tan.

Valkin Dragonknights possess the ability to mesmerize other beings with their gaze. Any living being caught by the gaze of a Valkin Dragonknight (which is any seeing being within Normal range of sight that rolls a 1 or 2 on a 1D6 while in sight of the Dragonknight) must make a successful Endurance Test against a Difficulty Value of 10 or become temporarily mesmerized. Mesmerized beings suffer a -1 Level penalty to all attributes for the duration of the Turn.

If a Valkin Dragonknight chooses, he may select only certain targets to be affected by his gaze. This is most necessary when the Valkin Dragonknight has allies in his midst that he doesn't want to be mesmerized.

Warlum Dragonknight

Warlum Dragonknights are very stocky and muscular. Their bodies are much shorter than the other Dragonknights. The greatest percentage of a Warlum Dragonknight's body is covered with large, sharp spikes which protrude about six to twelve inches out from the surface of their body. Any being engaging in melee combat with a Warlum Dragonknight risks being stabbed by these sharp spikes. Beings engaging in melee with a Warlum Dragonknight must roll 1D6. A result of 1 or 2 means that they are stabbed by one or more of the protruding spikes and suffer 1D6 +4 points of damage, whether or not the Warlum Dragonknight's attacks were successful or not, or whether or not he even attacks.

Warlum Dragonknights have extremely powerful jaws and their teeth are exceptionally long and sharp. When attacking with their jaws they receive a +1D4 point bonus to their attack value. The bite of a Warlum Dragonknight has a Damage Yield of Level 10.

The claws of the Warlum Dragonknight are of average size and like the other Dragonknights they are very sharp and deadly. The claws of a Warlum Dragonknight have a Damage Yield of Level 7.

Their tails are slightly shorter than that of the other Dragonknights and have a Damage Yield of Level 5. Their initial scale color is copper.

RELATION BETWEEN FORMS

Conjuring or projecting your character's essence is not possible while in Dragonknight form. Also, Mystical Attuning Points can not be used while in Dragonknight form.

Any damage to your character's Dragonknight form will transfer over to his ruling-race form at an increment of 10 points per hour. Fatigue Points will also transfer over at a rate of 1 point per hour. This damage will not begin transferring over until the sun turns dark (from the sixteenth to the twenty fifth hour). As long as the sun is giving light the damage that has been sustained in the Dragonknight form will remain there and will not affect your character's ruling-race form.

As damage is transferred from the Dragonknight form to the ruling-race form it is simply removed from the Dragonknight form. It does NOT bleed over so that both

forms eventually have equal amounts of damage.

Injuries do not carry over as injuries from Dragonknight to ruling-race; only the damage from injuries is transferred to the ruling-race form. Normal damage and injuries to your character's ruling-race form do not carry over to your character's Dragonknight form, however damage to the Dragonknight form will eventually transfer over to the ruling-race form if not healed.

As mentioned previously this transfer of damage only begins once the sun turns dark (the sixteenth hour) and will cease when it once again begins to burn (the twenty fifth hour). Damage sustained to a Korgathool's Dragonknight form transfers over to their ruling-race form in just the opposite manner that it does for Light-abiding Shinkai (their damage only transfers over while the sun is burning and ceases when it becomes dark).

If it is already dark when a Dragonknight returns to ruling-race form, 10 points of damage are transformed immediately at this time and then 10 more points per hour until all damage is transferred or until the twenty fifth hour.

Damage transferred from Dragonknight to ruling-race is reflective of the particular type and area of the damage inflicted.

Example, if a left arm is badly injured in Dragonknight form, the damage that transfers over to the ruling-race form will manifest as an equivalent wound to the equivalent body part; in this case, the character's left arm, but this does not automatically create another "Injury" to the ruling-race form.

Remember, only the damage carries over, not the actual injury itself, but if the amount of damage that comes over at one time (normally 10 points) is equal to or greater than the character's Injury Rating in ruling-race form, it will cause an injury.

Unlike injuries to a character's ruling-race form, injuries to the Dragonknight form do not take a certain number of days to heal. When enough damage is healed or transferred from the Dragonknight form the injuries are removed.

As with the ruling-race form, one point of damage is retained for each injury sustained. So, a Dragonknight with one injury will heal that injury when the last point of damage has either been healed or transferred. If a Dragonknight has two injuries, one injury will be healed when the next to last point of damage is healed or transferred, and the second injury will be healed when the last point of damage is healed or transferred.

The effects of Force-effects and mystical damage and poisons carry over instantly from one form to the other. So a Dragonknight who has "Weakness" placed upon him will still have it after returning to ruling race form and vice versa.

Characters are still able to utilize their innate abilities in Dragonknight. So a Valkin can still see in the dark when Dragonknight. A Brightling can still sense conjuring, etc.

Healing Damage

Damage to a Shinkai's Dragonknight form can be healed while in Dragonknight form or in ruling-race form, though healing the Dragonknight form while in ruling-race form is significantly slower.

If in ruling-race form, any healing received after the ruling-race form has healed all damage, including injury damage, carries over to the Dragonknight form, but this method requires 2 points of healing to cure 1 point of Dragonknight damage. So, if a character has no damage at all to their ruling-race form and they receive 10 points of healing their Dragonknight form will heal 5 points of damage. Because healing the Dragonknight form indirectly heals at a 2 point to 1 point ratio, at least 2 points of healing must be received in order to do any healing at all to the Dragonknight form.

Though usually unproductive, the same process can also be performed to heal damage to the ruling-race form while in Dragonknight form (though it would be easier to simply return to ruling-race form and receive healing point for point).

Healing damage to the Dragonknight form by means of normal Recovery Tests can be somewhat difficult. Recovery Tests can not be made in Dragonknight form unless your character was actually Dragonknight for the largest percentage of the recovery period (two hours). Since this is virtually impossible under normal circumstances (due to the amount of Force Energy required to maintain Dragonknight form), Recovery Tests can not be made while in Dragonknight, unless your character somehow manages to remain Dragonknight for the largest percentage of the recovery period (two hours).

Damage can be healed point for point in Dragonknight by the use of any mystical means of healing. Such methods may include Force-effects with healing properties or enchanted items with healing properties.

Your character's ruling-race form may be completely free from any current damage, including injury damage, even though his Dragonknight form may still have damage. But once the sun turns dark (the sixteenth hour) the damage will begin transferring over.

DRAGONKNIGHT ABILITIES

There are several different interesting and useful abilities that Dragonknight characters can acquire. The following will describe the details of how to gain and use these abilities.

FLYING

Flying is an ability that each of the five types of Dragonknights are capable of, though none are initially able to do so. The ability to fly must be learned. To learn how to fly the Shinkai Dragonknight simply spends 10 Light Points and informs the GM that he or she is doing so. At that instance their potential to fly is unleashed, and from that point on they are able to fly. When your character learns to fly in Dragonknight form mark the box to the left of "Maximum Flight Speed" and "Action Flight Movement" to indicate that your character's Dragonknight form is capable of flying.

The listed movement for the Dragonknight's Agility + Strength values is their Ground Movement. Their Flying Movement is double their Ground Movement. So a Dragonknight's Maximum Flight Speed is exactly double the Maximum Speed of their ruling-race form. The Action Flight Movement for their Dragonknight form can then be found by looking the Maximum Flight Speed up on the "MOVE/LIFT&CARRY" table and looking at the corresponding Action Movement for that speed, or by dividing the Maximum Flight Speed by three and rounding up.

For example, a Dragonknight whose Agility + Strength is 40 would have a Ground Movement of 130'\44'. The Maximum Flight Speed for this Dragonknight would be 260 feet per Turn (exactly double the Maximum Ground Speed). That Dragonknight's Action Flight Movement would be 87 feet (one third of the Maximum Flight Speed rounded up).

Your character may learn Technique Points in doing combat while flying in Dragonknight form (aerial combat). Aerial combat has a Maximum Technique of 2. This technique applies to any type of Dragonknight attack or Physical Defense made while in flight.

BREATHS

There are six different types of breaths (other than that used for normal breathing) that Dragonknights are capable of wielding. They are acid, darkness, fire, frost, paralysis, and poison. Dragonknights may learn any two of the six types of breath that they choose. Once a Dragonknight learns a particular type of breath it is permanent. You may not choose a new type of breath to replace one that your character has already learned.

Agility is the attribute used to perform attacks with all of the breath types.

Acid

This breath is a thick steaming blast of acid that brings blisters and burns to its unfortunate victims. The acid spreads slightly as it travels so that it is six feet wide at its maximum distance. Victims struck by this acid suffer Level 12 + 5 points of damage immediately and Level 6 damage on the Turn after exposure.

Learning Cost: 10 Light Points
Required Forces: *Water*
Maximum Range: 15 feet
Defense: Block (half-shield or larger) or Dodge

Darkness

This breath is a blast of impenetrable darkness that engulfs whatever it strikes. The darkness expands to a radius of ten feet from the area struck. The darkness moves with the object or being to which it struck, and remains for 1D4 Turns. This darkness breath sticks only to the object struck. Objects entering the darkened area around the target can't see, but it does not stick to them. Once they emerge from the darkened area they are not affected.

This darkness is impenetrable. No one, not even a Valkin, can see into or out of this darkness.

The blast of darkness spreads very little as it travels, covering a width of five feet at its maximum range.

Learning Cost: 8 Light Points
Required Forces: *Land* & *Spirit*
Maximum Range: 20 feet
Defense: Block (half-shield or larger) or Dodge

Fire

An extremely hot and forceful blast of flames that yields Level 12+5 points of damage to anything they come in contact with. The flames spread as they travel so that at their maximum range they cover an area eight feet wide.

Learning Cost: 7 Light Points
Required Forces: *Fire*
Maximum Range: 30 feet
Defense: Dodge

Frost

This freezing blast of icy breath bellows forth chilling any it comes in contact with. Beings struck with this frost suffer Level 10 damage and have a -2 Level penalty on any Test requiring movement. This penalty lasts for 2 Turns.

Multiple hits from this type of breath will render Level 10 damage each time that a successful hit is made, but additional hits from this breath to a being that is already under the effects from it only render a -1 Level penalty to Tests requiring movement, not -2 Levels.

The frost spreads as it travels, so that it is six feet wide at its maximum range.

Learning Cost: 7 Light Points

Required Forces: *Air & Water*
Maximum Range: 30 feet
Defense: Block (full-shield only) or Dodge

Paralysis

This type of breath is nearly invisible, noticeable only by the vague silver flashes throughout it. Beings struck with this breath must immediately make a Sixth Sense/Performance Test against a Difficulty Value of 9 or be completely paralyzed for the duration of the Turn. This is not a Mystical Defense, so Mystical Defense Bonus points can not be used to increase the results of this Test.

Those who pass the Sixth Sense/Performance Test are still partially paralyzed, having their movement decreased by half (rounded up), and all Tests requiring movement receive a -4 point penalty for 1 Turn.

Multiple hits from this type of breath will not add additional penalties to the beings movement or Tests requiring movement.

This breath does not spread out much as it travels, being only three feet wide at its maximum range.
Learning Cost: 8 Light Points
Required Forces: *Spirit*
Maximum Range: 30 feet
Defense: Block (half-shield or larger) or Dodge

Poison

A clear blast of foul smelling mist engulfs those in the path of this pungent breath, causing them to become increasingly weak. On the second Turn after exposure to this breath the victim's Strength drops 3 Levels. On the third Turn it will drop another 2 Levels where it will remain (unless altered by some other means) for 5 Turns. After this fifth Turn the victim's Strength will raise by 1 Level per Turn until it has returned to normal.

Multiple hits from this type of breath will render the penalties described above on top of the penalties that remain from previous hits, but only up to a maximum of three hits. Additional hits from this type of breath beyond the third have no additional effects.

This poisonous mist spreads out as it travels so that it is ten feet wide at its maximum range.
Learning Cost: 8 Light Points
Required Forces: *Land & Spirit*
Maximum Range: 15 feet
Defense: Dodge

SCALE GROWTH

Dragonknights are capable of growing various types of scales that offer protection in the same way that armor does for their ruling-race form. So red scales will absorb the first 5 points of damage rendered to it and the remaining damage is applied to the Dragonknight himself.

There are five types of scales which can be grown in addition to a Dragonknight's initial scales. The five types of scales in the order of lowest to highest Protection Ratings (P.R.) are white, red, emerald, blue, and gold.

Growing the various types of scales is simply a matter of spending the appropriate amount of Light Points listed under "Growth Cost" on the following "SCALES" table, and informing the GM that you are doing so.

It takes five days for the new scales to replace the old. At the first hour of the fifth day after the scales are purchased they will be fully developed and the new Protection Rating may then be applied. The scale types must be grown in consecutive order, thus in order to grow red scales your Dragonknight must have white scales, and in order to grow emerald scales he must first have red scales, etc.

The following "SCALES" table gives all of the needed information regarding each of the scale types.

As your Dragonknight form takes damage his scales become damaged and can even be destroyed to the point that they no longer offer any protection. The Reduced Protection value (R.P.) for each particular scale type is the number of points of damage that can be received before the scale's Protection Rating is decreased by 1 point. By paying the Light Point cost listed under "Regrowth Cost" for your Dragonknight's particular type of scales, he can regrow damaged scales and renew their Protection Rating.

Scales can only be regrown once every three hours, and the maximum number of damage points that are regrown within those three hours is a number equal to that particular scale type's R.P. value.

Example; A Dragonknight with Blue scales can only regrow 27 points worth of damaged scales every three hours, for a cost of 5 Light Points. Each such regrowth restores 1 point to the scale's P.R.

Note: Even if a Dragonknight has current damage to a given scale type, when the next type of scales fully form the damage to the previous type is erased; the damage does not carry over to the new scales.

SCALES				
Scale Type	Growth Cost	P.R	R.P.	Regrowth Cost
Initial	NA	3	every 10	1 Light Pt.
White	3 Light Pts.	4	every 12	2 Light Pts.
Red	6 Light Pts.	5	every 15	3 Light Pts.
Emerald	9 Light Pts.	7	every 21	4 Light Pts.
Blue	12 Light Pts.	9	every 27	5 Light Pts.
Gold	14 Light Pts.	12	every 36	6 Light Pts.

Advanced Combat

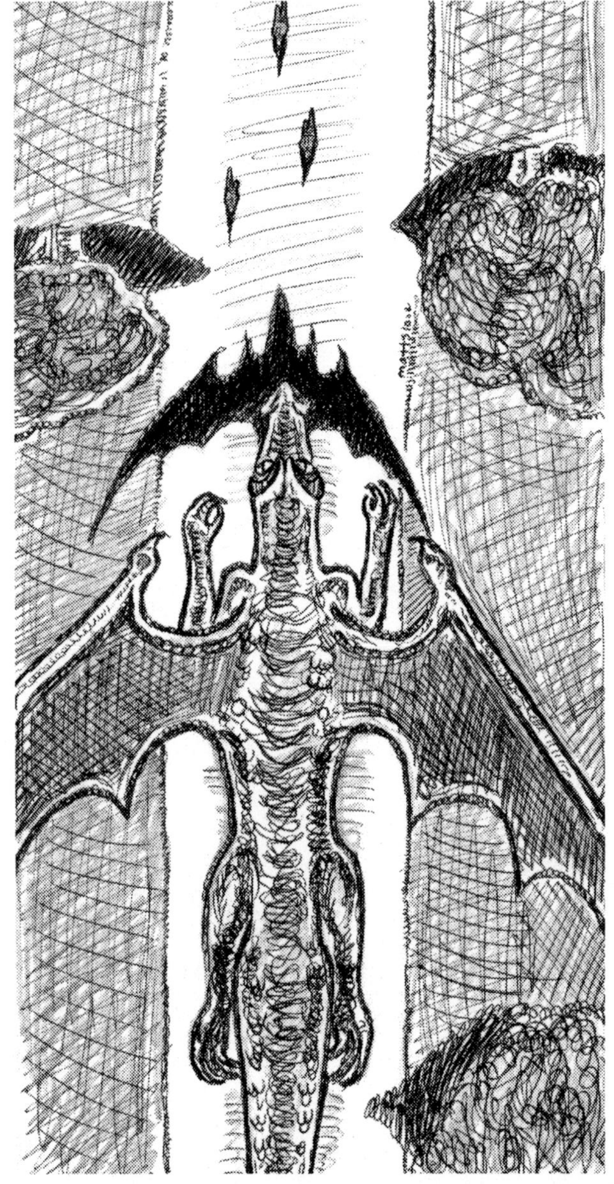

Dragonknights have the option if increasing their combat abilities, which is a skill known as Advanced Combat. Learning this skill costs 7 Light Points. A Dragonknight who has learned Advanced Combat may make two attacks per Turn. These attacks may be a combination of attack types or two attacks of the same type, but they must occur in rapid succession; no delay between the two attacks. Both attacks are considered a single Major Action.

Example; a Dragonknight with Advanced Combat may make one tail attack and one bite attack in the same Turn, or one bite attack and one claw attack, or two bite attacks, etc.

This second attack is treated as a separate attack. Separate attack rolls, damage rolls, etc. The Initiative for the second attack is 1 point lower than the Initiative of the first.

Advanced Combat may not be used in ruling-race while utilizing "Controlled Transformation".

When your character learns Advanced Combat simply place a check or an x in the box beside of "Advanced Combat" in the Dragonknight section of your Character Sheet to indicate that he has that ability.

Types of Attacks

There are basically four types of attacks that Dragonknights can employ. They are bite, breath, claw, and tail. The following gives an overview of each of these four types of attacks. If there is information about an attack type that is specific to one type of Dragonknight, that information will be given with the particular Dragonknight's description.

Bite

The powerful jaws and teeth of a Dragonknight are very effective weapons. The bite of most Dragonknights has a Damage Yield of Level 9.

A maximum of 2 Technique Points can be learned with bite attacks. Technique Points that your character may have with his head in ruling-race form do not apply to your Dragonknight's bite attacks.

Breath

Each particular type of breath attack has its own unique effects, each of which are described in detail under "Breath" in the "Dragonknight Abilities" part of this Section.

A maximum of 3 Technique Points can be learned with breath attacks. Technique Points that your character may have with his head in ruling-race form do not apply to your Dragonknight's breath attacks.

Claw

The arms and legs of a Dragonknight are equipped with very sharp talons capable of tearing an enemy to shreds. The claws of most Dragonknights have a Damage Yield of Level 7.

A maximum of 4 Technique Points can be learned with claw attacks. Technique Points that your character may have with his arms in ruling-race form do not apply to his Dragonknight's claw attacks.

Tail

Dragonknights are all equipped with fairly long muscular tails, which can be used to club their enemies. The tails of most Dragonknights have a Damage Yield of Level 5.

Brightlings, Grak, and Valkin have additional abilities in regards to their tails; these are described in detail under their Dragonknight description.

A maximum of 5 Technique Points can be learned with tail attacks.

MAGIC

"What is magic you ask? Magic is the embodiment of the most powerful forces in existence. Magic is a gift from the Light that should be looked upon with the highest of respect.

To be among the select few that have been blessed with the ability control the Mystic Forces is the highest honor that can be bestowed upon a being. Sadly there are those who have perverted the gift of the Light and use magic for evil purposes. This is the deepest and most vile form of treachery and betrayal of the Light that I can imagine.

Though the Shadow and its evil spawn plague Oryathar and though some use magic to further their cause, it will be magic wielded by those faithful to the Light that will bring about the demise of the Shadow and once again restore balance and peace to all the lands."

Norkweylan Kelgar, 597 AA

"Magic" is a general term for any type of action or effect that is produced or is the product of the Mystic Forces. There are five known Mystic Forces. They are *Air*, *Fire*, *Land*, *Spirit*, and *Water*. The Mystic Forces can not be seen, smelled, heard, or touched by normal means. The Mystic Forces encompass all things, beings, and areas of the known universe. Though they are completely invisible and go undetected by all but the elite, they are always present.

There are basically three types of magic. Conjuring, natural magic, and enchantments. Each of these three types of magic will be discussed in detail in this Section.

CONJURING

Other than dragons, Shinkai are the only beings known to be able to conjure. Their ability to conjure comes from the presence of a mystical energy within them known as the *Gift*.

Conjuring is the process of drawing in the Mystic Forces and bonding them with the *Gift* where they are manipulated and altered into another form of energy and matter.

Conjuring is at the heart of the Shinkai's arsenal. Once a Shinkai masters this ability he is next to invincible.

The *Gift*

Shinkai have a manifestation of the Light, referred to as the "*Gift*", infused into their Life Force. This *Gift* is the sum of all five Mystic Forces. The presence of the *Gift* enables the Shinkai to feel the energies of the five Mystic Forces, though this ability doesn't manifest until the ruling-race is within two to three years of physical maturity (the ability to meditate upon and control the Mystic Forces does not manifest until the ruling-race has reached physical maturity.

The *Gift* has been given to Shinkai by the Light for the intended purpose of opposing the Shadow, though some have turned their back on the Light and use their Light-given abilities to promote the Shadow.

Through deep meditation and concentration Shinkai can allow themselves to become more aware of and receptive to the various Mystic Forces (only one at a time). This meditation helps them to gain a greater knowledge of the Mystic Forces and how they relate to the *Gift* within themselves. This process of meditation in turn increases the strength of the *Gift* within the Shinkai (greater knowledge leads to greater strength of the *Gift*).

Meditating on the Mystic Forces

The Shinkai relaxes and clears his mind. He now focuses upon the subtle hints of mystical energies that are the Mystic Forces. The Shinkai must now single out one of the Mystic Forces. After singling out one of the Mystic Forces the Shinkai concentrates as intently as he can upon it; allowing his *Gift* to become more sensitive to it, feeling it out, studying it. The Mystic Force upon which the Shinkai is meditat-

ing intensifies around the Shinkai and though it is not drawn into the Shinkai, the *Gift* reaches a level of sensitivity to it that allows it to absorb some of its energies (this same process restores the Shinkai's Force Energy) as well as giving the Shinkai a greater knowledge of the Mystic Force. The knowledge of the Mystic Forces that is gained in this way is known as Force Knowledge.

In order for your character to meditate on the Mystic Forces he must be able to completely concentrate and focus. He can not perform any other tasks while attempting to meditate. Average Shinkai and Shinkai Dragonknights require one hour of uninterrupted meditation in order to gain any Force Knowledge. Shinkai Enchanters only require half an hour of uninterrupted meditation in order to gain Force Knowledge.

At the end of the required meditation time your character must expend 1 Light Point. He now makes a Random-roll Intelligence Test and a Random-roll Sixth Sense Test. The lowest result of either of these two Tests is the amount of Force Knowledge and Unapplied Force Knowledge that your character gains in the Mystic Force that he meditated upon. If you happen to get the exact same result on both the Random-roll Intelligence Test and the Random-roll Sixth Sense Test (perhaps you got a result of 7 on both Tests), you may roll 1D6 and add the amount rolled to the result of the meditation session.

As a positive side-effect of meditating for Force Knowledge your character will recover an amount of Force Energy, up to his maximum, equal to two times the amount of Force Knowledge gained for the meditation session. So, if your character is a Shinkai Dragonknight and he meditates on *Fire* and has an Intelligence of Level 7 and a Sixth Sense of Level 9, you would roll 1D10 + 1D4 for the Random-roll Intelligence Test and 1D10 + 1D8 for the Random-roll Sixth Sense Test. Lets say that you got a result of 7 on the Random-roll Intelligence Test and a 10 on the Random-roll Sixth Sense Test. Your character would gain 7 Force Knowledge in *Fire* and would recover 14 points of Force Energy. If for any reason your character is interrupted during the meditation session he will get no Force Knowledge or Force Energy and must start all over.

Average Shinkai and Shinkai Dragonknights can meditate for Force Knowledge only once per day without receiving Fatigue Points. They will receive 1 Fatigue Point for each time that they meditate for Force Knowledge past the first time (within the same day). Shinkai Enchanters can meditate twice in the same day without receiving Fatigue Points. They will receive 1 Fatigue Point for each time that they meditate for Force Knowledge past the second time (within the same day).

If you choose, your character can meditate on a Mystic Force for the sole purpose of recovering Force Energy. When meditating for this purpose your character will single out one of the Mystic Forces upon which to meditate, just as

if he were meditating for Force Knowledge, and begin the meditation session. At the end of the meditation your character would make the Random-roll Intelligence and Sixth Sense just as he would if he had meditated for Force Knowledge. An amount of Force Energy equal to two times the amount of the lowest result of the two Tests is recovered. The benefits in meditating solely for the purpose of Force Energy recovery is that the meditation session doesn't cost any Light Points and whether your character is Shinkai Dragonknight or Shinkai Enchanter he can meditate as many time as he wants without receiving Fatigue Points. It still takes normal Shinkai and Shinkai Dragonknights one full hour for this type of meditation and Shinkai Enchanters only half an hour. The only drawback to this type of meditation is that your character doesn't get any actual Force Knowledge from the meditation.

Your character may have up to 50 Force Knowledge in any one of the Mystic Forces without actually controlling the Mystic Force. In order to obtain more than 50 Force Knowledge in a Mystic Force your character must first control that Mystic Force. Once your character actually controls a Mystic Force there is no limit to the amount of Force Knowledge that he can acquire in it.

Controlling the Mystic Forces

Eventually, after gaining enough Force Knowledge (minimum of 25), your character can actually control the Mystic Forces. Through this control he can learn to conjure and blend the Mystic Forces to create various magical effects, known as Force-effects.

The process by which a Shinkai is able to control the Mystic Forces is much the same as the process for gaining Force Knowledge. It requires an uninterrupted meditation session of one hour for normal Shinkai and Shinkai Dragonknights and half an hour for Shinkai Enchanters. At the end of the meditation sessions the Shinkai must expend 5 Light Points and must now make a successful Sixth Sense/Performance Test against a Difficulty Value derived from the following "MYSTIC FORCE CONTROL" table.

MYSTIC FORCE CONTROL	
Knowledge	**Difficulty Value**
25-30	14
31-35	12
36-40	10
41-45	8
46-50	6

The more Force Knowledge that the Shinkai has at the time he attempts to control the Mystic Force, the lower the Difficulty Value is and greater the odds of success.

Find your character's Force Knowledge, not Unapplied Force Knowledge, in the Mystic Force that he is attempting to learn to control in the "Knowledge" column. Straight across from this value in the "Difficulty Value" column is the Difficulty Value of the Sixth Sense/Performance Test for learning to control that particular Mystic Force.

If you roll a 1 on the Performance Die (feeble attempt) for this Test your character fails to gain control of the Mystic Force (regardless of the Test result) and in addition his Life Force is consumed by the Mystic Force that he is attempting to control instantly killing him. If your character fails the Test but you didn't roll a 1 on the Performance Die he will not gain control of the Mystic Force and will also receive 10 points of damage for each point that he missed the required Difficulty Value by. So if your character had a Force Knowledge of 38 in the Mystic Force that he is attempting to control the Difficulty Value of the Sixth Sense/Performance Test is 10. If he got a result of 7 on his Sixth Sense/Performance Test then he will receive 30 points of damage.

If your character fails the Test for learning to control a Mystic Force he can still try again whenever he wants. He can try again immediately or he can wait until he increases his Force Knowledge in that Mystic Force first (your character's Force Knowledge can be as high as 50 without actually controlling the Mystic Force).

No Unapplied Force Knowledge is expended on failed attempts to control a Mystic Force. Only when your character passes the Test and actually learns to control the Mystic Force is the Unapplied Force Knowledge spent. He will however, waste 5 Light Points for the failed attempt and sustain damage (10 points of damage for each point that he missed the required Difficulty Value by).

If your character passes the Test he has learned to control the Mystic Force. At this time your character must expend all Unapplied Force Knowledge in the Mystic Force that he just learned to control. As a confirmation, your character's eyes will immediately rage for a brief second in the color of the Mystic Force that he has just learned to control.

On the back of the Character Sheets there are boxes located to the left of each of the five Mystic Forces. When your character controls a Mystic Force simply place a check or an x in the box to indicate that your character now controls that Mystic Force.

Your character can now continue to gain Force Knowledge through meditation sessions and can begin learning Force-effects.

Though your character may control a Mystic Force he is considered novice with it until his Force Knowledge in that Mystic Force is 100 or higher. Your character can still utilize Mystic Forces that he is novice with but there are some dangers that accompany using a Mystic Force that he is still novice with. These dangers are discussed in the "FORCE-EFFECTS" Section of the rules.

It is very easy for a Shinkai to be killed in attempting to control a Mystic Force. For this reason it is customary among the Defenders of the Light to make sure that a

Shinkai that is attempting to gain control of a Mystic Force has one or more Shinkai around him who know the Force-effects "Heal" and "Ressurection".

THE RAGING

Whenever a Shinkai draws in a Mystic Force in which he is novice with his eyes will glow with a color that matches the Mystic Force that he is drawing in. *Air* will cause the Shinkai's eyes to glow white, *Fire* will cause them to glow red, *Land* will cause them to glow brown, *Spirit* will cause them to glow silver, and *Water* will cause them to glow blue. Drawing in more than one Mystic Force at a time, that the Shinkai is novice with, will cause the eyes to glow a color that is a mixture of the colors of the Mystic Forces being drawn in. If a Shinkai is novice with all five Mystic Forces and draws in all five at the same time his eyes will glow with a golden color. The more of the Mystic Forces that are drawn in (the more Force Energy expended) the more intense the glow will be. This glowing of the eyes due to drawing in the Mystic Forces is known as the Raging. Shinkai that draw in a Mystic Force in which they are novice with can not prevent the Raging. Once a Shinkai is no longer novice with a particular Mystic Force he can control whether or not he will experience the Raging while drawing in that Mystic Force.

The Raging is very useful in helping other Shinkai to learn Force-effects. A Shinkai that has the Universal Talent "Force Sight" that looks into the eyes of another Shinkai experiencing the Raging while conjuring a Force-effect is able to see how the Force-effect is created. The Shinkai viewing the creation of the Force-effect may now add a bonus to his Sixth Sense/Performance Test for learning the Force-effect if the Shinkai conjuring the Force-effect has more Technique Points in the Mystic Forces contained within the Force-effect than the observing Shinkai does. Refer to the "FORCE-EFFECTS" Section for more information on learning Force-effects.

Another use for the Raging is to determine how strong that a particular Shinkai, or Korgathool, is mystically. Any Shinkai, or Korgathool, that looks into the Raging of another Shinkai, or Korgathool, will know what how strong that they are with the Mystic Forces (you will know their Total Force Energy, which is basically representative of the strength of a being's *Gift*).

Learning Force-effects

Once your character is able to control one or more of the Mystic Forces he can begin learning Force-effects. Each Force-effect has different requirements that must be met before it can be learned. Different Force-effects require that your character control different Mystic Forces and have a minimum amount of Force Knowledge in those Mystic Forces. Your character must then spend the listed amount of Unapplied Force Knowledge and make a successful Sixth Sense/Performance Test against a set Difficulty Value.

For detailed information on the learning and use of Force-effects as well as a complete description of all of the Force-effects see the "FORCE-EFFECTS" Section.

The Conjuring Process

The process of turning the Mystic Forces into Force-effects is what is actually referred to as "Conjuring". Conjuring requires the Shinkai to use his *Gift* to draw the Mystic Forces into his body. The more complicated or powerful the Force-effect, the more of the Mystic Forces that must be drawn in to create it.

Depending upon which Force-effect is to be created the Shinkai must draw in different Mystic Forces and in varying amounts. Then by means of the *Gift*, which is controlled by the Shinkai's Sixth Sense, the Mystic Forces that are drawn into the Shinkai's body bond with the *Gift* inside of him. Once bonded with the *Gift*, the Mystic Forces can be combined and altered into a different form of energy and matter and become a Force-effect. In short, conjuring uses the *Gift* to alter one or more of the Mystic Forces into new energy and or matter that takes the form of Force-effects.

Many Shinkai describe the conjuring process to be like taking a piece of clay and imagining what you would like it to look like, then willing it to shape itself into that form. Only the clay is the Mystic Forces and the shaping of the clay is done by Sixth Sense and the *Gift* instead of with hands.

If a Shinkai draws in one or more of the Mystic Forces but doesn't actually conjure them into a Force-effect the Mystic Forces are instantly drawn back into their original sources as soon as the Shinkai ceases to draw upon them.

Drawing the Mystic Forces into their body produces strong sensations that can be felt by the Shinkai. The more deeply that the Shinkai draws upon the Mystic Forces the stronger the sensations will be. The following list shows the different sensations that are experienced by the Shinkai while drawing in the different Mystic Forces.

Air = light, cool, nimble
Fire = hot, invincible, aggressive
Land = strong, heavy, slow, tough
Spirit = vibrant, refreshed, immortal

Water = wet, cold, limber

When drawing in multiple Mystic Forces that have conflicting sensations, the sensations average out and each individual sensation is somewhat dulled and combined with the others. So a Shinkai that is drawing in *Fire* and *Water* at the same time would feel neither hot nor cold, the two Mystic Forces would cancel out those sensations. However, the Shinkai would still feel the sensations of invincibility, aggression, wetness, and limberness.

These sensations seem very strong to the novice Shinkai but after utilizing the Mystic Forces for a while the Shinkai gets accustomed to the sensations and hardly even notices them.

A word of caution to novice Shinkai, these sensations are just that; sensations. They are not real. Just because your character may feel invincible or immortal doesn't mean that he is. A spear through the heart will kill him just as easily while he is drawing in on the Mystic Forces of *Spirit* and *Fire* as it would any other time.

Force Energy

Conjuring or even drawing upon the Mystic Forces without actually creating a Force-effect requires the Shinkai to expend energy. This energy that is expended in order to draw in the Mystic Forces is referred to as "Force Energy". Even drawing in a Mystic Force in the smallest amount possible expends .5 points of Force Energy per Turn. The stronger a Shinkai's *Gift*, the stronger potential (Total Force Energy) they have in utilizing the Mystic Forces.

Drawing upon and conjuring the Mystic Forces temporarily depletes a Shinkai's Force Energy (drains the *Gift*). Though their potential, or Total Force Energy, remains the same, their Current Force Energy will decrease and increase as the Shinkai conjures and then regains Force Energy.

Your character's Total Force Energy is determined by adding up his Force Knowledge in all of the Mystic Forces and then dividing this value by 2 and rounding up. This value is now added to your character's Innate Force Energy which will determine his Total Force Energy. So a Shinkai that had a Force Knowledge of 56 in *Fire*, 29 in *Land*, and 32 in *Spirit* would add these together for a Total Force Knowledge of 117. This is divided by 2 and rounded up for a result of 59. If this Shinkai's Innate Force Energy was 11 we would add the 59 to it for a Total Force Energy of 70.

Your character's Total Force Energy will only increase (as he increases his Force Knowledge) but his Current Force Energy will go up and down as he expends Force Energy and then regains it. There are spaces provided on the backs of the Character Sheets for recording your character's Total Force Knowledge, Innate Force Energy, and Total Force Energy.

When a Shinkai depletes all of his Current Force Energy he can no longer conjure or draw in the Mystic Forces (their *Gift* is exhausted) until enough of their Force Energy has

returned to perform the desired task. Being completely deleted of Force Energy usually causes the Shinkai to experience extreme headaches and a feeling of exhaustion.

Recovering Force Energy

A Shinkai can regain expended Force Energy by meditating and allowing himself, or more technically his *Gift*, to become receptive to the Mystic Forces without actually drawing upon them (see "Meditation Upon the Mystic Forces" in the first of this Section for details on recovering Force Energy in this manner). Shinkai will also naturally regain 1D20 points of Force Energy with each new sun (first hour of each day). There are also a few Force-effects that can restore a Shinkai's Current Force Energy, namely "Healing" and the "Force Energy" rune.

Focused Conjuring

Aside from the basic type of conjuring there is a specialized type of conjuring known as focused conjuring. The difference in focused conjuring and normal conjuring is that with normal conjuring the Mystic Forces that are drawn into the Shinkai's body equally bond to all areas of the Shinkai's *Gift* and thus is equally diffused throughout the Shinkai's entire body. With focused conjuring the Mystic Forces are still diffused throughout the Shinkai's entire body but are gathered up in a higher concentration in one particular area of the Shinkai's body. The Shinkai, once he is able to utilize focused conjuring, is able to focus the Mystic Forces into any area of his body that he wishes, but only to one area of his body per Turn. Someone that has "Force Sight" who looks at a Shinkai utilizing focused conjuring would see the glow of the Mystic Forces around them but would notice that the glow is more intense in the area of the Shinkai's body where the Mystic Forces have been focused.

Another ability that is possible only through focused conjuring is the ability for the Shinkai to actually focus the Mystic Forces into an object or another being. The area of the Shinkai's body where he has focused the Mystic Forces must be in direct contact with the object or being in order for the Mystic Forces to be focused into it. This process of focusing the Mystic Forces into objects is the principle upon which enchanting is based.

Focusing the Mystic Forces into other beings has no negative effects and is almost exclusively done in order to test if a ruling-race is Dragonknight or Enchanter (see the "DRAGONKNIGHT" and/or "ENCHANTING" Sections for details on how focused conjuring is used for testing purposes).

Focused conjuring must be learned separately for each of the five Mystic Forces. Just because a Shinkai can utilize focused conjuring with the Mystic Force of *Fire* doesn't mean that he knows how to focus conjure any of the other Mystic Forces. In order for your character to utilize Force-effects that require focused conjuring your character must be able to focus all of the Mystic Forces contained within the

Force-effect.

Before your character can learn focused conjuring he must have a Minimum Force Knowledge of 50 in the Mystic Force that he wishes to learn how to focus conjure with and must also have at least 1 Technique Point in that Mystic Force. Your character must now meditate upon the Mystic Force that he wants to learn focused conjuring with (one hour for normal Shinkai and Shinkai Dragonknights and half an hour for Shinkai Enchanters). At the end of the meditation your character must immediately draw in the Mystic Force that he has meditated upon while spending 2 Light Points and making a Sixth Sense/Performance Test against a Difficulty Value of 12. If the Test is successful he has learned how to focus that Mystic Force. If your character fails the Test then he has failed to learn how to focus that Mystic Force. The Light Points are simply wasted. Your character may try again whenever he chooses; the Difficulty Value of the Test remains 12 regardless of how many attempts are made.

If for any reason your character is interrupted during the meditation session he may not attempt to learn how to focus that Mystic Force. He must start the meditation all over.

Full-focused Conjuring

Just as focused conjuring is a specialized method of conjuring there is a specialized method of focused conjuring known as full-focused conjuring. The difference in full-focused conjuring and focused conjuring is that with focused conjuring the Mystic Forces are diffused throughout the Shinkai's entire body but are gathered up in a higher concentration in one particular area of the Shinkai's body. With full-focused conjuring the Mystic Forces are only drawn into one particular area of the Shinkai's *Gift* and remain solely within that area of his body. The Shinkai can choose to have the Mystic Forces fully focused into any area of his body that he wishes, but only to one area of his body per Turn. Someone that has "Force Sight" who looks at a Shinkai utilizing full-focused conjuring would only be able to see the glow of the Mystic Forces around the area of the Shinkai's body where the Mystic Forces have been fully focused. If the Shinkai had fully focused the Mystic Forces into his hand someone with "Force Sight" who looked at him would not be able to see the glow of conjuring unless they could see his hand.

Full-focused conjuring is used mainly for the purpose of concealing conjuring from those who may be observing with "Force Sight". Full-focused conjuring can be used to perform all of the same tasks that normal focused conjuring can with the following exception. Because full-focused conjuring limits the Mystic Forces exclusively to one particular area of the Shinkai's body and *Gift* there is a limit to the amount of the Mystic Forces that can be drawn in at one time. No Force-effects or other tasks can be performed with full-focused conjuring that require more than 30 points of Force Energy expenditure at one time.

Like focused conjuring full-focused conjuring must be learned separately for each of the five Mystic Forces.

Before your character can learn full-focused conjuring he must have a Minimum Force Knowledge of 100 in the Mystic Force that he wishes to learn how to full-focus conjure with and must also have at least 2 Technique Points in that Mystic Force. Your character must now meditate upon the Mystic Force that he wants to learn full-focused conjuring with (one hour for normal Shinkai and Shinkai Dragonknights and half an hour for Shinkai Enchanters). At the end of the meditation your character must immediately draw in the Mystic Force that he has meditated upon while spending 4 Light Points and making a Sixth Sense/Performance Test against a Difficulty Value of 14. If the Test is successful he has learned how to fully focus that Mystic Force. If your character fails the Test then he has failed to learn how to fully focus that Mystic Force. The Light Points are simply wasted. Your character may try again whenever he chooses; the Difficulty Value of the Test remains 14 regardless of how many attempts are made.

If for any reason your character is interrupted during the meditation session he may not attempt to learn how to fully focus that Mystic Force. He must start the meditation all over.

MYSTICAL ATTUNING

There is a way for a Shinkai to adjust or "attune" their *Gift* so that it is able to more efficiently utilize the Mystic Forces. The process by which this is possible is known as mystical attuning.

Mystical attuning essentially allows a Shinkai to fine tune and sensitize his *Gift* so that he can more efficiently manipulate and use the Mystic Forces. There are several different bonuses that can be acquired by having your character's *Gift* mystically attuned. The extent of the bonuses vary according to the degree to which the Shinkai's *Gift* has been attuned. The following will explain how your character can attune his *Gift* and the bonuses that come from it.

Mystical attuning is not a necessary part of the game though it is an interesting aspect of the game as well as a way for characters to receive very useful bonuses. Until you become comfortable with the other aspects and rules of the game you should not try using the mystical attuning rules. As you get more comfortable and knowledgeable with the rules you can incorporate the mystical attuning aspect of the game.

Mystical Attuning Points

All characters automatically have 1 Mystical Attuning Point and receive 1 extra point for each Mystic Force that they control. So a character that controls all five Mystic Forces would have six Mystical Attuning Points.

Even without having their *Gift* attuned a Shinkai can spend Mystical Attuning Points to use certain Universal Talents as well as to receive instant bonuses. There are three different types of instant bonuses that can be received by spending Mystical Attuning Points. Each of these three types of instant bonuses can only be received once per day.

Instant Damage Recovery

By expending 1 Mystical Attuning Point your character can make an extra Recovery Test at any time that he wishes.

Instant Fatigue Removal

By expending 1 Mystical Attuning Point your character can instantly remove 1 Fatigue Point from all attributes at any time that he wishes.

Instant Force Energy Recovery

By expending 1 Mystical Attuning Point your character can instantly recover 1D20 points of Force Energy at any time that he wishes. If a character uses a Mystical Attuning Point to recover Force Energy in this way he does not receive the bonus 1D20 points of Force Energy recovery at the first hour of the following day.

As your character expends Mystical Attuning Points he deducts them from his Current Mystical Attuning Points (or Current M.A.P.) and must also remove one attuning counter from his Mystical Attuning Sheet for each Mystical Attuning Point that he spends. A character's Total M.A.P. remains unchanged by the expenditure of Mystical Attuning Points.

At the first hour of each day all expended Mystical Attuning Points are regained.

How to Accomplish Mystical Attuning

A Mystical Attuning Sheet is necessary in order to properly keep track of and utilize your character's degree of mystical attuning. Each player should have a copy of the Mystical Attuning Sheet located at the back of this rule book. This sheet will represent your character's *Gift*. Each player will also have a number of mystical attuning counters. These counters will be placed on the Mystical Attuning Sheet to keep track of how the character's *Gift* is currently attuned. Virtually any small object (coins, dice, etc.) can be used for an attuning counter but my favorite thing to use is the small glass counters that you can purchase at most any store that carries collectible card games or role-playing games. They come in a variety of colors and work very well as attuning counters.

Each player receives one mystical attuning counter for each Mystical Attuning Point that his character has. Each player then rolls 1D12 for each counter and places the counter on the Mystical Attuning Sheet in the circle that corresponds with the number rolled for that counter. You can not have more than one counter in the outer circles (circles 1 through 6) and can have no more than two counters in the middle circles (circles 7 through 11). If you roll a result that indicates that you will have to place a counter in a circle where there is already the maximum number of counters you will simply re-roll the D12 to determine its placement.

As soon as your character gains control over a Mystic Force he immediately receives an attuning counter and rolls 1D12 to determine its placement.

By moving the counters into the various patterns (known as power combinations) shown on the bottom of the Mystical Attuning Sheet your character is able to attune his *Gift* and receive bonuses. There is only a limited number of ways and times per day that attuning counters can be moved.

Attuning counters can only be moved along the lines on the Mystical Attuning Sheet. So if you had an attuning counter in the 5 circle and wanted to move it to the 9 circle you would have to first move it to the 11 circle and then to the 9 circle. You could not move it straight to the 9 circle because there is no line connecting the two. Moving a single attuning counter from one adjoining circle to another is considered one move. So if you had an attuning counter in the 1 circle and wanted to move it to the 12 circle that would take two moves. One move to go to the 7 circle and then another to go to the 12 circle.

At the first hour of each day you may make one move, unless your character is a Brightling in which case you may make two moves. Any time your character meditates upon one of the Mystic Forces to gain Force Knowledge he may spend 2 Light Points instead of 1 Light Point in order to move one attuning counter to an adjacent circle. The Universal Talent "Heightened Senses" allows you to make an extra move at the first hour of each day. Also, once a day, at any time you wish you can spend 5 Light Points in order to move one attuning counter.

All but one of the power combination patterns require you to have six attuning counters- it only requires five. If you have all six attuning counters and want your character to attune to the pattern that requires only five attuning counters you must first remove one of the attuning counters. Removing an attuning counter from your Mystical Attuning Sheet in this manner is considered one move, just as if you had moved it to an adjacent circle. Replacing a removed attuning counter is also considered one move. (There are circumstances that will require you to remove an attuning counter from you Mystical Attuning Sheet that does not count as a move. Such circumstances include using Mystical Attuning Points to remove Fatigue Points, recover damage, or regain Force Energy or by using a Universal Talent that requires the expenditure of a Mystical Attuning Point.)

At the first hour of each day every character must re-attune. At this point all expended Mystical Attuning Points are regained and all attuning counters that may have been removed from the Mystical Attuning Sheets are replaced. Every player must now roll 1D12 for each attuning counter

that they have on their Mystical Attuning Sheet and place them accordingly. All non-Brightling characters may also move one attuning counter at this time. Brightling characters may move two attuning counters (or the same one twice if they wish).

Mystical Attuning Bonuses

Generally speaking, the closer that you can concentrate your attuning counters to the inner circle (circle 12) the more powerful the bonuses that your character will receive, and depending upon the number of attuning counters that you have, placing your attuning counters in the 12 circle may be the only way to get bonuses.

For each attuning counter that you have in the center circle you may add +1 point to the result of any Sixth Sense/Performance Test that your character makes. However, once you get all six attuning counters in the center circle this is an actual power combination and you will get the bonuses described for that power combination instead of a +6 point bonus for having six attuning counters in the center circle.

Once you have five or six attuning counters your character is capable of attuning his *Gift* into one of the four power combinations. On the bottom of the Mystical Attuning Sheet you will see four miniature representations of the twelve circles that represents your characters *Gift*. The blackened circles represent where the attuning counters are and thus the necessary pattern of the attuning counters in order to obtain the power combination. The bonuses rendered from having attuning counters in the center circle or being attuned into a power combination only remain as long as the attuning counters remain in the center circle or in the power combination.

Power Combination #1

If you have all six attuning counters in circle 12 your character receives a +10 point bonus to any Sixth Sense/Performance Test that he makes. In addition his Life Force is doubled (Force Failure and Injury Rating are increased accordingly) as long as this power combination is maintained.

Power Combination #2

If you have an attuning counter in circles 7, 8, 9, 10 ,11, and 12 your character will automatically regain 1D20 +10 points of Force Energy per hour (not to exceed his Total Force Energy). In addition your character may totally disregard the Novice Factor as long as this power combination is maintained.

Power Combination #3

If you have an attuning counter in circles 7, 8, 9, 10, and 11 any damage from a purely mystical source that your character receives is cut in half (round down). Some examples of damage from pure mystical sources would be the Force-effects "Pain", "Lie Detection", "Real Touch", and "Freeze Animate", or damage from Force Burn or essence combat.

The GM has the final say as to whether a particular source of damage is considered to be purely mystical or not.

Power Combination #4

If you have an attuning counter in circles 1, 2, 3, 4, 5, and 6 your character receives a 1D8 +4 point bonus to every Mystical Defense that he sets.

ENCHANTMENTS

Enchantments are basically objects that have magical properties. Only a rare type of Shinkai known as Enchanters have the ability to create enchantments. The process of enchanting is basically an advanced form of focused conjuring that only Enchanters are capable of performing. They actually take one or more of the Mystic Forces and infuse them into the object to be enchanted.

The Enchanters of today are much more limited in the effects that the enchantments that they can make are capable of. The Enchanters that existed before the temporary extinction of Shinkai did not seem to have such limitations to the enchantments that they could create. The effects of their enchantments were much more diverse and powerful than the enchantments created by todays Enchanters. Many of these enchantments, referred to as relics, are still being discovered today. Some believe that with time the knowledge to create such powerful enchantments will once again return.

The details and limitations of creating enchantments will not be discussed in this Section because another Section of this rulebook has been dedicated for just that purpose. See the following "ENCHANTING" Section for details on enchantments.

NATURAL MAGIC

Because the Mystic Forces are the driving forces behind any type of magic and because they encompass all things it is inevitable that they will have an effect on their surroundings. Any type of mystical anomaly or phenomenon that is not caused by the manipulation of the Mystic Forces by Shinkai or other mystically gifted beings is referred to as natural magic.

Natural magic can take on many different forms. It could be in the form of Light or Shadow entities or perhaps objects or entire landscapes that become enchanted without the influence of Shinkai. It may be a Force surge or Force drain, or any other mystical phenomenon that occurs naturally.

For a complete description of many of the different mystical phenomenon that can occur as a result of natural magic refer to "Mystical Phenomenon" in the "ORYATHAR" Section.

ENCHANTING

"It is felt by some that an inherent danger lies in placing too much trust into magic and enchantments. Though this may be true to some extent, I have seen too many battles won due solely to the presence of powerful enchantments. Let us not forget that it was an enchantment that held the Shadow-kin at bay for three hundred sixty-two years."

Lieutenant Stapten

Some Shinkai are born with the ability to place enchantments upon inanimate items. Only ten percent of Shinkai are capable of enchanting. Because of the rarity of this gift, Shinkai who can enchant are greatly sought after. The Defenders of the Light as well as the King's Guard greatly value such Shinkai, and have been known to pay them great prices for rendering their services. Unfortunately there are some that serve the Shadow who also have the ability to enchant. Some of the most devastating battles ever fought were influenced by the use of enchanted items and weapons.

The ability to create enchantments, or magical items, still exists in the Shinkai today. However, the strength and range of abilities of the enchantments created by today's Shinkai are not comparable to the enchanted items created by the first generations of Shinkai. Battles were swayed and the outcome often totally determined by the possession, or lack of possession, of enchantments.

Though enchanted items are unquestionably powerful and beneficial, they should be used with caution. Not all enchanted items are created to have helpful properties, Korgathool are as capable of Shinkai in the are of creating enchantments. Also there is very often an inherent danger in having more than one enchanted item within close proximity of one another.

These issues and much more will be discussed within this Section. Read carefully and study well, for you never know when the fate of your character's comrades or perhaps all of Oryathar may be affected by an enchantment that your own character has created.

THE TESTING

Although you as a player know that your character is is an Enchanter, your character doesn't know until someone informs him of the fact or until he is able to find out on his own. It's the GM's choice as to whether or not new characters already know whether or not they are Enchanters.

As with discovering whether or not a Shinkai is Dragonknight, the Defenders of the Light have developed an accurate method for testing Shinkai to determine whether or not they are an Enchanter. The process requires that someone uses focused conjuring to direct any one of the Mystic Forces into the head of the Shinkai to be tested. A minimum of 20 points of Force Energy must be expended at this time in order for the testing to work properly. If the Shinkai being tested is Dragonknight their eyes will rage with a glow to match the color of the Mystic Force being focused into them.

Even though your character may have the potential to enchant, he must first control one or more of the Mystic Forces before he can begin enchanting. The exact effect of the enchantment determines which of the Mystic Forces must be controlled in order to create it. This is described in detail later in this Section.

Very little to nothing is written on the subject of enchanting because the exact way that it is performed varies so widely from Shinkai to Shinkai. The Shinkai that have been questioned about this gift have found it extremely difficult to describe the way in which they enchant, though one common description that all Enchanters do give is that they infuse the Mystic Forces into the item to be enchanted until they actually become part of the item. Perhaps the Light has created the gift of enchanting to be a sacred thing only understandable to those with the gift.

Though Enchanter characters do have the ability to enchant items, the enchantments that they can create are not nearly as powerful or versatile as the enchantments created by the Shinkai of old, that is the Shinkai that existed prior to the temporary extinction of all Shinkai immediately following the War of Betrayal. The enchantments created by those Shinkai are now referred to as "relics". The enchantments created by the Shinkai of today are called "modern enchantments" and only have the ability to affect Force-effects.

The relics created by the Shinkai of old had the ability to affect and alter much more than just Force-effects. There appears to have been no limit as to what a relic could do. The enchantments that the Enchanters today are capable of creating, "modern enchantments", are only able to modify the effects of Force-effects in a limited number of ways. For this reason, as well as the fact that relics can no longer be created, relics are considered to be much more powerful and are much more expensive than modern enchantments.

Because of the potential danger that enchantments can create if used improperly or if fallen into the wrong hands, detailed records are kept on every enchanted item that the King's Guard or Defenders of the Light come across. Such details include the enchantments effects, Class, Enchantment Rating, the Mystic Forces infused into it, and who created the enchantment. Whenever any Shinkai creates a new enchantment they are required by the laws of the Ellabrian Realms to report to a King's Guard post or a Defender of the Light fort city with the enchantment so that the necessary information about the enchantment can be recorded. Further, if the enchantment to be created will have an Enchantment Rating of Complex or Highly Complex, or if it will likely be rated as Class Three or Four then permission to create the enchantment must be granted by an officer of the King's Guard or Defenders of the Light. Failure to report the creation of an enchantment within one block of creating it or failing to get permission to create an enchantment, when necessary, may result in steep fines and or imprisonment.

Trial & Error

Characters with the ability to enchant must learn how to perfect their gift through trial and error. The first several attempts at enchanting an object are very likely to fail. Time and patience is needed to master the art of enchanting.

Use the following "ENCHANTMENT SUCCESS" table to determine what base percent chance of success that your character has for successfully creating an enchantment of any Enchantment Rating depending on the number of times that he has attempted an enchantment of that Rating.

ENCHANTMENT SUCCESS					
# of Tries	Very Simple	Simple	Average	Complex	Highly Complex
1st	30%	40%	50%	60%	70%
2nd	50%	60%	70%	80%	90%
3rd	70%	80%	90%	100%	100%
4th	90%	100%	100%	100%	100%
Beyond	100%	100%	100%	100%	100%

Under the "# of Tries" column find what number attempt that this will make for your character trying this Enchantment Rating of enchantment. Now move across to the column that matches the Enchantment Rating of the enchantment that your character is attempting. This is the percent chance of successfully creating the enchantment.

For example, if this is your character's second attempt at creating an Average enchantment you will go down to 2nd under the "# of Tries" column and then move across to the column labeled " Average". This shows that there is a seventy percent chance of successfully creating the enchantment on this attempt. After meeting all of the necessary requirements and expenditures for the particular enchantment that your character is attempting to create you will roll the percentile dice. If you roll a result of 70 or under your character has successfully created the enchantment and has mastered Average enchantments. Further Average enchantments that your character creates will automatically be successful.

There are nine major categories that apply to enchanting. They are Enchantment Rating, Class, Required Forces, Enchanting Strength, Force Energy, Light Points, Time, Properties, and Level of Mastery. Each of these categories will now be explained in detail.

Enchantment Rating

The Enchantment Rating is a measure of the complexity of an enchantment. There are five different Enchantment Ratings that an enchantment may be classified under. They are "Very Simple", "Simple", "Average", "Complex", and "Highly Complex".

The GM decides what Enchantment Rating that a given enchantment will be classified as. This is a fairly generalized method of categorizing enchantments and is likely to vary widely from GM to GM. Ultimately it is a matter of opinion as to what rating an enchantment should be classified as, though the guidelines and examples given later in this section should greatly aide in the process.

The Enchantment Rating of an enchantment determines the amount of Light Points, Force energy, and Enchanting Strength that it will take to create the enchantment.

Class

The Class to which an enchantment is assigned is similar to its Enchantment Rating except the Class refers to the enchantments potential for being dangerous or threatening whereas Enchantment Rating refers to the complexity of the enchantment itself. The Class to which an enchantment is assigned does not affect the difficulty of creating the enchantment in any way. Distinguishing an enchantment's Class is simply a role-playing aide as well as a way to assist in determining the coin value of an enchantment.

There are four different Classes that an enchantment can be categorized under. They are simply referred to as Class One, Class Two, Class Three, and Class Four.

The more dangerous or higher potential for harm or misuse that an enchantment has, the higher its Class. Class One and Two enchantments can be purchased by commoners, but Class Three and Four enchantments can only be purchased by members of the King's Guard, Defenders of the Light, or those approved by officials of either of these two organizations.

Class One and Two enchantments are those that have little to no harmful, or easily abused properties, such as a waterskin that keeps the water within it cool. Class Three enchantments often have dangerous properties, such as a battle-axe that erupts into a fiery glow that greatly increases the attacks made with it or a ring that doubles the damage of "Lightning". Class Four enchantments are normally extremely dangerous or have very dangerous or harmful potential, such as a bow that increases the Damage Yield of arrows shot from it by 6 Levels or a pendant that increases the damage from "Concussion Sphere" by three times.

If the enchantment has properties that are potentially dangerous or harmful, or if by falling into the wrong hands the enchanted item could prove to be a serious threat it should be classified as a Class Three or Four enchantment.

The GM decides what Class that a given enchantment will be classified under. As with determining Enchantment Rating this is a fairly generalized method of categorizing enchantments and is subject to vary widely from GM to GM. Ultimately it is a matter of opinion as to what Class an enchantment should be classified as. As usual the GM's word is final.

Required Forces

This is a list of which of the Mystic Forces that must be controlled and infused into the item in order to create the desired enchantment. Depending upon the exact nature of the enchantment different Mystic Forces will be required in order to complete the enchanting process. The Shinkai must know focused conjuring in order to be able to infuse the Mystic Forces into an object.

As a general rule of thumb if an enchantment adds speed to an attack or to an ability, such as adding bonuses to a character's attack or Physical Defense, or giving bonuses to a weapon's attack, the enchantment will require *Air*. If an enchantment displays any properties of heat or light it should require *Fire*. If an enchantment adds strength to a weapon or being in the form of increased damage, Damage Yield, or Destroyed Rating, then it should require *Land*. If an enchantment has any cooling properties or produces or affects any water-based elements, it should contain *Water*. Many of the above examples only apply to relics.

A single enchantment may contain several or even all five of the Mystic Forces.

As with determining Enchantment Rating, it is ultimately a matter of opinion as to which of the Mystic Forces any given enchantment will require, and as with any rule interpretation the GM has the final say in the matter. The following examples offer some guidelines as to which of the Mystic Forces should be used in an enchantment based on the effects of the enchantment.

Air

Relic

Increased Physical Defense, increased range of ranged weapons, increase to Agility, add bonuses to the attacks of weapons

Modern Enchantment

Increased range of Force-effects (ex. "Wind Missile", "Fireball"), increased intensity of *Air*-based Force-effects (ex. "Summon Wind")

Fire

Relic

Increase the Damage Yield of weapons, produce fire on

items (ex. A sword that erupts into flames), increase an items resistance to heat

Modern Enchantment

Increase the intensity, effectiveness, or Damage Yield of *Fire*-based Force-effects, decrease the intensity, effectiveness, or Damage Yield of ice or *Water*-based Force-effects

Land

Relic

Increase the Damage Yield of weapons, increase the Destroyed Rating of armor and weapons

Modern Enchantment

Increase the effectiveness of *Land*-based Force-effects (ex. the Destroyed Rating of "Wall of Land")

Spirit

Relic

Increased Life Force, countless other effects

Modern Enchantment

Increase the effectiveness or range of *Spirit*-based Force-effects

Water

Relic

Increased Agility, add bonuses to the attacks of weapons

Modern Enchantment

Increase the effectiveness of *Water*-based Force-effects, decrease the intensity, effectiveness, or Damage Yield of *Fire*-based Force-effects

Enchanting Strength

This is the amount of Enchanting Strength that must be expended at the end of enchanting process in order to finalize and activate the enchantment. If the required amount of Enchanting Strength is not spent, the enchantment automatically fails and has no effects at all. The Light Points and Force Energy are simply wasted.

On the back of Enchanter Character Sheets is a place to record Total and Current Enchanting Strength. Only Enchanter character's have Enchanting Strength.

For each 50 points of Total Force Energy that your character has he will have 1 Total Enchanting Strength. So a character with a Total Force Energy of 200 would have an Enchanting Strength value of 4. If a character has a Total Force Energy of 375 he would have an Enchanting Strength value of 7. As with Light Points, your character will only spend Enchanting Strength from his Current Enchanting Strength not his Total Enchanting Strength. Your character's Total Enchanting Strength will only increase (as your character increases his Total Force Energy), but his Current Enchanting Strength will go up and down as he expends Enchanting Strength to create enchantments and then regains it.

Enchanting Strength is regained through meditation. In order for a character to regain Enchanting Strength he must have his Current Force Energy at its maximum and then meditate for half an hour (completely uninterrupted) while expending 5 Light Points. This will recover 1 point of Enchanting Strength. This type of meditation does not give the character any type of Force Knowledge, it is only for the regaining of Enchanting Strength.

Force Energy

This is the total amount of Force Energy that must be expended in order to create the enchantment.

Force Energy is expended every Turn throughout the entire enchantment process at a rate of 1 point of Force Energy per Turn per Mystic Force being infused into the enchantment. So, the Force Energy expenditure of an enchantment that only requires 1 of the Mystic Forces will proceed at a rate of 1 point of Force Energy per Turn. An enchantment that requires 2 of the Mystic Forces will proceed at a rate of 2 points of Force Energy per Turn and so on. So the more Mystic Forces that are used to create an enchantment the faster the required Force Energy can be met.

Light Points

This is a range of the number of Light Points that must be spent in order to place the given enchantment. These Light Points must be spent at the beginning of the enchanting process.

The exact amount of Light Points that the enchantment will require is left up to the GM. If the GM feels that the enchantment barely qualifies for the Enchantment Rating that it will fall under, he may wish to assign the minimum Light Point cost for an enchantment of that Enchantment Rating. If the enchantment is pushing the upper borders of a particular Enchantment Rating, the GM may wish to assign the maximum Light Point cost for an enchantment of that Enchantment Rating.

Customizing an enchantment will usually cost more Light Points than the same enchantment would have cost had it not been customized. Customized means that the enchantment works only within specified parameters. For example, it may only work for you or for a certain type of ruling-race. Or maybe it will only work if a specific verbal command is given etc.

If the GM determines that an enchantment will cost more than 30 Light Points (only applies to Highly Complex) the creator of the enchantment will lose 1 point from their Life Force for each Light Point above 30 that the enchantment costs. This is due to the extremely powerful nature of the enchantment. It actually takes the power of a Shinkai's actual essence, and consequently their *Gift*, in order to create enchanted items of this magnitude.

These lost points of Life Force are permanently removed, though you can of course later increase your Life Force as

normal.

The following "ENCHANTMENT COST" table lists the normal range of Light Points that an enchantment of any given rating should cost. The GM has the final say as to the exact amount of Light Points that an enchantment will cost. This is purely up to the GM's discretion, though he should strive to be fair and consistent.

ENCHANTMENT COST				
Rating	Light Points	Force Energy	Enchanting Strength	Time
Very Simple	4 - 8	50	1	10-50 Turns
Simple	8.5 - 12	100	2	20-100 Turns
Average	12.5 - 16	150	3	30-150 Turns
Complex	16.5 - 20	200	4	40-200 Turns
Highly Complex	20.5 - up	250	5	50-250 Turns

Time

This is the amount of time required to place the enchantment. This time must be spent in uninterrupted meditation. Being interrupted for even a second will disrupt the entire enchanting process. Your character must then start all over. The Light Points and Force Energy are simply wasted.

Referring to the "ENCHANTMENT COST" table under the Time column you will see that the amount of time required to create any given Rating of enchantment is listed as a range. The number before the hyphen is the number of Turns to create the enchantment if all five of the Mystic Forces are contained within the enchantment. The number to the right of the hyphen is the number of Turns to create the enchantment if only one of Mystic Forces is contained within the enchantment.

To calculate the exact number of Turns that it will take to complete any enchantment simply divide the required Force Energy for that enchantment by the number of Mystic Forces to be contained within the enchantment (round up).

So as you can see, the more of the Mystic Forces that are used to create an enchantment the faster the enchantment can be completed.

Properties

This is a detailed explanation of how the enchantment works and exactly what it does.

One property that is universal to all enchantments is that the enchanting process gives the item that is enchanted a set Mystical Defense. The exact value of the Mystical Defense depends upon the Rating of the enchantment. "Very Simple" enchantments have a Mystical Defense of 5 and each successive Rating has an additional 5. So a "Simple" has a Mystical Defense of 10, an "Average" has 15, a "Complex" has 20, and a "Highly Complex" has 25. This Mystical Defense given through the enchanting process is in addition to any Mystical Defense that the item may already have. Green-steel has a natural Mystical Defense of 5 so enchant-ing it with a Highly Complex enchantment would yield an item with a set Mystical Defense of 30.

Another common property among all enchantments, with the exception of some relics, is that their abilities are only given to the one touching them (thin clothing or armor can be in between the enchanted item and the user without hindering its abilities). So an amulet that has been enchanted to increase the radius that the Force-effect "Ground Blast" will affect would only grant this ability to the one wearing it, not all Shinkai near it.

If two or more Shinkai are touching an enchanted item and attempt to use its abilities at the exact same time an adverse reaction will immediately occur (roll 1D4 and consult the "ADVERSE REACTION" table on page 160 to see the result of the reaction.

It is not uncommon for Shinkai to come across enchantments that were created by someone else. In order to learn the details of the properties of an enchantment the Shinkai Enchanter must hold the enchanted item and allow theirself to sense the Mystic Forces within the item. This requires deep meditation and intense focus. It takes approximately one hour of meditation for a Shinkai Enchanter to gain knowledge of one detailed effect or property of a single enchantment. Though the Force-effect "Magical Detection" can be used to determine the basic nature and Enchantment Rating of the enchantment, it can not give your character specific details.

For example, a Shinkai Enchanter uses "Magical Detection" to learn that a ring has two "Complex" enchantments upon it and that one of the enchantments has to do with a being's Life Force and the other effects ruling-race's vision. The Enchanter now decides to study the ring to learn details of its properties. After one hour of deep meditative study the Enchanter learns that the ring will instantly ressurect the wearer at the moment of their death. Another hour of studying the ring reveals that the ressurecting properties of the ring has limited uses (it will ressurect three times before losing that ability). Another hour of studying reveals that the ring increases the wearer's vision by three times the normal range.

It may take several hours to learn all of the details of a single enchantment, but it is well worth the time. No one wants to use an enchanted item that could have hidden dangerous properties and its always handy to know the limitations of an enchanted item that you plan to use.

Level of Mastery

This refers to how skilled a Shinkai is at the art of enchanting. The Level of Mastery is simply the highest Enchantment Rating that the Shinkai has mastered (performed successfully at least once). So if your character has successfully performed an "Average" enchantment, his Level of Mastery is Average.

MODERN ENCHANTMENTS

Modern enchantments are enchantments that the Shinkai of today, the player characters, are capable of creating. A single modern enchantment can only modify one of the effects of a single Force-effect, and only in one of five ways. Your character must first know a Force-effect before he can create an enchantment that affects it. Modern enchantments can not be used to modify runes.

Below is a list of the five ways that a modern enchantment can modify a Force-effect.

1. To increase or decrease the Force-effect's range.

For example, the enchantment could be a ring that increases the range of "Fireball" from 900 feet to 2,700 feet.

Your character can increase ranges listed as "Touch", but only by a small degree. As a "Very Simple" enchantment you could increase the range of a Force-effect from touch up to one foot. A "Simple" enchantment could increase the range of touch up to two feet. An "Average" enchantment up to three feet, "Complex" enchantment up to four feet, and a "Highly Complex" enchantment up to five feet.

Force-effects that previously required touch in order to be used that have their range increased by an enchantment should still require your character to have line of sight or at least be able to pin-point the target's location in order to use it.

2. To increase or decrease the damage yielded by the Force-effect.

For example, the enchantment could be an amulet that increases the Damage Yield of "Pain" by +12 points.

3. To increase the duration of the Force-effect (can only increase existing durations not add a duration to a Force-effect that has instant effects or must be maintained to continue).

For example, the enchantment might be a staff that causes "Breath of Life" to last for 2 hours instead of 1 hour.

4. To increase or decrease the result of the Sixth Sense/Performance Test made to use the Force-effect (this is normally the attack value).

For example, the enchantment could be a helm that gives its wearer a +5 point bonus to their attack Test (Sixth Sense/Performance Test) with "Lightning".

5. To increase or decrease the effectiveness of the Force-effect (other than range, damage, or attack). This includes any bonuses or penalties given by the Force-effect and the Difficulty Values of Tests that may be required to avoid the effects of the Force-effect. You can't add new abilities to a Force-effect, only increase or decrease existing properties or abilities.

For example, the enchantment could be a gauntlet that allows water created by the Force-effect "Healing Water" to heal 3D10 +10 points of damage instead of just 3D10.

Here are some guidelines to help in determining what Enchantment Rating that a particular enchantment should fall under. Keep in mind, however, that these are just guidelines. There are countless other possibilities for enchantments of any given Enchantment Rating. The exact effects of the enchantment, as well as its Enchantment Rating, is up to the GM and the player whose character is creating the enchantment.

The GM's word is final in the determining of an enchantment's Enchantment Rating, Light Point cost, Class, and Required Forces.

The following examples are given with modern enchantments in mind, however they may used as guidelines for relics as well.

Very Simple

Very Simple enchantments can generally add up to +2 points to a Force-effect's attack or damage. A Very Simple enchantment could also increase a Force-effect's range, effectiveness, or duration by as much as twenty five percent.

Simple

Simple enchantments can generally add up to +4 points to a Force-effect's attack or damage. A Simple enchantment could also increase a Force-effect's range, effectiveness, or duration by as much as fifty percent.

Average

Average enchantments can generally add up to +8 points to a Force-effect's attack or damage. An Average enchantment could also increase a Force-effect's range, effectiveness, or duration by as much as seventy five percent.

Complex

Complex enchantments can generally add up to +12 points to a Force-effect's attack or damage (or possibly double the results). A Complex enchantment could also double a Force-effect's range or effectiveness.

Highly Complex

Highly Complex enchantments can generally add up to +20 points to a Force-effect's attack or damage (or possibly triple the results). A Highly Complex enchantment could also increase a Force-effect's range, effectiveness, duration, or the Difficulty Value of Tests needed to resist the effects of the Force-effect by as much as three times.

Occasionally players will want to create an enchantment that is simply too powerful or would overthrow the balance of the game. The GM reserves the right to disallow the creation of any enchantment that he feels it is too powerful (the concept of exactly how to create the enchantment eludes your character).

RELICS

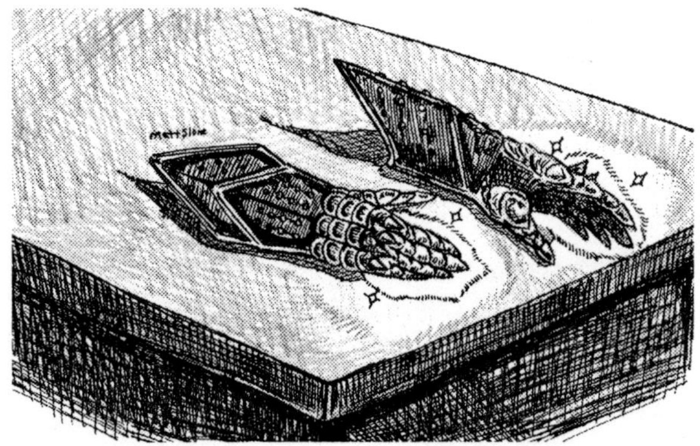

Relics are powerful and rare enchantments that were created by the Shinkai that lived before and during the War of Betrayal. No known Shinkai of today possesses the ability or knowledge of how to create relics. Some scholars believe that Shinkai today have the potential to create relics but simply lack the understanding of how to do it, and that with time the lost art will once again be relearned. Many Enchanters of today spend a great amount of their time trying to uncover and relearn the secrets of creating relics. The unlimited abilities and power of relics makes them a very valuable resource in the fight against the Shadow.

Relics can not be created by the player characters, but the GM may wish to add them into an adventure for the characters to find or buy.

Here are some examples of relics from each of the different Enchantment Ratings. The GM can use this as a guideline for placing relic enchantments into an adventure, or creating new ones.

Very Simple

A dagger handle that warms slightly when touched, an amulet that promotes feelings of confidence in the wearer, or a pair of boots that will never hurt your feet.

Simple

A waterskin that always keeps the water in it cool, a sword that does an additional +4 points of damage (or +4 points to its attacks), or a buckler that gives the wearer a +3 to their Physical (or perhaps Mystical) Defense.

Average

A sword that has an additional 4 Levels added to its Damage Yield, a steel chest and back guard that has double the normal Destroyed Rating, or a ring that gives the wearer a 1D4 +4 bonus to their Physical (or perhaps Mystical) Defense.

Complex

An amulet that increases the Damage Yield of a certain Force-effect by several Levels, a battle-axe whose blade erupts into a fiery glow on command the result of which increases attacks made with it by +11, or a helmet that allows the wearer to recover damage more easily by giving them an additional Recovery Test per day.

Highly Complex

A spear that will teleport itself back to its owners hand upon mental command, a bow that increases the Damage Yield of all arrows shot out of it by 6 Levels, or an item that allows the holder to conjure Force-effects with only expending half of the normally required Force Energy.

Another example of a Highly Complex relic that is commonly used among the Defenders of the Light and the King's Guard to question and simultaneously pass judgement on Shadow-sworn is an enchantment known as the "Judgement Stone". There are approximately ten of these relics known to exist on Oryathar. They look like smooth round stones that are dark brown in color with a light blend of red streaks throughout. Any living being that willfully speaks or otherwise tells a lie while touching a judgement stone will fall dead immediately.

Five of the judgement stones are in the hands of various Defenders of the Light across Oryathar, two are in King Lorsprit's possession, and three are lost.

Depending upon the exact effects of an enchantment, it will be classified into one of the five following Enchantment Ratings: Very Simple, Simple, Average, Complex, or Highly Complex. The GM will decide what Enchantment Rating that a particular enchantment will fall under.

A single object may have multiple enchantments placed upon it, but each single effect that is placed upon an item is considered to be a separate enchantment. You must be careful, however, not to place two separate enchantments upon the same item that have the exact same combination of Mystic Forces within them as this will create what is called conflicting enchantments. Conflicting enchantments are discussed later in this Section.

Enchantments can only be placed upon inanimate objects.

In addition, the object to be enchanted can not have a Bulk Value higher than 5.

When a Shinkai attempts to place an enchantment upon an item he must be very careful not to allow the object that is being enchanted to come in contact with another object during the enchanting process. The reason for this is because any objects that are touching an item during its enchantment process are considered to be part of the object as far as the enchantment is concerned. If two objects are enchanted as one and then one of the objects is separated from the other the enchantment is broken and ceases to work. This is called a breach in the Law of Containment.

LAW OF CONTAINMENT

The Law of Containment states, "An enchantment will cease to function as designed and be considered broken if the enchanted item's form significantly changes in shape or mass."

In simple language, if you bash, smash, break, melt, or drastically alter the form of the enchanted item, any enchantments that have been placed upon it will cease to function. This is called a breach in the Law of Containment.

An enchantment that ceases to function because of a breach in the Law of Containment, as described above, is considered *broken*. If the enchanted item can be restored to its original form (mass, shape, etc.) within a number of days equal to the Total Force Energy of the creator of the enchantment (at the time that he or she created it), it will return to normal and function as it did before it was broken; it is no longer considered broken.

If an enchantment remains broken longer than a number of days equal to the Total Force Energy of the creator of the enchantment (at the time that he or she created it), it is considered dead. A dead enchantment simply ceases to exist and no longer has any effects of any kind (it's gone). A dead enchantment can not be restored.

Here are some examples of broken enchantments.

Goldwyn has a ring that has been enchanted to give him bonuses to his attacks with the Force-effect "Fire Lightning". While scaling a gate Goldwyn snags his ring and it breaks. Its form is broken (altered) and the enchantment placed upon it is also considered broken and thus no longer works. Goldwyn's Total Force Energy was 230 at the time that he created the enchantment on the ring. If he can have the ring repaired so that it is returned to its original shape within 230 days the enchantment will be restored and work again. If not, the enchantment will die and be completely erased.

In many instances it may be impossible to restore the enchanted item to its original form. Say that the ring in the previous example was broken into several small fragments and only some of the fragments were recovered. Even if Goldwyn were to have a jeweler repair the ring with identical materials, it still wouldn't restore the enchantment. The ring would contain materials that it didn't when the enchantment was placed upon it, and wouldn't have enough of the original materials. For these reasons it would be considered a breach of the Law of Containment and remain broken.

Larstrom holds two coins in his hand and proceeds to place an enchantment upon them. After the enchantment has been successfully placed Larstrom separates the two coins. The enchantment is now broken and will not work unless the two coins are brought back together in the same position that they were when the enchantment was placed upon them.

If an object that is already in the process of being enchanted comes in contact with another object, for even one second, the enchantment is immediately neutralized. Force Energy and Light Points are wasted and you must start over. Also, if two objects are touching and are being enchanted as one, the enchanting process will immediately fail and the enchantment will be neutralized if the two objects significantly shift of change position or come out of contact with each other during the enchanting process.

Once an item is enchanted it is considered to be magical. The effects that an enchantment can have are nearly limitless, however modern enchantments are much more limited in what they are capable of than are relics.

In order to enchant an item, the Shinkai must physically touch the item for the entire duration of the enchanting process while using focused conjuring to infuse the required Mystic Forces into the item.

During the enchanting process the Shinkai enters into a deep meditation. If the Shinkai is interrupted for even 1 Turn while attempting to enchant an item, the enchantment is neutralized and must be started over. The Force Energy, Light Points, and Enchanting Strength required to create the enchantment are simply wasted.

The entire enchanting process must be performed in one continual enchanting session. Your character can not work on the enchantment for a few minutes here and a few minutes there to meet the required enchanting time.

The "ENCHANTMENT COST" table on page 155 shows the Light Point cost, required Force Energy, required Enchanting Strength, and time necessary for creating enchantments from each of the five Enchantment Ratings.

Sam wants to enchant one of his bracers to increase the effectiveness of "Spirit Shield" so that it increases his Mystical Defense by 10 instead of 7. The GM decides that this will be a "Simple" enchantment and will cost 10 Light

Points. And since "Spirit Shield" contains Air, Fire, and Spirit the GM decides that the enchantment that Sam is creating will also require Air, Fire, and Spirit. Since the effects of this enchantment are not of an aggressive or dangerous nature, but rather for defensive purposes the GM decides that this enchantment will be considered a Class Two enchantment.

Sam looks at the "ENCHANTMENT COST" table and finds the column titled "Simple" and sees that it will require the expenditure of 100 points of Force Energy as well as 2 points of Enchanting Strength to create this enchantment. Sam now takes the required Force Energy of 100 and divides it by the number of Mystic Forces to be contained within the enchantment (3) for a result of 33.3 which is rounded up to 34. It will take Sam 34 Turns to place this enchantment upon his bracer.

The first few times that your character tries to create an enchantment of any Enchantment Rating there is a chance that it will not work. The "ENCHANTMENT SUCCESS" table on page 152 shows the chance of success for enchanting an item based upon the Rating of the enchantment and the number of times that you have attempted an enchantment of that Enchantment Rating. Failing to create an enchantment will never result in a possible adverse reaction. Adverse reactions are only the result of attempting to alter an existing enchantment that was created by someone other than yourself.

After your character has met all of the requirements and expenditures for the enchantment you must roll the percentile dice. If you roll a value equal to or lower than the percent chance of success, your character has successfully created the enchantment. If you roll a value greater than the percent chance of success, the enchantment has completely failed. Your character must start from scratch and try again, if he so chooses.

Once your character has successfully performed an enchantment of a given Enchantment Rating, he has mastered it and may perform any further enchantments of that Enchantment Rating without chance of failure.

Sam has spent 34 Turns in deep meditation in an attempt to place a "Simple" enchantment upon one of his bracers. He has spent the necessary 10 Light Points that the GM determined that this particular enchantment will cost as well as the 100 points of Force Energy and 2 points of Enchanting Strength.

Because this is Sam's first attempt at a "Simple" enchantment, there is only a thirty percent chance that it will be successful. Sam rolls a 15 on the percentile die. He has successfully placed the enchantment upon the bracer. Had he rolled higher than 30, the enchantment would have failed. The Light Points, Force Energy, and Enchanting Strength would have been wasted and he would have to start over

again, but this time with a fifty percent chance of success (because it would be his second attempt at a "Simple" enchantment).

Enchanting is a very complicated process and requires practice in order to master the art. When your character performs his first enchantment, he must start with a "Very Simple" enchantment and work his way up to the more difficult Enchantment Ratings. Your character can not create a "Simple" enchantment until he has successfully created a "Very Simple" enchantment, or an "Average" enchantment until he has successfully created a "Simple" enchantment, and so on.

A character must control and be able to focus conjure different Mystic Forces for different types of enchantments. Which Mystic Forces are necessary for an enchantment depends upon the nature of the enchantment. A sword that is to be enchanted so that it receives bonuses to its Damage Yield should require your character to control either *Fire*, or *Land*. A bracer that increases the range of "Wind Missile" should require your character to control *Air*. Exactly which Mystic Forces are required for any particular enchantment is left to the GM's discretion.

Once an enchantment is created its effects are permanent. The enchantment can not be altered to either increase or decrease its effects. The only way that it can be altered is if it is completely disenchanted.

DISENCHANTING

Just as an item can be enchanted, it can also be disenchanted. Occasionally, for whatever reasons, characters may want to disenchant enchantments that they, or someone else, have created. In order to disenchant an enchantment the Shinkai wishing to remove the enchantment must have mastered (performed successfully at least once) the same Rating of enchantment. So a character that wishes to disenchant a shield with an "Average" enchantment upon it must have mastered "Average" enchantments himself. Also, the Shinkai wishing to disenchant an item must control all of the Mystic Forces that are contained within the enchantment to be disenchanted.

The process for disenchanting an item is essentially the same as for enchanting it, with the following exceptions.

Disenchanting does not require Light Point or Enchanting Strength expenditure. If the enchantment to be disenchanted is one that your character created himself, it requires one half the Force Energy (round down) to disenchant it as it took to create it. If the enchantment was placed by someone else, it will require twice the amount of Force Energy (round up) to disenchant it as it would for you to create it.

As with enchanting an item disenchanting requires deep meditation and concentration and requires your character to

physically touch the item to be disenchanted.

Difficulty of Disenchanting

If your character is the one who created the enchantment that he wants to disenchant disenchanting success is automatic. If the enchantment was created by someone else then there is only a percent chance that the enchantment will be disenchanted.

The following "DISENCHANTING" table gives the base percent chance of disenchanting an enchantment of any given Enchantment Rating that was created by someone other than your character.

DISENCHANTING	
Enchantment Rating	**Base Chance of Success**
Very Simple	70 %
Simple	60 %
Average	50 %
Complex	40 %
Highly Complex	30 %

To find out whether or not your character successfully disenchanted an enchantment first find its Rating in the left column of the "DISENCHANTING" table. Across from the Enchantment Rating you will find the base percent chance of disenchanting an enchantment of that Rating. You may add 2 percent the base percent chance of success for each Level of Sixth Sense that your character has and for each point of technique that he has in the Mystic Forces contained within the enchantment to be disenchanted.

Now roll the percentile die. If you roll a value equal to or lower than the percent chance of success, your character has successfully disenchanted the enchantment. If you roll a value greater than the percent chance of success, the disenchanting attempt has completely failed and may possibly cause an adverse reaction.

To determine whether or not a failed disenchanting attempt will cause an adverse reaction simply roll the percentile dice (this is done after the last of the Force Energy for the disenchanting has been expended. On a result of 20 or less an adverse reaction has occurred. Immediately roll 1D4 and consult the following "ADVERSE REACTION" table to find the result of the reaction.

ADVERSE REACTION	
Die Result	**Effect**
1	Energy surge
2	Neutralized
3	External effect
4	Thunder clap/blinding flash

Energy Surge

An energy surge is a blast of harmful energy that will inflict 5 points of damage per Rating of the enchantment to any living being within ten feet. So if the enchantment had a Rating of "Very Simple" a surge from it will cause 5 points of damage. If the Rating was "Average", a surge from it will cause 15 points of damage, etc.

An energy surge also knocks out all beings caught in it for 1D4 Turns unless they can make a successful Endurance Test against a Difficulty Value of 16. No type of natural armor can protect against the damage from an energy surge. If there is a surge between two enchantments with the same Mystic Force combination, the energy surge will inflict 5 points of damage per Enchantment Rating of the highest rated enchantment involved. So if an "Average" enchantment and a "Highly Complex" enchantment have an adverse reaction that results in an energy surge, all beings within ten feet will suffer 25 points of damage.

If your character has "The Mark" (see the "CHARACTER ADVANCEMENT" Section for more on the Mark) you can choose to have any enchantments that he creates to be immune to energy surges. This means that they will not surge or cause a surge when experiencing an adverse reaction, though they could still have another type of adverse reaction.

Neutralized

In this case all involved enchantments cease to exist just as if they never were.

If your character has "The Mark" you can choose to have any enchantments that he creates to be immune to being neutralized. This means that they will not be neutralized or cause another enchantment to be neutralized when experiencing an adverse reaction, though they could still have another type of adverse reaction.

External Effect

Any external effects that the enchantment or enchantments are capable of producing immediately occur. For example, if one of the enchantments causes the sword that it is on to glow red when the wielder is angry, then it will begin to glow red immediately. If the enchantment causes lightning to shoot from the enchanted item upon the wielder's mental command, then it will immediately shoot lightning from it (most likely in a random direction).

Thunder Clap/Blinding Flash

There is a brilliant flash of white-hot light that radiates from the enchantment or enchantments accompanied by a deafening boom like that of thunder. This thunder clap and blinding flash will completely deafen and blind anyone within thirty feet of the enchantment undergoing this reaction for 1D20 Turns. After the 1D20 Turns have lapsed the deafened and blinded being's hearing and sight will begin to return. It takes approximately five minutes for the effects to completely go away after the effects begin to wear off.

Disenchant Resistant

Sometimes the Shinkai who creates an enchantment may wish to make it so that it is much harder for someone to disenchant it. This must be done at the time the enchantment is being created. The player must state at the time his character is creating the enchantment whether or not they wish to make it more disenchant resistant.

If the enchantment is to be made disenchant resistant, two times the listed amount of Light Points must be expended in order to create it. There is no way to determine whether or not an enchantment has been made disenchant resistant in this manner until a Shinkai actually attempts to disenchant it. It will become clear at this time whether or not the enchantment has been made more resistant to disenchanting.

The percent chance of disenchanting an enchantment that has been made disenchant resistant is one half of that listed. So an "Average" enchantment that has been made disenchant resistant has only a twenty five percent base chance of being disenchanted.

CONFLICTING ENCHANTMENTS

Attempting to disenchant an enchantment created by someone else is not the only way of causing an adverse reaction. Having more than one enchantment containing the same combination of Mystic Forces within five feet of one another can possibly produce an adverse reaction. When the two similar enchantments approach five feet of one another both enchanted items will react and begin glowing red. If the two conflicting items remain within five feet of each other for 5 or more Turns roll the percentile dice. On a result of 20 or lower an adverse reaction has occurred. On a result of 21 or greater there is no immediate reaction but the two items will continue to glow red. If the two conflicting enchantments continue to remain within five feet of each other, then there is a twenty percent chance of an adverse reaction each hour on the hour.

It doesn't matter whether the enchantments are relics or modern enchantments. If the enchantments contain the same combination of Mystic Forces they will react and have a twenty percent chance of having an adverse reaction with each other. An object with a broken enchantment placed upon it will not react with other enchantments.

If more than two enchantments containing the exact same combination of Mystic Forces are brought within five feet of one another all enchanted items will immediately have an adverse reaction.

To determine exactly what the reaction is roll 1D4 and consult the "ADVERSE REACTION" table on the previous page.

ENCHANTMENT PRICING

It is often necessary, especially for the GM, to know the coin value of an enchantment. The higher the Class and Rating of an enchantment, the more coin it is worth. So a Class 1/ "Very Simple" enchantment has the lowest coin value and a Class 4/ "Highly Complex" enchantment has the highest value.

The "ENCHANTMENT PRICING" table can be used to find the average value of any given enchantment. This does not include the value of the item itself upon which the enchantment has been placed. The "ENCHANTMENT PRICING" table only lists the average prices for modern enchantments. Because of the rarity of relics and the limitless range of properties that they can possess, it is impossible to assign values that will accurately price the different Classes and Ratings of relics. Every individual owner of a relic will set his own price as to what he feels that the relic is worth.

ENCHANTMENT PRICING				
	Very Simple	**Simple**	**Average**	**Complex**	**Highly Complex**
Class 1	200 sc	400 sc	600 sc	800 sc	1000 sc
Class 2	300 sc	600 sc	900 sc	1200 sc	1500 sc
Class 3	NA	NA	1200 sc	1650 sc	2000 sc
Class 4	NA	NA	NA	2000 sc	2500 sc

As a general rule of thumb, however, relics are most always more expensive than modern enchantments.

To find the average value (in silver coins) of an enchantment start by finding its Class in the column on the left of the table. Now go across to the column that matches the Rating of the enchantment. The space where the enchantment's Class and Rating intersect is the average value of the enchantment.

FORCE-EFFECTS

Force-effects are magical effects that are produced through the conjuring of the Mystic Forces by Shinkai. There are one hundred Force-effects known to the Shinkai of today, however, it is believed that this is merely a fraction of the Force-effects that are possible.

Feel free to modify the Force-effects as needed to fit your particular gaming group or style of game play, or create your own Force-effects for that matter.

GENERAL FACTS ABOUT FORCE-EFFECTS

Damage from all Force-effects is considered lethal damage unless stated otherwise in the Force-effect's description.

Unless otherwise stated, your character must have visual contact with his target in order to use any Force-effect that directly targets another being or object.

Technique Points can be learned in each of the five Mystic Forces, each of which has a Maximum Technique of 3. Your character can not learn Technique Points in a Mystic Force that he is novice with.

There are several different categories of information pertaining to each Force-effect that precedes the description of the Force-effect. They are Learning Cost, Learning Difficulty, Required Forces, Minimum Knowledge, Force Energy, Defense, Difficulty, and Range. Each of these categories will now be explained in detail.

Learning Cost

If only one of the five Mystic Forces is required to learn and use the Force-effect there will simply be a value listed beside of the learning cost. This is the total amount of Unapplied Force Knowledge that your character must spend, or "apply", in order to learn the Force-effect. The Unapplied Force Knowledge that your character spends in this case will be from the Mystic Force required to learn and use the Force-effect.

If more than one of the Mystic Forces is required in order to learn and use the Force-effect there will be a value beside of the learning cost and then in parentheses there will be a list of values each beside of a letter representing a Mystic Force. A is for *Air*, F is for *Fire*, and so on. The value beside of each Mystic Force is the amount of Unapplied Force Knowledge from that particular Mystic Force that must be spent in order to learn the Force-effect. These values will add up to make the total amount of Unapplied Force Knowledge that your character will spend in his attempt to learn the Force-effect.

So, for a Force-effect that has the following listed for its Learning Cost; "Learning Cost: 25 (A-5, F-12, S-8)", your character will spend 5 points of Unapplied *Air* Knowledge, 12 points of Unapplied *Fire* Knowledge, and 8 points of Unapplied *Spirit* Knowledge for a total of 25 points of Unapplied Force Knowledge in an attempt to learn that particular Force-effect.

Whether your character's attempt at learning the Force-effect is successfully or not he still spends the listed amount of Unapplied Force Knowledge from each of the required Mystic Forces. When your character acquires the required amount of Unapplied Force Knowledge to learn the Force-effect he may try again.

Learning Difficulty

The value listed here is the Difficulty Value for learning the Force-effect. The Test required for learning any Force-effect is a Sixth Sense/Performance Test. You must get a result equal to or higher than the listed Learning Difficulty in order to learn the Force-effect.

The actual learning of a Force-effects is considered a Major Action and requires your character to draw in on all of the Mystic Forces contained within the Force-effect to be learned while spending the necessary amount of Unapplied Force Knowledge and making a Sixth Sense/Performance Test.

At this point the Shinkai is actually creating a mental image of the Force-effect that he is attempting to learn. He tries to visualize which of the Mystic Forces is necessary to create the Force-effect and how they must be conjured together in order to do so (of course if the Shinkai is looking into the raging of another Shinkai that is demonstrating the Force-effect for him he doesn't have to use his imagination as much as he simply has to pay attention to how the Shinkai demonstrating the Force-effect is conjuring). The Shinkai then draws in on all of the Mystic Forces contained within the Force-effect he is attempting to learn and allows his *Gift* to form the Mystic Forces into the Force-effect. If the Shinkai has successfully learned the Force-effect (met the Learning Difficulty for the Force-effect on a Sixth Sense/Performance Test) then his eyes will immediately rage for a brief second in the color, or mixture of colors, of the Mystic Forces contained within the Force-effect that he just learned. This temporary raging is the confirmation that the Force-effect was successfully learned.

At the moment that a Shinkai learns a Force-effect he can actually fully conjure and utilize the Force-effect (his *Gift* has already formed the Mystic Forces into the Force-effect) or he can release the Mystic Forces upon which he was drawing and allow the Force-effect to dissipate before it is fully conjured. If he fully conjures and utilizes the Force-effect he must then spend the required Force Energy for the Force-effect, but if he allows it to dissipate he expends no more energy than was necessary to draw in on the Mystic Forces (.5 Force Energy per Mystic Force drawn upon). Creating a Force-effect but allowing it to dissipate a split second before it is actually conjured is a very common technique employed by Shinkai who are demonstrating Force-effects for other Shinkai. In this way they can help the other Shinkai learn the Force-effect without actually having to expend the Force Energy for fully conjuring the Force-effect. Not to mention that in some circumstances it may not be desirable to actually fully conjure some Force-effects.

Enchantments, runes, or other mystical means of temporarily increasing your character's Sixth Sense can not be used to aid in the learning of Force-effects (it is based solely on your character's true potential and abilities).

Things that your character *may* use to aide in the Sixth Sense/Performance Test for learning Force-effects is the Skill "General Conjuring", Technique Points and mystical attuning bonuses. For each Technique Point that your character has in any of the Mystic Forces contained within the Force-effect that he is attempting to learn you may add +1 to the result of the Test. You may also add 1 point to the result of your character's Test for each mystical attuning counter that he has in the center circle (#12) on your Mystical Attuning Sheet.

If your character knows the Universal Talent "Force Sight" and looks into the raging of another Shinkai while they perform the Force-effect that your character is trying to learn, your character may receive additional bonuses to the learn-

ing Test. If the Shinkai that is demonstrating the Force-effect to your character has more Technique Points in the Mystic Forces contained within the Force-effect than your character does you may add +1 to the result of the Test for each Technique Point that he has beyond what your character does.

Your character must make the attempt to learn the Force-effect at the time that he observes it being performed through another Shinkai's raging in order to receive the bonuses.

For example, Artis is attempting to learn the Force-effect "Fire Lightning". This Force-effect contains the Mystic Forces of *Fire*, *Land*, and *Spirit*. Artis has 3 Technique Points in *Fire*, 1 in *Land*, and 1 in *Spirit*. Artis knows the Universal Talent "Force Sight" and looks into the raging of a fellow Shinkai while he actually performs "Fire Lightning". Artis' companion, who is demonstrating the Force-effect, has 3 Technique Points in *Fire*, 2 in *Land* and 3 in *Spirit*.

Artis will get to add at least +5 to the result of his Sixth Sense Performance Test because he has that many Technique Points in the Mystic Forces contained in "Fire Lightning". Now to see if he will get any additional bonuses from observing the Force-effect through Artis' raging while the attempt to learn it is made.

Artis' companion doesn't have any more Technique Points in *Fire* than he does so there is no additional bonuses received for his companion's Technique Points in *Fire*. Artis' companion has 1 more Technique Point in *Land* than he does so that will add +1 to his Test result. Artis' companion also has 2 more Technique Points in *Spirit* than he does so this will add an additional +2 to his Test result. Due to Technique Points alone Artis receives a bonus of +8 points to the result of his Sixth Sense/Performance Test for learning "Fire Lightning". He gets +5 because of his own Technique Points and an additional +3 because of his companion's additional Technique Points in the required Mystic Forces.

Required Forces

This is a list of the Mystic Forces that your character must control in order to learn and use the Force-effect. If a Mystic Force is listed that your character doesn't yet control he may not attempt to learn the Force-effect.

Minimum Knowledge

This is the minimum amount of Force Knowledge that your character must have in order to be able to learn the Force-effect.

If only a value is listed beside of Minimum Knowledge, that means that there is only one Mystic Force required to learn and use the Force-effect. The value listed is the minimum amount of Force Knowledge in the required Mystic Force that your character must have in order to attempt to learn the Force-effect.

If more than one of the Mystic Forces is required in order

to learn and use the Force-effect there will be a list of values beside of a letter representing a Mystic Force. L is for *Land*, S is for *Spirit*, and so on. The value listed beside of each Mystic Force is the minimum amount of Force Knowledge that your character must have in that particular Mystic Force in order to attempt to learn the Force-effect. So a Force-effect that has a Minimum Knowledge listing of S=31, W=37 means that your character must have a Force Knowledge of 31 or greater in *Spirit* and 37 or greater in *Water* before he can attempt to learn the Force-effect.

Force Energy

This is the amount of Force Energy required to create and utilize the Force-effect. Every time that your character utilizes a Force-effect he must subtract a number of points from his Current Force Energy equal to the listed Force Energy value of the Force-effect.

Maintaining a Force-effect

Some Force-effects can be maintained after they are created. This means that the effects of the Force-effect can be made to linger or continue. If there are two values listed beside of the Force-effect's Force Energy (18/14 for example) that means that the Force-effect can be maintained. The first value is the amount of Force Energy that must be expended in order to create the Force-effect and the second value is the amount of Force Energy that must be expended each Turn thereafter in order to maintain it or keep its effects going. As a general rule of thumb it requires less Force Energy to maintain a Force-effect than it does to initialize or create it.

Until your character is non-novice (has 100 or more Force Knowledge) in one or more of the Mystic Forces he can only create or maintain one Force-effect per Turn. For example, if your character is still novice in all of the Mystic Forces that he controls and is currently maintaining a fire weapon that he created via the Force-effect "Fire Weapon" he could not conjure another Force-effect until he ceased to maintain the fire weapon.

Once your character becomes non-novice with one of the Mystic Forces he may conjure a Force-effect while maintaining another Force-effect, or if he is not conjuring a new Force-effect he could maintain two Force-effects. For each Mystic Force that your character becomes non-novice with beyond the first he may maintain one additional Force-effect per Turn, even during the same Turn that he conjures a new Force-effect.

So if your character was non-novice with one of the Mystic Forces he could maintain one Force-effect while conjuring another Force-effect. If your character was non-novice in two of the Mystic Forces he could conjure a Force-effect while maintaining two other Force-effects (perhaps conjuring "Lightning" while maintaining a "Light Orb" and "Fire Weapon"). If your character was non-novice in all five of

the Mystic Forces he could maintain as many as five Force-effects in a single Turn, even while conjuring another new Force-effect or just maintain as many as six Force-effects.

Being non-novice in the Mystic Forces does not allow your character to *create* or *conjure* more than one Force-effect per Turn (conjuring a Force-effect is a Major Action and a character can only perform one Major Action per Turn), it only allows him to *maintain* multiple Force-effects, even while conjuring a new Force-effect.

One exception to this rule is if your character controls all five of the Mystic Forces. In this case your character may actually conjure two Force-effects per Turn and it is considered a single Major Action. Your character is NOT able to conjure one Force-effect and then perform one physical attack in the same Turn (even though he is non-novice in all five Mystic Forces). He may perform one physical type of Major Action or conjure two Force-effects as his single Major Action, not a combination of the two.

When performing two Force-effects per Turn as a single Major Action the first Force-effect will be conjured at your character's Mystical Initiative and the second Force-effect will be conjured 1 Initiative value below the first. So if your character is non-novice in all five Mystic Forces and wants to conjure two Force-effects in the same Turn, and has a Mystical Initiative of 12 his first Force-effect would be conjured at an Initiative of 12 and the second at an Initiative of 11.

Defense

Some Force-effects produce general effects or only affect inanimate objects, other Force-effects target living beings. If the Force-effect targets a being there will most always be a Defense listed under the Force-effect (sometimes inanimate objects, such as enchanted objects and items made from green-steel, will have Mystical Defenses).

The Defense is a listing of the types of defenses that are effective against the Force-effect. If "Mystical" is listed beside of Defense then that means that the target can set a Mystical Defense to attempt to avoid the effects of the Force-effect. If "Physical" is listed then that means that the target can set a Physical Defense to attempt to avoid the effects of the Force-effect.

If there is only a specific type of Physical Defense that is effective against the Force-effect it will be listed in parentheses. If dodging is the only type of Physical Defense that is effective against the Force-effect then the Defense for the Force-effect will be listed as "Physical (Dodge)". If dodging and blocking are both effective against the Force-effect then the Defense will be listed as "Physical (Block or Dodge)", etc.

If there is no Defense listed for the Force-effect that means that it either doesn't target a living being, the Shinkai must overcome a certain Difficulty Value (other than a Defense) to determine whether or not it succeeds, or the Force-effect suc-

ceeds automatically.

If there is an asterisk listed after Defense then that means there is special information pertaining to the Defenses that are effective against the Force-effect. This special information will be given in the Force-effect's description.

Difficulty

Any time that your character utilizes a Force-effect he must make a Sixth Sense/Performance Test. This Test is the attack value for the Force-effect and sometimes is also used to determine whether or not the Force-effect is created successfully. If the Force-effect has a Difficulty listed then that means that the Force-effect is not automatically created successfully. The value listed after the Difficulty is the minimum result required on the Sixth Sense/Performance Test made at the time the Force-effect is used. If the result of this Test is equal to or greater than the listed Difficulty then the Force-effect is created normally. If it is less than the listed Difficulty then the Force-effect fails completely. Regardless of whether or not the Force-effect is successfully conjured the required Force Energy is expended.

If there is an asterisk listed after Difficulty then that means there is special information that pertains to the use of the Force-effect. This special information will be given in the Force-effect's description.

Range

This is a listing of the effective range of the Force-effect. If the range is listed as "Self" that means that the Shinkai can only use the Force-effect on him or herself. If the range is listed as "Sight" that means that the Force-effect has an effective range that extends as far as the Shinkai conjuring it can see. If the range is listed as "Touch" that means that the Shinkai must be able to physically touch the target in order for the Force-effect to work.

If there is an asterisk listed after Range that means there is special information that pertains to it. This special information will be given in the Force-effect's description.

For additional information pertaining to the use of Force-effects, especially in combat, see "Mystical Combat" in the "COMBAT" Section.

USING FORCE-EFFECTS

To use a Force-effect you simply declare as part of you intended action which Force-effect that you would like for your character to use as well as any details in how he would like to use it (who he's aiming at for instance). At your character's Mystical Initiative he will use the Force-effect at which time he must expend the required amount of Force Energy and make a Sixth Sense/Performance Test (the attack Test for Force-effects). If your character is Novice in the Force-effect being used he must also roll the percentile dice at this time to see whether or not he succumbs to the Novice

Factor. A result of 20 or lower on the percentile dice means that your character has succumbed to the Novice Factor. A wide variety of possibilities can arrive from succumbing to the Novice Factor.

For a detailed description of the use of Force-effects see "Mystical Combat" in the "COMBAT" Section of the rules.

The following is a list of the one hundred known Force-effects. After each Force-effect's name is one or more letters in parentheses. These letters indicate which Mystic Forces that must be controlled in order to learn or use the Force-effect. A stands for *Air*, F stands for *Fire*, etc.

An asterisk after a Force-effect indicates that your character must know the art of focused conjuring before that particular Force-effect can be learned or used.

1. Acid Metal (F,W)
2. Acid Rain (W)
3. Air Bind (A)
4. Air Expansion (A)
5. Air Shield (A)
6. Air Talk (A,S)
7. Aura Sense (L,S)
8. Ball Lightning (A,F,S)
9. Beacon (A,S)
10. Bleeding Injury (F,W)
11. Breath of Life (L,S)
12. Concealed Force (A,F,L,S,W)
13. Concussion Sphere (A,F,S)
14. Confusion (S)
15. Cure (F,S,W)
16. Darkness (L,S)
17. Death Ward (A,F,L,S,W)
18. Decay (L,W)
19. Disintegrate (A,F,L,S,W)
20. Eagle Sight (A,S) *
21. Emotion Block (L)
22. Fear (S)
23. Fire & Ice (A,F,S,W)
24. Fireball (F) *
25. Fire Lightning (F,L,S) *
26. Fire Weapon (F) *
27. Flame (F)
28. Flame Rage (F)
29. Fog (A)
30. Force Block (L,S)
31. Force Sever (F,L,S)
32. Force Tying (L,S)
33. Freeze {Animate} (A,S)
34. Freeze {Inanimate} (A,W)
35. Frost Beam (A,W) *
36. Ground Blast (L)
37. Healing (S)
38. Healing Water (S)
39. Ice Weapon (A,W) *
40. Illusion {Large} (A,L,S)
41. Illusion {Self} (L,S)
42. Illusion {Small} (L,S)

43. Intense Heat (F)
44. Invincibility (A,F,L,S,W)
45. Invisibility {Other} (A,S)
46. Invisibility {Self} (A,S)
47. Landquake (L)
48. Land Vapors (L)
49. Levitation {Other} (A)
50. Levitation {Self} (A)
51. Lie Detection (S,W)
52. Life Bond (S)
53. Lightning (F,S) *
54. Light Orb (F,S)
55. Living Land (L)
56. Magical Detection (F,S)
57. Message Ward (L,S)
58. Metabolism (L,S)
59. Mutation (L,S)
60. Pain (F,S)
61. Possession (S)
62. Purify (F,S,W)
63. Quicksand (L,W)
64. Real Touch (A,L)
65. Regeneration (S,W)
66. Resurrection (F,L,S)
67. Rune Lore (A,F,L,S,W)
68. Rune Warding (A,F,L,S,W)
69. Shock Wave (A,F,L,S,W) *
70. Signal Ward (A,S)
71. Silence (A)
72. Sleep (S,W)
73. Sleep Ward (S,W)
74. Soft Stone (L) *
75. Speed Recovery (S,W)
76. Spirit Shield (A,F,S)
77. Storm (A,S,W)
78. Strength (L)
79. Suggestion (S)
80. Summon Air Creature (A,S)
81. Summon Fire Creature (F,S)
82. Summon Land Creature (L,S)
83. Summon Water (W)
84. Summon Water Creature (S,W)
85. Summon Wind (A)
86. Teleport (A,S)
87. Teleport Ward (A,S)
88. Tornado (A)
89. Unraveling (F,S)
90. Visioning (L,S)
91. Vitalize (S)
92. Wall of Land (L)
93. Wall of Fire (F)
94. Wall of Ice (A,W)
95. Water Blades (W)
96. Water Breathing (A,W)
97. Weakness (L)
98. Web (A,W)
99. Wind Missile (A) *
100. Wind Weapon {Melee} (A) *

ACID METAL

Learning Cost:20 (F-12, W-8)
Learning Difficulty: 12
Required Forces: *Fire & Water*
Minimum Knowledge: F=43, W=39
Force Energy: 22
Defense: *Mystical
Range: 60 feet

This Force-effect causes metal to sweat acid. This acid does not harm the metal, but does damage living tissue. If a living being's skin comes in contact with the acid they will suffer Level 8 damage per Turn until the acid is removed, neutralized, or 3 Turns have passed (after 3 Turns the acid neutralizes itself). Pouring water or other liquids directly on the affected area will remove the acid.

The largest area of metal that can be affected by one "Acid Metal" use is six feet. An individual can only suffer Level 8 damage per Turn from this acid regardless of how many separate sources of acid they come in contact with. So, if two separate Valkin conjure the Force-effect "Acid Metal" upon an enemies steel plate armor. This enemy would still only suffer Level 8 damage from the acid.

At the GM's discretion the Level of damage inflicted by "Acid Metal" may be reduced if the amount of acid that a being comes in contact with is minimal.

* Green-steel, as well as some enchanted items, has a Mystical Defense (all green-steel items inherently have a Mystical Defense of 5). In this case the Shinkai who is conjuring "Acid Metal" upon the item must have a higher Sixth Sense/Performance Test than the item's Mystical Defense value or it will have no effect.

The acid produced from this Force-effect is a different type than that produced by the Force-effect "Acid Rain". For this reason it is possible for a being to suffer damage from both of these Force-effects at the same time. The acid from the Force-effect "Acid Rain" will wash off the acid from "Acid Metal" after 1 full Turn, during which time the target will suffer damage from both of these separate sources of acid.

ACID RAIN

Learning Cost: 24
Learning Difficulty: 16
Required Forces: *Water*
Minimum Knowledge: 65
Force Energy: 30/15
Difficulty: 10
Range: The focal point can be a number of feet away no greater than the conjurer's Total Force Energy.

An acidic rain will pour down over a given area (up to a number of feet in diameter equal to the conjurer's Total *Water* Knowledge value), rendering Level 13 damage to any being whose body is exposed to the rain.

When maintained the rain can be moved once per Turn a number of feet no greater than the range of the rain. This movement is considered a Minor Action.

AIR BIND

Learning Cost: 35
Learning Difficulty: 17
Required Forces: *Air*
Minimum Knowledge: 80
Force Energy: 50/40
Defense: Mystical
Range: 300 feet

This Force-effect causes a selected area of air around a target to become as hard as stone, thereby binding the target. "Air Bind" can be used to bind a whole being or only selected areas of the target's body.

A binded being isn't held to the place where they are binded, rather the parts of their body that is binded simply aren't able to move.

If the face of a target is binded they are unable to breath as long as their face is binded.

The listed Force Energy required to use "Air Bind" is for binding only a single area of a target. The Force Energies (initial use and maintaining) are added in again for each additional area beyond the first that is binded.

So, to bind a being's entire body (head, both arms, and both legs) would expend 250 points of Force Energy to initiate and 200 per Turn to maintain. Adding or removing a zone from the bind is only a Minor Action.

A binded being can make a Strength Test against a Difficulty Value equal to the result of the Sixth Sense/Performance Test made by the Shinkai when he placed "Air Bind". If the result of the Strength Test is greater than that of the Sixth Sense/Performance Test, then the being breaks free. No matter how many different areas of a being that is binded, if they make a single successful Strength Test to break free the air bind is broken from all zones.

If the Shinkai using "Air Bind" wishes, he may raise the Difficulty Value of the Strength Test required to break free at any time (provided that "Air Bind" has not been tied off with "Force Tying") to a value no greater than his Total *Air* Knowledge. One point of damage, however, will be received for each point above the conjuring Shinkai's Sixth Sense/Performance Test result that the Difficulty Value is raised.

AIR EXPANSION

Learning Cost: 17
Learning Difficulty: 10
Required Forces: *Air*
Minimum Knowledge: 50
Force Energy: 20

Difficulty: *
Range: 60 feet

This Force-effect causes a given volume of air in an inanimate object to expand. Possible uses include busting open chests, locks, etc. (the target object must be hollow to some extent). Determining whether or not the object is forced apart or broken by the expansion is as simple as comparing the object's Shatter Threshold, or a Difficulty Value determined by the GM, to the conjurer's *Air* Knowledge value. If the latter is equal to or greater than the object's Shatter Threshold, then the object shatters or is forced apart.

"Air Expansion" can not be used to directly damage or expand living beings.

AIR SHIELD

Learning Cost: 20
Learning Difficulty: 10
Required Forces: *Air*
Minimum Knowledge: 52
Force Energy: 13/12
Range: Self

With this Force-effect a Shinkai can create an invisible shield of solidified air to appear attached to their desired arm. The shield may range in size from a buckler to a full shield, and no penalties to Agility or movement is given regardless of the size of the shield that is created.

The shield may not be created touching any other substance (other than the creator's arm); it may, however, be touched after created, as it is quite solid. The exact shape of the shield may be any shape which the creating Shinkai wishes.

Such shields have a Destroyed rating of 60 plus the Total *Air* Knowledge of the creator.

At the beginning of any Turn that "Air Shield" is maintained its damage is reduced to 0.

Attacks against an "Air Shield" which contain *Spirit* (such as "Lightning") yield double damage to the shield.

It is a Minor Action to use this Force-effect.

AIR TALK

Learning Cost: 15 (A-8, S-7)
Learning Difficulty: 9
Required Forces: *Air & Spirit*
Minimum Knowledge: A=40, S=40
Force Energy: 10/10
Difficulty: 6
Range: Sight

Using this Force-effect allows your character's voice to carry much farther than it normally would. Your character can also focus his voice upon one particular area or being and control how loud it is heard. He could gently whisper and make it heard by another being at the far edges of his sight. He can not, however, increase the volume of his voice to be any louder than it normally would be.

AURA SENSE

Learning Cost: 15 (L-6, S-9)
Learning Difficulty: 10
Required Forces: *Land & Spirit*
Minimum Knowledge: L=37, S=40
Force Energy: 12/10
Defense: Mystical -2
Range: 30 feet

The use of this Force-effect allows the Shinkai to sense the Aura (or Life Force) of another being, even if that being is hidden or obscured by a solid object such as a wall. The GM should limit the thickness that "Aura Sense" can penetrate. A good average is two feet.

The being's basic mood, race, gender, and health can be determined by using "Aura Sense".

BALL LIGHTNING

Learning Cost: 30 (A-6, F-14, S-10)

Learning Difficulty: 13
Required Forces: *Air, Fire, & Spirit*
Minimum Knowledge: A=40, F=55, S=45
Force Energy: 40/25
Defense: Physical (Dodge)
Range: 600 feet

The Shinkai summons a hovering ball of lightning anywhere within five feet of himself. The ball of lightning can be projected toward a target or it can be made to hover or float slowly in any desired direction.

When this ball of lightning is projected toward a target, the target receives a +3 bonus to their Defense due to the relatively slow movement of "Ball Lightning". The ball will discharge immediately upon contact with any solid or semi-solid object.

When made to float the ball lightning can pass through inanimate objects and discharges only when contacting a living being. Maximum float/hover speed is 10 feet per Turn. Causing the ball lightning to hover or float for longer than just the Turn it is created requires maintaining the Force-effect.

"Ball Lightning" does Level 16 damage. The victim will also be stunned for the remainder of the Turn unless they can make a successful Endurance Test against a Difficulty Value of 15.

BEACON

Learning Cost: 16 (A-8, S-8)
Learning Difficulty: 10
Required Forces: *Air & Spirit*
Minimum Knowledge: A=40, S=40
Force Energy: * 8
Defense: Mystical
Range: Touch (the beacon can be sensed a number of miles away equal to the Total Force Energy of the Shinkai who created the beacon)

This Force-effect allows your character to place a beacon on a being or object, allowing your character to sense the target of "Beacon", including its direction and distance from him.

If the object or being upon which "Beacon" was placed is destroyed or killed the Shinkai who placed the beacon will immediately know so. The beacon will also cease at this time.

The required Force Energy listed for beacon is the Force Energy required for the *first* "Beacon" that a Shinkai places. If an additional beacon is to be placed by the same Shinkai while another is still active, an additional 20 points of Force-Energy is required for each additional beacon that is created beyond the first.

The Shinkai who places a beacon can release it at will, at any time he or she desires.

BLEEDING INJURY

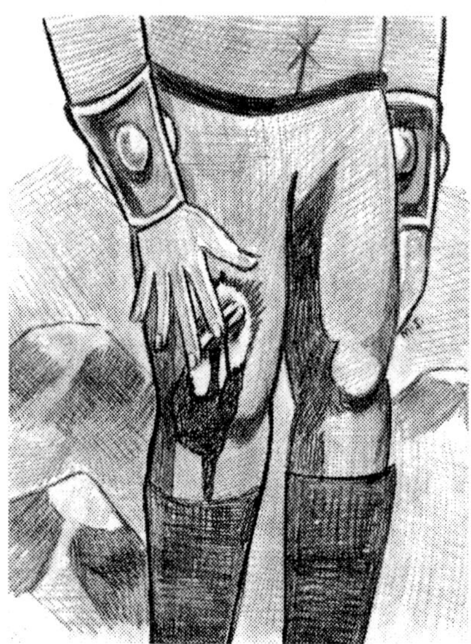

Learning Cost: 17 (F-10, W-7)
Learning Difficulty: 11
Required Forces: *Fire & Water*
Minimum Knowledge: F=45, W=40
Force Energy: 20
Defense: Mystical
Range: 300 feet

This Force-effect causes cuts or injuries of a target being to begin bleeding excessively. This loss of blood does 2 Levels of damage per Turn starting on the Turn in which "Bleeding Injury" is conjured. Every 2 Turns that this bleeding continues will also cause the victim's Strength and Agility to receive a 1 Level penalty.

The bleeding caused by this Force-effect can only be stopped by mystical means ("Healing", "Cure", "Regeneration", enchantments, etc.).

BREATH OF LIFE

Learning Cost: 22 (L-9, S-13)
Learning Difficulty: 12
Required Forces: *Land & Spirit*
Minimum Knowledge: L=40, S=45
Force Energy: 32
Defense: Mystical
Range: Touch

This Force-effect gives the target being an extra boost of life and physical endurance. The penalty from one injury may be ignored, unconsciousness due to Force Failure is avoided, and the recipient's Life Force is increased by 10 for the duration of "Breath of Life". This increase to Life Force also appropriately increases the being's Force Failure and Injury Rating.

"Breath of Life" lasts for one hour, in which time the same being may not be the recipient of another "Breath of Life". The same being may benefit by no more than 2 "Breath of

Life" Force-effects in the same day.

CONCEALED FORCE

Learning Cost: 32 (A-5, F-7, L-6, S-9, W-5)
Learning Difficulty: 25
Required Forces: *Air, Fire, Land, Spirit, & Water*
Minimum Knowledge: A=80, F=100, L=100, S=115, W=80
Force Energy: Variable
Difficulty: * 12
Range: 30 feet

A Shinkai using "Concealed Force" can make tied off flows of the Mystic Forces invisible to "Force Sight"; this includes wards. Concealing a Force-effect that another Shinkai has tied requires a successful Sixth Sense/Performance Test against a Difficulty Value of 12. Concealing a Force-effect that a Shinkai has tied himself does not have a set Difficulty Value in order to be successful.

The required Force Energy varies according to the number of Mystic Forces in the Force-effect being concealed. The required Force Energy for concealing a Force-effect containing only one of the Mystic Forces is 20. The required Force Energy is increased by 10 for each additional Mystic Force contained in the Force-effect to be concealed. "Concealed Force" lasts as long as the Force-effect that it is concealing lasts.

CONCUSSION SPHERE

Learning Cost: 40 (A-20, F-11, S-9)
Learning Difficulty: 22
Required Forces: *Air, Fire, & Spirit*
Minimum Knowledge: A=80, F=70, S=45
Force Energy: 60x2
Defense: Physical (Dodge)
Range: * 150 feet (1D10 x 30 feet)

This Force-effect is among the most deadly that can be learned, however it is also one of the most unpredictable. As soon as the Shinkai begins conjuring "Concussion Sphere" a glowing sphere of red and yellow light appears up to 150 feet away (Shinkai's choice as to where the sphere will manifest). This glowing sphere is approximately six inches in diameter and immediately begins to pulse and grow in size and intensity.

"Concussion Sphere", unlike any other Force-effect, requires 2 Turns of conjuring before it will produce its final effect. If the Shinkai continues conjuring the "Concussion Sphere" for 2 consecutive Turns (expending 60 points of Force Energy per Turn), the sphere will explode 1D4 seconds into the second Turn. This second Turn of conjuring is not considering maintaining the Force-effect, but is full conjuring (a Major Action). The Shinkai conjuring "Concussion Sphere" must stay within the 150 foot range of it in order to continue conjuring it on the second Turn.

The explosion sends a hot and forceful blast of red energy for 1D10 x 30 feet in all directions from the sphere inflicting 4D20 +20 points of damage to anything caught in its path.

No normal types of armor can protect against this damage. Solid barriers such as hills, large boulders, "Land Wall" or "Ice Wall", will absorb and stop "Concussion Sphere's" energy.

If the Shinkai does not continue conjuring "Concussion Sphere" into the second Turn the sphere will simply vanish with no effect.

CONFUSION

Learning Cost: 25
Learning Difficulty: 14
Required Forces: *Spirit*
Minimum Knowledge: 60
Force Energy: 30/25
Defense: Mystical
Range: 600 feet

The target of this Force-effect becomes very confused and disoriented. This confusion results in all Tests requiring any degree of concentration or agility (all attributes with the exceptions of Strength and Endurance) to be random-roll Tests. It also gives a -4 penalty to both Physical and Mystical Initiative.

At the beginning of each Turn the confused being can make a random-roll Willpower Test against a Difficulty Value of 10 to attempt to free themselves from the effects of the confusion. If they are successful "Confusion" ceases to work and must be placed on anew (can no longer be maintained because it has ceased).

A single being can not be affected by more than one "Confusion" at a time, and only one being can be targeted per use of this Force-effect.

CURE

Learning Cost: 30 (F-8, S-14, W-8)
Learning Difficulty: 15
Required Forces: *Fire, Spirit, & Water*
Minimum Knowledge: F=60, S=80, W=60
Force Energy: 70
Difficulty: *
Range: Touch

With this Force-effect a Shinkai can instantly cure most any illness, poison, or paralysis.
* Unless a Difficulty Value is listed for the particular illness attempting to be cured, consider "Cure" to automatically succeed. The specific conditions on which "Cure" will work is up to the GM.

DARKNESS

Learning Cost: 15 (L-8, S-7)
Learning Difficulty: 12
Required Forces: *Land & Spirit*
Minimum Knowledge: L=45, S=45
Force Energy: 20/15
Range: * the focal spot is 20 feet

An impenetrable blanket of darkness is summoned to cover any given area up to thirty feet in diameter from the focal spot of "Darkness". The darkness clings to the area over which it is conjured. Those inside of this blanket of darkness can not see out, neither can anyone outside see in. Torches, flames or any other natural source of light can not penetrate this darkness. Beings can enter and exit the area of darkness without the darkness clinging to them. It only clings to the initial area on which is was conjured, not the beings in the area (or later entering the area).

If the Force-effect "Light Orb" is conjured upon the same area as "Darkness", then the Shinkai with the highest Total Force Energy will overpower the other and his or her Force-effect will remain.

DEATH WARD

Learning Cost: 50 (A-7, F-16, L-9, S-12, W-6)
Learning Difficulty: 26
Required Forces: *Air, Fire, Land, Spirit, & Water*
Minimum Knowledge: A=100, F=130, L=100, S=120, W=100
Force Energy: 125
Difficulty: 16
Range: 25 feet

This ward can be placed on an area as large as twenty five feet in diameter. Any being entering the warded area will trigger the ward. Non-Shinkai beings that enter the ward have an automatic ninety percent chance of dying at this time.

If the beings that entered the "Death Ward" are Shinkai then they must make a successful Sixth Sense/Performance Test against a Difficulty Value of 15 at this time. If this Test is passed the Shinkai only receive Level 15 damage. If this Test is failed then they will instantly die.

Shinkai with a Total Force Energy higher than that of the creator of the ward (at the time the ward was created) may add 1D6 points to the result of their Sixth Sense/Performance Test to resist the ward's effects.

Note: Normally once a ward is triggered it ceases to exist, but there is a way to make a ward reset itself for use again. When creating the ward the Shinkai can expend twice the listed Force Energy for that particular ward, thus allowing the ward to reset itself one time after it is triggered. If three times the listed Force Energy is expended, then the ward can reset itself twice, if four times the listed Force Energy is expended it can reset three times, etc..

Wards can be created to target only specific targets or beings, but the required Force Energy increases by 5 for each type of target specification added. So, a ward that targets only natural creatures and ruling-races would require 10 more points of Force Energy than the same ward with no target specifications.

Any Shinkai who creates a ward can also destroy that same ward by simply reversing the flows. This expends no Force Energy and is considered to be a Minor Action. The only way to destroy a ward created by another Shinkai is to use the Force-effect "Unravelling".

DECAY

Learning Cost: 15 (L-8, W-7)
Learning Difficulty: 8
Required Forces: *Land & Water*
Minimum Knowledge: L=40, W=40
Force Energy:
Range: 150 feet

With this Force-effect a Shinkai can cause food, small plants, and organic materials (GM's discretion) to rapidly decay. Most items will completely decay within 3 Turns. If "Decay" is used on deceased beings, they will rot away to the bone within 5 Turns.

"Decay" has no known effect on living beings.

DISINTEGRATE

Learning Cost: 45 (A-5, F-17, L-7, S-12, W-4)
Learning Difficulty: 25
Required Forces: *Air, Fire, Land, Spirit, & Water*
Minimum Knowledge: A=65, F=100, L=70, S=100, W=60
Force Energy: 100
Defense: Mystical
Range: 150 feet

With this Force-effect a Shinkai can cause a living being's body to explode into charred bits of flesh and bone.

The Shinkai using "Disintegrate" must have a higher Total Force Energy than the target being or "Disintegrate" will automatically fail, only inflicting Level 10 damage instead

of disintegrating them.

If the Shinkai using "Disintegrate" *does* have a higher Total Force Energy than the target being, he must still overcome their Mystical Defense. Even then, the target being is allowed to make a Sixth Sense/Performance Test against a Difficulty Value of 14 to resist disintegrating. If the Test is successful the target feels only extreme discomfort and suffers Level 10 damage. If not successful, they are disintegrated.

If the target's Mystical Defense is sufficient against the attack then they do not have to make the Sixth Sense/Performance Test.

EAGLE SIGHT

Learning Cost: 15 (A-8, S-7)
Learning Difficulty: 9
Required Forces: *Air & Spirit*
Minimum Knowledge: A=40, S=40
Force Energy: 8/8
Range: Self

When using "Eagle Sight" the Shinkai focuses the Mystic Forces of *Air* and *Spirit* to his eyes. The Shinkai's eyes change to a golden color and his normal ranges of vision increase by three times. Any Force-effects or abilities that are based upon or limited by ranges of vision are also increased accordingly.

EMOTION BLOCK

Learning Cost: 20
Learning Difficulty: 11
Required Forces: *Land*
Minimum Knowledge: 55

Force Energy: 15/7
Range: Self

A being using "Emotion Block" is able to hide any sense of emotion that they might be experiencing. Anyone trying to sense or read this being's emotions will find it impossible to do so. "Emotion Block" also makes the user immune to "Lie Detection", "Fear", "Pain", or any other type of emotion based sensing or provoking abilities; mystical or mundane.

"Emotion Block" does not protect against "Suggestion".

If a character is already being affected by Force-effects or abilities that "Emotion Block" is effective against, the use of "Emotion Block" will counter them immediately.

FEAR

Learning Cost: 20
Learning Difficulty: 10
Required Forces: *Spirit*
Minimum Knowledge: 55
Force Energy: 30
Defense: Mystical
Range: 100 feet

The use of this Force-effect evokes extreme fear in the target being or beings. This fear is irrational, but extremely strong and emanates from the Shinkai who conjured "Fear".

Anyone affected by "Fear" is unable to function normally for the duration of the fear. Any Major Actions or actions requiring concentration, such as climbing, attacking, swimming, setting a Defense, etc. receive a -1D8 point penalty to the appropriate Test. The affected being also receives a -2 point penalty to both their Physical and Mystical Initiatives. On top of this, there is also a fifty percent chance that the being or beings influenced by "Fear" will flee from the conjuring Shinkai. The fear emanates from the Shinkai conjuring this Force-effect.

At the beginning of each Turn the being affected by "Fear" can make a Random-roll Willpower Test against a Difficulty Value of 10 to attempt to overcome the fear. If they are successful, then "Fear" ceases to work and must be placed on anew (can no longer be maintained because it has ceased).

A being can only be influenced by one "Fear" at a time. One use of "Fear" can target up to four beings, and lasts for 2 Turns (without being maintained).

FIRE & ICE

Learning Cost: 40 (A-9, F-14, S-8, W-9)
Learning Difficulty: 23
Required Forces: *Air, Fire, Spirit, & Water*
Minimum Knowledge: A=105, F=120, S=75, W=105
Force Energy: 85
Defense: Physical (Block or Dodge)
Range: * 150 feet

A floating sphere of swirling fire and ice is summoned to appear anywhere within 150 feet of the Shinkai who created it. It must remain within 150 feet of the Shinkai or it will evaporate instantly.

Upon the Shinkai's mental command the sphere will explode sending streams of fire and ice toward the target beings. Up to six beings can be targeted with one "Fire & Ice". The sphere has an effective range of 150 feet in addition to the 150 feet in which the sphere itself can be moved. The streams of fire and ice that shoot out of the orb move extremely fast and thus the Shinkai conjuring "Fire & Ice" receives a +3 point bonus to the result of the attack Test (Sixth Sense/Performance Test).

Any being struck by "Fire & Ice" receives Level 16 +16 points of damage, a -2 Level penalty to their Agility for 2 Turns, and a -50 feet per Turn penalty to their movement for 2 Turns. Multiple hits from this Force-effect to a single target increase the penalty to the target's Agility by an additional -1 Level and their movement by an additional -25 feet per Turn for every additional "Fire & Ice" that they are the victim of beyond the first. Additional hits from this Force-effect do the full amount of damage as previously described.

The Shinkai who created the sphere can move it at will up to a speed of 60 feet per Turn. The sphere must be used in the same Turn in which it is created or it will evaporate.

Any armor struck by this Force-effect will take an amount of damage up to twice its Protection Rating instead of equal to its Protection Rating.

FIREBALL

Learning Cost: 20
Learning Difficulty: 10
Required Forces: *Fire*
Minimum Knowledge: 50
Force Energy: 20
Defense: Physical (Block, Dodge, or Parry)
Range: 900 feet

The Shinkai focuses the Mystic Force of *Fire* into the palm of either hand where a searing hot ball of fire manifests. The Shinkai then releases the ball of fire sending it streaking toward its target. Any being struck by one of these fireballs suffers Level 15 +5 points of damage. Only one fireball may be created per use of "Fireball".

Your character is not required to have a target in sight in order to use "Fireball".

Parrying a fireball will automatically disarm the being who performs the parry.

FIRE LIGHTNING

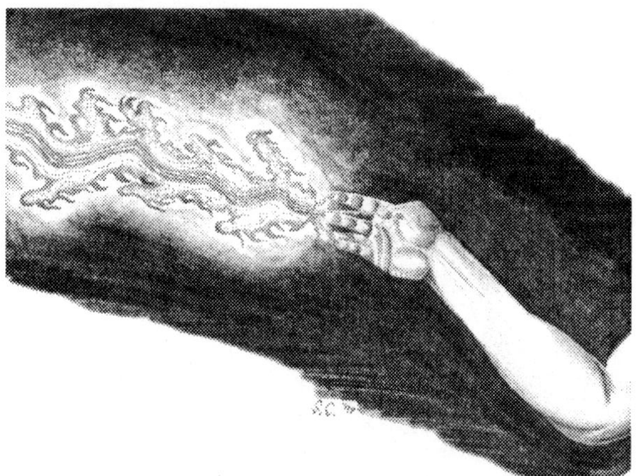

Learning Cost: 40 (F-22, L-7, S-11)
Learning Difficulty: 20
Required Forces: *Fire, Land, & Spirit*
Minimum Knowledge: F=120, L=75, S=75
Force Energy: 60
Defense: * Physical (Dodge)
Range: 800 feet

The Shinkai focuses the Mystic Forces of *Fire*, *Land*, and *Spirit* into the fingers of either hand. A streak of fiery lightning then shoots from the fingers uniting into one fiery bolt of lightning. Due to the incredible speed at which it travels the Shinkai attacking with "Fire Lightning" receives a +3 point bonus to the result of their attack Test (Sixth Sense/Performance Test). Any being struck by "Fire Lightning" receives Level 20 + 10 damage.

Beings struck by "Fire Lightning" must immediately make an Endurance Test against a Difficulty Value of 13 or be stunned for the remainder of the Turn.

Any non-metallic armor struck by "Fire Lightning" will take an amount of damage up to twice its Protection Rating instead of equal to its Protection Rating.

Your character is not required to have a target in sight in order to use "Fire Lightning".

FIRE WEAPON

Learning Cost: 23
Learning Difficulty: 12
Required Forces: *Fire*
Minimum Knowledge: 60
Force Energy: 22/12

The Shinkai focuses the Mystic Force of *Fire* into either hand and produces a melee weapon of his or her choice wrought completely of mystical fire.

The listed Force Energy is what is required to create a weapon with a Bulk Value of 1(or 1.5). The Required Force Energy and maintaining raises by 5 for each Bulk Value above 1 (or 1.5) of the fire weapon created.

Though it is made of fire, it will not burn the being that created it, and it is quite solid. If this fire weapon leaves the hand of the Shinkai that created it, it will instantly disappear.

These fire weapons do 6 Levels more damage than their mundane counterparts except to ice or water based objects or beings, in which case the fire weapon does 12 Levels more damage. Fire weapons can not be damaged except by water or ice-based means (GM's discretion as to how effective these sources are against fire weapons).

FLAME

Learning Cost: 12
Learning Difficulty: 7
Required Forces: *Fire*
Minimum Knowledge: 37
Force Energy: 5/2
Range: 3 feet

A small flame manifests and hovers within three feet of the summoning Shinkai. The Shinkai can move the flame at will but it must remain within three feet of him/her or it will vanish. The flame can not be created touching any living being, but can be moved into a living being after it is created.

The flame can be no larger than one foot in any direction and can not pass through solid objects. Contact with this flame will inflict the normal listed damage for fire of this size (Level 6).

FLAME RAGE

Learning Cost: 20
Learning Difficulty: 11
Required Forces: *Fire*
Minimum Knowledge: 55
Force Energy: 30
Range: 600 feet

This Force-effect causes an existing flame to suddenly and violently expand in all directions up to fifteen feet from the source. The Shinkai chooses how far the flame expands, up to the maximum range of fifteen feet. Anyone caught in this burst of fire will receive Level 11 damage. The raging fire only lasts for the Turn in which it is used after which time the flame or fire returns to its previous condition.

"Flame Rage" does not affect the weapons created by the Force-effect "Fire Weapon".

FOG

Learning Cost: 15
Learning Difficulty: 8
Required Forces: *Air*
Minimum Knowledge: 48
Force Energy: 20/12
Difficulty: 7
Range: * 200 feet

An extremely thick fog instantly manifests, covering an area up to two hundred feet in diameter from the focal point (focal point being anywhere within two hundred feet of the summoning Shinkai that he chooses). The Shinkai may choose how big of an area the fog will cover, not to exceed the maximum of two hundred feet. This fog will severely limit the vision of any one within it, and is nearly impossible to see into.

Any being within the fog will have their range of vision reduced to six feet and receive a -6 point penalty on any action normally requiring sight (GM's discretion).

FORCE BLOCK

Learning Cost: 30 (L-10, S-20)
Learning Difficulty: 14
Required Forces: *Land & Spirit*
Minimum Knowledge: L=45, S=75
Force Energy: 30/30
Defense: Mystical
Range: 600 feet

This Force-effect allows an invisible, mystical barrier to be placed between another being and the Mystic Forces, thereby keeping the target being from conjuring or even drawing

upon the Mystic Forces. "Force Block" cannot be placed on another being that is already drawing upon the Mystic Forces ("Force Sever" would be need in that situation).

The Shinkai using "Force Block" can tell whether or not their attempt to block their opponent was successful or not. A successfully binded target will immediately know they are blocked, even before they attempt to conjure.

It is possible for a being that is blocked by "Force Block" to break through the block and conjure. This requires the target being to make a Sixth Sense/Performance Test with a result higher than the Sixth Sense/Performance Test made by the Shinkai who placed the force block (the Sixth Sense/Performance made to initially use "Force Block"). If target's Sixth Sense/Performance Test *is* greater, then the block is shattered and the target can conjure normally.

A Shinkai may target more than one being with one use of "Force Block", but when used in this manner the Required Force Energy and maintenance is raised by 18 points for each additional being to be blocked.

The Sixth Sense/Performance Test made to determine if a target being can break through the force block is still made the same way as described above. All target being's make their own Sixth Sense/Performance Tests while the Shinkai who initiated the force block makes only one Sixth Sense/Performance Test (the one to initially use "Force Block"). Any being with a higher result on their Sixth Sense/Performance Test than the conjurer of "Force Block" breaks through the block.

If "Force Block" is tied off using "Force Tying" the Difficulty Value for breaking out of the block is a value equal to the result of the Sixth Sense/Performance Test made to tie off "Force Block".

If a Shinkai is blocked with "Force Block" by more than one Shinkai, he must break through all of his opponent's "Force Blocks" before he can conjure. It only takes one "Force Block" to keep a Shinkai from drawing upon the Mystic Forces. For each additional Shinkai using "Force Block" on another Shinkai, the Shinkai trying to break out of the block will receive a -1 penalty to their Sixth Sense/Performance Test to break out. So if five Shinkai are all using "Force Block" on one other Shinkai, the Shinkai getting blocked will receive a -4 point penalty to his Sixth Sense/Performance Test to break free (-4 because of the four additional "Force Blocks" being used).

It is a Major Action to attempt to break through "Force Block".

FORCE SEVER

Learning Cost: 50 (F-22, L-11, S-17)
Learning Difficulty: 18
Required Forces: *Fire, Land,* & *Spirit*
Minimum Knowledge: F=80, L=50, S=100
Force Energy: 50

Defense: * Mystical
Range: 600 feet

"Force Block" is required before a character can learn "Force Sever". "Force Sever" can cut the flows of the Mystic Forces off from a target being who is presently drawing upon them. In the instant that the flows are severed "Force Sever" will revert to "Force Block". So, for all Turns following the use of "Force Sever" the stats and regulations for "Force Block" apply.

A Shinkai may sever the flows of more than one being with a single use of "Force Sever", but will receive a -2 point penalty to their Sixth Sense/Performance Test for each additional target. When used in this manner the required Force Energy is raised by 20 for each additional target.

For example: Your character is faced off with two other Shinkai who he knows are already actively conjuring and he wants to use "Force Sever" on both of them. Since your character is targeting one additional target he will get a -2 penalty to his attack Test (Sixth Sense/Performance Test). In addition, the Force Energy that he must expend is raised from 40 to 60.

Any Shinkai that is severed from the Mystic Forces by "Force Sever" suffers what is known as backlash. Backlash yields 4 Levels of damage for every Mystic Force that was being drawn upon at the time of severing. So if a being was drawing on all five of the Mystic Forces at the time they were severed they would take Level 20 damage from the backlash.

If the target of this Force-effect isn't conjuring at the time it is used, then "Force Sever" works as "Force Block" instead and reverts to the cost of initiating and maintaining "Force Block" for all subsequent Turns.

Though "Force Sever" will temporarily act as "Force Block" when used on targets that aren't actively conjuring or drawing upon any of the Mystic Forces, the Force Energy that is expended is that listed for "Force Sever" not "Force Block".

"Force Sever" is ineffective against tied flows.

FORCE TYING

Learning Cost: 21 (L-9, S-12)
Learning Difficulty: 17
Required Forces: *Land & Spirit*
Minimum Knowledge: L=70, S=90
Force Energy: Variable
Difficulty: *
Range: same as the Force-effect to be tied

This Force-effect allows the flows of certain other Force-effects to be tied off, thus keeping the Force-effect active as if it were being maintained, but without the Shinkai actually maintaining it. Only certain Force-effects may be tied, and each that can be has its own specific limitations to being tied.

A Shinkai can only tie his own Force-effects. To tie off a

Force-effect requires the Shinkai to make a successful Sixth Sense/Performance Test against a Difficulty Value given by the following table or by the specific Force-effect. The Shinkai can not tie off a Force-effect in the same Turn that it is conjured, unless they are non-novice in all five of the Mystic Forces. On the following Turn the Shinkai simply ties off the Force-effect instead of maintaining it.

If the attempt to tie a Force-effect fails, then the Force-effect is released and must be re-conjured.

It is a Minor Action to tie off a Force-effect unless other Minor Actions are taken that Turn, in which case it is a Major Action.

One exception that will allow a Force-effect to be tied off as a Minor Action in the same Turn that other Minor Actions are made is if the other Minor Actions are performed *while* the Force-effect is being tied. For example, you may shout a command to a comrade while in the process of tying off a Force-effect, or draw a weapon while tying off a Force-effect. Only one Force-effect may be tied off in a single Turn.

The following table lists all of the Force-effects that can be tied off as well as the base Difficulty Values and required Force Energy for tying them off.

FORCE TYING			
Force-effect	Duration	Force Energy	Difficulty
Air Bind (per zone)	2 Turns	40	12
Air Shield	4 Turns	24	10
Darkness	4 Turns	30	10
Fire Weapon	5 Turns	32	10
Flame	11 Turns	11	9
Fog	4 Turns	24	9
Force Block	5 Turns	75	12
Ice Weapon	5 Turns	25	10
Illusion (Large)	4 Turns	60	12
Illusion (Self)	5 Turns	25	10
Illusion (Small)	5 Turns	50	11
Invisibility (Other)	4 Turns	60	11
Invisibility (Self)	4 Turns	40	11
Levitation (Other)	3 Turns	22	10
Levitation (Self)	3 Turns	15	9
Light Orb	11 Turns	55	9
Pain	3 Turns	37	11
Silence	3 Turns	30	9
Soft Stone	5 Turns	18	10
Spirit Shield	4 Turns	20	12
Tornado	3 Turns	75	11
Water Breathing	6 Turns	30	11
Wind Weapon	5 Turns	10	10

You may double the duration of the tie by doubling the amount of Force Energy expended at the time the Force-effect is tied off. The duration may not be extended for longer than double the listed duration. The duration of the tie is either as listed or double what's listed, not in increments between or beyond. So, to tie off "Air Bind" for 4 Turns would require the expenditure of 80 points of Force Energy.

Brightlings are unable to feel (via their Innate Ability of "Sense Conjuring") Force-effects that have been tied off, though "Force Sight" would still allow a being to see the tied Force-effect, unless "Concealed Force" had been used on it.

FREEZE (Animate)

Learning Cost: 20 (A-10, S-10)
Learning Difficulty: 13
Required Forces: *Air & Spirit*
Minimum Knowledge: A=55, S=55
Force Energy: 45
Defense: Mystical
Range: a number of feet equal to the Shinkai's Total Force Energy

Animate beings are instantly cooled to a dangerously low temperature. They are not actually frozen, but are brought very close to it. All actions and Tests requiring movement are penalized for 3 Turns. For the first Turn movement is reduced by fifty percent, round down, and the results of all Agility-based Tests are reduced by -4 points. On the second Turn movement is reduced by twenty five percent, round down, and all Agility-based Tests are reduced by -2 points. On the third Turn movement is normal but all Agility-based Tests are reduced by -1 point.

"Freeze" also does Level 5 damage to the target being. The same being can be "frozen" again before the previous "Freeze" wears off. This does not further increase the penalties or damage, but does renew the effects.

The damage rendered by this Force-effect is considered non-lethal damage.

FREEZE (Inanimate)

Learning Cost: 16 (A-8, W-8)
Learning Difficulty: 10
Required Forces: *Air & Water*
Minimum Knowledge: A=40, W=40
Force Energy: 20
Defense: Mystical
Difficulty: 6
Range: a number of feet equal to the Shinkai's Total Force Energy

Any inanimate object can be frozen with this Force-effect. The size of the object that can be frozen depends upon the Total Force Energy of the Shinkai conjuring the Force-effect.

The following table shows the approximate size of a target that can be frozen depending upon the Shinkai's Total Force Energy.

Total Force Energy	Diameter frozen
51	1'
71	5'
91	10'
111	15'

For every Force Energy value above 80 the number of feet that can be frozen increases by one foot.

Water can be frozen to a depth of one foot. Metal objects become easier to break when frozen. Armor is destroyed at its first Reduced Protection rating (R.P.), and weapons will be destroyed at their first Reduced Effectiveness rating (R.E.) instead of their Destroyed Rating.

Frozen objects take the same amount of time to unfreeze as it would for that object to unfreeze if frozen by normal means.

FROST BEAM

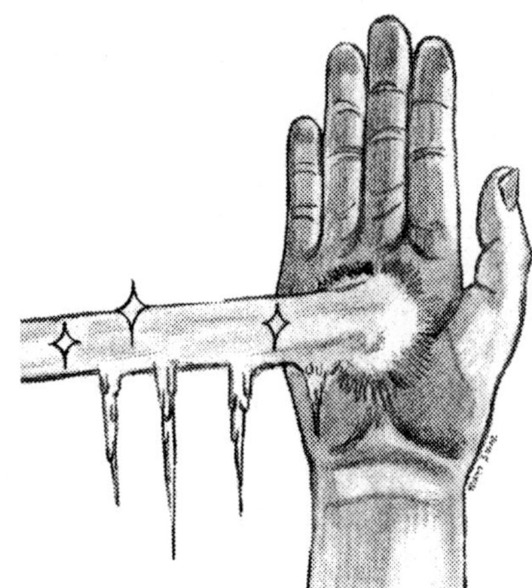

Learning Cost: 18 (A-9, W-9)
Learning Difficulty: 12
Required Forces: *Air & Water*
Minimum Knowledge: A=40, W=45
Force Energy: 30
Defense: Physical (Block or Dodge)
Range: 600 feet

The Shinkai focuses the Mystic Forces of *Air* and *Water* into either hand. A beam of sparkling frost then shoots out from the Shinkai's palm, inflicting Level 10 damage upon any living thing struck by it, as well as rendering a -4 Level penalty to their Agility for the duration of the Turn.

GROUND BLAST

Learning Cost: 30
Learning Difficulty: 16
Required Forces: *Land*
Minimum Knowledge: 80
Force Energy: 40
Difficulty: 9
Range: * 150 feet

If the target of "Ground Blast" is not natural ground, such as a stone floor, the Difficulty Value increases to 13.

A section of land sixteen feet in diameter will explode violently, sending rock and land from depths of up to one foot flying into the air. Anyone occupying the section of ground in which "Ground Blast" is used is immediately knocked down and stunned, and receives Level 12 damage.

Beings occupying the space upon which "Ground Blast" is used are allowed to make a Random-roll Sixth Sense Test to sense the building of explosive forces beneath them.

The base Difficulty Value to sense the explosion is 10. If successful, the target senses the danger and may attempt to jump or move out of the area of the "Ground Blast". The GM will determine the Difficulty Value of the Agility/Performance Test needed to jump out of harms way. The average base Difficulty Value for such a feat is 16.

If a being struck by "Ground Blast" was standing, the damage goes to their legs. If the being was lying down, the damage goes to their chest and/or back (torso). If the being was sitting, the damage goes to their pelvis.

HEALING

Learning Cost: 40
Learning Difficulty: 17
Required Forces: *Spirit*
Minimum Knowledge: 75
Force Energy: 50
Difficulty: 9
Range: Touch

This Force-effect instantly heals a number of points of damage up to the Total Force Energy of the Shinkai using "Healing", as well as restoring a number of Force Energy points equal to half the number of points of damage removed (round down).

This Force-effect does not heal damage from injuries when used on a being with damage beyond injury damage. When used on someone with no damage beyond injury damage it will heal one injury, even a Critical Injury, (the closest injury to being healed) and the damage from that injury.

If a being does not have *any* Life Force remaining (they are dead), then this Force Effect is useless.

A Shinkai may not use "Healing" on him/herself.

HEALING WATER

Learning Cost: 44
Learning Difficulty: 18
Required Forces: *Spirit*
Minimum Knowledge: 80
Force Energy: 50
Difficulty: 10
Range: 2 feet

A Shinkai can turn a small amount of water (1 standard-bottle) into water with healing properties. When this water is ingested it will heal 3D10 +10 points of damage and restore a number of points of Force Energy equal to half the amount of damage recovered (round down). The effects of the healing water take place 1D4 Turns after drinking it.

If a being with no damage ingests this water, it will heal one injury, even a Critical Injury, but will not restore any Force Energy). One standard-bottle of this water is enough for one use.

This "healing" water will return to normal water on the first nightfall after it is created.

ICE WEAPON

Learning Cost: 18 (A-9, W-9)
Learning Difficulty: 11
Required Forces: *Air & Water*
Minimum Knowledge: A=50, W=40
Force Energy: * 16/10

The Shinkai focuses the Mystic Forces of *Air* and *Water* into either hand and produces a melee weapon wrought completely of mystical ice. These weapons are not cold to the touch to the Shinkai who create them, and though made of ice these weapons are surprisingly durable (being wrought straight from the Mystic Forces and bound in a unique fashion). Ice weapons can withstand a great amount of abuse without being damaged.

The listed Force Energy is what is required to create an ice weapon with a Bulk Value of 1to 1.5. For each Bulk Value increase beyond 1.5 of the weapon created the required Force Energy for creating and maintaining it increases by 3.

Ice weapons yield 5 Levels more damage than their mundane counter-parts, except to fire based objects or beings to which they render 10 Levels more damage. A cut from an ice weapon sends an unnatural shock of cold through the victim stunning them for the remainder of the Turn unless they can make a successful Endurance Test against a Difficulty Value of 12.

In order to maintain an ice weapon it must remain in the grasp of the Shinkai who created it. When an ice weapon is destroyed or released it simply vanishes into mist.

Stats for ice weapons are as follows:
Weight: 3 lb.
Size: variable
Destroyed Rating: 200 (Ice weapons have no Reduced Effectiveness ratings)

ILLUSION (Large)

Learning Cost: 30 (A-7, L-11, S-12)
Learning Difficulty: 20

Required Forces: *Air, Land, & Spirit*
Minimum Knowledge: A=40, L=60, S=70
Force Energy: 40/30
Difficulty: 12
Range: * 75 feet

The Shinkai can create a very large illusion that can completely mask both animate and inanimate objects within the area of the illusion. Any thing or being within the range of the illusion can be masked (made to appear differently than it actually is). An exception to this rule is that illusion can not turn an area invisible. It can only change the appearance of an area, not cause it to become invisible. The illusion must take on the form of some sort of matter. When any being or object moves or is moved out of the affected area they will again appear as they were.

"Illusion (Large)" affects all of the senses except touch. Illusions created with "Illusion (Large)" may have motion.

The size of the illusion can be no larger in any direction (from the focal point) than a number of feet equal to the Shinkai's Total Force Energy.

The Learning Cost listed above does not apply if "Illusion (Small)" is already known. For those who already know "Illusion (Small)", the Learning Cost for "Illusion (Large)" is only 15 (A-7, L-3, S-5).

Changing an existing illusion requires a new use of "Illusion" and is considered a Major Action, not maintaining. Changing an illusion includes the adding or taking away of any elements from the illusion, or noticeably altering any of the elements of the illusion.

If another illusion of any type is used on the same area as an existing illusion, the illusion created by the Shinkai with the highest Total Force Energy will remain.

Beings with a Sixth Sense of Level 10 or higher have a twenty percent chance of seeing through the illusion the first time they see it. They will still see the illusion, but will also be able to see through it to the true surroundings or elements within it.

If the illusion is changed or another illusion is created, beings viewing them may roll percentile dice again to see if they realize they are viewing an illusion.

ILLUSION (Self)

Learning Cost: 14 (L-6, S-8)
Learning Difficulty: 15
Required Forces: *Land & Spirit*
Minimum Knowledge: L=40, S=50
Force Energy: 20/10
Difficulty: 6
Range: Self

A Shinkai can mask himself to seemingly take on the appearance of any other being or object that is roughly the same size and shape as himself. All of the senses except touch are affected, so anyone looking at the Shinkai under the effects of "Illusion (Self)" would see and smell whatever resemblance that the Shinkai had taken on and his voice would also sound like that of the mocked form. As with "Illusion (Large)" this Force-effect can not make an area to be invisible. It can only change the appearance of an area, not cause it to become invisible. The illusion must take on the form of some sort of matter.

Changing the illusion is considered another use of "Illusion (Self)", not maintaining. Changing an illusion includes the adding or taking away of any elements from the illusion, or noticeably altering any of the elements of the illusion.

Beings with a Sixth Sense of Level 10 or higher have a twenty five percent chance of seeing through the illusion the first time they see it. They will still see the illusion, but will also be able to see through it to the true surrounding or element within it.

If the illusion is changed or another illusion is created, beings viewing them may roll percentile dice again to see if they realize they are viewing an illusion.

ILLUSION (Small)

Learning Cost: 20 (L-8, S-12)
Learning Difficulty: 17
Required Forces: *Land & Spirit*
Minimum Knowledge: L=50, S=60
Force Energy: 30/20
Difficulty: 9
Range: 300 feet

The Shinkai can partially mask an area (make it appear differently than it actually is) up to a number of feet in any direction (from the focal point) equal to his or her Total Force Energy. Only inanimate objects within the affected area will be masked by the illusion.

Animate beings are not affected by "Illusion (Small)". They continue to appear as they normally would, only their surroundings changing. As with the other forms of illusion this Force-effect can not turn an area invisible. It can only *change* the appearance of an area, not cause it to become invisible. The illusion must take on the form of some sort of matter.

Illusions created by "Illusion (Small)" affect only sight and sound, and do not contain motion as in "Illusion (Large)".

Changing the illusion is considered another use of "Illusion (Small)", not maintaining. Changing an illusion includes adding or taking away of any elements from the illusion, or noticeably altering any of the elements of the illusion.

Beings with a Sixth Sense of Level 10 or higher have a twenty five percent chance of seeing through the illusion the first time they see it. They will still see the illusion, but will also be able to see through it to the true surrounding or element within it.

If the illusion is changed or another illusion is created, beings viewing them may roll percentile dice again to see if

they realize they are viewing an illusion.

INTENSE HEAT

Learning Cost: 16
Learning Difficulty: 12
Required Forces: *Fire*
Minimum Knowledge: 50
Force Energy: 26
Defense: Mystical
Difficulty: *
Range: 75 feet

Inanimate objects are instantly brought to a red-hot temperature (at the GM's discretion some materials/objects may ignite when subjected to "Intense Heat"). The Shinkai must overcome the appropriate Difficulty Value *and* any Mystical Defense the target may have in order to heat the object.

The size of the objects which can be heated with this Force-effect is dependent upon the Total Fire Knowledge of the Shinkai using "Intense Heat". In general, the Damage Yield from touching any object that has been heated by "Intense Heat", that is still hot of course, is Level 7.

The following chart shows the size of objects that can be heated based on the different Total Fire Knowledge values of the conjuring Shinkai. Also listed is the Difficulty Value for heating objects according to their size. It may take several Turns (GM's discretion) for the heated object to cool.

Total Fire Knowledge	Size of Target	Difficulty Value
50-55	1 foot	4
56-61	3 feet	8
62-67	7 feet	12
68-73	13 feet	16
74-79	21 feet	32
80-85	31 feet	45

* For each 20 points of Fire Knowledge above 85, 1 foot is added to size of target that can be heated, and 5 points are added to the Difficulty Value.

INVINCIBILITY

Learning Cost: 76 (A-12, F-15, L-17, S-20, W-12)
Learning Difficulty: 27
Required Forces: *Air, Fire, Land, Spirit, & Water*
Minimum Knowledge: A=80, F=110, L=125, S=150, W=90
Force Energy: 100/100
Range: Self

For the duration of "Invincibility" the Shinkai can not be harmed by any known means, however there are some drawbacks to using this Force-effect. The drawbacks are as follows:

1. The instant that the Shinkai ceases using "Invincibility" all of their remaining Force Energy is expended.

2. On the Turn that the Shinkai ceases to use "Invincibility"

he receives 4 Fatigue Points to all attributes.

3. After using this Force-effect the Shinkai is unable to recovery any Force Energy until first hour (if it is already the first hour when the Shinkai uses "Invincibility" he can not recover any more Force Energy until the first hour of the next day).

INVISIBILITY (Other)

Learning Cost: 20 (A-10, S-10)
Learning Difficulty: 22
Required Forces: *Air & Spirit*
Minimum Knowledge: A=140, S=80
Force Energy: 60/30
Range: 150 feet

In order to learn this Force-effect the Shinkai must first know "Invisibility (Self)".

With the use of "Invisibility", a Shinkai can cause a target being (only living beings are affected) to become completely invisible. The target will remain invisible as long as "Invisibility" is maintained, tied, or until they move out of the effective range.

Items touching the being under the influence of this Force-effect that do not have a Bulk Value greater than 3, and are not protruding more than five feet from the affected being's body, will also become invisible. If they move beyond five feet from the being under the influence of this Force-effect, the portion of the item extending beyond five feet will become visible.

INVISIBILITY (Self)

Learning Cost: 40 (A-20, S-20)
Learning Difficulty: 21
Required Forces: *Air & Spirit*
Minimum Knowledg*e*: A=130, S=70
Force Energy: 50/20
Range: Self

The Shinkai can make himself totally invisible for as long as he maintains this Force-effect (or for as long as he may have tied it off for).

Someone with the Universal Talent "Force Sight" can see the glow of conjuring around the invisible being, unless they had tied off the Force-effect and used "Concealed Force".

Items touching the Shinkai using this Force-effect that do not have a Bulk Value greater than 3, and are not protruding more than five feet from the Shinkai's body, will also become invisible. If they move beyond five feet from the Shinkai using this Force-effect, the portion of the item extending beyond five feet will become visible.

LANDQUAKE

Learning Cost: 40
Learning Difficulty: 17
Required Forces: *Land*
Minimum Knowledge: 200
Force Energy: 80
Difficulty: 10
Range: * The focal point is a number of feet away no greater than the conjuring Shinkai's Total Force Energy.

This Force-effect causes the ground to quake violently. The ground will shake violently for "x" number of feet in every direction from "Landquake's" focal point, where "x" is equal to a number of feet no greater than the conjuring Shinkai's Total *Land* Knowledge value.

At the beginning of any Turn that anyone is standing on this shaking ground, they must make an Agility/Performance Test against a Difficulty Value of 37 or be knocked down. It is a Major Action for a being to get back onto their feet as long as they remain in the area undergoing the quaking.

Needless to say these landquakes can render serious damage to buildings and structures within their range, making "Landquake" a very powerful Force-effect for the amount of Force Energy required. Average structures in an area undergoing a landquake have a thirty percent chance each Turn of toppling or collapsing.

"Landquake" lasts for 3 Turns. If more than one "Landquake" is cast upon the same section of ground at the same time, the Difficulty Value of the Agility/Performance Test to remain standing is raised by 5 for each additional "Landquake" used.

LAND VAPORS

Learning Cost: 15
Learning Difficulty: 12
Required Forces: *Land*
Minimum Knowledge: 50
Force Energy: 30
Difficulty: 8
Range: * 150 feet

The Shinkai can cause a section of ground (must be actual ground not solid stone, or stone floors, etc.) up to fifty feet in diameter, and up to one hundred and fifty feet away, to release toxic fumes. These fumes are barely visible and have only a slight smell. They spread ten feet per Turn from the focal point until they dissipate, which is three Turns after they appear.

Inhaling these fumes will cause temporary paralysis for 1D4 Turns (unless the victim makes a successful Endurance Test against a Difficulty Value of 10, or 14 if the Shinkai conjuring "Land Vapors" is not novice with Land). While paralyzed the victim is not capable of any more movement than blinking their eyes and speaking.

A Random-roll Intelligence Test should be given to targets of "Land Vapors". On a result of 12 or better they spot the fumes and may respond accordingly before they are affected.

LEVITATION (Other)

Learning Cost: 10
Learning Difficulty: 16
Required Forces: *Air*
Minimum Knowledge: 60
Force Energy: 35/15
Defense: * Mystical +2
Range: * 60 feet

"Levitation (Self)" must be known before this Force-effect can be learned.

The rules and use of this Force-effect, unless stated otherwise, are the same as for "Levitation (Self)" except "Levitation (Other)" levitates other beings instead of one's self.

The maximum amount of weight that can be lifted with "Levitation (Other)" is equal to the conjuring Shinkai's Total Force Energy + 50.

* The target of this Force-effect must be within sixty feet of the conjuring Shinkai in order to be used, but after it is initiated the target can be levitated further than sixty feet away from the Shinkai using "Levitation".

LEVITATION (Self)

Learning Cost: 20
Learning Difficulty: 14
Required Forces: *Air*
Minimum Knowledge: 50
Force Energy: 25/10
Range: * Self

Using this Force-effect allows a Shinkai to levitate him/herself into the air. The maximum number of feet the Shinkai can levitate is equal to one foot for every 2 Total *Air* Knowledge points of the levitating Shinkai.

The Shinkai may levitate (without Fatigue) as long as he/she and all carried items weigh no more than the

Shinkai's weight + a value equal to his or her Total Force Energy. For every pound above this that the Shinkai levitates, 1 Fatigue Point will be received.

The maximum amount of weight that can be levitated with is a number of pounds no greater than the Shinkai's weight + a value equal to his or her Total Force Energy value + 50.

Movement in the horizontal plane is very slow while levitating. A levitating Shinkai can only move (horizontally) at a rate of 5 feet per Turn, while the actual vertical levitation may be as fast as 60 feet per Turn.

LIE DETECTION

Learning Cost: 17 (S-9, W-8)
Learning Difficulty: 15
Required Forces: *Spirit & Water*
Minimum Knowledge: S=45, W=45
Force Energy: 20/20
Defense: Mystical
Range: 5 feet

While using this Force-effect a Shinkai can sense untruthfulness in a target being (only one being at a time may be targeted). Any intentional untruthful statement from the target being while being observed with "Lie Detection" will cause them to suffer Level 1 damage and a significant amount of pain. The Shinkai using "Lie Detection" will immediately recognize the untruthful statement.

The target being will feel no pain, nor will the Shinkai sense the lie, if the target is unaware that they are lying.

It is important to mention that for unknown reasons Loremek are often unaffected by the use of this Force-effect. So using this Force-effect on a Loremek often proves useless (GM's discretion as to whether or not a particular Loremek is immune to this Force-effect).

LIFE BOND

Learning Cost: 20
Learning Difficulty: 18
Required Forces: *Spirit*
Minimum Knowledge: 60
Force Energy: 40
Defense: Mystical
Range: Touch (to bond), there is no limit to the range between the two bonded beings

Using "Life Bond", a Shinkai can bond his Life Force to that of another being. When this Shinkai receives damage in excess of their Life Force value, the excess points of damage are added to the other being with whom the Shinkai was bonded. This Force-effect can be used on animals and ruling races but does not work on Shadow-kin.

Kuldar has a Life Force of 30 and decides to use "Life Bond" on Matusu, who has a Life Force of 46. Later that day Kuldar does battle with a wretchin. The wretchin inflicts 40 points of damage to Kuldar. Matusu suddenly receives 10 points of damage and Kuldar continues to live by using Matusu's Life Force, though he is unconscious.

The bond can work both ways so that the bonded individual could also take damage greater than his/her Life Force by using the Shinkai's Life Force to absorb the excess damage. The Shinkai using "Life Bond" must determine whether or not the bond is two-way at the moment of bonding.

A bonded being feels a drain of energy when he is receiving the bonding Shinkai's damage (vice versa), but does not feel the pain associated with that damage. The Shinkai can also sense the death of a being with which he was bonded, and vice versa if the bond was two-way.

A Shinkai may only have one being bonded at any one time, and may not be bonded himself while bonded to someone else. This bond will only last for 8 hours before terminating.

LIGHTNING

Learning Cost: 32 (F-22, S-10)
Learning Difficulty: 16
Required Forces: *Fire & Spirit*
Minimum Knowledge: F=55, S=50
Force Energy: 40
Defense: * Physical (Dodge)
Range: 1800 feet

The Shinkai focuses the Mystic Forces of *Fire* and *Spirit* into the fingers of either hand and summons a bolt of lightning that arcs from his fingertips. This bolt of lightning can be directed toward a target, that if struck, will suffer Level 18 +10 points of damage.

Due to the incredible speed at which lightning travels, the Shinkai attacking with "Lightning" receives a +3 point bonus to his attack Test (Sixth Sense/Performance).

Beings struck by "Lightning" must immediately make an Endurance Test against a Difficulty Value of 11 or be stunned for the remainder of the Turn.

It is not necessary to have a target in sight in order to use "Lightning".

LIGHT ORB

Learning Cost: 15 (F-8, S-7)
Learning Difficulty: 8
Required Forces: *Fire & Spirit*
Minimum Knowledge: F=40, S=40
Force Energy: 15/10
Range: * 20 feet

A radiant orb of light approximately eight inches in diameter is created in mid-air up to twenty feet away. The Shinkai (who created it) can control its movements mentally, even willing it to pass through solid objects (inanimate only). The orb of light can be moved at a maximum speed

of 50 feet per Turn.

The intensity of the light can be changed by the creating Shinkai at any time and can illuminate a maximum area of fifty feet in diameter.

If "Darkness" is cast upon the same area as a "Light Orb", then the Force-effect whose controlling Shinkai has the highest Total Force Energy will prevail.

LIVING LAND

Learning Cost: 18
Learning Difficulty: 11
Required Forces: *Land*
Minimum Knowledge: 55
Force Energy: 20/16
Difficulty: 9
Range: 75 feet

With this Force-effect a Shinkai can cause large plants, vines, trees, and their roots to slither and attack a selected target or targets. These plants, vines, and trees will obey the mental commands of the Shinkai who is using "Living Land" on them. Only one plant, vine, root, etc. can be affected with a single use of "Living Land".

These vines and roots, etc.. have an average Strength of Level 8 and an average Agility of Level 5. The exact strength of a plant depends upon its type and size (GM's discretion). Most plants have an average Damage Yield of Level 5.

Unless the GM decides otherwise all plants, vines, etc. have the ability to grapple a target (see the "Grappling" Talent for details on grappling).

These plants and vines can not uproot and chase targets,

therefore the target must be within their reach. These vines and roots make an Agility/Performance Test to attack. Damage is determined in the same way that characters with weapons do (a number of points equal to two times the Level of Strength applied plus the result of the dice rolled for the vine's Damage Yield; Level 5).

The exact abilities of the plants, vines, trees, etc. are left up to the GM.

As a good baseline for GM use, a wrist-thick vine must receive 30 points of cutting damage, or 60 points of crushing damage, before it is severed.

MAGICAL DETECTION

Learning Cost: 16 (F-7, S-9)
Learning Difficulty: 12
Required Forces: *Fire* & *Spirit*
Minimum Knowledge: F=40, S=45
Force Energy: 16/8
Range: Sight

This Shinkai focuses the Mystic Forces of *Fire* and *Spirit* into his eyes. The Shinkai's eyes then turn a soft, mystical blue color. The Shinkai is now able to see whether or not an item is enchanted (magical). Any enchanted object will appear to glow blue to a Shinkai viewing them with "Magical Detection". The deeper blue that an object glows, the stronger the enchantment upon it.

The Shinkai will also immediately sense the basic nature and effect of the enchantment. Different shades of blue in a single item represent the presence of multiple enchantments.

An "Enchanter" who uses this Force-effect will also immediately know the Enchantment Rating ("Very Simple", "Simple", "Average", etc.) of the enchantment, or enchantments.

MESSAGE WARD

Learning Cost: 28 (L-12, S-16)
Learning Difficulty: 12
Required Forces: *Land* & *Spirit*
Minimum Knowledge: L=60, S=50
Force Energy: 28
Difficulty: 7
Range: * 10 feet

This type of ward can be placed on an area as large as ten feet in diameter, but can be no further away from the creating Shinkai (at the time of creation) than five feet. Any being who enters this area will trigger the ward, which will then cause a message left by the creating Shinkai to be heard. The message must be spoken aloud as the ward is created. If the message is longer than 1 Turn then the creating Shinkai must maintain the Force-effect until the message is completed.

Note: Normally once a ward is triggered it ceases to exist,

but there is a way to make a ward reset itself for use again. When creating the ward the Shinkai can expend twice the listed Force Energy for that particular ward, thus allowing the ward to reset itself one time after it is triggered. If three times the listed Force Energy is expended, then the ward can reset itself twice, if four times the listed Force Energy is expended it can reset three times, etc..

Wards can be created to target only specific targets or beings, but the required Force Energy increases by 5 for each type of target specification added. So, a ward that targets only Shadow-kin and Brightlings would require 10 more points of Force Energy than the same ward with no target specifications.

Any Shinkai who creates a ward can also destroy that same ward by simply reversing the flows. This expends no Force Energy and is considered to be a Minor Action. The only way to destroy a ward created by another Shinkai is to use the Force-effect "Unravelling".

METABOLISM

Learning Cost: 16 (L-8, S-8)
Learning Difficulty: 10
Required Forces: *Land & Spirit*
Minimum Knowledge: L=40, S=40
Force Energy: 18
Defense: Mystical
Range: Touch

The Shinkai can increase or decrease the metabolism of him/herself or a target being. When decreased, a being can go twice as long without food or water as they other wise could have. When increased, twice as much food and/or water is required. "Metabolism" will last for 1 day, in which time a single target may not be influenced by another "Metabolism" Force-effect.

See the "ADVENTURING" Section for details of food and water requirements.

MUTATION

Learning Cost: 32 (L-15, S-17)
Learning Difficulty: 16
Required Forces: *Land & Spirit*
Minimum Knowledge: L=55, S=75
Force Energy: 38
Defense: Mystical
Range: 30 feet

With this Force-effect a Shinkai can grossly mutate another being's body, crippling and severely maiming them. Only one body part can be mutated per use of this Force-effect (one arm, one leg, etc.). A list of the specific body areas which can be mutated and the effects of the mutation are given below.

Face: Creatures that bite receive a -4 penalty to bite attacks and only do fi damage with their bite.

Arm (or Wing): The results of all Tests requiring the use of the affected arm are reduced by half rounded down. Mutating a beings wing or wings renders them incapable of flying.

Leg: If only one leg is affected, the results of all Agility-based Tests are reduced by half, and movement is decreased by twenty five percent. If both legs are affected, the results of all Agility-based Tests are reduced by half with an additional -1D10 penalty, and movement is decreased by fifty percent.

The penalties for mutation to the legs only apply if the mutated being is moving on the ground or performing an action than would normally require the use of legs. It would not penalize the Agility of a flying creature if you mutated its legs, at least not while it is flying. Also a being that wishes to throw a dagger would receive no penalties to their attack for having one or more legs mutated, even though throwing a dagger is an Agility-based action.

The effects of "Mutation" are permanent; but can, however, be removed with "Cure" or another equally effective means (GM's discretion).

More than one use of "Mutation" at a time upon a single part of a target will have no additional effects.

PAIN

Learning Cost: 22 (F-9, S-13)
Learning Difficulty: 12
Required Forces: *Fire & Spirit*
Minimum Knowledge: F=50, S=60
Force Energy: 30/25
Defense: Mystical
Range: 225 feet

Extreme pain is inflicted upon the victim of this Force-effect. The victim's entire body is racked with a horrible pain that is nearly unbearable. "Pain" inflicts Level 8 damage as well as a -2 point penalty to both Physical and Mystical Initiatives. All Tests (attribute/Performance and regular attribute Tests) become Random-roll Tests for the

duration of "Pain".

At the beginning of each Turn the being under the influence of "Pain" can make a Random-roll Willpower Test against a Difficulty Value of 10 to attempt to ignore and overcome the pain. If they are successful they may ignore all effects of "Pain" for the remainder of the Turn, but must make a new Random-roll Willpower Test each subsequent Turn that "Pain" is maintained on them to be able to continue to ignore it.

POSSESSION

Learning Cost: 27
Learning Difficulty: 17
Required Forces: *Spirit*
Minimum Knowledge: 130
Force Energy: 30
Defense: Mystical
Range: 300 feet

The use of this Force-effect allows a Shinkai to possess the body of an animal. This takes 2 Turns to achieve. The Shinkai makes the Sixth Sense/Performance Test to determine the success of the Force-effect on the second Turn. Full concentration must be maintained for these 2 Turns or the possession will automatically fail. The Shinkai must be able to see the animal he is attempting to possess.

While in possession of an animal's body the Shinkai has all senses and sensations of that particular animal. The Shinkai is in complete control of the animal's body, but has no control over their own body until the possession has ended (the Shinkai's body will be in a sleep like state). The Shinkai is, however, slightly aware of his/her body and will know immediately if anything disturbs it. It is not possible for a Shinkai to conjure while in possession of an animal.

A Shinkai who fails an attempt to possess an animal can't attempt to possess that same animal again until his or her Total Force Energy is increased.

The Shinkai may stay in possession of an animal for a maximum number of Turns equal to his Sixth Sense value. The Shinkai can end the possession at will at any time. It takes the Shinkai 1 full Turn to end the possession and return to his or her body. If the animal dies while possessed by a Shinkai, the Shinkai will return to his/her own body, but much slower than normal (1D8 Turns). During the transition from the animal's body to their own the Shinkai's Life Force is suspended in a state of limbo during which time they are not able to see, hear, or otherwise sense anything.

Any damage done to a possessed animal does not carry over to the Shinkai.

PURIFY

Learning Cost: 17 (F-4, S-8, W-5)
Learning Difficulty: 10
Required Forces: *Fire*, *Spirit*, & *Water*
Minimum Knowledge: F=35, S=40, W=35
Force Energy: 15
Difficulty: *
Range: 2 feet

With this Force-effect inanimate substances can be cleansed. The size and/or amount which can be cleansed varies according to the Total Force Energy of the Shinkai using "Purify". For every 70 points of Total Force Energy of the conjuring Shinkai solid objects to be purified may be as large as one foot in any direction and up to one gallon of liquids may be purified.

Different objects may have varying Difficulty Values in order to be purified. The GM assigns the Difficulty Values as he/she sees fit. Whether or not "Purify" will affect a particular object or substance is also up to the GM's discretion.

Some examples of a few common objects and substances which can be purified and their Difficulty Values are listed below. The Difficulty Values are treated the same as a Mystical Defense (a Sixth Sense/Performance Test is made when the Shinkai uses "Purify" the result of which must exceed the Difficulty Value in order to be successful).
Stagnant Water: 8
Spoiled Rations: 9
Poisoned Food/Water: 12

QUICKSAND

Learning Cost: 22 (L-11, W-11)
Learning Difficulty: 13
Required Forces: *Land & Water*
Minimum Knowledge: L=65, W=65
Force Energy: 35
Difficulty: 8
Range: 75 feet

The Shinkai can cause an area of ground up to ten feet in diameter to turn into quicksand. This quicksand can be any

depth the Shinkai wishes up to ten feet deep. Anyone caught in this quicksand must make three consecutive Agility/Performance Tests to escape. The base Difficulty Value for this Test is 12. No "escape" Tests can not be made on the same Turn that the being enters the quicksand. Every 5 Turns that a being struggles to free themselves from quicksand they will receive 1 Fatigue Point.

It takes an individual 20 Turns, under normal circumstances, before they will sink completely under.

REAL TOUCH

Learning Cost: 18 (A-9, L-9)
Learning Difficulty: 12
Required Forces: *Air & Land*
Minimum Knowledge: A=40, L=40
Force Energy: 3 to 83
Range: 225 feet

The Shinkai can cause a target being to feel a pinch, slap, punch, etc. as if he were actually being touched or struck. An extreme amount of force can not be applied in this manner, but it is possible to yield up to Level 8 damage in this manner. If no damage is to be dealt to the target the Force Energy required is 3. For each Level of damage to be inflicted the required Force Energy is increased by 10.

REGENERATION

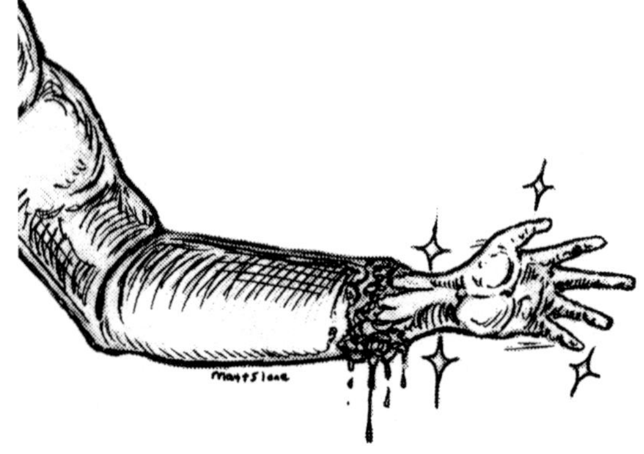

Learning Cost: 40 (S-25, W-15)
Learning Difficulty: 22
Required Forces: *Spirit & Water*
Minimum Knowledge: S=120, W=60
Force Energy: 65
Difficulty: 12
Range: Touch

"Regeneration" is a type of healing, but without as much damage curing properties as the Force-effect "Healing" (1D12 points of damage is recovered by "Regeneration"). "Regeneration" can cause a target being to re-grow any missing or severely mangled limbs or body parts within one day. Scars can also be removed with "Regeneration".

If a being has suffered extensive mutilation, from a source such as the Force-effect "Disintegration" for example, the GM may rule that "Regeneration" will have no effect.

RESURRECTION

Learning Cost: 50 (F-13, L-15, S-22)
Learning Difficulty: 28
Required Forces: *Fire, Land, & Spirit*
Minimum Knowledge: F=120, L=140, S=160
Force Energy: 150/50
Difficulty: 20
Range: Touch

This is an extremely powerful Force-effect that when used improperly is considered to be an act of the Shadow.

When used on a being who has been dead for 2 Turns or less it will bring that being back to life, 1 damage point away from their Life Force. When used in this manner "Resurrection" is not considered to be an act of the Shadow.

The trouble comes when it is used on a being who has been dead for *more* than 2 Turns. When used on a being dead for more than 2 Turns, it will merely animate that being, not truly give back their life. The resurrected being will only be semi-aware of who or what they were. They must obey any commands given by the Shinkai who resurrected them. This type of resurrection only lasts as long as the Shinkai maintains the flows of "Resurrection".

A Shinkai resurrected after being dead for more than 2 Turns no longer has the ability to conjure. Also, any beings or creatures with magical or innate abilities no longer possess those abilities after this type of resurrection.

Any Shinkai who uses "Resurrection" to bring back beings whose Life Force is completely gone (dead for more than 2 Turns) should receive a minimum of 2 Shadow Points, unless special circumstances prevail or the GM decides otherwise.

If a being has suffered mass mutilation, such as from the Force-effect "Disintegrate", the GM may determine that "Resurrection" has no effect.

RUNE LORE

Learning Cost: 50 (A-10, F-10, L-10, S-10, W-10)
Learning Difficulty: 20
Required Forces: *Air, Fire, Land, Spirit, & Water*
Minimum Knowledge: A=100, F=100, L=100, S=100, W=100
Force Energy: variable
Difficulty: *
Range: * Touch

This Force-effect gives the Shinkai the proper knowledge to be able to learn and draw runes, as well as kill them. There are many different types of runes with a wide variety of effects, all of which are discussed in detail in the "RUNE

LORE" Section .

RUNE WARDING

Learning Cost: 25 (A-5, F-5, L-5, S-5, W-5)
Learning Difficulty: 15
Required Forces: *Air, Fire, Land, Spirit, & Water*
Minimum Knowledge: A=130, F=130, L=130, S=130, W=130
Force Energy: variable
Range: Touch

This Force-effect is a companion to the Force-effect "Rune Lore". By using "Rune Warding" a Shinkai can protect the runes he or she creates from being killed, or at least from being easily killed.

Anyone attempting to kill a rune that has been warded must make a successful Sixth Sense/Performance Test against a base Difficulty Value of 20 instead of 10 in order to kill the rune. "Rune Warding" also allows a Shinkai to expend an extra amount of Force Energy at the creation of a rune in order to add damage yielding qualities to the rune which will affect anyone who tries to kill it.

While using this Force-effect every point of Force Energy expended (beyond the listed Force Energy for the particular rune) into the tracing of a rune, either at creation or at a later time, yields 1 point of damage to any individual who attempts to kill that rune. The damage yielded by a warded rune is given all at once just as the Force Energy is expended for the attempt to kill that rune. A maximum of 50 points of energy can be stored in a rune for the purpose of warding.

Once a warded rune releases the Force Energy placed into it (in the form of damage to an unfortunate victim) it is no longer warded, and may then be dealt with as it normally would be without any warding.

All of the Force Energy placed into a rune for the purpose of warding can only be done by the same Shinkai who created that particular rune, and must be placed in a single Turn.

SHOCK WAVE

Learning Cost: 35 (A-8, F-7, L-6, S-9, W-5)
Learning Difficulty: 18
Required Forces: *Air, Fire, Land, Spirit, & Water*
Minimum Knowledge: A=100, F=100, L=100, S=100, W=100
Force Energy: 40
Defense: Physical (Dodge)
Range: 300 feet

This Force-effect allows a Shinkai to release a wave of energy that severely interferes with the conjuring of other Shinkai. This wave of energy originates directly in front of the Shinkai's chest, where he or she has focused all five of the Mystic Forces, and spreads slightly as it travels. At its maximum range of three hundred feet it is seven feet wide; wide enough to strike up to three people if they are standing side by side. A shock wave gives off a faint blue glow that is only visible to beings with "Force Sight". To those who do not have "Force Sight" it is completely invisible.

If the target being, or beings, do not have "Force Sight" there is a seventy percent chance of an automatic hit. This is due to the shock wave's invisibility and incredible speed. If the opponent sets a Defense against "Shock Wave", and they are not automatically hit, they still receive a -6 point penalty to their Defense. It is extremely hard to dodge what you do not see.

Only Shinkai are affected by "Shock Wave". Any Shinkai struck by one of these shock waves suffers the following for the duration of the Turn in which they are struck, as well as the following Turn. A -5 Level penalty to their Sixth Sense and a fifty percent chance of failure for all Force-effects that do not require a Sixth Sense/Performance Test. Also Level 5 damage is inflicted for each Mystic Force drawn upon, every time they are drawn upon (for the duration of "Shock Wave").

At the moment the Shinkai is struck with one of these shock waves, they will feel as if a cold breeze has just washed over them. It lasts only for a second.

A Shinkai hit with more than one "Shock Wave" at a time will suffer no additional effects.

SIGNAL WARD

Learning Cost: 22 (A-12, S-10)
Learning Difficulty: 11
Required Forces: *Air & Spirit*
Minimum Knowledge: A=40, S=50
Force Energy: 14
Difficulty: 6
Range: * 100 feet

This ward can be placed on an area as large as one hundred feet in diameter. The Shinkai creating this ward must be within ten feet of the area to be warded in order to set the ward.

Any being entering this area will trigger the ward, at which

time the Shinkai who created the ward will immediately know that someone has entered the warded area. The Shinkai will also know how many and what type of beings entered the warded area, but the Shinkai must be no farther from the ward than a number of miles equal to his or her Total Force Energy in order to sense these things.

Note: Normally once a ward is triggered it ceases to exist, but there is a way to make a ward reset itself for use again. When creating the ward the Shinkai can expend twice the listed Force Energy for that particular ward, thus allowing the ward to reset itself 1 time after it is triggered. If three times the listed Force Energy is expended, then the ward can reset itself twice, if four times the required Force Energy is expended it can reset three times, etc..

Wards can be created to target only specific targets or beings, but the required Force Energy increases by 5 for each type of target specification added. So, a ward that targets only Brightlings and Loremek would require 10 more points of Force Energy than the same ward with no target specifi-cations.

Any Shinkai who creates a ward can also destroy that same ward by simply reversing the flows. This expends no Force Energy and is considered a Minor Action.

SILENCE

Learning Cost: 15
Learning Difficulty: 14
Required Forces: *Air*
Minimum Knowledge: 50
Force Energy: 20/20
Range: 100 feet

The Shinkai can cause all sound within one hundred feet of him or herself to be inaudible to all other beings within this range. *All* sound may be muted or only particular sounds (Shinkai's choice). For example: a Shinkai in a crowd of people could mute the voices and sounds of all other beings other than himself.

This Force-effect can not create sounds, it can only mute existing sounds.

SLEEP

Learning Cost: 40 (S-25, W-15)
Learning Difficulty: 22
Required Forces: *Spirit & Water*
Minimum Knowledge: S=150, W=65
Force Energy: 60
Defense: Mystical
Range: 75 feet

The Shinkai can cause one being to instantly fall asleep for 1 to 2 Turns (roll 1D4. A result of 1 or 2 = 1 Turn, 3 or 4 = 2 Turns). Even if the target's Defense is beat, they are still allowed to make a Willpower Test against a Difficulty Value

of 17 to avoid the effects. Success means they avoid the effects of "Sleep".

SLEEP WARD

Learning Cost: 50 (S-30, W-20)
Learning Difficulty: 25
Required Forces: *Spirit & Water*
Minimum Knowledge: S=160, W=75
Force Energy: 70
Difficulty: 12
Defense: Mystical
Range: 25 feet

This ward can be placed on an area as large as twenty five feet in diameter. The Shinkai creating this ward must be within ten feet of the area to be warded in order to set the ward.

Any being entering this area triggers the ward. If the Sixth Sense/Performance Test made by the Shinkai at the time he created the ward exceeds the target's Mystical Defense, then the target being must immediately make a successful Willpower Test against a Difficulty Value of 17 or fall asleep for 1 to 2 Turns (roll 1D4. A result of 1 or 2 = 1 Turn, 3 or 4 = 2 Turns).

Note: Normally once a ward is triggered it ceases to exist, but there is a way to make a ward reset itself for use again. When creating the ward the Shinkai can expend twice the listed Force Energy for that particular ward, thus allowing the ward to reset itself one time after it is triggered. If three times the listed Force Energy is expended, then the ward can reset itself twice, if four times the listed Force Energy is expended it can reset three times, etc..

Wards can be created to target only specific targets or beings, but the required Force Energy increases by 5 for each type of target specification added. So, a ward that targets only mundane animals and Shadow-sworn would require 10 more points of Force Energy than the same ward with no tar-get specifications.

Any Shinkai who creates a ward can also destroy that same

ward by simply reversing the flows. This expends no Force Energy and is considered a Minor Action. The only way to destroy a ward created by another Shinkai is to use the Force-effect "Unravelling".

SOFT STONE

Learning Cost: 20
Learning Difficulty: 13
Required Forces: *Land*
Minimum Knowledge: 70
Force Energy: 20/7
Difficulty: 9
Range: Touch

The Shinkai focuses the Mystic Force of *Land* into any part of his or her body that he wishes to use to soften stone. With a touch the Shinkai can cause stone to become soft and pliable. The stone turns soft at the area where the Shinkai touches and then spreads outward in all directions from that area. The stone could then be cut, shaped, have objects pushed into it, etc.

The largest amount of stone that can be affected by one use of "Soft Stone" can be no larger than 1 inch in any direction for each point of Total *Land* Knowledge of the Shinkai using "Soft Stone".

The listed Force Energy for initiating and maintaining this Force-effect is accurate only up to areas as large as thirty six inches in diameter. Beyond this the Force Energy required (initiating and maintaining) increases by 1 for each additional inch in diameter of stone to be affected. Basically 12 points of Force Energy for each additional 1 foot in diameter once beyond 3 feet in diameter.

SPEED RECOVERY

Learning Cost: 30 (S-20, W-10)
Learning Difficulty: 14
Required Forces: *Spirit & Water*

Minimum Knowledge: S=60, W=50
Force Energy: 35
Defense: Mystical
Range: Touch

The recipient of this Force-effect may now heal two injuries per day and has all Recovery Tests increased by 2 Levels. A Shinkai may use this Force-effect on him or herself. These effects last for two days.

A being may only benefit from one "Speed Recovery" at a time.

SPIRIT SHIELD

Learning Cost: 40 (A-10, F-10, S-20)
Learning Difficulty: 18
Required Forces: *Air, Fire, & Spirit*
Minimum Knowledge: A=60, F=60, S=125
Force Energy: 30/10
Defense: Mystical
Range: 30 feet

A Shinkai may place this shield on himself or another being. The shield is nearly invisible, giving off only a light red glow. The shield surrounds the target being's entire body and moves with him.

This shield is effective against any mystical based powers, whether it be Force-effects, enchantments, or the innate abilities of a creature. Some examples include; "Pain", "Suggestion", "Freeze (Animate)", "Weakness", "Metabolism", "Life Bond", "Concussion Sphere", a blast from a "Guardian" rune, etc.

As for Force-effects, if it a Mystical Defense is effective against it, it is a mystical based attack. The GM has the final say as to whether or not a particular attack is mystical-based.

A "Spirit Shield" has a Protection Rating (P.R.) of 20 against mystical attacks, and also gives the target being a +7 point bonus to any Mystical Defense they set while under the effects of this Force-effect.

A single being can not benefit from more than one use of "Spirit Shield" at a time.

STORM

Learning Cost: 45 (A-15, S-15, W-15)
Learning Difficulty: 20
Required Forces: *Air, Spirit, & Water*
Minimum Knowledge: A=125, S=85, W=125
Force Energy: 60
Difficulty: 14
Range: * The focal point is a number of feet away no greater than the summoning Shinkai's Total Force Energy x2.

A fierce storm of high winds, rain, hail, and lightning is summoned to an area of the Shinkai's choice. This storm takes 3 Turns to manifest and can cover an area as large as 1,000 feet in diameter from the focal point.

Each Turn that anyone remains within the storming area they will receive Level 15 +12 points of damage and must make an Agility/Performance Test against a Difficulty Value of 15 to remain standing. The storm lasts for 4 Turns or until the Shinkai who summoned it dismisses it.

This Force-effect can not create storms indoors. If you are inside of a building or structure when you use "Storm", the storm will manifest outside of the building.

STRENGTH

Learning Cost: 35
Learning Difficulty: 18
Required Forces: *Land*
Minimum Knowledge: 110
Force Energy: *
Defense: Mystical
Range: 300 feet

With this Force-effect a Shinkai can give himself or another being a temporary boost of strength. For every 25 points of Force Energy expended the recipient's Strength is increased by 1 Level. A single being may not have their Strength in-creased by more than 10 Levels by the use of this Force-effect.

The same being may benefit from multiple uses of "Strength" (maximum of five), but no more than one from the same Shinkai. So, up to five Shinkai with the "Strength" Force-effect could all use it on the same being at the same time.

This enhanced strength will last for a number of Turns equal to the Sixth Sense Level of the Shinkai who placed this Force-effect. This Force-effect can not be used to aide in the learning of Skills. Any Progress Tests made while under the effects of this Force-effect will automatically fail.

SUGGESTION

Learning Cost: 30
Learning Difficulty: 17
Required Forces: *Spirit*
Minimum Knowledge: 150
Force Energy: 40/30
Defense: Mystical +3
Range: 75 feet

A Shinkai can use this Force-effect to plant strong suggestions into the mind of other intelligent beings. However, the target being can still possibly resist the suggestion even if his Mystical Defense is not sufficient against the Force-effect. There is a twenty-five percent chance that the suggestion will be ignored, even if the target's Mystical Defense is overcome. Any suggestion for the target to perform any action that will directly bring harm to him or herself or someone whom they care about will always be ignored, unless the conjuring Shinkai's Total Force Knowledge is 250 or higher.

If the Shinkai using this Force-effect has a Total Force Knowledge value in *Spirit* of 250 or higher, the suggestion can bring harm and even death to the target. The suggestion need not be verbal, the Shinkai can merely will the suggestion upon the target and achieve the same results.

In short, a Shinkai using this Force-effect with a Force Knowledge value in *Spirit* of 250 or higher could suggest that a being jump off of a cliff, and there would only be a twenty-five percent chance that they would not comply. Of course if the target's Mystical Defense was not overcome then there is no chance that they will follow the suggestion.

The percent chance that the suggestion will be followed may be changed by the GM if he feels that the particular circumstance warrants it.

SUMMON *AIR* CREATURE

Learning Cost: 50 (A-28, S-22)
Learning Difficulty: 20
Required Forces: *Air & Spirit*
Minimum Knowledge: A=50, S=50
Force Energy: 25, 50, 100
Difficulty: * 7, 12, 17
Range: 1D10 feet

The result of this Force-effect is that an *Air* creature appears within 1D10 feet of the summoning Shinkai. The Shinkai can choose what type of *Air* creature that they are attempting to summon (they must, however, have enough Force Knowledge in the appropriate Mystic Force to do so). For summoning *Air* creatures the appropriate Mystic Force is *Air*.

There are three different types of *Air* creatures that are strong enough to survive out of their element for any length of time. In order of relative strength they are the grovling, chief, and boss.

A Shinkai with 50 to 74 points of Force Knowledge in the appropriate Mystic Force is capable of summoning a grovling. A Total Force Knowledge of 75 to 99 makes the Shinkai capable of summoning a chief, and 100 or higher allows a boss to be summoned. The Difficulty Value that must achieved on the Sixth Sense/Performance Test is 7 for summoning a grovling, 12 for chief, and 17 for a boss. The Force Energy required for summoning a grovling is 25, 50 for a chief, and 100 for a boss.

After being summoned the creature may move any distance from the Shinkai that it is told. The creature will follow any orders given by the summoning Shinkai (these orders must be spoken aloud) as long as the Shinkai continues to maintain this Force-effect. As soon as the Shinkai ceases to maintain the summoning the *Air* creature will vanish, returning to its home realm.

Grovlings can remain on Oryathar for no longer than 1D4 Turns, chiefs can remain for no longer than 1D4+1 Turns, and a boss can remain for no longer than 1D6+1 Turns

before they will return to their home realm (regardless of the summoning Shinkai's commands). The summoning Shinkai can dismiss the creature upon verbal command at any time he or she wishes, at which time the creature will simply disappear.

See "*Air* Creatures" in the "CREATURE LORE" Section for a listing of each specific *Air* creature's stats.

SUMMON *FIRE* CREATURE

Learning Cost: 50 (F-28, S-22)
Learning Difficulty: 20
Required Forces: *Fire* & *Spirit*
Minimum Knowledge: F=50, S=50
Force Energy: 25, 50, 100
Difficulty: * 7, 12, 17
Range: 1D10 feet

The result of this Force-effect is that a *Fire* creature appears within 1D10 feet of the summoning Shinkai. The Shinkai can choose what type of *Fire* creature that they are attempting to summon (they must, however, have enough Force Knowledge in the appropriate Mystic Force to do so). For summoning Fire creatures the appropriate Mystic Force is *Fire*.

There are three different types of *Fire* creatures that are strong enough to survive out of their element for any length of time. In order of relative strength they are the grovling, chief, and boss.

A Shinkai with 50 to 74 points of Force Knowledge in the appropriate Mystic Force is capable of summoning a grovling. A Force Knowledge of 75 to 99 makes the Shinkai capable of summoning a chief, and 100 or higher allows a boss to be summoned. The Difficulty Value that must achieved on the Sixth Sense/Performance Test is 7 for summoning a grovling, 12 for chief, and 17 for a boss. The Force Energy required for summoning a grovling is 25, 50 for a chief, and 100 for a boss.

After being summoned the creature may move any distance from the Shinkai that it is told. The creature will follow any orders given by the summoning Shinkai (these orders must be spoken aloud) as long as the Shinkai continues to maintain this Force-effect. As soon as the Shinkai ceases to maintain the summoning the *Fire* creature will vanish, returning to its home realm.

Grovlings can remain on Oryathar for no longer than 1D4 Turns, chiefs can remain for no longer than 1D4+1 Turns, and a boss can remain for no longer than 1D6+1 Turns before they will return to their home realm (regardless of the summoning Shinkai's commands). The summoning Shinkai can dismiss the creature upon verbal command at any time he or she wishes, at which time the creature will simply disappear.

See "*Fire* Creatures" in the "CREATURE LORE" Section for a listing of each specific *Fire* creature's stats.

SUMMON *LAND* CREATURE

Learning Cost: 50 (L-28, S-22)
Learning Difficulty: 20
Required Forces: *Land* & *Spirit*
Minimum Knowledge: L=50, S=50
Force Energy: 25, 50, 100
Difficulty: * 7, 12, 17
Range: 1D10 feet

The result of this Force-effect is that a *Land* creature appears within 1D10 feet of the summoning Shinkai. The Shinkai can choose what type of *Land* creature that they are attempting to summon (they must, however, have enough Force Knowledge in the appropriate Mystic Force to do so). For summoning *Land* creatures the appropriate Mystic Force is *Land*.

There are three different types of *Land* creatures that are strong enough to survive out of their element for any length of time. In order of relative strength they are the grovling, chief, and boss.

A Shinkai with 50 to 74 points of Force Knowledge in the appropriate Mystic Force is capable of summoning a grovling. A Force Knowledge of 75 to 99 makes the Shinkai capable of summoning a chief, and 100 or higher allows a boss to be summoned. The Difficulty Value that must achieved on the Sixth Sense/Performance Test is 7 for summoning a grovling, 12 for chief, and 17 for a boss. The Force Energy required for summoning a grovling is 25, 50 for a chief, and 100 for a boss.

After being summoned the creature may move any distance from the Shinkai that it is told. The creature will follow any orders given by the summoning Shinkai (these orders must be spoken aloud) as long as the Shinkai continues to maintain this Force-effect. As soon as the Shinkai ceases to main-

tain the summoning the *Land* creature will vanish, returning to its home realm..

Grovlings can remain on Oryathar for no longer than 1D4 Turns, chiefs can remain for no longer than 1D4+1 Turns, and a boss can remain for no longer than 1D6+1 Turns before they will return to their home realm (regardless of the summoning Shinkai's commands). The summoning Shinkai can dismiss the creature upon verbal command at any time he or she wishes, at which time the creature will simply disappear.

See *"Land* Creatures" in the "CREATURE LORE" Section for a listing of each specific *Land* creature's stats.

SUMMON WATER

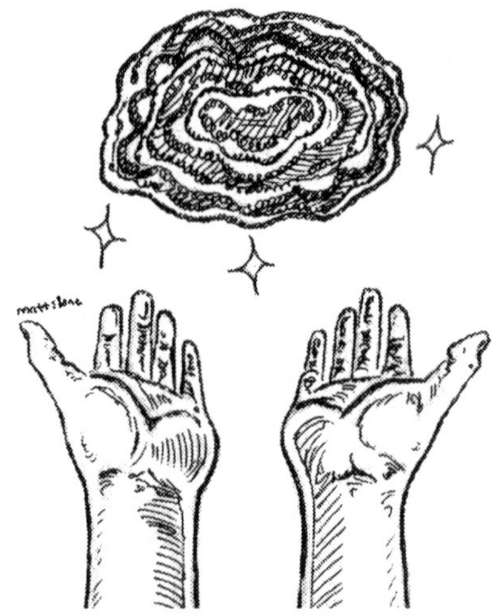

Learning Cost: 12
Learning Difficulty: 7
Required Forces: *Water*
Minimum Knowledge: 45
Force Energy: 10
Range: 3 feet

This Force-effect allows the Shinkai to summon small amounts of water. If the Shinkai is in an area where water is very sparse, such as a desert, then the amount of water summoned is much less than it would be in a moist area. The water is pulled from the moisture in the air, ground, other objects, or all three. If the area is not deprived of moisture up to two standard-bottles of water can be summoned per use. In a dry area only half of a standard-bottle of water can be summoned per use.

When a Shinkai uses "Summon Water" the water will appear in a spherical shape in mid-air within three feet of the summoning Shinkai. It will float for approximately 1 Turn before splashing to the ground.

The water summoned by this Force-effect will not appear inside of living beings, however if your character's Total *Water* Knowledge is over 100 he may cause the water to manifest inside of inanimate objects such as waterskins

instead of simply hovering in the air.

SUMMON *WATER* CREATURE

Learning Cost: 50 (S-28, W-22)
Learning Difficulty: 20
Required Forces: *Spirit* & *Water*
Minimum Knowledge: S=50, W=50
Force Energy: 25, 50, 100
Difficulty: * 7, 12, 17
Range: 1D10 feet

The result of this Force-effect is that a *Water* creature appears within 1D10 feet of the summoning Shinkai. The Shinkai can choose what type of *Water* creature that they are attempting to summon (they must, however, have enough Force Knowledge in the appropriate Mystic Force to do so). For summoning *Water* creatures the appropriate Mystic Force is *Water*.

There are three different types of *Water* creatures that are strong enough to survive out of their element for any length of time. In order of relative strength they are the grovling, chief, and boss.

A Shinkai with 50 to 74 points of Force Knowledge in the appropriate Mystic Force is capable of summoning a grovling. A Force Knowledge of 75 to 99 makes the Shinkai capable of summoning a chief, and 100 or higher allows a boss to be summoned. The Difficulty Value that must achieved on the Sixth Sense/Performance Test is 7 for summoning a grovling, 12 for chief, and 17 for a boss. The Force Energy required for summoning a grovling is 25, 50 for a chief, and 100 for a boss.

After being summoned the creature may move any distance from the Shinkai that it is told. The creature will follow any orders given by the summoning Shinkai (these orders must be spoken aloud) as long as the Shinkai continues to maintain this Force-effect. As soon as the Shinkai ceases to maintain the summoning the *Water* creature will vanish, returning to its home realm..

Grovlings can remain on Oryathar for no longer than 1D4 Turns, chiefs can remain for no longer than 1D4+1 Turns, and a boss can remain for no longer than 1D6+1 Turns before they will return to their home realm (regardless of the summoning Shinkai's commands). The summoning Shinkai can dismiss the creature upon verbal command at any time he or she wishes, at which time the creature will simply disappear.

See *"Water* Creatures" in the "CREATURE LORE" Section for a listing of each specific *Water* creature's stats.

SUMMON WIND

Learning Cost: 15
Learning Difficulty: 9
Required Forces: *Air*
Minimum Knowledge: 40
Force Energy: variable/variable
Range: 100 feet

Using this Force-effect a Shinkai can summon wind ranging from a slight breeze to a full gale. If the summoning Shinkai has a Total Force Knowledge in *Air* of at least 80 he can produce strong winds. Anything less than 80 means he can produce only a small breeze. The stronger winds can hinder movement of beings (base movement penalty of -20 feet per Turn) and even knock them down (Agility/Performance Test against a base Difficulty Value of 12 to resist strong winds).

The required Force Energy for summoning and maintaining a breeze is 5, for strong winds the required Force Energy begins at 30 and can be much higher.

As mentioned above, a minimum *Air* Knowledge of 80 is needed to produce strong winds. Shinkai with an *Air* Knowledge greater than 80 can increase the strength of the wind.

For every 10 *Air* Knowledge points above 80 of the conjuring Shinkai, the base Difficulty Value for resisting knockdown from the wind may be increased by 1, and the movement penalty may be increased by -5 feet per Turn. The amount of Force Energy required also increases by 10 for every 1 point increase to the wind's strength. This Force-effect does, however, have a limit to the strength of the winds it can produce. The highest that the Agility/Performance Test to resist being knocked down can be increased to is 20.

A character with an *Air* Knowledge of 93 could produce winds that require an Agility/Performance Test result of 13 in order to remain standing and yield a movement modifier of -25 feet per Turn. It would require 40 points of Force Energy to produce or hold this wind. If this same Shinkai had an *Air* Knowledge of 130 and expended 80 points of Force Energy, he could produce winds that would require an Agility/Performance Test result of 17 to avoid being

"slammed" as well as slowing the movement of anyone in this wind by 45 feet per Turn.

The source of this wind originates directly in front of the summoning Shinkai and blows in the direction that the Shinkai's body is facing. It is only two feet wide at the source and twenty feet wide at its maximum range of one hundred feet. Beyond one hundred feet the wind simply becomes a strong breeze and renders no penalties to other beings within it.

TELEPORT

Learning Cost: 40 (A-19, S-21)
Learning Difficulty: 18
Required Forces: *Air & Spirit*
Minimum Knowledge: A=180, S=90
Force Energy: 55
Defense: Mystical +2 (none for a Shinkai to teleport himself)
Range: * 75 feet

Shinkai using this Force-effect can disappear or cause another living being to disappear from one place and then reappear in another. The actual teleportation takes place in less than one second. The number of feet away that the Shinkai can teleport to can be no farther than a number of feet equal to his Total Force Energy. The target being of "Teleport", if it isn't the Shinkai using "Teleport", can be no farther than seventy five feet away in order to be teleported.

A being may not teleport or be teleported to reappear in the air or on any other insubstantial substance, or within a solid object. An attempt to do so will result in automatic failure of the Force-effect (no effect at all except wasted Force Energy and time).

Any items touching or otherwise attached to a teleporting being (as long as the sum of the items are no larger than the teleporting being) will be teleported with them.

Only one living being may be teleported per use of this Force-effect.

TELEPORT WARD

Learning Cost: 45 (A-21, S-24)
Learning Difficulty: 20
Required Forces: *Air & Spirit*
Minimum Knowledge: A=200, S=100
Force Energy: 65
Defense: Mystical +2
Difficulty: 10
Range: 25 feet

A Shinkai can place this ward on an area as large as twenty five in diameter. The Shinkai creating this ward must be within ten feet of the area to be warded.

Any being that enters this area after the ward is placed will trigger the ward. If the Sixth Sense/Performance Test made by the Shinkai at the time he created the ward exceeds the

target's Mystical Defense +2, then the being or beings that entered the warded area (whose Mystical Defenses were insufficient) will be teleported to an area predetermined by the Shinkai who created the ward. A maximum number of five beings can be teleported by a single "Teleport Ward" (any beings beyond five that simultaneously enter the warded area are unaffected).

The distance which the target can be teleported is a number of feet no farther away than a value equal to the Total Force Energy of the Shinkai who created the ward.

As with the Force-effect "Teleport", a being may not be teleported to reappear in the air or on any other insubstantial substance, and any items touching or otherwise attached to a teleported being (as long as the sum of the items are no larger than the teleporting being) will be teleported with him/her.

Note: Normally once a ward is triggered it ceases to exist, but there is a way to make a ward reset itself for use again. When creating the ward the Shinkai can expend twice the listed Force Energy for that particular ward, thus allowing the ward to reset itself one time after it is triggered. If three times the listed Force Energy is expended, then the ward can reset itself twice, if four times the listed Force Energy is expended it can reset three times, etc..

Wards can be created to target only specific targets or beings, but the required Force Energy increases by 5 for each type of target specification added. So, a ward that targets only Grak and Warlum would require 10 more points of Force Energy than the same ward with no target specifications.

Any Shinkai who creates a ward can also destroy that same ward by simply reversing the flows. This expends no Force Energy and is considered a Minor Action. The only way to destroy a ward created by another Shinkai is to use the Force-effect "Unravelling".

TORNADO

Learning Cost: 45
Learning Difficulty: 19
Required Forces: *Air*
Minimum Knowledge: 220
Force Energy: 80/50
Difficulty: 14
Range: 300 feet *

This Force-effect allows a Shinkai to create a tornado which will appear anywhere within three hundred feet of him or herself. The tornado can move extremely fast (600 feet per Turn) and unless controlled will move randomly, wreaking havoc upon everything in its path.

In order to control a tornado the Shinkai who summoned it must maintain the Force-effect. Full concentration must be kept to control the tornado, meaning no other Major Actions may be taken while controlling one; not even if the Shinkai can maintain more than one Force-effect at a time. If he/she ties the flows off or simply neglects to control it, the tornado will run wild in a random state of chaos.

A tornado does Level 13 + 40 points of damage per Turn to anything in its path (which is within one hundred feet of it), and also makes it very hard to stand for any one or thing near it. Average structures within one hundred feet of a tornado have a twenty percent chance each Turn of toppling, collapsing, or simply being torn to shreds.

Any being within the following ranges of a tornado must make the appropriate Agility/Performance Test to remain standing and avoid flying debris.

# of Feet Away	Needed Agility/ Performance Test
0-20	Impossible
21-40	46
41-60	37
61-80	28
81-100	19
101-up	N/A

UNRAVELLING

Learning Cost: 30 (F-13, S-17)
Learning Difficulty: 20
Required Forces: *Fire & Spirit*
Minimum Knowledge: F=80, S=115
Force Energy: Variable/Variable
Difficulty: *
Range: 30 feet +3 feet for every Sixth Sense Level beyond 3 of the Shinkai using this Force-effect

A Shinkai can unravel and destroy a Force-effect that has been tied off (which destroys the Force-effect), the most common of which are wards. In order to unravel tied off Force-effect the Shinkai must first have "Force Sight" and know "Force Tying", and be within the listed range of "Unraveling".

If the Shinkai knows the Force-effect that he is attempting to unravel then the base Difficulty Value for unraveling is 15 on a Sixth Sense/Performance Test. If the Shinkai doesn't know the Force-effect that he is attempting to unravel then the base Difficulty Value for unraveling is 30 on a Sixth Sense/Performance Test. For every Level that the Sixth Sense of the creator of the tied Force-effect exceeds that of the Shinkai attempting to unravel the Force-effect 1 additional point is added to the Difficulty Value for the unraveling. Also, if the Shinkai using "Unraveling" has the higher Sixth Sense, 1 point is subtracted from the Difficulty Value for every Level of difference.

The required Force Energy depends upon the number of different Mystic Forces that are tied into the Force-effect. If there is only one Mystic Force in the tied Force-effect, then the required Force Energy is 40. Add 10 more to the required Force Energy for each additional Mystic Force contained.

VISIONING

Learning Cost: 40
Learning Difficulty: 23
Required Forces: *Spirit*
Minimum Knowledge: 200
Force Energy: * 80
Difficulty: *8
Range: 300 feet

This powerful Force-effect allows a Shinkai to look into the past events that occurred in the immediate area. The Shinkai closes his or her eyes while conjuring this Force-effect in order to envision a detailed replay of events of a particular area.

The maximum size of the area in which the past can be seen is three hundred feet, and the Shinkai must be standing in this area for it to work. The required Force Energy and Difficulty listed above is if the Shinkai is attempting to envision an event that occurred within the last day. For every day farther into the past that the Shinkai wishes to envision he or she must expend 20 more points of Force Energy, and the Difficulty Value will increase by 4 points. Approximately two minutes of the past event can be seen with one use of "Visioning".

At the GM's discretion, events that were of little overall importance or lacked intense emotion can not be envisioned and some events can't be envisioned for unknown reasons.

VITALIZE

Learning Cost: 13
Learning Difficulty: 7
Required Forces: *Spirit*
Minimum Knowledge: 38
Force Energy: 12

Range: Touch

This Force-effect gives a character some relief from injuries and heals a small amount of damage. "Vitalize" instantly removes 1D10 +3 points of damage, and restores 1D10 points of Force Energy. It also allows the recipient to ignore the -2 Level attribute penalty rendered by one injury for the next four hours. The same being may not be the recipient of more than one "Vitalize" at a time.

A Shinkai may not use "Vitalize" on their self.

WALL OF FIRE

Learning Cost: 20
Learning Difficulty: 14
Required Forces: *Fire*
Minimum Knowledge: 50
Force Energy: 30
Difficulty: 8
Range: 5 feet

A one-foot thick, semi-solid wall of fire is produced. It may be as high and wide as ten feet. The shape of the wall can be altered slightly in such that it may curve or bend to form a concave or convex shape. Beings on the inside of the wall feel no heat and receive no damage from the wall, but anyone within five feet of the "hot side" of the wall will receive Level 7 damage. Those touching the wall will receive Level 15 damage.

Since this wall is not completely solid, any being or object pressing into with a Strength Test result of more than 14 will pass through it, though this yields Level 18 +20 points of damage. Objects made of ice or water can not pass through this type of wall, and will receive double the normal damage for nearing and/or touching one.

These walls of fire have a Protection Rating of 14 and a

Destroyed Rating of 75, and can only be damaged by ice or water based means. They will disappear into smoke 6 Turns after they are created.

WALL OF ICE

Learning Cost: 18 (A-8, W-10)
Learning Difficulty: 14
Required Forces: *Air & Water*
Minimum Knowledge: A=50, W=55
Force Energy: 27
Difficulty: 8
Range: 5 feet

A solid one-foot thick wall of ice up to eight feet high and wide is produced. The shape of the wall can be altered slightly in such that it may curve or bend to form a concave or convex shape.

These walls have a Protection Rating of 50 and a Destroyed Rating of 200. They can not be produced in extremely dry surroundings, such as a desert or the Lake of Fire. These ice walls will dissolve into vapors 15 Turns after they are created.

WALL OF LAND

Learning Cost: 16
Learning Difficulty: 14
Required Forces: *Land*
Minimum Knowledge: 50
Force Energy: 25
Difficulty: 8
Range: 5 feet

A solid wall of land and rock is formed, rising straight up out of the ground. This wall can be as high and wide as eight feet, and one foot thick. The shape of the wall can be altered slightly in such that it may curve or bend to form a concave shape, or convex shape.

Land walls have a Protection Rating of 40 and a Destroyed Rating of 350. There must be a reasonable amount of dirt or rock present in order to create a land wall (it would not be possible to created one on a ship in the middle of the sea). These walls will crumble back to the land 10 Turns after they are created.

WATER BLADES

Learning Cost: 30
Learning Difficulty: 17
Required Forces: *Water*
Minimum Knowledge: 60
Force Energy: 30
Defense: Physical (Dodge or Parry)
Difficulty: 10
Range: 150 feet

The Shinkai focuses the Mystic Force of *Water* into either hand and releases a jet of water that is semi-solid and travels extremely fast. This jet of water has razor-sharp blades of water sticking out at all angles. The water spirals and spins around the target's body upon impact, cutting and slicing them for Level 10 +10 points of damage.

"Water Blades" spirals and assaults its victim for the full duration of the Turn in which the victim is struck. While being assaulted by "Water Blades" the victim receives a -1D10 point penalty to any Test performed.

If the attack is a Flawless Performance "Water Blades" lasts for 2 full Turns instead of 1. The victim would take Level 10 +10 points of damage on the second Turn as well as the first.

WATER BREATHING

Learning Cost: 20 (A-10, W-10)
Learning Difficulty: 16
Required Forces: *Air & Water*
Minimum Knowledge: A=75, W=75
Force Energy: 25/10
Range: Self

The use of this Force-effect allows a Shinkai to breathe under water as comfortably and easily as on land.

WEAKNESS

Learning Cost: 35
Learning Difficulty: 16
Required Forces: *Land*
Minimum Knowledge: 80
Force Energy: *
Defense: Mystical
Range: 300 feet

With this Force-effect a Shinkai can cause a being to

become considerably weakened. For every 15 points of Force Energy expended 1 Level may be temporarily subtracted from the target's Strength.

The same being may suffer from multiple uses of "Weakness", (maximum of 5), but not more than one at a time from the same Shinkai. So, up to five Shinkai with the "Weakness" Force-effect could all use it on the same being at the same time. However, a single being may not have their Strength decreased by more than 10 Levels by the use of this Force-effect.

This weakness will last for a number of Turns equal to the Sixth Sense Level of the Shinkai who placed the "Weakness".

WEB

Learning Cost: 15 (A-7, W-8)
Learning Difficulty: 12
Required Forces: *Air & Water*
Minimum Knowledge: A=45, W=45
Force Energy: 25
Difficulty: 7
Range: 600 feet

A frost covered web of solidified air manifests anywhere within range that the Shinkai wishes, as long as their is something for the web to attach itself to. This could be a being, object, or a combination of the two. The web can be as large as ten feet in diameter (large enough to trap four ruling race sized beings).

Anything that comes in contact with the web is held fast to it. To break free from the web requires a Strength Test with a result of 16 or better.

The web will fall apart and lose its stickiness a number of Turns after creation equal to the creating Shinkai's Total *Air + Water* Knowledge values.

WIND MISSILE

Learning Cost: 18
Learning Difficulty: 15
Required Forces: *Air*
Minimum Knowledge: 55
Force Energy: 15
Defense: * Physical (Block, Dodge, or Parry)
Range: 600 feet

The Shinkai focuses the Mystic Force of *Air* into the palm of either hand. The Shinkai then emits a completely in-visible blast of solidified air from the palm of the chosen hand.

This blast of air is very powerful and needle thin, doing Level 10 damage to anything which it strikes. There is a seventy percent chance that an attack with "Wind Missile" will automatically hit its target. If the automatic hit fails, the target still receives a -8 penalty to their Defense due to the invisibility and high speed of "Wind Missile".

Attempting to parry against this Force-effect is extremely difficult. In addition to the normal -5 point penalty for attempting to parry a ranged attack there is an additional -8 point penalty due to the invisibility and high speed of "Wind Missile" which gives a -13 point penalty to anyone attempting to parry it.

WIND WEAPON (Melee)

Learning Cost: 16
Learning Difficulty: 12
Required Forces: *Air*
Minimum Knowledge: 50
Force Energy: 10/4

The Shinkai focuses the Mystic Force of *Air* into either hand and produces a melee weapon of his choice wrought completely of solidified.

The listed Force Energy is what is required to create a weapon with a Bulk Value of 1. The Required Force Energy and maintaining raises by 3 for each Bulk Value above 1 (or 1.5) of the wind weapon created.

Though they are made of air, these weapons are quite solid. If a wind weapon leaves the hand of the Shinkai who created it, it will instantly disappear.

These wind weapons do 2 Levels more damage than their mundane counterparts. Wind weapons can not be damaged by any means and are completely invisible.

Because such weapons are invisible it is very hard to set a proper defense against an attack with one. Due to this fact any opponent attacked with a wind weapon receives a -6 point penalty to their Defense (against the wind weapon attack only).

RUNE LORE

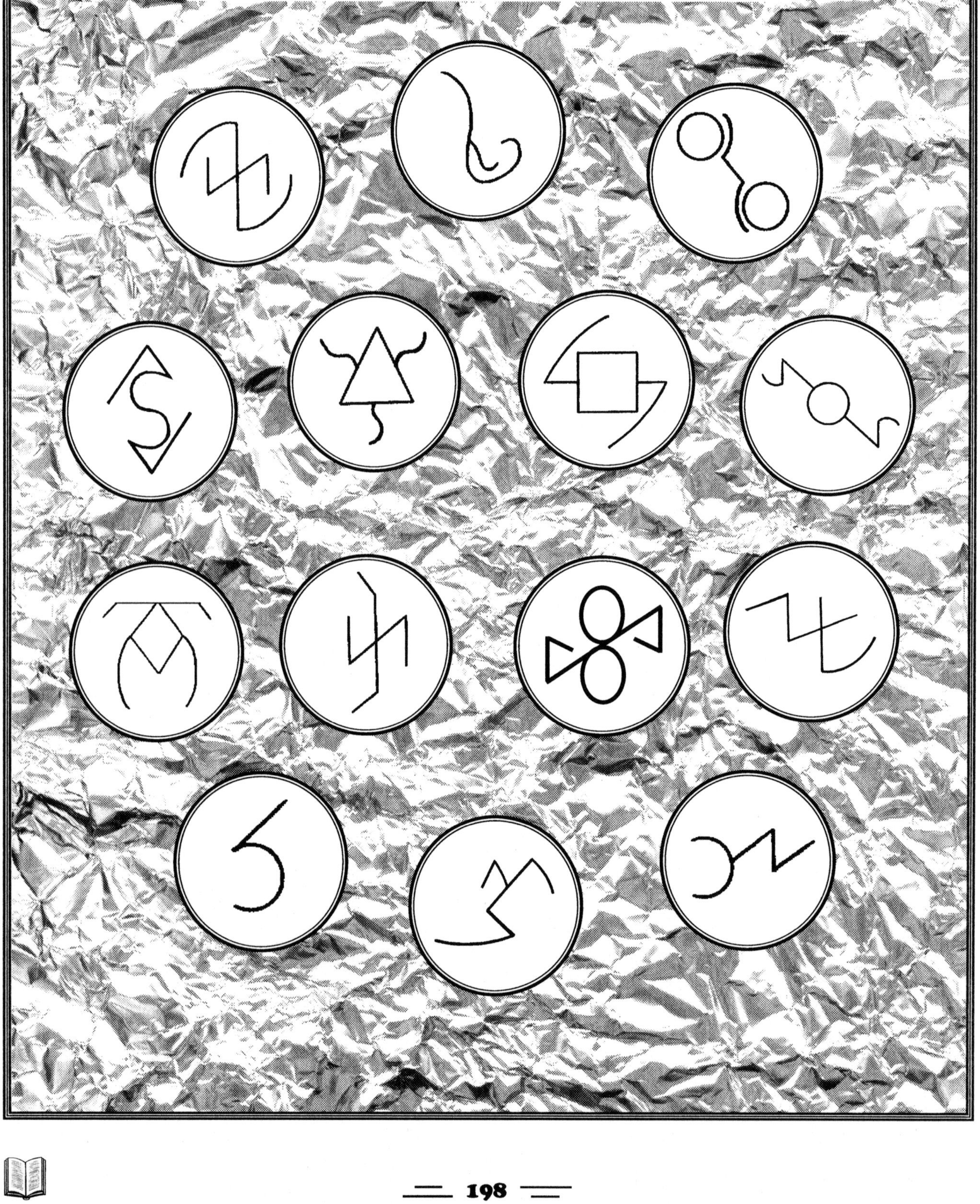

In the early days of the Shinkai it was discovered that the drawing of certain symbols (runes) by skilled Shinkai could produce various mystical effects. The Shinkai would actually conjure intricate flows of the Mystic Forces into the rune's pattern, thereby empowering the rune with mystical abilities. With the passing of years many different runes were learned, each having their own specific effects. The study and utilization of runes is now known as Rune Lore.

The fort cities of the Defenders of the Light have records of many different runes in their libraries where Shinkai with the necessary abilities can come to study and learn them. As with any ability or gift, the power of the rune is one to be used with great caution and respect.

There are four different categories included in the description of each rune that represent important values and information about the rune. They are Learning Difficulty, Required Forces, Drawing Sensitivity, Force Energy, and Life. Each of these categories is described in detail below.

Learning Difficulty

Once your character has learned the art of focused conjuring (which is required to draw any rune) and the Force-effect "Rune Lore" he may then begin learning the different runes. Every rune is different in appearance and in effect, and in how difficult they are to learn.

The simplest way of learning a particular rune is to have the Universal Talent "Force Sight". If a Shinkai with "Force Sight" has and and is able to study an active rune or can watch it being drawn (an active rune is a rune which is empowered and ready to perform the effect for which it was designed) it is much simpler to learn how to recreate the rune.

Though many active runes are also visible to those without "Force Sight", the Mystic Forces that are infused into the rune and the pattern in which they are woven into the rune is not seen. This is why "Force Sight" is recommended to any Shinkai wishing to learn "Rune Lore". "Force Sight" allows your character to see the different Mystic Forces in a rune. This aids in the studying and learning of the rune, as well as helping to determine the effects of an unknown rune.

With an active rune available for study your character must make two Tests to determine whether or not he learns the particular rune. The "Learning Difficulty" lists the Difficulty Value of these two Tests. The two Tests are an Intelligence Test and a Sixth Sense/Performance Test. The Difficulty Values for the Tests are different for each rune and are listed in the rune's description beside of "Learning Difficulty".

Both Tests must be made consecutively (one Test per Turn). If either Test is failed then the rune was not learned and a whole new attempt must be made (your character must repeat both Tests). Also, the Difficulty Value for each Test increases by 1 point for each failed attempt. Technique with

the Mystic Forces does not aide in the learning of runes. General Conjuring, however, can be used to aide the Sixth Sense/Performance Test for the learning of runes.

For example, Onar, who has "Force Sight", is attempting to learn the "Impact" rune which has a Learning Difficulty of Intelligence = 9, Sixth Sense = 10. Onar gets a result of 7 on his Intelligence Test and an 11 on the Sixth Sense/Performance Test. His attempt to learn the rune is unsuccessful because he failed one of the Tests.

Onar tries again to learn the "Impact" rune this time the Learning Difficulty is Intelligence = 10, Sixth Sense = 11. He makes an Intelligence Test with a result of 10 and gets an 8 on his Sixth Sense/Performance Test. The Sixth Sense/Performance Test is unsuccessful, so the attempt to learn the rune is again unsuccessful.

Onar again attempts to learn the same rune for the third time. The Learning Difficulty is now Intelligence = 11, Sixth Sense = 12. Onar makes another Intelligence Test with a result of 12 and a Sixth Sense/Performance Test with a result of 13. He has successfully learned the "Impact" rune.

Even if a rune has been dead for years their will most always be a trace of the Mystic Forces that were infused into the rune lingering on the object where the rune was drawn. This lingering concentration of the Mystic Forces is known as a residual pattern. A Shinkai with "Force Sight" observing a dead rune while simultaneously focusing the Mystic Force of *Spirit* into his eyes can see the residual pattern of the rune and use this information to study and learn the rune just as if he were studying an active rune. Studying the residual pattern of a rune is not quite as accurate or as easy as studying an active rune. For this reason the Learning Difficulty for learning runes in this manner is doubled.

Not all runes leave a residual pattern. Some runes are designed to completely disappear when they die, leaving no trace of their existence.

Another method of learning runes is utilized when your character does not have the Universal Talent "Force Sight" or can not obtain a sample rune to study. In this case your character must have someone to guide him through an example of the rune (or must have a very detailed description of the rune and how it is created), instructing with great time, and difficulty, the proper manner, sequence, amount, and location of which flows of the Mystic Forces that must be placed into the rune. This process of learning a rune is much more complicated and time consuming than if your character had "Force Sight". The Learning Difficulty for learning runes in this manner is doubled.

So, as you can see "Force Sight" is a wise investment for anyone wishing to practice "Rune Lore".

Note: Runes can not be used to enhance a character's attributes to aide in the learning of other runes, Skills, or Technique Points. So, for example, you could not draw a rune on your character to increase his Agility so that he could more easily pass a Progress Test or any of the Tests required

for learning other runes or Technique Points.

If a character is under the effects of any rune that increases an attribute that is involved in the learning of a Skill, other rune, or Technique Point, the Test for the learning of the Skill, rune, etc. automatically fails.

Required Forces

Though your character must control all five of the Mystic Forces before he can learn the "Rune Lore" Force-effect, not all runes require the actual conjuring of all five of the Mystic Forces. The "Required Forces" for a particular rune lists the Mystic Forces that must be focused into the rune as it is being drawn in order for it to be created successfully.

Drawing Sensitivity

Different runes require different consistencies of drawing media in order to be drawn successfully. Some runes must be drawn with a very dark and legible substance while some runes need no physical media at all, being able to be traced out with a bare fingertip.

Every rune will have a value ranging from 0 to 3 which represents the degree of its Drawing Sensitivity. The following table defines the sensitivity of each value.

DRAWING SENSITIVITY	
Value	**Sensitivity**
0	Needs no physical media to be drawn/can be traced with finger tip.
1	Very light, visible media needed such as a sketch in dirt or a very light drawing of the rune.
2	Significant visibility needed such as a charcoal drawing of the rune.
3	Very dark, visible media needed such as paint or heavy charcoal.

Blood is never to be used as the drawing media for runes. Using blood to create runes is considered an act of the Shadow, as they often employ this method to establish links to their evil kind and to gain unnatural, dark abilities. Any character who uses blood (of any kind) to draw runes should immediately be awarded a minimum of 2 Shadow Points.

The use of blood in drawing runes or for any type of writing at all is forbidden by the laws of most every king on Oryathar as well as all Defenders of the Light.

There is no limit to how small or large that a rune can be drawn. As long as the shape of the rune is accurately drawn and the proper Mystic Forces are correctly focused into the rune its doesn't matter. Runes are traditionally drawn very small. This practice most likely originated due to the fact that the Shinkai utilizing runes wanted to keep their runes a secret from others and having them drawn small made it easy to conceal them.

Force Energy

This is the amount of Force Energy that must be expended to draw the rune and make it active. In some situations, as in the use of "Rune Warding", more Force Energy will be expended than what is actually necessary for the creation of the rune.

The required Force Energy for the creation of any rune is spent at the beginning of the Turn in which the drawing of the rune begins. If the drawing of the rune lasts for more than 1 Turn (which it usually does, as the minimum time in which a rune can be drawn without a chance of dying is 3 Turns), then the required Force Energy is divided evenly among the number of Turns that the drawing of the rune lasts. If a Shinkai begins drawing a rune and then stops for 1 Turn or more or performs a Major Action, then the rune will die and must be started again. The Force Energy spent on the previous Turns is simply lost.

You can change the number of Turns that your character will spend on the drawing of a rune even after he begins drawing it and Force Energy expenditure has begun.

For example, Rothic wishes to draw the "Impact" rune which requires 24 points of Force Energy. Rothic wishes to spend 3 Turns drawing the rune, thus spending 8 points of Force Energy per Turn and finishing the rune at the end of the third Turn.

At the beginning of the second Turn, however, Rothic decides that he must finish the rune this Turn. He would at this time (the beginning of the second Turn) expend the remaining 16 points of Force Energy to finish the rune.

Life

The Life of a rune is the amount of time in which the rune remains active or alive. The Life of any particular rune can range from 1 Turn to several days, or even weeks. It is rumored that there are some runes with a Life of several years, though this remains *just* a rumor.

In **Mystic Forces** the duration of Force-effects, runes, or anything else for that matter, is often listed as a number of days or Turns. If something has a Life or duration of 1 day it will only last until the first hour of the next day (the first hour marks a new day). A rune, for example, that has a Life of 1 day that is drawn during the night would die at the first hour (one day is considered to have passed). If the duration was listed as 25 hours then it would live until the same hour on the following day that it was drawn. So technically, in **Mystic Forces**, a day is marked by the arrival of first light (the first hour) not necessarily a twenty-five hour period. If the duration is to be for 25 hours then it should be listed as such and not as 1 day.

Likewise, durations listed as a number of Turns operate in the same manner. If something has a duration of 1 Turn the Turn in which it becomes active or in use counts as the 1 Turn of its duration. For example, being stunned normally lasts for 1 Turn. The Turn in which the being is stunned is

the 1 Turn duration (at the beginning of the following Turn the effects of the stun would be over).

The creation/drawing of any rune takes a minimum of 1 full Turn. The drawing of a rune is considered using a Force-effect and is thus a Major Action. A rune becomes active at the end of the Turn that the last of the required Force Energy is expended.

Some runes may be alive but are not active until certain other actions are performed. For example, the "Fire" rune is alive once successfully drawn, but remains inactive until the creating Shinkai commands it to activate, at which time it bursts into a white-hot flame. This activation of runes that are alive but dormant is not considered conjuring, and thus the activation of such a rune can not be sensed by a Brightling's innate ability to sense conjuring. The actual creation of a rune, however, is conjuring and can be sensed by Brightlings just like any other type of conjuring.

There is no limit to the number of Turns which can be spent drawing any one rune, though 3 Turns is enough time to guarantee that the rune does not die immediately upon completion. Any rune drawn in less than 3 Turns will have a chance of dying (or becoming inactive) before any of its effects or abilities ever manifest. A rune drawn in 2 Turns has a twenty-five percent chance of immediate death while a rune drawn in 1 Turn has a fifty percent chance.

If a Shinkai is novice with any of the Mystic Forces required to draw a particular rune, then they are novice with that rune. Drawing a rune in which your character is novice requires that he face the Novice Factor just as when utilizing Force-effects which he is novice with.

It is possible for an active rune to be killed (made permanently inactive) by another Shinkai with "Rune Lore". In order to kill an active rune your character must know "Rune Lore" as well as the particular rune to be killed. Your character must then physically trace the rune, normally with a finger, while using focused conjuring in a manner that basically reverses the same process as that used to create the rune. Twice the Force Energy must be expended to kill a rune than to create that same rune. After the Force Energy is expended the Shinkai must make a Sixth Sense/Performance Test to determine whether or not his attempt to kill the rune was successful. If the rune is one that he created himself he does not have to make a Sixth Sense/Performance Test (the rune is automatically killed after the Force Energy is expended). If the rune was created by another Shinkai then the Difficulty Value of the Test is 10. It only takes 1 Turn (a single Major Action) in order to kill a rune. A result equal to or greater than 10 means that the rune was killed. A result less than 10 means that the rune remains active and unharmed.

Attempting to erase, smear, or rub away an active rune by physical means has no effect. As long as the rune is active the drawing media is mystically fixed to the object upon which the rune is drawn. However, if the object upon which the rune is drawn is shattered or broken so that the rune itself is broken apart the rune is immediately killed. Killing runes in this manner can be very dangerous. When a rune is killed in this manner a blast of energy is released from the rune inflicting a number of points of damage to any being within ten feet of the rune equal to the number of points of Force Energy expended to create the rune.

A Shinkai with "Rune Lore" can reactivate runes that are inactive for whatever reason, providing that the rune still meets the Writing Sensitivity criteria and still retains its proper form. Reactivating a rune requires physically tracing the rune while using focused conjuring to infuse the appropriate Mystic Forces into it.

Unless otherwise stated in a rune's description, only one rune of a particular type may be active at the same time, if drawn by the same Shinkai. In other words your character can not draw the same rune over and over. Whenever your character draws a rune that he has already drawn once (and is still alive) then the new rune kills the old one, thus only one of the same type of rune may be active at one time (if drawn by the same Shinkai). If the description of a rune says that it may be drawn multiple times, then it may be drawn by the same Shinkai as many times as the description of that particular rune says it may.

If the description of a rune says that it may be drawn multiple times, but does not say that there is a limit to how many times it may be duplicated, then it may be drawn as many times as you wish.

Any rune created by the same Shinkai (past the maximum number of allowable multiples) will kill the rune of the same type with the shortest remaining life. For example, your character has drawn the "Force Energy" rune which has a Life of three days and can be drawn twice. On the following day he draws a second "Force Energy" rune. If he were to now draw a third "Force Energy" rune it will immediately kill the one he had drawn the day before (the one with the shortest remaining Life).

Some runes do not glow or give any obvious signs that they are active. Only a Shinkai with "Force Sight" can perceive whether or not these types of runes are active (without actually touching or triggering the rune of course), and as far as it is known no one can detect whether or not a rune has been warded.

Any other information which is vital to the drawing of, or use of any particular rune will be given with the description of that particular rune.

Below is a compilation of thirty-three known runes, listed in alphabetical order.

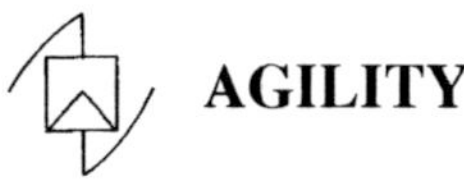 **AGILITY**

Learning Difficulty: Intelligence = 14, Sixth Sense = 15
Required Forces: *Air & Spirit*

Writing Sensitivity: 2
Force Energy: 30
Life: 1 hour

Having this rune drawn on the skin or worn directly against the skin (such as on one's armor or an amulet) adds 3 Levels to that being's Agility.

Regardless of the drawing media, when active this rune changes to light yellow in color and reverts to the initial drawing media when inactive.

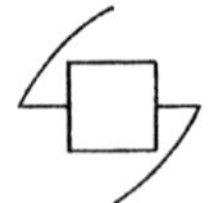 ## *AIR* PORTAL

Learning Difficulty: Intelligence = 21, Sixth Sense = 22
Required Forces: *Air*
Writing Sensitivity: 0
Force Energy: 250
Life: 10 Turns

When drawn on any object this rune expands into a portal seven feet in diameter that opens into the mystical realm of *Air*. The portal will remain open for 10 Turns at which time it will contract back and close. Though all of the mystical elements of the *Air* realm are visible and lay just beyond the threshold of the portal, none of the realm's material or substance will come through the portal on its own (opening the portal doesn't cause the realm's contents to come pouring out into Oryathar).

Any object that is within the entrance to the portal as it closes will be completely and cleanly severed. The object upon which an "*Air* Portal" rune is drawn will not be affected and will be left in the same state that it was before the rune was drawn. This rune can not be drawn on a living being.

At the time that your character draws an "*Air* Portal" rune he may increase the number of Turns that the portal will remain open by expending additional Force Energy into the rune. For each additional 5 points of Force Energy beyond that listed that your character places into the rune at creation the portal will remain open for 1 additional Turn.

This rune will glow a radiant white color for an instant before it expands into the portal, and will also glow for an instant after the portal closes, at which time it will vanish leaving no trace that it was ever drawn.

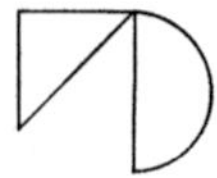 ## ANIMAL WARD

Learning Difficulty: Intelligence = 10, Sixth Sense = 11
Required Forces: *Fire* & *Spirit*
Writing Sensitivity: 1

Force Energy: 24
Life: 1 hour

Each of these runes can keep one mundane animal from approaching within six feet of it. So, if three animals are to be kept from a particular spot there must be three of these runes present.

This rune appears the same during and after inactivity as it does when first drawn. This rune may be drawn multiple times.

 ## COOLING

Learning Difficulty: Intelligence = 10, Sixth Sense = 11
Required Forces: *Air* & *Water*
Writing Sensitivity: 2
Force Energy: 10 *
Life: 1 day

This rune can not be drawn on living beings (it will immediately die as soon as it is drawn). As soon as this rune is alive it will become cool and the object upon which it is drawn will consequently be cooled. This cooling effect will slowly spread out from the rune and will cool the object that it is drawn on up to two feet in any direction from the rune itself.

The listed Force Energy for the "Cooling" rune is the Force Energy needed to make the rune and the object it is drawn upon cool. Doubling the Force Energy placed into the "Cooling" rune upon creation will cause the rune and the object it is drawn upon to become cold instead of just cool. Tripling the Force Energy placed into the "Cooling" rune upon creation will cause the rune and the object it is drawn upon to become extremely cold, nearly to the point of freezing (excellent for drawing on your waterskin and keeping your water ice-cold on those hot Light season days).

This Rune may be drawn multiple times up to a maximum of three times.

 ## ENDURANCE

Learning Difficulty: Intelligence = 14, Sixth Sense = 15
Required Forces: *Land*
Writing Sensitivity: 2
Force Energy: 30
Life: 1 hour

Having this rune drawn on the skin or worn directly against the skin (such as on one's armor or an amulet) adds 3 Levels to that being's Endurance.

Regardless of the drawing media, when active, this rune

changes to light brown in color and reverts to the initial drawing media when inactive.

ENHANCED ESSENCE

Learning Difficulty: Intelligence = 10, Sixth Sense = 18
Required Forces: *Air*, *Fire*, *Land*, *Spirit*, & *Water*
Writing Sensitivity: 0
Force Energy: 40
Life: 4 hours

When drawn upon the skin this rune will allow your character to target two beings in essence combat instead of just one.

This rune also allows your character to force a single target being into essence combat (if that being is capable of projecting their essence).

The target to be forced into combat and the Shinkai using "Enhanced Essence" both make Sixth Sense/Performance Tests. If the target being's result is higher, then they aren't forced into essence combat. If the Shinkai using "Enhanced Essence" has the higher result, then the target will be forced into their essence form (though they can return to their body at any time, after the first Turn).

Using this rune's effects is a Minor Action.

While active this rune glows with a silvery radiance and returns to the color of the drawing media when inactive. The recipient's essence form will also display this rune.

FIRE

Learning Difficulty: Intelligence = 14, Sixth Sense = 15
Required Forces: *Fire*
Writing Sensitivity: 2
Force Energy: 20
Life: 1 day

This rune is capable of bursting into white-hot flames whenever it is mentally willed to do so by the Shinkai who drew it; regardless of his/her distance from the rune. These flames reach out one foot in all directions from the rune.

A Shinkai who draws multiple "Fire" runes can set them off individually, but has no mystical means of telling them apart. For example, your character has drawn ten of these runes on ten separate arrows. Your character now decides that he wants to set one of them off that has just been shot into a Shadow-kin. He had better recognize the arrow to which the proper "Fire" rune was drawn or he may ignite one that is still on an arrow in his quiver.

This rune will burn for 4 Turns and will yield Level 9 damage to any being coming in contact with its flames, as well as yielding fire damage to the object upon which it is drawn.

After the rune quits burning it will become inactive, regardless of its remaining Life.

This rune doesn't change in appearance while active but the inactive remains of this rune appear as a black charred replica of the original.

This Rune may be drawn multiple times up to a maximum of ten times.

FIRE PORTAL

Learning Difficulty: Intelligence = 21, Sixth Sense = 22
Required Forces: *Fire*
Writing Sensitivity: 0
Force Energy: 250
Life:10 Turns

When drawn on any object this rune expands into a portal seven feet in diameter that opens into the mystical realm of *Fire*. The portal will remain open for 10 Turns at which time it will contract back and close. Though all of the mystical elements of the *Fire* realm are visible and lay just beyond the threshold of the portal, none of the realm's material or substance will come through the portal on its own (opening the portal doesn't cause the realm's contents to come pouring out into Oryathar).

Any object that is within the entrance to the portal as it closes will be completely and cleanly severed. The object upon which a "*Fire* Portal" rune is drawn will not be affected and will be left in the same state that it was before the rune was drawn. This rune can not be drawn on a living being.

At the time that your character draws a "*Fire* Portal" rune he may increase the number of Turns that the portal will remain open by expending additional Force Energy into the rune. For each additional 5 points of Force Energy beyond that listed that your character places into the rune at creation the portal will remain open for 1 additional Turn.

This rune will glow a radiant red color for an instant before it expands into the portal, and will also glow for an instant after the portal closes, at which time it will vanish leaving no trace that it was ever drawn.

FORCE-ENERGY

Learning Difficulty: Intelligence = 16, Sixth Sense = 18
Required Forces: *Air*, *Fire*, *Land*, *Spirit*, & *Water*
Writing Sensitivity: 0
Force Energy: 24

Life: 3 days

This rune is able to store up to 100 points of Force Energy. While active (of course) any Shinkai, whether they know "Rune Lore" or not, can add or take Force Energy from this rune by simply tracing it with a finger. A Shinkai can even draw Force Energy out of this rune while in essence form, but can not place energy into it while they are in essence.

A Shinkai can only place as much Force Energy into the rune as he has in Current Force Energy. Life Force, unlike with Force-effects, can not be substituted for Force Energy for the purpose of loading a Force-Energy rune.

The number of points to be taken from the rune is up to the being receiving them. A Shinkai can not receive more points of Force Energy than his Total Force Energy.

It is a Major Action to draw Force Energy from or place it into this rune.

This rune glows when active, changing colors every few minutes. The colors are white, red, emerald, blue, and gold. This rune completely disappears after it dies, leaving no trace of its existence.

This rune may be drawn multiple times up to a maximum of two times.

GUARDIAN

Learning Difficulty: Intelligence = 12, Sixth Sense = 14
Required Forces: *Air & Fire*
Writing Sensitivity: 1
Force Energy: 25 *
Life: 10 days

This rune is mainly used to guard valuable items. It can be drawn on most any surface. The object or item on which it is drawn is considered to be "guarded". The maximum size of an object that can be guarded with this rune is twenty feet in any direction.

Any living being, other than the Shinkai who drew the "Guardian" rune, who comes within one foot of a guarded item will receive a stinging blast of energy from the rune. This blast of energy yields 1D20 damage and is capable of emitting a number of blasts equal to the creating Shinkai's Sixth Sense Level before becoming inactive. For each blast of energy that your character wishes the rune to be capable of emitting, beyond the first, he must place an additional 10 points of Force Energy into the rune at its creation. No normal armor protects against this damage.

Even if this rune has not reached the end of its normal Life it will become inactive after emitting all of its energy blasts.

At the creation of this rune your character may make exceptions as to who or what the rune will guard against. For example, your character may choose to have the rune only protect against Shadow-kin, Shadow-sworn,

Korgathool, or any and all living beings.

This rune glows a soft red while active and appears normally (whatever media was used to draw it) when inactive.

HEALING HOLD

Learning Difficulty: Intelligence = 15, Sixth Sense = 18
Required Forces: *Spirit*
Writing Sensitivity: 0
Force Energy: 60
Life: 2 days

This rune is able to store up to 60 points of healing. While active (of course) any Shinkai who knows the force effect "Healing" can add points of healing to this rune by simply placing an amount of Force Energy into the rune equal to the number of points of healing to be added.

Any Shinkai (whether they know "Healing" or not) can receive points of healing from this rune by simply touching and tracing its outline. The number of points to be taken from the rune is up to the being receiving them, however a being can not receive more points than their Life Force.

The healing received from this rune can not heal injuries, just current damage other than injury damage. This rune will not restore any Force Energy at all.

It is a Major Action to draw healing out of this rune or to place it into it.

This rune periodically glows a faint yellow while active, but usually remains invisible. Whenever a living being approaches within two feet a "Healing Hold" rune it will begin to glow. If no drawing media was used to draw this rune it will completely disappear after dying. If drawing media was used to draw this rune it will simply return to the color of the drawing media.

This rune may be drawn multiple times up to a maximum of three times.

IMMORTALITY

Learning Difficulty: Intelligence = 14, Sixth Sense = 20
Required Forces: *Fire, Land, Spirit, & Water*
Writing Sensitivity: 1
Force Energy: 40 *
Life: half an hour *

This rune is quite possibly the most powerful rune ever to be discovered. This rune must be drawn directly on the skin in order to work. The "Immortality" rune is not active as soon it is successfully drawn. The person upon whom this rune is drawn must have the Mystic Force of *Spirit* focused into the rune via focused conjuring in order to activate it. As soon as the rune is activated the being will be enveloped with a blue aura, as well as any object that he is holding (up to a Bulk Value of 3). This blue glow is the sign of the empowerment of the "Immortality" rune. Any being actively empowered by the "Immortality" rune (denoted by the blue glow) is totally immune to any harm from another being empowered by an "Immortality" rune.

If a being with an active "Immortal" rune is killed by another being with an active "Immortal" rune they will immediately be resurrected, healed, and regenerated to the state they were in before their "Immortality" rune was activated.

A character doesn't have to be killed in order for this rune to restore him to the condition that he was in before it was activated. At any time that he wants he can mentally cause the "Immortality" rune (if he drew it) to restore him to the condition he was in before it was activated, at which time the rune dies.

One exception to this total restoration is Force Energy. Any and all Force Energy expended while under the influence of the "Immortality" rune must be regained as normal.

A single Shinkai can not have more than two "Immortality" runes alive at any one time. Drawing a third "Immortality" rune will simply kill and replace the first one.

This rune is used by the Defenders of the Light as well as the King's Guard for use in elite training exercises. The immortality granted by this rune allows soldiers to engage in lethal, true-to-life combat without fear of killing the other combatants. Such training will prove invaluable when encountering powerful Shadow-kin and Shadow-sworn Shinkai.

This rune will live for half an hour if it is not activated. Once activated it will keep the recipient enveloped in the immortal glow for 5 Turns, but if the Shinkai wishes he can add up to 10 more Turns to the rune's duration by expending an extra 10 points of Force Energy for each additional Turn the rune is to live.

This rune may be drawn multiple times up to a maximum of two times. The same being can not have more than one "Immortality" rune active upon himself at any one time (the second will not activate until the first dies).

IMPACT

Learning Difficulty: Intelligence = 10, Sixth Sense = 12
Required Forces: *Air, Fire, & Spirit*
Writing Sensitivity: 2
Force Energy: 24
Life: 7 hours

When drawn upon an object this rune will increase the Damage Yield of that object by 3 Levels (if the object is thrown or used as a weapon of course). The object may be of any material and size.

This rune doesn't change in appearance during or after activation.

This rune may be drawn multiple times up to a maximum of two times, but it may only be drawn once per item, by the same Shinkai. The same item could have a dozen "Impact" runes on it as long as each one was drawn by a different Shinkai.

INTELLIGENCE

Learning Difficulty: Intelligence = 14, Sixth Sense = 15
Required Forces: *Spirit*
Writing Sensitivity: 2
Force Energy: 30
Life: 1 hour

Having this rune drawn on the skin or worn directly against the skin (such as on one's armor or an amulet) adds 3 Levels to that being's Intelligence.

Regardless of the drawing media, when active, this rune changes to light red in color and reverts to the initial drawing media when inactive.

LAND PORTAL

Learning Difficulty: Intelligence = 21, Sixth Sense = 22
Required Forces: *Land*
Writing Sensitivity: 0
Force Energy: 250
Life: 10 Turns

When drawn on any object this rune expands into a portal seven feet in diameter that opens into the mystical realm of *Land*. The portal will remain open for 10 Turns at which time it will contract back and close. Though all of the mystical elements of the *Land* realm are visible and lay just beyond the threshold of the portal, none of the realm's material or substance will come through the portal on its own (opening the portal doesn't cause the realm's contents to come pouring out into Oryathar).

Any object that is within the entrance to the portal as it closes will be completely and cleanly severed. The object upon which a "*Land* Portal" rune is drawn will not be affected and will be left in the same state that it was before the rune was drawn. This rune can not be drawn on a living being.

At the time that your character draws a "*Land* Portal" rune

he may increase the number of Turns that the portal will remain open by expending additional Force Energy into the rune. For each additional 5 points of Force Energy beyond that listed that your character places into the rune at creation the portal will remain open for 1 additional Turn.

This rune will glow a radiant brown color for an instant before it expands into the portal, and will also glow for an instant after the portal closes, at which time it will vanish leaving no trace that it was ever drawn.

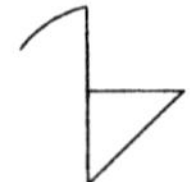 ## LIFE KEEPER

Learning Difficulty: Intelligence = 11, Sixth Sense = 14
Required Forces: *Spirit*
Writing Sensitivity: 0
Force Energy: 25
Life: 1 hour

Having this rune drawn directly on the skin will add 38 Turns to the safe resurrection time of that being. This rune will still work if drawn on a being after they are dead, as long as they have not been dead for more than 2 Turns at the time the rune becomes active.

This rune has a bright golden glow when active and returns to the media that it was drawn in when inactive (it disappears if no drawing media was used).

LIGHTNING FORK

Learning Difficulty: Intelligence = 13, Sixth Sense = 17
Required Forces: *Fire & Spirit*
Writing Sensitivity: 0
Force Energy: 50
Life: 50 Turns (5 minutes)

Having this rune drawn on the skin or worn directly against the skin (such as on one's clothing) enhances that being's ability to use the Force-effects "Lightning" and "Fire-Lightning". Instead of producing one bolt of lightning per use, that Shinkai can now produce two bolts of lightning or fire-lightning with a single use. These two bolts of lightning can both be directed at a single target or two separate targets. A single Sixth Sense/Performance Test is made for both bolts, but damage for each bolt is rolled separately.

This rune glows bright silver while active. If no drawing media was used to draw this rune it will disappear when inactive. If drawing media was used, it will simply return to the color of the drawing media.

 ## MIND SIGHT

Learning Difficulty: Intelligence = 11, Sixth Sense = 11
Required Forces: *Air & Spirit*
Writing Sensitivity: 1
Force Energy: 40
Life: 3 days

This rune must be drawn twice in order to produce the desired effect. This is the exception to the rule that states that a rune that is not to be drawn multiple times will replace the previous version of that rune when drawn a second time.

The first time this rune is drawn it is normally on an object in an area where the Shinkai has some future interest. The second time it is drawn the Shinkai concentrates on the first rune while tracing and using focused conjuring to infuse *Air* and *Spirit* into the second. The Shinkai (who created both runes) will then be able to see a mental picture of everything within four hundred-fifty feet of the first rune. Once the runes are activated in this manner they will live for 30 Turns before dying.

These runes appear normally until they are used, at which time they glow soft blue.

 ## SHADOW SIGNAL

Learning Difficulty: Intelligence = 10, Sixth Sense = 10
Required Forces: *Fire & Spirit*
Writing Sensitivity: 1
Force Energy: 25
Life: 12 hours

This rune will glow bright red as well as emitting a loud shrilling noise whenever any type of Shadow-kin come within three hundred feet of it.

This rune doesn't change in appearance during or after being active.

 ## SHADOW SUMMON

Learning Difficulty: Intelligence = 11, Sixth Sense = 12
Required Forces: *Spirit*
Writing Sensitivity: 2
Force Energy: 30
Life: 6 hours

This rune sends out a wave of telepathic energy for ten miles in every direction that causes any Shadow-kin within its range to be drawn to it. The higher the Shadow-kin's

Aggression Rating, the faster they will seek out the rune.

This rune doesn't change in appearance during or after being active.

 ## SHADOW WARD

Learning Difficulty: Intelligence = 9, Sixth Sense = 12
Required Forces: *Fire & Spirit*
Writing Sensitivity: 0
Force Energy: 15
Life: 8 hours

Each of these runes can keep one Shadow-kin from approaching within six feet of it. So, if four Shadow-kin are to be kept from a particular spot there must be four of these runes present.

While active this rune glows a faint golden color and returns to the media that it was drawn in when inactive (it disappears if no drawing media was used).

This rune may be drawn multiple times up to a maximum of ten.

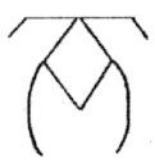 ## SHINKAI'S DEMISE

Learning Difficulty: Intelligence = 18, Sixth Sense = 20
Required Forces: *Air*, *Fire*, *Land*, *Spirit*, & *Water*
Writing Sensitivity: 2
Force Energy: 80
Life: 6 hours

No drawing upon or conjuring of any of the Mystic Forces is possible while within thirty feet of this rune (it paralyzes the *Gift*). Any one, Shinkai or Korgathool, that is already drawing upon the Mystic Forces or conjuring at the time they come in range of this rune will be immediately severed from the Mystic Forces and will suffer the appropriate backlash damage (see the Force-effect "Force Sever" in the "FORCE-EFFECTS" Section for details backlash).

This rune has no effect on Force-effects that are already tied off before they come within range of it.

This rune appears the same during and after inactivity as it does when first drawn.

This rune may be drawn multiple times up to a maximum of three times.

 ## SHINKAI SIGNAL

Learning Difficulty: Intelligence = 11, Sixth Sense = 11
Required Forces: *Fire & Spirit*
Writing Sensitivity: 1
Force Energy: 30
Life: 12 hours

This rune will glow bright blue as well as emitting a loud shrilling noise whenever any Shinkai, other than the creator of the rune, come within one hundred yards of it. Though the name only implies Shinkai, this rune is equally effective in detecting Korgathool.

This rune appears the same during and after inactivity as it does when first drawn.

 ## SIXTH SENSE

Learning Difficulty: Intelligence = 14, Sixth Sense = 15
Required Forces: *Air*, *Fire*, *Land*, *Spirit*, & *Water*
Writing Sensitivity: 2
Force Energy: 30
Life: 1 hour

Having this rune drawn on the skin or worn directly against the skin (such as on one's armor or clothing) temporarily adds 3 Levels to that being's Sixth Sense.

Regardless of the drawing media, when active, this rune changes to light blue in color and reverts to the initial drawing media when inactive.

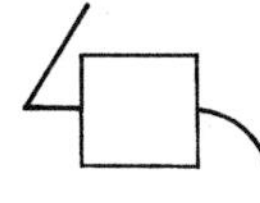 ## SPIRIT EYE

Learning Difficulty: Intelligence = 10, Sixth Sense = 10
Required Forces: *Spirit*
Writing Sensitivity: 2
Force Energy: 18
Life: * 3 Turns

This rune will cause any inanimate object it is drawn upon to become transparent. The area that can be made transparent can be no larger than four feet in diameter and four feet thick. The Shinkai may choose at the creation of the rune how large of an area that the rune will affect. Changing the size of the transparency once the rune is drawn requires the rune to be redrawn.

The transparency only affects one side of the object (the side that the Shinkai drew the rune upon). The other side will appear normally.

This rune is completely invisible while active, even to beings with "Force Sight".

If 36 points of Force Energy is expended into the creation of the rune instead of 18 the Life of the rune is extended to

6 Turns. This rune will completely disappear when it becomes inactive.

SPLIT FIRE

Learning Difficulty: Intelligence = 11, Sixth Sense = 15
Required Forces: *Fire*
Writing Sensitivity: 0
Force Energy: 30
Life:50 Turns (5 minutes)

Having this rune drawn on the skin or worn directly against the skin (such as on one's armor or an amulet) enhances that being's ability to use the Force-effect "Fireball". Instead of producing one fireball per use, that Shinkai can now produce two fireballs with a single use of "Fireball". These two fireballs can both be directed at a single target or two separate targets. A single Sixth Sense/Performance Test is made for both fireballs, but damage for each fireball is rolled separately.

This rune glows bright orange while active. If no drawing media was used to draw this rune it will disappear when inactive. If drawing media was used, it will simply return to the color of the drawing media.

STONE SKIN

Learning Difficulty: Intelligence = 13, Sixth Sense = 14
Required Forces: *Land*
Writing Sensitivity: 3
Force Energy: 40
Life: 3 hours

The skin of any living being that this rune is drawn on will instantly become thick and tough, taking on a stone-like appearance similar to that of Warlum skin but tougher. This new skin gives the being, or adds in the case of Warlum, a Protection Rating of 7. Armor can still be worn over this skin as normal.

This rune appears the same during and after inactivity as it does when first drawn.

STRENGTH

Learning Difficulty: Intelligence = 14, Sixth Sense = 15
Required Forces: *Land*
Writing Sensitivity: 2

Force Energy: 30
Life:1 hour

Having this rune drawn on the skin or worn directly against the skin (such as on a bracer or pendant) temporarily adds 3 Levels to that being's Strength.

Regardless of the drawing media, when active, this rune appears light maroon in color and reverts to the initial drawing media when inactive.

STRENGTHENED STEEL

Learning Difficulty: Intelligence = 9, Sixth Sense = 9
Required Forces: *Fire & Land*
Writing Sensitivity: 2
Force Energy: 18
Life: 7 hours

Any metal item on which this rune is drawn receives a +3 point increase to its Protection Rating as well as increasing its Destroyed Rating and Reduced Effectiveness (Reduced Protection for armor) by 20 points.

This rune looks like polished silver as long as it remains active. Once inactive its appearance reverts back to the natural look of the media in which it is drawn.

This rune may be drawn multiple times up to a maximum of three times, but it may only be drawn once per item, by the same Shinkai. The same item could have a dozen "Strengthened Steel" runes on it as long as each one was drawn by a different Shinkai.

TRAVELING PORTAL

Learning Difficulty: Intelligence = 18, Sixth Sense = 20
Required Forces: *Air & Spirit*
Writing Sensitivity: 2
Force Energy: 75
Life: *

This rune allows living beings to travel from one point to another without covering the space in between. This rune must be drawn in pairs in order to be effective. The first one is drawn on an object where the Shinkai wishes to return. When the Shinkai draws a second one of these runes on any object, both runes expand into shimmering silver portals a number of feet in diameter equal to the creating Shinkai's Sixth Sense Level. Any living being stepping into one portal will step out through the other. Any items touching or otherwise attached to a being that steps into one of these portals (as long as the sum of the items are no larger than the being himself) will be transported with them.

The portals are not transparent, so looking into one portal will not allow a being to see into the area surrounding the other.

This rune has a Life equal to a number of days equal to the creating Shinkai's Sixth Sense Level. But once the second rune is drawn and the traveling portals appear they will only remain open for 20 Turns, after which time they will fade away and both runes die.

Anyone mid-way through one of these portals when it fades out may end up in either location where the two runes were drawn (determined by any random method or by the GM).

Your character may only create one "Traveling Portal" at a time, so he can not have "Traveling Portal" runes drawn for more than one place at a time (drawing a second "Traveling Portal" rune will immediately open a portal to the first).

WARMING

Learning Difficulty: Intelligence = 10, Sixth Sense = 11
Required Forces: *Fire*
Writing Sensitivity: 2
Force Energy: 10 *
Life: 1 day

This rune can not be drawn on living beings (it will immediately die as soon as it is drawn). As soon as this rune is alive it will become warm and the object upon which it is drawn will consequently be warmed. This warming effect will slowly spread out from the rune and will warm the object that it is drawn on up to two feet in any direction from the rune itself.

The listed Force Energy for the "Warming" rune is the Force Energy needed to make the rune and the object it is drawn upon warm. Doubling the Force Energy placed into the "Warming" rune upon creation will cause the rune and the object it is drawn upon to become hot instead of just warm. Tripling the Force Energy placed into the "Warming" rune upon creation will cause the rune and the object it is drawn upon to become extremely hot, hot enough to burn for an average of Level 2 damage.

This rune is commonly used by alchemists to keep certain ingredients warm, such as lava lizard eggs, or to heat ingredients.

Writing Sensitivity: 0
Force Energy: 250
Life:10 Turns

When drawn on any object this rune expands into a portal seven feet in diameter that opens into the mystical realm of *Water*. The portal will remain open for 10 Turns at which time it will contract back and close. Though all of the mystical elements of the *Water* realm are visible and lay just beyond the threshold of the portal, none of the realm's material or substance will come through the portal on its own (opening the portal doesn't cause the realm's contents to come pouring out into Oryathar).

Any object that is within the entrance to the portal as it closes will be completely and cleanly severed. The object upon which a "*Water* Portal" rune is drawn will not be affected and will be left in the same state that it was before the rune was drawn. This rune can not be drawn on a living being.

At the time that your character draws a "*Water* Portal" rune he may increase the number of Turns that the portal will remain open by expending additional Force Energy into the rune. For each additional 5 points of Force Energy beyond that listed that your character places into the rune at creation the portal will remain open for 1 additional Turn.

This rune will glow a radiant blue color for an instant before it expands into the portal, and will also glow for an instant after the portal closes, at which time it will vanish leaving no trace that it was ever drawn.

WILLPOWER

Learning Difficulty: Intelligence = 14, Sixth Sense = 15
Required Forces: *Land* & *Spirit*
Writing Sensitivity: 2
Force Energy: 30
Life:1 hour

Having this rune drawn on the skin or worn directly against the skin (such as on a bracelet) adds 3 Levels to that being's Willpower.

Regardless of the drawing media, when active, this rune changes to light green in color and reverts to the initial drawing media when inactive.

WATER PORTAL

Learning Difficulty: Intelligence = 21, Sixth Sense= 22
Required Forces: *Water*

WEAPONS & ARMOR

In order to prepare your character to do battle with the many minions of the Shadow, you will need to properly equip him, or her, with the necessary weapons and armor.

In order to better assist you with that task, this Section will describe the various types of weapons and armor that your character may use and any special rules or information that pertains to them.

Following is a description of the various types of weapons and armor available to characters as well as tables listing detailed facts and information about each weapon or piece of armor.

This Section is divided into four main areas. They are Melee Weapons, Ranged Weapons, Armor, and Shields. Most all types of metal weapons and types of armor are available in green-steel, but at four times the cost of the same weapon made of normal steel. Green-steel is favorable because it is lighter, stronger and sharper than normal steel and doesn't rust.

The various weapons, armor, and shields tables at the end of this Section contain much of the needed information about each weapon, type of armor, or shield arranged in a very compact and convenient manner. These tables are an invaluable resource for the players and GM.

MELEE WEAPONS

Designed for the grueling punishment of close combat, these weapons are strong and durable. Never knowing when your character may find himself face to face with a an opponent, melee weapons are an essential part of any adventurer's arsenal.

Battle-axe

The battle-axe is a very heavy and deadly weapon. Designed for use in melee, this weapon has a long handle with a large, curved blade at one end. Some battle-axes have a single blade on one side with a spike on the opposite side while others have blades on both sides. Either type is a truly formidable weapon more than capable of taking on the fiercest of enemies.

Most battle-axes are around two and a half to three feet in length.

Club

This is a very simple type of weapon designed from a large piece of wood. It has a comfortably carved handle usually wrapped with leather, and a very large and heavy body designed for smashing. Some clubs have metal bands around them for added strength and durability.

Clubs are usually around three feet in length.

Dagger

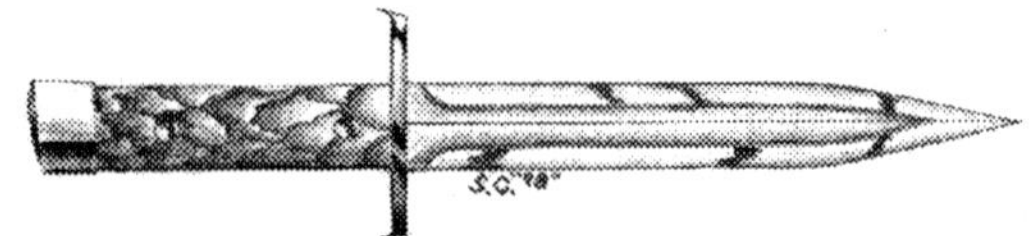

The dagger is a very common weapon among adventurers. Double-edged with a very fine point, a dagger can cut or stab its way through most anything.

Some daggers are designed for use in melee while others are balanced for throwing. Generally speaking, daggers designed for melee are more durable.

Most daggers have a blade of five to ten inches in length.

Double-flail

This weapon is identical to a normal flail with the exception that it has two separate chains and steel balls coming from the handle rather than just one. Some of these steel balls have small knots or ridges covering their surface.

A double-flail can only be used in conjunction with "Single-Strike" attacks. Also, a double-flail can not be used to parry with.

Flail

This weapon consists of an eight to ten inch handle with a length of chain attached to it. On the end of the chain is a heavy steel ball designed to smash its way through opponents. When this weapon starts swinging foes had better beware. Some of these steel balls have small knots or ridges over their surface.

The average flail is approximately three and a half feet in length.

A flail can only be used in conjunction with "Single-Strike"

attacks. Also, a flail can not be used to parry with.

Halberd

This is the most lethal and feared of all edged melee weapons. It is a massive cruelly-edged blade, similar to that of a battle-axe, mounted on the end of a very long shaft.

Halberds are very heavy and require a good amount of strength to wield, but to those with the ability a fiercer weapon is seldom found.

Most halberds are an average of six to seven feet in length.

Knife

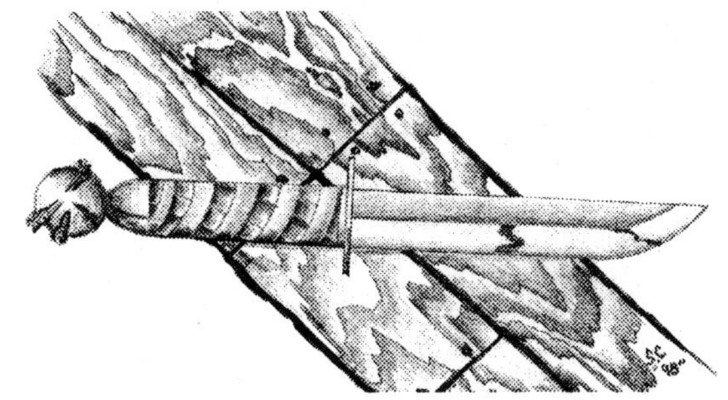

Probably the most common of all weapons, the knife has endless uses. The sturdy blade is sharp only on one side and usually ranges from three to twelve inches in length.

Some knives are designed for use in melee while others are balanced for throwing. Generally speaking, knives designed for melee are more durable.

Lance

This weapon is a very long spear like weapon designed specifically for use on mounts. Its primary use is for jousting and is not actually designed for use in real combat. For this reason its tip is somewhat blunt and it does not have a very high Damage Yield.

Lances have cone shaped guards near their base to protect the hand holding the handle.

Mace

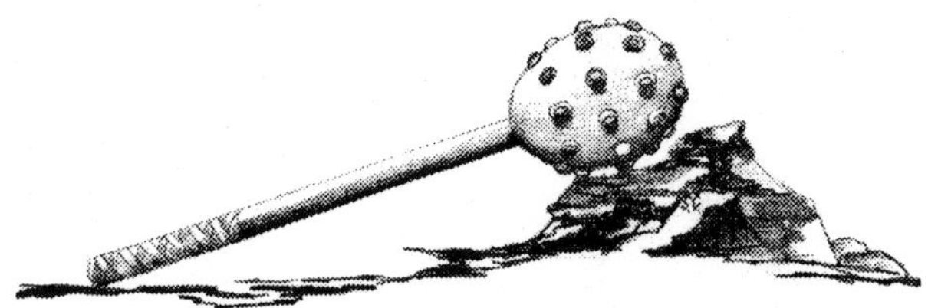

This weapon is a very popular non-edged melee weapon. It consists of a long handle with a heavy steel ball mounted at the end. Some of these steel balls have small knots or ridges over their surface to increase their effectiveness.

Pike

A pike is a very long and heavy spear-like weapon designed for use on a mount. Unlike a lance, it is designed for use in combat. Its tip is very sharp and strong and designed for piercing through armor and the tough hides of Shadow-kin.

A pike can only be used in conjunction with "Single-Strike" attacks.

Quarterstaff

This weapon is simply a long, round wooden pole. Its light weight and even balance makes it an excellent weapon for parrying attacks, but unfortunately it isn't able to withstand a large amount of damage.

Quarterstaffs are designed to be wielded with two hands, but can be wielded with only one hand. When using only one hand to wield a quarterstaff you must subtract 4 points from any attacks made with it, and subtract 2 points from your character's Physical Defense if you parry with it.

When using a quarterstaff to parry, you may add +2 to your character's Physical Defense, but only if both hands are used. If only one hand is used your character doesn't get the +2 point bonus but rather a -2 point penalty.

If your character has all 3 possible Technique Points with the quarterstaff, he can make two attacks with them in a single Turn. The two attacks occur one immediately after the other (if the first occurs at an Initiative value of 9 then the second must occur at an Initiative value of 8, or not at all). Both of these attacks are considered a single Major Action. Both hands must be used in order to make two attacks per Turn with a quarterstaff.

Scimitar

Scimitars are very similar to broadswords, but instead of a straight blade the blade of a scimitar is curved. All scimitars are only single-edged. Scimitars are generally lighter than most common types of swords, but are also slightly easier to wield. For this reason attacks made with scimitars receive a +1D4 point bonus but consequently the damage of attacks with them receive a -1D4 point penalty.

Most scimitars are an average of two and a half to three feet in length.

Spear

These weapons are excellent for hunting as well as for use in actual combat. Their design is simple; a long shaft with a sharp, pointed blade attached to one end.

Some spears are designed for the abuse of melee combat while others are balanced and designed for throwing.

Most spears are an average of five to six feet in length.

Spiked Double-flail

Spiked double-flails are identical to normal double-flails with the exception that the spiked double-flail has long, razor-sharp spikes protruding from the steel balls. Because of these spikes, this weapon has a higher Damage Yield than its non-spiked counter-part.

The spiked double-flail is an extremely lethal weapon capable of piercing through steel as well as the toughest of hides.

Spiked double-flails can only be used in conjunction with "Single-Strike" attacks, and can not be used to parry with.

Spiked Flail

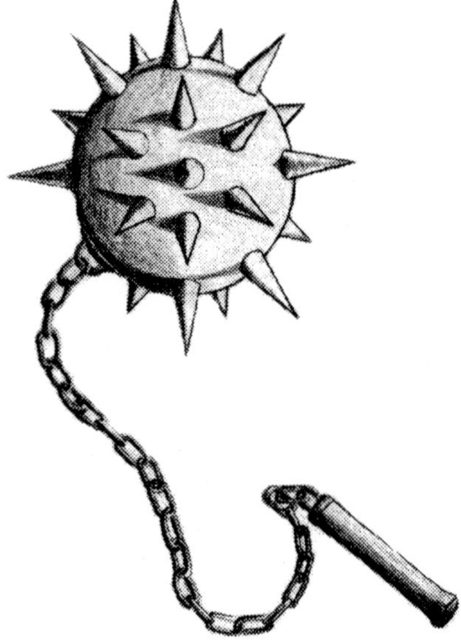

This weapon is identical to its non-spiked counterpart, with the exception that it has long, sharp spikes covering it instead of small ridged or knots.

Due to the spikes, this weapon has a higher Damage Yield than its non-spiked counter-part.

As with normal flails, spiked-flails can only be used in conjunction with "Single-Strike" attacks, and can not be used to parry with.

Spiked Mace

This weapon consists of a long handle with a heavy steel ball mounted at one end. The steel ball is covered with sharp, steel spikes. Though somewhat less convenient to carry than a normal mace, a spiked mace has a higher Damage Yield.

Spiked War Hammer

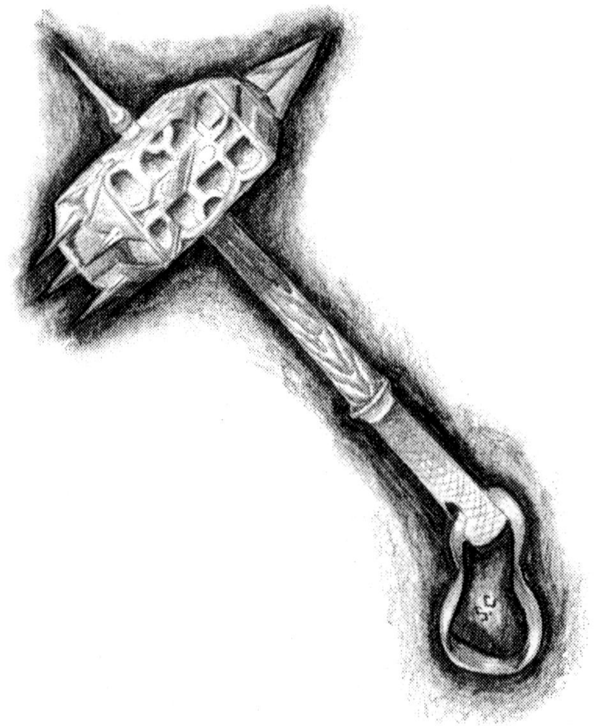

This is the deadliest of all non-edged melee weapons. It consists of a two to three foot long handle with a very large and heavy steel head attached to it that has spikes decorating its surface. Designed for a combination of stabbing and crushing this weapon can quickly mame or kill.

Though the spiked war hammer is quite cumbersome and heavy it is worth its weight in gold in battle for those who can wield it.

"Single-Strike" attacks made with spiked war hammers add 10 points of damage to the attack instead of the normal 6 points.

Sword

The sword is undoubtedly the most common and trusted of all melee weapons. A significant length of well-balanced, razor-edged steel attached to a short handle the sword is simple in design yet a weapon of stunning effectiveness in the hands of a Blade Master.

The three most common types of swords are the broadsword, short-sword, and two-handed sword.

Broadsword

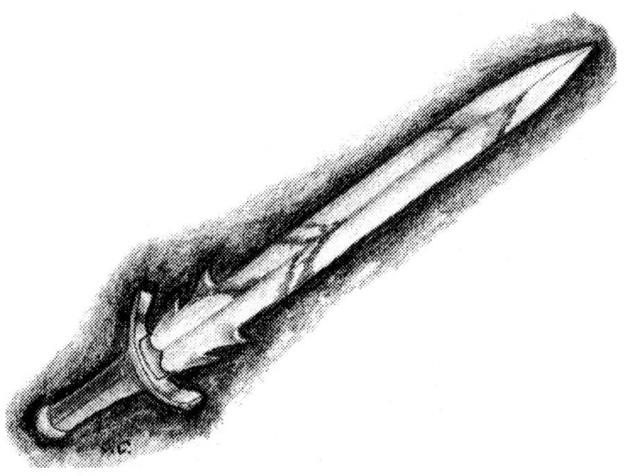

A very large sword with a broad blade designed more for cutting than stabbing, often with an edge on both sides. The broadsword is perhaps the most popular type of sword among soldiers and adventurers.

Most broadswords are around three to three and a half feet in length.

Shortsword

Short-swords gain their popular name due to the simple fact that they are somewhat short, at least in comparison to other types of swords. As far as design and shape, short-swords are no different than broadswords. Somewhat more compact than other swords but still very effective, the short-sword is a quite popular weapon.

Most short-swords are an average of two feet in length.

Two-handed Sword

The two-handed sword is the largest and most lethal of swords. It gets its name because its handle is long enough to accommodate two hands, which is required by most in order to be wielded properly. This awesome weapon has an impressive Damage Yield to match its impressive size.

Most two-handed swords are double-edged, though some are single-edged.

Most two-handed swords are around three and a half to four feet in length.

Trident

This weapon is essentially a spear, but with three separate tips instead of one. The three tips are often designed in different shapes and positions on the head of the shaft.

Some tridents are designed for the abuse of melee combat, while others are balanced and designed for throwing.

Most tridents are an average of five to six feet in length.

War Hammer

This weapon is virtually the same as the spiked war hammer except it doesn't have spikes.

Though the Damage Yield for this weapon isn't quite as high as that of its spiked counterpart, it is still a fearsome weapon with a lot to offer to those with the strength to wield it.

"Single Strike" attacks made with war hammers add 9 points of damage to the attack instead of the normal 6 points.

Whip

This weapon is a simple handle, usually leather wrapped, with a long braided leather cord attached to it. Some whips have sharp metal shards attached to their end for increased effectiveness (whips with metal shards on their ends receive a +1 point bonus to their Damage Yield).

The whip can be used to attack opponents up to seven feet away. This is the exception to the range of five feet, which is normally considered the maximum melee distance.

Another interesting ability of the whip is that it can be used to disarm opponents. On a successful attack to an opponents arm the whip may actually wrap around the opponent's arm, or weapon, and disarm them. This requires a Performance Die result of 8 or higher, and the player must state in his or her intended action that their character is attempting to disarm with the whip. When attacking to disarm with a whip the attack does one half of the damage that would normally

be rendered (determine damage as normal and then cut it in half). Once a character attempts to disarm with a whip the damage of the attack will be cut in half whether or not the attack actually disarms the opponent or not.

If the attack to disarm is successful (meaning the Performance Die result was 8 or higher and the attack hit the opponent's arm or weapon) the weapon is thrown 1D8 feet in the general direction of the character wielding the whip.

Most whips are seven to eight feet in length.

RANGED WEAPONS

Ranged weapons are extremely useful and effective weapons. They allow the user the safety of making attacks at a safe distance from their opponent, ending most confrontations without ever having to engage in melee.

Arc-dagger

This particular type of dagger, especially designed to be used as a throwing weapon, has a unique shape compared to other types of daggers. The arc-dagger has a blade like that of a normal dagger that is typically between twelve and sixteen inches in length, and has curved eight inch blades extending outward on either side of the main blade. Even if the tip misses, the side blades will slice through the target as long as the dagger passes within close proximity.

Arc-daggers are considered by many to be the deadliest of all throwing weapons.

Bola

This weapon is designed more for entangling opponents than inflicting damage upon them. It is a length of cord with steel weights attached to its ends. When it strikes an opponent it wraps around them and entangles them. The steel weights also do a small amount of damage as they strike the opponent, but their main purpose is to entangle.

When an opponent is successfully hit with a bola, and the Performance Die result of the attack is at least 6, the opponent is entangled. If the legs of a moving opponent are entangled, they will fall.

An opponent who's head or neck is entangled with a bola has a fifty percent chance of being knocked out for 1D4 Turns.

It is a Major Action for someone to untangle themselves from a bola.

Most bolas range in length from three to four feet.

Bow

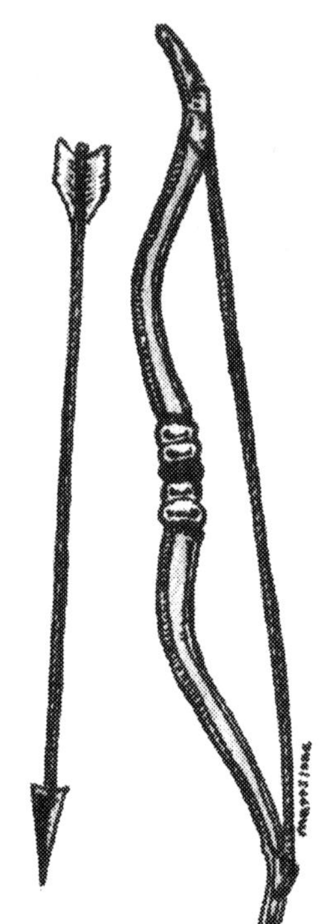

A bow is simply a long and somewhat curved piece of flexible wood with a string tightly strung between its two ends. It is balanced and fashioned into an accurate instrument capable of hurdling deadly-tipped arrows with incredible force and speed.

Heavy Bow

This extremely heavy and fierce bow is exceptionally thick and strong with the potential to send an arrow blasting through even the best of armor.

The heavy bow requires more strength to wield than the normal bow, but for those with the ability to wield it, it is definitely the bow of choice.

Normal Bow

The common bow of choice, the normal bow is light and less cumbersome than its larger counter-part, the heavy bow. With impressive damage yielding capability and easy handling, the normal bow is an excellent choice for the novice as well as experienced bowman.

Crossbow

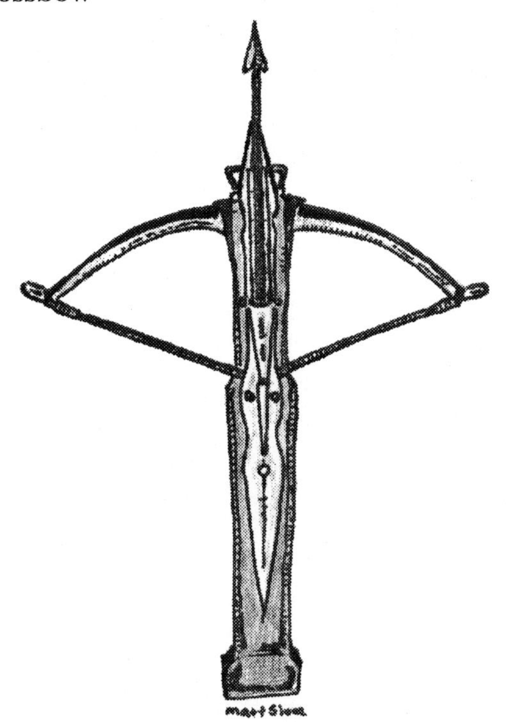

These weapons are very useful archery weapons for cavalrymen as they can be wielded and fired with one hand, making them easy to use while riding.

The crossbow shoots a short type of arrow called a bolt. The crossbow is like a small bow that is fixed horizontally to a length of wood with a hand grip. The crossbow's string is pulled back to full draw position and locked in place by a small lever. The bolt is placed in a small groove on the crossbow's top side. There is a trigger mechanism that the shooter can pull to release the string and launch the bolt.

Crossbows are generally less accurate than regular bows and have a shorter range as well. Though it is possible to aim and fire a crossbow with one hand, it is much harder to keep the crossbow steady and to be accurate if used in this manner (a -1D6 penalty is applied to crossbow attacks if only one hand is used to aim and fire them).

Pulling the string of a crossbow to full draw and locking it in place is somewhat difficult and normally requires two hands, especially for the heavy crossbow. Cocking and loading a crossbow is considered a single Major Action.

Heavy Crossbow

The heavy crossbow can hurl arrows much farther and faster than normal or one-handed crossbows. It is also significantly larger and heavier than other crossbows, but for those looking for maximum damage yield from a crossbow, this is the weapon.

The heavy crossbow is about three feet in length and width.

Normal Crossbow

The normal crossbow is the most commonly used type of crossbow. It is significantly larger and more powerful than the one-handed crossbow but is much lighter and easier to wield than the heavy crossbow. It is a fine choice for the ruling-race looking for a strong crossbow but not willing to pack the brutish heavy crossbow.

The normal crossbow is about two feet in length and width.

One-handed Crossbow

This crossbow is quite a bit smaller than the other types of crossbows. It is only around nine inches in length and width making it very easy to conceal inside of a cloak or coat. Though significantly less powerful than the other types of crossbows, the one-handed crossbow is more than capable of delivering lethal attacks to smaller foes, or even large foes if the shots are carefully placed.

The one-handed crossbow is an excellent back-up weapon and is a common part of most any battle-seasoned warrior's arsenal.

Shuriken

The shuriken is a flat piece of metal that has several sharp points protruding from it. Many have given the nickname "throwing star". It is designed so that when thrown it will spin through the air and regardless of how it strikes its target (as long as it hits on edge) one or more of the spikes will impale the target. Some shuriken have as few as three spikes and others have as many as eight.

The exact shape and design of shurikens varies widely.

Spiked Ball

This weapon is a small iron ball with thin, sharp spikes covering its surface. The spiked balls are thrown by hand and inflict impact damage as well as stabbing the victim with their numerous spikes. Spiked balls are sometimes thrown on the ground in the path of approaching enemies so that they might step on them, impaling their feet.

Spiked balls are about three inches in diameter with around twenty one inch spikes protruding from them.

Throwing Hatchet

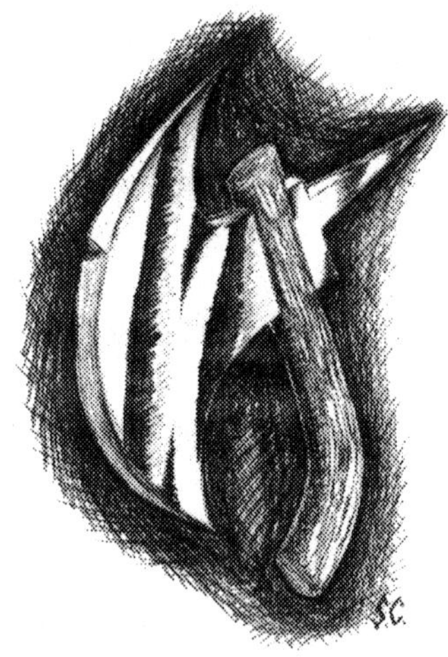

This weapon is a favorite among those who prefer throwing weapons. It is a light-weight hatchet that is balanced for throwing. It usually has a single curved blade on one side with a sharp spike on the opposite side of the blade. These hatchets are also often equipped with a sharp spike protruding from the bottom of the handle. As the hatchet whirls toward its target one of its three deadly ends is bound to strike home.

The throwing hatchet is an average of two feet in length.

WEAPON RANGES

The following table lists the ranges for the various types of ranged weapons. All ranges are listed in feet.

RANGED WEAPONS	
Weapon	**Range (Normal/Long)**
Arc-dagger	60/110
Bola	60/100
Normal Bow	150/300
Heavy Bow	175/350
One-hand Crossbow	60/120
Normal Crossbow	110/200
Heavy Crossbow	150/275
Shuriken	50/90
Spear	60/120
Spiked Ball	40/70
Throwing Dagger	55/110
Throwing Hatchet	35/60
Throwing Knife	50/110
Trident	60/110

Under the "Range" column there are two sets of numbers. Then number before the slash is the maximum range for the weapon that is still considered Normal range. The number after the slash is the maximum range for the weapon that is considered Long range. Attacks at targets that are beyond a weapon's Long range are not normally permitted, but the GM can make exceptions if he feels it is appropriate.

For details on the bonuses and penalties that accompany the various ranges that a weapon is used see "Ranged Combat" in the "COMBAT" Section.

ARMOR

The following is a list of the different types of body armor that you can equip your character with. They are listed in order of lowest Protection Ratings to the greatest.

Though shields are considered a type of armor, they are listed in a category by themselves.

Wearing armor reduces the amount of damage that your character receives from attacks but it can also become quite cumbersome. Some types of armor give Agility and or movement penalties to the wearer. When wearing more than one piece of armor you add the penalties of each piece of armor together to determine your character's total penalty. For example, if your character is wearing a chain-mail shirt, which has an Agility penalty of -1 Level and a -5 feet per Turn movement penalty, and chain-mail breeches, which have an Agility penalty of -1 Level and a -20 feet per Turn movement penalty, he would have a total Agility penalty of -2 Levels and a total movement penalty of -25 feet per Turn.

It is possible to wear more than one type of armor over the same area of the body at one time, but no more than two. So, your character may wear a chain-mail hood under a steel helm but couldn't wear a leather hood, chain-mail hood, and steel helm all at the same time. Your character could also, for example, wear cloth armor under any other type of armor, or wear chain-mail armor under steel plate armor, but can't wear more than two types over the same area.

When wearing two pieces or types of armor that have no penalties over the same area of the body, your character will receive a -1 penalty to Agility.

So as you can see, stacking cumbersome pieces of armor on may give your character a high degree of protection, but it will also slow him down significantly. Is the trade-off worth it? That's up to you.

An exception to wearing multiple types of armor at the same time is steel plate. Your character can not wear two pieces of the same type of steel plate at the same time. Such as two steel helms, two steel plate chest and back-guards, etc.

Cloth

This type of armor consists of thick, padded cloth. It offers minimal protection, but it's light weight and flexibility makes it preferable to some.

Cloth armor generally comes in two parts. One part is very similar to a coat and protects the torso and often the arms. The other part is the breeches which protect the pelvis and legs.

Leather Hood

This is a hood made of thick leather that protects the head as well as the neck. It is very light weight and comfortable and can be worn under a chain-mail hood or steel helm for added protection, or can be worn by itself.

Leather

This armor is made of tough, flexible leather. It comes in various pieces that can be worn separately or buckled together to form an entire suit of armor. The various pieces of leather armor available is arm-guards, chest and back-guard, and breeches. The chest and back-guard can be purchased with an extension (pelvis skirt) long enough to cover the pelvis as well as the torso area.

The arm-guards protect the entire arms, the chest and back-guard protects the entire torso area, and the breeches protect the pelvis and legs.

Padded Leather

Padded leather is the same type and design as normal leather armor but also has thick padding on the inside for additional protection.

Padded leather is slightly heavier and more cumbersome than normal leather and renders slight penalties to the wearer's Agility.

Chain Mail Hood

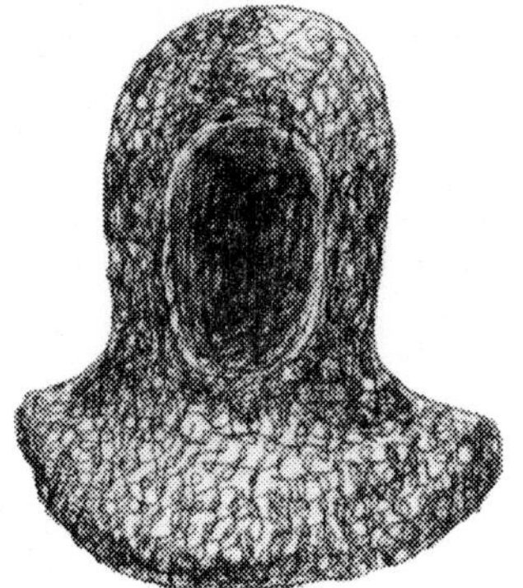

This hood is made of interconnecting rings of steel. It covers the head and neck area and offers a significant amount of protection while remaining fairly lightweight and flexible.

The chain-mail hood can be worn under a steel helm for added protection, but is more commonly worn over a thin cloth hood or by itself.

Chain Mail

This type of armor is made up of interconnecting rings of steel. The end result is a very tough yet flexible type of armor.

The various pieces of chain mail armor available to characters are a shirt with or without sleeves, long-shirt (which is long enough to cover the pelvis area as well as the torso) with or without sleeves, and breeches.

Chain mail is fairly abrasive and tough on the skin. Often cloth armor, or just a layer of thick clothing, is worn under it, for comfort.

Gauntlets

Gauntlets are protective gloves made of overlapping steel plates. They cover the entire hands and the lower half of the forearm. Because they are made of steel the Damage Yield from a punch from someone wearing gauntlets is increased by +2 points.

Spiked Gauntlets

Spike gauntlets are the same as normal gauntlets except they have half-inch to one-inch long spikes protruding from the knuckle area. These spikes further increase the damage done by a successful punch from the gauntlets. The Damage Yield from a punch from someone wearing spiked gauntlets is increased by 1 Level and +2 points.

Plate & Chain

This type of armor is simply a combination of steel plate and chain mail armor that has been combined. It offers a great deal of protection and still retains much of its mobility. The chest and back of this type of armor is steel plate with connected sleeves of chain mail. The lower half of the armor has steel plates covering the front of the thigh and shin areas connected to chain mail which makes up the remainder of the armor.

Steel Helm

This is simply a one-piece helm constructed of steel plate and shaped to conform to the head. Some steel helms are designed to wrap around and cover the jaw and also have a guard over the nose, and some have a hinged face guard that can be raised or lowered to provide protection for the face as needed. Helms with hinged face guard have small holes in them for ease of breathing and a small eye slit to see through. Some helms only protect the skull, leaving the face and jaw completely exposed.

Steel Plate

This type of armor is the strongest and offers the most protection, but it is also the heaviest and most cumbersome of all types of armor. Steel plate armor consists of heavy pieces of steel plating connected by metal buckles or heavy leather cords. It takes a minimum of 10 Turns for someone accustomed to wearing steel plate to suit up in an entire steel plate suit of armor.

Many don't like steel plate armor due to its heaviness and bulk, but to those with the agility and strength to properly use it steel plate armor offers the ultimate protection.

SHIELDS

Shields make an excellent addition to any warriors armory. Usually the first line of defense against attacks, shields are designed to withstand severe abuse. Due to their portability and the fact that they don't significantly hinder mobility shields are commonly used even when actual body armor isn't desirable. Any veteran to combat will be quick to point out the value of a good shield.

Shields, unlike normal types of armor, absorb the entire damage from the attacks that they intercept (normal types of armor only absorb an amount of damage up to their Protection Rating). In some instances shields may not absorb all of the damage from an attack.

The three main types of shields are bucklers, half-shields, and full-shields.

Buckler

Bucklers are the smallest type of shields and are designed to be worn on the forearm. They are normally constructed out of wood with metal slats on and around them, though some are made out of solid steel. Most bucklers are round in shape and are approximately one foot or less in diameter. They have a heavy leather strap on the back into which the user can slide his forearm.

Because of their small size and the fact that they fasten to the users forearm and don't require the use of the hands to hold them, bucklers don't hinder the arm on which they are attached. Weapons can still be used freely with the same arm to which a buckler is attached.

Half-Shield

Half-shields are probably the most commonly used type of shield. They are large enough to offer a good amount of protection yet small enough that they don't greatly hinder the movement and range of motion of the wearer. Most half-shields are acorn-shaped but do come in varying shapes and designs.

The most common size for a half-shield is approximately two feet in length and a foot and a half wide. Some half-shields are slightly smaller or larger but not normally by more than a few inches.

Full-Shield

Full-shields are the largest and strongest type of shields, but are also the heaviest and most cumbersome. When mobility is not as much of a priority as protection the full-shield is the way to go. Like half-shields, most full-shields are acorn-shaped but also come in varying shapes and designs.

The most common size for a full-shield is four to four and a half feet in length and two to two and a half feet wide. Some full-shield are slightly smaller or larger but not normally by more than a few inches.

WEAPONS, ARMOR, & SHIELDS TABLES

Each of the following tables has a number of categories of information. In order to properly utilize the information on these tables each of these categories and their significance is explained in detail.

Agility Penalty

Due to the weight and/or restriction to movement some types of armor render penalties to those wearing them. The "Agility Penalty" is the penalty that is given to the character's Agility as long as he is wearing the armor.

Record the penalties to your character's Agility on the front of your Character Sheet in the appropriate spaces. Record the Level of the Agility penalty under "Penalty" across from Agility and write "armor" under "Penalty Type" so that you will know what the Agility penalty is for. When your character removes the armor that is causing the penalty simply remove the penalty and penalty type information.

Agility penalties are cumulative. So if your character is wearing one piece of armor that has an Agility Penalty of -1 Level and another piece of armor that has an Agility Penalty of -3 Levels, your character's Agility would be penalized by a total of -4 Levels.

Bulk Value

This is a rating of how bulky the particular weapon or piece of armor is. Characters can only have a certain Total Bulk Value, so it is important to know the Bulk Value of any piece of equipment or item that a character is carrying so that the player can keep up with his or her character's Total Bulk Value. The Equipment Sheets have designated areas for recording the Bulk Value of all of your character's equipment and items.

Coin

This is the average amount of silver coin that the particular weapon or piece of armor costs. Sometimes characters may be able to find an item for sale for less than this listed price or may be able to bargain or haggle the price down (GM's discretion).

Dmg. Yield (Damage Yield)

This is the Level of damage that the particular weapon inflicts.

Destroyed Rating

This is the number of points of cumulative damage that it takes to destroy the weapon, armor, or shield. Every item also has what is known as a Shatter Threshold. The Shatter Threshold of any item is equal to half of its Destroyed Rating. If an item receives a number of points of damage at one time that equals or exceeds its Shatter Threshold it is immediately destroyed.

All types of armor and shields, as well as most any object, has a Destroyed Rating. Though a Destroyed Rating is not listed with the descriptions of average items and equipment they too can only sustain so much damage before they are destroyed. The GM can decide what the Destroyed Rating for any particular item is when and if it becomes necessary. Normally it is not necessary to keep up with the damage of normal items and pieces of equipment.

Max. Tech. (Maximum Technique)

This is the maximum number of Technique Points that can be learned with the particular weapon or shield.

Minimum Strength

Due to their weight and/or design some weapons and shields require the character to have a minimum Strength Level before they can use them. "Minimum Strength" is the minimum Strength Level that a character must have in order to properly wield the weapon or shield.

At the GM's discretion characters that don't have a Strength Level high enough to meet the minimum that is required for a weapon or shield may still be able to use it but with severe penalties (GM's choice as to the extent of the penalties).

Move Penalty

Due to the weight and/or restriction to movement some types of armor render penalties to those wearing them. The "Move Penalty" is the penalty that is given to the character's movement as long as he is wearing the armor. The penalty is the number of feet per Turn that the character's Maximum Speed is reduced by. Their Action Movement is then calculated as normal from their adjusted Maximum Speed.

Movement penalties are cumulative. So if your character is wearing one piece of armor that has a Move Penalty of -20 feet per Turn and another piece of armor that has a Move Penalty of -10 feet per Turn, your character would have a total movement penalty of -30 feet per Turn.

Protection Rating

This is the number of points of damage that the armor can absorb at one time. If the amount of damage rendered exceeds the armors Protection Rating then the amount of damage beyond the armor's Protection Rating is inflicted to the being wearing the armor.

So lets say that your character is wearing a piece of armor that has a Protection Rating of 8 and he receives an attack that renders 20 points of damage. The armor would absorb the first 8 points of damage and your character would receive the remaining 12 points of damage. In the appropriate area of your Character Sheet you would note that your character's armor received 8 points of damage and on your Combat Sheet you would note that your character received 12 points of damage.

If your character is wearing multiple layers of armor over the same area the damage is dealt to, then the outer layer takes damage first and if it can not absorb all of the damage dealt then the next layer will take damage. If the second layer of armor can not absorb the remainder of the damage then the being wearing the armor would take the remaining damage.

For example, your character is wearing a leather chest/back-guard under a chain mail shirt. Your character takes a hit in the chest with a battle-axe. The damage rendered by the attack is 32 points. The chain mail has a Protection Rating of 6 so it is able to absorb 6 points of the damage. That leaves 26 more points of damage that will go past the protection of the chain mail shirt. The leather chest/back-guard will now absorb some of the damage. Since leather armor has a Protection Rating of 3 it will absorb 3 more points of the damage leaving 23 points of damage unabsorbed. Your character receives 23 points of damage, his chain mail shirt receives 6 points of damage and his leather chest/back-guard receives 3 points of damage.

If the damage from an attack does not exceed the Protection Rating of the armor then that means that the armor absorbed all of the damage and the wearer of the armor will receive no damage at all, though the armor will still be damaged by an amount equal to the damage value of the attack.

At the GM's discretion certain types of attacks may not be able to damage certain types of armor. For example, if your character was wearing chain mail armor and was hit with a quarter staff the GM may determine that the chain mail will receive no actual damage from the attack. Or if your character was wearing steel-plate armor and was hit with a normal leather whip the armor would not sustain any damage. In such cases the armor may absorb, or deflect, the entire amount of the damage yielded by the weapon or may still only absorb a number of points of damage up to its Protection Rating (leaving the wearer of the armor to receive the remainder of the damage). Whether or not the armor will offer complete protection against a particular type of attack or will be damaged from the attack are both decisions that are left up to the GM.

R.E. (Reduced Effectiveness)

As weapons sustain damage they may become dull, warped, and overall less effective. The "Reduced Effectiveness" (or R.E.) of a weapon is the number of points of cumulative damage that it takes to lower the weapon's Damage Yield by 1 Level. So a weapon that has a R.E. of 20 would lose 1 Level from its Damage Yield for every 20 points of damage that it has accumulated. When the weapon accumulates a number of points of damage equal to or greater than its Destroyed Rating then it has a Damage Yield of 0 and is useless (it is destroyed at this point).

If N/A is listed as the weapon's R.E. that means that it only has a Damage Yield of Level 1 to start with. If it takes enough damage to drop its effectiveness by 1 Level it is destroyed.

R.P. (Reduced Protection)

As armor sustains damage it may warp and tear and develop holes or weak spots. After enough damage has been sustained to a piece of armor it begins to lose its ability to protect the wearer. The "Reduced Protection" (or R.P.) of a piece of armor is the number of points of cumulative damage that it takes to lower the armor's Protection Rating by 1 point. So a piece of armor that has a R.P. of 22 would lose 1 point from its Protection Rating for every 22 points of damage that it has accumulated. When the armor accumulates a number of points of damage equal to or greater than its Destroyed Rating then it has a Protection Rating of 0 and is useless (it is destroyed at this point).

Shields do not have a Reduced Protection Rating. They only have a Destroyed Rating. They either completely

absorb the damage from an attack or they do not. They will offer their full protection and function normally until their Destroyed Rating is equaled or exceeded, at which time they are completely destroyed.

If N/A is listed as the R.P. for a piece of armor that means that it only has a Protection Rating of 1 to start with. If it takes enough damage to drop its Protection Rating by 1 point it is destroyed.

Repair Cost

For weapons and normal types of armor the "Repair Cost" is listed as a single value. This value is the cost in silver coin that a blacksmith will normally charge to repair the item if it has sustained enough damage to drop one Reduced Effectiveness rating or one Reduced Protection rating. If the item has sustained enough damage that it has dropped by two Reduced Effectiveness ratings or Reduced Protection ratings then the cost to repair it will double that listed.

For shields the "Repair Cost" is listed as two sets of values. The value before the slash, which is followed by "sc" for silver coins, is the cost to repair the shield if has sustained no more points of damage than the value listed after the slash. So to repair a shield that has 8sc/15 listed as its Repair Cost would cost your character eight silver coins for every 15 points of damage that it has sustained.

If N/A is listed as the Repair Cost for an item that means that it really can't be repaired because if it sustains enough damage to drop its effectiveness or Protection Rating by even 1 Level or 1 point it is destroyed. Your character would simply have to buy a new one.

Type

This is simply the name (type) of the weapon, piece of armor, or shield.

Weight (lbs)

This is how much that the particular item weighs. Most all weight is given in pounds, but a few select items are listed in ounces.

Since characters can only carry a certain amount of weight before he begins receiving penalties, it is important to keep track of the weight of all items that your character is carrying. The Equipment Sheets have designated areas for recording the weight of all of your character's equipment and items.

MELEE WEAPONS

EDGED MELEE WEAPONS									
Type	Coin	Minimum Strength	Dmg. Yield	Max. Tech.	Bulk Value	Weight (lbs)	Repair Cost	Destroyed Rating	R.E.
*Battle Axe	175	Level 4	5	5	4	9	30	70	14
Broad Sword	100	Level 3	4	4	3	5	22	40	10
Dagger	10	Level 1	2	2	1	1	2	16	8
*Halberd	350	Level 4	6	5	5	13	55	72	12
Knife	8	Level 1	2	2	1.5	1	2	16	8
*Pike	50	Level 2	4	3	4	4	11	20	5
Scimitar	120	Level 3	4-1D4	3	3	5	25	40	10
Short Sword	60	Level 2	3	3	2	4	18	30	10
Spear	22	Level 2	3	3	4	2	5	21	7
Trident	45	Level 2	4	4	4	4	10	24	6
*Two Hand Sword	210	Level 3	5	5	4	8	40	50	10

WEAPONS & ARMOR

NON-EDGED MELEE WEAPONS

Type	Coin	Minimum Strength	Dmg. Yield	Max. Tech.	Bulk Value	Weight (lbs)	Repair Cost	Destroyed Rating	R.E.
Club	2	Level 1	2	1	2	2	N/A	12	3
Double-Flail	150	Level 3	5	5	4	7	25	60	12
Flail	75	Level 3	4	3	2	4	21	40	10
Lance	80	Level 3	2	2	6	12	12	30	5
Mace	70	Level 2	4	2	2	3	17	40	10
*Quarter Staff	5	Level 2	2	3	4	2	N/A	15	3
Spiked Double-Flail	175	Level 4	6	5	5	8	28	72	12
Spiked Flail	130	Level 3	5	4	3	5	38	50	10
Spiked Mace	100	Level 2	5	3	3	4	20	50	10
*Spiked War Hammer	275	Level 5	6	5	5	12	45	120	20
*War Hammer	200	Level 4	5	4	4	10	34	100	20
Whip	6	Level 1	2	3	1	2	2	6	3

RANGED WEAPONS

ARCHERY WEAPONS

Type	Coin	Minimum Strength	Dmg. Yield	Max. Tech.	Bulk Value	Weight (lbs)	Repair Cost	Destroyed Rating	R.E.
* Normal Bow	150	Level 3	7	4	3	3	N/A	15	N/A
* Heavy Bow	250	Level 4	8	5	3	5	N/A	20	N/A
1 Hand Crossbow	75	Level 1	5	1	1	2	13	15	3
Normal Crossbow	200	Level 2	7	2	2	8	25	28	4
* Heavy Crossbow	250	Level 4	8	2	3	12	30	32	4

THROWING WEAPONS

Type	Coin	Minimum Strength	Dmg. Yield	Max. Tech.	Bulk Value	Weight (lbs)	Repair Cost	Destroyed Rating	R.E.
Arc-Dagger	85	Level 3	5	4	3	3	15	40	8
Bola	2	Level 1	1	3	1	1	N/A	6	N/A
Shuriken	4	Level 1	2 (+1)	2	.5	4 oz	1	10	5
Spear	22	Level 2	3 (+1)	3	4	2	5	15	5
Spiked Ball	3	Level 1	2 (+1)	1	.5	4 oz	N/A	16	8
Throwing Dagger	11	Level 1	2 (+1)	2	1	1	2	12	6
Throwing Hatchet	35	Level 2	3	2	2	3	12	60	20
Throwing Knife	9	Level 1	2 (+1)	2	1	1.5	2	12	6
Trident	45	Level 2	4 (+1)	4	4	4	10	20	5

GREEN-STEEL WEAPONS

Type	Coin	Minimum Strength	Dmg. Yield	Max. Tech.	Bulk Value	Weight (lbs)	Repair Cost	Destroyed Rating	R.E.
GREEN-STEEL WEAPONS									
Edged Melee									
* Battle Axe	700	Level 3	6	5	4	5	100	96	16
Broadsword	400	Level 2	5	4	3	3	70	60	12
Dagger	40	Level 1	3	2	1	8 oz	10	21	7
*Halberd	1300	Level 3	7	5	5	7	160	98	14
Knife	32	Level 1	3	2	1	8 oz	9	21	7
*Pike	200	Level 2	5	3	4	2	35	30	6
Scimitar	480	Level 2	5 -1D4	3	3	3	85	60	12
Shortsword	240	Level 1	4	3	2	2	52	44	11
Spear	100	Level 2	4	3	4	1.5	20	32	8
Trident	180	Level 2	5	4	4	2	32	40	8
*Two-Hand Sword	840	Level 3	6	5	4	5	125	78	13
Non-Edged Melee									
Double-Flail	600	Level 2	6	5	4	4	90	90	15
Flail	300	Level 3	5	3	1	2	60	60	12
Lance	1200	Level 2	7	2	6	6	150	49	7
Mace	280	Level 1	5	2	2	2	50	60	12
Spiked Double-Flail	700	Level 2	7	5	5	4	90	105	15
Spiked Flail	520	Level 3	6	4	3	3	80	78	13
Spiked Mace	400	Level 1	6	3	4	2	60	78	13
*Spiked War Hammer	1100	Level 3	7	5	5	6	140	182	26
*War Hammer	800	Level 3	6	4	4	5	115	150	25
Throwing									
Arc-Dagger	340	Level 3	6	4	2	1.5	50	60	10
Shuriken	16	Level 1	3 (+1)	2	.5	2 oz	4	15	5
Spear	88	Level 2	5 (+1)	3	4	1	15	30	6
Throwing Dagger	44	Level 1	3 (+1)	2	1	12 oz	11	21	7
Throwing Hatchet	70	Level 1	4	2	2	1.5	36	90	30
Throwing Knife	36	Level 1	3 (+1)	2	1	8 oz	10	21	7
Trident	180	Level 2	5 (+1)	4	4	4	10	24	4

WEAPONS & ARMOR

Type	Coin	Protect Rating	Bulk Value	Weight (lbs)	Repair Cost	Destroyed Rating	R.P.	Agility Penalty	Move Penalty
Cloth									
Shirt (no sleeves)	10	1	1	1.5	N/A	10	N/A	0	0
Shirt (sleeves)	15	1	1	2	N/A	10	N/A	0	0
Breeches	15	1	1	2	N/A	10	N/A	0	0
Leather									
Arm-guards	30	3	2	6	9	24	8	0	0
Chest/Back-guard	60	3	2	10	18	24	8	0	0
(with Pelvis Skirt)	+20		3	13					
Breeches	40	3	2	8	12	24	8	0	-10'/Turn
Padded Leather									
Arm-guards	50	4	2	12	9	40	10	-1 Level	0
Chest/Back-guard	90	4	3	16	18	40	10	-1 Level	0
(with Pelvis Skirt)	35		4	19					
Breeches	60	4	2	14	12	40	10	-1 Level	-20'/Turn
Chain Mail									
Shirt (no sleeves)	240	6	2	14	44	84	14	-1 Level	0
Shirt (sleeves)	360	6	3	20	44	84	14	-1 Level	0
Long Shirt (no sleeves)	360	6	3	25	44	84	14	-2 Levels	0
Long Shirt (sleeves)	460	6	4	31	44	84	14	-2 Levels	0
Breeches	160	6	2	18	22	84	14	-1 Level	-15'/Turn
Plate & Chain									
Chest Plate & Sleeves	700	8	4	30	80	152	19	-2 Levels	0
(with Pelvis Skirt)	+100		5	40					
Breeches	350	8	3	26	42	152	19	-2 Levels	-15'/Turn
Gr.-St. Plate & Chain									
Chest Plate & Sleeves	2800	10	3	15	240	220	22	-1 Level	0
(with Pelvis Skirt)	+400		4	20					
Breeches	1400	10	2	13	42	220	22	-1 Level	-10'/Turn
Steel Plate									
Arm-guards	880	10	3	16	80	220	22	-3 Level	0
Gauntlets (each)	200	10	1	3	45	220	22	-1 Level	0
Spiked Gauntlets (each)	250	10	1	4	50	220	22	-1 Levels	0
Chest/Back Plate	200	10	3	20	17	220	22	-1 Level	0
Pelvis-guard	160	10	3	18	22	220	22	-2 Levels	-15'/Turn
Leggings	920	10	3	22	87	220	22	-3 Levels	-40'/Turn
Gr.-Steel Plate									
Arm-guards	3400	12	3	9	250	312	26	-2 Levels	0
Gauntlets (each)	800	12	1	1.5	140	312	26	0	0
Spiked Gauntlets (each)	1000	12	1	2	160	312	26	0	0
Chest/Back Plate	800	12	3	10	55	312	26	0	0
Pelvis-guard	640	12	2	9	70	312	26	-1 Level	-10'/Turn
Leggings	3800	12	3	11	280	312	26	-2 Levels	-25'/Turn
Leather Hood	12	2	1	2	4	14	7	0	0
Chain Mail Hood	50	3	1	3	14	21	7	0	0
Steel Helm	70	5	1	7	12	60	12	0	0
Gr.-St. Helm	280	7	1	3.5	35	112	16	0	0

SHIELDS

SHIELDS								
Type	Coin	Minimum Strength	Maximum Technique	Bulk Value	Weight (lbs)	Repair Cost	Destroyed Rating	Agility Penalty
Buckler	20	Level 1	1	2	4	2 sc/10	160	0
Gr.- Steel Buckler	80	Level 1	1	2	2	8 sc/40	240	0
Half-Shield	75	Level 3	2	3	8	8 sc/15	300	0
Gr.- Steel Half-Shield	300	Level 2	2	3	4	30 sc/20	450	0
Full-Shield	150	Level 4	3	5	12	15 sc/20	360	-10'/Turn
Gr.- Steel Full-Shield	600	Level 3	3	5	6	70 sc/90	540	-5'/Turn

After a shield receives an amount of damage equal to or greater than 1/2 of its Destroyed Rating, 1/2 of the damage rendered to it (round down) will be received by the being wielding the shield.

EQUIPMENT

There are a multitude of different items and equipment that your character must have in order to embark on his many dangerous quests, as well as simply living from day to day. This Section lists and describes many of the more common items and pieces of equipment that a character may have need of. At the end of this Section there is a table with additional information on all of the equipment that your character may purchase.

Adventurer's Kit

This is a pre-packaged kit of items that most adventurers would find useful and/or needful. Instead of having to purchase and record each item separately you can simply purchase an adventurer's kit for your character and condense much of the purchasing and Equipment Sheet recording into one simple step. It is most often cheaper to purchase an adventurer's kit than to individually purchase all of the items that an adventurer's kit contains.

The common adventurer's kit consists of one waterskin, two torches, one flint & steel, three days rations, one poison poultice, one healing herb, one shovel, one blanket, a whetstone, and a small sac. All of the items of the adventurer's kit come neatly packed into the small sac, which is part of the kit.

The GM can modify and customize the contents and price of any adventurer's kit as he sees fit.

Anvil

These are large blocks of steel used by blacksmiths and farriers as a platform for working and shaping heated metals.

Arrow

Arrows are long shafts of wood with feathers attached to one end to help the them fly straight and a steel point on the other end designed to be shot from a bow. Some arrows are designed with heavy tips for penetrating armor and others have wide broadheads made to inflict maximum damage on the target.

Axe

A heavy piece of sharpened steel attached to a short wooden handle. Some axes have a single blade and others are doubled-bladed. Though there are some axes designed for use as weapons, the common axe is mainly used for chopping wood.

Backpack

This is a large leather container with a flap on it that can be fastened shut. It has straps on it for the arms to be placed through so that it can be worn on one's back. Backpacks can hold a significant amount of equipment and are particularly useful because they can be strapped to the back where they don't get in the way. Backpacks are most commonly used during long travels on foot.

Most backpacks can hold up to a Total Bulk Value of 24 and no single item within can have a Bulk Value higher than 2. If the Bulk Value of all of the contents in a backpack add up to 12 or less then the backpack and all of its contents are considered to have a single Bulk Value of 2 (an empty backpack is also considered to have a Bulk Value of 2). If the Bulk Value of all of the contents in the backpack adds up to 13 or more then the backpack and all of its contents are considered to have a single Bulk Value of 4.

Blacksmith's Tools

This is a kit that contains many of the basic tools that a blacksmith needs to operate a forge. Included is a pair of long metal tongs, a bellows, a metal punch, a small shaping hammer, and a file.

Blanket

Commonly made of wool or cotton, blankets are commonly four feet wide by six feet in length. No traveler's equipment list is complete without a warm blanket to curl up into on those cold nights out on the trail.

Bleyk

The Defenders of the Light and the King's Guard commonly use these large animals for battle steeds. Some people also use them as work animals for plowing and pulling carts and wagons. Most bleyk are very calm and easily trained. For a more complete description of bleyk see the "CREATURE LORE" Section.

Boots

Most boots are made of strong leather and cover the entire foot up past the ankles. Strong rope or leather laces are used to tightly secure them to the feet. Though most Loremek prefer not to wear anything on their feet there are boots that are designed especially for them.

Bottles

These small glass containers are most commonly used to store liquids. Alchemists often use them to store their products and ingredients. Bottles are most always shaped with a flat bottom so that they can be stood upright. They have small openings on their tops to accommodate a cork for sealing the contents and keeping them airtight.

There are two different basic sizes of bottles; the half-bottle and the standard-bottle. In regards to volume both types of bottles are always made to standard specifications to ensure consistency in measurement. Half-bottles are smaller than standard-bottles and can hold 6,000 drops. Standard-bottles can hold 12,000 drops.

Bowstring

These slender strings are made of braided hemp or cotton fibers. They have loops at either end designed to fit onto the ends of a bow. The string is used to draw the limbs of the bow back and send the arrow into flight. Regardless of the quality of the bowstring they will eventually wear out and break. No experienced archer will be caught without at least one or two spare bowstrings.

Breeches

Made to cover the pelvis and both legs breeches are easy to slip on and off, usually having a single button in the front to fasten them together and a draw-string in the waste to tighten them to the desired fit. Most breeches are made of strong cloth, wool, or cotton.

Bridle

This is a leather harness designed to fit onto the head of a horse or bleyk. It has a metal bit attached to it that is inserted into the horse or bleyk's mouth with two long leather reins attached to it by which the rider can control the animal's movement and direction.

Canisters

These small containers are most commonly made of wood but some are made of glass or stone. Canisters are round and have a flat bottom and top. The lid is slightly larger than the base so that it will tightly slip down over the base to seal the ingredients inside. Though not normally airtight, well-crafted canisters do a good job of keeping the ingredients within fresh. They are usually used to store small dry objects. Alchemists often use them to store powdered or granulated products and ingredients.

There are three different basic sizes of canisters. They are the coin-canister, the flat-canister, and the standard canister. In regards to volume all three types of canisters are always made to standard specifications to ensure consistency in measurement.

Coin-canisters are the smallest of the three types of canisters. They get their name from the fact that their size, in diameter, is almost the same as that of a coin. Coin-canisters can hold as much as 60 pinches. The flat-canister is the next size up from the coin-canister. It can hold as much as 600 pinches. The largest of the three types of canisters is the standard-canister, which can hold as much as 2,400pinches.

Canoe

A small wooden vessel capable of seating up to four ruling-races, canoes are commonly used to float down small rivers and streams.

Canoe Paddle

A wide and flat paddle on a three to four foot handle used for steering and maneuvering canoes.

Cart

A small wooden box with wheels is the easiest way to describe this item. Some have handles on them so that they can be pulled by hand and other are designed to be hitched up to a horse. Carts are used to transport supplies for short distances (most commonly to and from areas within a city or town).

Carving Tools

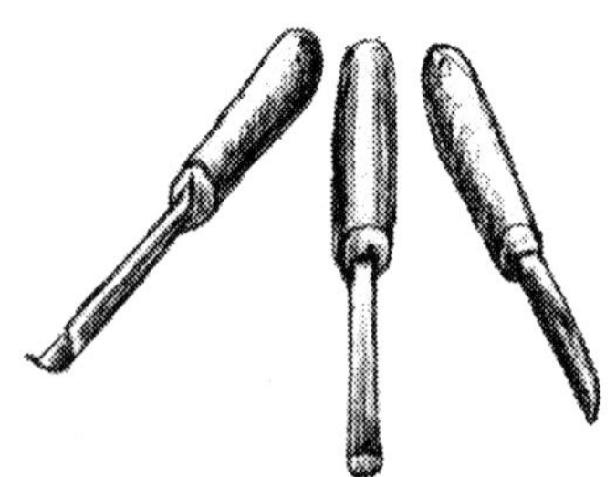

Carving tools generally consist of three to four different sizes of knives designed for carving wood. One or more wood chisels and a small wooden mallet are also common carving tools.

Chain

Heavy steel rings interconnected to form a long and flexible rope of steel. Chains come in varying sizes and lengths.

Cloak

A long piece of cloth, wool, or silk, tailored to drape over the shoulders and cover the body, usually hanging down to one's ankles. Most cloaks have strings or buttons in the front to tie them on. Some cloaks have hoods on them but most do not.

Cloth and wool cloaks are worn more by commoners while silk cloaks are worn more commonly by the wealthy.

Coat

Most coats are made of cotton, wool, or silk and have thick padded linings for warmth. Though mainly a wardrobe accessory for the Shadow season there are some coats that do not have the padded linings and are designed more for a sophisticated appearance than for warmth.

Compass

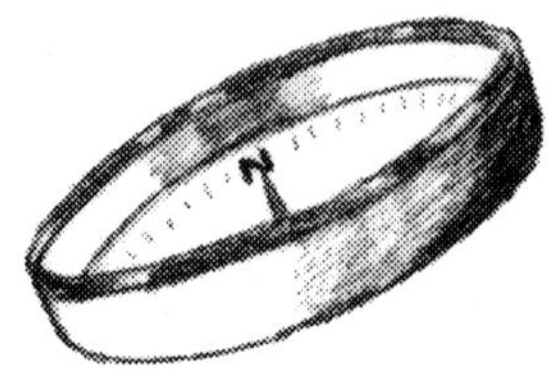

This device is essentially a bubble of glass filled with water that has a magnetized needle on a spindle within it. The glass is mounted in a wooden or metal case for protection as well as to make it easier to hold on to and to hold level. The magnetized needle within the compass is attracted to the northern-most region of Oryathar (land of fire) and will always point in that direction thus allowing one to determine their direction in any given area of Oryathar.

Crossbow Bolt

The crossbow bolt is essentially the same as a normal arrow but it is designed to be shot from a crossbow instead of a regular bow. Crossbow bolts are significantly shorter than normal arrows and their shafts are slightly larger in diameter.

Dress

Designed as a one-piece covering for the female gender dresses come in varying lengths. Some hang down to the ankles and others barely clear the thighs. Dresses are made of a wide variety of materials from plain coarse canvas to luxurious silk.

Farrier's Tools

This is an assortment of tools that are commonly used by farriers to shape horseshoes and to shoe horses. Farrier's tools often include a rasp, small hammer, cutters, and pliers.

Flasks

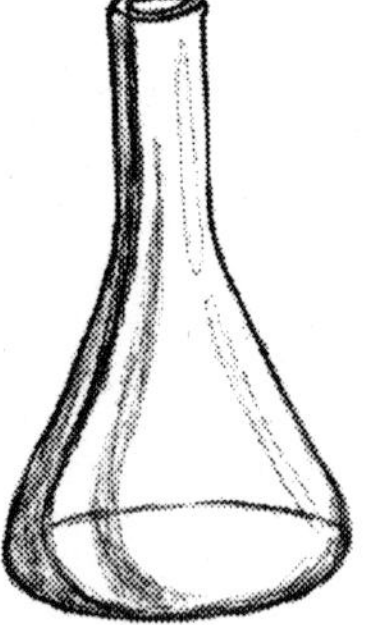

These glass containers are used to store liquids. Most flasks have wide bases to help keep them from tipping over and taper significantly toward their top. Alchemists often use them to store their products and ingredients. Some flasks are made with green-steel melted into the glass. This enables the flasks to be heated to extreme temperatures without cracking or shattering. This makes them an ideal container for heating up alchemy ingredients. The mouths of flasks are designed with a groove that aids in the pouring of ingredients. Wooden corks are used to seal the ingredients inside. Nearly airtight, well-crafted flasks do an excellent job of keeping the ingredients within fresh.

There are three different basic sizes of flasks. They are the half-flask, standard-flask, and the head-flask. In regards to volume all three types of flasks are always made to standard specifications to ensure consistency in measurement.

Half-flasks are the smallest of the three types of flasks. Half-flasks can hold as much as 6,000 drops. The standard-flask is the next size up from the half-flask. It can hold as much as 12,000 drops. The largest of the three types of flasks is the head-flask. It gets its name because the diameter of its base is the same size of the diameter of an average adult Brightling's head. Head-flasks can hold as much as 48,000 drops.

Flint & Steel

This item is fairly self-explanatory; one small piece of flat steel and a piece of flint usually sold in a small wooden box. The flint is struck against the piece of steel to produce sparks that can be used to ignite a torch or start a campfire.

Grappling Hook

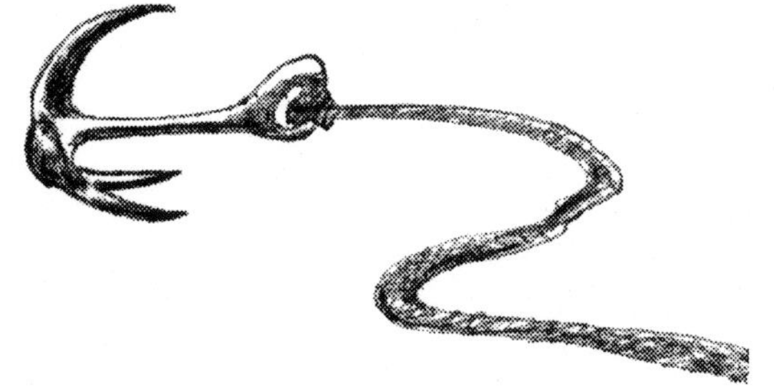

This is a heavy piece of steel with three hooks. It is fixed to a length of rope and can be thrown over a wall or similar structure where it will catch and anchor itself thus allowing someone to climb the rope.

Hammer

This is a small barrel shaped piece of steel attached to a short wooden handle, most commonly used for driving nails or shaping metal.

Hatchet

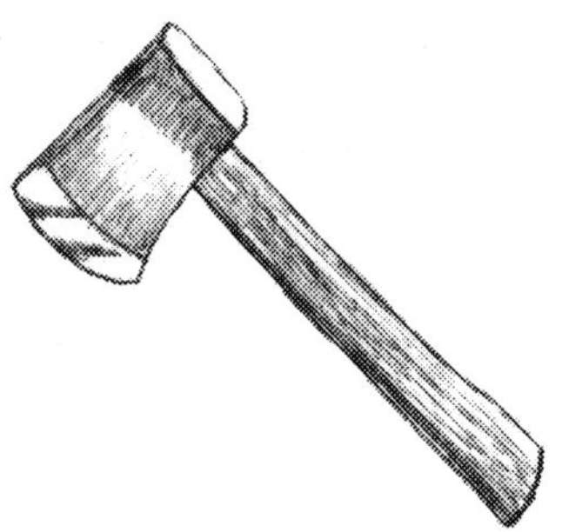

This tool is very similar to a hammer except the metal head is flattened on one side to form a blade. Hatchets are most commonly used for chopping small pieces of wood.

Healing Herb

Healing herb is the common name given to the root of the blue-briar plant. Eating this root speeds up the body's natural healing process.

Beings who eat one of these healing herbs may add 1D10 points to the result of their character's next Recovery Test, if it is made within two hours of eating the healing herb. Eating more than one healing herb at a time does not increase the bonuses to the being's next Recovery Test but may make them ill.

Horse Feed

A mixture of corn and grains ground up to form a nutritious feed for horses.

Ink

Commonly sold by the half-bottle this is a black liquid used to load writing quills. Ink is extremely hard to remove from clothes and similar items and is usually permanent.

Lantern

Lanterns are essentially a hollow metal container that has

oil placed into it with a cloth wick protruding from it. The oil container is encased in a metal frame with glass sides. Once lit the wick burns fairly bright allowing the lantern to efficiently light up an area as large as sixty feet in diameter.

Life Water

This is a thick liquid that is made of water and several different types of vegetables and herbs. Though not particularly tasty it is a very good source of rations for long journey. Life water serves as both water and a meal all in one.

Lock Picking Kit

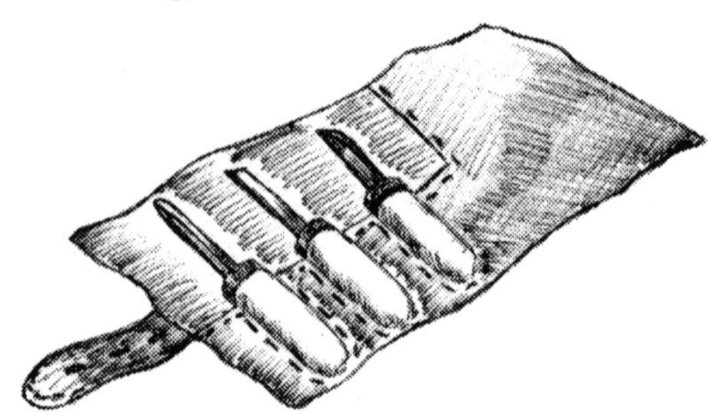

This kit consists of several small metal pins and picks designed for picking locks. The picks usually come in a handy leather pouch that can be rolled up and neatly tucked away.

Map

Maps of the various regions of Oryathar can be purchased in the larger cities and town. Most maps are very crude in nature and are only vaguely accurate, however there are some maps that are much more accurate than others. Purchasing maps is a buyer beware venture.

Mirror

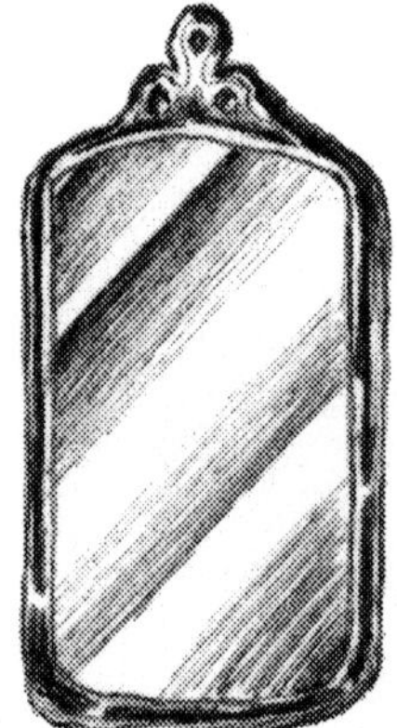

This is a piece of very smooth reflective metal or glass usu-

ally mounted in a wooden or metal frame with a handle.

Nails

Thin pointed pieces of steel with flat heads on one end to make an easy surface for striking and driving them into wood or other surfaces. There are different types of nails designed for different purposes. Some nails are made for use in holding shoes to horses feet and other nails are used for woodworking projects such as wagons, doors, cabinets, etc. Most nails are sold by the pound.

Oil

This is a thick flammable liquid that is used as fuel in lanterns and is also used to soak the cloth of torches in to make them burn longer. Oil is normally sold in bottles or flasks, but can be purchased by the barrel.

Pain Block Herb

This is a small piece of dried out root from several different types of select plants. It has the ability to greatly reduce pain from most any type of injury or other source of intense pain.

Parchment

Made from animal skins or trees parchment is sold in small rectangular sheets that can be easily written on with a writing quill. Most sheets of parchment are very smooth and hold ink well but some of the more poorly designed pieces of parchment are rough and fragile and tend to fade easily.

Poison Poultice

This is a blend of special herbs crushed and worked into a paste and rolled up in a piece of thin cloth. The poultice can be applied and held to areas of the body where poison has been injected and it will draw out much of the poison and greatly reduce the effects and duration of the poison.

There are some poisons that poison poultices are not effective against but they are effective against a great many of the more common poisons that one may encounter in Oryathar.

Pouch

Most pouches are made of leather with a draw-string to pull them shut, others have flaps for closing that buckle or tie shut. Pouches are most commonly used for carrying coin in but can be used for just about anything.

Most pouches are very small and can not hold anything that has a Bulk Value higher than .5. The Total Bulk Value of all the contents of a pouch may not exceed 2.5. Regardless of whether or not a pouch is empty or full, it and all of its contents are considered to have a Bulk Value of .5.

Quiver

This is a round tube usually made of rawhide and often covered with animal fur for decoration, and to reduce noise from the quiver rubbing against one's body. Quivers are designed to hold arrows or crossbow bolts. Most quivers will hold up to ten arrows or crossbow bolts before becoming too tightly packed.

Rations

Rations, commonly referred to as trail rations, are simply dried out packages of various foods designed to keep good for days or weeks and often used as a food source for adventurers or soldiers that are out on the trail and don't have access to any other food source. A normal ration pack often contains a small portion of dried beef, cheese, bread, and a piece of dried fruit (usually apple or pear).

Rope

Rope is nothing more than long pieces of braided hemp. Rope is sold in varying thicknesses depending upon its intended use. It is also normally sold by the foot. A good solid length of rope has numerous uses from tying up captured foes to scaling down a cliff face. Every serious adventurer's equipment should include rope.

Sac

Sacs are normally made of tough cloth and are handy for packing or dragging just about anything. Sacs come in two main sizes, small and large. Small sacs can hold up to a Total Bulk Value of 12 with no single item within having a Bulk Value higher than 2. Large sacs can hold up to a Total Bulk Value of 24 with no single item within having a Bulk Value higher than 3.

If the Bulk Value of all of the contents in a small sac add up to 6 or less (12 or less for a large sac) then the sac and all of its contents is considered to have a single Bulk Value of 1 (2 for large sacs). An empty small sac is also considered to have a Bulk Value of 1 (and an empty large sac still has a Bulk Value of 2). If the Bulk Value of all of the contents in a small sac adds up to 7 or more (12 or more for a large sac), meaning it is more than half full, then the small sac and all of its contents is considered to have a single Bulk Value of 2 (4 for a large sac).

Saddle

This piece of equipment is generally made up of wood and leather and is designed to be fitted onto the back of a horse or bleyk to support a rider. Many saddles have metal rings and clips on them designed for attaching weapons or equipment.

Saddles come in many different sizes and designs.

Saddle Bags

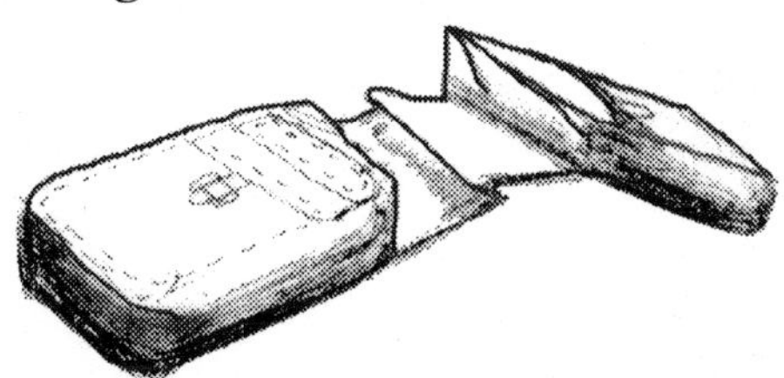

Saddles bags normally come as a joined pair. They consist of two leather pouches with a length of flat leather connecting them that can be thrown across a horse or bleyk's back so that the pouches hang down on either side of the animal. Each pouch has a flap for closing them that can be buckled and/or tied shut.

Saddle bags are extremely useful for long travels. They are often used to store waterskins, rations, torches, and a multitude of miscellaneous items.

Each saddle bag (each pouch) can hold up to a Total Bulk Value of 12 with no single item within having a Bulk Value higher than 2. If the Bulk Value of all of the contents in a saddle bag add up to 6 or less then the saddle bag and all of its contents is considered to have a single Bulk Value of 1.

Sandals

Sandals are a type of shoe that have a flat wooden or thick rawhide bottom with flat leather straps that attach to it on one side and wrap across the top of the foot and buckle on

the other side. Sandals are a lightweight and more comfortable alternative to boots, but are not very suitable for climbing or long travel.

Scroll Case

This is a short hollow tube that is made of either hollowed out wood or the bones of animals. It is made to store rolled up scrolls, maps, or other important parchments. Most scroll cases have a cap on one end that can be used to seal the contents, keeping them free of dirt and moisture.

Sheath

Sheaths are hollow wooden or metal sleeves that are shaped to accommodate the blade of a dagger, knife or sword. Most sheaths have loops attached to them so that they can be attached to a belt or tied to one's waist. Sheaths help protect their wearer from the sharp tips and edges of their weapons, allowing them to be carried in safety.

Shirt

A piece of clothing that can be made of a wide variety of materials ranging from plain cloth to fine silk that is designed to be worn over the torso. Some shirts have sleeves long enough to cover the entire arm and others have no sleeves at all. Shirts have leather strings laced up the front of them so that they can be snugly secured to the wearer.

Shovel

A variable length wooden handle with a wide metal head attached to one end. Some shovels have square ends used for shoveling across flat surfaces such as stable floors and others have a spade shape for digging. Some shovels have very short handles and a small blade designed for the traveler. These compact shovels can easily fit into a backpack or sac.

Skillet

A round iron pan with a handle on it used for frying or baking food. Most skillets are very heavy and durable and come in a wide range of sizes. A small skillet is very useful to have on the trail to warm up rations or fry up a fresh kill.

Soap

Most soaps are made from animal fats and plant fibers and are condensed into small blocks for easy handling and portability. Some types of soap are stronger than others but most all are good enough for a descent cleaning and freshening up.

Steel Spikes

Basically nails on a larger scale steel spikes are just what they sound like, spikes made of steel. Most steel spikes are around one inch in diameter and about three to six inches in length. They have a wide range of uses from construction to use as anchors for climbing.

Sun Crystal

The sun crystal is a colorful crystal found in mountainous regions all across Oryathar. Sun crystals change colors as Oryathar's golden sun increases and decreases in intensity. Sun crystals are black when the sun is at its lowest energy level (twentieth and a half hour) and bright gold when the sun is at its highest energy level (seventh and a half hour). This unique ability of the sun crystal has proven to be a very accurate method of keeping track of time and is widely used among the ruling-races for just this purpose.

Sun crystals are commonly shaped into round flat disks and attached to a leather cord so they can be worn around the neck as an amulet.

Sunsfane

Sunsfane is a granular blue powder that is created by the means of Stage Two alchemy.

Sprinkling this powder over the burning coals of a forge fire will turn the coals and the fire a mystical blue color. This blue fire is necessary in order to forge green-steel.

Telescope

This item is essentially a length of metal tubing with a glass lens at either end. One end of the telescope is slightly larger in diameter than the other. Some telescopes are larger than others, but most range from six inches to one foot in length.

Looking through the telescope gives the user a significantly magnified view. Objects visualized through a telescope

are magnified to three times their normal size (essentially increasing the viewer's range of vision by three times).

Tent

Most tents are made of large sheets of tough canvas and have a few wooden rods and lengths of thin rope that help support the tent and allow it to stand.

Tents come in various sizes though the most common type of tents are designed to accommodate only one person. Tents are designed to be easily and quickly folded up and transported and can be unfolded and put up fairly quickly (usually no more than ten minutes is required to throw up a tent). Some tents do a good job of keeping out rain and others allow the water to soak right through. A good inspection of the tent is recommended before making a purchase.

Torch

The most common type of torch consists of a short length of wood with an oil-soaked rag wrapped and tied around one end. They are fairly easy to light and will burn continuously for up to one hour.

The average torch will sufficiently light up an area up to thirty feet in diameter, and though it will actually give off light for farther than this the amount of illumination and details of what can be seen is very minimal beyond this distance.

Traveler's Kit

This is a pre-packaged kit of items that most travelers would find useful. Instead of having to purchase and record each item separately you can simply purchase a traveler's kit for your character and condense much of the purchasing and Equipment Sheet recording into one simple step. It is most often cheaper to purchase a traveler's kit than to individually purchase all of the items that a traveler's kit contains.

The common traveler's kit consists of one shirt, one pair of breeches, one belt, one pair of boots, one set of underclothes, a blanket, one block of soap, one skillet, one compass, one

sun crystal, and a backpack. All of the items of the traveler's kit come neatly packed into the backpack, which is part of the kit.

The GM can modify and customize the contents and price of any traveler's kit as he sees fit.

Underclothes

Underclothes, as the name implies, are clothes designed to be worn under one's normal clothing. Standard underclothes consist of a thin shirt and a pair of shorts. Both are usually made of cotton, regular cloth, or even silk.

Vials

These small glass containers are most commonly used to store liquids. Alchemists often use them to store their products and ingredients as well as for measuring out proper amounts of ingredients. Vials are thin round tubes with a rounded bottom, so they are not able to be stood upright. The single opening on their tops can accommodate a quark for sealing the contents and keeping them airtight.

There are two different basic sizes of vials; the thumb-vial and the standard-vial. In regards to volume both types of vials are always made to standard specifications to ensure consistency in measurement.

Thumb-vials are smaller than standard-vials, one fourth the size to be exact, and can hold 60 drops. Standard-vials can hold 240 drops.

Wagon

Basically the same as a cart but much larger wagons are used to transport large quantities of goods. They are most often pulled by two or more horses or bleyks. Some wagons are very luxurious in design and are used by the wealthy, but most are very plain and practical.

Waterskin

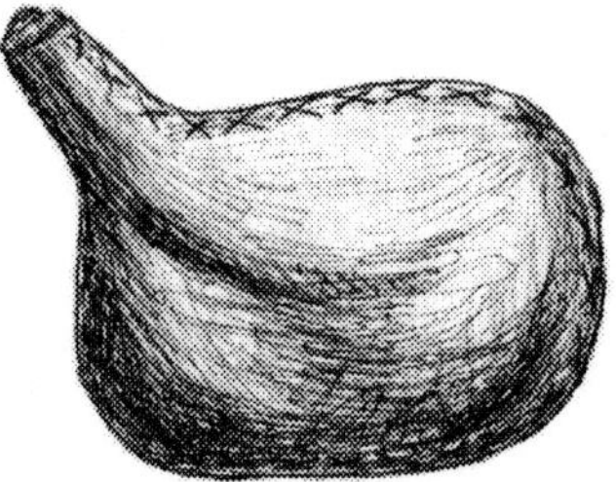

Waterskins are waterproof containers made from animal bladders or from leather. They are designed for storing small amounts of water. Most waterskins are basically oval-shaped with a tapered spout-like end, and can hold four stan-

dard-bottles of water (a four-day supply for the average ruling-race under normal conditions).

Whetstone

The whetstone is a piece of hard stone, usually small and in the shape of a block, with a fairly smooth surface. They are used for sharpening knives, daggers, and any other type of blade. Whetstones of varying sizes and coarseness are available, depending upon the size of the blade to be sharpened.

Writing Quill

This is a large quill (feather) that has had its tip cut at an angle to produce a point for writing. The shaft of the feather is hollow and when dipped into ink it will soak a small portion of it up into this shaft. You can then write with the quill, re-dipping it into ink as necessary.

EQUIPMENT & MERCHANDISE TABLE

The following table has several categories of information pertaining to the various items and pieces of equipment listed in it. In order to properly utilize the information on this table each of these categories and their significance is explained in detail.

Though this table doesn't contain all of the possible items of interest or need that a character may acquire through the course of gameplay, it does contain most of the more commonly used and needful items. Feel free to make up any items or pieces of equipment that you need. You can use the "EQUIPMENT & MERCHANDISE" table as a guide for determining the cost, Bulk Value, and weight of the equipment or merchandise that you may add.

Bulk Value

This is a rating of how bulky the particular item or piece of equipment is. Characters can only have a certain Total Bulk Value, so it is important to know the Bulk Value of any piece of equipment or item that a character is carrying so that the player can keep up with his or her character's Total Bulk Value. The Equipment Sheet (provided at the end of this rulebook) has designated areas for recording the Bulk Value of all of your character's equipment and items.

Coin

This is the average amount of silver coin that the particular item or piece of equipment costs. Sometimes characters may be able to find an item for sale for less than this listed price or may be able to bargain or haggle the price down (GM's discretion).

Weight (lbs)

This is how much that the particular item weighs. Most all weight is given in pounds, but a few select items are listed in ounces.

Since characters can only carry a certain amount of weight before considered to be encumbered and begin receiving penalties, it is important to keep track of the weight of all items that your character is carrying. The Equipment Sheet has designated areas for recording the weight of all of your character's equipment and items.

EQUIPMENT & MERCHANDISE

Type	Coin	Bulk Value	Weight (lbs.)	Type	Coin	Bulk Value	Weight (lbs.)
Adventurer's Kit	55	4	12 lb, 5 oz	Lantern	9	1	2
Anvil	40	3	10-50	Life Water	2	1	5
Arrow	2	1	4 oz	Lock Picking Kit	6	.5	9 oz
Axe	10	3	3	Map	3	.5	N/A
Backpack	30	2	1	Mirror	3	1	1
Belt	2	.5	8 oz	Nails (per pound)	1	.5	1
Black Smith's Tools	85	2	20	Oil (standard-flask)	2	1	1 lb, 12 oz
Blanket	4	2	2	Pain Block Herb	3	.5	3 oz
Bleyk	800	9	1500-2000	Parchment (per sheet)	3 cc	N/A	N/A
Boots	11	2	2	Poison Poultice	6	.5	1
Bottle				Pouch			
(Half-bottle)	1	.5	8 oz	(Cloth)	1	.5	N/A
(Standard-bottle)	2	1	1	(Leather)	3	.5	5 oz
Bow String	7 cc	N/A	N/A	(Silk)	5	.5	N/A
Breeches	6	1	1	Pulley	9	1	3
Bridle	25	1	2	Quiver	4	2	1
Candle	5 cc	.5	4 oz	Rations (per day)	1	1	9 oz
Canister				Rope (per foot)	3 cc	.5	8 oz
(Coin-canister)	1	.5	3 oz	Sac			
(Flat-canister)	2	.5	8 oz	(Large)	1	2	6 oz
(Standard-canister)	3	1	2	(Small)	5 cc	1	N/A
Canoe	125	4-8	20-35	Saddle	200	5	30
Canoe Paddle	7	3	3	Saddle Bags	35	2	5
Cart	280	5-9	75-200	Sandals	3	1	8 oz
Carving Tools				Scroll Case	2	1	6 oz
(Stone)	7	2	2	Sheath			
(Wood)	4	1	10 oz	(Broadsword/Scimitar)	7	2	2
Chain	1/ft	.5/ft	1	(Dagger/Knife)	2	1	8 oz
Cloak				(Shortsword)	5	1	1
(Cloth)	6	2	1 lb, 8 oz	(Two-handed Sword)	9	3	3
(Silk)	26	1	8 oz	Shirt	5	.5	8 oz
(Wool)	16	2	4	Shovel	7	3	2
Coat	32	3	3	Skillet	3	1	2
Compass	11	.5	8 oz	Soap	2	.5	5 oz
Crossbow Bolt	15 cc	1	3 oz	Steel Spikes	8 cc	.5	1
Dress	7	2	1	Sun Crystal	20	.5	6 oz
Farrier's Tools	75	2	10	Sunsfane	80	.5	8 oz
Flask				Telescope	50	1.5	2
(Half-flask)	1	.5	8 oz	Tent	15	2	2
(Head-flask)	5	2	3	Torch	5 cc	1	1
(Standard-flask)	2	1	1	Traveler's Kit	55	2	9 lb, 3 oz
Flint & Steel	15 cc	.5	7 oz	Underclothes	2	.5	N/A
Grappling Hook	13	2	3	Vial			
Hammer	6	2	2	(Standard-vial)	1	.5	8 oz
Hatchet	6	2	2	(Thumb-vial)	8 cc	.5	3 oz
Healing Herb	10	.5	3 oz	Wagon	1500	10-15	800-1500
Horse	600	6	800	Waterskin	1	1	4 (full)
Horse Feed	1/day	2	4	Whetstone	2	.5	4 oz
Ink (half-bottle)	1	.5	1	Writing Quill	5 cc	.5	N/A

SURVIVING ORYATHAR

The lands of Oryathar are wrought with danger and opposition. Knowing how to handle yourself in battle is only a portion of the skills and knowledge that you will need to survive. In this Section a majority of the skills, abilities, and information that you will need in order for your character to make it in Oryathar will be discussed.

Pay close attention, because you never know when one of these basic skills, tasks, or bits of knowledge will mean the difference between life and death. May the Light guide you to your destiny.

COIN

In order to buy anything your character will have to have some coin. Small oval coins are the common type of currency used all across Oryathar. The most common material that coins are made of is silver. Though some coins are made of gold and others are made of copper. Gold is the most expensive of these three types of materials, silver is second-most expensive and copper is the least expensive. It takes ten copper coins to equal the value of one silver coin, and it takes twenty silver coins to equal the value of one gold coin. Most merchants prefer to deal with silver coins and rarely carry more than a handful of gold coins at any one time.

All of the current coins in the Ellabrian Realms are molded in Helmsrink, the king's city, and bear the likeness of King Lorsprit on one side and a cloud-capped mountain on the other side. These coins have been in circulation since 580 AA, when King Lorsprit assumed the throne. All coins previous to this date, as far back as the year 500 AA have the likeness of the sun on one side and a waterfall on the other side.

All silver coins produced between the years 500 AA and 580 AA have a slight bit more silver in them than do the current silver coins. For this reason they are slightly more valuable, but not every merchant or trader will actually give the extra value that these coins are actually worth. It only takes eighteen of these silver coins to equal the value of a gold coin and it takes eleven copper coins to equal the value of one of these silver coins.

GENERAL CONCERNS

There are several general concerns and factors that may come into play during your character's various quests and adventures that can have a significant impact on the game. A few of the more common concerns and their impact on your character are addressed here.

Encumbered

There is only a certain amount of weight that your character can carry at any given time without receiving penalties. Simply put, if your character is packing too much weight it will slow him down.

Your character is capable of carrying an amount of weight equal to two times his listed Carrying Capacity. However, once your character exceeds his listed Carrying Capacity he is considered to be encumbered and will begin receiving penalties. For each 10 pound increment of weight over your character's Carrying Capacity that he carries his Agility will drop by 1 Level and his Maximum Speed is decreased by 10'/Turn. If your character's Agility ever becomes Level 1 due to an excessive load of weight he can not move until his load is lightened. Also, if your character remains encumbered for more than thirty minutes he will begin receiving Fatigue Points to every attribute at a rate of 1 point every thirty minutes until he is no longer encumbered.

Over-bulked

If your character is carrying too much bulky equipment, weapons, or items he will receive penalties to his Agility and movement. Brightlings can carry a Total Bulk Value of 25 without penalties and all other ruling-races can carry up to a Total Bulk Value of 30 without penalties.

For each Bulk Value of 1 beyond the maximum that your character is allowed to carry (25 for Brightlings and 30 for all other ruling-races) his Agility will drop by 1 Level and his Maximum Speed is decreased by 10'/Turn. If your character's Agility ever becomes Level 1 due to excessive bulk he can not move until his Total Bulk Value is decreased.

All of the afore mentioned penalties will remain until your character's Total Bulk Value is decreased to within normal limits, at which time the penalties may be removed.

Poor Judgement

There are several different potential situations where a character may make a mistake or do something that he may later regret because of poor judgment on his behalf. For instance, your character may perform an action based upon what he sees or hears and may find out after the fact that he has made a mistake. Perhaps he heard wrong or perhaps that wretchin that he thought he saw behind the bush and consequently used "Lightning" on happened to be a neighbor's dog.

One of many that poor judgement can be incorporated in to the game is by allowing a margin of error for player characters or NPCs that attempt to approximate or guess at a certain distance to move to or to aim for. For instance, a character states to the GM, "I want to stop fifty feet short of that large bush and then take a shot at it with the flaming arrow that's in my one-hand crossbow." The GM may choose to simply say that the player's character stops at exactly fifty feet from the bush, or he could allow for a little bit of miscalculation (or "poor judgment") on the character's part.

Miscalculating distances when using ranged weapons can have a serious impact on the success of the attack (it can easily mean the difference between being within "Normal" range of the weapon and getting a -4 point penalty to the attack or being within "Long" range of the weapon and getting a -8 point penalty to the attack).

The following is a very good method for determining the amount of miscalculation when a character is trying to approximate distances.

For relatively short distances (one hundred feet or less) the GM may have the player roll 1D20 and 1D4. The result of the D20 is the number of feet that the character miscalculated the distance by. The D4 determines whether it was an overcalculation or undercalculation. Results of 1 or 3 on the D4 means that the character *over*calculated the distance by a number of feet equal to the result of the D20. Results of 2 or 4 on the D4 means that the character *under*calculated the dis-

tance by a number of feet equal to the result of the D20.

For especially long distances the result of the D20 may be double or even tripled. The exact potential for under or overcalculation of any given distance is ultimately up to the GM. Feel free to modify this method to whatever works best for you or the particular situation at hand.

The GM can use the poor judgment concept to add flavor and a bit of realism into any event or situation that he desires. Poor judgment can take the form of any number of mistakes. The GM should feel free to incorporate this concept in whatever manner that he feels would add to a particular situation or event, but should be careful not to make it a too common part of the game.

HEALTH

Maintaining your character's health is vital in a world where he is regularly pushed to his physical limits. It is inevitable that from time to time you will find your character injured, fatigued, or going without food and water. We will now discuss the effects of such conditions and how to recover from them as well as how to prevent them.

Fatigue

Fatigue normally occurs when your character is pushed too hard or he hasn't had sufficient rest. Fatigue Points are assigned to attributes to represent your character's fatigued condition. Normally when Fatigue Points are awarded they affect every attribute, but on some occasions only specific attributes may receive Fatigue Points. Each Fatigue Point lowers the attribute to which it is applied by 1 Level.

Though there are several actions listed throughout this rulebook that will give your character Fatigue Points, it would be impossible to list every circumstance or action that would fatigue your character. The GM can award Fatigue Points to a character for any action that he feels would warrant it.

There are several ways to remove Fatigue Points. Every Recovery Test that your character makes will remove 1 Fatigue Point from all attributes. After five consecutive hours of rest 2 Fatigue Points are automatically removed from all attributes. There are also some Force-effects, such as "Healing" and "Vitalize" that will also remove 1 Fatigue Point.

If your character accumulates 5 or more Fatigue Points to any attribute, other than Intelligence or Sixth Sense, he will collapse and be non-functional until he has less than 5 Fatigue Points to any single attribute (other than Intelligence or Sixth Sense).

Food & Water Requirements

Your character must eat and drink in order to survive. If he neglects eating or drinking for very long he will begin to receive penalties. Most ruling-races, with the exception of Grak, must eat at least one small meal a day and drink at least one standard-bottle of water (1/4 of a normal waterskin) per day.

If your character goes one whole day without meeting the food or water requirements he will receive 1 Fatigue Point to all attributes on the following morning (first hour). If your character continues to neglect to meet the food or water requirements for a second day he will receive 2 more Fatigue Points to all attributes on the next morning and will only get 2 Recovery Tests to use for the entire following day. If your character continues to neglect food and water requirements after this second day he will continue to get 2 Fatigue Points per day and will lose 1 Recovery Test per day until he has no Recovery Tests available. Your character will eventually collapse from fatigue if he doesn't eat or drink (remember, 5 Fatigue Points or more to a single attribute, other than Intelligence or Sixth Sense, will cause your character to collapse).

When your character meets the food and water requirements he will cease to accumulate Fatigue Points and on the first hour of the next day he will get all 3 Recovery Tests back as normal.

Depending upon the type of climate that characters are in the food and water requirements may be higher or lower than normal (GM's discretion).

Damage

It is unavoidable that your character at one point or another will sustain damage. Damage to your character should be recorded on a scrap piece of paper or on a Combat Sheet (provided in the back of this rulebook). There are several ways that damage can affect your character's performance. This could be in the form of injuries or causing your charac-

ter to black out (Force Failure), or even death.

There are several ways in which your character can recover from damage. Understanding the most efficient way of utilizing these methods may make the difference in your character surviving to meet the next challenge or retiring to an early grave.

Recovering from Damage

The normal method for removing damage is by Recovery Tests. Whenever your character has any damage he is considered to be in recovery. Every two hours that your character is in recovery he may make a Recovery Test. This is done by rolling the dice indicated on your Character Sheet beside of "Recovery". The result of your dice roll is the number of points of damage that your character recovered. Your character gets 3 normal Recovery Tests per day and 1 instant Recovery Test that he can make at any time that he wants by spending a Mystical Attuning Point.

There are times that your character will have damage but he won't be in recovery. This occurs when your character has one or more injuries. For each injury that your character has there is 1 point of damage (2 points of damage for critical injuries) that can't be healed until the proper number of days have passed for the injury to heal. So if your character has an injury that can't be healed for another two days and he has healed all damage except for the 1 point that is held because of the injury, he is not considered to be in recovery. Once the two days have passed your character will go into recovery again (at the first hour of the day that the required time has elapsed) and the 1 point of damage held from the injury may now be healed (by making a normal Recovery Test). In summation, an injury can only be healed by making a Recovery Test after all damage other than the damage being held by the injury has been healed and the appropriate healing time for the injury has elapsed.

Mark's character Webgray has just finished battling three wretchin. Though he survived the encounter he has sustained some serious damage. The wretchin inflicted a total of 42 points of damage to him and inflicted two injuries. One injury is applied to his Agility and will take four days to heal and the other injury is applied to his Endurance and will take two days to heal.

Two hours after the encounter Webgray makes a Recovery Test. His Recovery dice are 1D10 + 1D4. Mark rolls a 9 and a 3. His character has healed 12 points of damage and has 30 points of damage remaining.

Approximately an hour later Webgray walks into the camp of his companions. One of his companions knows the Force-effect "Healing" and uses it on him. Webgray instantly heals all damage other than injury damage. Since he has two injuries there are 2 points of damage that he can't heal until the injuries are healed.

Webgray and his companions set out to return to their fort.

On the first hour of the second day after receiving his injuries Webgray has no current damage other than the 2 points of damage being held by the injuries and so goes into recovery. He immediately makes a Recovery Test with a result of 8 which is more than enough to remove the 1 point of damage being held by that injury. Webgray has healed one of the injuries and now has one more injury that can be healed in two more days.

Just before daybreak (the first hour) on the fourth day after receiving his injuries Webgray and his companions are attacked by a pack of bristle wolves. They are able to fight off and defeat all of the bristle wolves, but all of them received damage in the process. Webgray received 7 points of damage during the battle. Webgray is now in recovery again and has Recovery Tests remaining, so he immediately makes a Recovery Test with a result of 9. Since the healing time for his remaining injury will not be up until the first hour, the 1 point of damage being held by the injury can not be healed by this Recovery Test. Mark's Recovery Test heals all damage except for the 1 point of injury damage so he is no longer in recovery (he has no current damage other than injury damage).

When the first hour comes the healing time for his injury is up and Webgray immediately goes into recovery again. Since this is a new day Webgray gets all 3 Recovery Tests back and immediately uses the first one at this time. He gets a result of 6 on his Recovery Test. He has healed the remaining injury and its 1 point of damage. Webgray now has no damage whatsoever and is no longer in recovery. He still has two Recovery Tests remaining for this day.

There are several Force-effects that can heal damage but there are limitations to the amount of mystical healing that your character can receive in a single day. Your character may not receive more than three types of mystical healing in a single day and may not receive the exact same type of mystical healing more than twice in a single day.

See "Perils of Combat" in the "COMBAT" Section for more on injuries.

Sleep

Sleep is a necessary part of life and if your character doesn't get enough he will receive penalties. Ruling-races must get at least five hours of consecutive uninterrupted sleep per day. If your character doesn't get five hours of consecutive sleep he will receive 1 Fatigue Point to all attributes at the first hour of the following morning as well as only getting 2 Recovery Tests for the day instead of 3. If your character doesn't get five hours of consecutive sleep for a second day in a row he will receive 2 more Fatigue Points to all attributes at the first hour and will only get 1 Recovery Test for the day. If your character goes without the proper amount of sleep for a third day he will get another 2 Fatigue Points to all attributes at the first hour and will have no Recovery

Tests. Each day beyond this point that your character doesn't receive at least five hours of consecutive sleep he will get another 2 Fatigue Points to all attributes. Unless your character has found a way to remove his Fatigue Points faster than he is getting them he will eventually collapse from lack of sleep (5 Fatigue Points or more to a single attribute, other than Intelligence or Sixth Sense, will cause your character to collapse).

At the first hour of the day after your character gets five or more hours of sleep he will get all 3 Recovery Tests back.

MUNDANE SKILLS

The following is a compilation of several of the more mundane skills that your character will need to have in order to survive his life-long quest of restoring balance to Oryathar. Chances are that your character will have to perform one or more of these mundane skills on a regular basis; perhaps just for fun, or perhaps to save his life.

COMMON TASK DIFFICULTY	
Task	**Difficulty Value**
Climbing	Agility-9
Disarming Traps	Agility-12
Fishing	Agility-9/Intelligence-9
Hunting	Agility-9/Intelligence-9
Locating Traps	Intelligence-12
Lock Picking	Agility-12/Intelligence-10
Swimming	Agility-9
Tracking	Intelligence-11

The "COMMON TASK DIFFICULTY" table is a convenient listing of the average Difficulty Values for many of the common tasks that your character may need to perform. In the "Task" column is the names of these common tasks. Across from each task under "Difficulty Value" is an attribute followed by a value. All tasks that have "Agility" listed beside of them means that they require an Agility/Performance Test to be performed. All tasks that have "Intelligence" listed beside of them means that they require an Intelligence Test to be performed. If both Agility and Intelligence are listed, then an Agility/Performance Test and an Intelligence Test both must be made in order to perform the task. The value beside of the attribute is the base Difficulty Value for that task.

Climbing

Under normal conditions your character can climb a number of feet per Turn equal to his Agility Level. An Agility/Performance Test against a base Difficulty Value of 9 is required to climb average surfaces and obstacles. The GM may lower or raise the Difficulty Value for any climbing Test to any value that he feels is appropriate.

Failure of a climbing Test means that your character has faltered or slipped and has a fifty percent chance of falling at that point. When your character fails a climbing Test he doesn't climb the normal distance that he normally would have for that Turn. How far below the Difficulty Value that the result of your character's climbing Test is determines how far he climbed before he slipped, and possibly fell.

For example, let's say that your character attempts to climb a surface with an Average climbing difficulty (9). If the result of your character's climbing Test is 3 or less that means he slipped within the first few feet of his climb, 4 to 6 and he slipped at approximately half way through his climbing movement for that Turn, 7 or 8 means he nearly completed his full climbing movement for that Turn before faltering. Let's say that the result of your character's climbing Test is 7 and he can climb five feet per Turn. Since a result of 7 is very close to meeting the Difficulty Value of the climbing Test (9), the GM determines that your character almost made it his full climbing distance of five feet before faltering. It is the GM's decision as to exactly how far your character travels during the Turn in which he fails a climbing Test.

The GM states that your character was at a height of four feet when he faltered. Your character now has a fifty percent chance of falling at this point (a result of 50 or lower on the percentile means that he fell). You roll the percentile dice and get a result of 25. Your character falls at a height of four feet. Looking to the "FALLING DAMAGE" table on page 242 you see that falling from a height of four feet will yield Level 4 damage. You roll the dice for Level 4 (1D8) for a result of 5. Your character sustains 5 points of damage from the fall.

Had you rolled above 50 on the percentile dice your character wouldn't have fallen but would have ended his climb for the Turn at a height of four feet.

Fishing

An Agility/Performance Test and Intelligence Test are both required in order to make a single fishing Test. The base Difficulty Value for a fishing Test is 9/9 (9 for the Agility/Performance Test and a 9 on the Intelligence Test as well). If successful, then your character has caught enough fish to provide one small meal for 1D4 people.

A minimum of thirty minutes must be spent fishing in order to make a fishing Test. The Difficulty Value of either Test required for a fishing Test is subject to change depending upon the abundance of fish in the area, the time of day, bait used, etc.

Holding Your Breath

Your character can only hold his breath for a short period of time before he will begin to take damage and eventually pass out. The amount of time that your character is able to hold his breath depends upon his Endurance Level and whether or not he is active or at rest at the time he is holding his breath.

If your character is calm and at rest while holding his breath he can hold it for a number of Turns equal to his Endurance Level times two (his normal limit) before he begins to suffer damage. If your character is physically active or undergoing strenuous activity (being beaten for example) he can only hold his breath for a number of Turns *equal* to his Endurance Level before he begins to suffer damage.

On the Turn following your character's limit for holding his breath he will receive 1D4 points of suffocation damage and will continue to receive 1D4 points of damage per Turn until he breaths. On the beginning of the third Turn that a character takes suffocation damage they must also make an Endurance Test against a base Difficulty Value of 10 or blackout for 1D4 Turns. If the character continues to hold his breath past this point he will continue to receive the suffocation damage and must continue making the Endurance Test to resist blacking out. In addition, the Difficulty Value of the Endurance Test increases by 1 point with each successive Turn.

Once a character blacks out they will automatically begin to breath and will no longer receive the 1D4 points of suffocation damage.

Hunting

An Agility/Performance Test and Intelligence Test are both required in order to make a single hunting Test. The base Difficulty Value for a hunting Test is 9/9 (9 for the Agility/Performance Test and a 9 on the Intelligence Test as well). If successful, then your character has killed enough game to provide one small meal for 1D4 people.

A minimum of one hour must be spent hunting in order to make a hunting Test. The Difficulty Value of either Test required for a hunting Test is subject to change depending upon the abundance of game in the area hunted, the time of day, the type of weapon being used, etc.

Jumping

In order to jump the maximum horizontal distance possible (listed as Horizontal Leap on your Character Sheet) your character must have at least a thirty-five foot running start to build up his speed. Having the proper running start of thirty-five feet does not guarantee that your character will jump his maximum distance. Every jump will be slightly different and the actual distance that your character jumps will be different. Sometimes your character may not get as good a foothold as other times, or he may have sloppy form one time and perform flawlessly the next.

To determine how far your character actually jumps he must make an Agility/Performance Test. The result of this Test is the number of feet that he jumped. If the result of your character's Agility/Performance Test ends up being a negative value he will still jump one foot, and even if the result of the Agility/Performance Test is greater than your character's listed Horizontal Leap he will actually only jump a distance equal to his listed Horizontal Leap. Your character can not jump farther than the Horizontal Leap distance listed on your Character Sheet, at least not by natural means.

To determine how high your character can jump vertically he will make an Agility/Performance Test as if you were determining a horizontal jump and then divide the result by 4, rounding up to the next half foot. However, if the result of the Agility/Performance Test is less than 4 you would round down to a half foot. So if the result of your character's vertical jump Test (Agility/Performance Test) is 9, he actually jumped a height of two and a half feet. If the result of the Test was 1, 2, or 3 he would only jump a half of a foot.

Running

Running at high speeds takes a lot out of your character and he can only keep up high running speeds for a very limited amount of time. Your character can only run at half or more or his Maximum Speed for a number of Turns equal to his Endurance Level before he will begin to receive Fatigue Points. Your character will continue to receive 1 Fatigue Point to every attribute for each Turn beyond this point that he continues to run at half or more of his Maximum Speed.

In order to stop gaining the Fatigue Points your character must rest or slow down to below half of his Maximum Speed for at least 10 Turns. If your character continues to run at speeds half or more of his Maximum Speed before he has rested or slowed for 10 Turns he will immediately begin accumulating Fatigue Points again at a rate of 1 point per Turn. Once your character has accumulated 5 or more Fatigue Points to any single attribute, other than Intelligence or Sixth Sense, he will collapse.

Swimming

Under normal conditions your character can swim a number of feet per Turn equal to his Agility Level. An Agility/Performance Test against a base Difficulty Value of 9 is required to swim in calm water under normal conditions. The GM may lower or raise the Difficulty Value for any swimming Test to any value that he feels is appropriate.

Failure of a swimming Test means that your character swam poorly for that Turn and maybe even begins to go under a bit. When your character fails a swimming Test he

doesn't swim the normal distance that he normally would have for that Turn. How far below the Difficulty Value that the result of your character's swimming Test is determines how far he swam before he faltered.

For example, let's say that your character attempts to swim in waters and conditions that the GM assigns a swimming Difficulty Value of 9 to. If the result of your character's swimming Test is 3 or less that means he began to falter within the first few feet of his swim for that Turn, 4 to 6 and he faltered at approximately half way through his swimming movement for that Turn, 7 or 8 means he nearly completed his full swimming movement for that Turn before faltering.

Let's say that the result of your character's swimming Test is 8 and your character can swim six feet per Turn. Since a result of 8 is very close to meeting the Difficulty Value of the swimming Test, the GM determines that your character almost made it his full swimming distance of six feet before faltering (perhaps five feet). It is the GM's decision as to exactly how far your character traveled during the Turn in which he fails a swimming Test.

If your character fails two swimming Tests in a row he will take 1D4 points of drowning damage at the beginning of the next Turn. Your character will continue to take 1D4 points of drowning at the beginning of each Turn thereafter until he passes the swimming Test or gets out of the water. Once your character passes the swimming Test the drowning damage will cease (until he fails two more consecutive swimming Tests).

If your character fails six consecutive swimming Tests he will black out on the beginning of the Turn in which the sixth swimming Test is failed. He will remain unconscious and continue to take 1D4 points of drowning damage per Turn thereafter until he dies or is rescued from the water.

It is a Major Action each Turn to swim so if your character attempts to make an attack or perform another Major Action while he is swimming he is not able to make a swimming Test that Turn (not making a swimming Test is treated the same as failing a swimming Test) and he will begin to sink. Also, any types of physical actions (attacking, setting a Defense, etc.) performed by a being that is under water is cut in half (round down).

OBSTACLES & STRUCTURES

There will be times that your character will encounter obstacles or structures that he may have to bash his way through or destroy. The following "COMMON OBSTACLES/STRUCTURES" table lists the average Destroyed Ratings for many of the common obstacles or structures that your character may encounter. Though your character may encounter many more structures than just those listed on this table, you can use this table as a guideline to determine the Destroyed Ratings of other structures based on their similarities to those listed on the table.

The Destroyed Rating is the cumulative amount of damage that an object can sustain before being destroyed. There is also something known as Shatter Threshold. The Shatter Threshold of any object is the amount of damage, given in one blow, that will cause the object to shatter. The Shatter Threshold for any object is equal to one half of the object's Destroyed Rating. So, looking to the following "COMMON OBSTACLES/STRUCTURES" table we can see that a normal wooden door has a Destroyed Rating of 80. That means that it has a Shatter Threshold of 40. If a normal wooden door sustains 80 or more points of damage it is destroyed. If a normal wooden door sustains 40 or more points of damage in a single blow it will shatter, in which case it is also destroyed.

Depending upon exactly what a particular object is made of and what weapon or object is used to inflict the damage to it, the GM may rule that it will take more or less damage than that listed in order to destroy it.

COMMON OBSTACLES/STRUCTURES

Obstacle/Structure	Destroyed Rating
Normal Wooden Door	80
Heavy Wooden Door	240
Wooden Gate	50
Thick Ice	200
Normal Stone Wall or Door	300
Heavy Stone Wall or Door	1200
Normal Steel Wall or Door	500
Heavy Steel Wall or Door	2000

NATURAL PERILS

Besides the influence of the Shadow, Shadow-kin, and Korgathool there are a multitude of natural perils that can befall adventurers. Below is a list of twenty random natural events or situations that can befall someone unfortunate enough to be in the wrong place at the wrong time.

1. **Avalanche**
2. **Rock-slide**
3. **Volcanic Eruption**
4. **Storm (hail, etc.)**
5. **Tornado**
6. **Landquake**
7. **Quicksand**
8. **Falling Tree**
9. **Pit**
10. **Hunter's Trap/Snare**
11. **Lost**
12. **Twisted Ankle**
13. **Slip on Rocks or Roots**
14. **Poisonous Plants**
15. **Ice Break**
16. **Force Surge**
17. **Force Drain**
18. **Natural Sickness**
19. **Falling**
20. **Fire**

GMs may use this list to add random events into their adventures by rolling 1D20 and then incorporating the event that matches the result of the dice roll into the adventure. Or perhaps they would just like to choose an event from the list that they feel would be appropriate for the current situation. The exact effects of each natural peril is ultimately up to the GM, though the effects of many of these perils can be found in similar Force-effects. For instance, you can look at the Force-effect "Tornado" to see what the average effects of a tornado should be, or the Force-effect "Quicksand" to see the normal effects of getting into quicksand, etc.

Feel free to make up your own natural perils or events, and have fun in playing out the details of the various events. The main thing is that you have fun.

Falling

It is inevitable that your character will take a fall at one point or another. Depending upon how far your character falls the damage may be no more than a scrape or may be enough to permanently end his career. The surface upon which a character falls also plays a part in how much damage is sustained from the fall. The following table lists the average amounts of damage sustained from falls depending upon the distance fallen.

FALLING DAMAGE

# of Feet Fallen	Damage
1-2	Level 2
3-6	Level 4
7-10	Level 6
11-15	Level 8
16-19	Level 10
20-24	Level 12
25-30	Level 15
31-36	Level 18 + 5
37-42	Level 21 + 10
43-up	Level 24 + 20

If the GM rules that the surface landed on was exceptionally soft he may choose to lessen the amount of damage sustained from the fall. If the surface landed on was exceptionally hard or was full of jagged rocks or the like he may choose to increase the amount of damage sustained from the fall. In any case, the "FALLING DAMAGE" table is a useful guide in determining the damage sustained from a fall.

Fire

In your character's numerous quests and adventures he will no doubt have many encounters with fire. It may be a forest fire, fire from a torch, or fire resulting from any one of the many fire-based Force-effects. Regardless of the source or type of fire that a character or being may encounter, the following table can be used as a guide in determining the amount of damage that the fire will render.

FIRE DAMAGE	
Source	Level of Damage
Torch/ Small Flame	Level 6
Campfire	Level 8
Inferno/ Forest Fire	15 (contact) 8 (within 20 ft)
Lava	25 (contact) 16 (within 20 ft)

The damage listed for the different sources and types of fire is the average amount of damage rendered per Turn. So if your character is caught in a forest fire he will suffer Level 15 damage each Turn until he can get out of the fire.

SITUATION MODIFIERS

It's not very often that you will find your character battling Shadow-kin in his choice of terrain and conditions. Very often your character will be caught out in storms, or thrown into battle in the middle of the night, or in the midst of heavy fog, or countless other undesirable situations.

This section of "SURVIVING ORYATHAR" gives examples of many such undesirable situations or factors that can modify the outcome of your character's actions.

Outside Factors That May Penalize Attacks

There are a number of outside factors that can penalize and greatly effect the outcome of your character's, or his opponent's, attacks or actions. The following is a list of ten such outside factors. GMs should feel free to use these factors to add flavor and challenge to any situation. The exact effects of these factors are left up to the GM's discretion, though the "SITUATION MODIFIERS" table gives the average penalty for several of these factors.

1. **High winds**
2. **Sun in eyes**
3. **String break (bow or crossbow)**
4. **Darkness**
5. **Rain**
6. **Fog**
7. **Distractions (loud thunder-clap or flash of lightning, etc.)**
8. **Weapon breaks**
9. **Slippery terrain**
10. **Personal flaw (fear of closed-in spaces, etc.)**

Visibility

Having a clear look at your target or foe can greatly determine your character's success at attacking or defending. Visibility is vital for many of the tasks that your character will have to perform on a regular basis. Ranges of vision are divided into three main categories. They are Normal, Medium, and Maximum.

The following "RANGES OF VISION" table shows the normal distances that characters are able to see at the various ranges of vision as well as a basic description of how keen your character's sight is at those distances.

RANGES OF VISION	
Normal	0 to 99 yards (Most details can be seen)
Medium	100 to 299 yards (Few details can be seen)
Maximum	300 to 600 yards (No details seen. Only large objects are visible)

There are several different factors and conditions that can decrease your character's visibility and interfere with his actions. The following "SITUATION MODIFIERS" table shows the average penalties for many of the common conditions that can affect your character's vision.

SITUATION MODIFIERS	
Visibility	Level of Damage
Light Rain	-2 pts /-5 pts
Dusk	-2 pts /-6 pts
Hail	-3 pts /-8 pts
Light Fog	-3 pts /-8 pts
Heavy Rain	-4 pts /-10 pts
Heavy Fog	-5 pts /-12 pts
Darkness (minor star or moonlight)	-6 pts /-14 pts

The result of whatever type of Test that your character is making that requires sight in order to be performed normally is penalized by the number of points listed across from the condition that your character is currently in. The penalty value listed before the backslash is the penalty applied to actions in melee and the number after the backslash is the penalty to ranged actions.

So, if your character is in light rain any action that the GM deems would be affected by decreased visibility will be penalized by -2 points if he is interacting in melee and -5 points if he is interacting with someone or something that is ranged.

Perhaps your character is in a large field and there is a light rain falling. He is trying to look across the field to spot someone hiding in some bushes. The GM tells you that this will require an Intelligence Test against a Difficulty Value of

10 and according to the "SITUATION MODIFIERS" table he will penalize the result of this Test by -5 points. Or perhaps your character is fighting a creature in light fog. If he is engaged in melee with the creature all of his attack Tests (Agility/Performance Tests) will be penalized by -3 points. If your character was in a hail storm and trying to shoot someone forty feet away with a crossbow he would receive a -8 point penalty to his attack.

TRAVEL

During the course of your character's adventures he will have to travel to and from many regions of Oryathar. Some of these travels may take your character days or even weeks in order to reach his destination. Since the arrival of Shadow-kin traveling has become increasingly dangerous. Aside from the harsh terrains and elements that are often encountered characters must deal with the ever-present threat of being attacked by Shadow-kin or even Korgathool. Though Shinkai have mystical means of greatly increasing the ease and speed of travel, such mystical means of traveling are not always the wisest solution. It is inevitable that your character will end up braving the many dangers of a long journey across vast expanses of land in both charted and uncharted regions.

The three most commons means of travel are by foot, by horse or bleyk, or by boat.

Travel by Foot

Though slower than travel on horse or bleyk it is often necessary to travel by foot. Some reasons that traveling on foot may be preferred over other means of travel are when stealth is necessary. It is also much easier for a group of soldiers on foot to quietly move about than for a group of soldiers on horseback. Also the regions to be traveled to may be inaccessible on horse or bleyk, or there simply may not be opportunity to acquire horses or bleyk for the journey.

Depending upon the type of terrain the average ruling-race can cover approximately thirty miles a day on foot, assuming that he travels for at least ten hours a day. Traveling through dense forest or mountainous terrain may slow travel to eighteen miles per day. When roads are available traveling is much easier and quicker. On well-maintained roads it is possible to travel as many as forty miles a day, again assuming that at least ten hours a day are spent traveling.

Travel by Horse or Bleyk

Travel by horse or bleyk is the preferred means of traveling on land. It is significantly faster than travel on foot and horses and bleyks are able to stay on the move without fatiguing for much greater distances than ruling-races can. The Defenders of the Light and King's Guard have large stables of horses and bleyks. Horses are more preferred for long trips and bleyk are more preferred for short trips or where intense battle is expected. Bleyk are much more dependable and useful in combat than the average horse.

Depending upon the type of terrain most horses and bleyk can cover approximately forty-five miles in a single day, assuming that they travel for at least ten hours a day. Traveling through dense forest or mountainous terrain may slow travel to twenty-five miles per day. When roads are available traveling is much easier and quicker. On well-maintained roads it is possible to travel as many as sixty miles a day, again assuming that at least ten hours a day are spent traveling.

Travel by Boat

Long journeys often require the use of ships or boats. A good ship can travel as far as one hundred-ten miles in a single day. This is assuming that the ship travels twenty-five hours a day. There are numerous amounts of docks along the western coast of the Ellabrian Realms where travelers can purchase passage on a ship. Most ships charge a fee of ten silver coins per person for one day of passage, and five silver coins per horse or bleyk for one day of passage.

There are many small riverboats that travel the various rivers of the Ellabrian Realms bringing goods from abroad and also offering passage to paying customers. Passage on a riverboat is significantly cheaper than the larger ships that travel the seas. Most riverboat captains charge a fee of five silver coins per person for one day of passage, and two silver coins per horse or bleyk for one day of passage. A well-staffed riverboat can travel as much as eighty miles in a single day. This is assuming that the riverboat travels twenty-five hours a day.

CHARACTER ADVANCEMENT

Regardless of which Specialty that you choose or which race that your character is the ways in which you can proceed in developing and advancing your character are nearly endless. You choose the areas of your character that you want to develop. If you are more interested in the physical aspects of your character you may immediately begin developing those areas. If magic is your interest you may begin working toward the mystical aspects of developing your character. No matter what your goal for your character is you decide when and in what ways he will advance. Nearly all of the Talents, Skills, Force-effects, and other abilities in the game are obtainable to all races and characters of all Specialties.

When your character is first created he is far short of being ready to take on a horde of Shadow-kin or being a force to be reckoned with. There are many things that you will need to do in order to prepare your character for the many difficult challenges and tasks that lie ahead of him. Some of these preparations include increasing his attributes, learning to control the Mystic Forces, learning Force-effects, Talents, Skills, and so forth.

As your character continues to survive encounters with the Shadow and completes his many quests he will gain the Light Points and Character Points needed to increase his skills and abilities. This Section will discuss the various ways that you can increase your character's existing abilities as well as gain new abilities.

FINDING A THEME

There are a multitude of ways that you can go about advancing your character, such as learning Skills, Talents, Universal Talents, technique with weapons, Force-effects, learning to enchant, advancing your Dragonknight form, raising attributes, and the list goes on. It may be overwhelming to some players as to what is the best way to go about improving and advancing their character. The truth is, there is no one way that is best. There are many different ways and methods for advancing and progressing your character. A large part of the fun for most players is deciding exactly what they want their characters to learn or train for. The longer that you play **Mystic Forces** the more of the many little tricks and advantages that you will find in how to progress your character.

Though there is no one best way for advancing your character there are some fundamental concepts to keep in mind while doing so that can greatly increase your character's effectiveness.

Probably the single greatest tip to keep in mind while advancing your character is finding a theme. By that I mean that you should determine what aspect of your character that you would like to develop or advance first and then learn Skills, Talents, or other abilities that will complement that area. For example, if you want your character to be very good with the Mystic Forces you would probably want to spend your Light Points in increasing his Sixth Sense, learning Technique Points in the Mystic Forces, and perhaps learn the Universal Talent "Mind Focus". You wouldn't increase your character's Strength one time and then Willpower the next, and then maybe learn technique with a weapon and then learn technique in a Mystic Force. There is nothing wrong with this pattern of developing your character, but you will find that he is quickly becoming marginal in many areas and not really good in any one area.

Holding to a theme and strategically advancing your character often proves to be the most effective method, but feel free to experiment and advance your character in whatever manner that you wish. As long as you are having fun then you can't go wrong.

INCREASING ATTRIBUTES

Increasing your character's attributes is at the heart of character advancement. By increasing attributes you can improve many of the different aspects of your character. There are two methods by which you can increase an attribute. One method is to pay for the increase by spending Light Points and the other is a bonus increase given for each 20 Light Points earned.

Buying Attribute Increases

The amount of Light Points that your character must spend to increase an attribute depends upon how many times that the attribute has already been increased.

Every time that an attribute is increased you must draw a line in the box to the left of the attribute to indicate that it has been increased. The number of lines in the box will reflect the total number of times that the attribute has been

increased. Each attribute may be increased a maximum of sixteen times. It is up to you how to place the marks in the box to represent an attribute increase, but the suggested method is to draw your lines inside of the box so that when you make the sixteenth increase to a particular attribute the symbol for the Defenders of the Light will be the pattern that has been created by the box and the lines. The symbol on the bottom of page 67 is the symbol for the Defenders of the Light.

To determine how many Light Points that it will cost to increase an attribute find the number of times that this increase will make the attribute having been increased on the following "ATTRIBUTE" table.

ATTRIBUTE COST	
# of Increases	L.P. Cost
1	3
2	3
3	4
4	4
5	5
6	5
7	6
8	6
9	7
10	7
11	8
12	8
13	9
14	9
15	10
16	10

The Light Point cost for the increase is listed in the right column across from the number of increases that this increase will make. For example, if this will make the third increase to a particular attribute your character will have to spend 4 Light Points.

Deduct the proper amount of Light Points from your character's Current Light Points and increase the attribute by the following number of points. Roll 1D4. If the number rolled is a 1 or 2 the attribute increases by 1 point. If the number rolled is a 3 or 4 the attribute increases by 2 points. Place a line in the box to the left of the attribute and adjust the Level and Dice for the attribute as necessary, as well as any other factors or stats that the attribute affects.

Bonus Attribute Increases

Every time that your character earns 20 Light Points you may increase an attribute of your choice by 1 Level (5 points). So your character will raise an attribute by an entire Level once his Total Light Points reaches 20 and then again once it reaches 40, again at 60 and so on. Place a line in the box to the left of the attribute and adjust the Value, Level, and Dice for the attribute as necessary as well as any other factors or stats that the attribute affects.

Whether the increase to the attribute was only 1 or 2 points purchased by Light Points or an entire Level given because of earning 20 Light Points it is considered one increase each time that an attribute is raised.

A word of caution in regards to increasing your character's attributes. You should limit the number of times that you increase an attribute through purchasing the increases. Remember, you can only increase a single attribute sixteen times no matter if those increases consist of 1 point increases or 1 Level increases (5 points). If you use all of your character's sixteen increases by increasing his attributes a point or two at a time your character will quickly end up with an attribute Level that can not be increased further and may be far below the Level that you had hoped for. There is a Universal Talent, however, that can make purchasing attribute increases much more efficient. It is called "Blood of the Ancients". If your character has this Universal Talent you may increase his attributes by 1D4 +1 points each time that you pay for an increase, instead of 1 or 2 points as previously described.

As mentioned before, increasing your character's attributes is the heart of character advancement. Through increasing your character's attributes you are able to increase a lot of the other stats and aspects of your character. If you will refer back to the descriptions of each of the six attributes in the "CREATING A CHARACTER" Section you will be able to see what things that each attribute affects. Here are a few of the more common benefits and reasons for increasing your character's attributes.

Life Force

Your character's Life Force is extremely important to his survival. The higher your character's Life Force is the more damage that he is able to sustain and still survive. Since your character's Life Force, and subsequently Force Failure and Injury Rating, are comprised from the values of your character's Strength, Endurance, and Willpower, any time that you increase one of these three attributes you are in effect increasing your character's Life Force, Force Failure, and Injury Rating.

Any time that you increase either your character's Strength, Endurance, or Willpower you should immediately recalculate his Life Force, Force Failure, and Injury accordingly.

Initiative

Physical Initiative is based on your character's Agility and Mystical Initiative is based on your character's Sixth Sense. So by increasing either of these two attributes you are increasing your character's Initiative. Striking the first blow often determines the outcome of a battle.

Attacking

By increasing your character's Agility you are increasing the potential result of his attack Tests, and who doesn't want to have more effective attacks.

Defense

By increasing your character's Agility you are increasing the potential results of any Physical Defense that he sets, and by increasing his Sixth Sense you are increasing the potential results of any Mystical Defense that he sets. Being able to avoid attacks is definitely crucial to one's survival.

Defense Bonuses

By increasing your character's Agility you are able to increase his Physical Defense Bonus Points and by increasing Sixth Sense you can increase your character's Mystical Defense Bonus Points, both of which are very handy when his initial Defense isn't enough.

Damage Yield

By increasing your character's Strength you are able to increase the amount of damage that his physical attacks do. With the number of formidable creatures to be constantly wary of a strong arm is a welcomed ally.

Recovery Tests

It is inevitable that your character will sustain damage in the course of his many heroic quests. By increasing your character's Endurance you are able to increase the potential results of his Recovery Tests thereby increasing the speed in which he is able to recover from damage and heal injuries.

Meditation Results

By increasing your character's Intelligence and Sixth Sense you increase the potential results of his Meditation Tests for gaining Force Knowledge. When it comes to the Mystic Forces, knowledge is power.

Force Failure

When your character accumulates an amount of damage equal to or greater than his Force Failure he will normally black out. However, your character is allowed to make a Willpower Test to resist this blacking out. So, by increasing your character's Willpower you are increasing his odds of passing this Test and resisting Force Failure. Being able to hold on to consciousness for one more Turn can easily make the difference between life and death.

Movement

By increasing your character's Agility or Strength you are able to increase his Maximum Speed and Action Movement. Being able to run fast and cover larger areas during combat is extremely helpful. There are times to fight and times to run, and when it is time to run it is always desirable to be able to run faster than your pursuer.

Lifting Limit/Carrying Capacity

By increasing your character's Strength you are able to increase the amount of weight that he is able to lift and carry, both of which are very important when your character discovers that giant chest of gold.

These are just a few of the many things that increasing your character's attributes will affect. Your character's attributes affect most anything that he can do, from running and jumping to gaining Force Knowledge and learning Force-effects.

As you play and advance your character you will learn the best methods for increasing your character's attributes and the proper times to do so. A large part of the fun of playing **Mystic Forces** is experimenting with advancing your character.

REMOVING SHADOW POINTS

In the unfortunate event that you find your character in possession of a few Shadow Points, and odds are that you eventually will, you will need to remove them. The penalties that accompany the ownership of Shadow Points are not pleasant to say the least. The following "SHADOW POINT PENALTIES" table shows the penalties for the different amounts of Shadow Points that your character may possess.

SHADOW POINT PENALTIES	
Current Shadow Points	**Penalty**
.5 to 2	Unable to assume Dragonknight form or enchant
2.5 to 4	No bonus attribute Level increase for earning 20 L.P.
4.5 to 6	All attributes drop by 2 Levels (permanently)
6.5 to 8	A Shadow-kin of GM's choice seeks you out and invites you to join the Shadow. If you refuse, then it will attack
8.5 or higher	You completely forsake the Light and turn to the Shadow (you are now Shadow-sworn)

As your character moves into each new penalty category he retains the penalties from the previous categories as well as the one that he has just moved into. So if your character has 7 Current Shadow Points he will not get the 1 Level bonus attribute increase each time that he earns 20 Light Points and is also unable to transform into Dragonknight if he is a Dragonknight character or enchant if he is an Enchanter character.

All of the penalties that accompany the ownership of Current Shadow Points will remain until your character removes enough Current Shadow Points to take him out of that category. So the first category of Shadow Point penalties, which is given for having .5 to 2 Current Shadow Points, will remain until your character no longer has any Current Shadow Points. The second category of Shadow Point penalties, which is given for having 2.5 to 4 Current Shadow Points, will remain until your character has less than 2.5 Current Shadow Points, and so on.

If your character ever has 8.5 or more Current Shadow Points he has lost all ability to resist the temptations of the Shadow and becomes Korgathool. A character that becomes Korgathool is immediately removed from the game and becomes a non-player character (NPC). The GM could then use the character as a villain against the other player characters or could just simply discard it. Regardless, once your character becomes Korgathool you lose that character and must start a new one.

If the GM so wished, he could allow a player to play a Korgathool character, but the overall intent and design of **Mystic Forces** does not support such an option.

PROWESS RATING

Every character has what is known as a Prowess Rating. There are two types of Prowess Ratings; Physical Prowess and Mystical Prowess. Physical Prowess is essentially a measure of how physically competent and skilled that your character is and is determined from your character's Agility and Strength Levels. Mystical Prowess is a measure of how mystically competent and skilled that your character is and is determined from your character's Intelligence and Sixth Sense Levels.

Your character's Prowess Rating doesn't have any direct influence in the game. It is basically a way of categorizing your character's level of ability in physical and mystical aspects. Prowess Ratings are used more for a personal record and for keeping up with your character's status than for actual game purposes.

PROWESS RATING	
Level	**Rating**
2-14	Amateur
15-19	Average
20-24	Skilled
25-29	Advanced
30-up	Legendary

To determine your character's Physical Prowess Rating add his Agility and Strength Levels (of his ruling-race form) together. Find this Level in the left column of the "PROWESS RATING" table. Now go straight across to the "Rating" column to see what your character's current Physical Prowess Rating is.

Your character's Mystical Prowess Rating is determined in the same manner except you will add his Intelligence and Sixth Sense Levels together instead of his Agility and Strength Levels.

TECHNIQUE POINTS

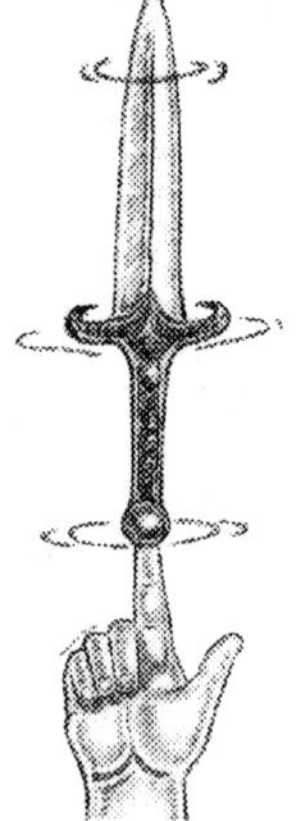

Technique is the extra skill that comes from intensive training and practice. Characters can learn Technique Points for

weapons, shields, the various aspects of their Dragonknight form, and the Mystic Forces.

Every weapon, shield, Mystic Force, etc. has a maximum number of Technique Points which can be achieved. The maximum number of Technique Points attainable for any particular weapon, shield, Mystic Force, etc. is listed along with the item's description in the appropriate table within the Section pertaining to the weapon or attack style that the Technique Points are being learned. For example, the information on the maximum number of Technique Points available for the different aspects of a character's Dragonknight form is given in the "DRAGONKNIGHT" Section. Nothing has a possible technique of more than 5 points (unless your character has the Universal Talent "Master's Touch").

Training

In order to obtain Technique Points a character must actually train and practice with the weapon, shield, Mystic Force, etc. in which the technique is to be learned.

The amount of training time needed to learn the first Technique Point with any weapon or shield is three hours. Each subsequent Technique Point requires double the training time as the last. So the second Technique Point for a particular weapon would require six hours training, the third would require twelve hours, and so on.

Characters may break the training time up into various smaller training sessions with the following exceptions. The character must train for no less than one hour at a time (with the exception of Technique Points for the different aspects of the Dragonknight form), and the time in between any two training sessions for a given Technique Point may be no longer than five days. If a character waits for more than five days in between training sessions for any given Technique Point all previous Training Time for that Technique Point is lost and the character must start over.

Learning Technique Points

After the required training time has been met the character makes an Agility/Performance Test, unless the Technique Points being learned is in one of the Mystic Forces in which case a Sixth Sense/Performance Test is made to determine how well they have been performing and whether or not they have acquired any Technique Points. Players may add +1 to the result of the roll if the weapon trained with is of their character's own Specialty.

Additionally if the character's training was instructed by another person who already has Technique Points with the same weapon, Mystic Force, etc. with which the character is training, the character may add a number of points equal to the difference in the trainer's total number of Technique Points with that particular weapon or Mystic Force and his. In order to receive the bonus from having a trainer, the trainer must assist the character for the entire duration of the training time.

A total result of 8 is required on the attribute/Performance Test for the first Technique Point of any weapon, shield, Mystic Force, etc., 11 for the second, 14 for the third, 17 for the fourth, and 20 for the fifth.

Unlike failing a Progress Test for a Skill, failing the attribute/Performance Test for obtaining any given Technique Point does not increase the Difficulty Value for obtaining that Technique Point on the next try. The time spent in training is simply wasted.

Nayrim is training for his second Technique Point with the broadsword. The Difficulty Value for the Agility/Performance Test to learn the second Technique Point is 11. The Training Time for the second Technique Point is six hours.

For then entire duration of the Training Time Nayrim is instructed and coached by a Blade Master who has 4 Technique Points with the broadsword. Since Nayrim has 1 Technique Point with the broadsword he may add +3 to the result of his Agility/Performance Test for learning his second Technique Point (Nayrim's instructor has 3 more Technique Points with the broadsword than he does).

At the end of the six hours of training Nayrim makes an Agility/Performance Test with a result of 9. To this he adds the +3 point bonus that he gains from his skilled instructor for a total Test result of 12. Nayrim has learned his second Technique Point with the broadsword. Had he failed the Test he could attempt it again after completing another six hours of training. The Difficulty Value for the Test would remain 11.

Benefits of Technique Points

For each Technique Point that a character has in a particular weapon, shield, Mystic Force, or Dragonknight attack type they may add 1 point to any attacks and/or Defenses made with that weapon, shield, Mystic Force, or Dragonknight attack type. Technique Points do not add to the damage of these attacks, only the attack value (or Defense).

Technique Points in the Mystic Forces aid in the learning of Force-effects (each point of Technique in any of the Mystic Forces contained within the Force-effect to be learned adds 1 point the Sixth Sense/Performance Test made to learn it) as well as the actual attacks made with the Force-effects. Technique Points do not give bonuses to meditation Tests.

Learning Technique Points in the various aspects of Dragonknight and for the Mystic Forces has some differences compared to the learning of Technique Points with weapons or shields.

The Training Time for all of the various aspects of Dragonknight in which Technique Points can be learned is as follows: 1st Technique Point = 5 Turns, the 2nd = 7 Turns, the 3rd = 9, the 4th = 11, and the 5th = 13. All of this train-

ing must be done in Dragonknight form in one continuous training session, and the Tests for learning Technique Points in any of the various aspects of the Dragonknight form is an Agility/Performance Test.

Learning Technique Points in the Mystic Forces requires that the Shinkai initiate and release conjuring, or draw upon and release a Mystic Force, 16 times per hour for the full duration of the Training Time (that is 8 points of Force Energy per hour). Characters can only learn Technique Points in one Mystic Force at a time.

THE MARK

Characters who do enough in service of the Light and have risked their lives in the attempt to vanquish the Shadow receive a reward from the Light known as "The Mark".

In order for a character to receive The Mark they must have 500 or more Total Light Points and can not have more than 4.5 Total Shadow Points. At the time that the character meets these requirements their entire body will glow with a bright golden light for a few moments and then The Mark and all of its accompanying abilities will immediately manifest.

The Mark appears as the image of a golden streak of lightning on one of the recipient's forearms. The benefits of The Mark are listed and discussed below.

1. The Shinkai's Life Force increases by 10 points (this affects their Force Failure and Injury Rating accordingly).

2. The Shinkai permanently gains a +5 point bonus on the results of all Random-roll Sixth Sense Tests and Sixth Sense/Performance Tests.

3. The Shinkai's natural lifespan is increased by fifty years.

4. This character now gets the attribute of your choice raised by 2 Levels for every 20 Light Points earned instead of by 1 Level.

5. The Shinkai has a positive effect on all other beings near him (generally ten feet or closer). These beings tend to become more friendly, display a strong concern for the well-being of others and the promotion of the Light, and seem to have an overall boost in morale. The effects are not severe, however, and wear off within minutes after leaving the presence of the Shinkai with The Mark.

6. The Mark is visible on a character's Dragonknight form as well as their ruling-race form. Dragonknight characters that receive The Mark instantly gain a new breath attack called "Silver Storm".

Silver Storm

This type of breath shoots forth a stream of thousands of silver energy particles. If a being is struck by this breath the silver energy particles explode into a violent rage of crackling energy that surrounds the being's entire body for 2 full Turns. This storm of energy causes severe burns to the victim and also directly attacks their Life Force.

Victims of this breath attack suffer Level 15 +15 points of damage for each of the 2 Turns that the silver storm lasts, and receive an automatic injury from the burns in addition to any injuries that the actual damage may have caused.

This type of breath doesn't spread out very much at all. It maintains an approximate one to two foot diameter throughout its range.

Maximum Range: 200 feet
Defense: Dodge

7. Enchanter characters now gain the permanent ability to have any enchantment that they create to be complete buffered from reacting with any other enchantments containing the same combination of Mystic Forces. This buffering eliminates all four types of adverse reactions that would normally occur when conflicting enchantments are brought together.

In order to play **Mystic Forces** you must have a group of players and a Game Master, or GM. Though the GM is not technically considered a player he is by no means left out of the game. Where each player only runs their one character, the GM runs every non-player character and creature that the characters can encounter within the game. The GM's responsibility is much greater than that of the average player, but so are the rewards.

This Section will describe many of the different aspects of the game that the GM will encounter and have to deal with. By the time you finish reading this Section you should know whether or not Game Mastering is for you as well as knowing the responsibilities that the GM has. Also discussed in this Section is many tips to help make your Game Mastering experience as enjoyable and efficient as possible, both for you and the players.

THE GAME MASTER'S JOB

The Game Master's primary job is to control the flow of events within the game. This includes resolving any actions that the players' characters take as well as controlling the actions of any non-player characters or creatures. The GM sets the mood for whatever situation or setting that the characters are in by describing what the characters see, hear, smell, etc. Good story-telling is also an essential part of the GM's arsenal.

The GM has many responsibilities in running a gaming session. Without him there is no one to referee the situations that the characters become involved in or to control the opposition and allies that the characters may meet. Simply put, without a GM there is no way to play **Mystic Forces** in its intended form.

Many of the responsibilities and jobs that a GM will face are described in this Section, along with many tips on how your Game Mastering can make the gaming experience more enjoyable for you as well as the players. Though the GM has the most difficult role within the game, he experiences rewards and an enjoyment that the players can not.

Is Game Mastering for Me?

A question that you may have is how do I know if I want to be the GM or a player. There are several ways in which you could answer this question. If you enjoy story-telling or being the one in control of events and knowing all of the behind-the-scenes details then you may want to consider Game Mastering. If you like being surprised or are the type that enjoys listening to stories rather than telling them, you may not want to be a GM.

A very common method of determining the GM of any gaming group is who owns the rulebook that you are reading right now. Chances are, if you are the one that has purchased this book you are going to be the one who has read the rules

first and you will be the one telling your friends about the game and asking them to play. This in itself will most likely draft you into being the GM.

If you try Game Mastering for a while and find that it is not for you, then let someone else give it a try. Game Mastering is not for everyone. I personally have more fun Game Mastering than being a player, but for many people the opposite is true. Bottom line; if you enjoy being a Game Mater then stick with it, if you don't then find someone else that does. The purpose of a game is to have fun and having a GM that enjoys being the GM greatly assists in that goal.

Hopefully by now you have decided whether or not you want to give Game Mastering a shot, and since you are still reading this Section it is a safe assumption that you do.

There are several jobs that you will have to perform regularly as part of your GM responsibilities. The rest of this Section will discuss these jobs as well as tips and tricks to make your job as GM as rewarding as possible.

AWARDING LIGHT POINTS

Light Points are necessary for many vital parts of progressing a character. Players love nothing more than to rake in the Light Points. Though it *is* nice to earn lots of Light Points you should make sure that the characters are actually earning them. Over-rewarding Light Points takes the appreciation and challenge out of the game. Players like to feel like they have accomplished something and that their character has advanced because they have played well and earned it. If the only reason that their characters have the number of Light Points that they do is because you have handed out Light Points like giving out candy they won't feel as if they've earned them, and eventually that will take a lot of the fun out of the game. On the other hand, you don't want to be too conservative in awarding Light Points. When players put long hours into a gaming session and don't get a decent reward for their efforts they will be disappointed and possibly discouraged from even playing. Learning to award an adequate number of Light Points is a vital part of good Game Mastering.

Vanquishing evil, promoting the Light, helping others, and self-sacrifice are the most common reasons for awarding Light Points.

Vanquishing evil includes such things as defeating Shadow-kin or other creatures that are a threat to the innocent or to the livelihood of Oryathar. In the "CREATURE LORE" Section of the rules the maximum number of Light Points that the defeat of any given creature is worth is listed with the creature's description.

Promoting the Light includes such things being a positive role-model for others, persuading and assisting others to follow the Light and standing against the Shadow.

Helping others includes such things as protecting and offering assistance to those in need and providing for those who

are in need.

Self-sacrifice includes things such as putting yourself at risk whenever it is necessary, going without so that others may have, and choosing the difficult path because it is the right thing though an easier, but corrupt, path is available.

Light Points are the most commonly awarded type of points within the game, so there will most likely be numerous instances throughout any gaming session that characters will be earning them. If you like you may award Light Points, and Character Points and Shadow Points for that matter, at the time that they are earned or only at the end of the gaming session or at a set point mid-way through the gaming session. Most players like to receive the Light Points as their character earns them so that they can immediately spend them, however this can greatly disrupt the flow of the game and waste time if you stop the game every thirty minutes to give out Light Points and allow the players to spend them. It is your decision as to when to award the various types of points that the characters earn, but you should try to choose a method that works well with your particular group of players and doesn't greatly distract from the mood of the game or flow of events.

AWARDING CHARACTER POINTS

Character Points are awarded for getting into character and for creative role-playing. Getting into character simply means that you are displaying the characteristics of the character that you are running or you attempt to make your dialogue the dialogue that your character is actually using. For example, if a player wants his character to ask a merchant for a better deal on a sword that he wants to buy he might say to the GM, "My character is going to ask the merchant if he can give me a better deal." Or he may look to the GM, who is playing the part of the merchant, and say in a voice imitative of his character's, "How about coming down a coin or two for an honest paying customer." The latter is a good example of getting into character and could be worth Character Points.

Creative role-playing may be coming up with a very clever or ingenious way of solving a problem or overcoming a situation. It could also be the use of a Talent, Skill, or Force-effect in a unique way.

Generally speaking, Character Points should be awarded in smaller amounts than Light Points. The only thing that Character Points can be spent on is Universal Talents, which should be somewhat challenging to obtain. So flooding your players with Character Points and allowing them to obtain Universal Talents too rapidly will take a lot of the fun and challenge out of the game. In most situations .5 Character Points is a fair amount to award for each exceptional display of getting into character or creative role-playing.

If players so choose they can trade their character's Character Points in for Light Points. For each 5 Character Points that they trade in they may receive 1 Light Point. They may not spend 2.5 Character Points for .5 Light Points or 7.5 Character Points for 1.5 Light Points. The Character Points can only be traded in 5 point increments.

AWARDING SHADOW POINTS

It is never a good thing to have to award someone's character with Shadow Points, but the concept of **Mystic Forces** and the ideas and beliefs that Shinkai stand for should be upheld to a high standard. If characters perform actions that are worthy of Shadow Points don't hesitate to award them. Just be careful not to award too many Shadow Points. Remember, if a character has 8.5 or more Current Shadow Points at any one time they become Korgathool and the character is removed from the game.

Shadow Points are awarded for performing any action that intentionally supports or promotes the Shadow or is counter-productive to serving the Light. Lying, stealing, attacking another ruling-race or innocent being without just cause, or acting in any manner that is considered negative are just a few examples.

Actions that would be considered to intentionally support or promote the Shadow or be counter-productive to serving the Light would include such actions as disrupting or resisting the laws and authorities of the land, refusing to help someone in need or preventing someone in need from receiving help, or assisting Shadow-sworn or Shadow-kin in their evil ventures. The other actions that are worthy of receiving Shadow Points, lying, stealing, attacking an innocent without just cause, etc., are fairly self-explanatory.

Just use your own judgement as to whether or not an action is worthy of Shadow Points. Most everyone is very much aware of what actions are considered good or positive and what types of actions are negative or "un-Lightworthy".

Minor infractions or actions that are Shadow Point worthy should typically be met with the awarding of .5 to 1 Shadow Points. Serious infractions or blatant attempts to serve the Shadow and/or resist the Light should be met with a minimum of 1.5 Shadow Points to as many as 4 Shadow Points for a single occurance.

TESTS

Tests are made to determine a character's success in performing various tasks as well as determining many other things throughout the game. The rules clearly state what type of Test, if any, is needed to perform most all of the common actions and tasks that your character may attempt. There may be times, however, when a player wants his character to do something that isn't covered in the rules and you may not know exactly what type of Test that he needs to make. In these situations just use your best judgment along with the examples laid out throughout this rulebook and you should have no problem in determining the type of Test that would best determine the outcome or success of the action.

There are three basic types of Tests that characters will have to make. Tests are performed by rolling dice and using the results in conjunction with the character's various attribute Levels. The three types of Tests are the Attribute/Performance Test, Attribute Test, and the Random-roll Attribute Test (the word "attribute" is substituted in place of one of the six actual attributes).

As an optional rule you may allow players to spend 1 Light Point before any Test is made in order to make any dice rolled for the Test re-rollable on a max roll.

Depending upon the attribute, only certain types of Tests can be made. The following list shows the different types of Tests that a character may make with the different attributes.

Agility
Agility/Performance Test or Random-roll Agility Test
Strength
Strength Test or Random-roll Strength Test
Endurance
Endurance Test or Random-roll Endurance Test
Willpower
Willpower Test or Random-roll Willpower Test
Intelligence
Intelligence Test or Random-roll Intelligence Test
Sixth Sense
Sixth Sense/Performance Test or Random-roll Sixth Sense Test

ATTRIBUTE/PERFORMANCE TEST

Attribute/Performance Tests (ie. Agility/Performance Test) are performed by rolling 1D12 (the Performance Die) and adding the current Level of the appropriate attribute to the result (only Agility & Sixth Sense have attribute/Performance Tests). So if your character's Agility is currently Level 7 and he makes an Agility/Performance Test you would roll 1D12 and add the result to 7 for the total result of the Test.

Attribute/Performance Tests are made for most any type of attack that your character makes or Defense that he sets as well as many other tasks. Any time that a 1 is rolled on the Performance Die this is called a "Feeble Attempt". The 1 is not added to the Test and the Test is also penalized by -1D4. Any time that a 12 is rolled on the Performance Die this is called a "Flawless Performance". The 12 is added to the Test and the Test also receives a +1D4 point bonus.

ATTRIBUTE TEST

Attribute Tests (ie. Strength Test) are performed by rolling the dice for the current Level of the appropriate attribute and adding the attribute's current Level to the result. So if your character's current Intelligence Level is Level 9 and he makes an Intelligence Test you would roll 1D10 + 1D8 (the dice for Level 9) and add the results of the dice rolls to a value of 9 (your character's current Intelligence Level) for the total result of the Test.

Attribute Tests are made for many common tasks such as attempting to locate traps or spot someone hiding in the distance, or to resist Force Failure or the effects of various poisons or Force-effects.

RANDOM-ROLL ATTRIBUTE TEST

Random-roll Attribute Tests (ie. Random-roll Intelligence Test) are performed in the same way that normal attribute Tests are performed except you may not add the Level of the attribute to the result of the dice roll. The results of the dice roll is the total result of the Test. So if your character had to make a Random-roll Sixth Sense Test and he had a current Sixth Sense of Level 11 you would roll 1D12 + 1D10 (the dice for Level 11). The total value of the dice rolls are the result of the Test.

Random-roll attribute Tests are made for many of the same reasons that normal attribute Tests or attribute/Performance Tests are made, but when the character may not be prepared for or concentrating on the task that he is trying to perform. For example, a character that is intentionally looking for someone trying to ambush them from some nearby weeds may be allowed to make an Intelligence Test in order to spot them, but if they were not specifically looking for the ambush and just out for a stroll the GM would most likely allow them to make a Random-roll Intelligence Test to see if they notice the ambush. Or lets say that a character is specifically attempting to notice if they can feel any hint of the presence of the Shadow. The GM may allow them to make a Sixth Sense/Performance Test to see if they can sense it (if it is present), but if they were not attempting to notice it the GM may simply allow them to make a Random-roll Sixth Sense Test to see if they happen to notice it.

Generally, you would not tell the players what they are making the Random-roll Tests for, unless they are successful at which point you might declare to them the outcome. For example, you wouldn't say to the player, "Make me a Random-roll intelligence Test to see if your character notices the creatures hiding in the nearby bushes". You would simply tell them to make the Test, then if they are successful you would inform them of what their character notices. If they were not successful then you could conclude the situation in any way that you like. Perhaps by letting them continue on and never informing them of what the Test was for, or by allowing them to be ambushed and attacked by the creatures.

SPECIAL TASKS

Mystic Forces is a very detailed game with many options and possibilities. Though there are rules for most all common types of actions and tasks that characters can attempt, it would be impossible to write a rule for every possible action that a player may come up with for his character to attempt. Whenever a character attempts an action or task that is not specifically covered by the rules it is called a special task.

The following "SPECIAL TASK DIFFICULTY" table is used to determine the difficulty of these special tasks. Take it from a long-time GM, players will frequently come up with things that they want their character's to do that there are no actual rules for. When such occasions arise you may simply decide to determine the outcome through role-playing, or you may want them to make a Test to determine if the success of the task. If the latter is your choice, then you will find the "SPECIAL TASK DIFFICULTY" table very helpful.

SPECIAL TASK DIFFICULTY	
Task Difficulty	**Difficulty Value**
Very Easy	2-4
Easy	5-9
Average	10-18
Challenging	19-27
Difficult	28-36
Very Difficult	37-45
Nearly Impossible	46-up

Let's say that a player wants his character to try to swing on a rope from the bridge of a ship and land on the dock while only holding on to the rope with his teeth. There is no rule in this book for grasping a rope in your teeth and swinging from it. This is where the "SPECIAL TASK DIFFI-CULTY" table comes in. The GM simply chooses how difficult that he feels that the task is from the seven levels of difficulty listed under the "Task Difficulty" column. He now goes straight across from the appropriate level of difficulty to the "Difficulty Value" column. The value listed here is the average range of Difficulty Values for a task of that difficulty.

The GM will now decide what type of Test will be required to perform the task. Tasks that require high levels of Agility should require an Agility/Performance Test or Random-roll Agility Test (Agility/Performance Test if the character was concentrating on the task and Random-roll Agility Test if he ended up performing the task off-guard or by surprise). Tasks that require high levels of reasoning or observation skills should require an Intelligence Test or Random-roll Intelligence Test (Intelligence Test if the character was concentrating on the task and Random-roll Intelligence Test if he ended up performing the task off-guard or was not actually concentrating on the task at hand), etc.

Using the example above, swinging on a rope by one's teeth, we will now use the "SPECIAL TASK DIFFICULTY" table to determine the Difficulty Value for such a task. The GM decides that such a task would at least be considered very difficult. Looking across from Very Difficult on the table we find that the proposed Difficulty Value is between 37 and 45. The GM decides that the Difficulty Value should be in the upper borders of the Very Difficult range so he assigns a Difficulty Value of 42 to the task.

Now to decide what type of Test is necessary to perform the task. The GM decides that swinging from a rope by your teeth is probably more agility related than anything else, and so determines that an Agility/Performance Test is required to perform such a task. The character must make a successful Agility/Performance Test against a Difficulty Value of 42 in order to successfully swing from the rope by his teeth and land on the dock.

The "SPECIAL TASK DIFFICULTY" table is simply a guideline for your convenience. Feel free to modify the difficulty ratings or Difficulty Values as needed.

GENERAL TIPS

There are many things that you can do as GM that will make it much easier to keep the game running smoothly and enjoyably. Though much of being a good GM will come only with time and experience, the following tips should be of some assistance in your journey to becoming the greatest Game Master of all time.

A. Know the Rules

One of the single largest factors that will affect how smoothly you are able to run a game session is your knowledge of the rules. Though it is not necessary that you know and memorize every detail of the rules in this book it *is* necessary that you at least have a general knowledge and understanding of all of the basic rules and concepts of the game. If you have to halt the game every time that a question arises and read through a section of the rules you are going to waste a lot of time and lose the attention of the players. Even if you don't know the exact answer to the question or what a particular rule states you should be familiar enough with the rules to know where to look for the answer.

Knowing the rules well will make your job as GM much easier and will also increase the enjoyment of the game and the amount of actual playing time of each game session.

B. Keep Order

The typical gaming session consists of around five players. As GM you will have to keep up with what each player wants their character to do, the actions of all of the characters, as well as determining which character's actions are resolved first. During every Turn of a gaming sessions there

will be of necessity a lot of talking going on. You must relay all information pertinent to the immediate setting to your players and they must relay to you what actions they want their characters to take. If you have all of the players at the table talking among themselves or trying to speak to you all at once you are going to find that it is very difficult to concentrate or keep up with who is doing what and when they are supposed to be doing it. Keeping order at the gaming table is therefore a must.

One of my favorite ways to keep down the level of chaos is to simply start with the player to either my left or right and then go around the table asking each player one at a time what their character's intended actions are. This allows me to focus on each individual player and also keeps down the commotion so that the other players can be aware of what each of their comrades is going to do.

Everybody wants to have fun and be able to joke and cut up with each other during the game, but unless you find some way of keeping everyone in order you will spend a large part of each gaming session being frustrated and trying to determine what everyone is doing instead of actually playing.

C. Be Fair

This is self-explanatory. It is not the GM's job to try and kill all of the characters, neither is it his job to alter situations so that the characters always prevail. A good GM will be impartial and play by the rules. If you fudge your dice rolls to give one a character a break you will have to do it for all of them and before long you have taken all of the challenge and risk out of the game. It is best to let the chips fall where they may.

You also want to to be careful not to place characters in situations that you know are overwhelming for them. You want encounters to be challenging but at the same time you don't want to put characters in situations where the odds are slim that they will survive. Most GMs will do their best to be fair and helpful to the players and their characters but if a player has his character do something foolish and gets it killed by all means the GM should not fudge the rules and allow his character to survive.

D. Be consistent

There will be many times that you will have to make decisions on events or actions for which there are no rules. Use your best judgement in determining how to resolve the situation and above all else be consistent. Don't interpret a rule one way for one player and then change it for another. If you come up with a ruling for any aspect of the game stick to it. If you constantly alter how you interpret rules or make judgment calls your players may feel that you are showing favoritism or simply being unfair. So, if you are consistent and a situation arises where you have to make a ruling that may not be how a player would like it to be you can always

say, "This is the way I always determine this", or "This is how I have determined this before and I don't think I should change it". This will take a lot of the pressure off of you and make for a smoother and more fair gaming session.

E. Keep it Fun

Sometimes it is easy to get too caught up in trying to keep the rules straight and make sure that everything is running smooth and that you are doing everything that you are supposed to be doing. Try not to become so stressed and engrossed with the technical aspects of the game that you or the other players are no longer having fun. Remember, this is a game and it is meant to be fun. Relax and enjoy the game, if there are rules that you are unsure of don't worry about it, just do the best that you can with it and above all else have fun.

F. Don't Be a Rules Cop

Though it is extremely important that you understand the rules and make sure that all of the players are playing by the rules, you don't want to be what some refer to as a rules cop. Your main priority in playing and Game Mastering **Mystic Forces** is to have fun. If your main goal is to point out every little mistake or pick out every detail of the rules that someone may be doing wrong you are going to lose out on the fun that the game is meant to be, not to mention you are going to make a lot of people mad. Now I'm not saying that you don't try to enforce the rules, for without rules the game would be nothing but a meaningless assembly of words, but you don't want to overdo it. If a player makes a small mistake or oversight in the rules don't make a big deal out of it. After the game session is over you can go over the rules with the player and help them to correct any errors they may have made.

G. Don't Be Predictable

It's very easy to find a certain type of setting or certain types of encounters that you like to run, but avoid becoming predictable. Players should have to wonder what awaits them over the next hill or in the next town. If you always have every stranger that the characters meet to be a villain who tries to rob them, or if every adventure is about rescuing someone the players will quickly become bored with the game. Do your best to keep the game as exciting and unpredictable as possible. Most players enjoy being challenged and not knowing exactly what the next encounter will bring.

H. Improvise and Customize Rules

There will be many situations and circumstances that will eventually arise during game play that you will not know exactly how it should be handled. There will also no doubt be situations where players try to use elements of the game in an unusual manner and you may not know exactly how the situation should be resolved. There may be times that you

find certain rules in conflict because of a specific action taken. In these circumstances you should feel free to improvise and customize the rules to handle the situation. Simply use your own judgment and the principals laid out in the rules to come up with the most logical method of resolving the situation.

I. Announce Test Difficulties

Consider announcing to players the Difficulty Values that they must achieve in order to pass any given Test. For example, if a character walks by a bush where a creature is hiding and you want to give them a chance of spotting, it you may have them make a Random-roll Intelligence Test. After you have determined what Difficulty Value is necessary to spot the creature announce to the player what value they must get in order to pass the Test. You don't need to tell them why they are making the Test in this case, but you could still announce to them the Difficulty Value for the Test that they are making. Something like, "You will need to get a result of 12 or higher on this Test in order to be successful."

Announcing the Difficulty Values of Tests before the players actually roll the dice give the players a solid goal to shoot for and takes away any doubt that you may be altering the Difficulty Values or unfairly determining whether they pass or fail the Test.

There will be instances where you may not want to announce the Difficulty Value required for a Test, but generally it is good to do so.

J. Prepare in Advance

Be prepared in advance for your gaming sessions. Make sure that you know what events and encounters are coming up in the adventure and be sure that you understand any and all details of the adventure that the characters may possibly face in the coming gaming session. No one likes to sit at the table and wait while the GM digs through his notes or the adventure to try to figure out exactly what is going on and how he is supposed to run each encounter. You may also want to get all of the supplements and items that you will need for the gaming session together ahead of time. This includes pencils, dice, character sheets, rulebook, etc. If you do your homework ahead of time you will find that the gaming session will go much smoother and you and the players spend more time actually playing the game and enjoying the adventure instead of just sitting at the table and waiting while you are trying to get organized.

K. Don't Overdo Your Adventures With Too Many Meaningless Choices

One flaw that many adventures have is that they are filled with too many meaningless and distracting options. Adventures should be challenging and detailed, but players should feel like their choices are important and should be able to keep up with the events of the adventure. One example of overdoing it is what I like to call the endless maze. It

goes something like this;

GM: "As you turn the corner you see a long hallway stretching out before you. There are four doors on the left side of the hall and five on the right."

Player: "My character will go through the first door on the right."

GM: "When you open the door you see a short hallway before you with one door on the left and two on the right. The hallway ends in a large room that has two doors in the east wall, one in the south wall and three in the west wall."

Player: "Being careful not to make too much noise my character will slowly enter the large room at the end of the hall and go through the door in the south wall."

GM: "When you go through the door in the south wall you find yourself in another room with one door in its east wall, two in the south wall, and two in the west wall."

You get the point. When you present players with too many choices that have little to no real importance they quickly get confused and bored with the game. Players want choices, but not so many that they can't remember them all or keep them straight. Also players like to feel that there is importance in the choices that their characters make, and there should be, but when you have so many random decisions and useless options it takes the strategy and excitement out of the game. Players will develop the attitude of, "Oh well, I'll just go through the first door that I see. It doesn't matter anyway, there will just be a dozen more doors in the next room I enter."

You want to put a lot of detail and options into the adventures that you run, but be careful not to overdo it.

L. Don't Over-empower the Characters

One pitfall that many GMs fall into is allowing the characters to become too powerful too quickly. All players love earning Light Points and finding those powerful and ancient relics, but be careful not to award too many Light Points too fast or to place too many powerful enchanted items into your adventures. If you do, you will find that in a very short time all of the characters are far too powerful and you will have a hard time creating and running adventures that are challenging to them. This is not to say that you should never be generous with awarding Light Points or that you should never allow the characters to discover interesting and powerful enchanted items, but do so with moderation. The players will appreciate it more when they have to work hard to build up their characters and you will find that the gaming sessions run smoother when you don't have a group of players whose characters are so loaded with magical items and extreme abilities that they can't be stopped.

M. Keep the Number of NPCs to a Minimum

Non-player characters (NPCs) are a vital part of any

Mystic Forces adventure. They are the villains, allies, and all other beings and creatures that the player characters will encounter. As GM you have complete control over what type and how many NPCs to place into an adventure. Pre-designed adventure modules will already have all recommended NPCs included, but you may wish to change or add to these. And if you are writing your own adventures it will be entirely up to you as to how many and what type of NPCs to include.

One thing that you want to be wary of in regards to the use of NPCs in an adventure is having too many in any one encounter. If you have five player characters in an encounter with say ten or twelve wretchin then you have fifteen to seventeen different characters to keep up with. This can be extremely frustrating and time consuming, especially if you've not been playing long enough to be comfortable with all of the rules. If you are trying to give a group of advanced characters a challenge you have other options than simply piling on a large number of creatures or NPCs as opposition. You may want to consider one or two larger or more powerful foes instead of a dozen smaller or less powerful foes.

N. Use Miniatures to Help Players Visualize Situations

It is very helpful to use miniatures to represent the characters, creatures and non-player characters in any given situation, especially combat. When you have five or six players doing combat with five or six creatures it can be exceptionally difficult to keep track of where the characters and creatures are and who is fighting who. Using miniatures to represent the position of each character and creature can make it much easier to keep track of complex situations.

Most any hobby store has a variety of miniatures from which you can choose, but you can use virtually anything to represent the characters or creatures. It adds more realism to the game when you use miniatures that resemble the actual characters and creatures, but it's more of a convenience than a necessity. You may also want to consider using game mats with grid lines to help you more accurately determine distances between characters and other objects and beings within the game. Terrain models also make an interesting and colorful addition to the use of miniatures. These also can be found in most hobby stores.

O. Use Music to Enhance the Setting or Mood

The use of music can greatly enhance the mood of a gaming session. I prefer music without words such as ambience music. There are a few companies that sale ambience music designed just for use with role-playing games. Having a specific piece of music to match certain events in the game can greatly add to the mood and excitement. If you find that the use of music is too distracting then don't use it. There are times when I find it enjoyable and times that I don't. To each his own.

P. Role-Play

Though Gms are not awarded Character Points for getting into character they should always do their best to do so. When the GM gets into role-playing out the NPCs it encourages the players to do the same with their characters. Some people don't like to actually get into character as much as they just like playing the game for its mechanics and combat. Other players, however, really enjoy taking on the role of their character and talking and acting in the manner they want their character to behave. I find that it usually makes for a much more interesting and realistic gaming session when you do your part in role-playing out your NPCs. If you are running a creature in a combat situation that is capable of talking don't just say, "Ok i'm attacking you now", or "The wretchin will try to bite you now". Actually change your voice to mimic what you think that creature would sound like and shout out your threats and growls as the creature that you are controlling makes its attacks. Try to make all of the creatures and NPCs that you run seem as realistic as possible, giving them a personality of their own and you'll find that your gaming sessions will be much more captivating and exciting. After all, that is why they call them role-playing games.

Q. Create Your Own Adventures

Though you may purchase pre-constructed adventures with the plot, scenarios, and events already laid out and ready to go, you will also most likely want to create your own adventures. Feel free to improvise the pre-constructed **Mystic Forces** adventures as well as write your own. Creating your own adventures is very fun and interesting and gives you complete control over how the plot proceeds, what kinds of creatures and NPCs that you would like to include, and the level of difficulty that the characters will face. When you create your own adventures feel free to create your own creatures or treasures, or enchanted items to include. Some of the most interesting and enjoyable adventures that I have ever played were written by friends of mine rather than pre-constructed adventures. With a little practice you too will be writing and running adventures that are just as challenging and fun to play as pre-constructed adventures.

SUMMATION

There is no way that anyone or any set of rules can tell you how to be a good GM. That only comes through experience. But it is hoped that the information given in this Section will help you to better yourself as a GM and assist you in running smoother and overall more enjoyable game sessions. The main thing to remember is that you are playing a game. There will undoubtedly be situations where you will have to make judgment calls and come up with rules on the fly, but keep in mind that you are playing a game and if you do make a mistake or don't have an answer for a particular question or situation it's no big deal. Just do the best you can and go on with it.

CREATURE LORE

"It is said by some that knowledge is power. I also agree with this reasoning. Knowing one's enemies is an unparalleled advantage on the field of battle. Some thought it foolish for me to spend so much of my time studying the creatures of Oryathar. Many of my comrades who shared this opinion are now dead. No my friend, make no mistake. Knowledge is power!"

Oryathar is home to an abundant number of creatures. Some are natural creatures, some are mystical creatures with magical abilities, and others are Shadow-kin spawned from the Shadow itself. In any area of Oryathar your character is likely to run into one or more of any of these three main types of creatures. Various scholars and Naturalists have compiled a great deal of information on many of the creatures that inhabit Oryathar. The information that they have gathered has been copied and passed from city to city in the forms of books and scrolls. The study and knowledge of Oryathar's many creatures has become known as creature lore. Most all of the cities and major towns of Oryathar have collected creature lore information. Such information has proved invaluable to the Kingsguard and Defenders of the Light in their fight to restore balance to the land.

Regardless of what type of creature that your character's creature lore studies bring him across there are several categories of information used to describe them that he will need to become familiar with. They are Aggression Rating, Attack, Damage Yield, Attribute and Level, Health, Value, Natural Protection Rating (P.R.), Bulk, Move, and Description. Each of these categories will now be explained in detail.

Aggression Rating

This is a general measure of how aggressive that the creature typically is. Sometimes creatures may behave more or less aggressively than their listed Aggression Rating may imply, but normally the Aggression Rating very accurately describes the creature's temperament.

There are four categories of Aggression Ratings. They are Passive, Moderate, High, and Extreme. Passive creatures will generally avoid conflict and will very rarely attack unless heavily threatened or provoked. They tend to be very shy and elusive.

Creatures with a Moderate Aggression Rating don't normally attack unless provoked or threatened and generally tend to mind their own business.

Creatures with a High Aggression Rating seem to enjoy conflict and will not hesitate to attack anything that invades their territory or poses the least indication of a threat.

Creatures with an Extreme Aggression Rating are by far the most dangerous type of creatures. They need not feel imposed on or threatened to be prompted to attack. They will often go out of their way to attack other beings and most always fight to the death with no regard to pain or personal injury.

Attack

Beside of the "Attack" category is a listing of the different types of attacks that the creature normally uses. When a creature has more than one type of attack that it can employ, the attack types that it uses most frequently will be listed first followed by the second most frequent, etc.

Beside of each type of attack is a positive value, such as +6. This value is the number of points added to the creature's attack value when making that type of attack. It is sort of the equivalent to the bonuses that your character would receive from Talents, Skills, technique, etc.

If there is an asterisk (*) in front of the value for an attack, that means that there is special information in regards to the attack. This information will be given in the creature's description.

Some creatures are able to make more than one attack per Turn. This will be indicated by a number in parentheses beside of "Attack", such as (x2). So a creature that has the following listed for its attack, "Attack: (x3)", can make three attacks per Turn. A creature with "Attack: (x2)" can make two attacks per Turn, etc.

Regardless of the number of attacks that a creature can make per Turn they are all considered one Major Action. All of a creature's multiple attacks take one right after the other. If the creature's first attack occurs at an Initiative value of 10, the second will occur at an Initiative value of 9 and so on.

Damage Yield

Beside of the "Damage Yield" category there is a value listed beside of an L, such as L6. The L stands for Level. This is a listing of the Damage Yield Level that each of the creature's attacks will do. If a positive value is given after the Damage Yield Level, such as L10 +10, that means that after the dice for the listed Level have been rolled you will add that value to it. So for an attack that has L10 +10 listed as its Damage Yield you will roll the dice for Level 10, which is 2D10 and then add 10 points to the result. Sometimes the Damage Yield for an attack is listed as the actual dice to be rolled for the attack instead of as a Level.

Unless stated otherwise in the creature's description, the damage from a physical attack from a creature is determined in the same manner as the damage from a physical attack that you may make. You will roll the dice that match the Level for the Damage Yield of the particular type of attack made and then add that value to a value equal to two times the current Strength Level of the creature. So a creature that has a current Strength of Level 7 that makes a successful attack with its claws that have a Damage Yield of L4 would have the damage value of the attack determined by rolling 1D8 (the dice for Level 4) and then adding the result to a value of 14 (two times its Strength Level).

If there is an asterisk (*) in front of the the listed Damage Yield Level for an attack that means that there is special information in regards to the damage of the attack. This information will be given in the creature's description.

Attribute and Level

Beneath the "Attribute" category is a listing of the creature's six attributes. Across from each attribute under the "Level" category is the creature's normal Level for that

attribute. Attribute Tests for creatures are made in the same way as those for ruling-races.

With ruling-races the attributes themselves are used to calculate many factors such as Life Force, Movement, Lifting Limit & Carrying Capacity. With creatures the attributes are normally not used in determining these values. The Life Force and Move for creatures are predetermined based on the creature's anatomy, size, and other factors. You will notice that there is no Lifting Limit or Carrying Capacity listed for creatures. This is because it is rare that such information will be necessary (most creatures don't carry equipment or items and their capacity for lifting and carrying is not a big factor within the game). If you do find it necessary to know how much that a particular creature can lift or carry the GM may assign any value that he feels is appropriate for the given creature.

The Levels for the Intelligence of creatures means something slightly different than it does for ruling-races. The "RULING-RACE INTELLIGENCE" table commonly describes the various Levels of a ruling-race's Intelligence by their ability to read or write. No creatures are able to read or write therefore the definitions of their various Levels of Intelligence are described somewhat differently than those for ruling-races.

The following "CREATURE INTELLIGENCE" table briefly describes the meaning of of a creature's intelligence based on its Intelligence Level.

CREATURE INTELLIGENCE	
Intelligence	**Description**
Level 1-2	Extremely poor logic & slow witted
Level 3-4	Poor logic & slow witted
Level 5-6	Average intelligence
Level 7-8	Above average intelligence. Crafty and has good sense of logic
Level 9-up	Highly intelligent. Extremely sharp-witted and cunning.

Health

This category contains the creature's Life Force, Force Failure, Injury Rating, and Recovery, all of which work in exactly the same way as they do for the ruling-races.

The value listed beside of "Life Force" is the amount of damage that the creature must accumulate before it is killed.

"Force Failure" is the amount of damage that the creature must accumulate before it will possibly black out (creatures can also make a Willpower Test against a Difficulty Value of 10 to resist blacking out due to accumulated damage).

"Injury Rating" is the amount of damage that the creature must receive at one time in order for it to be injured.

Lastly "Recovery" gives the dice rolled to determine how much damage the creature can naturally recover (Recovery Test). Creatures, like ruling-races, recover damage once every two hours and receive three Recovery Tests per day.

Life Force, Force Failure, and Injury Ratings for creatures are not calculated in the same way that they are for ruling-races. For one thing only the Levels are listed for creatures' attributes, and if they were adding the values for the creature's Strength, Endurance, and Willpower Levels still will not add up to give you the creature's Life Force. Creatures are designed totally different than ruling-races and their Life Force is not necessarily based on their attributes.

When making up your own creatures simply choose a Life Force value that you think is appropriate for the type of creature that you have created. The Force Failure and Injury Rating are then calculated from the Life Force value as normal (Injury Rating is one fourth of the Life Force, rounded up, and the Force Failure is the difference between the Injury Rating and the Life Force).

Value

Beside of "Value" is a number of Light Points (L.P.). This is the maximum number of Light Points that should be awarded for defeating that particular creature. Each player should be awarded an amount of Light Points, up to the maximum that the creature is worth, based upon how much they assisted or participated in the defeat of that creature. For example, Kardan has been battling it out with a kicker for 4 Turns and has the kicker almost defeated, and then on the fourth Turn Arkus steps out from behind his hiding spot and shoots the kicker with his bow and kills it. The maximum Light Points to be awarded for a kicker is 7. Because Kardan fought the kicker from the beginning and did the most to defeat it the GM decides that he will award him with the maximum Light Points that the kicker is worth, 7. Because Arkus' participation and assistance was minimal the GM decides that he will only award him 3 of the possible 7 Light Points that the kicker is worth.

Though the value for most creatures is listed as Light Points it may be that the GM will reward your character with Shadow Points instead of Light Points. Shadow-kin are always worth Light Points when defeated, but natural creatures and mystical creatures are a different story. If your character attacks a natural or mystical creature without cause or provocation the GM should award him with 1 to 2 Shadow Points.

The number of Shadow Points to be awarded for attacking a creature without just cause is not the same as the number of Light Points that it is worth if your character defeats it due to necessary circumstances. Though the creature may be worth 5 or 6 Light Points, the number of Shadow Points given for attacking or killing the creature without just cause will still only be 1 or 2.

A few creatures, such as white wolves and unicorns for example, are only worth Shadow Points for being defeated. This is because such creatures are pure in intentions and will never attack those who follow the Light without a justified reason.

Natural P.R. (Protection Rating)

Many creatures have tough hides or skins that offer them protection much in the same manner that armor offers protection to the ruling-races. Even one of the ruling-races, Grak, have a Natural Protection Rating.

The value beside of the "Natural P.R." category is the amount of protection that the creature's hide or skin offers them. Like armor, this value is subtracted from the damage rendered to the creature. So, a creature with a Natural P.R. of 4 that gets hit with an attack that renders 25 points of damage will actually only receive 21 points of damage. Its own skin absorbed 4 points of the damage.

Bulk Value

"Bulk Value" represents the general bulkiness and size of the creature. The greater the value the larger and bulkier the creature is.

Bulk Values are often used to determine what bonuses or penalties are rendered to those trying to attack a creature with a ranged weapon (see the "COMBAT" section for information on how Bulk Value effects ranged attacks).

Move

Beside of this category is one or two sets of values. A set of values in parentheses is the creature's flight movement and a set of values with no parentheses is the creature's ground movement. So a creature that has a set of movement values in parentheses and a set of movement value without parentheses is capable of moving on the ground as well as flying. A creature that only has a set of movement values without parentheses is not capable of flying. And a creature that only has a set of movement values inside of parentheses can fly but is incapable of measurable movement on the ground.

With each set of numbers there will be a value before and after a backslash (/). The value before the backslash is the creature's Maximum Speed and the value after the backslash is the creature's Action Movement.

Maximum Speed is just what it sounds like. It is the fastest speed, in feet per Turn, that the creature is capable of moving. Action Movement on the other hand does not represent a speed but rather a distance. It is the maximum number of feet that the creature can move in a single Turn and still perform a Major Action, unless the Major Action is actually performed while the creature is moving.

A creature can move its Action Movement at any speed that it wishes. So a creature with a Move of 330/110 that has already performed a Major Action and then wishes to run toward another target can only cover 110 feet during that Turn, but may cover that 110 feet at a speed of 330 feet per Turn (330'/T).

Movement for creatures is not determined in the same way that it is for ruling-races. It is not solely based on the creature's Agility and Strength. Much of the creature's body structure and composition determine how quickly it can move.

When making up your own creatures simply choose Move values that you think are appropriate for the type of creature that you have created.

Description

This is a detailed description of the creature's physical traits, special information about its attacks, and any other information felt to be useful about the creature.

NATURAL CREATURES

Many of the creatures that inhabit Oryathar are quite harmless but some are extremely dangerous. Some of the natural creatures of Oryathar are very efficient predators, and though they may not intentionally seek out ruling-races some of these creatures will not hesitate to attack ruling-races if their territory is invaded or if they feel threatened.

A large number of the natural creatures of Oryathar are hunted and killed by the ruling-races as food sources as well as for clothing. Bear, rabbit, and deer are just a few examples of creatures that are hunted by the ruling-races.

Some breeds of natural creatures have been domesticated by the ruling-races to be used for transportation, work animals, and even pets. Some such creatures include horses, bleyk, and dogs.

The following is a compilation of many of the natural creatures that inhabit Oryathar.

BAT

Aggression Rating: Passive
Attack: Bite = +6
Damage Yield: Bite = * L2

Attribute	Level	Health
Agility	30	Life Force: 12
Strength	2	Force Failure: 9
Endurance	2	Inj. Rating: 3
Willpower	3	Recovery: 1D4
Intelligence	2	
Sixth Sense	2	Value: 1 L.P.

Natural P.R.: 0
Bulk Value: .5
Move: (330/110)

Description

Bats are small nocturnal creatures with thin leathery wings. They are extremely agile. Though they feed strictly on insects some bats have been known to attack livestock and even ruling-races.

Anyone bitten by a bat runs a risk of acquiring a severe sickness from the saliva that is transmitted during the bite. A

bitten being has a seventy five percent chance of acquiring the sickness. The sickness manifests on the third day after being bitten. It causes the victim to lose 1 point of Strength per day until their Strength Value reaches 0, at which point they die. The only two known means of curing this sickness is ingesting the root of the vyourin plant and the Force-effect "Cure".

BEAR

Aggression Rating: Moderate
Attack: Claws = +4, Bite = +3
Damage Yield: Claws = L4, Bite = L6

Attribute	Level	Health
Agility	8	Life Force: 220
Strength	32	Force Failure: 146
Endurance	10	Inj. Rating: 74
Willpower	6	Recovery: 2D10
Intelligence	5	
Sixth Sense	3	Value: 6 L.P.

Natural P.R.: 4
Bulk Value: 8
Move: 330/110

Description

The bear is a very common animal found mostly in wooded areas. They are approximately six feet in height and weigh an average of four hundred pounds. Bears are very strong and also very agile for their size. They have sharp claws on their paws and their crushing bite is powerful enough to snap bones. The most common color of bears is dark brown and black although a few grey bears have been spotted from time to time.

Bears often feed on berries but will also hunt and kill other animals such as deer. Unless provoked or threatened bears are not generally a threat to the ruling-races, but they have been known to attack and kill ruling-races on rare occasions.

Bears are often hunted by the ruling-races as a source of food and their thick fur makes their hides valuable for making clothing.

BLEYK

Aggression Rating: Moderate
Attack: Horn = +3, Feet = +2
Damage Yield: Horn = L5, Feet = L2

Attribute	Level	Health
Agility	7	Life Force: 160
Strength	26	Force Failure: 120
Endurance	10	Inj. Rating: 40
Willpower	8	Recovery: 2D10
Intelligence	4	
Sixth Sense	3	Value: 3 L.P.

Natural P.R.: 8
Bulk Value: 10
Move: 220/74

Description

Bleyk are massive horse-like creatures. They have a large, curved horn that protrudes from their forehead. Their feet are not single-hoofed like that of a horse, but rather are made more like the feet of an elephant. The skin of a bleyk is a tan color sometimes with grey patches throughout. This skin is extremely tough and thick offering them a great deal of protection against any predator foolish enough to tangle with them.

Bleyk are an average of six feet tall at the shoulders and weigh an amazing eighteen hundred pounds or more. They can be found most anywhere across Oryathar but are found in greater numbers to the far East. They often are found in herds of five to thirty.

Bleyk make excellent battle steeds and are commonly raised and trained for just that purpose. The bleyk's immense strength and physical endurance have earned them a favored and respected position among the King's Guard and the Defenders of the Light.

DOG

Aggression Rating: Moderate
Attack: Bite = +2
Damage Yield: Bite = L3

Attribute	Level	Health
Agility	8	Life Force: 36
Strength	4	Force Failure: 27
Endurance	4	Inj. Rating: 9
Willpower	3	Recovery: 1D8
Intelligence	6	
Sixth Sense	3	Value: 2 L.P.

Natural P.R.: 1
Bulk Value: 4
Move: 260/87

<u>Description</u>

The common dog is found throughout Oryathar. Often running in packs of six to twenty in the wild, they survive by hunting game such as deer and wild pigs. Wild dogs are generally not a threat to the ruling-races and will normally avoid them. Dogs average about two feet in height at the shoulders and weigh an average of seventy to one hundred pounds. Their most common colors are dark brown and tan.

Many of the ruling-races have domesticated dogs for use as guards, pets, or to train to hunt.

EAGLE

Aggression Rating: Passive
Attack: Claws = +10, Bite = +3
Damage Yield: Claws = L5, Bite = L2

Attribute	Level	Health
Agility	15	Life Force: 50
Strength	5	Force Failure: 37
Endurance	4	Inj. Rating: 13
Willpower	3	Recovery: 1D8
Intelligence	3	
Sixth Sense	4	Value: 4 L.P.

Natural P.R.: 1
Bulk Value: 3
Move: 70/24 (450/150)

<u>Description</u>

This massive and regal bird has a wingspan of approximately five feet. The eagle has extremely sharp and long talons and a hooked beak that is very sharp and powerful as well. The eagle's primary food source is fish and small field animals such as rabbits. The eagle has extremely keen vision which assists it greatly in spotting it prey as it soars high above.

Though the eagle is somewhat slow and clumsy on the ground its grace and speed in the air is extremely impressive. Most eagles are a dark brown in color with some white markings.

FINGAR

Aggression Rating: Extreme
Attack: Bite = +3, Fin = +1
Damage Yield: Bite = L5, Fin = L3

Attribute	Level	Health
Agility	10	Life Force: 40
Strength	7	Force Failure: 30
Endurance	4	Inj. Rating: 10
Willpower	4	Recovery: 1D8
Intelligence	6	
Sixth Sense	5	Value: 5 L.P.

Natural P.R.: 0
Bulk Value: 5
Move: 340/114

Description

The fingar is found exclusively in large bodies of fresh water such as lakes and rivers. It resembles a shark with very sharp, oversized teeth. It has two large fins that run down the length of its back that have razor sharp edges.

Fingar weigh an average of three hundred pounds are grow to an average of four feet in length.

Fingar often travel in schools of three to eight and will eat nearly anything. They fear nothing and attack with reckless abandon and once they've tasted blood they will travel any length to pursue their prey.

GIANT HORNED BEETLE

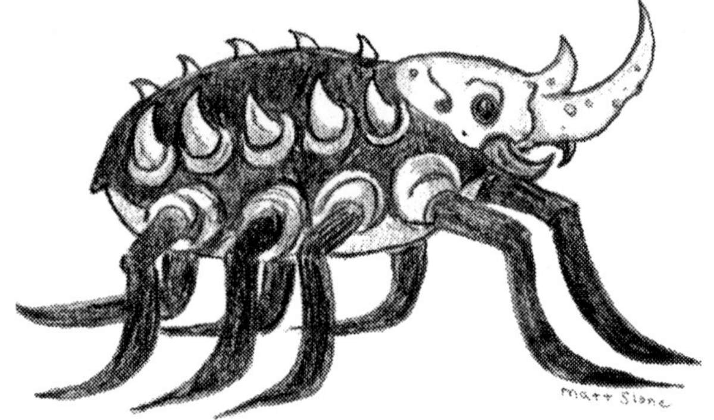

Aggression Rating: Moderate
Attack: Horn = +5, Bite = +2
Damage Yield: Horn = L6, Bite = L5

Attribute	Level	Health
Agility	7	Life Force: 112
Strength	9	Force Failure: 84
Endurance	5	Inj. Rating: 28
Willpower	4	Recovery: 1D10
Intelligence	3	
Sixth Sense	3	Value: 5 L.P.

Natural P.R.: 7
Bulk Value: 7
Move: 160/54

Description

These creatures are very large and tough. They resemble a normal beetle, except they are about six feet long and four feet high and weigh an average of four hundred pounds. They have a long curved horn protruding from the front of their head. Along the bottom edge and top of their shells they have small curved spikes.

HORSE

Aggression Rating: Passive
Attack: Hooves = +2, Bite = +1
Damage Yield: Hooves + L4, Bite = L2

Attribute	Level	Health
Agility	8	Life Force: 130
Strength	11	Force Failure: 97
Endurance	8	Inj. Rating: 33
Willpower	6	Recovery: 1D10 + 1D6
Intelligence	4	
Sixth Sense	3	Value: 2 L.P.

Natural P.R.: 3
Bulk Value: 8
Move: 350/117

Description

Horses were domesticated by the ruling-races hundreds of years ago. They are often used to pull wagons and carts or ridden by themselves. They have proven to be a very reliable source of transportation and some of the larger breeds have even been trained to use as mounts during battle.

Most horses are are an average of four to five feet in height and weigh around eight hundred pounds. They come in a variety of colors and breeds. Though domesticated and raised by the ruling-races, wild horses are a common sight in the open plains of Oryathar.

KING SCORPION

Aggression Rating: High
Attack: Pinchers = +10, Stinger = +8
Damage Yield: Pinchers = L8, Stinger = * L7

Attribute	Level	Health
Agility	15	Life Force: 360
Strength	18	Force Failure: 270
Endurance	14	Inj. Rating: 90
Willpower	12	Recovery: 1D20 + 1D8
Intelligence	5	
Sixth Sense	10	Value: 12 L.P.

Natural P.R.: 9
Bulk Value: 8
Move: 200/67

Description

The king scorpion resembles a normal scorpion with the exceptions that it is extremely large and has very sharp spikes lining the insides of its pinchers. The king scorpion is an average of five feet in length and weighs three to four hundred pounds. Their tough exoskeleton is generally black or dark red in color.

King scorpions prefer very dry and hot areas and often make their burrows in the sand. They are strictly carnivores and will eat most any type of meat, including ruling-races.

The king scorpion's massive pinchers are capable of crushing and impaling a ruling-race with ease and the massive needle-sharp stinger on the end of its tail is full of a very deadly poison.

The venom of the king scorpion takes effect on the Turn after being stung and lasts for several days. It has a crippling and damage yielding effect on its victims. On the Turn after being stung the victim will suffer 1D10 points of damage and will continue to take 1D10 points of damage each Turn for a total of 10 Turns. Also starting on the Turn following a sting the victim's Agility will drop by 2 Levels and will continue to drop by 2 Levels each Turn thereafter until it reaches Level 0, at which time the victim is totally paralyzed except for breathing and minor eye movement. This paralysis will last for 1D4 days unless mystical intervention, such as the Force-effect "Cure", is used. Using "Cure" any time after after being stung will immediately halt the damage rendered by the venom as well as stopping the loss of Agility Levels.

POISON LEECH

Aggression Rating: High
Attack: Bite *
Damage Yield: Bite = * Poison

Attribute	Level	Health
Agility	5	Life Force: 12
Strength	1	Force Failure: 9
Endurance	2	Inj. Rating: 3
Willpower	2	Recovery: 1D4
Intelligence	1	

Sixth Sense	2	Value: .5 L.P.

Natural P.R.: 0
Bulk Value: .5
Move: 20/7

Description

This is a slimy leech with small razor sharp teeth in its circular mouth which it uses to latch onto its unsuspecting victims. The poison leech has two distinguishing white streaks down its back. They lie in wait in slow-moving streams or ponds and wait for hapless victims to wade or swim through. They then attach themselves to the victim, who is unaware of their presence, and feed on their blood.

While feeding the poison leech also secretes a venom into their victim. This venom causes the victim to become very weak and disoriented. Within one hour of attaching themselves the poison leeches' venom will cause the victim's Agility Level to drop by 3 Levels and will also cause them to experience extreme dizziness. The lost Agility Levels and dizziness will remain until the leeches are removed, after which point it usually takes a couple of hour for the victim to recover.

ROCK VIPER

Aggression Rating: High
Attack: Bite = +6
Damage Yield: Bite = * L3

Attribute	Level	Health
Agility	12	Life Force: 20
Strength	4	Force Failure: 10
Endurance	4	Inj. Rating: 5
Willpower	4	Recovery: 1D6
Intelligence	2	
Sixth Sense	2	Value: 3 L.P.

Natural P.R.: 1
Bulk Value: 2
Move: 110/34

Description

The rock viper is a highly aggressive and highly poisonous snake. It has dark brown and sometime grey skin and prefers rocky and mountainous environments. Most adult rock vipers reach an average of eighteen inches in length and weigh around two pounds. Rock vipers will very often attack without provocation and will even chase their victims.

The venom of the rock viper is exceptionally strong. Poison poultices have no effect in treating this venom and even the Force-effect "Cure" only counters the venom fifty percent of the time.

The venom takes effect extremely fast (on the same Turn as the bite). Victims of a rock viper bite suffer excruciating pain throughout their entire body which last for hours and will also immediately suffer 1D20 points of poison damage. The skin around the area of the bite will turn black and begin to die within minutes of being bitten. On the second Turn after being bitten the victim will suffer and additional 1D20 +20 points of poison damage. Approximately twenty minutes after being bitten the victim will run a very high fever and begin to shake violently. It is at this point where most victims succumb to the venom and die. The victim must at this point make an Endurance Test against a Difficulty Value of 15. If they pass there is only a twenty percent chance that they will die at this time. If they fail the Endurance Test there is an eighty percent chance that they will die at this point.

THORN SNAKE

Aggression Rating: High
Attack: Bite = +9, Squeeze = N/A
Damage Yield: Bite = L2, Squeeze = L4

Attribute	Level	Health
Agility	8	Life Force: 40
Strength	6	Force Failure: 30
Endurance	3	Inj. Rating: 10
Willpower	3	Recovery: 1D6
Intelligence	3	
Sixth Sense	7	Value: 2 L.P.

Natural P.R.: 4
Bulk Value: 3
Move: 80/27

Description

This peculiar snake gets its name due to the fact that its entire body is covered with thorn-like spikes. The thorn snake is grey in color and does an excellent job of blending in with thorn thickets and vines where it lies in wait for its victims. Thorn snakes usually climb high into thorn thickets

or into trees and wait for their prey to pass by under them. They will then drop down onto their prey, wrapping around them and squeezing them to death before swallowing them whole.

Though the typical diet of thorn snakes is other snakes, rabbits, piglets and the like, they have been known to attack ruling-races.

Thorn snakes can be found in most any are with lots of vegetation, especially thorns. They range in length from eighteen to twenty four inches and weigh an average of four pounds.

TIGER

Aggression Rating: Moderate
Attack: Claw = +6, Bite = +3
Damage Yield: Claw = L5, Bite = L6

Attribute	Level	Health
Agility	11	Life Force: 60
Strength	11	Force Failure: 45
Endurance	6	Inj. Rating: 15
Willpower	4	Recovery: 1D12
Intelligence	7	
Sixth Sense	2	Value: 7 L.P.

Natural P.R.: 2
Bulk Value: 5
Move: 300/100

Description

The tiger is a very large cat-like predator that roams the forest and open plains of Oryathar. Most adult tigers stand three to four feet tall at the shoulders and weigh in at around three hundred pounds. They have extremely sharp claws and very long, sharp teeth. The tiger is an excellent hunter and moves with surprising stealth. Most tigers are tan or orange in color but a rare few are black.

WHITE WOLF

Aggression Rating: Passive
Attack: Bite = +7
Damage Yield: Bite = L7

Attribute	Level	Health
Agility	18	Life Force: 220
Strength	13	Force Failure: 145
Endurance	9	Inj. Rating: 55
Willpower	10	Recovery: 1D10 + 1D8
Intelligence	10	
Sixth Sense	12	Value: 3 S.P.

Natural P.R.: 3

Bulk Value: 5
Move: 260/87

Description

The white wolf is a rare type of wolf found only in high mountain ranges. True to their name, the white wolf is solid white in color. The white wolf is much larger and more muscular than common wolves and possesses a level of intelligence and compassion unheard of among other types of wolves. An adult white wolf is generally around four feet in height at the shoulders and weighs an average of two hundred and eighty to three hundred pounds.

Many ruling-races believe that the white wolf is an animal created by the light itself and that their original home is on the Dream Star. This belief springs from the fact that many white wolves have been known to rescue ruling-races from danger and even risk their own lives to protect them. Killing a white wolf, to many ruling-races, is an act only considered by those who serve the Shadow.

WOLF

Aggression Rating: Moderate
Attack: Bite = +3
Damage Yield: Bite = L4

Attribute	Level	Health
Agility	9	Life Force: 52
Strength	6	Force Failure: 39
Endurance	6	Inj. Rating: 13
Willpower	5	Recovery: 1D12
Intelligence	6	
Sixth Sense	3	Value: 5 L.P.

Natural P.R.: 2
Bulk Value: 4
Move: 240/80

Description

The wolf is common to all regions of Oryathar. They generally make their homes in mountainous terrain but are also commonly found in the lowlands. Wolves travel and hunt in packs of four to eight and though they do not commonly hunt ruling-races there have been many cases of ruling-races being killed and eaten by packs of wolves.

Most wolves are about two to two and a half feet tall at the shoulders and weigh around a hundred to a hundred and fifty pounds. Their common colors are black, grey, and brown.

WULVRIN SCORPION

Aggression Rating: High
Attack: Sting = +8, Pincher = +1
Damage Yield: Sting = * L1, Pincher = L1

Attribute	Level	Health
Agility	5	Life Force: 20
Strength	2	Force Failure: 15
Endurance	2	Inj. Rating: 5
Willpower	3	Recovery: 1D4
Intelligence	2	
Sixth Sense	4	Value: 1 L.P.

Natural P.R.: 1
Bulk Value: .5
Move: 30/10

Description

The wulvrin scorpion is a light tan colored scorpion with thin white bristles covering its back. The wulvrin scorpion is slightly larger than most other species of scorpions. It ranges in length from twelve to eighteen inches.

The wulvrin scorpion is feared and renowned for its very peculiar and potent venom. Victims of a wulvrin scorpion sting suffer excruciating pain throughout their entire bodies and especially around the area of the sting. Nothing eases this pain and it remains a constant torment day and night. In addition to the terrible pain that the venom causes it also causes the victim's muscles to slowly weaken until they are unable to walk or even move. After this point the victim's heart ceases to function and they die. The entire process takes about two blocks. The only known cure for wulvrin scorpion venom is ingesting the root of a rare plant known as the vyourin.

Wulvrin scorpions prefer very dark and cool areas such as caves. They often nest within the deep cracks and crevices in the cave walls.

MYSTICAL CREATURES

There are a great many creatures of Oryathar that are not considered Shadow-kin nor natural creatures. These are the mystical creatures. They possess mystical abilities that are not found among the natural creatures of Oryathar.

The ruling-races believe the mystical creatures of Oryathar are protected by the Light. For this reason mystical creatures are never hunted or attacked without just cause, at least not by those who follow the Light.

The following is a compilation of many of the know mystical creatures that inhabit or frequent Oryathar.

AIR CREATURES

Air creatures exist solely on an alternate, mystical realm of existence known as the *Air* realm. They appear occasionally on Oryathar for reasons unknown. *Air* creatures are not able to survive indefinitely on Oryathar and thus normally only remain for short periods of time.

Air creatures have been known to materialize by their own will all across Oryathar.

As with the other types of mystical creatures that exist in alternate realms, *Air* creatures are often summoned by Shinkai to combat Shadow-kin and other forces of darkness. When appearing by means of their own will they are generally avoided at all cost, as Shinkai have no control over mystical creatures that they have not summoned.

There are three distinct types of *Air* creatures known to be able to manifest and survive outside of their natural realm of existence. In order of relative strength and ability they have been named the grovling, chief, and boss. Each is described in detail below.

GROVLING

Aggression Rating: Moderate
Attack: Claws = +4, Bite = +3
Damage Yield: Claws = L2, Bite = L3

Attribute	Level	Health
Agility	12	Life Force: 32
Strength	3	Force Failure: N/A
Endurance	4	Inj. Rating: 8
Willpower	3	Recovery: 1D8
Intelligence	3	
Sixth Sense	5	Value: 6 L.P.

Natural P.R.: 0
Bulk Value: 4
Move: (210/70)

Description

This *Air* grovling possesses impressive speed but is not very strong or durable. A very strong advantage that it possesses is its near invisibility. The *Air* grovling, as well as most other *Air* creatures, is almost completely invisible. It only displays a very faint vapor-like form. Because of their near invisibility *Air* creatures receive a +4 bonus to their Physical Defense and all opponents receive a -4 penalty to their Physical Defense.

The *Air* grovling has a slender body of about three to four feet in height. Its arms are very long and slender and end in small hands that have three-inch long talons. Their heads are somewhat flat looking with a wide, gaping mouth that runs from one side of their head to the other.

The *Air* grovling, and all other types of *Air* creatures for that matter, are not restricted to moving upon the ground. *Air* creatures can move in any direction through the air and cannot be knocked down. They are also immune to the Force-effect "Air Bind".

CHIEF
Aggression Rating: Moderate
Attack: (x2) Wind Blast = +9, Claws = +5, Bite = +4
Damage Yield: Wind Blast = L9, Claws = L3, Bite = L4

Attribute	Level	Health
Agility	18	Life Force: 64
Strength	6	Force Failure: N/A
Endurance	6	Inj. Rating: 16
Willpower	5	Recovery: 1D12
Intelligence	4	
Sixth Sense	9	Value: 15 L.P.

Natural P.R.: 0
Bulk Value: 6
Move: (260/87)

<u>Description</u>

Air chiefs are considerably quicker and physically tougher than the *Air* grovling. They also possess the same near invisible nature that the grovling does, which gives them the same bonuses to their Physical Defense and the same penalty to their opponent's Physical Defense.

The *Air* chief has an ability that the *Air* grovling doesn't. Air chiefs can emit a very powerful and focused blast of wind from their mouths. This wind blast has an effective range of fifty feet. Any being struck by this blast of wind must make a successful Agility/Performance Test against a Difficulty Value of 12 or be knocked off of their feet and stunned, as well as receiving Level 9 damage. Because this wind is invisible there is an automatic seventy percent chance that it will automatically hit its target. The *Air* chief's Agility is used to perform the wind blast attack (Agility/Performance Test).

The *Air* chief's body is very similar to that of the *Air* grovling except they are larger and their head has long snake-like tentacles.

The *Air* chief is able to move in all directions just as the *Air* grovling, and is also immune to being knocked down and is unaffected by the Force-effect "Air Bind".

BOSS
Aggression Rating: Moderate
Attack: (x3) Wind Blast = +13, Claws = +8, Bite = +10
Damage Yield: Wind Blast = L12, Claws = L6, Bite = L8

Attribute	Level	Health
Agility	24	Life Force: 90
Strength	10	Force Failure: N/A
Endurance	8	Inj. Rating: 23
Willpower	7	Recovery: 1D10 + 1D6
Intelligence	5	
Sixth Sense	12	Value: 25 L.P.

Natural P.R.: 0
Bulk Value: 8
Move: (400/134)

<u>Description</u>

The *Air* boss is the largest and fastest of all types of *Air* creatures. They can perform lightning quick attacks, and are large enough to inflict a serious amount of damage. Like the *Air* grovling and chief, the boss is nearly invisible. They receive the same bonuses from this ability as the grovling and chief. The *Air* boss can also emit the same type of wind blast that the *Air* chief is capable of except it is much more powerful. The Difficulty Value of the Agility/Performance needed to keep from being knocked down and stunned is 16 instead of 12. The *Air* boss's wind blast also inflicts more damage than that of the *Air* chief. The *Air* boss's Agility is used to perform the wind blast attack (Agility/Performance Test).

In addition to the abilities of the grovling and chief, the *Air* boss has the ability to teleport itself. It can teleport itself up to three hundred feet away as a Minor Action, though this can only be done once every 3 Turns.

The *Air* boss looks quite different than the grovling or chief. They have bodies that are very wide and they walk on four long and agile legs. Their heads are huge and the largest part of their head consists of a grotesque mouth lined with jagged teeth. Snake-like tendrils hang all along their back.

Like the *Air* grovling and chief, the *Air* boss is able to move in all directions and is immune to being knocked down and is completely unaffected by the Force-effect "Air Bind".

CRYSTAL SERPENT

Aggression Rating: Moderate
Attack: Shards = +15, Bite = +9
Damage Yield: Shards = L20 + 30, Bite = L6

Attribute	Level	Health
Agility	25	Life Force: 240
Strength	13	Force Failure: 180
Endurance	9	Inj. Rating: 60
Willpower	16	Recovery: 1D10 + 1D8
Intelligence	5	
Sixth Sense	22	Value: 16 L.P.

Natural P.R.: 8
Bulk Value: 3
Move: 180/60

Description

The crystal serpent resembles a fat snake of about three feet in length with two front legs. The crystal serpent's entire body appears to be made of a white crystal-looking substance. Their skin is very hard and offers them a great deal of protection.

Along the crystal serpents back grows dozens of very jagged and sharp crystalline spikes. Each of these spikes are about three inches in length. At will the crystal serpent can cause several of these spikes to explode, sending shards of razor-sharp crystals flying in all directions. These shards are capable of cutting an opponent to shreds. The crystal serpent can regrow its crystal spikes within 2 Turns.

The crystal serpent weighs an average of one hundred and twenty pounds. They are generally found in high altitudes where the temperatures remain fairly low. Icy caves and cliffs are a common home for these creatures.

The crystal serpent's eggs are often sought after for use in alchemy.

DRAGON

Aggression Rating: Moderate
Attack: Breath = +40, Tail = +30, Bite = +25, Claws = +22
Damage Yield: Breath = *, Tail = L25 +200, Bite = L25 +400, Claw = L25 +250

Attribute	Level	Health
Agility	30	Life Force: 1500
Strength	80	Force Failure: 1000
Endurance	38	Inj. Rating: 500
Willpower	32	Recovery: 3D20 +20
Intelligence	30	
Sixth Sense	70	Value: 100 L.P.

Natural P.R.: 50
Bulk Value: 100
Move: 380/127 (2000/667)

Description

Dragons are the greatest and most deadly of all creatures. The dragon is a giant reptile-like creature with huge wings and a long tail. Their scales are very large and strong and can fend off most any type of attack. Dragon's scales change color as they get older, changing into a new color every five hundred years. The scale colors in the order in which they change are white, red, emerald, blue, and finally gold.

Dragon's mouths are full of razor-sharp, dagger-like teeth. Their bodies are extremely large and powerful. Most dragons are an average of seventy feet in length and weigh several thousand pounds. They usually have sharp, long horns protruding from their heads.

Dragons live an average of three thousand years. They spend the largest part of their lives asleep, usually hidden deep within mountainous catacombs. Dragons keep to themselves and rarely if ever interfere or accept the company of the ruling-races.

Dragons are extremely intelligent and have an ability that is unheard of in any other type of creature. They have the ability to conjure and enchant. Dragons know all Force-effects known to the ruling-races as well as some that are unknown. There is a saying written about dragons; "Only the bravest of souls stand alone against an army, only a fool challenges a dragon."

There are some types of dragons known as Shadow dragons. There are not nearly as large or strong as natural dragons and lack the ability to conjure or enchant. Shadow dragons are extremely evil and often attack villages and towns for the pleasure of destroying as well as feeding on the ruling-races.

Dragons can fluently speak Oryatharian as well as all five ruling-race languages.

FAMILIAR

Aggression Rating: Variable
Attack: Claws = +4, Bite = +2

Damage Yield: Claws = L3, Bite = L2

Attribute	Level	Health
Agility	8	Life Force: 100
Strength	3	Force Failure: 75
Endurance	4	Inj. Rating: 25
Willpower	7	Recovery: 1D8 +20
Intelligence	5	
Sixth Sense	10	Value: 4 L.P.

Natural P.R.: 2
Bulk Value: 1.5
Move: 110/34 (320/107)

Description

Familiars are very unusual and rare type of creature. They are an evolved form of a creature known as dragonids, which are themselves an evolved form of dragons. Dragonids were approximately one fourth the size of dragons and lacked the ability to conjure. Dragonids are now extinct but before they became completely extinct Shinkai made an attempt at capturing and taming them for use as guardians. The dragonids proved to be too wild and dangerous to be tamed, but through mystical intervention the dragonid eventually evolved into a much smaller creature that was much more suited to ruling-race companionship. This evolved creature became known as the familiar.

Familiars are very rare creatures and are found exclusively in large forested areas. They nest in hollow trees by night and during the day they hunt for food. Their main diet consists of rabbit, squirrel and the like.

Familiars are hatched from eggs and normally hatch no more than two eggs per year. The average lifespan for a familiar is a hundred years.

Familiars have accepted the companionship of ruling-races to the point that they will bond with one ruling-race, usually whoever spends time with the familiar when it is very young. Once bonded with a ruling-race the familiar becomes extremely loyal to that individual and will risk their life to protect them. Another curious fact about familiars is that they tend to take on some of the physical characteristics of the ruling-race to which they are bonded. Such characteristics include skin color, eye color, and ear shape. Many familiars also adopt the attitude and disposition of the one they are bonded to. So if you are extremely hateful and grouchy, a familiar that bonds with you will also be hateful and grouchy.

A familiar's attributes can be as much as three times higher than that listed. Their Life Force, Natural P.R., and Move can also be increased. Without the aid of ruling-races however their stats will remain as listed.

To increase a familiar's attribute by 1 point, 3 Light Points must be expended while simultaneously infusing the proper Mystic Forces into the familiar by way of focused conjuring.

Depending upon which attribute is to be increased different Mystic Forces must be focused into the familiar. To increase Agility *Air* or *Water* must be infused into the familiar. For Strength and Endurance *Land* must be used. For Willpower *Fire* must be used. For Intelligence and Sixth Sense *Spirit* must be used. 50 points of Force Energy (per point of increase) must be expended at the time the proper Mystic Forces are infused into the familiar.

To increase a familiar's Life Force the bonded Shinkai must focus conjure *Land* and *Spirit* into the familiar while spending 10 Light points. 50 points of Force Energy must be expended at the time that *Land* and *Spirit* are infused into the familiar. This will increase the familiar's Life Force by 5 points (Force Failure and Injury Rating are increased accordingly).

A drawback to increasing your familiar's Life Force is that each time you increase their Life Force *your* Life Force will drop by 2 Points (Force Failure and Injury Rating are decreased accordingly). This loss is permanent. Increasing a familiar's Strength, Endurance, or Willpower will not affect their Life Force.

To increase a familiar's Natural P.R. by 1 point 5 Light Points must spent while simultaneously infusing *Land* into the familiar by means of focused conjuring. 50 points of Force Energy must be expended (per point increase) at the time that *Land* is infused into the familiar.

To increase a familiar's Movement 5 Light Points must be spent while simultaneously infusing *Air* into the familiar by means of focused conjuring. Each 50 points of Force Energy expended at the time that *Air* is infused into the familiar will increase the familiars Movement by 10 feet per Turn. Increasing a familiar's Agility or Strength will not affect their Move.

All of the processes for increasing a familiar's stats are Major Actions and take only 1 Turn to perform.

FIRE BAT

Aggression Rating: High
Attack: Bite = +7
Damage Yield: Bite = L5

Attribute	Level	Health
Agility	25	Life Force: 24
Strength	2	Force Failure: 18
Endurance	3	Inj. Rating: 6
Willpower	5	Recovery: 1D6
Intelligence	2	
Sixth Sense	12	Value: 6 L.P.

Natural P.R.: 0
Bulk Value: 1
Move: (460/154)

Description

Extremely agile, the fire bat resembles a large bat, except that its body consists entirely of partially solidified fire. They are very aggressive and will attack most anything that threatens them or their habitat, which is commonly in and around volcanoes.

Fire bats are not nearly as common as natural bats, but where found their numbers have been no less impressive. As many as ten thousand fire bats have been found in a single volcano.

Fire bats hate the cold and will never wander far from a source of heat, such as a volcano.

FIRE CREATURES

The following three types of *Fire* creatures exist solely on an alternate, mystical realm of existence, the *Fire* realm. They appear occasionally on Oryathar for reasons unknown. *Fire* creatures are not able to survive indefinitely on Oryathar and thus normally only remain for short periods of time.

Fire creatures that materialize on Oryathar by their own will most always do so in areas of intense heat, such as in or near volcanoes or deserts. All types of *Fire* creatures are vulnerable to water or ice-based attacks. Damage from water or ice-based sources will yield double damage to *Fire* creatures.

As with the other types of mystical creatures that exist in alternate realms of existence, *Fire* creatures are often summoned by Shinkai to combat Shadow-kin and other forces of darkness. When appearing by means of their own will they are generally avoided at all cost, as Shinkai have no control over mystical creatures that they have not summoned.

There are three distinct types of *Fire* creatures known to be able to manifest and survive outside of their natural realm of existence. In order of relative strength and ability they have been named the grovling, chief, and boss. Each is described in detail below.

GROVLING

Aggression Rating: High
Attack: Claws = +3, Bite = +2
Damage Yield: Claws = L5, Bite = L8

Attribute	Level	Health
Agility	9	Life Force: 44
Strength	6	Force Failure: N/A
Endurance	7	Inj. Rating: 11
Willpower	5	Recovery: 1D10 + 1D4
Intelligence	3	
Sixth Sense	5	Value: 6 L.P.

Natural P.R.: 1
Bulk Value: 4
Move: 180/60

Description

The *Fire* grovling resembles a Brightling for size and general body shape, except their bodies are composed entirely of blazing mystical *Fire*. They also have exceptionally long claws and a mouth full of dagger-like teeth.

Easily provoked and always eager to fight, this creature, as well as the other types of *Fire* creatures, are more commonly summoned by Shinkai for the purpose of combat than the creatures from the other three mystical realms.

CHIEF

Aggression Rating: Extreme
Attack: (x2) Fire Breath = +7, Claws = +4, Bite = +3
Damage Yield: Fire Breath = L10 +10, Claws = L7, Bite = L10

Attribute	Level	Health
Agility	15	Life Force: 88
Strength	10	Force Failure: 66
Endurance	11	Inj. Rating: 22
Willpower	7	Recovery: 1D12 + 1D10
Intelligence	4	
Sixth Sense	9	Value: 18 L.P.

Natural P.R.: 2
Bulk Value: 6
Move: 220/74

Description

The *Fire* chief looks much like the *Fire* grovling except it is slightly larger and has a somewhat elongated neck. The *Fire* chief is the most aggressive of the *Fire* creatures. It will fight most anything on sight without reason or provocation.

The *Fire* chief is capable of emitting a blast of fire from its mouth that can travel up to fifteen feet away and will cover an area up to six feet wide. The *Fire* chief's Agility is used to perform its breath attack (Agility/Performance Test).

BOSS

Aggression Rating: High
Attack: (x2) Fire Breath = +11, Claws = +6, Bite = +5
Damage Yield: Fire Breath = L13 +20, Claw = L11, Bite = L13

Attribute	Level	Health
Agility	20	Life Force: 88
Strength	14	Force Failure: 66
Endurance	16	Inj. Rating: 22
Willpower	9	Recovery: 1D12
Intelligence	5	
Sixth Sense	12	Value: 23 L.P.

Natural P.R.: 3
Bulk Value: 8
Move: 360/120

Description

The *Fire* boss is the largest and most lethal of the *Fire* creatures. It looks nothing like the *Fire* grovling or chief. The *Fire* boss walks upright on two huge legs and has two exceptionally long arms that equipped with very long and sharp talons. It has a long serpentine neck protruding from its chest at the end of which its thin head is attached. The shape of the *Fire* boss's head resembles that of a crocodile with short pointed teeth lining their mouth. Most *Fire* bosses stand around six feet in height.

Fire bosses have the ability to breath fire just like the *Fire* chief but their fire breath has a range of thirty feet instead of fifteen and has a higher Damage Yield. The *Fire* boss' Agility is used to perform its breath attack (Agility/Performance Test).

Fire bosses also have the ability to teleport to any source of fire within one thousand feet of them. This teleportation is a Minor Action.

FIRE FLOAT

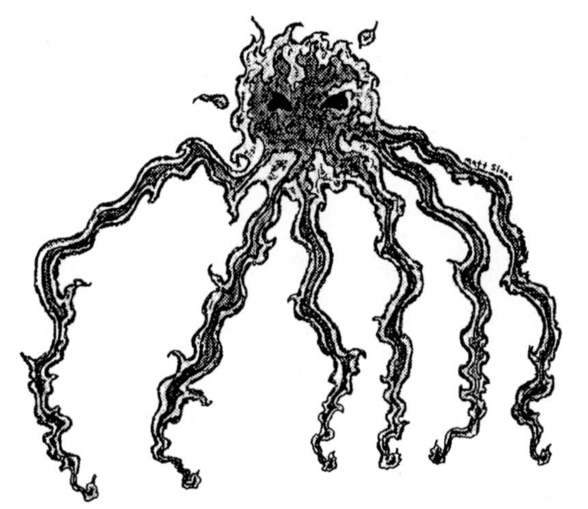

Aggression Rating: High
Attack: (x2) Tail = +4
Damage Yield: Tail = L9

Attribute	Level	Health
Agility	8	Life Force: 70
Strength	6	Force Failure: N/A
Endurance	5	Inj. Rating: 18
Willpower	4	Recovery: 1D12
Intelligence	2	
Sixth Sense	10	Value: 5 L.P.

Natural P.R.: 0
Bulk Value: 3
Move: (180/60)

Description

The fire float is a very dangerous type of mystical creature that inhabits Oryathar. It is usually found within and around volcanoes and sources of lava. The Lake of Fire is home to hundreds of fire floats.

Fire floats resemble a floating ball of fire about two feet in diameter with six long snake-like appendages of fire writhing from their bodies. Fire floats actually float through the air without any apparent means of propulsion. It is not known by what means they propel themselves.

Fire floats use their long appendages, or tails, to lash out and strike down their prey. They then pull their victims into their bodies where they are absorbed and consumed. Fire floats generally feed on small creatures such as birds, bats, and rabbits, but they will not hesitate to attack ruling-races that invade their territory.

One interesting and useful fact to know about fire floats is that their lava-like blood has an extreme reaction on metals, excluding green steel). Any metal object that is exposed to a fire float's blood will ignite into flames and rapidly begin to melt down. Their blazing blood can not be washed off or removed from the metal by any known means. The metal will take 1D20 +10 points of damage per Turn until it is destroyed.

LAND CREATURES

The following three types of *Land* creatures exist solely on an alternate, mystical realm of existence, the *Land* realm. They appear occasionally on Oryathar for reasons unknown. *Land* creatures are not able to survive indefinitely on Oryathar and thus normally only remain for short periods of time.

Land creatures that materialize on Oryathar by their own will most always do so in very mountainous and rocky areas.

As with the other types of mystical creatures that exist in alternate realms of existence, *Land* creatures are often summoned by Shinkai to combat Shadow-kin and other forces of

darkness. When appearing by means of their own will they are generally avoided at all cost, as Shinkai have no control over mystical creatures that they have not summoned.

There are three distinct types of *Land* creatures known to be able to manifest and survive outside of their natural realm of existence. In order of relative strength and ability they have been named the grovling, chief, and boss. Each is described in detail below.

GROVLING

Aggression Rating: Passive
Attack: Claw = +2, Bite = +1
Damage Yield: Claws = L4, Bite = L5

Attribute	Level	Health
Agility	5	Life Force: 90
Strength	10	Force Failure: N/A
Endurance	10	Inj. Rating: 23
Willpower	7	Recovery: 2D10
Intelligence	3	
Sixth Sense	5	Value: 5 L.P.

Natural P.R.: 6
Bulk Value: 5
Move: 120/40

Description

The *Land* grovling stands on two legs and is about three feet in height. Its arm are extremely large in proportion to the rest of its body, and its strength is truly amazing for its size. Their entire bodies appear to made of actual rock and land. Their mouths have short squared off teeth and they have small jagged claws on the ends of their stubby fingers. *Land* grovlings are very solid and heavy weighing an average of three hundred pounds.

Land grovlings are very passive creatures and are not very fond of combat, and beyond this they are fairly slow which makes them an undesirable candidate for assisting in battle. They are generally summoned by Shinkai for use in brute labor, such as clearing away rubble from a collapsed corridor or packing heavy objects. *Land* grovlings can carry approximately four hundred pounds with minimal effort. Some *Land* grovlings have been known to be able to carry as much as six hundred pounds.

CHIEF

Aggression Rating: Moderate
Attack: Boulder = +6, Claw = +3, Bite = +2
Damage Yield: Boulder = L20 +20, Claws = L6, Bite = L7

Attribute	Level	Health
Agility	7	Life Force: 180
Strength	15	Force Failure: N/A
Endurance	15	Inj. Rating: 45
Willpower	9	Recovery: 1D20 + 1D10
Intelligence	4	
Sixth Sense	9	Value: 11 L.P.

Natural P.R.: 9
Bulk Value: 7
Move: 170/57

Description

The *Land* chief looks very much like the *Land* grovling except that it is about five feet tall and has a large jagged boulder attached to its chest. The *Land* chief can cause this boulder to launch from its chest at incredible speeds. The boulder has an effective range of one hundred feet and can inflict serious damage to anything that it strikes. A new boulder will form on the *Land* chief's chest at the beginning of every Turn. The *Land* chief's Agility is used to make this form of attack (Agility/Performance Test).

Land chiefs are also extremely strong for their size. They can carry approximately five hundred pounds with minimal effort. Some *Land* chiefs have been known to be able to carry as much as eight hundred pounds.

BOSS

Aggression Rating: Moderate
Attack: (x2) Boulder = +10, Claw = +5, Bite = +4
Damage Yield: Boulder = L20 +35, Claws = L9, Bite = L12

Attribute	Level	Health
Agility	9	Life Force: 270
Strength	23	Force Failure: N/A
Endurance	23	Inj. Rating: 68
Willpower	11	Recovery: 1D6
Intelligence	5	
Sixth Sense	11	Value: 18 L.P.

Natural P.R.: 13
Bulk Value: 10
Move: 250/84

Description

Land bosses look very much like *Land* chiefs except they are larger and have four arms instead of two. They have the same ability to project and reform jagged boulders from their chest as the chiefs do but the boulders projected by a *Land* boss have an effective range of three hundred feet instead of one hundred feet. The *Land* boss's boulder also does a bit more damage.

Land bosses also have the ability to move through land and rock as easily as we can wade or swim in water. At any time that a *Land* boss wishes it can sink into the ground, move, and then come up out of the ground wherever it wishes. Moving through solid rock is no problem for the *Land* boss either.

Land bosses, like the other types of *Land* creatures, are extremely strong. They can carry approximately eight hundred pounds with minimal effort. Some *Land* bosses have been known to be able to carry as much as fifteen hundred pounds.

LAVA LIZARD

Aggression Rating: High
Attack: Claws = +10, Bite = +10
Damage Yield: Claws = L8, Bite = * L21

Attribute	Level	Health
Agility	30	Life Force: 300
Strength	18	Force Failure: 225
Endurance	22	Inj. Rating: 75
Willpower	18	Recovery:
Intelligence	4	
Sixth Sense	30	Value: 17 L.P.

Natural P.R.: 5
Bulk Value: 4
Move: 260/87

Description

Lava lizards are highly aggressive creatures that inhabit areas of intense heat such as the mouths of volcanoes or around streams and pools of lava. The lava lizard is about three feet in length and has six legs. They weigh an average of one hundred pounds. They have extremely hard and razor-sharp claws on all of their feet and have a short, blunt tail. Their hide is a dark red color and is very tough.

The lava lizard's mouth is full of long, sharp teeth that inject a fiery red liquid into their victims when bitten. This liquid is extremely hot and causes immediate burns and internal damage to those who are injected with it. On the Turn that a being is bitten by a lava lizard and for the next 3

Turns they must make Endurance Tests. The result of these Endurance Tests is subtracted from a value of 50. The end result is the number of points of damage that the lava lizard's fiery liquid venom has inflicted for that Turn.

The eggs of the lava lizard are often sought after for use in alchemy products.

UNICORN

Aggression Rating: Passive
Attack: Light Ray = +12, Horn = +8, Hooves = +5
Damage Yield: Light Ray = 6D20 +100, Horn = L10, Hooves = L7

Attribute	Level	Health
Agility	22	Life Force: 250
Strength	17	Force Failure: 167
Endurance	16	Inj. Rating: 83
Willpower	20	Recovery: 1D12
Intelligence	20	
Sixth Sense	35	Value: 4 S.P.

Natural P.R.: 5
Bulk Value: 7
Move: 460/154

Description

Unicorns are considered to be a very sacred animal. They are pure and untainted by all of the Shadows influence on the rest of the world. They look like white horses with a long

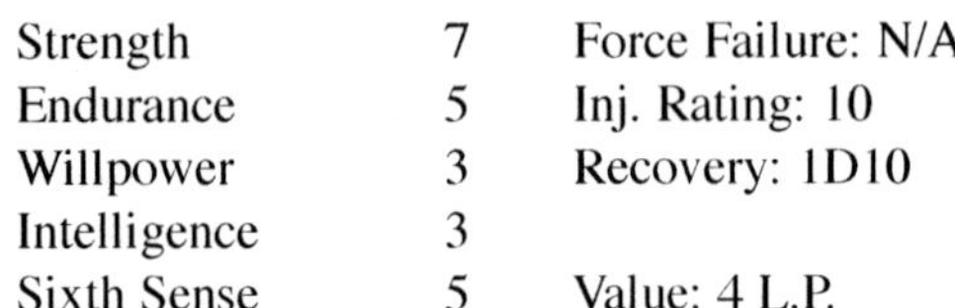

spiraled horn of gold protruding from their forehead. Their mane and tale have a lustrous golden shine and their eyes are a pure sky-blue. Unicorns are very docile creatures and are rarely spotted. They appear most commonly at dawn. Many ruling-races believe that the unicorn's home is on the Dream Star and that it only teleports onto Oryathar for brief visits. Though this belief seems to be very popular, no one has ever witnessed a unicorn teleport farther than a mile at a time.

Unicorns may teleport at will as many times per day as they wish, but must wait for 10 turns in between teleportations. They are also able to project a ray of blinding golden light from their horns which has an astonishing range of three thousand feet. Anything struck by this ray will suffer 6D20 +100 points of damage. There has been no armor known, green-steel included, that could protect against this ray of light.

The average weight of a Unicorn is around eight hundred pounds and the average height is five feet to the top of their back.

Unicorns do not speak, but are able to fully understand Oryatharian and all five ruling-race languages.

WATER CREATURES

The following three types of *Water* creatures exist solely on an alternate, mystical realm of existence, the *Water* realm. They appear occasionally into Oryathar for reasons unknown. *Water* creatures are not able to survive indefinitely on Oryathar and thus normally only remain for short periods of time.

Water creatures that materialize on Oryathar by their own will most always do so in or around large bodies of water, such as ponds, lakes, or the sea, etc. All types of *Water* creatures are vulnerable to fire-based attacks. Damage from fire-based sources will yield double damage to *Water* creatures.

As with the other types of mystical creatures that exist in alternate realms of existence, *Water* creatures are often summoned by Shinkai to combat Shadow-kin and other forces of darkness. When appearing by means of their own will they are generally avoided at all cost, as Shinkai have no control over mystical creatures that they have not summoned.

There are three distinct types of *Water* creatures known to be able to manifest and survive outside of their natural realm of existence. In order of relative strength and ability they have been named the grovling, chief, and boss. Each is described in detail below.

GROVLING

Aggression Rating: Moderate
Attack: Claws = +3, Bite = +2
Damage Yield: Claws = L3, Bite = L4

Attribute	Level	Health
Agility	8	Life Force: 38
Strength	7	Force Failure: N/A
Endurance	5	Inj. Rating: 10
Willpower	3	Recovery: 1D10
Intelligence	3	
Sixth Sense	5	Value: 4 L.P.

Natural P.R.: 1
Bulk Value: 4
Move: 150/50

Description

Water grovlings look like three foot long worms made completely of shimmering blue water. Their bodies are about one foot in diameter and have two long tentacles coming out of either side. These tentacles actually have clawed hands at the ends of them. At the end of the *Water* grovling's head is a rounded mouth full of jagged teeth.

Water grovlings move across the ground much in the same manner that a worm crawls, leaving trails of water to mark their passing.

CHIEF

Aggression Rating: Moderate
Attack: Water Blast = +6, Claws = +4, Bite = +3
Damage Yield: Water Blast = L9, Claws = L5, Bite = L6

Attribute	Level	Health
Agility	11	Life Force: 70
Strength	11	Force Failure: N/A
Endurance	7	Inj. Rating: 18
Willpower	5	Recovery: 1D10 + 1D4
Intelligence	4	
Sixth Sense	9	Value: 10 L.P.

Natural P.R.: 2
Bulk Value: 6
Move: 180/60

Description

The *Water* chief is shaped much like the *Water* grovling except it is slightly larger and instead of crawling across the ground they remain upright as they move. They appear to glide smoothly across the surface of the ground, and like the grovling they leave a wet trail behind them.

The *Water* chief is capable of emitting a very powerful blast of water from its mouth. This jet of water has an effective range of fifty feet and can strike with enough force to cause significant damage. Beings struck with this blast of water must immediately make a random-roll Agility Test against a Difficulty Value of 8 or be knocked down.

BOSS

Aggression Rating: High
Attack: (x2) Water Blast = +10, Claws = +6, Bite = +5

Damage Yield: Water Blast = L11 +15, Claws = L7, Bite = L8

Attribute	Level	Health
Agility	16	Life Force: 110
Strength	15	Force Failure: N/A
Endurance	9	Inj. Rating: 28
Willpower	6	Recovery: 1D10 + 1D8
Intelligence	5	
Sixth Sense	12	Value: 16 L.P.

Natural P.R.: 4
Bulk Value: 8
Move: 220/74

Description

The *Water* boss is the largest of the *Water* creatures. It stands at approximately six and a half feet high and has six long tentacles attached to its body, all of which are equipped with long hooked talons at their ends. The shape of the *Water* boss' body is the same as that of the grovling and chief, and like the chief it moves upright with a gliding type of motion.

Just like the *Water* chief the boss can also emit a powerful blast of water from its mouth. The *Water* boss' water blast has an effective range of one hundred feet and also does a significant greater amount of damage. Beings hit with the water blast from a *Water* boss must make random-roll Agility Test against a Difficulty Value of 12 in order to resist being knocked down.

The *Water* boss has another interesting ability. Any metal, other than green-steel, that comes in contact with the water from one of their blasts will immediately begin to rust away at a rate of 1D20 +20 points of damage per Turn until it is completely destroyed. There is no known means of stopping or preventing this rusting.

SHADOW-KIN

Shadow-kin are the most evil and bloodthirsty creatures on Oryathar. They exist only to kill and destroy. They have no respect for life and their appetite for destruction seems to be limitless.

There are a multitude of different breeds and types of Shadow-kin. Each type is unique and possesses its own particular abilities and skills. Some Shadow-kin are very difficult to distinguish from natural creatures, others are easily recognizable as evil creations of the Shadow, and others possess obvious mystical properties and abilities. One common link between all Shadow-kin, however, is their lust for killing. Some Shadow-kin devour their prey and others kill for the simple joy of kill, leaving their victims lying, but all Shadow-kin have an inherent passion for killing.

Though many Shadow-kin are very mystical in nature and possess many mystical abilities, the fact that they are Shadow-kin places them in a different category than other mystical creatures. For that reason, all Shadow-kin whether they are mystical in nature or not are described in this section of the creature lore logs.

ACID MOG

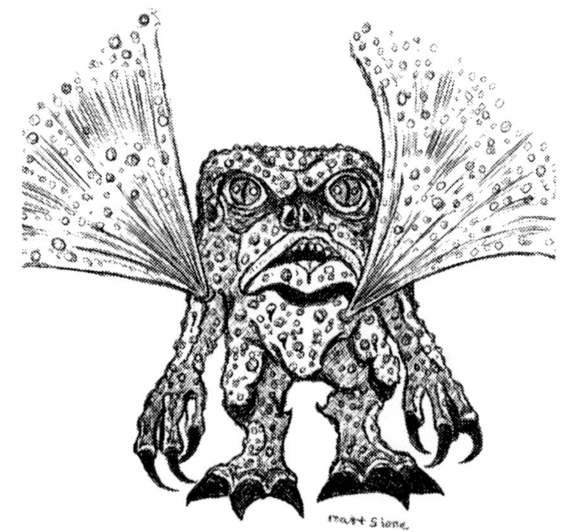

Aggression Rating: High
Attack: Acid = +5, Claws = +3, Bite = +2
Damage Yield: Acid = * L4, Claws = L2, Bite = L3

Attribute	Level	Health
Agility	5	Life Force: 32
Strength	3	Force Failure: 24
Endurance	3	Inj. Rating: 8
Willpower	3	Recovery: 1D6
Intelligence	2	
Sixth Sense	3	Value: 3 L.P.

Natural P.R.: 0
Bulk Value: 4
Move: 130/44

Description

These creatures are small, hairless, and slimy with dozens of oozing pores covering their bodies. They have very long and sharp claws and their mouths are lined with tiny razor-sharp teeth. They range from two to three feet in height and weigh an average of seventy pounds.

The acid mog is normally a very dark green color but some are brown with green blotches. They normally travel in groups of five to ten.

The acid mog is capable of spraying an acidic mist out of the pores on its skin. This acid sprays out with tremendous speed and force and can strike any thing within ten feet of the acid mog. Agility is the attribute used for the acid mog to use its acid attack (Agility/Performance Test).

Exposure to this acid will yield Level 4 damage for 3 Turns unless the acid is washed off sooner. Any metal that is sprayed by this acid will sustain 2D20 points of damage on the Turn following exposure.

Acid mogs generally prefer moist and damp environments such as caves and swamps, and tend to avoid moving about in the daylight. They often travel in groups of five to eight members.

BLADE BEAST

Aggression Rating: Extreme
Attack: Blood-fire = *, Blades = +10
Damage Yield: Blood-fire = * 1D100 +50/50, Blades = L12

Attribute	Level	Health
Agility	28	Life Force: 300
Strength	30	Force Failure: 225
Endurance	22	Inj. Rating: 75
Willpower	25	Recovery: 1D6
Intelligence	13	
Sixth Sense	40	Value: 38 L.P.

Natural P.R.: 12
Bulk Value: 5
Move: 520/174

Description

The blade beast is one of the deadliest of all Shadow-kin. They are extremely intelligent, capable of fluently speaking not only Oryatharian but all five ruling-race languages as well. Their cunning is unmatched among Shadow-kin.

The blade beast gets its name from the fact that its body, arms, and legs all appear to be thin metallic-looking blades. The basic design of the blade beast's body is similar to that of a ruling-race in that they stand upright on two legs and have two arms and one head. The similarities end there.

The blade-beast's entire body is solid black in color and its arms look like the curved blades of a scimitar. Their torso and legs look the blades of a massive broadsword. On the ends of their legs are small clawed feet. Their mouths have six long teeth that have serrated edges for ease in cutting through the flesh and bones of their prey.

The exterior of the blade beast not only looks like metal blades but is also as hard as metal. But despite its solid metallic appearance the blade beast is extremely quick and agile. They are capable of leaping as high as thirty feet into the air from a standing position.

*The blade beast has a very lethal and devastating attack known as blood-fire. The blade beast can only make one blood-fire attack for each time that it engorges on a fresh kill. The blade beast spews the blood from its last kill into the air

and as the mist of blood ascends it explodes into a vortex of fire. Anything within one hundred feet of the blade beast when it performs the blood-fire attack will suffer 1D100 +50 points of damage and will also suffer 50 points of damage on the following Turn.

If the damage from a blood-fire attack causes an injury it will automatically cause two additional injuries. If the first injury is applied to Agility then the additional two injuries are applied to Strength and Endurance. If the first injury is applied to Strength then the additional two injuries are applied to Agility and Endurance, so on and so forth.

BORB

Aggression Rating: Moderate
Attack: Claws = +2, Bite = +3
Damage Yield: Claws = L2, Bite = L4

Attribute	Level	Health
Agility	3	Life Force: 24
Strength	3	Force Failure: 18
Endurance	2	Inj. Rating: 6
Willpower	2	Recovery: 1D4
Intelligence	5	
Sixth Sense	3	Value: 1 L.P.

Natural P.R.: 1
Bulk Value: 3
Move: 240/80

Description

Borbs are small creatures with dark skin (usually black or dark grey), no hair, and short stubby fingers. Their oddest feature is that they have four eyes spaced evenly around their head. They are only about two feet in height and weigh around sixty pounds. Borbs do not normally travel in groups of more than two or three and can often be found traveling alone, most commonly in forests and dense swampland.

Borbs are relatively weak and are poor in combat. They are generally employed as scouts and spies for other

Shadow-kin. They are exceptionally fast runners, which lends further to their spying abilities.

BRECKON

Aggression Rating: Extreme
Attack: Claws = +4, Bite = +3
Damage Yield: Claws = L2, Bite = L3

Attribute	Level	Health
Agility	10	Life Force: 80
Strength	9	Force Failure: 60
Endurance	7	Inj. Rating: 20
Willpower	12	Recovery: 1D10 + 1D4
Intelligence	2	
Sixth Sense	5	Value: 7 L.P.

Natural P.R.: 2
Bulk Value: 3
Move: 280/94

<u>Description</u>

These small Shadow-kin resemble a cross between a wolverine and a wolf. They have coarse black fur, large feet with sharp claws, and sharp canines for shredding meat. Most breckon are about two feet in length, stand around one foot tall, and weigh an average of seventy pounds.

Breckon thrive in thickly forested areas where there are plenty of small shrubs and dense undergrowth. They are extreme loners and never travel in packs.

BRISTLE WOLF

Aggression Rating: High
Attack: Bite = +3
Damage Yield: Bite = L4, Bristles = * L2

Attribute	Level	Health
Agility	7	Life Force: 120
Strength	6	Force Failure: 90
Endurance	5	Inj. Rating: 30
Willpower	5	Recovery: 1D10
Intelligence	6	
Sixth Sense	6	Value: 5 L.P.

Natural P.R.: 4
Bulk Value: 5
Move: 220/74

<u>Description</u>

The bristle wolf is an extremely ferocious and dangerous predator. It is built like a normal wolf but with long quills, like that of a porcupine, covering its entire body. The bristle wolf's hair and bristles are almost always a faded brown color.

Bristle wolves most often travel in packs. These packs may consist of as many as thirty bristle wolves and rarely contain fewer than four.

The bristle wolf's favorite habitat is thickly wooded forests and thickets. They have a remarkable ability to blend into their surroundings and are usually not spotted until it is too late.

The bristles, or quills, of a bristle wolf are extremely sharp. Anything that is successfully struck or bitten by a bristle wolf will be stuck with 1D10 of these quills. The quills themselves, regardless of how many the target is stuck with at a time, inflict Level 2 damage to the being struck. The quills are lined with tiny barbs that make them difficult to pull out. As long as a being has even one of these quills stuck in them they receive a -2 Level penalty to their Agility until all quills are removed.

As a general rule of thumb, a character should be able to remove approximately one quill per Turn as a Minor Action and 1D4 quills per Turn as a Major Action. The removal of each quill inflicts Level 1 damage.

CLAWED CRAWLER

Aggression Rating: High
Attack: Bite = +3, Claws = +1

Damage Yield: Bite = L7, Claw = L4

Attribute	Level	Health
Agility	7	Life Force: 88
Strength	12	Force Failure: 66
Endurance	6	Inj. Rating: 22
Willpower	5	Recovery: 1D12
Intelligence	2	
Sixth Sense	4	Value: 5 L.P.

Natural P.R.: 4
Bulk Value: 7
Move: 130/44

Description

This creature looks a lot like a giant turtle, but without its shell. Its skin is black and covered with hard knots that serve as a type of armor. The clawed crawler has six legs, each with large, four-toed feet that have very long and sharp claws designed for tearing prey apart. Their heads have two giant pincher-like hooks that it uses to latch onto its prey and hold it while its claws finish them off. Their mouth is actually very small with many small dagger-like teeth.

Clawed crawlers are generally about five feet in length and weigh around four hundred pounds.

Clawed crawlers tend to travel and hunt alone, but most always lair with other clawed crawlers. They prefer caves and dense brush for their lairs. As many as ten clawed crawlers will lair together during the day, preferring to move about at night.

CRADLE ROBBER

Aggression Rating: Extreme
Attack: Claw = +6, Tail = +5, Bite = +3
Damage Yield: Claw = L5, Tail = * L5, Bite = L6

Attribute	Level	Health
Agility	14	Life Force: 100
Strength	13	Force Failure: 75
Endurance	7	Inj. Rating: 25
Willpower	6	Recovery: 1D12
Intelligence	8	
Sixth Sense	9	Value: 11 L.P.

Natural P.R.: 4
Bulk Value: 5
Move: 340/114

Description

Cradle robbers are large tiger-like Shadow-kin. They are solid black with very long tails that have thin needle-like spikes on their ends. Cradle robbers get their name because they very often sneak into huts and snatch young babies from their cradles and run off with them. Cradle robbers stand three to four feet tall at the shoulders and weigh in at around three hundred and fifty pounds. They have extremely sharp claws and very long and sharp teeth. They prefer to hunt at night and seem to have an appetite for ruling-races.

Beings struck by a cradle robber's tail will have several of the needle-like spikes stuck in their flesh. These spikes are poisonous and will cause the victim stuck by them to black out for 1D6 +2 Turns unless they make a successful Endurance Test against a Difficulty Value of 10. The unfortunate thing is that after being stuck with the cradle robbers spikes the victim must continue making Endurance Tests each Turn to resist blacking out, and to make matters worse the Difficulty Value of the Test increases by 1 point each Turn. So on the Turn that a being is stuck by the spikes the Endurance Test's Difficulty Value is 10, on the second Turn it is 11, on the third Turn it is 12, and so on. Eventually the victim *will* black out. The only thing that will prevent the victim from having to make the Endurance Tests and eventually blacking out is the Force-effect "Cure".

FOWLEN

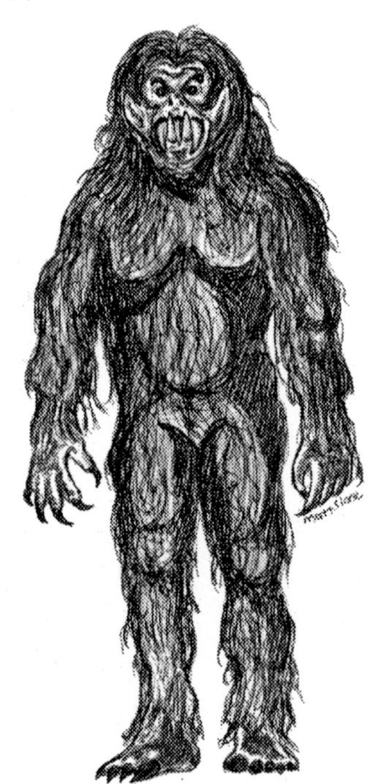

Aggression Rating: High
Attack: Claw = +5, Bite = +3
Damage Yield: Claws = L3, Bite = L5

Attribute	Level	Health
Agility	5	Life Force: 60
Strength	6	Force Failure: 45
Endurance	3	Inj. Rating: 15
Willpower	4	Recovery: 1D6
Intelligence	3	

Sixth Sense   3   Value: 3 L.P.

Natural P.R.: 2
Bulk Value: 7
Move: 160/54

Description

This disgusting creature walks upright on two legs just as a ruling-race would. They have long, black hair covering their entire body. Their eyes are a menacing red and they have four large saber-teeth that can bite large holes into their prey. Fowlen stand an average of six feet in height and generally weigh around two hundred pounds. They can be found in any climate or area and are often found in groups of two or three.

The fowlen's primary weapon is the foul stench that it gives off. This putrid smell is very strong and can be smelled from great distances. The closer to the fowlen, of course, the stronger the stench. Anyone within twenty feet of a fowlen must make a successful Endurance Test against a Difficulty Value of 9 each Turn to resist the intoxicating effect of the odor. Beings that fail the Test are overcome by the powerful odor and become intoxicated for 1D6 Turns. Victims of the intoxication suffer a -2 Level penalty to all attributes until the intoxication wears off.

If a being is still within twenty feet of a fowlen when the effects of the intoxication wear off, they must immediately make another Endurance Test or become intoxicated again.

HIPTOTRIKT

Aggression Rating: High
Attack: Claw = +5, Bite = +2
Damage Yield: Claw = L3, Bite = * L5

Attribute	Level	Health
Agility	10	Life Force: 36
Strength	6	Force Failure: 25
Endurance	3	Inj. Rating: 9
Willpower	3	Recovery: 1D6
Intelligence	2	
Sixth Sense	6	Value: 5 L.P.

Natural P.R.: 2
Bulk Value: 3
Move: 240/80

Description

These little creatures are only about two feet in length and walk on three hind legs. They also have to front legs that they can use like arms. Their bodies are covered with a short, dark fur. They have no ears and have a very long snout that is full of very small, but razor sharp teeth. They have very short and stubby tails and their feet are small with very sharp claws that can extend and contract like that of a cat. Hiptotrikts are very quick and are excellent climbers. They weigh an average of 30 pounds.

The bite of a hiptotrikt is very poisonous. Victims of a hiptotrikt bite begin suffering extreme hallucination within two hours of being bitten. On the second day after being bitten by a hiptotrikt there is a fifty percent chance that the victim will die. If the player rolls above 50 on the percentile dice, then his character has fought off the poison and has no further chance of dying. The hallucinations will end by the next morning and the character will fully recover.

There is no cure for those bitten by a hiptotrikt other than killing the hiptotrikt that bit them, or simply being able to fight it off on your own. Killing the hiptotrikt that bit them will cause the hallucination to immediately cease and will stop any chance of dying due to the poison.

HORNED MONKEY

Aggression Rating: Extreme
Attack: Bite = +3, Claw = +5
Damage Yield: Bite = L4, Claw = L3

Attribute	Level	Health
Agility	11	Life Force: 44
Strength	7	Force Failure: 33
Endurance	4	Inj. Rating: 11
Willpower	4	Recovery: 1D8
Intelligence	3	

Sixth Sense   5   Value: 2.5 L.P.

Natural P.R.: 4
Bulk Value: 3
Move: 260/87

Description

  These creatures are black-haired monkeys with long tails nd very sharp teeth. They have sharp claws on their hands and feet.

  Horned monkeys have a set of horns that protrude straight forward out of their foreheads (about five inches long). They are very quick and ferocious and often move about in the tree tops in order to drop down and get the surprise on their victims.

  Horned monkeys can be found in most any forested area throughout Oryathar. They range in length from two to three feet, not including their tail, and weigh an average of fifty pounds.

JAHOOK

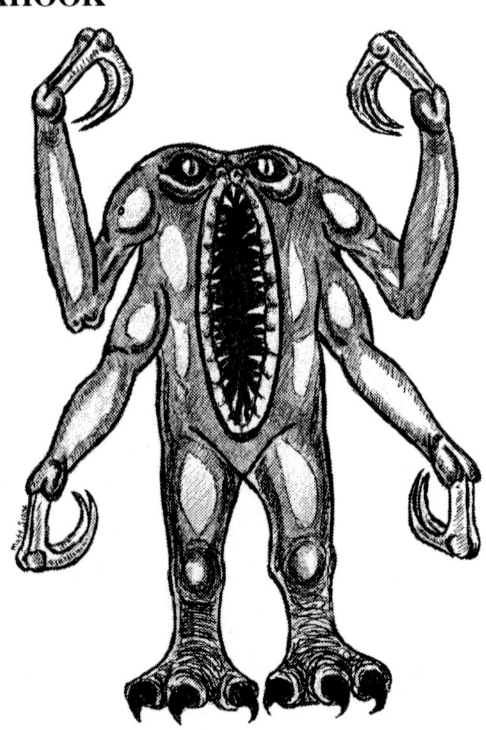

Aggression Rating: Extreme
Attack: (x2) Hooks = +10, Bite = +3
Damage Yield: Hooks = L8, Bite = L10

Attribute	Level	Health
Agility	15	Life Force: 240
Strength	12	Force Failure: 180
Endurance	10	Inj. Rating: 60
Willpower	9	Recovery: 2D10

Intelligence   5
Sixth Sense   11   Value: 15 L.P.

Natural P.R.: 8
Bulk Value: 8
Move: 320/107

Description

  The jahook is a large, stout Shadow-kin with two arms on each side of its body. The arms are fairly long with two sharp hooks at their ends used for hooking their victims and pulling them into the huge vertical mouth in the middle of their chest. Their mouth is huge and full of jagged razor sharp teeth.

  Most jahook stand about six feet in height and weigh around two hundred and fifty pounds. They can be found in almost any type of environment in all regions of Oryathar. Jahook seem to have an appetite for bleyk and often hunt down wipe out entire herds of bleyk in a single day.

KICKER

Aggression Rating: High
Attack: Tail = +3, Bite = +2, Kick = +2
Damage Yield: Tail = L4, Bite = L5, Kick = L10

Attribute	Level	Health
Agility	7	Life Force: 80
Strength	10	Force Failure: 60
Endurance	6	Inj. Rating: 20
Willpower	5	Recovery: 1D12
Intelligence	4	
Sixth Sense	4	Value: 7 L.P.

Natural P.R.: 5
Bulk Value: 6

Move: 260/87

Description

These Shadow-kin are very powerful and dangerous combatants. Their head resembles that of a large fox with unusually long teeth. Their bodies are short and stout with extremely muscular legs that allow them to leap up to twenty feet in a single bound. Their short arms and powerful legs are both equipped with long razor sharp talons. They also have a long muscular tail that they often use to lean back on to support their body; from this position they can unleash a powerful kick with both legs capable of killing large prey instantly.

Kicker skin is very tough and leathery and is usually dark brown, grey, or black in color. The average height of a kicker is five feet, though some have been know to reach seven feet. Their average weight is two hundred pounds. Kickers prefer the open plains and often travel in groups of three to five.

KREEJA

Aggression Rating: High
Attack: Tongue = +7, Claw = +5, Bite = +4,
Damage Yield: Tongue = N/A, Claw = L4, Bite = L5

Attribute	Level	Health
Agility	7	Life Force: 140
Strength	9	Force Failure: 105
Endurance	6	Inj. Rating: 35
Willpower	5	Recovery: 1D12
Intelligence	3	
Sixth Sense	9	Value: 6 L.P.

Natural P.R.: 3
Bulk Value: 5
Move: 260/87

Description

Kreeja look like dogs with wet fur matted against their bodies. Their front legs are much larger in proportion to their hind legs and they have huge front feet to match. They have very long, sharp claws on both their front and hind feet, but those on the front are considerably larger.

Kreeja have extremely long frog-like tongues that can lash out of their mouths and strike their victims, sticking them to their tongue and holding them while they move in and claw them to shreds with their powerful front legs. Beings that are entangled by a kreeja's tongue receive a -1D10 point penalty to any Agility-based action that they make.

It takes a minimum of 20 points of damage inflicted in a single blow to sever the tongue of a kreeja. The tongue of a kreeja will regenerate on the second Turn after it is severed.

KRUELIN

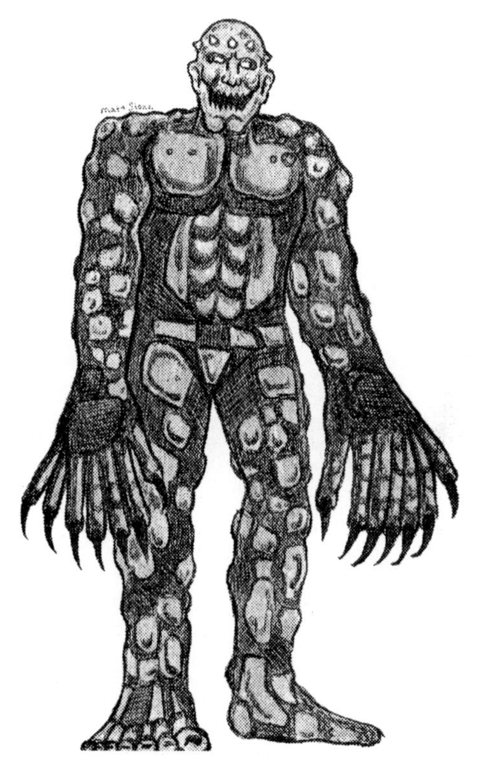

Aggression Rating: Extreme
Attack: (x2) Claw = +10, Bite = +5
Damage Yield: Claw = L11, Bite = L7

Attribute	Level	Health
Agility	13	Life Force: 320
Strength	20	Force Failure: 240
Endurance	14	Inj. Rating: 80
Willpower	11	Recovery: 1D20 + 1D8
Intelligence	7	
Sixth Sense	18	Value: 18 L.P.

Natural P.R.: 12
Bulk Value: 10
Move: 380/127

<u>Description</u>

Kruelin are very strong and powerful creatures that stand around eight feet tall and weigh around four hundred pounds. Their skin looks like it is made of black stone. Short spikes of about an inch in length protrude all around their head. The kruelin has a strong bottom jaw that can snap down like a steel trap. Their hands are extremely long with seven fingers on each hand. The fingers themselves are also very long with sharp claws at their ends.

Kruelin are very cruel and merciless and prefer the flesh of ruling-races over any other food source. They are found most commonly in and around deep caves.

Most all kruelin are capable of speaking very basic Oryatharian.

PACKWAN

Aggression Rating: Extreme
Attack: (x3) Bite = +5
Damage Yield: Bite = L5

Attribute	Level	Health
Agility	9	Life Force: 180
Strength	9	Force Failure: 135
Endurance	6	Inj. Rating: 45
Willpower	7	Recovery: 1D12
Intelligence	4	
Sixth Sense	7	Value: 11 L.P.

Natural P.R.: 3
Bulk Value: 6
Move: 270/90

<u>Description</u>

This creature is a giant three headed wolf with two small, sharp horns on each head. They are about five feet high at the shoulders and weigh an average of three hundred pounds.

An interesting fact about packwan is that although they have three heads, only one of those heads has a brain. The single brain controls all three heads. Due to this fact, only one of the heads, the one containing the packwan's brain, is considered a vital area. Lethal damage to either of the two heads that does not contain the brain will not necessarily kill the packwan. Which head contains the brain varies from one packwan to another and their is no obvious way to tell which one it is.

Packwan are extremely ferocious and will always fight to the death. Even when they are greatly outnumbered they will fight as if they have the upper hand. Packwan live mainly in forested areas and usually make dens in the dense underbrush. Packwans often travel in small packs of three to six members.

QUAMAN

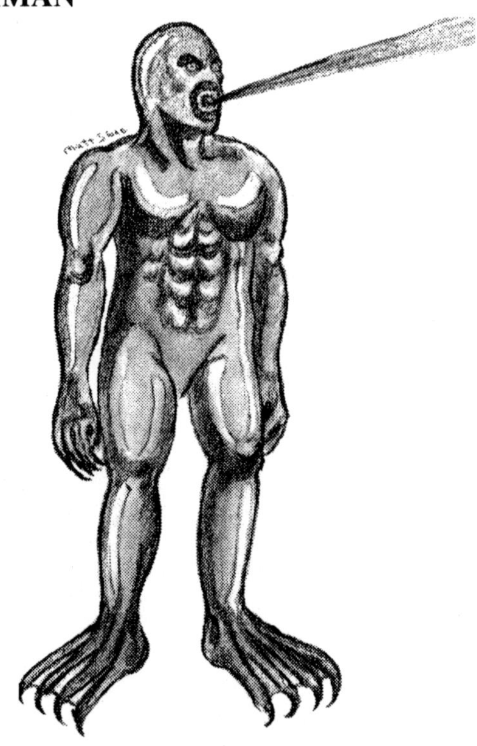

Aggression Rating: Extreme
Attack: (x2) Spit = +6, Claw = +5
Damage Yield: Spit = * L10, Claw = L4

Attribute	Level	Health
Agility	9	Life Force: 110
Strength	7	Force Failure: 72
Endurance	6	Inj. Rating: 28

Willpower	10	Recovery: 1D12
Intelligence	5	
Sixth Sense	7	Value: 9 L.P.

Natural P.R.: 2
Bulk Value: 7
Move: 200/67

Description

These slimy Shadow-kin slightly resemble one of the ruling races, but without any distinctive facial features. They are extremely ferocious and deadly fighters that stop at nothing to kill anyone or anything that gets in their path. Their bodies are covered with a wet frog-like skin that is usually a deep gray color. They usually live in moist and dark environments such as caves. Perfectly adapted to their dark habitats, Quaman have perfect vision in complete darkness, and avoid sunlight at all times.

Quaman are capable of spitting a stream of poison up to thirty feet away. If this poison comes in contact with the skin of a living being they will suffer the following penalties; the area of contact with the poison is burned into a festering blister which yields Level 10 damage. This blister is a two-day Critical Injury. On the Turn after exposure the victim's Agility will be penalized by -1 Level, the following Turn their Strength is penalized by -1 Level, the Turn after that Endurance, then Agility is penalized another -1 Level, and finally Strength is penalized another -1 Level. These penalties remain until the Critical Injury is healed. Quaman can spit poison once per Turn.

Their average weight is one hundred seventy pounds, and the average height is six feet.

RASP WORM

Aggression Rating: Moderate
Attack: Bite = +7, Hooks = +12
Damage Yield: Bite = L25, Hooks = L10

Attribute	Level	Health
Agility	12	Life Force: 380
Strength	25	Force Failure: 285
Endurance	16	Inj. Rating: 95
Willpower	10	Recovery: 1D20 + 1D12

Intelligence	3	
Sixth Sense	14	Value: 14 L.P.

Natural P.R.: 20
Bulk Value: 12
Move: 130/44

Description

Rasp worms are very large and deadly Shadow-kin. They resemble giant worms with sharp curved barbs covering their entire body. Their mouths are full of hundreds of dagger-like teeth. They burrow underground and sense their prey by vibration- they have no eyes. Their skin is very tough and rock-like.

Rasp Worms are an average of eight feet in length and two feet in diameter. They weigh as much as several hundred pounds. They live mainly in desert areas where the terrain consists mainly of sand or loose soil.

ROCKLING (SHINKAI KILLER)

Aggression Rating: High
Attack: Bite = +2
Damage Yield: Bite = L7

Attribute	Level	Health
Agility	4	Life Force: 80
Strength	6	Force Failure: 60
Endurance	3	Inj. Rating: 20
Willpower	3	Recovery: 1D6
Intelligence	5	
Sixth Sense	9	Value: 8 L.P.

Natural P.R.: * 10/6
Bulk Value: 3
Move: 120/40

Description

The rockling is a most peculiar and dangerous Shadow-kin. They resemble small boulders roughly two feet in diameter. Their small legs and arms are concealed by holding them tight against their bodies. The outer layer of their body is very tough and rock-like with a Natural Protection Rating of 10 while their front side, concealed by their arms and legs when crouched, is somewhat softer having a Natural Protection Rating of 6. The rockling has a large mouth full of jagged teeth. Their arms are not suitable for grabbing or attacking prey. The rockling attacks simply by running into the prey and biting into them with their sharp teeth.

The rockling has a couple of very interesting and dangerous innate abilities. They can emit a very loud, shrilling scream that will paralyze the lungs of any living being within one hundred feet of them, unless those beings can make an Endurance Test against a Difficulty Value of 12. The paral-

ysis lasts for 1D10 times 2 Turns. During this time the victims are totally unable to breathe.

The other innate ability which is responsible for the rockling's nickname "Shinkai Killer" is perhaps the most peculiar. Different rocklings have the ability to be completely immune to the effects of different Mystic Forces. This includes Force-effects ("Fireball", "Freeze (Animate)", "Air Bind", "Lightning", etc.), enchantments, or any other effects or abilities directly created by the Mystic Forces.

The color pattern on each individual rockling determines which of the Mystic Forces to which they are immune. White indicates *Air*, red indicates *Fire*, brown indicates *Land*, silver indicates *Spirit*, and blue indicates *Water*. The different colors appear as vague streaks or blotches along the rockling's back.

Each rockling may be immune to one or more, possibly all, of the Mystic Forces (GM's choice per each individual rockling).

SERPENT-WOLF

Aggression Rating: High
Attack: (x2) Bite = +8
Damage Yield: Bite = * L6

Attribute	Level	Health
Agility	11	Life Force: 200
Strength	9	Force Failure: 150
Endurance	7	Inj. Rating: 50
Willpower	6	Recovery: 1D10
Intelligence	6	
Sixth Sense	9	Value: 14 L.P.

Natural P.R.: 4
Bulk Value: 5
Move: 300/100

Description

The serpent-wolf is a very large wolf-like creature with the neck and head of a large snake. The neck of the serpent-wolf is approximately four feet in length and is capable of performing lightning quick attacks. Serpent-wolves are almost always black in color, this also includes their neck and head. Their eyes are an eerie yellow color with dark vertical pupils. They normally travel in packs of three to six and reside mostly in the higher elevations of mountains.

In the top of the serpent-wolf's mouth are two very long and sharp fangs capable of injecting venom into its victims. The bottom of the serpent-wolf's mouth is lined with sharp canines.

Any one bitten by a serpent-wolf is poisoned and suffers the following penalties. The victim's Agility and Strength both drop by 5 Levels on the Turn following the bite. The bite is extremely painful and the venom creates a burning pain throughout the victim's entire body. Additional serpent-wolf bites received while still being affected by previous bites will only further lower the victim's Agility and Strength by -1 Level.

The effects of the venom will begin to fade away six hours after it is injected, at which time the victim's Agility and Strength will regain 1 Level per hour until all 5 Levels are recovered.

There is no known method of removing the effects of the serpent-wolf's venom other than simply allowing them to wear off. Not even the Force-effect "Cure" has an effect. This fact makes the serpent-wolf a very formidable and feared foe.

SHADOW DEMON

Aggression Rating: High
Attack: (x2) Shadow Fire = +33, Claw = +11

Damage Yield: Shadow Fire = 6D20 + 150, Claw = L12

Attribute	Level	Health
Agility	25	Life Force: 400
Strength	28	Force Failure: 300
Endurance	16	Inj. Rating: 100
Willpower	15	Recovery: 1D20 + 1D12
Intelligence	14	
Sixth Sense	44	Value: 35 L.P.

Natural P.R.: 20
Bulk Value: 9
Move: 300/100 (600/200)

Description

These creatures are spawned directly from the Shadow itself. They are tall beings (seven feet tall) that weigh an average of two hundred and fifty pounds. They are extremely muscular and quick. Their skin is smooth, and black as night, and is very tough. They have a huge pair of dark wings that resemble those of a bat that attach between their shoulders. Their eyes are like that of a huge cat. Their noses are very short and pointed. They have very sharp teeth about two inches in length each. Their hands are slightly long with long sharp talons at the end of each of their five fingers. Their ears are tall and pointed.

Shadow demons can breath a blast of black fire-laced fog from their mouths known as shadow-fire. Shadow fire has a range of six hundred feet and covers an area up to ten feet wide at that distance. There is no know type of armor that can protect against shadow-fire, though the Force-effect "Spirit Shield" does offer protection. Shadow-fire is an extremely lethal attack that few opponents are able to survive.

Shadow demons regenerate extremely fast, healing 2D20 +30 points of damage per Turn.

Shadow demons reside within the mystical Shadow realm. They only appear on Oryathar for short periods of time, entering and exiting through portals which they are able to open and close at will. Only Shadow demons are able to pass through these portals.

SHAWLESH

Aggression Rating: Extreme
Attack: (x2) Claw = +16, Bite = +15
Damage Yield: Claw = L8 +5, Bite = L10 +5

Attribute	Level	Health
Agility	28	Life Force: 320
Strength	40	Force Failure: 240
Endurance	12	Inj. Rating: 80
Willpower	16	Recovery: 1D12
Intelligence	9	

Sixth Sense   18   Value: 30 L.P.

Natural P.R.: 20
Bulk Value: 14
Move: 250/84 (410/134)

Description

Shawlesh are very large and muscular creatures with an unstoppable craving for death and destruction. They have black and grey skin and leather wings that are approximately 6 feet in length each. Their bodies are shaped somewhat like that of a lion, but with very long muscular ruling-race-like arms in the front. They have deadly talons on their hands and feet and have a set of curved horns on their head. Their eyes glow with an evil red glare. Their mouth is full of long canine teeth used for tearing into the flesh of their prey. Their tail is long and thin with sharp spikes all over it. Shawlesh stand approximately eight feet in height and weigh well over two thousand pounds.

Shawlesh have the ability to emit a pulse of dark energy that will effect any living being within one hundred feet of them. This dark energy is referred to as a shadow pulse. The shadow pulse instantly inflicts 1D20 +20 points of damage to any living being within its range (one hundred feet). This damage is essentially the Life Force being pulled from the unfortunate beings caught within the shadow pulse. If the shawlesh has any current damage, the Life Force drained from the beings within its shadow pulse is given to the shawlesh in the form of instant healing. So if three beings are within the range of a shawlesh's shadow pulse and each suffer 30 points of damage, the shawlesh instantly heals 90 points of damage at that time. Shawlesh can only shadow pulse once every 3 Turns.

SHUFFLE-WING

Aggression Rating: Moderate
Attack: Wings = +6, Bite = +3

Damage Yield: Wings = * L2, Bite = L4

Attribute	Level	Health
Agility	8	Life Force: 32
Strength	8	Force Failure: 24
Endurance	6	Inj. Rating: 8
Willpower	6	Recovery: 1D8
Intelligence	2	
Sixth Sense	7	Value: 6 L.P.

Natural P.R.: 3
Bulk Value: 4
Move: 120/40

Description

Shuffle Wings are Shadow-kin that resemble giant featherless vultures with long bat-like wings that drag the ground. The rest of their body is covered with a lizard-like hide. Shuffle Wings are unable to fly; they use their wings as a means of attack. They drop to the ground upon their bellies and shuffle their wings in a scissor-type movement, clipping their opponent's feet out from under them, this maneuver is known as the wing shuffle. When they use the wing shuffle to attack, the damage yielded is only an amount equal to the strength the shuffle wing applies, but if the attack is successful the opponent is automatically knocked down and stunned. Shuffle wings prefer to knock their victims down with a wing shuffle and then attack them with their razor-sharp beak.

The average weight of a shuffle wing is a hundred and ten pounds and the average height is four feet.

STEEL SPIDER

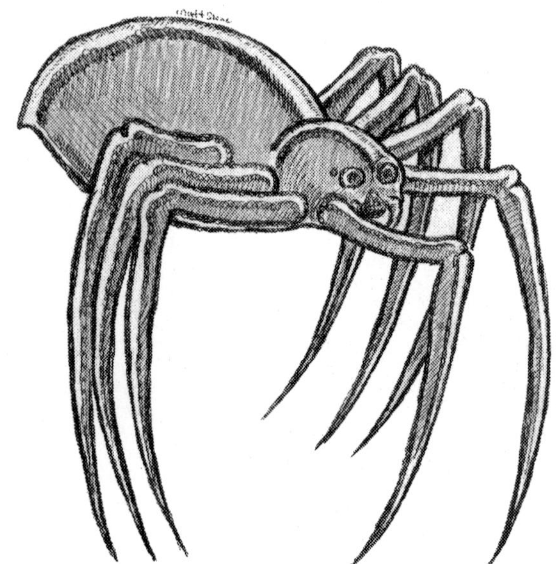

Aggression Rating: High
Attack: Legs = +12, Bite = +8

Damage Yield: Legs = L12 +20, Bite = L8 +10

Attribute	Level	Health
Agility	25	Life Force: 400
Strength	20	Force Failure: 300
Endurance	14	Inj. Rating: 100
Willpower	10	Recovery: 1D20 + 1D8
Intelligence	5	
Sixth Sense	12	Value: 20 L.P.

Natural P.R.: 12
Bulk Value: 8
Move: 300/100

Description

The steel spider is a giant black spider with a very hard exterior much like that of steel. The steel spider stands about four feet tall and has legs that are approximately four feet long each. The steel spider weighs a hefty seven hundred pounds.

The steel spider's legs, like the rest of its body, are extremely hard and end in sharp sword-like points. They use their legs to strike out at their prey and impale them. Their mouth has several very long and sharp teeth that they use to bite into their prey and suck out all of their body fluids.

Steel spiders live mostly in very rocky hillsides and caves. The feed off of nearly any and all types of creatures and beings.

WHIP-TAIL

Aggression Rating: High
Attack: Tail = +6, Bite = +3
Damage Yield: Tail = * L3, Bite = L4

Attribute	Level	Health
Agility	8	Life Force: 60
Strength	6	Force Failure: 45
Endurance	4	Inj. Rating: 15
Willpower	5	Recovery: 1D8
Intelligence	2	
Sixth Sense	6	Value: 7 L.P.

Natural P.R.: 2
Bulk Value: 7
Move: (260/87)

Description

These flying creatures resemble a giant bat with three long, whip-like tails (about six feet in length each) dangling from their posterior. They use these whip-like tails to lash out and entangle their victims, then drag them to their death, or fly high into the air and drop them.

It takes a Strength Test result of 14 in order to pull a whip-tail's tail loose or it must receive 30 points of damage in a single cutting blow in order to be severed.

As long as a whip-tail has an opponent entangled it will receive a -1D10 point penalty to the result of any Physical Defense that it sets. If the whip-tail is flying with and has its entangled victim completely off of the ground the -1D10 penalty does not apply.

WORM THORNS

Aggression Rating: Extreme
Attack: +20
Damage Yield: * L3

Attribute	Level	Health
Agility	2	Life Force: 8
Strength	1	Force Failure: 6
Endurance	2	Inj. Rating: 2
Willpower	3	Recovery: 1D4
Intelligence	2	
Sixth Sense	5	Value: .5 L.P.

Natural P.R.: 0
Bulk Value: .5
Move: 20/7

Description

Worm thorns are small black thorns with with blood-thirsty worms inside of them. Worm thorns reside within large grey pods that look very much like rocks. Whenever a being comes near the pods the subtle vibrations of their steps causes the pods to explode, sending the worm thorns flying out in all directions. Any being within ten feet of a worm thorn pod that explodes will be impaled with 1D4 worm thorns.

Immediately upon penetrating the skin of a victim the worms emerge from their thorns and enter the victim's body where they will feed for 3 Turns. The worms can be cut out of the skin, but it is a Major Action action to cut a single worm out and it inflicts 1D4 points of damage. The worms themselves inflict 1D6 points of damage per Turn as they feed. On the third Turn of being in the victim they emerge from the skin, fall to the ground, and burrow beneath the surface. There they will lay eggs that will form new pods and new worm thorns.

On normal terrain it takes an Agility/Performance Test against a base Difficulty Value of 20 to walk within ten feet of a worm thorn pod without causing enough vibration to set it off.

The worms themselves are solid black and have very small razor-sharp teeth. Worm thorns are about one inch in length.

WRETCHIN

Aggression Rating: High
Attack: Dagger = +4, Claw = +3, Bite = +2
Damage Yield: Dagger = L2, Claw = L3, Bite = L4

Attribute	Level	Health
Agility	7	Life Force: 60
Strength	7	Force Failure: 45
Endurance	6	Inj. Rating: 15
Willpower	6	Recovery: 1D12
Intelligence	4	
Sixth Sense	8	Value: 3 L.P.

Natural P.R.: 2
Bulk Value: 4
Move: 170/57

Description

These creatures are an average of four feet in height and weigh an average of one hundred pounds. They walk upright. Their head is very similar to that of a dog with small spiked ridges sticking out along the length of their muzzle. Their entire bodies are covered with a thick dog-like hair. They normally wear the skins of other animals around their waste. Their fingers have short claws much like that of a dog. They usually pack small daggers as weapons and often use the sharpened bones of victims to make daggers with.

ZOMBIE

Aggression Rating: Variable
Attack: +3
Damage Yield: Variable (Weapon Dependent)

Attribute	Level	Health
Agility	5	Life Force: N/A
Strength	8	Force Failure: N/A
Endurance	10	Inj. Rating: 30
Willpower	11	Recovery: N/A
Intelligence	1	
Sixth Sense	4	Value: 6 L.P.

Natural P.R.: 0 (Warlum = 2)
Bulk Value: 5-8
Move: 100/34

Description

Zombies are the unnatural result of a being that has been brought back to life beyond the safe resurrection time. Some zombies seem to be resurrected without any ruling-race involvement, but most are a result of Korgathool using the Force-effect "Resurrection" beyond the safe resurrection time.

Zombies are completely mindless beings that are bound to obey those who resurrect them. Though somewhat alive, they continue to decay as a normal body would, but in spite of this they display surprising strength and endurance.

Creating zombies is considered an evil act and should be worth a penalty of no less than 2 Shadow Points.

The common method used to kill zombies is to inflict two injuries to their head/neck area as well as two injuries to their Torso or Pelvis area. This will destroy the zombie and put an end to their artificial life. Though injuring the legs and arms, or even cutting them off, will slow a zombie down, they will not cease to live until the proper number of injuries are caused to the proper areas of their body.

ZORVEEL

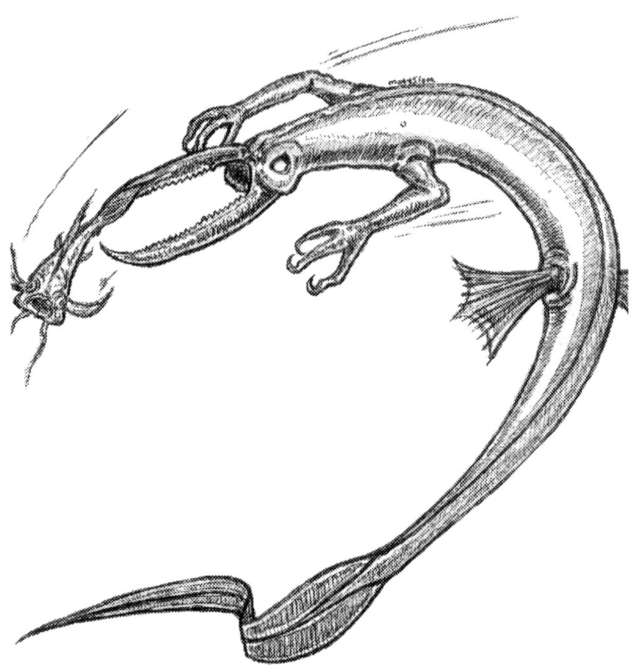

Aggression Rating: High
Attack: Bite = +10, Claw = +6
Damage Yield: Bite = L15 +20, Claw = L10

Attribute	Level	Health
Agility	20	Life Force: 600
Strength	20	Force Failure: 450
Endurance	9	Inj. Rating: 150
Willpower	10	Recovery: 1D10 + 1D8
Intelligence	4	
Sixth Sense	11	Value: 20 L.P.

Natural P.R.: 8
Bulk Value: 13
Move: 1200/400

Description

Zorveel are a very large and deadly type of Shadow-kin found only in the sea. They have a tail much like that of an eel and have two fins on their sides like that of a normal fish. They have two long arms that end in a three-clawed hand that is used for tearing apart their prey. They have two very long and powerful pinchers lined with razor sharp teeth that they use to latch onto and crush their prey while their clawed hands begin tearing them apart.

Zorveel prefer the deep waters but have been found in shallow waters on occasion. They mainly hunt and kill sharks and large fish but will not hesitate to feed on a ruling-race. The powerful tail and fins of the zorveel make them extremely fast swimmers.

Player Name:________________________   Specialty:__________________

Character Name:________________   Gender:___________

Race:________________   Innate Abilities: *Dragonknight*
____

Mystic Forces

	Attribute	Value	Level	Dice	Penalty	Penalty Type
☐	**Agility**	_____	_____	_____	_____	__________
☐	**Strength**	_____	_____	_____	_____	__________
☐	**Endurance**	_____	_____	_____	_____	__________
☐	**Willpower**	_____	_____	_____	_____	__________
☐	**Intelligence**	_____	_____	_____	_____	__________
☐	**Sixth Sense**	_____	_____	_____	_____	__________

Health
Life Force:________
Force Failure:________
Injury Rating:________
Recovery:________

Prowess Rating
Physical:____________
Mystical:____________

Total M.A.P.________

Defense Bonus
Physical:________
Mystical:________

Current M.A.P.________

Total Light Points:________
Current Light Points:________
Character Points:________
Total Shadow Points:________
Current Shadow Points:________

Protection Rating
Head/Neck:________
Arms:________   Torso:________
Pelvis:________   Legs:________

Maximum Speed:________ft/T
Action Movement:________ft
Lifting Limit:________
Carrying Capacity:________

Coin
Gold:________
Silver:________
Copper:________

Weapon Statistics

Weapon Type	Tech.	Attack	Dmg. Yield	Dmg. Received
__________	____	____	____	____
__________	____	____	____	____
__________	____	____	____	____
__________	____	____	____	____
__________	____	____	____	____
__________	____	____	____	____
__________	____	____	____	____

Armor Statistics

Armor Type	Tech.	P.R./ Destroy	Move/Agil. Penalty	Dmg. Received
__________	____	____	____	____
__________	____	____	____	____
__________	____	____	____	____
__________	____	____	____	____
__________	____	____	____	____
__________	____	____	____	____
__________	____	____	____	____

Mystic Forces   Force Knowledge   Unapplied Force Knowledge   Technique

- ☐ Air
- ☐ Fire
- ☐ Land
- ☐ Spirit
- ☐ Water

Total Force Knowledge:__________   Innate Force Energy:__________   Total Force Energy:__________

Notes	**Talents**	**Skills**	**Universal Talents**

Character Description

Height:_______   Skin:____________   Max. Horizontal Leap:__________

Weight:_______   Eyes:____________   Max. Vertical Leap:_________

Age:_______   Hair:____________

Other:_______________________________

____

DRAGONKNIGHT FORM

Attribute	Value	Level	Dice	Penalty	Penalty Type
Agility	____	____	____	____	________
Strength	____	____	____	____	________
Endurance	____	____	____	____	________
Willpower	____	____	____	____	________
Intelligence	____	____	____	____	________
Sixth Sense	____	____	____	____	________

Health

Life Force:______

Force Failure:______

Injury Rating:______

Advanced Combat ☐

Scale Color:__________

Protection Rating:______

Scale Damage:______

Defense Bonus

Physical:______

Mystical:______

Breath

____

____

Horizontal Leap:______

Vertical Leap:______

Lifting Limit:________

Carrying Capacity:_________

Maximum Ground Speed: __________

Action Ground Movement: __________

☐ Maximum Flight Speed: __________

☐ Action Flight Movement: __________

Player Name:______________________

Character Name:________________

Race:________________

Specialty:__________________

Gender:___________

Innate Abilities: *Enchanting*
____

MYSTIC FORCES

	Attribute	Value	Level	Dice	Penalty	Penalty Type
☐	Agility	_____	_____	_____	_____	__________
☐	Strength	_____	_____	_____	_____	__________
☐	Endurance	_____	_____	_____	_____	__________
☐	Willpower	_____	_____	_____	_____	__________
☐	Intelligence	_____	_____	_____	_____	__________
☐	Sixth Sense	_____	_____	_____	_____	__________

Health
Life Force:________
Force Failure:________
Injury Rating:________
Recovery:________

Prowess Rating
Physical:____________
Mystical:____________
Total M.A.P.________

Defense Bonus
Physical:________
Mystical:________
Current M.A.P.________

Total Light Points:________
Current Light Points:________
Character Points:________
Total Shadow Points:________
Current Shadow Points:________

Protection Rating
Head/Neck:________
Arms:________   Torso:________
Pelvis:________   Legs:________

Maximum Speed:________ft/T
Action Movement:________ft
Lifting Limit:________
Carrying Capacity:________

Coin
Gold:_________
Silver:________
Copper:________

Weapon Statistics

Weapon Type	Tech.	Attack	Dmg. Yield	Dmg. Received
____________	____	____	____	____
____________	____	____	____	____
____________	____	____	____	____
____________	____	____	____	____
____________	____	____	____	____
____________	____	____	____	____
____________	____	____	____	____

Armor Statistics

Armor Type	Tech.	P.R./ Destroy	Move/Agil. Penalty	Dmg. Received
____________	____	____	____	____
____________	____	____	____	____
____________	____	____	____	____
____________	____	____	____	____
____________	____	____	____	____
____________	____	____	____	____
____________	____	____	____	____

Mystic Forces	**Force Knowledge**	**Unapplied Force Knowledge**	**Technique**
☐ Air	_______________	_______________	_________
☐ Fire	_______________	_______________	_________
☐ Land	_______________	_______________	_________
☐ Spirit	_______________	_______________	_________
☐ Water	_______________	_______________	_________

Total Force Knowledge:__________   Innate Force Energy:__________   Total Force Energy:__________

Notes	**Talents**	**Skills**	**Universal Talents**
_____________	_____________	_____________	_____________
_____________	_____________	_____________	_____________
_____________	_____________	_____________	_____________
_____________	_____________	_____________	_____________
_____________	_____________	_____________	_____________
_____________	_____________	_____________	_____________
_____________	_____________	_____________	_____________
_____________	_____________	_____________	_____________
_____________	_____________	_____________	_____________
_____________	_____________	_____________	_____________
_____________	_____________	_____________	_____________
_____________	_____________	_____________	_____________
_____________	_____________	_____________	_____________
_____________	_____________	_____________	_____________
_____________	_____________	_____________	_____________
_____________	_____________	_____________	_____________

Character Description

Height:________   Skin:_____________

Weight:________   Eyes:_____________

Age:________   Hair:_____________

Other:__________________________________

____

Max. Horizontal Leap:__________

Max. Vertical Leap:__________

ENCHANTMENT COST				
Rating	**Light Points**	**Force Energy**	**Enchanting Strength**	**Time**
Very Simple	4 - 8	50	1	10-50 Turns
Simple	8.5 - 12	100	2	20-100 Turns
Average	12.5 - 16	150	3	30-150 Turns
Complex	16.5 - 20	200	4	40-200 Turns
Highly Complex	20.5 - up	250	5	50-250 Turns

COMBAT SHEET

Character Name:_______________________

Current Damage:_____________

Current Force Energy:_____________

Current M.A.P.:_____________

Injuries

Affected Attribute:_____________   **Number of Days to Heal:**_________

Affected Attribute:_____________   **Number of Days to Heal:**_________

Affected Attribute:_____________   **Number of Days to Heal:**_________

Affected Attribute:_____________   **Number of Days to Heal:**_________

Affected Attribute:_____________   **Number of Days to Heal:**_________

Notes

____
____
____
____
____
____
____
____
____
____
____
____
____
____
____
____

EQUIPMENT SHEET

Character Name:_________________________________

	Equipment	Bulk Value	Weight

Total Bulk Value:___________   **Load:**___________

✔ = in sac or backpack   **X** = not on character

FORCE-EFFECT RECORD SHEET

Character Name:_________________________________

Force-Effect	**Force Energy**	**Comments**
1.		
2.		
3.		
4.		
5.		
6.		
7.		
8.		
9.		
10.		
11.		
12.		
13.		
14.		
15.		
16.		
17.		
18.		
19.		
20.		
21.		
22.		
23.		
24.		
25.		
26.		
27.		
28.		
29.		
30.		
31.		
32.		
33.		
34.		
35.		
36.		
37.		
38.		
39.		
40.		
41.		
42.		
43.		
44.		
45.		
46.		
47.		
48.		

ENCHANTMENT LOG SHEET

Character Name:_________________________________

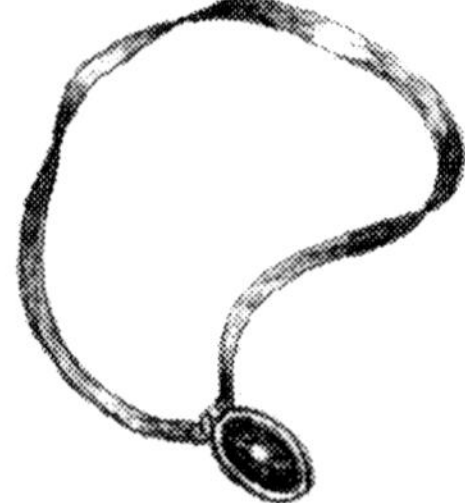

# of Tries	Very Simple	Simple	Average	Complex	Highly Complex
		ENCHANTMENT SUCCESS			
1st	30%	40%	50%	60%	70%
2nd	50%	60%	70%	80%	90%
3rd	70%	80%	90%	100%	100%
4th	90%	100%	100%	100%	100%
Beyond	100%	100%	100%	100%	100%

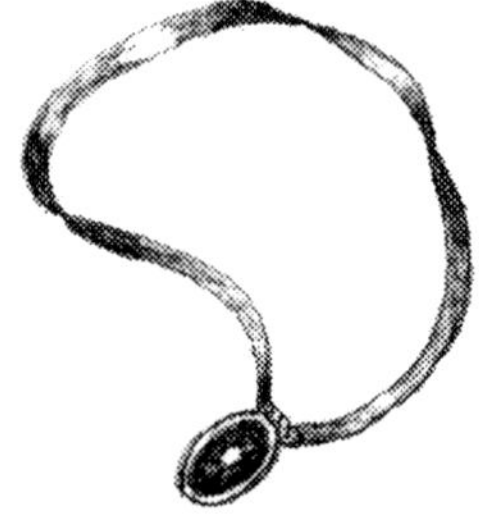

Item	Mystic Forces	Rating	Class	Enchantment Description

MYSTICAL ATTUNING SHEET

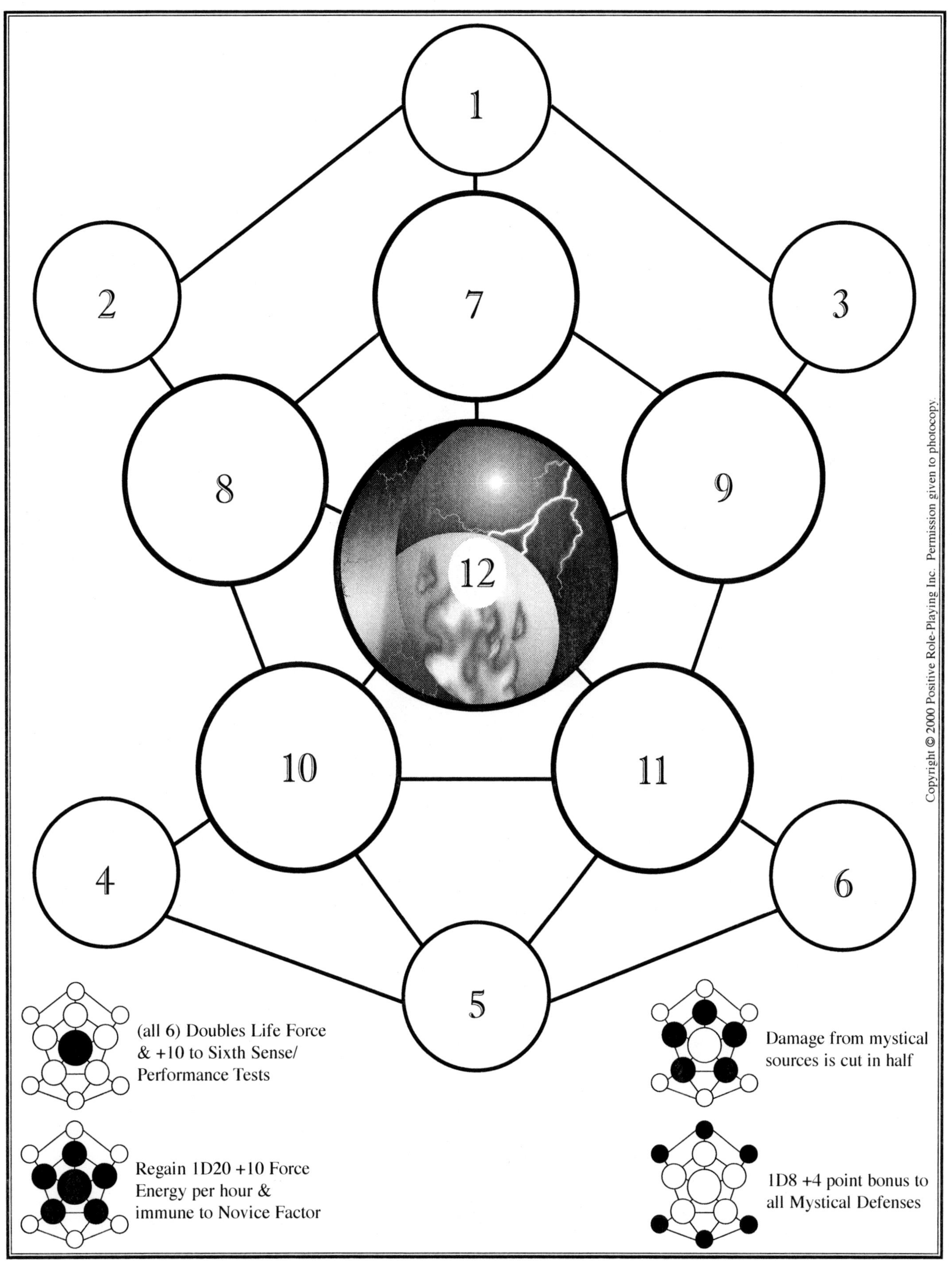

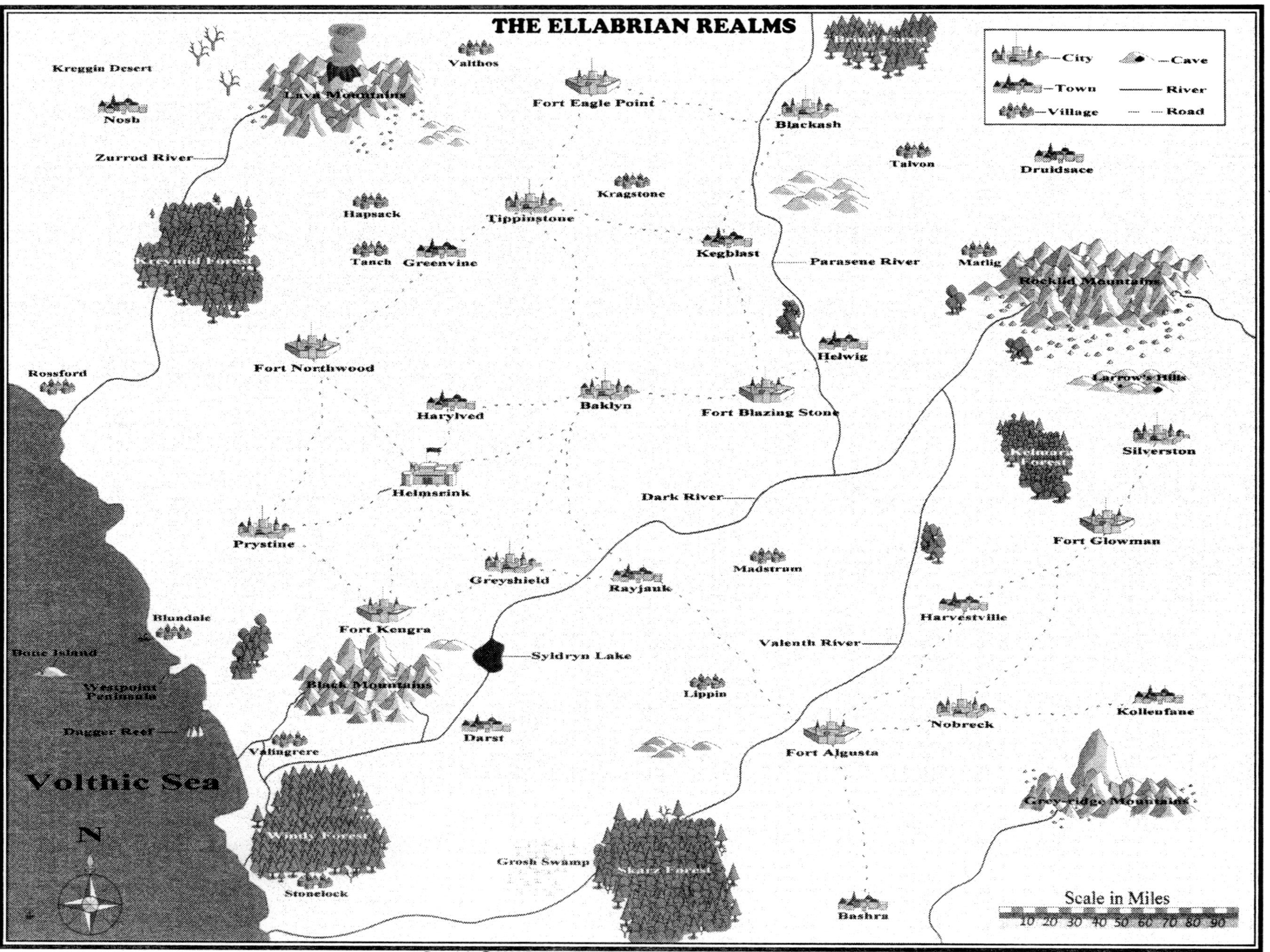

Copyright © 2000 Positive Role-Playing Inc. Permission given to photocopy.